SHIFTING HISTORIES

Transforming Schools for Social Change

Edited by

GLADYS R. CAPELLA NOYA
KATHRYN GEISMAR
GUITELE NICOLEAU

REPRINT SERIES NO. 26 • HARVARD EDUCATIONAL REVIEW

Library of Congress Catalog Card Number 95-076371

ISBN 0-916690-28-8

Harvard Educational Review
Gutman Library Suite 349
6 Appian Way
Cambridge, MA 02138

Cover Design: Kathryn Geismar
Cover Photographs: Dody Riggs
Typesetting: Sheila Walsh
Editorial Production: Dody Riggs

Contents

ON TRANSFORMATION:
FROM A CONVERSATION WITH MEL KING
141

Education is an act of love, and thus an act of courage.

— Paulo Freire
Education for Critical Consciousness

Introduction

The ability of schools to participate effectively in preparing young people to meet the challenges of the future is a subject of significant concern for all of U.S. society. How can teachers, administrators, policymakers, parents, children, and young people bridge the gaps that impede the learning and teaching process for today's youth? What would be included in the portrait of a school that successfully builds on the strengths that children bring to their classroom learning from their experiences in homes and communities that are shaped by the complex dynamics of history, ethnicity, race, class, gender, physical ability, and sexual orientation? What are the curricular practices that can increase students' ability to perceive and practice their roles as contributors to society? These are some of the questions addressed by the authors whose chapters appear in this book. *Shifting Histories: Transforming Schools for Social Change* is a collection of nineteen articles published in the *Harvard Educational Review* between 1989 and 1995. It brings under one cover the expert and timely writing of researchers in the field of education, along with the voices of practitioners who are struggling to reform their classrooms in order to reach and teach the diverse students who populate U.S. schools. We have brought these articles together to bring to light the ways in which educators and researchers are shifting the discourse of educational research, classroom innovation, and community involvement to create greater resonance between children's and young people's lives and the content of educational curricula and policies.

The volume is divided into three parts, preceded by an introductory chapter by Sonia Nieto, Professor of Education at the University of Massachusetts, Amherst. We have chosen Nieto's piece to frame the chapters that follow because it touches on all aspects of the book's core themes: diversity of ethnic, racial, linguistic, and social-class backgrounds within schools; the potential to promote change through curricular innovation; and the power of inviting personal experience into the classroom setting. In this beginning chapter, "Lessons from Students on Creating a Chance to Dream," Nieto attempts to articulate an understanding of multicultural education that is anti-racist, comprehensive, based on critical pedagogy, and rooted in social justice. Drawing on the voices and wisdom of students as well as educational research, she focuses on both practice and policy within the school setting, with an eye towards changing existing structures that often silence and ignore those who most need to be heard and acknowledged.

Part One of *Shifting Histories*, "Shifting Histories: Movement from the Inside Out," is comprised of six chapters. These contributors explore the importance of bringing one's own identity, culture, and history to discussions with disenfranchised communities — in raising questions about the meaning and power of knowledge and helping to develop constructions that can create changes in the relations between families and schools. The contributors to Part Two, entitled

"Histories of Institutional Change," explore the historical dissonance between the cultural experiences of historically oppressed groups, such as African Americans and the Maori in New Zealand, and the Eurocentric values that permeate the curricula of the schools that educate them. In their exploration, the authors raise important policy questions that can force open newly informed debates about the value of separate schools, parental and community roles in schools, inclusiveness in curricular practices, equity, multiculturalism and biculturalism. Part Three, "Changing Classrooms," brings the reader into the classroom, where innovative teachers and teacher researchers describe the transformative potential of personal experience when it is integrated into the learning environment. Describing their belief in students' capacities to engage in difficult conversations that challenge the cultural status quo, these authors offer compelling examples of the ways in which pedagogy and practice can help sow seeds for social change.

PART ONE

Part One, entitled "Shifting Histories: Movement from the Inside Out," highlights the personal dimension inherent in processes of institutional change within the field of education. This dimension is illuminated by the six different perspectives presented in the chapters comprising this section. This section begins with Lilia Bartolomé's call for teachers to develop political clarity. In "Beyond the Methods Fetish: Toward a Humanizing Pedagogy," Bartolomé, a former classroom teacher and current professor of anti-racist and multicultural education courses, challenges prevailing efforts to improve linguistic minority education that focus on specific methods of instruction. Bartolomé, who is a Chicana, argues that this focus perceives the underachievement of culturally and linguistically subordinated students as a technical problem and that it rests on three wrong assumptions: 1) teachers are fine, and do not need to identify, interrogate, or change their biased beliefs and fragmented views about subordinated students; 2) schools, as institutions, are basically fair and democratic sites where all students are provided with similar, if not equal, treatment and learning conditions; and 3) children who experience academic difficulties require some form of "special" instruction since they obviously have not been able to succeed under "regular" or "normal" instructional conditions (p. 40). Alternatively, Bartolomé argues that fundamental to schools' historical "mistreatment" and "miseducation" of linguistic and cultural minorities is the discrimination and denial of their humanity to which members of these groups have been *and continue to be* subjected. Therefore, the focus that perceives their underachievement as a technical problem must shift. Efforts must transcend the narrow, mechanistic perspective that leads to ineffective technical "solutions," and move to examine the historical and political dimensions of education. Bartolomé discusses salient issues regarding these dimensions, including the need for teachers to develop "political clarity" (p. 43); how schools have traditionally reproduced asymmetrical power relations among different social groups; and the too often unmentioned antagonistic relations between subordinated students and White school personnel. In essence, Bartolomé argues that when teachers develop political clarity, they are then able to implement teaching methods in critical and cultur-

ally responsive ways. Such personal and pedagogical changes can offset potentially unbalanced relations and discriminatory structures and practices, thus humanizing teaching and learning experiences for all involved, particularly for
members of subordinated groups for whom schooling has traditionally been a
*de*humanizing experience.

In "Giving Voice to the Voiceless," Beverly McElroy-Johnson weaves together
her own experiences as an African American child and adolescent, as an African
American woman teacher, and the experiences of her junior high school students to convey the fundamental responsibility that teachers and schools have
to support the development of voice among African American students. She
defines voice as "a strong sense of identity within an individual, an ability to
express a personal point of view, and a sense of personal well-being" (p. 61),
and maintains that African Americans have been denied their voice through
their collective oppressive history — a history of slavery and persistent racism.
The disproportionate number of African Americans who are not successful in
schools reflects this denial within the educational system. McElroy-Johnson
maintains that teachers *can* foster significant change in this prevailing situation,
that they *can* play a crucial role in educating students, in leading them forth "to
the source — to themselves and to their inner understandings of identity, culture, responsibility, and self-worth" (p. 70). However, teachers can achieve this
goal of "giving voice to the voiceless" *only* if they have a critical consciousness
and solid understanding that African Americans have been historically perceived
and treated as inferior to others "by the forces of White supremacy" (p. 71). This
force of White supremacy is embedded, for example, in the Eurocentric curriculum that has been imposed in U.S. schools. Therefore, it is imperative that
teachers move away from that monolithic perspective, which excludes so many
students, and view each child and adolescent within their whole personal, cultural, and ethnic context. Only then will teachers be supporting the development of voice, and thus the success, of African American students. Otherwise,
teachers and the educational system are only contributing to the silencing of
African American students, and thus to their failure.

In the chapter entitled "Challenging Venerable Assumptions: Literacy Instruction for Linguistically Different Students," María de la Luz Reyes challenges
"venerable assumptions" underlying *process instruction* as an approach to developing literacy among linguistic minorities in the United States. "Process instruction" refers to whole language and writing process, or literature-based, instruction. The four assumptions that Reyes challenges are that 1) English is the only
legitimate medium for learning and instruction; 2) linguistic minorities must be
immersed in English as quickly as possible if they are to succeed in school; 3) a
"one size fits all" teaching approach is good for *all* students; and 4) error correction in process instruction hampers learning. At the heart of her challenge
is that by failing to recognize and acknowledge the importance of cultural and
linguistic diversity as a fundamental dimension of teaching and learning, process
instruction discriminates against linguistically different students and privileges
mainstream ones. By failing to address the need to modify teaching programs
to meet the needs and validate the strengths of linguistically different children,
process instruction misguides teachers into believing that such programs are

inherently good for all students. Reyes challenges each of the four assumptions through concrete examples that she has documented in her research. All of the examples portray teachers using process instruction without questioning the "venerable assumptions," and the negative consequences that such uncritical implementation has for linguistically different children. At the end of the chapter, Reyes presents an alternative to the previous examples by portraying a teacher who — by making culturally and linguistically sensitive adaptations to process instruction — was able to implement this approach successfully with mainstream as well as linguistically different students. This example illustrates how teachers must rise above the assumptions underlying process instruction and challenge them in ways that acknowledge and validate each student's cultural and linguistic background. Reyes argues that such challenges and adaptations are indispensable if teachers are to be successful in teaching literacy among linguistically different learners.

In "A Curious Plan: Managing on the Twelfth," Patricia Clifford and Sharon Friesen, team teachers engaged in action research in an open-area, multi-aged elementary school classroom in Alberta, Canada, share their commitment "to developing a classroom where teachers and children are passionate, robust learners" (p. 101). This commitment comes alive through the stories they tell about their practice, the voices of the children that they include, and through their reflections on both of these. Clifford and Friesen understand the importance of listening to the children in order to recognize who they really are, and thus being able to construct with these children a curriculum in harmony with their connections to the world. They believe in the value of using traditional stories to prompt children to ask "big questions" that touch the essence of the human spirit. For example, when children in their classroom were discussing *Rumpelstiltskin,* questions such as whether "people have the right to ask for help without pledging something in return" (p. 105) emerged. Clifford and Friesen believe in the importance of inviting children to go beyond "school math" and to explore ideas like space and balance that have been explored by passionate learners throughout history. For example, when exploring the concept of time, children asked questions like "was there time before there was a universe?" (p. 114). At the heart of this chapter is the notion that striving to interact with children in this way demands more than new programs or methods. The authors ask, rather, that teachers grow into a philosophy of education that allows them to embrace children's authentic realities and questions and that leads them to be less focused on "planning" lessons and more on being "prepared" to perceive the wonderful possibilities that inevitably arise in the daily experiences with children and that allow them to recognize "human relationships as a fundamental source of knowledge" (p. 104). Finally, Clifford and Friesen discuss their conviction that teachers, because of their close contact with children, are in a privileged position to "make change happen" (p. 116) once they transcend traditional conceptions of children, teaching, learning, and knowledge.

In "Researching Change and Changing the Researcher," Concha Delgado-Gaitan, an ethnographic researcher of Mexican immigrant heritage, describes her research of a Latino community in California and discusses her evolving role throughout the course of her study. Although the initial focus of her research was family literacy practices, eliciting participants' feedback about her data directed her elsewhere. She began to focus on community empowerment as she learned from parents about their own understandings of literacy and about their concerns regarding communication with schools. This significant change in focus presented a major challenge to Delgado-Gaitan, as she had to decide about the extent of her own involvement within such process of empowerment. With much honesty and deep reflection, Delgado-Gaitan tells how her determination to validate participants' knowledge and to respect their struggles forced her to examine her own identity and, ultimately, to allow herself to change. After much internal debate, and supported by the work of Freire and the Cornell University Empowerment Group (p. 132), Delgado-Gaitan chose to become actively involved in this community's process of empowerment while simultaneously researching that process. Her story is a forceful illustration of the need to reflect upon one's identity, and upon the relationships that are established between researchers and researched as an integral dimension of engaging in responsible research.

"On Transformation: From a Conversation with Mel King" is an edited version of a five-hour conversation between Mel King and three former *Review* Board Members (Alexander Goniprow, Victoria Borden Munoz, and Jacquelyn Ramos). Originally published in a *Review* special issue on community-based education, the conversation presents King's insights on several topics, including the principles of community-based education and where to begin such a process; how community organizing works; King's formal and informal education; and working with young people to help them determine their own destinies. The richness of King's experiences as an activist, politician, and educator makes this conversation a powerful document that invites reflection, and is also a call to action, to transformation. Among the salient ideas that run through the piece are that the fundamental reason for community education is to facilitate building community, that *really* listening means being willing to change, and that raising political consciousness is an integral dimension of community education. The piece ends with a story of transformation from each of the three editors who took part in the conversation with King. The editors end by expressing their hope that their conversation with King will invite educators to "really listen" to young people. We join them in that hope.

PART TWO

In Part Two of *Shifting Histories,* entitled "Histories of Institutional Change," we present four articles that explore the changes that have occurred in the history of schooling for African Americans, from curricular orientations to shifts in the relationships between communities and schools. We include a fifth chapter that addresses similar themes, but in the context of New Zealand's efforts to restructure its schools to create greater equity, equality, and biculturalism. The section opens with William H. Watkins's article, "Black Curriculum Orientations: A Preliminary Inquiry." Situating his inquiry as an attempt to lay a foundation for further research, Watkins identifies and describes six orientations that have framed the curricula used to educate African Americans in the United States from the era of slavery to current times. He begins with the argument that "Black social, political, and intellectual development in all cases evolved under socially oppressive and politically repressive circumstances involving physical and intellectual duress and tyranny" (p. 160), thus creating a socio-eductional response that "runs the gamut from capitulation to accommodation to outright defiance" (p. 160). With a sociopolitical and historical analysis as his framework, Watkins proposes the tenets and rationale for the six orientations, which he labels the functionalist, accommodationist, liberal, reconstructionist, Black Nationalist, and Afrocentrist. He finds that while the accommodationist and functionalist orientations accepted the concept of racial subservience for Blacks, the liberal curriculum "acknowledged that slavery, not race, impeded Black education and it assumed Blacks learned by the same modality as Whites" (p. 165). Aligned with traditional liberal thought, Black liberal education "was designed to develop the students' analytical and critical faculties and to help students become worldly, tolerant, and capable of significant societal participation" (p. 166). Occurring in several incarnations since the 1800s, the Black Nationalist orientation is, for Watkins, the "most extreme reaction to American racism" (p. 168). Black Nationalists shun assimilation, focus on separatism, and stress the value of the school curriculum as a "vehicle through which Black values can be imparted to young learners, who are expected to go forth and contribute to the building of a Black civilization" (p. 168). The Afrocentrists, in the late twentieth century, pick up on the nationalist and separatist ideas by reclaiming traditional African cultural values and placing them at the center of historical, social, communicative, and pedagogical dialogue. Rejecting the rationalism and empiricism of Eurocentric models of inquiry, the Afrocentrists "seek interpretation, expression, and understanding without preoccupation for verification" (p. 168). Watkins observes that as the Afrocentric movement launches its curriculum and its own schools, several questions can be raised: "Will this model lead to resegregation? How should Afrocentric models fit with current proposals of 'globalism' and 'internationalism' and 'cultural diversity' in the curriculum?" (p. 173).

We pick up on the theme of separate schools in "Caswell County Training School, 1933–1969: Relationships between Community and School," wherein Emilie V. Siddle Walker offers a reading of the educational experience of an African American community in rural North Carolina during the days of segregated schooling. Siddle Walker premises her article on the idea that "segregated schools that were valued by their communities did exist, and that understanding more about the nature of those schools is important for historical accuracy and for educational reform" (p. 179). Being careful not to validate the inequities or minimize the discrimination that existed during this period of segregation, Siddle Walker analyzes why schools like the Caswell County Training School (CCTS) live on in the memory of former teachers, principals, parents, and students as "good" schools. She focuses her ethnographic explorations of the educational activities of CCTS on the relationship between the school and the community in order to fill an important lacuna in the analysis of segregated schools. Walker's findings reveal that the characterization of CCTS as a "good" school was contingent upon several factors related to the interaction between the school and the community. For example, the participants shared common expectations about the roles of the principal, teachers, students, and parents as defined by "mutually accepted boundaries of authority" (p. 191); the parents and the school had a " 'collective stake in the educational process of the youth in the community' " (p. 188); parents were engaged in many aspects of the school's life, including being advocates for the school with the White school board; the teachers and principal were very visible and made themselves known to the community; and, the principal and the teachers communicated with the parents in accessible language about the progress and problems that were being manifested in their children's educational experience.

While recognizing that "since that era, the nature of problems confronting children has changed as has the structure of families" (p. 195), Siddle Walker proposes that the CCTS case "provides an important framework within which to consider current problems of school reform" (p. 195) — a framework that allows researchers to ask new questions, such as, "How do African American parents currently view schools? Are there still invisible ways they support the school that are generally unknown and unappreciated? Are African American parents and schools operating from the same expectations about appropriate community-school interactions? . . . Do African American parents have a mode of advocacy that creates dissonance, rather than collaboration between parents and administrators?" (p. 195). With these questions, Walker seeks to push the margins of the current discourse that dominates the characterization of African American parents' involvement in their children's education. For her, answers to these questions would "[restore] voice to African American educators and parents, whose knowledge has been devalued and whose opinions have been silenced since the onset of integration" (p. 196).

The theme of the relationship between the school and the community is explored in "When the Walls Come Tumbling Down." In this piece, Paula Lawrence Wehmiller takes us back to a time in her educational experience as a young African American girl growing up in rural New York state, when there "were no walls around our two-room schoolhouse" (p. 199), when the dreams and hopes of a range of students with diverse names, histories, looks, fears, and temperaments found their place inside of the school. But now, as she travels the country visiting schools, she is "almost always met with a wall" (p. 201) — a stone wall, a brick wall, and sometimes a seemingly invisible yet perceivable wall. In these instances, "the school is one world and the community around it is another" (p. 201).

In this revised keynote speech to educators from independent schools, Wehmiller uses the image of the wall and its separatist purposes to talk about the systemic structures that create divisions between students, schools, and communities. She recalls that over the past ten years, in pursuing goals of diversity, independent schools have invited students of different races, cultures, religions, economic groups, and neighborhoods to "come through the gate and inside the wall" (p. 201). But, she contends, the walls that have distinguished insiders from outsiders have also been erected inside of the schools via "ritual and symbol and language and habits" that include some and exclude others (p. 202). She exhorts the members of her audience to contemplate what it means to bring those walls down, and suggests that the effort to do so will require hard work, courage, and strength. She proposes that as independent schools attempt to meet the demands of educating youth for the twenty-first century, they will have to build covenants, "a promise to carry the gifts, the stories, the histories, the visions, the dreams of all people inside the schools. It is a promise to take down the walls of exclusion" (p. 207).

In "Reading the World of School Literacy: Contextualizing the Experience of a Young African American Male," Arlette Ingram Willis reflects on the unspoken barriers inside the schools and classrooms that push her nine-year-old son to create a distance between "the cultural images and nuances" (p. 214) he experiences in his community life and the life he leads in school. She observes, "It seems that he has come to understand that as an African American he must constantly make a mediating effort to help others understand events that appear to be commonplace on the surface, but are in fact culturally defined" (p. 212). She recounts various incidents in the life of her son's schooling and in her own experience as a teacher of multicultural literature in which she witnesses how non-mainstream students are challenged to "choose between cultural assimilation and accommodation, or resistance" (p. 213). As argued by Watkins in this section, Willis ascertains that her son's internal struggle to express his "real self" within the school curriculum is "framed by the sociohistorical and sociocultural inequities of U.S. society" (p. 214). For her, educators are complicit in perpetuating the "sin of omission'" (p. 214) that allows the "cultural knowledge of culturally and linguistically diverse children to be ignored, devalued, and unnurtured as valid sources of literacy acquisition" (p. 214). She argues that while social constructivists have made significant contributions to the understanding of culture in literacy acquisition, they have not explicitly addressed the multilayered complexity of the cultures of historically oppressed groups such as African Americans. Willis suggests that the systemic changes that would have to occur to attend to the plurality and diversity in the United States would have to include a teacher education agenda that "makes explicit the relationship among culture, language, literacy, and power" and "that trains teachers to use cultural information to support and nurture the literacy development of all students who enter their classroom" (pp. 220).

With the final article in this section, while we make a geographical shift to New Zealand, the issues of separatism and inclusiveness tackled by the first four authors are echoed in the struggle in New Zealand to implement goals of equity, equality, and cultural inclusiveness in their school restructuring efforts. In "Equity, Equality, and Biculturalism in the Restructuring of New Zealand Schools: A Life-History Approach," Sue Middleton uses life-history interviews to document and analyze the reaction of school board members (parents, teachers, and administrators) to the school restructuring initiatives in three different school settings — a predominantly Maori (the indigenous Polynesian population) urban school, a predominantly *Pakeha* (the White descendants of British and other European colonists) rural primary school, and a small-town secondary school with a mixed Maori and *Pakeha* population. Cast in the context of politically charged meanings of "biculturalism," "multiculturalism," and "equity," Middleton's research focused on "how board members positioned themselves with respect to the various, changing, and often contradictory equity discourses — the debates then raging in the mass media, in parliament, on *marae* (Maori tribal or family meeting places), and in other public and private spaces" (p. 240). The data from the interviews "depicted school communities that embodied wide differences of opinion and perspectives on biculturalism and multiculturalism" (p. 240). School board members in the predominantly Maori school placed a "high priority on Maori language and culture" (p. 240); and while the board members of the predominantly *Pakeha* school did not see the relevance of immersion and bicultural education policies to their schools, they "supported the rights of access of Maori pupils to such an education" (p. 240). Middleton states, "Board members of one multicultural school (a school with many pupils from families of recent immigrants) were generally supportive of multiculturalism in the sense of learning about other cultures, but only if such learning were within the framework of the dominant New Zealand *Pakeha* culture" (p. 241). Though these positions on biculturalism and multiculturalism differed, spanning a range from "supportive to indifferent to hostile" (p. 241), Middleton found that with few exceptions, people "expressed high opinions of their children's schooling, preferring it greatly to their own" (p. 248), and "most expressed liberal rather than conservative views [favoring] some degree of [Maori] and/or multicultural experiences in their schools' curriculum" (p. 240).

However, this discourse of biculturalism and multiculturalism, which was spurred by the Labour Government's agenda to bring about social equity through the schools, gave way to the discourse of schooling for increased competitiveness in the global economy that was introduced with the newly elected rightist government of the New Zealand National Party. Middleton suggests that *Pakeha* and Maori board members' desire to have their children become "well-rounded individuals" (p. 248) and their support for some form of equity policy and biculturalism in their schools might enable the wave of change to persist beyond the political shifts that have occurred. She expresses her hope that by taking a life-history approach that makes "the protagonists in the debates both audible and visible to one another" (p. 248), educational researchers can assist them in the task of sustaining their commitments to bring about necessary systemic changes.

PART THREE

In Part Three, "Changing Classrooms," the focus shifts to the classroom. The themes of *Shifting Histories* — addressing issues of difference and multiculturalism, challenging the social status quo, and the transformative potential of personal experience — are taken up here by educators and researchers alike. Specifically, the seven chapters in Part Three offer varying accounts of the classroom experience and its potential to address difference, promote dialogue, and, ultimately, to change existing social systems. The authors whose work comprises this section believe that students have a capacity to engage in difficult — and *transformative* — conversations, and they describe programs, curricula, and research that foster (or document) such dialogues between students of all ages in elementary and high schools.

Eric Rofes's chapter, "Opening Up the Classroom Closet: Responding to the Educational Needs of Gay and Lesbian Youth," is a call to educators to learn about the needs of their gay and lesbian students. Rofes makes it clear that the results of years of public education that ignores the identities of gay and lesbian people can be devastating: significantly low self-esteem, emotional difficulties, suicide attempts, and substance abuse are all markedly high among gay and lesbian youth. Rofes looks at possible reasons why schools have failed these students, and then discusses two initiatives aimed at making a difference: Project 10, a program in Los Angeles aimed at serving gays and lesbians through providing support services, educating gay and lesbian students about positive role models, providing support for school safety, and emphasizing drop-out prevention strategies; and the Harvey Milk School in New York City, a school founded to meet the specific educational and social needs of gay and lesbian youth. Rofes sees a need for many more such programs and provides a list of changes that must happen if U.S. schools are to become truly accessible to self-identified gay and lesbian youth. Among these changes are: focusing on students' needs rather than on the demands of parents or the larger community; moving issues of sexuality into the fore of public discourse; educating teachers to become better acquainted and more comfortable with gay and lesbian issues; developing school curricula that integrate historical contributions of gays and lesbians, as well as "literature that reflects the experiences and culture of gay and lesbian writers" (p. 261); and shedding the belief that open discussion of gay and lesbian issues will persuade young people to become gay.

Like Rofes, Patricia Saylor writes about a population, and indeed a culture, that has often gone unacknowledged. In "A Hearing Teacher's Changing Role in Deaf Education," Saylor describes a program called BRIDGES (not an acronym) created with the goal of "building understanding between two cultures, the Deaf culture and the hearing culture" (footnote, p. 263). BRIDGES is a bilingual, bicultural day-care and family service organization that serves both deaf children and hearing children with Deaf family members.[1] The program was founded with the belief that "the developmental delays typically experienced by deaf children are entirely preventable. What deaf children need for normal social and linguistic development is to mingle daily in a community of Deaf, fluent signers" (p. 265). Saylor created the program in 1990 with the belief that, given the proper supports, all deaf children can thrive. The article combines theory-driven beliefs about Deaf children and the language and social delays that they typically experience along with Saylor's experiences with Deaf children in her role as the founder of BRIDGES. She believes that a successful program must draw upon the strengths of the cultural heritage that members of the Deaf community hold — "a wealth of knowledge about how to cope in a sometimes hostile (or at least unaccommodating) environment," as well as "a rich heritage of folklore, literature, customs, and values that can be a source of pride and self-esteem for young deaf children" (p. 272).

While Saylor's chapter uses a rather broad stroke in describing the program and the need for greater awareness about Deaf culture, Cynthia Ballenger's article, "Because You Like Us: The Language of Control," looks into cross-cul-

---

[1] Saylor makes a distinction between the words "deaf" and "Deaf" that is common within the Deaf Community. The word "deaf" refers to someone who does not hear or does not hear well, and "Deaf" refers to a cultural identification with members of the American Deaf Community.

tural encounters in a focused and concentrated way. Ballenger, a White teacher with fifteen years' experience in preschools, recounts her efforts to learn how to manage the behavior of Haitian preschoolers she was teaching in Dorchester, Massachusetts. Finding that the techniques of behavior management that had worked with children brought up in North American culture were not successful with her Haitian students, Ballenger turned the experience into a fruitful period of self-reflection and teacher research. As a member of the Brookline Teacher-Researcher Seminar, Ballenger came to focus her interest on the different languages of control used by Haitian teachers and by herself. Offering transcripted interactions between teachers and students and parents and students, Ballenger came to see some fundamental differences that deeply affected her practice and effectiveness as a teacher of children of a different culture. Through numerous "conversations" with Haitian teachers and parents at the day-care center, with her teacher-research group, and through her work in a child development class, Ballenger learns about Haitian culture and comes to question the assumptions that shape her own experience — and practice — as a North American teacher.

Like Ballenger, Adrienne Alton-Lee, Graham Nuthall, and John Patrick take a focused, in-depth look at children's worlds — and the way culture impacts those worlds — in "Reframing Classroom Research: A Lesson from the Private World of Children." The lessons in this chapter are derived from conducting research in a sixth-grade classroom in New Zealand as part of ongoing research by the Understanding Learning and Teaching Project. Citing the work of Courtney Cazden, the authors talk about "two interpenetrating worlds: the official world of the teachers' agenda, and the unofficial world of the peer culture" (p. 289). The authors, like Cazden, assert that while the official world of teachers and teaching has been much studied, the unofficial, private world of children has remained unexplored. Guiding the research are two questions: How do children experience these two worlds? and What can be learned from the private utterances of children about the process of learning? Children being studied were chosen because they represented different achievement levels and different genders. They wore individual microphones that picked up their utterances while they learned about New York City via a standardized social studies curriculum. The authors then developed "a framework within which utterances [were] interpreted as a source of information about the ways in which children [respond] to the classroom context" (p. 297). Looking at the interaction between the culture of the classroom and the how the children's cultural perspectives were shaped by their race, class, and gender, the authors came to see that "these cultural perspectives influence [the children's] negotiation of the classroom culture and their public and private participation in curriculum enactment" (p. 297).

Cultural context is a critical force in "Promoting the Success of Latino Language-Minority Students: An Exploratory Study of Six High Schools" by Tamara Lucas, Rosemary Henze, and Rubén Donato. These authors open their chapter with a description of the ways in which minority students have historically been viewed through a deficit model lens. The authors offer the alternative belief that all children should be seen as educable — a shift in ideology that places the responsibility for schooling on schools rather than on the students. Further, they claim that there needs to be a shift in perspective to a focus on children's strengths. The authors show that secondary language-minority students bring not only the diversity of their cultural heritages to U.S. schools, but also a diversity of strengths and experiences with formal education. Asking what makes some schools more successful than others in educating language minority students, Lucas et al. look at what has worked in six high schools in California and Arizona. Common elements of a successful school include a "positive attitude towards the students, a willingness to question conventional practices, a strong and competent leadership, a highly committed teaching staff, high expectations and standards, and an emphasis on high achievement and academics" (p. 324). Although the authors warn that there is no clear method or recipe for success, they provide charts that outline and explicate some features of the high schools that successfully promoted achievement in language-minority students, focusing the majority of their article on describing these features.

Taking up the thread of issues of difference within the classroom context, Melinda Fine explores a particular curriculum in her article " 'You Can't Just Say That the Only Ones Who Can Speak Are Those Who Agree with Your Position': Political Discourse in the Classroom." By providing her readers with a detailed portrait of a class in the process of facing volatile issues, Fine builds a compelling case for her belief that "one cannot possibly avoid bringing into the classroom issues over which society is . . . divided because students . . . are well aware of these issues and hungry to discuss them with their peers" (p. 366). She focuses on the experience of Marysa Gonzalez's seventh-/eighth-grade class in Cambridge, Massachusetts, as they grapple with the curricular content of the program "Facing History and Ourselves." This program, Fine explains, is "an interdisciplinary social studies unit" that "seeks to provide a model for teaching history in a way that helps students reflect critically upon a variety of contemporary social, moral, and political issues" (p. 348). Using the Nazi rise to power and the holocaust as a focal point of the curriculum, Fine says that this program "guides students back and forth between in-depth historical case study and reflection on the causes and consequences of present-day prejudice, intolerance, violence, and racism" (p. 348).

While Fine, in keeping with Facing History's philosophy, provides a rationale for focusing on a historical rather than a present-day event in the curriculum, the power of the subject matter and the passionate and difficult discussions it engenders are clearly evident in the vivid class portrait she provides. Focusing on this group of students and their teacher, Fine details the often constructive and illuminating power of these difficult and often heated discussions. Using a day-by-day, diary-like account of her classroom observations, she shows the students' changing attitudes and their capacity to speak about difficult and painful subjects such as free speech, multiculturalism and cultural homogeneity, racism, and prejudice, among others. Fine builds a strong case for her belief that adolescents are capable of grappling with the most thorny and difficult topics and are able to engage each other in open debate. Further, she believes and shows that these students were able to fully engage with such material and still maintain a sense of community, under the guidance of their skilled teacher. This, Fine believes, is critical if students are to "learn to tolerate more fully the conflicts they will inevitably encounter in the world beyond the classroom" and to acknowledge the different perspectives and communities around them. Helping students to learn the important task of building connections between these communities — rather than creating a single, ideal one — is, Fine states, "essential to education in a democracy" (p. 367).

Like Fine, Paul Skilton Sylvester offers a detailed class portrait of the extraordinary work that students can accomplish in a classroom that allows them to use their full range of experiences and knowledge. In "Elementary School Curricula and Urban Transformation," Sylvester describes how his third-grade class explored multiple facets of the "real world" through the creation of "Sweet Cakes Town," a "child-sized, red-brick neighborhood . . . created out of cardboard boxes in [his] classroom" (p. 369). Children ran all aspects of Sweet Cakes — the businesses, the government, the union — and in this chapter, Sylvester vividly portrays how his curriculum was used to address the "inequality of a post-industrial society" (p. 370). Students used money earned from jobs in the classroom to buy goods in stores owned and run by classmates. As Sylvester describes it: "They could buy and manage businesses, rent a chess board at the toy store, rent paints at the Art Supply Store, borrow a book from the Free Library, plant seeds at the Wonderful World of Plants Store, sell one of their own paintings at the Art Gallery" (p. 369), and so on. With his belief in the power of education to change entrenched social systems and the children's creative powers as learners, community builders, and citizens, Sylvester offers a striking example of the practice of critical pedagogy.

The Sweet Cakes economy grew out of a larger study of the neighborhood surrounding the school. Through living the "real" situations of everyday business and trade, justice and power, and money and homelessness, students encountered education as a means to explore societal conditions and the possibility of social transformation. Sylvester first offers a description of the creation of Sweet Cakes and its evolution as a community, and then the changing roles of three students in the class. In discussing the implications of this particular curriculum's potential for social transformation, he clearly shows that students in his class found that they could indeed change their roles in Sweet Cakes Town and, through this change, could alter the town's social structures. This experience, Sylvester states, offered his students a striking example that "the society of the future need not be what the students have seen but what they can imagine" (p. 388).

We believe that *Shifting Histories: Transforming Schools for Social Change* will be a valuable resource for teachers, teacher educators, school administrators, and policymakers alike. As a substantial number of the book's chapters are written from the perspective of teachers, they address issues of differences with the wisdom and knowledge grounded in reflective practice. In this sense, schoolteachers will see themselves, their students, and their struggles in the stories and studies that the chapters present. Teacher educators will value this collection as an important source of theories and practices that can engender deep reflection and fertile discussions about difficult issues, and also provoke constructive actions that educators might take to address these issues. School administrators and policymakers will value the opportunity to listen to and reflect, along with students, teachers, and researchers, on the systemic challenges of building schools that honor the diversity of their constituents. It is our hope that *Shifting Histories* will make a dynamic contribution to the efforts of educators to construct schools that value the voices and experiences of all their members, and that promote the possibility for personal and professional, as well as systemic, change.

GLADYS R. CAPELLA NOYA • KATHRYN GEISMAR • GUITELE NICOLEAU
Harvard Graduate School of Education

BEGINNINGS

Creating a Chance to Dream

Lessons from Students on Creating a Chance to Dream

SONIA NIETO

*For the most part, discussions about developing strategies to solve educational prob-
lems lack the perspectives of one of the very groups they most affect — students,
especially those students who are categorized as "problems" and are most oppressed
by traditional educational structures and procedures. In this article, Sonia Nieto uses
interviews to develop case studies of young people from a wide variety of ethnic, racial,
linguistic, and social-class backgrounds who at the time interviewed were attending
and successfully completing junior or senior high school. By focusing on students'
thoughts about a number of school policies and practices and on the effects of racism
and other forms of discrimination on their education, Nieto explores what characteristics of these students' specific experiences helped them remain and succeed in
school, despite the obstacles. In essence, these are lessons from students, and Nieto
believes that in order to reflect critically on school reform, students need to be included
in the dialogue. She sets about developing an understanding of multicultural education that is basic for everyone, and is anti-racist, comprehensive, pervasive in the
curriculum and pedagogy, based on critical pedagogy, and rooted in social justice.*

> How does it come about that the one institution that is said to be the gateway
> to opportunity, the school, is the very one that is most effective in perpetuat-
> ing an oppressed and impoverished status in society? (Stein, 1971, p. 178)

The poignant question above was posed in this very journal almost a quarter of
a century ago by Annie Stein, a consistent critic of the schools and a relentless
advocate for social justice. This question shall serve as the central motif of this
article because, in many ways, it remains to be answered and continues to be a
fundamental dilemma standing in the way of our society's stated ideals of equity
and equal educational opportunity. Annie Stein's observations about the New
York City public schools ring true today in too many school systems throughout
the country and can be used to examine some of the same policies and practices
she decried in her 1971 article.

It is my purpose in this article to suggest that successfully educating all students in U.S. schools must begin by challenging school policies and practices
that place roadblocks in the way of academic achievement for too many young
people. Educating students today is, of course, a far different and more complex
proposition than it has been in the past. Young people face innumerable personal, social, and political challenges, not to mention massive economic structural changes not even dreamed about by other generations of youth in the
twentieth century. In spite of the tensions that such challenges may pose, U.S.

Harvard Educational Review Vol. 64 No. 4 Winter 1994, 392–426

society has nevertheless historically had a social contract to educate *all* young-sters, not simply those who happen to be European American, English speaking, economically privileged, and, in the current educational reform jargon, "ready to learn."[1] Yet, our schools have traditionally failed some youngsters, especially those from racially and culturally dominated and economically oppressed back-grounds. Research over the past half century has documented a disheartening legacy of failure for many students of all backgrounds, but especially children of Latino, African American, and Native American families, as well as poor Euro-pean American families and, more recently, Asian and Pacific American immi-grant students. Responding to the wholesale failure of so many youngsters within our public schools, educational theorists, sociologists, and psychologists devised elaborate theories of genetic inferiority, cultural deprivation, and the limits of "throwing money" at educational problems. Such theories held sway in particular during the 1960s and 1970s, but their influence is still apparent in educational policies and practices today.[2]

The fact that many youngsters live in difficult, sometimes oppressive con-ditions is not at issue here. Some may live in ruthless poverty and face the challenges of dilapidated housing, inadequate health care, and even abuse and neglect. They and their families may be subject to racism and other oppressive institutional barriers. They may have difficult personal, psychological, medical, or other kinds of problems. These are real concerns that should not be dis-counted. But, despite what may seem to be insurmountable obstacles to learning and teaching, some schools are nevertheless successful with young people who live in these situations. In addition, many children who live in otherwise onerous situations also have loving families willing to sacrifice what it takes to give their children the chance they never had during their own childhoods. Thus, poverty, single-parent households, and even homelessness, while they may be tremen-dous hardships, do not in and of themselves doom children to academic failure (see, among others, Clark, 1983; Lucas, Henze, & Donato, 1990; Mehan & Vil-lanueva, 1993; Moll, 1992; Taylor & Dorsey-Gaines, 1988). These and similar studies point out that schools that have made up their minds that their students deserve the chance to learn do find the ways to educate them successfully in spite of what may seem to be overwhelming odds.

Educators may consider students difficult to teach simply because they come from families that do not fit neatly into what has been defined as "the main-stream." Some of them speak no English; many come from cultures that seem to be at odds with the dominant culture of U.S. society that is inevitably reflected in the school; others begin their schooling without the benefit of early experi-ences that could help prepare them for the cognitive demands they will face. Assumptions are often made about how such situations may negatively affect

[1] I recognize that overarching terms, such as "European American," "African American," "Latino," etc., are problematic. Nevertheless, "European American" is more explicit than "White" with regard to culture and ethnicity, and thus challenges Whites also to think of themselves in ethnic terms, something they usually reserve for those from more clearly identifiable groups (generally, people of color). I have a more in-depth discussion of this issue in chapter two of my book, *Affirming Diversity* (1992).

[2] The early arguments for cultural deprivation are well expressed by Carl Bereiter and Siegfried Englemann (1966) and by Frank Reissman (1962). A thorough review of a range of deficit theories can be found in Herbert Ginsburg (1986).

student achievement and, as a consequence, some children are condemned to failure before they begin. In a study by Nitza Hidalgo, a teacher's description of the students at an urban high school speaks to this condemnation: "Students are generally poor, uneducated and come from broken families who do not value school. Those conditions that produce achievers are somewhere else, not here. We get street people" (Hidalgo, 1991, p. 58). When such viewpoints guide teachers' and schools' behaviors and expectations, little progress can be expected in student achievement.

On the other hand, a growing number of studies suggest that teachers and schools need to build on rather than tear down what students bring to school. That is, they need to understand and incorporate cultural, linguistic, and experiential differences, as well as differences in social class, into the learning process (Abi-Nader, 1993; Hollins, King, & Hayman, 1994; Lucas et al., 1990; Moll & Díaz, 1993). The results of such efforts often provide inspiring examples of success because they begin with a belief that all students deserve a chance to learn. In this article, I will highlight these efforts by exploring the stories of some academically successful young people in order to suggest how the policies and practices of schools can be transformed to create environments in which all children are capable of learning.

It is too convenient to fall back on deficit theories and continue the practice of blaming students, their families, and their communities for educational failure. Instead, schools need to focus on where they *can* make a difference, namely, their own instructional policies and practices. A number of recent studies, for example, have concluded that a combination of factors, including characteristics of schools as opposed to only student background and actions, can explain differences between high- and low-achieving students. School characteristics that have been found to make a positive difference in these studies include an enriched and more demanding curriculum, respect for students' languages and cultures, high expectations for all students, and encouragement for parental involvement in their children's education (Lee, Winfield, & Wilson, 1991; Lucas et al., 1990; Moll, 1992). This would suggest that we need to shift from a single-minded focus on low- or high-achieving students to the conditions that create low- or high-achieving schools. If we understand school policies and practices as being enmeshed in societal values, we can better understand the manifestations of these values in schools as well. Thus, for example, "tracked" schools, rather than reflecting a school practice that exists in isolation from society, reflect a society that is itself tracked along racial, gender, and social-class lines. In the same way, "teacher expectations" do not come from thin air, but reflect and support expectations of students that are deeply ingrained in societal and ideological values.

Reforming school structures alone will not lead to substantive differences in student achievement, however, if such changes are not also accompanied by profound changes in how we as educators think about our students; that is, in what we believe they deserve and are capable of achieving. Put another way, changing policies and practices is a necessary but insufficient condition for total school transformation. For example, in a study of six high schools in which Latino students have been successful, Tamara Lucas, Rosemary Henze, and

Rubén Donato (1990) found that the most crucial element is a shared belief among teachers, counselors, and administrators that all students are capable of learning. This means that concomitant changes are needed in policies and practices *and* in our individual and collective will to educate all students. Fred Newmann (1993), in an important analysis of educational restructuring, underlines this point by emphasizing that reform efforts will fail unless they are accompanied by a set of particular commitments and competencies to guide them, including a commitment to the success of all students, the creation of new roles for teachers, and the development of schools as caring communities.

Another crucial consideration in undertaking educational change is a focus on what Jim Cummins (1994) has called the "relations of power" in schools. In proposing a shift from coercive to collaborative relations of power, Cummins argues that traditional teacher-centered transmission models can limit the potential for critical thinking on the part of both teachers and students, but especially for students from dominated communities whose cultures and languages have been devalued by the dominant canon.[3] By encouraging collaborative relations of power, schools and teachers can begin to recognize other sources of legitimate knowledge that have been overlooked, negated, or minimized because they are not part of the dominant discourse in schools.

Focusing on concerns such as the limits of school reform without concomitant changes in educators' attitudes towards students and their families, and the crucial role of power relationships in schools may help rescue current reform efforts from simplistic technical responses to what are essentially moral and political dilemmas. That is, such technical changes as tinkering with the length of the school day, substituting one textbook for another, or adding curricular requirements may do little to change student outcomes unless these changes are part and parcel of a more comprehensive conceptualization of school reform. When such issues are considered fundamental to the changes that must be made in schools, we might more precisely speak about *transformation* rather than simply about reform. But educational transformation cannot take place without the inclusion of the voices of students, among others, in the dialogue.

WHY LISTEN TO STUDENTS?

One way to begin the process of changing school policies and practices is to listen to students' views about them; however, research that focuses on student voices is relatively recent and scarce. For example, student perspectives are for the most part missing in discussions concerning strategies for confronting educational problems. In addition, the voices of students are rarely heard in the debates about school failure and success, and the perspectives of students from disempowered and dominated communities are even more invisible. In this article, I will draw primarily on the words of students interviewed for a previous research study (Nieto, 1992). I used the interviews to develop case studies of young people from a wide variety of ethnic, racial, linguistic, and social-class

---

[3] "Critical thinking," as used here, is not meant in the sense that it has come to be used conventionally to imply, for example, higher order thinking skills in math and science as disconnected from a political awareness. Rather, it means developing, in the Freirian (1970) sense, a consciousness of oneself as a critical agent in learning and transforming one's reality.

6

backgrounds who were at the time students in junior or senior high school. These ten young people lived in communities as diverse as large urban areas and small rural hamlets, and belonged to families ranging from single-parent households to large, extended families. The one common element in all of their experiences turned out to be something we as researchers had neither planned nor expected: they were all successful students.[4]

The students were selected in a number of ways, but primarily through community contacts. Most were interviewed at home or in another setting of their choice outside of school. The only requirement that my colleagues and I determined for selecting students was that they reflect a variety of ethnic and racial backgrounds, in order to give us the diversity for which we were looking. The students selected self-identified as Black, African American, Mexican, Native American, Black and White American (biracial), Vietnamese, Jewish, Lebanese, Puerto Rican, and Cape Verdean. The one European American was the only student who had a hard time defining herself, other than as "American" (for a further analysis of this issue, see Nieto, 1992). That these particular students were academically successful was quite serendipitous. We defined them as such for the following reasons: they were all either still in school or just graduating; they all planned to complete at least high school, and most hoped to go to college; they had good grades, although they were not all at the top of their class; they had thought about their future and had made some plans for it; they generally enjoyed school and felt engaged in it (but they were also critical of their own school experiences and that of their peers, as we shall see); and most described themselves as successful. Although it had not been our initial intention to focus exclusively on academically successful students, on closer reflection it seemed logical that such students would be more likely to want to talk about their experiences than those who were not successful. It was at that point that I decided to explore what it was about these students' specific experiences that helped them succeed in school.

Therefore, the fact that these students saw themselves as successful helped further define the study, whose original purpose was to determine the benefits of multicultural education for students of diverse backgrounds. I was particularly interested in developing a way of looking at multicultural education that went beyond the typical "Holidays and Heroes" approach, which is too superficial to have any lasting impact in schools (Banks, 1991; Sleeter, 1991).[5] By exploring such issues as racism and low expectations of student achievement, as well as school policies and practices such as curriculum, pedagogy, testing, and tracking, I set about developing an understanding of multicultural education as anti-

---

[4] I was assisted in doing the interviews by a wonderful group of colleagues, most of whom contacted the students, interviewed them, and gave me much of the background information that helped me craft the case studies. I am grateful for the insights and help the following colleagues provided: Carlie Collins Tartakov, Paula Elliott, Haydée Font, Maya Gillingham, Mac Lee Morante, Diane Sweet, and Carol Shea.

[5] "Holidays and Heroes" refers to an approach in which multicultural education is understood as consisting primarily of ethnic celebrations and the acknowledgment of "great men" in the history of particular cultures. Deeper structures of cultures, including values and lifestyle differences, and an explicit emphasis on power differentials as they affect particular cultural groups, are not addressed in this approach. Thus, this approach is correctly perceived as one that tends to romanticize culture and treat it in an artificial way. In contrast, multicultural education as empowering and liberating pedagogy confronts such structural issues and power differentials quite directly.

racist, comprehensive, pervasive, and rooted in social justice. Students were interviewed to find out what it meant to be from a particular background, how this influenced their school experience, and what about that experience they would change if they could. Although they were not asked specifically about the policies and practices in their schools, they nevertheless reflected on them in their answers to questions ranging from identifying their favorite subjects to describing the importance of getting an education. In this article, I will revisit the interviews to focus on students' thoughts about a number of school policies and practices and on the effects of racism and other forms of discrimination on their education.

The insights provided by the students were far richer than we had first thought. Although we expected numerous criticisms of schools and some concrete suggestions, we were surprised at the depth of awareness and analysis the students shared with us. They had a lot to say about the teachers they liked, as well as those they disliked, and they were able to explain the differences between them; they talked about grades and how these had become overly important in determining curriculum and pedagogy; they discussed their parents' lack of involvement, in most cases, in traditional school activities such as P.T.O. membership and bake sales, but otherwise passionate support for their children's academic success; they mused about what schools could do to encourage more students to learn; they spoke with feeling about their cultures, languages, and communities, and what schools could do to capitalize on these factors; and they gave us concrete suggestions for improving schools for young people of all backgrounds. This experience confirmed my belief that educators can benefit from hearing students' critical perspectives, which might cause them to modify how they approach curriculum, pedagogy, and other school practices. Since doing this research, I have come across other studies that also focus on young people's perspectives and provide additional powerful examples of the lessons we can learn from them. This article thus begins with "lessons from students," an approach that takes the perspective proposed by Paulo Freire, that teachers need to become students just as students need to become teachers in order for education to become reciprocal and empowering for both (Freire, 1970).

This focus on students is not meant to suggest that their ideas should be the final and conclusive word in how schools need to change. Nobody has all the answers, and suggesting that students' views should be adopted wholesale is to accept a romantic view of students that is just as partial and condescending as excluding them completely from the discussion. I am instead suggesting that if we believe schools must provide an equal and quality education for all, students need to be included in the dialogue, and that their views, just as those of others, should be problematized and used to reflect critically on school reform.

SELECTED POLICIES AND PRACTICES AND STUDENTS' VIEWS ABOUT THEM

School policies and practices need to be understood within the sociopolitical context of our society in general, rather than simply within individual schools' or teachers' attitudes and practices. This is important to remember for a number of reasons. First, although "teacher bashing" provides an easy target for complex problems, it fails to take into account the fact that teachers function within particular societal and institutional structures. In addition, it results in placing an inordinate amount of blame on some of those who care most deeply about students and who struggle every day to help them learn. That some teachers are racist, classist, and mean-spirited and that others have lost all creativity and caring is not in question here, and I begin with the assumption that the majority of teachers are not consciously so. I do suggest, however, that although many teachers are hardworking, supportive of their students, and talented educators, many of these same teachers are also burned out, frustrated, and negatively influenced by societal views about the students they teach. Teachers could benefit from knowing more about their students' families and experiences, as well as about students' views on school and how it could be improved.

How do students feel about the curriculum they must learn? What do they think about the pedagogical strategies their teachers use? Is student involvement a meaningful issue for them? Are their own identities important considerations in how they view school? What about tracking and testing and disciplinary policies? These are crucial questions to consider when reflecting on what teachers and schools can learn from students, but we know very little about students' responses. When asked, students seem surprised and excited about being included in the conversation, and what they have to say is often compelling and eloquent. In fact, Patricia Phelan, Ann Locke Davidson, and Hanh Thanh Cao (1992), in a two-year research project designed to identify students' thoughts about school, discovered that students' views on teaching and learning were remarkably consistent with those of current theorists concerned with learning theory, cognitive science, and the sociology of work. This should come as no surprise when we consider that students spend more time in schools than anybody else except teachers (who are also omitted in most discussions of school reform, but that is a topic for another article). In the following sections, I will focus on students' perceptions concerning the curriculum, pedagogy, tracking, and grades in their schools. I will also discuss their attitudes about racism and other biases, how these are manifested in their schools and classrooms, and what effect they may have on students' learning and participation in school.

Curriculum

The curriculum in schools is at odds with the experiences, backgrounds, hopes, and wishes of many students. This is true of both the tangible curriculum as expressed through books, other materials, and the actual written curriculum guides, as well as in the less tangible and "hidden" curriculum as seen in the bulletin boards, extracurricular activities, and messages given to students about their abilities and talents. For instance, Christine Sleeter and Carl Grant (1991) found that a third of the students in a desegregated junior high school they studied said that *none* of the class content related to their lives outside class. Those who indicated some relevancy cited only current events, oral history, money and banking, and multicultural content (because it dealt with prejudice) as being relevant. The same was true in a study by Mary Poplin and Joseph Weeres (1992), who found that students frequently reported being bored in school and seeing little relevance in what was taught for their lives or their futures. The authors concluded that students became more disengaged as the curriculum, texts, and assignments became more standardized. Thus, in contrast to Ira Shor's (1992) suggestion that "What students bring to class is where learning begins. It starts there and goes places" (p. 44), there is often a tremendous mismatch between students' cultures and the culture of the school. In many schools, learning starts not with what students bring to class, but with what is considered high-status knowledge; that is, the "canon," with its overemphasis on European and European American history, arts, and values. This seldom includes the backgrounds, experiences, and talents of the majority of students in U.S. schools. Rather than "going elsewhere," their learning therefore often goes nowhere.

That students' backgrounds and experiences are missing in many schools is particularly evident where the native language of most of the students is not English. In such settings, it is not unusual to see little or no representation of those students' language in the curriculum. In fact, there is often an insistence that students "speak only English" in these schools, which sends a powerful message to young people struggling to maintain an identity in the face of overpowering messages that they must assimilate. This was certainly the case for Marisol, a Puerto Rican girl of sixteen participating in my research, who said:

> I used to have a lot of problems with one of my teachers 'cause she didn't want us to talk Spanish in class and I thought that was like an insult to us, you know? Just telling us not to talk Spanish, 'cause they were Puerto Ricans and, you know, we're free to talk whatever we want, . . . I could never stay quiet and talk only English, 'cause sometimes . . . words slip in Spanish. You know, I think they should understand that.

Practices such as not allowing students to speak their native tongue are certain to influence negatively students' identities and their views of what constitutes important knowledge. For example, when asked if she would be interested in taking a course on Puerto Rican history, Marisol was quick to answer: "I don't think [it's] important. . . . I'm proud of myself and my culture, but I think I know what I should know about the culture already, so I wouldn't take the course." Ironically, it was evident to me after speaking with her on several occasions that Marisol knew virtually nothing about Puerto Rican history. However, she had already learned another lesson well: given what she said about the courses she needed to take, she made it clear that "important" history is U.S. history, which rarely includes anything about Puerto Rico.

Messages about culture and language and how they are valued or devalued in society are communicated not only or even primarily by schools, but by the media and community as a whole. The sociopolitical context of the particular city where Marisol lived, and of its school system, is important to understand: there had been an attempt to pass an ordinance restricting the number of Puerto Ricans coming into town based on the argument that they placed an undue burden on the welfare rolls and other social services. In addition, the "English Only" debate had become an issue when the mayor had ordered all municipal workers to speak only English on the job. Furthermore, although the school system had a student body that was 65 percent Puerto Rican, there was only a one-semester course on Puerto Rican history that had just recently been approved for the bilingual program. In contrast, there were two courses, which although rarely taught were on the books, that focused on apartheid and the Holocaust, despite the fact that both the African American and Jewish communities in the town were quite small. That such courses should be part of a comprehensive multicultural program is not being questioned; however, it is ironic that the largest population in the school was ignored in the general curriculum.

In a similar vein, Nancy Commins's (1989) research with four first-generation Mexican American fifth-grade students focused on how these students made decisions about their education, both consciously and unconsciously, based on their determination of what counted as important knowledge. Her research suggests that the classroom setting and curriculum can support or hinder students' perceptions of themselves as learners based on the languages they speak and their cultural backgrounds. She found that although the homes of these four students provided rich environments for a variety of language uses and literacy, the school did little to capitalize on these strengths. In their classroom, for instance, these children rarely used Spanish, commenting that it was the language of the "dumb kids." As a result, Commins states: "Their reluctance to use Spanish in an academic context also limited their opportunities to practice talking about abstract ideas and to use higher level cognitive skills in Spanish" (p. 35). She also found that the content of the curriculum was almost completely divorced from the experiences of these youngsters, since the problems of poverty, racism, and discrimination, which were prominent in their lives, were not addressed in the curriculum.

In spite of teachers' reluctance to address such concerns, they are often compelling to students, particularly those who are otherwise invisible in the curriculum. Vinh, an 18-year-old Vietnamese student attending a high school in a culturally heterogeneous town, lived with his uncle and younger brothers and sisters. Although grateful for the education he was receiving, Vinh expressed concern about what he saw as insensitivity on the part of some of his teachers to the difficulties of adjusting to a new culture and learning English:

> [Teachers] have to know about our culture. . . . From the second language, it is very difficult for me and for other people.

Vinh's concern was echoed by Manuel, a nineteen-year-old Cape Verdean senior who, at the time of the interviews, was just getting ready to graduate, the first in his family of eleven children to do so:

> I was kind of afraid of school, you know, 'cause it's different when you're learning the language. . . . It's kind of scary at first, especially if you don't know the language and like if you don't have friends here.

In Manuel's case, the Cape Verdean Crioulo bilingual program served as a linguistic and cultural mediator, negotiating difficult experiences that he faced in school so that, by the time he reached high school, he had learned enough English to "speak up." Another positive curricular experience was the theater workshop he took as a sophomore. There, students created and acted in skits focusing on their lived experiences. He recalled with great enthusiasm, for example, a monologue he did about a student going to a new school, because it was based on his personal experience.

Sometimes a school's curriculum is unconsciously disrespectful of students' cultures and experiences. James, a student who proudly identified himself as Lebanese American, found that he was invisible in the curriculum, even in supposedly multicultural curricular and extracurricular activities. He mentioned a language fair, a multicultural festival, and a school cookbook, all of which omitted references to the Arabic language and to Lebanese people. About the cookbook, he said:

> They made this cookbook of all these different recipes from all over the world. And I would've brought in some Lebanese recipes if somebody'd let me know. And I didn't hear about it until the week before they started selling them. . . . I asked one of the teachers to look at it and there was nothing Lebanese in there.

James made an effort to dismiss this oversight, and although he said that it didn't matter, he seemed to be struggling with the growing realization that it mattered very much indeed:

> I don't know, I guess there's not that many Lebanese people in . . . I don't know; you don't hear really that much . . . Well, you hear it in the news a lot, but I mean, I don't know, there's not a lot of Lebanese kids in our school. . . . I don't mind, 'cause I mean, I don't know, just I don't mind it. . . . It's not really important. It *is* important for me. It would be important for me to see a Lebanese flag.

Lebanese people were mentioned in the media, although usually in negative ways, and these were the only images of James's ethnic group that made their way into the school. He spoke, for example, about how the Lebanese were characterized by his peers:

> Some people call me, you know, 'cause I'm Lebanese, so people say, "Look out for the terrorist! Don't mess with him or he'll blow up your house!" or some stuff like that. . . . But they're just joking around, though. . . . I don't think anybody's serious 'cause I wouldn't blow up anybody's house — and they know that. . . . I don't care. It doesn't matter what people say. . . . I just want everybody to know that, you know, it's not true.

Cultural ambivalence, both pride and shame, were evident in the responses of many of the students. Although almost all of them were quite clear that their culture was important to them, they were also confronted with debilitating messages about it from society in general. How to make sense of these contradictions was a dilemma for many of these young people.

Fern, who identified herself as Native American, was, at thirteen, one of the youngest students interviewed. She reflected on the constant challenges she faced in the history curriculum in her junior high school. Her father was active in their school and community and he gave her a great deal of support for defending her position, but she was the only Native American student in her entire school in this mid-size city in Iowa. She said:

> If there's something in the history book that's wrong, my dad always taught me that if it's wrong, I should tell them that it is wrong. And the only time I ever do is if I

know it's *exactly* wrong. Like we were reading about Native Americans and scalping. Well, the French are really the ones that made them do it so they could get money. And my teacher would not believe me. I finally just shut up because he just would not believe me.

Fern also mentioned that her sister had come home angry one day because somebody in school had said "Geronimo was a stupid chief riding that stupid horse." The connection between an unresponsive curriculum and dropping out of school was not lost on Fern, and she talked about this incident as she wondered aloud why other Native Americans had dropped out of the town's schools. Similar sentiments were reported by students in Virginia Vogel Zanger's (1994) study of twenty Latinos from a Boston high school who took part in a panel discussion in which they reflected on their experiences in school. Some of the students who decided to stay in school claimed that dropping out among their peers was a direct consequence of the school's attempts to "monoculture" them.

Fern was self-confident and strong in expressing her views, despite her young age. Yet she too was silenced by the way the curriculum was presented in class. This is because schools often avoid bringing up difficult, contentious, or conflicting issues in the curriculum, especially when these contradict the sanctioned views of the standard curriculum, resulting in what Michelle Fine has called "silencing." According to Fine: "Silencing is about who can speak, what can and cannot be spoken, and whose discourse must be controlled" (1991, p. 33). Two topics in particular that appear to have great saliency for many students, regardless of their backgrounds, are bias and discrimination, yet these are among the issues most avoided in classrooms. Perhaps this is because the majority of teachers are European Americans who are unaccustomed, afraid, or uncomfortable in discussing these issues (Sleeter, 1994); perhaps it is due to the pressure teachers feel to "cover the material"; maybe it has to do with the tradition of presenting information in schools as if it were free of conflict and controversy (Kohl, 1993); or, most likely, it is a combination of all these things. In any event, both students and teachers soon pick up the message that racism, discrimination, and other dangerous topics are not supposed to be discussed in school. We also need to keep in mind that these issues have disparate meanings for people of different backgrounds, and are often perceived as particularly threatening to those from dominant cultural and racial groups. Deidre, one of the young African American women in Fine's 1991 study of an urban high school, explained it this way: "White people might feel like everything's over and OK, but we remember" (p. 33).

Another reason that teachers may avoid bringing up potentially contentious issues in the curriculum is their feeling that doing so may create or exacerbate animosity and hostility among students. They may even believe, as did the reading teacher in Jonathan Kozol's 1967 classic book on the Boston Public Schools, *Death at an Early Age,* that discussing slavery in the context of U.S. history was just too complicated for children to understand, not to mention uncomfortable for teachers to explain. Kozol writes of the reading teacher:

She said, with the very opposite of malice but only with an expression of the most intense and honest affection for the children in the class: "I don't want these children to have to think back on this year later on and to have to remember that we were the ones who told them they were Negro. (p. 68)

More than a quarter of a century later, the same kinds of disclaimers are being made for the failure to include in the curriculum the very issues that would engage students in learning. Fine (1991) found that although over half of the students in the urban high school she interviewed described experiences with racism, teachers were reluctant to discuss it in class, explaining, in the words of one teacher, "It would demoralize the students, they need to feel positive and optimistic — like they have a chance. Racism is just an excuse they use to not try harder" (p. 37). Some of these concerns may be sincere expressions of protectiveness towards students, but others are merely self-serving and manifest teachers' discomfort with discussing racism.

The few relevant studies I have found concerning the inclusion of issues of racism and discrimination in the curriculum suggest that discussions about these topics can be immensely constructive if they are approached with sensitivity and understanding. This was the case in Melinda Fine's description of the "Facing History and Ourselves" (FHAO) curriculum, a project that started in the Brookline (Massachusetts) Public Schools almost two decades ago (Fine, 1993). FHAO provides a model for teaching history that encourages students to reflect critically on a variety of contemporary social, moral, and political issues. Using the Holocaust as a case study, students learn to think critically about such issues as scapegoating, racism, and personal and collective responsibility. Fine suggests that moral dilemmas do not disappear simply because teachers refuse to bring them into the schools. On the contrary, when these realities are separated from the curriculum, young people learn that school knowledge is unrelated to their lives, and once again, they are poorly prepared to face the challenges that society has in store for them.

A good case in point is Vanessa, a young European American woman in my study who was intrigued by "difference" yet was uncomfortable and reluctant to discuss it; although she was active in a peer education group that focused on such concerns as peer pressure, discrimination, and exclusion, these were rarely discussed in the formal curriculum. Vanessa, therefore, had no language with which to talk about these issues. In thinking about U.S. history, she mused about some of the contradictions that were rarely addressed in school:

> It seems weird . . . because people came from Europe and they wanted to get away from all the stuff that was over there. And then they came here and set up all the stuff like slavery, and I don't know, it seems the opposite of what they would have done.

The curriculum, then, can act to either enable or handicap students in their learning. Given the kind of curriculum that draws on their experiences and energizes them because it focuses precisely on those things that are most important in their lives, students can either soar or sink in our schools. Curriculum can provide what María Torres-Guzmán (1992) refers to as "cognitive empowerment," encouraging students to become confident, active critical thinkers who learn that their background experiences are important tools for further learning. The connection of the curriculum to real life and their future was mentioned by several of the students interviewed in my study. Avi, a Jewish boy of sixteen who often felt a schism between his school and home lives, for instance, spoke about the importance of school: "If you don't go to school, then you can't learn about life, or you can't learn about things that you need to progress [in] your life." And Vanessa, who seemed to yearn for a more socially conscious curriculum in her school, summed up why education was important to her: "A good education is like when you personally learn something . . . like growing, expanding your mind and your views."

Pedagogy

If curriculum is primarily the *what* of education, then pedagogy concerns the *why* and *how*. No matter how interesting and relevant the curriculum may be, the way in which it is presented is what will make it engaging or dull to students. Students' views echo those of educational researchers who have found that teaching methods in most classrooms, and particularly those in secondary schools, vary little from traditional "chalk and talk" methods; that textbooks are the dominant teaching materials used; that routine and rote learning are generally favored over creativity and critical thinking; and that teacher-centered transmission models prevail (Cummins, 1994; Goodlad, 1984; McNeil, 1986). Martin Haberman is especially critical of what he calls "the pedagogy of poverty," that is, a basic urban pedagogy used with children who live in poverty and which consists primarily of giving instructions, asking questions, giving directions, making assignments, and monitoring seat work. Such pedagogy is based on the assumption that before students can be engaged in creative or critical work, they must first master "the basics." Nevertheless, Haberman asserts that this pedagogy does not work and, furthermore, that it actually gets in the way of real teaching and learning. He suggests instead that we look at exemplary pedagogy in urban schools that actively involves students in real-life situations, which allows them to reflect on their own lives. He finds that good teaching is taking place when teachers welcome difficult issues and events and use human difference as the basis for the curriculum; design collaborative activities for heterogeneous groups; and help students apply ideals of fairness, equity, and justice to their world (Haberman, 1991).

Students in my study had more to say about pedagogy than about anything else, and they were especially critical of the lack of imagination that led to boring classes. Linda, who was just graduating as the valedictorian of her class in an urban high school, is a case in point. Her academic experiences had not always been smooth sailing. For example, she had failed both seventh and eighth grade twice, for a combination of reasons, including academic and medical problems. Consequently, she had experienced both exhilarating and devastating educational experiences. Linda had this to say about pedagogy:

> I think you have to be creative to be a teacher; you have to make it interesting. You can't just go in and say, "Yeah, I'm going to teach the kids just that; I'm gonna teach them right out of the book and that's the way it is, and don't ask questions." Because I know there were plenty of classes where I lost complete interest. But those were all because the teachers just, "Open the books to this page." They never made up problems out of their head. Everything came out of the book. You didn't ask

questions. If you asked them questions, then the answer was "in the book." And if you asked the question and the answer *wasn't* in the book, then you shouldn't have asked that question!

Rich, a young Black man, planned to attend pharmacy school after graduation, primarily because of the interest he had developed in chemistry. He too talked about the importance of making classes "interesting":

> I believe a teacher, by the way he introduces different things to you, can make a class interesting. Not like a normal teacher that gets up, gives you a lecture, or there's teachers that just pass out the work, you do the work, pass it in, get a grade, good-bye!

Students were especially critical of teachers' reliance on textbooks and blackboards, a sad indictment of much of the teaching that encourages student passivity. Avi, for instance, felt that some teachers get along better when they teach from the point of view of the students: "They don't just come out and say, 'All right, do this, blah, blah, blah.' . . . They're not so *one-tone voice.*" Yolanda said that her English teacher didn't get along with the students. In her words, "She just does the things and sits down." James mentioned that some teachers just don't seem to care: "They just teach the stuff. 'Here,' write a couple of things on the board, 'see, that's how you do it. Go ahead, page 25.' " And Vinh added his voice to those of the students who clearly saw the connection between pedagogy and caring: "Some teachers, they just go inside and go to the blackboard. . . . They don't care."

Students did more than criticize teachers' pedagogy, however; they also praised teachers who were interesting, creative, and caring. Linda, in a particularly moving testimony to her first-grade teacher, whom she called her mentor, mentioned that she would be "following in her footsteps" and studying elementary education. She added:

> She's always been there for me. After the first or second grade, if I had a problem, I could always go back to her. Through the whole rest of my life, I've been able to go back and talk to her. . . . She's a Golden Apple Award winner, which is a very high award for elementary school teachers. . . . She keeps me on my toes. . . . When I start getting down . . . she peps me back up and I get on my feet.

Vinh talked with feeling about teachers who allowed him to speak Vietnamese with other students in class. Vinh loved working in groups. He particularly remembered a teacher who always asked students to discuss important issues, rather than focusing only on learning what he called "the word's meaning" by writing and memorizing lists of words. The important issues concerned U.S. history, the students' histories and cultures, and other engaging topics that were central to their lives. Students' preference for group work has been mentioned by other educators as well. Phelan et al. (1992), in their research on students' perspectives concerning school, found that both high- and low-achieving students of all backgrounds expressed a strong preference for working in groups because it helped them generate ideas and participate actively in class.

James also appreciated teachers who explained things and let everybody ask questions because, as he said, "There could be someone sitting in the back of the class that has the same question you have. Might as well bring it out." Fern contrasted classes where she felt like falling asleep because they're just "blah," to chorus, where the teacher used a "rap song" to teach history and involve all the students. And Avi, who liked most of his teachers, singled out a particular math teacher he had had in ninth grade for praise:

> 'Cause I never really did good in math until I had him. And he showed me that it wasn't so bad, and after that I've been doing pretty good in math and I enjoy it.

Yolanda had been particularly fortunate to have many teachers she felt understood and supported her, whether they commented on her bilingual ability, or referred to her membership in a folkloric Mexican dance group, or simply talked with her and the other students about their lives. She added:

> I really got along with the teachers a lot. . . . Actually, 'cause I had some teachers, and they were always calling my mom, like I did a great job. Or they would start talking to me, or they kinda like pulled me up some grades, or moved me to other classes, or took me somewhere. And they were always congratulating me.

Such support, however, rarely represented only individual effort on the part of some teachers, but rather was often manifested by the school as a whole; that is, it was integral to the school's practices and policies. For instance, Yolanda had recently been selected "Student of the Month" and her picture had been prominently displayed in her school's main hall. In addition, she received a certificate and was taken out to dinner by the principal. Although Linda's first-grade teacher was her special favorite, she had others who also created an educational context in which all students felt welcomed and connected. The entire Tremont Elementary School had been special for Linda, and thus the context of the school, including its leadership and commitment, were the major ingredients that made it successful:

> All of my teachers were wonderful. I don't think there's a teacher at the whole Tremont School that I didn't like. . . . It's just a feeling you have. You know that they really care for you. You just know it; you can tell. Teachers who don't have you in any of their classes or haven't ever had you, they still know who you are. . . . The Tremont School in itself is a community. . . . I love that school! I want to teach there.

Vanessa talked about how teachers used their students' lives and experiences in their teaching. For her, this made them especially good teachers:

> [Most teachers] are really caring and supportive and are willing to share their lives and are willing to listen to mine. They don't just want to talk about what they're teaching you; they also want to know you.

Aside from criticism and praise, students in this study also offered their teachers many thoughtful suggestions for making their classrooms more engaging places. Rich, for instance, said that he would "put more activities into the day that can make it interesting." Fern recommended that teachers involve students more actively in learning: "More like making the whole class be involved, not making only the two smartest people up here do the whole work for the whole class." Vanessa added, "You could have games that could teach anything that they're trying to teach through notes or lectures." She suggested that in learning Spanish, for instance, students could act out the words, making them easier to remember. She also thought that other books should be required "just to show some points of view," a response no doubt to the bland quality of so many of the textbooks and other teaching materials available in schools. Avi thought that teachers who make themselves available to students ("You know, I'm here after school. Come and get help.") were most helpful.

Vinh was very specific in his suggestions, and he touched on important cultural issues. Because he came from Vietnam when he was fifteen, learning English was a difficult challenge for Vinh, and he tended to be very hard on himself, saying such things as "I'm not really good, but I'm trying" when asked to describe himself as a student. Although he had considered himself smart in Vietnam, he felt that because his English was not perfect, he wasn't smart anymore. His teachers often showered him with praise for his efforts, but Vinh criticized this approach:

> Sometimes, the English teachers, they don't understand about us. Because something we not do good, like my English is not good. And she say, "Oh, your English is great!" But that's the way the American culture is. But my culture is not like that. . . . If my English is not good, she has to say, "Your English is not good. So you have to go home and study." And she tell me what to study and how to study and get better. But some Americans, you know, they don't understand about myself. So they just say, "Oh! You're doing a good job! You're doing great! Everything is great!" Teachers talk like that, but my culture is different. . . . They say, "You have to do better."

This is an important lesson not only because it challenges the overuse of praise, a practice among those that María de la Luz Reyes (1992) has called "venerable assumptions," but also because it cautions teachers to take into account both cultural and individual differences. In this case, the practice of praising was perceived by Vinh as hollow, and therefore insincere. Linda referred to the lesson she learned when she failed seventh and eighth grade and "blew two years":

> I learned a lot from it. As a matter of fact, one of my college essays was on the fact that from that experience, I learned that I don't need to hear other people's praise to get by. . . . All I need to know is in here [pointing to her heart] whether I tried or not.

Students have important messages for teachers about what works and what doesn't. It is important, however, not to fall back on what Lilia Bartolomé (1994) has aptly termed the "methods fetish," that is, a simplistic belief that particular methods will automatically resolve complex problems of underachievement. According to Bartolomé, such a myopic approach results in teachers avoiding the central issue of why some students succeed and others fail in school and how political inequality is at the heart of this dilemma. Rather than using this or that method, Bartolomé suggests that teachers develop what she calls a "humanizing pedagogy" in which students' languages and cultures are central. There is also the problem that Reyes (1992) has called a "one-size-fits all" approach, where students' cultural and other differences may be denied even if teachers' methods are based on well-meaning and progressive pedagogy. The point here is that no method can become a sacred cow uncritically accepted and used simply because it is the latest fad. It is probably fair to say that teachers who use more traditional methods but care about their students and believe they deserve the chance to dream may have more of a positive effect than those who know the latest methods but do not share these beliefs. Students need more than such innovations as heterogeneous grouping, peer tutoring, or cooperative groups. Although these may in fact be excellent and effective teaching methods, they will do little by themselves unless accompanied by changes in teachers' attitudes and behaviors.

The students quoted above are not looking for one magic solution or method. In fact, they have many, sometimes contradictory, suggestions to make about pedagogy. While rarely speaking with one voice, they nevertheless have similar overriding concerns: too many classrooms are boring, alienating, and disempowering. There is a complex interplay of policies, practices, and attitudes that cause such pedagogy to continue. Tracking and testing are two powerful forces implicated in this interplay.

Tracking/Ability Grouping/Grades and Expectations of Student Achievement

> It is not low income that matters but low status. And status is always created and imposed by the ones on top. (Stein, 1971, p. 158)

status

In her 1971 article, Annie Stein cited a New York City study in which kindergarten teachers were asked to list in order of importance the things a child should learn in order to prepare for first grade. Their responses were coded according to whether they were primarily socialization or educational goals. In the schools with large Puerto Rican and African American student populations, the socialization goals were always predominant; in the mixed schools, the educational goals were first. Concluded Stein, "In fact, in a list of six or seven goals, several teachers in the minority-group kindergartens forgot to mention any educational goals at all" (p. 167). A kind of tracking, in which students' educational goals were being sacrificed for social aims, was taking place in these schools, and its effects were already evident in kindergarten.

Most recent research on tracking has found it to be problematic, especially among middle- and low-achieving students, and suggestions for detracking schools have gained growing support (Oakes, 1992; Wheelock, 1992). Nevertheless, although many tracking decisions are made on the most tenuous grounds, they are supported by ideological norms in our society about the nature of intelligence and the distribution of ability. The long-term effects of ability grouping can be devastating for the life chances of young people. John Goodlad (1984) found that first- or second-grade children tracked by teachers' judgments of their reading and math ability or by testing are likely to remain in their assigned track _for the rest of their schooling_. In addition, he found that poor children and children of color are more likely to face the negative effects of tracking than are other youngsters. For example, a recent research project by Hugh Mehan and Irene Villanueva (1993) found that when low-achieving high school students are detracked, they tend to benefit academically. The study focused on low-achieving students in the San Diego City Schools. When these students, mostly Latinos and African Americans, were removed from a low track and placed in college-bound courses with high-achieving students, they benefitted in a number of ways, including significantly higher college enrollment. The researchers concluded that a rigorous academic program serves the educational and social interests of such students more effectively than remedial and compensatory programs.

Most of the young people in my study did not mention tracking or ability grouping by name, but almost all referred to it circuitously, and usually in negative ways. Although by and large academically successful themselves, they were quick to point out that teachers' expectations often doomed their peers to failure. Yolanda, for instance, when asked what suggestions she would give teachers. said, "I'd say to teachers, 'Get along more with the kids that are not really into themselves. . . . Have more communication with them.' " When asked what she would like teachers to know about other Mexican American students, she quickly said, "They try real hard, that's one thing I know." She also criticized teachers for having low expectations of students, claiming that materials used in the classes were "too low." She added, "We are supposed to be doing higher things. And like they take us too slow, see, step by step. And that's why everybody takes it as a joke." Fern, although she enjoyed being at the "top of my class," did not like to be treated differently. She spoke about a school she attended previously where "you were all the same and you all got pushed the same and you were all helped the same. And one thing I've noticed in Springdale is they kind of teach 25 percent and they kinda leave 75 percent out." She added that, if students were receiving bad grades, teachers did not help them as much: "In Springdale, I've noticed if you're getting D's and F's, they don't look up to you; they look down. And you're always the last on the list for special activities, you know?"

These young people also referred to expectations teachers had of students based on cultural or class differences. Vanessa said that some teachers based their expectations of students on bad reputations, and found least helpful those teachers who "kind of just move really fast, just trying to get across to you what they're trying to teach you. Not willing to slow down because they need to get in what they want to get in." Rich, who attended a predominately Black school, felt that some teachers there did not expect as much as they should from the Black students: "Many of the White teachers there don't push. . . . Their expectations don't seem to be as high as they should be. . . . I know that some Black teachers, their expectations are higher than White teachers. . . . They just do it, because they know how it was for them. . . . Actually, I'd say, you have to be in Black shoes to know how it is." Little did Rich know that he was reaching the same conclusion as a major research study on fostering high achievement for African American students. In this study, Janine Bempechat determined that "across all schools, it seems that achievement is fostered by high expectations and standards" (Bempechat, 1992, p. 43).

Virginia Vogel Zanger's research with Latino and Latina students in a Boston high school focused on what can be called "social tracking." Although the students she interviewed were high-achieving and tracked in a college-bound course, they too felt the sting of alienation. In a linguistic analysis of their comments, she found that students conveyed a strong sense of marginalization, using terms such as "left out," "below," "under," and "not joined in" to reflect their feelings about school (Zanger, 1994). Although these were clearly academically successful students, they perceived tracking in the subordinate status they were assigned based on their cultural backgrounds and on the racist climate established in the school. Similarly, in a study on dropping out among Puerto Rican students, my colleague Manuel Frau-Ramos and I found some of the same kind of language. José, who had dropped out in eleventh grade, explained, "I was alone. . . . I was an outsider" (Frau-Ramos & Nieto, 1993, p. 156). Pedro, a young man who had actually graduated, nevertheless felt the same kind of alienation. When asked what the school could do to help Puerto Ricans stay in school, he said, *"Hacer algo para que los boricuas no se sientan aparte"* (Do something so that the Puerto Ricans wouldn't feel so separate) (p. 157).

Grading policies have also been mentioned in relation to tracking and expectations of achievement. One study, for example, found that when teachers de-emphasized grades and standardized testing, the status of their African American and White students became more equal, and White students made more cross-race friendship choices (Hallinan & Teixeira, 1987). In my own research, I found a somewhat surprising revelation: although the students were achieving successfully in school, most did not feel that grades were very helpful. Of course, for the most part they enjoyed receiving good grades, but it was not always for the expected reason. Fern, for instance, wanted good grades because they were one guarantee that teachers would pay attention to her. Marisol talked about the "nice report cards" that she and her siblings in this family of eight children received, and said, "and, usually, we do this for my mother. We like to see her the way she wants to be, you know, to see her happy."

But they were also quick to downplay the importance of grades. Linda, for instance, gave as an example her computer teacher, who she felt had been the least helpful in her high school:

> I have no idea about computer literacy. I got A's in that course. Just because he saw that I had A's, and that my name was all around the school for all the "wonderful things" I do, he just automatically assumed. He didn't really pay attention to who I was. The grade I think I deserved in that class was at least a C, but I got A just because everybody else gave me A's. . . . He didn't help me at all because he didn't challenge me.

She added,

> To me, they're just something on a piece of paper. . . . [My parents] feel just about the same way. If they ask me, "Honestly, did you try your best?" and I tell them yes, then they'll look at the grades and say okay.

Rich stated that, although grades were important to his mother, "I'm comfortable setting my own standards." James said, without arrogance, that he was "probably the smartest kid in my class." Learning was important to him and, unlike other students who also did the assignments, he liked to "really get into the work and stuff." He added,

> If you don't get involved with it, even if you do get, if you get perfect scores and stuff . . . it's not like really gonna sink in. . . . You can memorize the words, you know, on a test . . . but you know, if you memorize them, it's not going to do you any good. You have to *learn* them, you know?

Most of the students made similar comments, and their perceptions challenge schools to think more deeply about the real meaning of education. Linda was not alone when she said that the reason for going to school was to "make yourself a better person." She loved learning, and commented that "I just want to keep continuously learning, because when you stop learning, then you start dying." Yolanda used the metaphor of nutrition to talk about learning: "[Education] is good for you. . . . It's like when you eat. It's like if you don't eat in a whole day, you feel weird. That's the same thing for me." Vanessa, also an enthusiastic student, spoke pensively about success and happiness: "I'm happy. Success is being happy to me, it's not like having a job that gives you a zillion dollars. It's just having self-happiness."

Finally, Vinh spoke extensively about the meaning of education, contrasting the difference between what he felt it meant in the United States and what it meant in his home culture:

> In Vietnam, we go to school because we want to become educated people. But in the United States, most people, they say, "Oh, we go to school because we want to get a good job." But my idea, I don't think so. I say, if we go to school, we want a good job *also,* but we want to become a good person.
>
> [Grades] are not important to me. Important to me is education. . . . I not so concerned about [test scores] very much. . . . I just know I do my exam very good. But I don't need to know I got A or B. I have to learn more and more.
>
> Some people, they got a good education. They go to school, they got master's, they got doctorate, but they're just helping *themselves.* So that's not good. I don't care much about money. So, I just want to have a normal job that I can take care of myself and my family. So that's enough. I don't want to climb up compared to other people.

RACISM AND DISCRIMINATION

> The facts are clear to behold, but the BIG LIE of racism blinds all but its victims. (Stein, 1971, p. 179)

An increasing number of formal research studies, as well as informal accounts and anecdotes, attest to the lasting legacy of various forms of institutional discrimination in the schools based on race, ethnicity, religion, gender, social class, language, and sexual orientation. Yet, as Annie Stein wrote in 1971, these are rarely addressed directly. The major reason for this may be that institutional discrimination flies in the face of our stated ideals of justice and fair play and of the philosophy that individual hard work is the road to success. Beverly Daniel Tatum, in discussing the myth of meritocracy, explains why racism is so often denied, downplayed, or dismissed: "An understanding of racism as a system of advantage presents a serious challenge to the notion of the United States as a just society where rewards are based solely on one's merits" (Tatum, 1992, p. 6).

Recent studies point out numerous ways in which racism and other forms of discrimination affect students and their learning. For instance, Angela Taylor found that, to the extent that teachers harbor negative racial stereotypes, the African American child's race *alone* is probably sufficient to place him or her at risk for negative school outcomes (Taylor, 1991). Many teachers, of course, see it differently, preferring to think instead that students' lack of academic achievement is due solely to conditions inside their homes or communities. But the occurrence of discriminatory actions in schools, both by other students and by teachers and other staff, has been widely documented. A 1990 study of Boston high school students found that while 57 percent had witnessed a racial attack and 47 percent would either join in or feel that the group being attacked deserved it, only a quarter of those interviewed said they would report a racial incident to school officials (Ribadeneira, 1990). It should not be surprising, then, that in a report about immigrant students in California, most believed that Americans felt negatively and unwelcoming toward them. In fact, almost every immigrant student interviewed reported that they had at one time or another been spat upon, and tricked, teased, and laughed at because of their race, accent, or the way they dressed. More than half also indicated that they had been the victims of teachers' prejudice, citing instances where they were punished, publicly embarrassed, or made fun of because of improper use of English. They also reported that teachers had made derogatory comments about immigrant groups in front of the class, or had avoided particular students because of the language difficulty (Olsen, 1988). Most of the middle and high school students interviewed by Mary Poplin and Joseph Weeres (1992) had also witnessed incidents of racism in school. In Karen Donaldson's study in an urban high school where students used the racism they experienced as the content of a peer education program, over 80 percent of students surveyed said that they had perceived racism to exist in school (Donaldson, 1994).

Marietta Saravia-Shore and Herminio Martínez found similar results in their ethnographic study of Puerto Rican young people who had dropped out of school and were currently participating in an alternative high school program. These adolescents felt that their former teachers were, in their words, "against Puerto Ricans and Blacks" and had openly discriminated against them. One reported that a teacher had said, "Do you want to be like the other Puerto Rican women who never got an education? Do you want to be like the rest of your family and never go to school?" (Saravia-Shore & Martínez, 1992, p. 242). In Virginia Vogel Zanger's study of high-achieving Latino and Latina Boston high school students, one young man described his shock when his teacher called him "spic" right in class; although the teacher was later suspended, this incident had left its mark on him (Zanger, 1994). Unfortunately, incidents such as these are more frequent than schools care to admit or acknowledge. Students, however, seem eager to address these issues, but are rarely given a forum in which such discussions can take place.

How do students feel about the racism and other aspects of discrimination that they see around them and experience? What effect does it have on them? In interviews with students, Karen Donaldson found three major ways in which they said they were affected: White students experienced guilt and embarrassment when they became aware of the racism to which their peers were subjected; students of color sometimes felt they needed to overcompensate and overachieve to prove they were equal to their White classmates; and students of color also mentioned that discrimination had a negative impact on their self-esteem (Donaldson, forthcoming). The issue of self-esteem is a complicated one and may include many variables. Children's self-esteem does not come fully formed out of the blue, but is *created* within particular contexts and responds to conditions that vary from situation to situation, and teachers' and schools' complicity in creating negative self-esteem certainly cannot be discounted. This was understood by Lillian, one of the young women in Nitza Hidalgo's study of an urban high school, who commented, "That's another problem I have, teachers, they are always talking about how we have no type of self-esteem or anything like that. . . . But they're the people that's putting us down. That's why our self-esteem is so low" (Hidalgo, 1991, p. 95).

The students in my research also mentioned examples of discrimination based on their race, ethnicity, culture, religion, and language. Some, like Manuel, felt it from fellow students. As an immigrant from Cape Verde who came to the United States at the age of eleven, he found the adjustment difficult:

> When American students see you, it's kinda hard [to] get along with them when you have a different culture, a different way of dressing and stuff like that. So kids really look at you and laugh, you know, at the beginning.

Avi spoke of anti-Semitism in his school. The majority of residents in his town were European American and Christian. The Jewish community had dwindled significantly over the years, and there were now very few Jewish students in his school. On one occasion, a student had walked by him saying, "Are you ready for the second Holocaust?" He described another incident in some detail:

> I was in a woods class, and there was another boy in there, my age, and he was in my grade. He's also Jewish and he used to come to the temple sometimes and went to Hebrew school. But then, of course, he started hanging around with the wrong people and some of these people were in my class, and I guess they were . . . making fun of him. And a few of them starting making swastikas out of wood. . . . So I saw one and I said to some kid, "What are you doing?" and the kid said to me, "Don't worry. It's not for you, it's for him." And I said to him, "What?!"

Other students talked about discrimination on the part of teachers. Both Marisol and Vinh specifically mentioned language discrimination as a problem. For Marisol, it had happened when a particular teacher did not allow Spanish to be spoken in her room. For Vinh, it concerned teachers' attitudes about his language: "Some teachers don't understand about the language. So sometimes, my language, they say it sounds funny." Rich spoke of the differences between the expectations of White and Black teachers, and concluded that all teachers should teach the curriculum *as if they were in an all-White school,* meaning that then expectations would be high for everybody. Other students were the object of teasing, but some, including James, even welcomed it, perhaps because it at least made his culture visible. He spoke of Mr. Miller, an elementary teacher he had been particularly fond of, who had called him "Gonzo" because he had a big nose and "Klinger" after the *M.A.S.H.* character who was Lebanese. James said, "And then everybody called me Klinger from then on. . . . I liked it, kind of . . . everybody laughing at me."

It was Linda who had the most to say about racism. As a young woman who identified herself as mixed because her mother was White and her father Black, Linda had faced discrimination or confusion on the part of both students and teachers. For example, she resented the fact that when teachers had to indicate her race, they came to their own conclusions without bothering to ask her. She explained what it was like:

[Teachers should not] try to make us one or the other. And God forbid you should make us something we're totally not. . . . Don't write down that I'm Hispanic when I'm not. Some people actually think I'm Chinese when I smile. . . . Find out. Don't just make your judgments. . . . If you're filling out someone's report card and you need to know, then ask.

She went on to say:

I've had people tell me, "Well, you're Black." I'm not Black; I'm Black and White. I'm Black and White American. "Well, you're Black!" No, I'm not! I'm both. . . . I mean, I'm not ashamed of being Black, but I'm not ashamed of being White either, and if I'm both, I want to be part of both. And I think teachers need to be sensitive to that.

Linda did not restrict her criticisms to White teachers, but also spoke of a Black teacher in her high school. Besides Mr. Benson, her favorite teacher of all, there was another Black teacher in the school:

The other Black teacher, he was a racist, and I didn't like him. I belonged to the Black Students Association, and he was the advisor. And he just made it so obvious: he was all for Black supremacy. . . . A lot of times, whether they deserved it or not, his Black students passed, and his White students, if they deserved an A, they got a B. . . . He was insistent that only Hispanics and Blacks be allowed in the club. He had a very hard time letting me in because I'm not all Black. . . . I just really wasn't that welcome there. . . . He never found out what I was about. He just made his judgments from afar.

It was clear that racism was a particularly compelling issue for Linda, and she thought and talked about it a great deal. The weight of racism on her mind was evident when she said, "It's hard. I look at history and I feel really bad for what some of my ancestors did to some of my other ancestors. Unless you're mixed, you don't know what it's like to be mixed." She even wrote a poem about it, which ended like this:

But all that I wonder is who ever gave
them the right to tell me
What I can and can't do
Who I can and can't be
God made each one of us
Just like the other
the only difference is,
I'm darker in color.

IMPLICATIONS OF STUDENTS' VIEWS FOR
TRANSFORMATION OF SCHOOLS

Numerous lessons are contained within the narratives above. But what are the implications of these lessons for the school's curriculum, pedagogy, and track-ing? How can we use what students have taught us about racism and discrimina-tion? How can schools' policies and practices be informed through dialogue with students about what works and doesn't work? Although the students in my study never mentioned multicultural education by name, they were deeply concerned with whether and in what ways they and their families and communities were respected and represented in their schools. Two implications that are inherently multicultural come to mind, and I would suggest that both can have a major impact on school policies and practices. It is important that I first make explicit my own view of multicultural education: It is my understanding that multicultural education should be *basic for all students, pervasive in the curriculum and pedagogy, grounded in social justice, and based on critical pedagogy* (Nieto, 1992). Given this interpretation of multicultural education, we can see that it goes beyond the "tolerance" called for in numerous proclamations about diversity. It is also a far cry from the "cultural sensitivity" that is the focus of many professional development workshops (Nieto, 1994). In fact, "cultural sensitivity" can become little more than a condescending "bandaid" response to diversity, because it often does little to solve deep-seated problems of inequity. Thus, a focus on cultural sensitivity in and of itself can be superficial if it fails to take into account the structural and institutional barriers that reflect and reproduce power differentials in society. Rather than promoting cultural sensitivity, I would suggest that multicultural education needs to be understood as "arrogance reduction"; that is, as encompassing *both* individual *and* structural changes that squarely confront the individual biases, attitudes, and behaviors of educators, as well as the policies and practices in schools that emanate from them.

Affirming Students' Languages, Cultures, and Experiences

Over twenty years ago, Annie Stein reported asking a kindergarten teacher to explain why she had ranked four of her students at the bottom of her list, noting that they were "mute." "'Yes,' she said, 'they have not said one word for six months and they don't appear to hear anything I say.' 'Do they ever talk to the other children?' we asked. 'Sure,' was her reply. 'They cackle to each other in Spanish all day.'" (Stein, 1971, p. 161). These young children, although quite vocal in their own language, were not heard by their teacher because the language they spoke was bereft of all significance in the school. The children were not, however, blank slates; on the contrary, they came to school with a language, culture, and experiences that could have been important in their learning. Thus, we need to look not only at the individual weaknesses or strengths of particular students, but also at the way in which schools assign status to entire groups of students based on the sociopolitical and linguistic context in which they live. Jim Cummins addressed this concern in relation to the kinds of superficial antidotes frequently proposed to solve the problem of functional illiteracy among students from culturally and economically dominated groups: "A remedial focus only on technical aspects of functional illiteracy is inadequate because the causes of educational underachievement and 'illiteracy' among subordinated groups are rooted in the systematic devaluation of culture and denial of access to power and resources by the dominant group" (1994, pp. 307–308). As we have seen in many of the examples cited throughout this article, when culture and language are acknowledged by the school, students are able to reclaim the voice they need to continue their education successfully.

Nevertheless, the situation is complicated by the competing messages that students pick up from their schools and society at large. The research that I have reviewed makes it clear that, although students' cultures are important to them personally and in their families, they are also problematic because they are rarely valued or acknowledged by schools. The decisions young people make about their identities are frequently contradictory and mired in the tensions and struggles concerning diversity that are reflected in our society. Schools are not immune to such debates. There are numerous ways in which students' languages and cultures are excluded in schools: they are invisible, as with James, denigrated, as in Marisol's case, or simply not known, as happened with Vinh. It is no wonder then that these young people had conflicted feelings about their backgrounds. In spite of this, all of them spoke about the strength they derived from family and culture, and the steps they took to maintain it. James and Marisol mentioned that they continued to speak their native languages at home; Fern discussed her father's many efforts to maintain their Native American heritage; Manuel made it clear that he would always consider himself first and foremost Cape Verdean. Vinh spoke movingly about what his culture meant to him, and said that only Vietnamese was allowed in the home and that his sisters and brothers wrote to their parents in Vietnamese weekly. Most of these young people also maintained solid ties with their religion and places of worship as an important link to their heritage.

Much of the recent literature on educating culturally diverse students is helping to provide a radically different paradigm that contests the equation *education = assimilation* (Trueba, 1989). This research challenges the old assumptions about the role of the school as primarily an assimilationist agent, and provides a foundation for policy recommendations that focus on using students' cultural background values to promote academic achievement. In the case of Asian Pacific American youth, Peter Kiang and Vivian Wai-Fun Lee state the following:

> It is ironic that strengths and cultural values of family support which are so often praised as explanations for the academic achievement of Asian Pacific American students are severely undercut by the lack of programmatic and policy support for broad-based bilingual instruction and native language development, particularly in early childhood education. (Kiang & Lee, 1993, p. 39)

A study by Jeannette Abi-Nader of a program for Hispanic youth provides an example of how this can work. In the large urban high school she studied, students' cultural values, especially those concerned with *familia,* were the basis of everyday classroom interactions. Unlike the dismal dropout statistics prevalent in so many other Hispanic communities, up to 65 percent of the high school graduates in this program went on to college. Furthermore, the youth attributed their academic success to the program, and made enthusiastic statements about it, including this one written on a survey: "The best thing I like about this class is that we all work together and we all participate and try to help each other. We're family!" (Abi-Nader, 1993, p. 213).

The students in my research also provided impassioned examples of the effect that affirming their languages and cultures had on them and, conversely, on how negating their languages and cultures negated a part of them as well. The attitudes and behaviors of the teachers in Yolanda's school, for example, were reflected in policies that seemed to be based on an appreciation for student diversity. Given the support of her teachers and their affirmation of her language and her culture, Yolanda concluded, "Actually, it's fun around here if you really get into learning. . . . I like learning. I like really getting my mind working." Manuel also commented on how crucial it was for teachers to become aware of students' cultural values and backgrounds. This was especially important for Manuel, since his parents were immigrants unfamiliar with U.S. schools and society, and although they gave him important moral support, they could do little to help him in school. He said of his teachers:

> If you don't know a student there's no way to influence him. If you don't know his background, there's no way you are going to get in touch with him. There's no way you're going to influence him if you don't know where he's been.

Fern, on the other hand, as the only Native American student in her school, spoke about how difficult it was to discuss values that were different from those of the majority. She specifically mentioned a discussion about abortion in which she was trying to express that for Native Americans, the fetus is alive: "And, so, when I try to tell them, they just, 'Oh, well, we're out of time.' They cut me off, and we've still got half an hour!" And Avi, although he felt that teachers tried to be understanding of his religion, also longed for more cultural affirmation. He would have welcomed, for example, the support of the one Jewish teacher at school who Avi felt was trying to hide his Jewishness.

On the contrary, in Linda's case, Mr. Benson, her English teacher, who was also her favorite teacher, provided just that kind of affirmation. Because he was racially mixed like Linda, she felt that he could relate to the kinds of problems she confronted. He became, in the words of Esteban Díaz and his colleagues, a "sociocultural mediator" for Linda by assigning her identity, language, and culture important roles in the learning environment (Díaz, Flores, Cousin, & Soo Hoo, 1992). Although Linda spoke English as her native language, she gave a wonderful example of how Mr. Benson encouraged her to be "bilingual," using what she referred to as her "street talk." Below is her description of Mr. Benson and the role he played in her education:

> I've enjoyed all my English teachers at Jefferson. But Mr. Benson, my English Honors teacher, he just threw me for a whirl! I wasn't going to college until I met this man. . . . He was one of the few teachers I could talk to . . . 'cause Mr. Benson, he says, I can go into Harvard and converse with those people, and I can go out in the street and "rap with y'all." It's that type of thing. I love it. I try and be like that myself. I have my street talk. I get out in the street and I say "ain't" this and "ain't" that and "your momma" or "wha's up?" But I get somewhere where I know the people aren't familiar with that language or aren't accepting that language, and I will talk properly. . . . I walk into a place and I listen to how people are talking and it just automatically comes to me.

Providing time in the curriculum for students and teachers to engage in discussions about how the language use of students from dominated groups is discriminated against would go a long way in affirming the legitimacy of the discourse of *all* students (Delpit, 1992). According to Margaret Gibson (1991), much recent research has confirmed that schooling may unintentionally contribute to the educational problems of students from culturally dominated groups by pressuring them to assimilate against their wishes. The conventional wisdom that assimilation is the answer to academic underachievement is thus severely challenged. One intriguing implication is that the more students are involved in resisting assimilation while maintaining their culture and language, the more successful they will be in school. That is, maintaining culture and language, although a conflicted decision, seems to have a positive impact on academic success. In any case, it seems to be a far healthier response than adopting an oppositional identity that effectively limits the possibility of academic success (Fordham & Ogbu, 1986; Skutnabb-Kangas, 1988). Although it is important not to overstate this conclusion, it is indeed a real possibility, one that tests the "melting pot" ideology that continues to dominate U.S. schools and society.

We know, of course, that cultural maintenance is not true in all cases of academic success, and everybody can come up with examples of students who felt they needed to assimilate to be successful in school. But the question remains whether this kind of assimilation is healthy or necessary. For instance, in one large-scale study, immigrant students clearly expressed a strong desire to maintain their native languages and cultures and to pass them on to their children (Olsen, 1988). Other research has found that bilingual students specifically appreciate hearing their native language in school, and want the opportunity to learn in that language (Poplin & Weeres, 1992). In addition, an intriguing study of Cambodian refugee children by the Metropolitan Indochinese Children and Adolescent Service found that the more successful they became at modeling their behavior to be like U.S. children, the more their emotional adjustment worsened (National Coalition, 1988). Furthermore, a study of Southeast Asian students found a significant connection between grades and culture: in this research, higher grade point averages correlated with the *maintenance* of traditional values, ethnic pride, and close social and cultural ties with members of the same ethnic group (Rumbaut & Ima, 1987).

All of the above suggests that it is time to look critically at policies and practices that encourage students to leave their cultures and languages at the schoolhouse door. It also suggests that schools and teachers need to affirm, maintain, and value the differences that students bring to school as a foundation for their learning. It is still too common to hear teachers urging parents to "speak only English," as my parents were encouraged to do with my sister and me (luckily, our parents never paid attention). The ample literature cited throughout this article concerning diverse student populations is calling such practices into question. What we are learning is that teachers instead need to encourage parents to speak their *native* language, not English, at home with their children. We are also learning that they should emphasize the importance of family values, not in the rigid and limiting way that this term has been used in the past to create a sense of superiority for those who are culturally dominant, but rather by accepting the strong ethical values that all cultural groups and all kinds of families cherish. As an initial step, however, teachers and schools must first learn more about their students. Vinh expressed powerfully what he wanted teachers to know about him by reflecting on how superficial their knowledge was:

> They understand something, just not all Vietnamese culture. Like they just understand something *outside*. . . . But they cannot understand something inside our hearts.

Listen to Students

Although school is a place where a lot of talk goes on, it is not often student talk. Student voices sometimes reveal the great challenges and even the deep pain young people feel when schools are unresponsive, cold places. One of the students participating in a project focusing on those "inside the school," namely students, teachers, staff, and parents, said, "This place hurts my spirit" (Poplin & Weeres, 1992, p. 11). Ironically, those who spend the most time in schools and classrooms are often given the least opportunity to talk. Yet, as we saw in the many examples above, students have important lessons to teach educators and we need to begin to listen to them more carefully. Suzanne Soo Hoo captured the fact that educators are losing a compelling opportunity to learn from students while working on a project where students became coresearchers and worked on the question, "What are the obstacles to learning?" a question that, according to Soo Hoo, "electrified the group" (1993, p. 386). Including students in addressing such important issues places the focus where it rightfully belongs, said Soo Hoo: "Somehow educators have forgotten the important connection between teachers and students. We listen to outside experts to inform us, and consequently, we overlook the treasure in our very own backyards: our students" (p. 390). As Mike, one of the coresearchers in her project, stated, "They think just because we're kids, we don't know anything" (p. 391).

When they are treated as if they do know something, students can become energized and motivated. For the ten young people in my study, the very act of speaking about their schooling experiences seemed to act as a catalyst for more critical thinking about them. For example, I was surprised when I met Marisol's mother and she told me that Marisol had done nothing but speak about our interviews. Most of the students in the study felt this enthusiasm and these feelings are typical of other young people in similar studies. As Laurie Olsen (1988) concluded in an extensive research project in California in which hundreds of immigrant students were interviewed, most of the students were gratified simply to have the opportunity to speak about their experiences. These findings have several implications for practice, including using oral histories, peer interviews, interactive journals, and other such strategies. Simply providing students with time to talk with one another, including group work, seems particularly helpful.

The feeling that adults do not listen to them has been echoed by many young people over the years. But listening alone is not sufficient if it is not accompanied by profound changes in what we expect our students to accomplish in school. Even more important than simply *listening* is *assisting* students to become agents of their own learning and to use what they learn in productive and critical ways. This is where social action comes in, and there have been a number of eloquent accounts of critical pedagogy in action (Peterson, 1991; Torres-Guzmán, 1992). I will quote at length from two such examples that provide inspiring stories of how listening to students can help us move beyond the written curriculum.

Iris Santos Rivera wrote a moving account of how a Freirian "problem-posing" approach was used with K-6 Chicano students in a summer educational program of the San Diego Public Schools in 1975 (Santos Rivera, 1983–1984). The program started by having the students play what she called the "Complain, Moan, and Groan Game." Using this exercise, in which students dialogued about and identified problems in the school and community, the young people were asked to identify problems to study. One group selected the school lunch program. This did not seem like a "real" problem to the teacher, who tried to steer the children toward another problem. Santos Rivera writes: "The teacher found it hard to believe in the problem's validity as an issue, as the basis for an action project, or as an integrating theme for education" (p. 5). She let the children talk about it for awhile, convinced that they would come to realize that this was not a serious issue. However, when she returned, they said to her, "Who is responsible for the lunches we get?" (p. 6). Thus began a summer-long odyssey in which the students wrote letters, made phone calls, traced their lunches from the catering truck through the school contracts office, figured out taxpayers' cost per lunch, made records of actual services received from the subcontractors, counted sandwiches and tested milk temperatures, and, finally, compared their findings with contract specifications, and found that there was a significant discrepancy. "We want to bring in the media," they told the teacher (p. 6). Both the local television station and the major networks responded to the press releases sent out by the students, who held a press conference to present the facts and answer reporters' questions. When a reporter asked who had told them all this, one nine-year old girl answered, "We found this stuff out. Nobody had to tell us anything. You know, you adults give yourselves too much credit" (p. 7). The postscript to this story is that state and federal laws had to be amended to change the kinds of lunches that students in California are served, and tapes from the students in this program were used in the state and federal hearings.

In a more recent example, Mary Ginley, a student in the doctoral program at the School of Education at the University of Massachusetts and a gifted teacher in the Longmeadow (Massachusetts) Public Schools, tries to help her second-graders develop critical skills by posing questions to them daily. Their responses are later discussed during class meeting time. Some of these questions are fairly straightforward ("Did you have a good weekend?"), while others encourage deeper thinking; the question posed on Columbus Day, "Was Columbus a hero?" was the culmination of much reading and dialogue that had previously taken place. Another activity she did with her students this year was to keep a daily record of sunrise and sunset. The students discovered to their surprise that December 21 was *not* the shortest day of the year. Using the daily almanac in the local newspaper, the students verified their finding and wrote letters to the editor. One, signed by Kaolin, read (spelling in original):

Dear Editor,

Acorting to our chart December 21 was not the shotest day of the year. But acorting to your paper it is. Are teacher says it happens evry year! What's going on?

As a result of this letter, the newspaper called in experts from the National Weather Service and a local planetarium. One of them said, "It's a fascinating question that [the pupils] have posed. . . . It's frustrating we don't have an adequate answer."(Kelly, 1994, p. 12). Katie, one of the students in Mary's class, compared her classmates to Galileo, who shook the scientific community by saying that the earth revolved around the sun rather than the other way around. Another, Ben, said, "You shouldn't always believe what you hear," and Lucy asserted, "Even if you're a grown-up, you can still learn from a second-grader!"

In the first part of this article, I posed the question, "Why listen to students?" I have attempted to answer this question using numerous comments that perceptive young people, both those from my study and others, have made concerning their education. In the final analysis, the question itself suggests that it is only by first listening *to* students that we will be able to learn to talk *with* them. If we believe that an important basis of education is dialogue and reflection about experience, then this is clearly the first step. Yolanda probably said it best when she commented, "'Cause you learn a lot from the students. That's what a lot of teachers tell me. They learn more from their students than from where they go study."

CONCLUSION

I have often been struck by how little young people believe they deserve, especially those who do not come from economically privileged backgrounds. Although they may work hard at learning, they somehow believe that they do not deserve a chance to dream. This article is based on the notion that all of our students deserve to dream and that teachers and schools are in the best position for "creating a chance" to do so, as referred to in the title. This means developing conditions in schools that let students know that they have a right to envision other possibilities beyond those imposed by traditional barriers of race, gender, or social class. It means, even more importantly, that those traditional barriers can no longer be viewed as impediments to learning.

The students in my study also showed how crucial extracurricular activities were in providing needed outlets for their energy and for teaching them important leadership skills. For some, it was their place of worship (this was especially true for Avi, Manuel, and Rich); for others, it was hobbies (Linda loved to sing); and for others, sports were a primary support (Fern mentioned how she confronted new problems by comparing them to the sports in which she excelled: "I compare it to stuff, like, when I can't get science, or like in sewing, I'll look at that machine and I'll say, 'This is a basketball; I can overcome it'"). The schools' responsibility to provide some of these activities becomes paramount for students such as Marisol, whose involvement in the Teen Clinic acted almost like a buffer against negative peer pressure.

These students can all be characterized by an indomitable resilience and a steely determination to succeed. However, expecting all students, particularly those from subordinated communities, to be resilient in this way is an unfair burden, because privileged students do not need this quality, as the schools generally reflect their backgrounds, experiences, language, and culture. Privileged students learn that they are the "norm," and although they may believe this is inherently unfair (as is the case with Vanessa), they still benefit from it.

Nevertheless, the students in this research provide another important lesson about the strength of human nature in the face of adversity. Although they represented all kinds of families and economic and social situations, the students were almost uniformly upbeat about their future and their lives, sometimes in spite of what might seem overwhelming odds. The positive features that have contributed to their academic success, namely, caring teachers, affirming school climates, and loving families, have helped them face such odds. "I don't think there's anything stopping me," said Marisol, whose large family lived on public assistance because both parents were disabled. She added, "If I know I can do it, I should just keep on trying." The determination to keep trying was evident also in Fern, whose two teenage sisters were undergoing treatment for alcohol and drug abuse, but who nevertheless asserted, "I succeed in everything I do. If I don't get it right the first time, I always go back and try to do it again," adding, "I've always wanted to be president of the United States!" And it was evident as well in the case of Manuel, whose father cleaned downtown offices in Boston while his mother raised the remaining children at home, and who was the first of the eleven children to graduate from high school: "I can do whatever I want to do in life. Whatever I want to do, I know I could make it. I believe that strongly." And, finally, it was also clear in the case of Rich, whose mother, a single parent, was putting all three of her children through college at the same time. Rich had clearly learned a valuable lesson about self-reliance from her, as we can see in this striking image: "But let's not look at life as a piece of cake, because eventually it'll dry up, it'll deteriorate, it'll fall, it'll crumble, or somebody will come gnawing at it." Later he added, "As they say, self-respect is one gift that you give yourself."

Our students have a lot to teach us about how pedagogy, curriculum, ability grouping, and expectations of ability need to change so that greater numbers of young people can be reached. In 1971, Annie Stein expressed the wishes and hopes of students she talked with, and they differ little from those we have heard through the voices of students today: "The demands of high school youth are painfully reasonable. They want a better education, a more 'relevant' curriculum, some voice in the subject matter to be taught and in the running of the school, and some respect for their constitutional and human rights" (1971, p. 177). Although the stories and voices I have used in this article are primarily those of individual students, they can help us to imagine what it might take to transform entire schools. The responsibility to do so cannot be placed only on the shoulders of individual teachers who, in spite of the profound impact they can have on the lives of particular students, are part of a system that continues to be unresponsive to too many young people. In the final analysis, students are asking us to look critically not only at structural conditions, but also at individual attitudes and behaviors. This implies that we need to undertake a total transformation not only of our schools, but also of our hearts and minds.

REFERENCES

Abi-Nader, J. (1993). Meeting the needs of multicultural classrooms: Family values and the motivation of minority students. In M. J. O'Hair & S. Odell (Eds), *Diversity and teaching: Teacher education yearbook 1* (pp. 212–236). Fort Worth, TX: Harcourt Brace Jovanovich.

Banks, J. A. (1991). *Teaching strategies for ethnic studies* (6th ed.). Boston: Allyn & Bacon.

Bartolomé, L. (1994). Beyond the methods fetish: Toward a humanizing pedagogy. *Harvard Educational Review, 64,* 173–194.

Bempechat, J. (1992). *Fostering high achievement in African American children: Home, school, and public policy influences.* New York: ERIC Clearinghouse on Urban Education, Teachers College, Columbia University.

Bereiter, C., & Englemann, S. (1966). *Teaching disadvantaged children in the preschool.* Englewood Cliffs, NJ: Prentice Hall.

Clark, R. M. (1983). *Family life and school achievement: Why poor Black children succeed or fail.* Chicago: University of Chicago Press.

Commins, N. L. (1989). Language and affect: Bilingual students at home and at school. *Language Arts, 66,* 29–43.

Cummins, J. (1994). From coercive to collaborative relations of power in the teaching of literacy. In B. M. Ferdman, R-M. Weber, & A. G. Ramírez (Eds.), *Literacy across languages and cultures* (pp. 295–331). Albany: State University of New York Press.

Delpit, L. (1992). The politics of-teaching literate discourse. *Theory into Practice, 31,* 285–295.

Díaz, E., Flores, B., Cousin, P. T., & Soo Hoo, S. (1992, April). *Teacher as sociocultural mediator.* Paper presented at the Annual Meeting of the AERA, San Francisco.

Donaldson, K. (1994). Through students' eyes. *Multicultural Education, 2(2),* 26–28.

Fine, M. (1991). *Framing dropouts: Notes on the politics of an urban public high school.* Albany: State University of New York Press.

Fine, M. (1993). "You can't just say that the only ones who can speak are those who agree with your position": Political discourse in the classroom. *Harvard Educational Review, 63,* 412–433.

Fordham, S., & Ogbu, J. (1986) Black students' school success: Coping with the "burden of acting White." *Urban Review, 18,* 176–206.

Frau-Ramos, M., & Nieto, S. (1993). "I was an outsider": Dropping out among Puerto Rican youths in Holyoke, Massachusetts. In R. Rivera & S. Nieto (Eds.), *The education of Latino students in Massachusetts: Research and policy considerations* (pp. 143–166). Boston: Gastón Institute.

Freire, P. (1970). *Pedagogy of the oppressed.* New York: Seabury Press.

Gibson, M. (1991). Minorities and schooling: Some implications. In M. A. Gibson & J. U. Ogbu (Eds.), *Minority status and schooling: A comparative study of immigrant and involuntary minorities* (pp. 357–381). New York: Garland.

Ginsburg, H. (1986). The myth of the deprived child: New thoughts on poor children. In U. Neisser (Ed.), *The school achievement of minority children: New perspectives.* Hillsdale, NJ: Lawrence Erlbaum.

Goodlad, J. I. (1984). *A place called school.* New York: McGraw-Hill.

Haberman, M. (1991). The pedagogy of poverty versus good teaching. *Phi Delta Kappan, 73,* 290–294.

Hallinan, M., & Teixeira, R. (1987). Opportunities and constraints: Black-White differences in the formation of interracial friendships. *Child Development, 58,* 1358–1371.

Hidalgo, N. M. (1991). *"Free time, school is like a free time": Social relations in City High School classes.* Unpublished doctoral dissertation, Harvard University.

Hollins, E. R., King, J. E., & Hayman, W. C. (Eds.). (1994). *Teaching diverse populations: Formulating a knowledge base.* Albany: State University of New York Press.

Kelly, R. (1994, January 11). Class searches for solstice. *Union News,* p. 12.

Kiang, P. N., & Lee, V. W-F. (1993). Exclusion or contribution? Education K-12 policy. In *The State of Asian Pacific America: Policy Issues to the Year 2020* (pp. 25–48). Los Angeles: LEAP Asian Pacific American Public Policy Institute and UCLA Asian American Studies Center.

Kohl, H. (1993). The myth of "Rosa Parks, the tired." *Multicultural Education, 1(2),* 6–10.

Kozol, J. (1967). *Death at an early age: The destruction of the hearts and minds of Negro children in the Boston Public Schools.* New York: Houghton Mifflin.

Lee, V. E., Winfield, L. F., & Wilson, T. C. (1991). Academic behaviors among high-achieving African-American students. *Education and Urban Society, 24(1),* 65–86.

Lucas, T., Henze, R., & Donato, R. (1990). Promoting the success of Latino language-minority students: An exploratory study of six high schools. *Harvard Educational Review, 60,* 315–340.

McNeil, L. M. (1986). *Contradictions of control: School structure and school knowledge.* New York: Routledge & Kegan Paul.

Mehan, H., & Villanueva, I. (1993). Untracking low achieving students: Academic and social consequences. In *Focus on Diversity* (Newsletter available from the National Center for Research on Cultural Diversity and Second Language Learning, 399 Kerr Hall, University of California, Santa Cruz, CA 95064).

Moll, L. (1992). Bilingual classroom studies and community analysis: Some recent trends. *Educational Researcher, 21*(2), 20–24.

Moll, L., & Díaz, S. (1993). Change as the goal of educational research. In E. Jacob & C. Jordan (Eds.), *Minority education: Anthropological perspectives* (pp. 67–79). Norwood, NJ: Ablex.

National Coalition of Advocates for Students. (1988). *New voices: Immigrant students in U.S. public schools.* Boston: Author.

Newmann, F. M. (1993). Beyond common sense in educational restructuring: The issues of content and linkage. *Educational Researcher, 22*(2), 4–13, 22.

Nieto, S. (1992). *Affirming diversity: The sociopolitical context of multicultural education.* White Plains, NY: Longman.

Nieto, S. (1994). Affirmation, solidarity, and critique: Moving beyond tolerance in multicultural education. *Multicultural Education, 1*(4), 9–12, 35–38.

Oakes, J. (1992). Can tracking research inform practice? *Educational Researcher, 21*(4), 12–21.

Olsen, L. (1988). *Crossing the schoolhouse border: Immigrant students and the California public schools.* San Francisco: California Tomorrow.

Peterson, R. E. (1991). Teaching how to read the world and change it: Critical pedagogy in the intermediate grades. In C. E. Walsh (Ed.), *Literacy as praxis: Culture, language, and pedagogy* (pp. 156–182). New Jersey: Ablex.

Phelan, P., Davidson, A. L., & Cao, H. T. (1992). Speaking up: Students' perspectives on school. *Phi Delta Kappan, 73,* 695–704.

Poplin, M., & Weeres, J. (1992). *Voices from the inside: A report on schooling from inside the classroom.* Claremont, CA: Claremont Graduate School, Institute for Education in Transformation.

Reissman, F. (1962). *The culturally deprived child.* New York: Harper & Row.

Reyes, M. de la Luz (1992). Challenging venerable assumptions: Literacy instruction for linguistically different students. *Harvard Educational Review, 62,* 427–446.

Ribadeneira, D. (1990, October 18). Study says teen-agers' racism rampant. *Boston Globe,* p. 31.

Rumbaut, R. G., & Ima, K. (1987). *The adaptation of Southeast Asian refugee youth: A comparative study.* San Diego: Office of Refugee Resettlement.

Santos Rivera, I. (1983–1984, October-January). Liberating education for little children. In *Alternativas* (Freirian newsletter from Río Piedras, Puerto Rico, no longer published).

Saravia-Shore, M., & Martínez, H. (1992). An ethnographic study of home/school role conflicts of second generation Puerto Rican adolescents. In M. Saravia-Shore & S. F. Arvizu (Eds.), *Cross-cultural literacy: Ethnographies of communication in multiethnic classrooms* (pp. 227–251). New York: Garland.

Shor, I. (1992). *Empowering education: Critical teaching for social change.* Chicago: University of Chicago Press.

Skutnabb-Kangas, T. (1988). Resource power and autonomy through discourse in conflict: A Finnish migrant school strike in Sweden. In T. Skutnabb-Kangas & J. Cummins (Eds.), *Minority education: From shame to struggle* (pp. 251–277). Clevedon, England: Multilingual Matters.

Sleeter, C. E. (1991). *Empowerment through multicultural education.* Albany: State University of New York Press.

Sleeter, C. E. (1994). White racism. *Multicultural Education, 1*(4), 5–8, 39.

Sleeter, C. E., & Grant, C. A. (1991). Mapping terrains of power: Student cultural knowledge vs. classroom knowledge. In C. E. Sleeter (Ed.), *Empowerment through multicultural education* (pp. 49–67). Albany: State University of New York Press.

Soo Hoo, S. (1993). Students as partners in research and restructuring schools. *Educational Forum, 57,* 386–393.

Stein, A. (1971). Strategies for failure. *Harvard Educational Review, 41,* 133–179.

Tatum, B. D. (1992). Talking about race, learning about racism: The application of racial identity development theory in the classroom. *Harvard Educational Review, 62,* 1–24.

Taylor, A. R. (1991). Social competence and the early school transition: Risk and protective factors for African-American children. *Education and Urban Society, 24*(1), 15–26.

Taylor, D., & Dorsey-Gaines, C. (1988). *Growing up literate: Learning from inner-city families.* Portsmouth, NH: Heinemann.

Torres-Guzmán, M. (1992). Stories of hope in the midst of despair: Culturally responsive education for Latino students in an alternative high school in New York City. In M. Saravia-Shore & S. F. Arvizu (Eds.), *Cross-cultural literacy: Ethnographies of communication in multiethnic classrooms* (pp. 477–490). New York: Garland.

Trueba, H. T. (1989). *Raising silent voices: Educating the linguistic minorities for the twenty-first century.* Cambridge, MA: Newbury House.

Wheelock, A. (1992). *Crossing the tracks: How "untracking" can save America's schools.* New York: New Press.

Zanger, V. V. (1994). Academic costs of social marginalization: An analysis of Latino students' perceptions at a Boston high school. In R. Rivera & S. Nieto (Eds.), *The education of Latino students in Massachusetts: Research and policy considerations* (pp. 167–187). Boston: Gastón Institute.

PART ONE

Shifting Histories:
Movement from the Inside Out

Beyond the Methods Fetish:
Toward a Humanizing Pedagogy

LILIA I. BARTOLOME

In this article, Lilia Bartolomé argues that the current focus on finding the right "methods" to improve the academic achievement of students who have historically been oppressed hides the less visible but more important reasons for their performance: the asymmetrical power relations of society that are reproduced in the schools, and the deficit view of minority students that school personnel uncritically, and often unknowingly, hold. Bartolomé argues instead for a humanizing pedagogy that respects and uses the reality, history, and perspectives of students as an integral part of educational practice. Discussing two approaches in particular that show promise when implemented within a humanizing pedagogical framework — culturally responsive education and strategic teaching — Bartolomé emphasizes the need for teachers' evolving political awareness of their relationship with students as knowers and active participants in their own learning.

Much of the current debate regarding the improvement of minority student academic achievement occurs at a level that treats education as a primarily technical issue (Giroux, 1992).[1] For example, the historical and present day academic underachievement of certain culturally and linguistically subordinated student populations in the United States (e.g., Mexican Americans, Native Americans, Puerto Ricans) is often explained as resulting from the lack of cognitively, culturally, and/or linguistically appropriate teaching methods and educational programs.[2] As such, the solution to the problem of academic underachievement tends to be constructed in primarily methodological and mechanistic terms dislodged from the sociocultural reality that shapes it. That is, the solution to the current underachievement of students from subordinated cultures is often reduced to finding the "right" teaching methods, strategies, or prepackaged curricula that will work with students who do not respond to so-called "regular" or "normal" instruction.

Recent research studies have begun to identify educational programs found to be successful in working with culturally and linguistically subordinated minority student populations (Carter & Chatfield, 1986; Lucas, Henze, & Donato,

---

[1] The term "technical" refers to the positivist tradition in education that presents teaching as a precise and scientific undertaking and teachers as technicians responsible for carrying out (preselected) instructional programs and strategies.

[2] "Subordinated" refers to cultural groups that are politically, socially, and economically subordinate in the greater society. While individual members of these groups may not consider themselves subordinate in any manner to the White "mainstream," they nevertheless are members of a greater collective that historically has been perceived and treated as subordinate and inferior by the dominant society.

Harvard Educational Review Vol. 64 No. 2 Summer 1994, 173–194

1990; Tikunoff, 1985; Webb, 1987). In addition, there has been specific interest in identifying teaching strategies that more effectively teach culturally and linguistically "different" students and other "disadvantaged" and "at-risk" students (Knapp & Shields, 1990; McLeod, in press; Means & Knapp, 1991; Tinajero & Ada, 1993). Although it is important to identify useful and promising instructional programs and strategies, it is erroneous to assume that blind replication of instructional programs or teacher mastery of particular teaching methods, in and of themselves, will guarantee successful student learning, especially when we are discussing populations that historically have been mistreated and miseducated by the schools.

This focus on methods as solutions in the current literature coincides with many of my graduate students' beliefs regarding linguistic minority education improvement. As a Chicana professor who has taught anti-racist multicultural education courses at various institutions, I am consistently confronted at the beginning of each semester by students who are anxious to learn the latest teaching methods — methods that they hope will somehow magically work on minority students.[3] Although my students are well-intentioned individuals who sincerely wish to create positive learning environments for culturally and linguistically subordinated students, they arrive with the expectation that I will provide them with easy answers in the form of specific instructional methods. That is, since they (implicitly) perceive the academic underachievement of subordinated students as a technical issue, the solutions they require are also expected to be technical in nature (e.g., specific teaching methods, instructional curricula and materials). They usually assume that: 1) they, as teachers, are fine and do not need to identify, interrogate, and change their biased beliefs and fragmented views about subordinated students; 2) schools, as institutions, are basically fair and democratic sites where all students are provided with similar, if not equal, treatment and learning conditions; and 3) children who experience academic difficulties (especially those from culturally and linguistically low-status groups) require some form of "special" instruction since they obviously have not been able to succeed under "regular" or "normal" instructional conditions. Consequently, if nothing is basically wrong with teachers and schools, they often conclude, then linguistic minority academic underachievement is best dealt with by providing teachers with specific teaching methods that promise to be effective with culturally and linguistically subordinated students. To further complicate matters, many of my students seek *generic* teaching methods that will work with a variety of minority student populations, and they grow anxious and impatient when reminded that instruction for any group of students needs to be tailored or individualized to some extent. Some of my students appear to be seeking what María de la Luz Reyes (1992) defines as a "one size fits all" instructional recipe. Reyes explains that the term refers to the assumption that instructional methods

Thus it is not entirely accurate to describe these students as "minority" students, since the term connotes numerical minority rather than the general low status (economic, political, and social) these groups have held and that I think is important to recognize when discussing their historical academic underachievement.

[3] "Chicana" refers to a woman of Mexican ancestry who was born and/or reared in the United States.

that are deemed effective for mainstream populations will benefit *all* students, no matter what their backgrounds may be.[4] She explains that the assumption is

> similar to the "one size fits all" marketing concept that would have buyers believe that there is an average or ideal size among men and women. . . . Those who market "one size fits all" products suggest that if the article of clothing is not a good fit, the fault is not with the design of the garment, but those who are too fat, too skinny, too tall, too short, or too high-waisted. (p. 435)

I have found that many of my students similarly believe that teaching approaches that work with one minority population should also fit another (see Vogt, Jordan, & Tharp, 1987, for an example of this tendency). Reyes argues that educators often make this "one size fits all" assumption when discussing instructional approaches, such as process writing. For example, as Lisa Delpit (1988) has convincingly argued, the process writing approach that has been blindly embraced by mostly White liberal teachers often produces a negative result with African-American students. Delpit cites one Black student:

> I didn't feel she was teaching us anything. She wanted us to correct each other's papers and we were there to learn from her. She didn't teach anything, absolutely nothing.
> Maybe they're trying to learn what Black folks knew all the time. We understand how to improvise, how to express ourselves creatively. When I'm in a classroom, I'm not looking for that, I'm looking for structure, the more formal language.
> Now my buddy was in a Black teacher's class. And that lady was very good. She went through and explained and defined each part of the structure. This [White] teacher didn't get along with that Black teacher. She said she didn't agree with her methods. But *I* don't think that White teacher *had* any methods. (1988, p. 287)

The above quote is a glaring testimony that a "one size fits all" approach often does not work with the same level of effectiveness with all students across the board. Such assumptions reinforce a disarticulation between the embraced method and the sociocultural realities within which each method is implemented. I find that this "one size fits all" assumption is also held by many of my students about a number of teaching methods currently in vogue, such as cooperative learning and whole language instruction. The students imbue the "new" methods with almost magical properties that render them, in and of themselves, capable of improving students' academic standing.

One of my greatest challenges throughout the years has been to help students to understand that a myopic focus on methodology often serves to obfuscate the real question — which is why in our society, subordinated students do not generally succeed academically in schools. In fact, schools often reproduce the existing asymmetrical power relations among cultural groups (Anyon, 1988; Gibson & Ogbu, 1991; Giroux, 1992; Freire, 1985). I believe that by taking a sociohistorical view of present-day conditions and concerns that inform the lived experi-

---

[4] "Mainstream" refers to the U.S. macroculture that has its roots in Western European traditions. More specifically, the major influence on the United States, particularly on its institutions, has been the culture and traditions of White, Anglo-Saxon Protestants (WASP) (Golnick & Chinn, 1986). Although the mainstream group is no longer composed solely of WASPs, members of the middle class have adopted traditionally WASP bodies of knowledge, language use, values, norms, and beliefs.

ences of socially perceived minority students, prospective teachers are better able to comprehend the quasi-colonial nature of minority education. By engaging in this critical sociohistorical analysis of subordinated students' academic perform-ance, most of my graduate students (teachers and prospective teachers) are better situated to reinterpret and reframe current educational concerns so as to develop pedagogical structures that speak to the day-to-day reality, struggles, concerns, and dreams of these students. By understanding the historical speci-ficities of marginalized students, these teachers and prospective teachers come to realize that an uncritical focus on methods makes invisible the historical role that schools and their personnel have played (and continue to play), not only in discriminating against many culturally different groups, but also in denying their humanity. By robbing students of their culture, language, history, and values, schools often reduce these students to the status of subhumans who need to be rescued from their "savage" selves. The end result of this cultural and linguistic eradication represents, in my view, a form of dehumanization. There-fore, any discussion having to do with the improvement of subordinated stu-dents' academic standing is incomplete if it does not address those discrimina-tory school practices that lead to dehumanization.

In this article, I argue that a necessary first step in reevaluating the failure or success of particular instructional methods used with subordinated students calls for a shift in perspective — a shift from a narrow and mechanistic view of in-struction to one that is broader in scope and takes into consideration the socio-historical and political dimensions of education. I discuss why effective methods are needed for these students, and why certain strategies are deemed effective or ineffective in a given sociocultural context. My discussion will include a sec-tion that addresses the significance of teachers' understanding of the political nature of education, the reproductive nature of schools, and the schools' con-tinued (yet unspoken) deficit views of subordinated students. By conducting a critical analysis of the sociocultural realities in which subordinated students find themselves at school, the implicit and explicit antagonistic relations between students and teachers (and other school representatives) take on focal impor-tance.

As a Chicana and a former classroom elementary and middle school teacher who encountered negative race relations that ranged from teachers' outright rejection of subordinated students to their condescending pity, fear, indiffer-ence, and apathy when confronted by the challenges of minority student educa-tion, I find it surprising that little minority education literature deals explicitly with the very real issue of antagonistic race relations between subordinated stu-dents and White school personnel (see Ogbu, 1987, and Giroux, 1992, for an in-depth discussion of this phenomenon).

For this reason, I also include in this article a section that discusses two in-structional methods and approaches identified as effective in current education literature: culturally responsive education and strategic teaching. I examine the methods for pedagogical underpinnings that — under the critical use of politi-cally clear teachers — have the potential to challenge students academically and intellectually while treating them with dignity and respect. More importantly, I examine the pedagogical foundations that serve to humanize the educational process and enable both students and teachers to work toward breaking away from their unspoken antagonism and negative beliefs about each other and get on with the business of sharing and creating knowledge. I argue that the informed way in which a teacher implements a method can serve to offset potentially unequal relations and discriminatory structures and practices in the classroom and, in doing so, improve the quality of the instructional process for both student and teacher. In other words, politically informed teacher use of methods can create conditions that enable subordinated students to move from their usual passive position to one of active and critical engagement. I am convinced that creating pedagogical spaces that enable students to move *from object to subject position* produces more far-reaching, positive effects than the implementation of a particular teaching methodology, regardless of how technically advanced and promising it may be.

The final section of this article will explore and suggest the implementation of what Donaldo Macedo (1994) designates as an

> anti-methods pedagogy that refuses to be enslaved by the rigidity of models and methodological paradigms. An anti-methods pedagogy should be informed by a critical understanding of the sociocultural context that guides our practices so as to free us from the beaten path of methodological certainties and specialisms. (p. 8)

Simply put, it is important that educators not blindly reject teaching methods across the board, but that they reject uncritical appropriation of methods, materials, curricula, etc. Educators need to reject the present methods fetish so as to create learning environments informed by both action and reflection. In freeing themselves from the blind adoption of so-called effective (and sometimes "teacher-proof") strategies, teachers can begin the reflective process, which allows them to recreate and reinvent teaching methods and materials by always taking into consideration the sociocultural realities that can either limit or expand the possibilities to humanize education. It is important that teachers keep in mind that methods are social constructions that grow out of and reflect ideologies that often prevent teachers from understanding the pedagogical implications of asymmetrical power relations among different cultural groups.

THE SIGNIFICANCE OF TEACHER POLITICAL CLARITY[5]

In his letter to North American educators, Paulo Freire (1987) argues that technical expertise and mastery of content area and methodology are insufficient to ensure effective instruction of students from subordinated cultures. Freire contends that, in addition to possessing content area knowledge, teachers must possess political clarity so as to be able to effectively create, adopt, and modify teaching strategies that simultaneously respect and challenge learners from diverse cultural groups in a variety of learning environments.

---

[5] "Political clarity" refers to the process by which individuals achieve a deepening awareness of the sociopolitical and economic realities that shape their lives and their capacity to recreate them. In addition, it refers to the process by which individuals come to better understand possible linkages between macro-level political, economic, and social variables and subordinated groups' academic performance at the micro-level classroom. Thus, it invariably requires linkages between sociocultural structures and schooling.

Teachers working on improving their political clarity recognize that teaching is not a politically neutral undertaking. They understand that educational institutions are socializing institutions that mirror the greater society's culture, values, and norms. Schools reflect both the positive and negative aspects of a society. Thus, the unequal power relations among various social and cultural groups at the societal level are usually reproduced at the school and classroom level, unless concerted efforts are made to prevent their reproduction. Teachers working toward political clarity understand that they can either maintain the status quo, or they can work to transform the sociocultural reality at the classroom and school level so that the culture at this micro-level does not reflect macro-level inequalities, such as asymmetrical power relations that relegate certain cultural groups to a subordinate status.

Teachers can support positive social change in the classroom in a variety of ways. One possible intervention can consist of the creation of heterogeneous learning groups for the purpose of modifying low-status roles of individuals or groups of children.[6] Elizabeth Cohen (1986) demonstrates that when teachers create learning conditions where students, especially those perceived as low status (e.g., limited English speakers in a classroom where English is the dominant language, students with academic difficulties, or those perceived by their peers for a variety of reasons as less able), can demonstrate their possession of knowledge and expertise, they are then able to see themselves, and be seen by others, as capable and competent. As a result, contexts are created in which peers can learn from each other as well.

A teacher's political clarity will not necessarily compensate for structural inequalities that students face outside the classroom; however, teachers can, to the best of their ability, help their students deal with injustices encountered inside and outside the classroom. A number of possibilities exist for preparing students to deal with the greater society's unfairness and inequality that range from engaging in explicit discussions with students about their experiences, to more indirect ways (that nevertheless require a teacher who is politically clear), such as creating democratic learning environments where students become accustomed to being treated as competent and able individuals. I believe that the students, once accustomed to the rights and responsibilities of full citizenship in the classroom, will come to expect respectful treatment and authentic estimation in other contexts. Again, it is important to point out that it is not the particular lesson or set of activities that prepares the student; rather, it is the teacher's politically clear educational philosophy that underlies the varied methods and lessons/activities she or he employs that make the difference.

Under ideal conditions, competent educators simultaneously translate theory into practice *and* consider the population being served and the sociocultural reality in which learning is expected to take place. Let me reiterate that command of a content area or specialization is necessary, but it is not sufficient for effectively working with students. Just as critical is that teachers comprehend that their role as educators is a political act that is never neutral (Freire, 1985,

---

[6] Elizabeth Cohen (1986) explains that in the society at large there are status distinctions made on the basis of social class, ethnic group, and gender. These status distinctions are often reproduced at the classroom level, unless teachers make conscious efforts to prevent this reproduction.

1987, 1993; Freire & Macedo, 1987). In ignoring or negating the political nature of their work with these students, teachers not only reproduce the status quo and their students' low status, but they also inevitably legitimize schools' discriminatory practices. For example, teachers who uncritically follow school practices that unintentionally or intentionally serve to promote tracking and segregation within school and classroom contexts continue to reproduce the status quo. Conversely, teachers can become conscious of, and subsequently challenge, the role of educational institutions and their own roles as educators in maintaining a system that often serves to silence students from subordinated groups.

Teachers must also remember that schools, similar to other institutions in society, are influenced by perceptions of socioeconomic status (SES), race/ethnicity, language, and gender (Anyon, 1988; Bloom, 1991; Cummins, 1989; Ogbu, 1987). They must begin to question how these perceptions influence classroom dynamics. An important step in increasing teacher political clarity is recognizing that, despite current liberal rhetoric regarding the equal value of all cultures, low SES and ethnic minority students have historically (and currently) been perceived as deficient. I believe that the present methods-restricted discussion must be broadened to reveal the deeply entrenched deficit orientation toward "difference" (i.e., non-Western European race/ethnicity, non-English language use, working-class status, femaleness) that prevails in the schools in a deeply "cultural" ideology of White supremacy. As educators, we must constantly be vigilant and ask how the deficit orientation has affected our perceptions concerning students from subordinated populations and created rigid and mechanistic teacher-student relations (Cummins, 1989; Flores, Cousin, & Diaz, 1991; Giroux & McLaren, 1986). Such a model often serves to create classroom conditions in which there is very little opportunity for teachers and students to interact in meaningful ways, establish positive and trusting working relations, and share knowledge.

OUR LEGACY: A DEFICIT VIEW OF SUBORDINATED STUDENTS

As discussed earlier, teaching strategies are neither designed nor implemented in a vacuum. Design, selection, and use of particular teaching approaches and strategies arise from perceptions about learning and learners. I contend that the most pedagogically advanced strategies are sure to be ineffective in the hands of educators who implicitly or explicitly subscribe to a belief system that renders ethnic, racial, and linguistic minority students at best culturally disadvantaged and in need of fixing (if we could only identify the right recipe!), or, at worst, culturally or genetically deficient and beyond fixing.[7] Despite the fact that various models have been proposed to explain the academic failure of certain subordinated groups — academic failure described as *historical, pervasive,* and *disproportionate* — the fact remains that these views of difference are deficit-based and deeply imprinted in our individual and collective psyches (Flores, 1982, 1993; Menchaca & Valencia, 1990; Valencia, 1986, 1991).

---

[7] For detailed discussions regarding various deficit views of subordinated students over time, see Flores, Cousin, and Diaz, 1991; also see Sue and Padilla, 1986.

The deficit model has the longest history of any model discussed in the education literature. Richard Valencia (1986) traces its evolution over three centuries:

> Also known in the literature as the "social pathology" model or the "cultural deprivation" model, the deficit approach explains disproportionate academic problems among low status students as largely being due to pathologies or deficits in their sociocultural background (e.g., cognitive and linguistic deficiencies, low self-esteem, poor motivation). . . . To improve the educability of such students, programs such as compensatory education and parent-child intervention have been proposed. (p. 3)

Barbara Flores (1982, 1993) documents the effect this deficit model has had on the schools' past and current perceptions of Latino students. Her historical overview chronicles descriptions used to refer to Latino students over the last century. The terms range from "mentally retarded," "linguistically handicapped," "culturally and linguistically deprived," and "semilingual," to the current euphemism for Latino and other subordinated students: the "at-risk" student.

Similarly, recent research continues to lay bare our deficit orientation and its links to discriminatory school practices aimed at students from groups perceived as low status (Anyon, 1988; Bloom, 1991; Diaz, Moll, & Mehan, 1986; Oaks, 1986). Findings range from teacher preference for Anglo students, to bilingual teachers' preference for lighter skinned Latino students (Bloom, 1991), to teachers' negative perceptions of working-class parents as compared to middle-class parents (Lareau, 1990), and, finally, to unequal teaching and testing practices in schools serving working-class and ethnic minority students (Anyon, 1988; Diaz et al., 1986; Oaks, 1986; U.S. Commission on Civil Rights, 1973). Especially indicative of our inability to consciously acknowledge the deficit orientation is the fact that the teachers in these studies — teachers from all ethnic groups — were themselves unaware of the active role they played in the differential and unequal treatment of their students.

The deficit view of subordinated students has been critiqued by numerous researchers as ethnocentric and invalid (Boykin, 1983; Diaz et al., 1986; Flores, 1982; Flores et al., 1991; Sue & Padilla, 1986; Trueba, 1989; Walker, 1987). More recent research offers alternative models that shift the source of school failure away from the characteristics of the individual children, their families, and their cultures, and toward the schooling process (Au & Mason, 1983; Heath, 1983; Mehan, 1992; Philips, 1972). Unfortunately, I believe that many of these alternative models often unwittingly give rise to a kinder and more liberal, yet more concealed version of the deficit model that views subordinated students as being in need of "specialized" modes of instruction — a type of instructional "coddling" that mainstream students do not require in order to achieve in school. Despite the use of less overtly ethnocentric models to explain the academic standing of subordinated students, I believe that the deficit orientation toward difference, especially as it relates to low socioeconomic and ethnic minority groups, is very deeply ingrained in the ethos of our most prominent institutions, especially schools, and in the various educational programs in place at these sites.

It is against this sociocultural backdrop that teachers can begin to seriously question the unspoken but prevalent deficit orientation used to hide SES, racial/ethnic, linguistic, and gender inequities present in U.S. classrooms. And it is against this sociocultural backdrop that I critically examine two teaching approaches identified by the educational literature as effective with subordinated student populations.

POTENTIALLY HUMANIZING PEDAGOGY: TWO PROMISING TEACHING APPROACHES

Well-known approaches and strategies such as cooperative learning, language experience, process writing, reciprocal teaching, and whole language activities can be used to create humanizing learning environments where students cease to be treated as objects and yet receive academically rigorous instruction (Cohen, 1986; Edelsky, Altwerger, & Flores, 1991; Palinscar & Brown, 1984; Pérez & Torres-Guzmán, 1992; Zamel, 1982). However, when these approaches are implemented uncritically, they often produce negative results, as indicated by Lisa Delpit (1986, 1988). Critical teacher applications of these approaches and strategies can contribute to discarding deficit views of students from subordinated groups, so that they are treated with respect and viewed as active and capable subjects in their own learning.

Academically rigorous, student-centered teaching strategies can take many forms. One may well ask, is it not merely common sense to promote approaches and strategies that respect, recognize, utilize, and build on students' existing knowledge bases? The answer would be, of course, yes, it is. However, it is important to recognize, as part of our effort to increase our political clarity, that these practices have *not* typified classroom instruction for students from marginalized populations. The practice of learning from and valuing student language and life experiences *often* occurs in classrooms where students speak a language and possess cultural capital that more closely matches that of the mainstream (Anyon, 1988; Lareau, 1990; Winfield, 1986).[8]

Jean Anyon's (1988) classic research suggests that teachers of affluent students are more likely than teachers of working-class students to utilize and incorporate student life experiences and knowledge into the curriculum. For example, in Anyon's study, teachers of affluent students often designed creative and innovative lessons that tapped students' existing knowledge bases; one math lesson, designed to teach students to find averages, asked them to fill out a possession survey inquiring about the number of cars, television sets, refrigerators, and games owned at home so as to teach students to average. Unfortunately, this practice of tapping students' already existing knowledge and language bases is not commonly utilized with student populations traditionally perceived as deficient. Anyon reports that teachers of working-class students viewed them as

---

[8] "Cultural capital" refers to Pierre Bourdieu's concept that certain forms of cultural knowledge are the equivalent of symbolic wealth in that these forms of "high" culture are socially designated as worthy of being sought and possessed. These cultural (and linguistic) knowledge bases and skills are socially inherited and are believed to facilitate academic achievement. See Lamont and Lareau, 1988, for a more in-depth discussion regarding the multiple meanings of cultural capital in the literature.

lacking the necessary cultural capital, and therefore imposed content and behavioral standards with little consideration and respect for student input. Although Anyon did not generalize beyond her sample, other studies suggest the validity of her findings for ethnic minority student populations (Diaz et al., 1986; Moll, 1986; Oaks, 1986).

The creation of learning environments for low SES and ethnic minority students, similar to those for more affluent and White populations, requires that teachers discard deficit notions and genuinely value and utilize students' existing knowledge bases in their teaching. In order to do so, teachers must confront and challenge their own social biases so as to honestly begin to perceive their students as capable learners. Furthermore, they must remain open to the fact that they will also learn from their students. Learning is not a one-way undertaking.

It is important for educators to recognize that no language or set of life experiences is inherently superior, yet our social values reflect our preferences for certain language and life experiences over others. Student-centered teaching strategies such as cooperative learning, language experience, process writing, reciprocal teaching, and whole language activities (if practiced consciously and critically) can help to offset or neutralize our deficit-based failure and recognize subordinated student strengths. Our tendency to discount these strengths occurs whenever we forget that learning only occurs when prior knowledge is accessed and linked to new information.

Beau Jones, Annemarie Palinscar, Donna Ogle, and Eileen Carr (1987) explain that learning *is* the act of linking new information to prior knowledge. According to their framework, prior knowledge is stored in memory in the form of knowledge frameworks. New information is understood and stored by calling up the appropriate knowledge framework and then integrating the new information. Acknowledging and using existing student language and knowledge makes good pedagogical sense, and it also constitutes a humanizing experience for students traditionally *de*humanized and disempowered in the schools. I believe that strategies identified as effective in the literature have the potential to offset reductive education in which "the educator as *the one who knows* transfers existing knowledge to the learner as *the one who does not know*" (Freire, 1985, p. 114, emphasis added). It is important to repeat that mere implementation of a particular strategy or approach identified as effective does not guarantee success, as the current debate in process writing attests (Delpit, 1986, 1988; Reyes, 1991, 1992).

Creating learning environments that incorporate student language and life experiences in no way negates teachers' responsibility for providing students with particular academic content knowledge and skills. It is important not to link teacher respect and use of student knowledge and language bases with a laissez-faire attitude toward teaching. It is equally necessary not to confuse academic rigor with rigidity that stifles and silences students. The teacher is the authority, with all the resulting responsibilities that entails; however, it is not necessary for the teacher to become authoritarian in order to challenge students intellectually. Education can be a process in which teacher and students mutually participate in the intellectually exciting undertaking we call learning. Students *can* become active subjects in their own learning, instead of passive objects waiting to be filled with facts and figures by the teacher.

I would like to emphasize that teachers who work with subordinated populations have the responsibility to assist them in appropriating knowledge bases and discourse styles deemed desirable by the greater society. However, this process of appropriation must be additive, that is, the new concepts and new discourse skills must be added to, not subtracted from, the students' existing background knowledge. In order to assume this additive stance, teachers must discard deficit views so they can use and build on life experiences and language styles too often viewed and labeled as "low class" and undesirable. Again, there are numerous teaching strategies and methods that can be employed in this additive manner. For the purposes of illustration, I will briefly discuss two approaches currently identified as promising for students from subordinated populations. The selected approaches are referred to in the literature as culturally responsive instructional approaches and strategic teaching.

CULTURALLY RESPONSIVE INSTRUCTION:
THE POTENTIAL TO EQUALIZE POWER RELATIONS

Culturally responsive instruction grows out of cultural difference theory, which attributes the academic difficulties of students from subordinated groups to cultural incongruence or discontinuities between the learning, language use, and behavioral practices found in the home and those expected by the schools. Ana María Villegas (1988, 1991) defines culturally responsive instruction as attempts to create instructional situations where teachers use teaching approaches and strategies that recognize and build on culturally different ways of learning, behaving, and using language in the classroom.

A number of classic ethnographic studies document culturally incongruent communication practices in classrooms where students and teachers may speak the same language but use it in different ways. This type of incongruence is cited as a major source of academic difficulties for subordinated students and their teachers (see Au, 1980; Au & Mason, 1983; Cazden, 1988; Erickson & Mohatt, 1982; Heath, 1983; Philips, 1972). For the purposes of this analysis, one form of culturally responsive instruction, the Kamehameha Education Project reading program, will be discussed.

The Kamehameha Education Project is a reading program developed as a response to the traditionally low academic achievement of native Hawaiian students in Western schools. The reading program was a result of several years of research that examined the language practices of native Hawaiian children in home and school settings. Observations of native Hawaiian children showed them to be bright and capable learners; however, their behavior in the classroom signaled communication difficulties between them and their non-Hawaiian teachers. For example, Kathryn Hu-Pei Au (1979, 1980) reports that native Hawaiian children's language behavior in the classroom was often misinterpreted by teachers as being unruly and without educational value. She found that the children's preferred language style in the classroom was linked to a practice used by adults in their homes and community called "talk story." She discusses the

49

talk story phenomenon and describes it as a major speech event in the Hawaiian community, where individuals speak almost simultaneously and where little attention is given to turn taking. Au explains that this practice may inhibit students from speaking out as individuals because of their familiarity with and preference for simultaneous group discussion.

Because the non-Hawaiian teachers were unfamiliar with talk story and failed to recognize its value, much class time was spent either silencing the children or prodding unwilling individuals to speak. Needless to say, very little class time was dedicated to other instruction. More important, the children were constrained and not allowed to demonstrate their abilities as speakers and possessors of knowledge. Because the students did not exhibit their skills in mainstream accepted ways (e.g., competing as individuals for the floor), they were prevented from exhibiting knowledge via their culturally preferred style. However, once the children's interaction style was incorporated into classroom lessons, time on task increased and, subsequently, students' performance on standardized reading tests improved. This study's findings conclude that educators can successfully employ the students' culturally valued language practices while introducing the student to more conventional and academically acceptable ways of using language.

It is interesting to note that many of the research studies that examine culturally congruent and incongruent teaching approaches also inadvertently illustrate the equalization of previous asymmetrical power relations between teachers and students. These studies describe classrooms where teachers initially imposed participation structures upon students from subordinated linguistic minority groups and later learned to negotiate with them rules regarding acceptable classroom behavior and language use (Au & Mason, 1983; Erickson & Mohatt, 1982; Heath, 1983; Philips, 1972). Thus these studies, in essence, capture the successful negotiation of power relations, which resulted in higher student academic achievement and increased teacher effectiveness. Yet there is little explicit discussion in these studies of the greater sociocultural reality that renders it perfectly normal for teachers to automatically disregard and disrespect subordinated students' preferences and to allow antagonistic relations to foment until presented with empirical evidence that legitimizes the students' practices. Instead, the focus of most of these studies rests entirely on the cultural congruence of the instruction and not on the humanizing effects of a more democratic pedagogy. Villegas (1988) accurately critiques the cultural congruence literature when she states:

> It is simplistic to claim that differences in languages used at home and in school are the root of the widespread academic problems of minority children. Admittedly, differences do exist, and they can create communication difficulties in the classroom for both teachers and students. Even so, those differences in language must be viewed in the context of a broader struggle for power within a stratified society. (p. 260)

Despite the focus on the cultural versus the political dimensions of pedagogy, some effort is made to link culturally congruent teaching practices with equalization of classroom power relations. For example, Kathryn Au and Jana Mason

(1983) explain that "one means of achieving cultural congruence in lessons may be to *seek a balance between the interactional rights of teachers and students,* so that the children can participate in ways comfortable to them" (p. 145, emphasis added). Their study compared two teachers and showed that the teacher who was willing to negotiate with students either the topic of discussion or the appropriate participation structure was better able to implement her lesson. Conversely, the teacher who attempted to impose both topic of discussion *and* appropriate interactional rules was frequently diverted because of conflicts with students over one or the other.

Unfortunately, as mentioned earlier, interpretations and practical applications of this body of research have focused on the *cultural* congruence of the approaches. I emphasize the term *cultural* because in these studies the term "culture" is used in a restricted sense devoid of its dynamic, ideological, and political dimensions. Instead, culture is treated as synonymous with ethnic culture, rather than as "the representation of lived experiences, material artifacts and practices *forged within the unequal and dialectical relations* that different groups establish in a given society at a particular point in historical time" (Giroux, 1985, p. xxi, emphasis added). I use this definition of culture because, without identifying the political dimensions of culture and subsequent unequal status attributed to members of different ethnic groups, the reader may conclude that teaching methods simply need to be ethnically congruent to be effective — without recognizing that not all ethnic and linguistic cultural groups are viewed and treated as equally legitimate in classrooms. Interestingly enough, there is little discussion of the various socially perceived minority groups' subordinate status vis-à-vis White teachers and peers in these studies. All differences are treated as ethnic cultural differences and not as responses of subordinated students to teachers from dominant groups, and vice versa.

Given the sociocultural realities in the above studies, the specific teaching strategies may not be what made the difference. Indeed, efforts to uncritically export the Kamehameha Education Project reading program to other student populations resulted in failure (Vogt et al., 1987). It could well be that the teachers' effort to negotiate and share power by treating students as equal participants in their own learning is what made the difference in Hawaii. Just as important is the teachers' willingness to critically interrogate their deficit views of subordinated students. By employing a variety of strategies and techniques, the Kamehameha students were allowed to interact with teachers in egalitarian and meaningful ways. More importantly, the teachers also learned to recognize, value, use, and build upon students' previously acquired knowledge and skills. In essence, these strategies succeeded in creating a comfort zone so students could exhibit their knowledge and skills and, ultimately, empower themselves to succeed in an academic setting. Teachers also benefitted from using a variety of student-centered teaching strategies that humanized their perceptions of treatment of students previously perceived as deficient. Ray McDermott's (1977) classic research reminds us that numerous teaching approaches and strategies can be effective, so long as trusting relations between teacher and students are established and power relations are mutually set and agreed upon.

STRATEGIC TEACHING: THE SIGNIFICANCE OF TEACHER-STUDENT INTERACTION AND NEGOTIATION

Strategic teaching refers to an instructional model that explicitly teaches students learning strategies that enable them consciously to monitor their own learning. This is accomplished through the development of reflective cognitive monitoring and metacognitive skills (Jones, Palinscar, Ogle, & Carr, 1987). The goal is to prepare independent and metacognitively aware students. This teaching strategy makes explicit for students the structures of various text types used in academic settings and assists students in identifying various strategies for effectively comprehending the various genres. Although text structures and strategies for dissecting the particular structures are presented by the teacher, a key component of these lessons is the elicitation of students' knowledge about text types and their own strategies for making meaning before presenting them with more conventional academic strategies.

Examples of learning strategies include teaching various text structures (i.e., stories and reports) through frames and graphic organizers. *Frames* are sets of questions that help students understand a given topic. Readers monitor their understanding of a text by asking questions, making predictions, and testing their predictions as they read. Before reading, frames serve as an advance organizer to activate prior knowledge and facilitate understanding. Frames can also be utilized during the reading process by the reader to monitor self-learning. Finally, frames can be used after a reading lesson to summarize and integrate newly acquired information.

Graphic organizers are visual maps that represent text structures and organizational patterns used in texts and in student writing. Ideally, graphic organizers reflect both the content and text structure. Graphic organizers include semantic maps, chains, and concept hierarchies, and assist the student in visualizing the rhetorical structure of the text. Beau Jones and colleagues (1987) explain that frames and graphic organizers can be "powerful tools to help the student locate, select, sequence, integrate and restructure information — both from the perspective of understanding and from the perspective of producing information in written responses" (p. 38).

Although much of the research on strategic teaching focuses on English monolingual mainstream students, recent efforts to study linguistic minority students' use of these strategies show similar success. This literature shows that strategic teaching improved the students' reading comprehension, as well as their conscious use of effective learning strategies in their native language (Avelar La Salle, 1991; Chamot, 1983; Hernandez, 1991; O'Malley & Chamot, 1990; Reyes, 1987). Furthermore, these studies show that students, despite limited English proficiency, were able to transfer or apply their knowledge of specific learning strategies and text structure to English reading texts. For example, Jose Hernandez (1991) reports that sixth-grade limited English proficient students learned, in the native language (Spanish), to generate hypotheses, summarize, and make predictions about readings. He reports:

> Students were able to demonstrate use of comprehension strategies even when they could not decode the English text aloud. When asked in Spanish about English texts

the students were able to generate questions, summarize stories, and predict future events in Spanish. (p. 101)

Robin Avelar La Salle's (1991) study of third- and fourth-grade bilingual students shows that strategic teaching in the native language of three expository text structures commonly found in elementary social studies and science texts (topical net, matrix, and hierarchy) improved comprehension of these types of texts in both Spanish and English.

Such explicit and strategic teaching is most important in the upper elementary grades, where students are expected to focus on the development of more advanced English literacy skills. Beginning at about third grade, students face literacy demands distinct from those encountered in earlier grades. Jeanne Chall (1983) describes the change in literacy demands in terms of stages of reading. She explains that at a stage three of reading, students cease to "learn to read" and begin "reading to learn." Students in third and fourth grade are introduced to content area subjects such as social studies, science, and health. In addition, students are introduced to expository texts (reports). This change in texts, text structures, and in the functions of reading (reading for information) calls for teaching strategies that will prepare students to comprehend various expository texts (e.g., cause/effect, compare/contrast) used across the curriculum.

Strategic teaching holds great promise for preparing linguistic minority students to face the new literacy challenges in the upper grades. As discussed before, the primary goal of strategic instruction is to foster learner independence. This goal in and of itself is laudable. However, the characteristics of strategic instruction that I find most promising grow out of the premise that teachers and students must interact and negotiate meaning as equals in order to reach a goal.

Teachers, by permitting learners to speak from their own vantage points, create learning contexts in which students are able to empower themselves throughout the strategic learning process. Before teachers attempt to instruct students in new content or learning strategies, efforts are made by the teacher to access student prior knowledge so as to link it with new information. In allowing students to present and discuss their prior knowledge and experiences, the teacher legitimizes and treats as valuable student language and cultural experiences usually ignored in classrooms. If students are encouraged to speak on what they know best, then they are, in a sense, treated as experts — experts who are expected to refine their knowledge bases with the additional new content and strategy information presented by the teacher.

Teachers play a significant role in creating learning contexts in which students are able to empower themselves. Teachers act as cultural mentors of sorts when they introduce students not only to the culture of the classroom, but to particular subjects and discourse styles as well. In the process, teachers assist the students in appropriating the skills (in an additive fashion) for themselves so as to enable them to behave as "insiders" in the particular subject or discipline. Jim Gee (1989) reminds us that the social nature of teaching and learning must involve apprenticeship into the subject's or discipline's discourse in order for students to do well in school. This apprenticeship includes acquisition of particular content matter, ways of organizing content, and ways of using language (oral and written). Gee adds that these discourses are not mastered solely

through teacher-centered and directed instruction, but also by "apprenticeship into social practices through scaffolded and supported interaction with people who have already mastered the discourse" (p. 7). The apprenticeship notion can be immensely useful with subordinated students if it facilitates the acceptance and valorization of students' prior knowledge through a mentoring process.

Models of instruction, such as strategic teaching, can promote such an apprenticeship. In the process of apprenticing linguistic minority students, teachers must interact in meaningful ways with them. This human interaction not only assists students in acquiring new knowledge and skills, but it also often familiarizes individuals from different SES and racial/ethnic groups, and creates mutual respect instead of the antagonism that so frequently occurs between teachers and their students from subordinated groups. In this learning environment, teachers and students learn from each other. The strategies serve, then, not to "fix" the student, but to equalize power relations and to humanize the teacher-student relationship. Ideally, teachers are forced to challenge implicitly or explicitly held deficit attitudes and beliefs about their students and the cultural groups to which they belong.

BEYOND TEACHING STRATEGIES: TOWARDS A HUMANIZING PEDAGOGY

When I recall a special education teacher's experience related in a bilingualism and literacy course that I taught, I am reminded of the humanizing effects of teaching strategies that, similar to culturally responsive instruction and strategic teaching, allow teachers to listen, learn from, and mentor their students. This teacher, for most of her career, had been required to assess her students through a variety of closed-ended instruments, and then to remediate their diagnosed "weaknesses" with discrete skills instruction. The assessment instruments provided little information to explain why the student answered a question either correctly or incorrectly, and they often confirmed perceived student academic, linguistic, and cognitive weaknesses. This fragmented discrete skills approach to instruction restricts the teacher's access to existing student knowledge and experiences not specifically elicited by the academic tasks. Needless to say, this teacher knew very little about her students other than her deficit descriptions of them.

As part of the requirements for my course, she was asked to focus on one Spanish-speaking, limited-English-proficient special education student over the semester. She observed the student in a number of formal and informal contexts, and she engaged him in a number of open-ended tasks. These tasks included allowing him to write entire texts, such as stories and poems (despite diagnosed limited English proficiency), and to engage in "think-alouds" during reading.[9] Through these open-ended activities, the teacher learned about her student's English writing ability (both strengths and weaknesses), his life experiences and world views, and his meaning-making strategies for reading. Consequently, the teacher constructed an instructional plan much better suited to her student's

---

[9] "Think-alouds" refers to an informal assessment procedure where readers verbalize all their thoughts during reading and writing tasks. See J. A. Langer, 1986, for a more in-depth discussion of think-aloud procedures.

academic needs and interests. And even more important, she underwent a humanizing process that allowed her to recognize the varied and valuable life experiences and knowledge her student brought into the classroom.

This teacher was admirably candid when she shared her initial negative and stereotypic views of the student and her radical transformation. Despite this teacher's mastery of content area, her lack of political clarity blinded her to the oppressive and dehumanizing nature of instruction offered to linguistic minority students. Initially, she had formed an erroneous notion of her student's personality, worldview, academic ability, motivation, and academic potential on the basis of his Puerto Rican ethnicity, low SES background, limited English proficiency, and moderately learning-disabled label. Because of the restricted and closed nature of earlier assessment and instruction, the teacher had never received information about her student that challenged her negative perceptions. Listening to her student and reading his poetry and stories, she discovered his loving and sunny personality, learned his personal history, and identified academic strengths and weaknesses. In the process, she discovered and challenged her deficit orientation. The following excerpt from this student's writing exemplifies the power of the student voice for humanizing teachers:

My Father

I love my father very much. I will never forget what my father has done for me and my brothers and sisters. When we first came from Puerto Rico we didn't have food to eat and we were very poor. My father had to work three jobs to put food and milk on the table. Those were hard times and my father worked so hard that we hardly saw him. But even when I didn't see him, I always knew he loved me very much. I will always be grateful to my father. We are not so poor now and so he works only one job. But I will never forget what my father did for me. I will also work to help my father have a better life when I grow up. I love my father very much.

The process of learning about her student's rich and multifaceted background enabled this teacher to move beyond the rigid methodology that had required her to distance herself from the student and to confirm the deficit model to which she unconsciously adhered. In this case, the meaningful teacher-student interaction served to equalize the teacher-student power relations and to humanize instruction by expanding the horizons through which the student demonstrated human qualities, dreams, desires, and capacities that closed-ended tests and instruction never captured.

I believe that the specific teaching methods implemented by the teacher, in and of themselves, were not the significant factors. The actual strengths of methods depend, first and foremost, on the degree to which they embrace a humanizing pedagogy that values the students' background knowledge, culture, and life experiences, and creates learning contexts where power is shared by students and teachers. Teaching methods are a means to an end — humanizing education to promote academic success for students historically under-served by the schools. A teaching strategy is a vehicle to a greater goal. A number of vehicles exist that may or may not lead to a humanizing pedagogy, depending on the sociocultural reality in which teachers and students operate.

The critical issue is the degree to which we hold the moral conviction that we must humanize the educational experience of students from subordinated populations by eliminating the hostility that often confronts these students. This process would require that we cease to be overly dependent on methods as technical instruments and adopt a pedagogy that seeks to forge a cultural democracy where all students are treated with respect and dignity. A true cultural democracy forces teachers to recognize that students' lack of familiarity with the dominant values of the curriculum "does not mean . . . that the lack of these experiences develop in these children a different 'nature' that determines their absolute incompetence" (Freire, 1993, p. 17).

Unless educational methods are situated in the students' cultural experiences, students will continue to show difficulty in mastering content area that is not only alien to their reality, but is often antagonistic toward their culture and lived experiences. Further, not only will these methods continue to fail students, particularly those from subordinated groups, but they will never lead to the creation of schools as true cultural democratic sites. For this reason, it is imperative that teachers problematize the prevalent notion of "magical" methods and incorporate what Macedo (1993) calls an anti-methods pedagogy, a process through which teachers 1) critically deconstruct the ideology that informs the methods fetish prevalent in education, 2) understand the intimate relationships between methods and the theoretical underpinnings that inform these methods, and 3) evaluate the pedagogical consequences of blindly and uncritically replicating methods without regard to students' subordinate status in terms of cultural, class, gender, and linguistic difference. In short, we need

> an anti-methods pedagogy that would reject the mechanization of intellectualism . . . [and] challenge teachers to work toward reappropriation of endangered dignity and toward reclaiming our humanity. The anti-methods pedagogy adheres to the eloquence of Antonio Machado's poem, "Caminante, no hay camino, se hace camino al andar." (Traveler, there are no roads. The road is created as we walk it [together])." (Macedo, 1993, p. 8)

REFERENCES

Anyon, J. (1988). Social class and the hidden curriculum of work. In J. R. Gress (Ed.), *Curriculum: An introduction to the field* (pp. 366–389). Berkeley, CA: McCutchan.

Au, K. H. (1979). Using the experience text relationship method with minority children. *The Reading Teacher, 32,* 677–679.

Au, K. H. (1980). Participant structures in a reading lesson with Hawaiian children: Analysis of a culturally appropriate instructional event. *Anthropology and Educational Quarterly, 11,* 91–115.

Au, K. H., & Mason, J. M. (1983). Cultural congruence in classroom participation structures: Achieving a balance of rights. *Discourse Processes, 6,* 145–168.

Avelar La Salle, R. (1991). *The effect of metacognitive instruction on the transfer of expository comprehension skills: The interlingual and cross-lingual cases.* Unpublished doctoral dissertation, Stanford University.

Bloom, G. M. (1991). *The effects of speech style and skin color on bilingual teaching candidates' and bilingual teachers' attitudes toward Mexican American pupils.* Unpublished doctoral dissertation, Stanford University.

Boykin, A. W. (1983). The academic performance of Afro-American children. In J. T. Spence (Ed.), *Achievement and achievement motives: Psychological and sociological approaches* (pp. 322–369). San Francisco: W. H. Freeman.

Carter, T. P., & Chatfield, M. L. (1986) Effective bilingual schools: Implications for policy and practice. *American Journal of Education, 95,* 200–232.

Cazden, C. (1988). *Classroom discourse: The language of teaching and learning.* Portsmouth, NH: Heinemann.

Chall, J. (1983). *Stages of reading development.* New York: McGraw-Hill.

Chamot, A. U. (1983). How to plan to transfer curriculum from bilingual to mainstream instruction. *Focus, 12.* (A newsletter avialable from The George Washington University National Clearinghouse for Bilingual Education, 1118 22nd St NW, Washington, DC 20037)

Cohen, E. G. (1986). *Designing groupwork: Strategies for the heterogeneous classroom.* New York: Teachers College Press.

Cummins, J. (1989). *Empowering minority students.* Sacramento: California Association of Bilingual Education.

Delpit, L. (1986). Skills and other dilemmas of a progressive black educator. *Harvard Educational Review, 56,* 379–385.

Delpit, L. (1988). The silenced dialogue: Power and pedagogy in educating other people's children. *Harvard Educational Review, 58,* 280-298.

Diaz, S., Moll, L. C., & Mehan, H. (1986). Sociocultural resources in instruction: A context-specific approach. In *Beyond language: Social and cultural factors in schooling language minority students* (pp. 187–230). Los Angeles: California State University, Evaluation, Dissemination and Assessment Center.

Edelsky, C., Altwerger, B., & Flores, B. (1991). *Whole language: What's the difference?* Portsmouth, NH: Heinemann.

Erickson, F., & Mohatt, G. (1982). Cultural organization of participation structures in two classrooms of Indian students. In G. Spindler (Ed.), *Doing the ethnography of schooling: Educational anthropology in action* (pp. 133–174). New York: Holt, Rinehart and Winston.

Flores, B. M. (1982). *Language interference or influence: Toward a theory for Hispanic bilingualism.* Unpublished doctoral dissertation, University of Arizona at Tucson.

Flores, B. M. (1993, April). *Interrogating the genesis of the deficit view of Latino children in the educational literature during the 20th century.* Paper presented at the American Educational Research Association Conference, Atlanta.

Flores, B., Cousin, P. T., & Diaz, E. (1991). Critiquing and transforming the deficit myths about learning, language and culture. *Language Arts, 68,* 369-379.

Freire, P. (1985). *The politics of education: Culture, power and liberation.* South Hadley, MA: Bergin & Garvey.

Freire, P. (1987). Letter to North-American teachers. In I. Shor (Ed.), *Freire for the classroom* (pp. 211–214). Portsmouth, NH: Boynton/Cook.

Freire, P. (1993). *A pedagogy of the city.* New York: Continuum Press.

Freire, P., & Macedo, D. (1987). *Literacy: Reading the word and the world.* South Hadley, MA: Bergin & Garvey.

Gee, J. P. (1989). Literacy, discourse, and linguistics: Introduction. *Journal of Education, 171,* 5–17.

Gibson, M. A., & Ogbu, J. U. (1991). *Minority status and schooling: A comparative study of immigrant and involuntary minorities.* New York: Garland.

Giroux, H. (1985). Introduction. In P. Freire, *The politics of education: Culture, power and liberation* (pp. xi-xxv). South Hadley, MA.: Bergin & Garvey.

Giroux, H. (1992). *Border crossing: Cultural workers and the politics of education.* New York: Routledge.

Giroux, H., & McLaren, P. (1986). Teacher education and the politics of engagement: The case for democratic schooling. *Harvard Educational Review, 56,* 213–238.

Golnick, D. M., & Chinn, P. C. (1986). *Multicultural education in a pluralistic society.* Columbus, OH: Merrill.

Heath, S. B. (1983). *Ways with words.* New York: Cambridge University Press.

Hernandez, J. S. (1991). Assisted performance in reading comprehension strategies with non-English proficient students. *Journal of Educational Issues of Language Minority Students, 8,* 91–112.

Jones, B. F., Palinscar, A. S., Ogle, D. S., & Carr, E. G. (1987). *Strategic teaching and learning: Cognitive instruction in the content areas.* Alexandria, VA: Association for Supervision and Curriculum Development.

Knapp, M. S., & Shields, P. M. (1990). *Better schooling for the children of poverty: Alternatives to conventional wisdom: Vol. 2. Commissioned papers and literature review.* Washington, DC: U.S. Department of Education.

Lamont, M., & Lareau, A. (1988). Cultural capital-allusions, gaps and glissandos in recent theoretical developments. *Sociological Theory, 6,* 153–168.

Langer, J. A. (1986). *Children reading and writing: Structures and strategies.* Norwood, New Jersey: Ablex.

Lareau, A. (1990). *Home advantage: Social class and parental intervention in elementary education.* New York: Falmer Press.

Lucas, T., Henze, R., & Donato, R. (1990). Promoting the success of Latino language-minority students: An exploratory study of six high schools. *Harvard Educational Review, 60,* 315–340.

Macedo, D. (1994). Preface. In P. McLaren & C. Lankshear (Eds.), *Conscientization and resistance* (pp. 1–8). New York: Routledge.

McDermott, R. P. (1977). Social relations as contexts for learning in school. *Harvard Educational Review, 47,* 198–213.

McLeod, B. (Ed.). (in press). *Cultural diversity and second language learning.* Albany: State University of New York Press.

Means, B., & Knapp, M. S. (1991). *Teaching advanced skills to educationally disadvantaged students.* Washington, DC: U.S. Department of Education.

Mehan, H. (1992). Understanding inequality in schools: The contribution of interpretive studies. *Sociology of Education, 65*(1), 1-20.

Menchaca, M., & Valencia, R. (1990). Anglo-Saxon ideologies in the 1920s–1930s: Their impact on the segregation of Mexican students in California. *Anthropology and Education Quarterly, 21,* 222–245.

Moll, L. C. (1986). Writing as communication: Creating learning environments for students. *Theory Into Practice, 25,* 102–110.

Oaks, J. (1986). Tracking, inequality, and the rhetoric of school reform: Why schools don't change. *Journal of Education, 168,* 61–80.

Ogbu, J. (1987). Variability in minority responses to schooling: Nonimmigrants vs. immigrants. In G. Spindler & L. Spindler (Eds.), *Interpretive ethnography of education* (pp. 255–280). Hillsdale, NJ: Lawrence Erlbaum Associates.

O'Malley, J., & Chamot, A. U. (1990). *Learning strategies in second language acquisition.* New York: Cambridge University Press.

Palinscar, A. S., & Brown, A. L. (1984). Reciprocal teaching of comprehension fostering and comprehension-monitoring activities. *Cognition and Instruction, 1*(23), 117–175.

Pérez, B., & Torres-Guzmán, M. E. (1992). *Learning in two worlds: An integrated Spanish/English biliteracy approach.* New York: Longman.

Philips, S. U. (1972). Participant structures and communication competence: Warm Springs children in community and classroom. In C. B. Cazden, V. P. John, & D. Hymes (Eds.), *Functions of language in the classroom* (pp. 370–394). New York: Teachers College Press.

Reyes, M. de la Luz. (1987). Comprehension of content area passages: A study of Spanish/English readers in the third and fourth grade. In S. R. Goldman & H. T. Trueba (Eds.), *Becoming literate in English as a second language* (pp. 107–126). Norwood, NJ: Ablex.

Reyes, M. de la Luz. (1991). A process approach to literacy during dialogue journals and literature logs with second language learners. *Research in the Teaching of English, 25,* 291–313.

Reyes, M. de la Luz. (1992). Challenging venerable assumptions: Literacy instruction for linguistically different students. *Harvard Educational Review, 62,* 427–446.

Sue, S., & Padilla, A. (1986). Ethnic minority issues in the U.S.: Challenges for the educational system. In *Beyond language: Social and cultural factors in schooling language minority students* (pp. 35–72). Los Angeles: California State University, Evaluation, Dissemination and Assessment Center.

Tikunoff, W. (1985). *Applying significant bilingual instructional features in the classroom.* Rosslyn, VA: National Clearinghouse for Bilingual Education.

Tinajero, J. V., & Ada, A. F. (1993). *The power of two languages: Literacy and biliteracy for Spanish-speaking students.* New York: Macmillan/McGraw-Hill.

Trueba, H. T. (1989). Sociocultural integration of minorities and minority school achievement. In *Raising silent voices: Educating the linguistic minorities for the 21st century* (pp. 1–27). New York: Newbury House.

U. S. Commission on Civil Rights. (1973). *Teachers and students: Report V. Mexican-American study: Differences in teacher interaction with Mexican-American and Anglo students.* Washington, DC: Government Printing Office.

Valencia, R. (1986, November 25). *Minority academic underachievement: Conceptual and theoretical considerations for understanding the achievement problems of Chicano students.* Paper presented to the Chicano Faculty Seminar, Stanford University.

Valencia, R. (1991). *Chicano school failure and success: Research and policy agendas for the 1990s.* New York: Falmer Press.

Villegas, A. M. (1988). School failure and cultural mismatch: Another view. *Urban Review, 20,* 253–265.

Villegas, A. M. (1991). *Culturally responsive pedagogy for the 1990s and beyond.* Paper prepared for the Educational Testing Service, Princeton, NJ.

Vogt, L. A., Jordan, C., & Tharp, R. G. (1987). Explaining school failure, producing school success: Two cases. *Anthropology & Education Quarterly, 18,* 276–286.

Walker, C. L. (1987). Hispanic achievement: Old views and new perspectives. In H. T. Trueba (Ed.), *Success or failure: Learning and the language minority student* (pp. 15–32). New York: Newbury House.

Webb, L. C. (1987). *Raising achievement among minority students.* Arlington, VA: American Associates of School Administrators.

Winfield, L. F. (1986). Teachers' beliefs toward academically at risk students in inner urban schools. *Urban Review, 18,* 253–267.

Zamel, V. (1982). Writing: The process of discovering meaning. *TESOL Quarterly, 16,* 195–209.

Giving Voice to the Voiceless

BEVERLY McELROY-JOHNSON

In this article, Beverly McElroy-Johnson weaves together memories of her early experiences as a young African American encountering prejudice in school with reflections on her current practice as a junior high school English teacher. Through this intimate narrative, she expresses concerns about the development of today's African American students. She believes today's African American youth continue to face many of the same obstacles that she faced as a young girl — low self-esteem, lack of validation in society and in the classroom, and, consequently, poor motivation and a lack of confidence in their ability to succeed. McElroy-Johnson emphasizes the need for significant improvements in teacher awareness and advocacy that celebrates African American culture and provides the necessary academic and social education that the next generation must have in order to succeed.

Every person has a different voice, just as every person has a different genetic inheritance. A person's voice is like a fingerprint, an identifying mark. There are squeaky, low, cheerful, harsh, angry, strident, weak, and sweet voices — all different kinds. In fact, most people have two voices — an outer voice that other people hear when they speak, and an inner voice that other people may not hear at all. There are people who have a particularly difficult time making contact with their inner voice with any confidence, and thus often take the authority of external voices as their own. Some people are so used to hearing their own voices that they hardly hear anything else, while others have been silenced or unheard for so long that they either never learned to speak or have forgotten how.

When I use the term *voice*, I am thinking of a strong sense of identity within an individual, an ability to express a personal point of view, and a sense of personal well-being that allows a student to respond to and become engaged with the material being studied, the other students in the classroom, and the teacher. Voice, in this sense, is having a place within the academic setting, other than just a desk and a book. Voice is the student's participation in and acceptance of the academic and intellectual process. It is the student's desire to express ideas in a clear, coherent way, because that student understands that his or her thoughts are important. It is the solid understanding of why an individual must communicate clearly and effectively, the recognition of self within the student that gives that student the ability to express with confidence the answers to important questions within the academic setting. Voice is identity, a sense of self, a sense of relationship to others, and a sense of purpose. Voice is power — power to express ideas and convictions, power to direct and shape an individual life towards a productive and positive fulfillment for self, family, community, nation, and the world.

Harvard Educational Review Vol. 63 No. 1 Spring 1993, 85–104

The students I teach have different voices. They come from thirty-nine different countries and speak twenty-nine different languages. I teach eighth- and ninth-grade English classes (and previously seventh-grade English class as well) at Westlake Junior High School, which is located in the central section of Oakland, California, close to the downtown business district. The school's student population consists of three major groups: 44 percent African American; 42 percent Asian (including Chinese, Vietnamese, Laotian, Thai, and other Pacific groups, mostly immigrant); and 12 percent Hispanic (mostly Mexican). The remaining 2 percent are made up of other diverse groups from around the world. The school is divided into two sections, one devoted primarily to English as a Second Language students, which is called the International Department. The other section, which has no official name, is for native English speakers, primarily African Americans. Our faculty is predominantly European American; the support staff is predominantly African American.

Since arriving at Westlake Junior High School, I've had only one Caucasian student. Most of my students are Asian, African American, and Hispanic. Because their inner and outer voices have often been historically muted and stifled, they have little sense of security when they speak during class discussions.

In this article, I will focus on the educational status of African American students and my connection to them culturally and ethnically. My concerns stem from my own personal observations and experience, which is supported by statistical information collected within my district. These statistics, compiled by the District Curriculum and Instruction Department, show that African American students are unable to: 1) complete high school disproportionately to other groups; 2) function within certain classrooms (88% of suspensions at my school are of African American students, mostly males); 3) read and write at a level that enables them to be socially and economically successful within the school environment and in the larger work world; 4) have a sense of personal power and worth.

The fact that I am an African American teacher and a woman is obviously a strength for me in teaching African American students, because of our shared historical connections and collective experience in this country. I was brought up to believe in the significance of the ancestral African role of woman, her significance as mother and teacher in the beginning years of a young person's life. Some may ask, "Can you teach other children as well?" This question is misguided at best and racist at worst, and reveals an underlying negative assumption. My response is simple: Does anyone ever ask the many White teachers all over the world who teach non-White children, including African American children, if they (Whites) can teach them as well as Blacks, or if their whiteness somehow limits their work with "other" people's children?

As a teacher, my dedication to teach all students as they are is essential to my instructional practices. However, recognition of my own background as a woman and as an African American contributes to my strong sense of self, my personal/cultural history, and my identity. It is this personal sense of strength that makes me a credible person and teacher.

Like all human beings, I am affected by my cultural/ethnic condition and gender. By acknowledging and accepting my own identity, I am able to accept others and assist my students, whoever they are, in building their own identities as readers, writers, and human beings. I am also able to study what I do not know about others, to do research, to ask for assistance from more knowledgeable sources, and, thereby, to encourage student progress in learning.

To me, successful students are those who are able to master the necessary tools, whatever they may be, to ensure their completion of high school, college, vocational school, and/or apprenticeships in order to make positive lives for themselves. Success especially involves the ability to read and write, so that students have the power of communication and the necessary proficiencies for seeking employment. Success also means students being able to navigate, in a disciplined way, within a diverse society that is sometimes hostile to them, without falling apart and/or being self-destructive.

However, as an observer of student successes, I am disturbed that the failures of the educational system seem to be reflected disproportionately in the African American culture, and, more specifically, among African American males. Why is this? Perhaps part of the answer lies in the status of African Americans as a minority group and in their history. While Asians, for example — who are often referred to by the dominant culture as the "model minority" — voluntarily immigrated to the United States to seek a better life, African Americans were forcibly brought in chains. In his article "Minority Status and Literacy," John Ogbu (1990) points out that Asian immigrants

> have chosen to move to the United States or to some other society, in the belief that this change will lead to an improvement in their economic well-being or to greater political freedom. These expectations influence the way they perceive and respond to white Americans and to institutions controlled by whites. . . . Castelike or involuntary minorities are people initially brought into the United States through slavery, conquest or colonization. Resenting the loss of their former freedom and perceiving the social, political, and economic barriers against them as part of an undeserved oppression, American Indians, black Americans, Mexican Americans and native Hawaiians are characteristic American examples of these involuntary minorities. (p. 145)

The failure of the current urban educational system is that, in general, it does not address the needs of all those it serves. Educators who force a Eurocentric curriculum upon students from non-European backgrounds assume that these students: 1) want to be like European Americans; 2) understand this Eurocentric framework; and 3) bring with them the necessary knowledge and empowerment to navigate in such foreign waters.

The failure of the educational system extends further, in my opinion, into the political and psychological nature of the teaching body, primarily consisting of European American females who, for whatever reasons, are too often unaware of the non-European learners' needs, who ignore the need to translate curriculum and instruction into language readily accessible to these learners, and/or who rigidly oppose acknowledging diversity and instead work for the "oneness of all" in "their image" of what that is. This destroys the self-concept and individual power of non-European students, forcing them either into personal conduct that is destructive in nature or into a "white-washed" imitation of the European American ideal, an uneasy identity that is in opposition to their own natural cultural, ethnic, and racial identities.

Another way of addressing the reason for the failures of African American students within the U.S. educational system is to study in depth the collective history of African Americans, and the psychological implications of their history on this group of people. It has never ceased to amaze me that, when the subject of African American history is raised and the impact of slavery on this group is addressed, the response is often negative and resistant. If the subject were the dropping of the atomic bomb on innocent people at Hiroshima, one would select words carefully in raising any objection to the voicing of the terror of that deed and the effect it has had on the Japanese people and the world. If it were the Holocaust, one would be ill-advised to raise an objection to the constant reminders of these horrors in print, on television, and in film. We are encouraged to feel empathy and concern for the Southeast Asian people, who have fled oppression, or the Central American people, who are suffering from the ravages of war. Yet, when the subject of the psychological, moral, emotional, spiritual, and physical effects of slavery upon African American men, women, and children comes up, the responses are often very different, even hostile.

Since my sophomore year in high school, I have heard these negative attitudes and responses expressed, at times overtly and at other times more subtly. I attended Male High School in Louisville, Kentucky, and graduated with honors in 1965. The name of the school itself explains some of its limitations; previous to my enrollment, the school's student body had been all White and all male. I received no college counseling while there, even though I graduated second in a class of 500 students that was roughly 15 percent African American, second only to the valedictorian, a White male, who did receive such counseling.

However, my experience of this attitude extends into every aspect of my adult life, notably my professional and volunteer environments. When I was hired to be assistant manager of press relations at Kaiser Steel, I was told by the head of our department that I filled two quotas — "You're Black and a woman, and we need the federal subsidies that go with that." My personal accomplishments and abilities were not discussed. Whenever I expressed concerns about the racist/sexist overtones at work, including the hostile jokes or slanders, I was not taken seriously and was even told that I had "an axe to grind." Sometimes this attitude took the form of asking me questions like, "Don't you like being a woman?" or, "Do you have a problem being Black?"

After leaving that profession, I experienced similar attitudes in the volunteer work I did. European Americans would express prejudices that were often explicit and sometimes implicit, such as, "You're very intelligent. You're really different from most Black people. How did you turn out so well?" (shock) or, "My, you're so articulate" (surprise). Others would dwell on my physical appearance — "You're so attractive" or "You look nice" (condescending) — in situations where the issues being addressed had nothing to do with physical attributes. My intelligence and ideas were often ignored. When I complained that these comments and attitudes smacked of racism, sexism, or both, and were extremely painful for me to deal with, I was told, "Well, that's the past. Things have changed" or "Here we go again."

As far as I am concerned, those of us who have persisted in insisting that we be heard and that our voices be acknowledged have done so at great personal sacrifice. In the face of ridicule and denial, we still attempt to make contact with our brothers and sisters of different cultures, especially our European American coworkers in education, in this democratic society where individual voice is ostensibly supreme.

The African American experience over the past twenty-five years, including my own, has been a particularly painful one — an experience rooted in a past of great ancestral beauty in Africa and the sorrow of slavery in America. It involves the realization that the few of us who have passed through a window of time and opportunity have often done so at great personal cost and with the neglect of our own inner spirits as human beings. For me, poet Paul Laurence Dunbar (1990) eloquently captures this state of being in "Sympathy":

> I know why the caged bird sings, ah me,
> When his wing is bruised and his bosom sore, —
> When he beats his bars and would be free;
> It is not a carol of joy or glee,
> But a prayer that he sends from his heart's deep core,
> But a plea, that upward to Heaven he flings —
> I know why the caged bird sings!
> (p. 45)

I also identify with the words Dunbar (1990) expresses in "We Wear the Mask":

> We wear the mask that grins and lies,
> It hides our cheeks and shades our eyes, —
> This debt we pay to human guile;
> With torn and bleeding hearts we smile,
> And mouth with myriad subtleties.
>
> Why should the world be over-wise,
> In counting all our tears and sighs?
> Nay, let them only see us, while
> We wear the mask.
>
> We smile, but, O great Christ, our cries
> To thee from tortured souls arise.
> We sing, but oh the clay is vile
> Beneath our feet, and long the mile;
> But let the world dream otherwise,
> We wear the mask.
> (p. 251)

For me, the denial has ended. I can no longer tolerate the refusal of most European Americans to see that we African Americans are, independently of them, living, breathing, thinking human beings with a culture, a history, and an origin of our own. Our complaints are as real as those of our Japanese American brothers and sisters who have received recognition and restitution for their grievances. The genocide, the destruction of our will, the enslavement of our ancestors has been, for us, and I dare say for the rest of humanity, as vile as the Holocaust. I think we need to be heard and to be recognized, but not for revenge or restitution — there can be no restitution or revenge to equal the death and destruction of millions of African souls traversing the middle passage to the Americas in slave ships. We have no country but this one, no education but the one offered here, no language but English, no nationality but the one we have here.

> Everything of Africa that we had including language was taken away from us. All we had left was our skin. So, I guess my ethnic background is the Black-American ethnic culture which has built itself on half-remembered scraps of things from Africa and been incorporated with the new American experience from the plantations. I am not African and I am not accepted as being American, yet. Have I no ethnicity? I think not. (Gandesbery, 1970, p. 10)

We must have full recognition and participation. We cannot be dismissed. And yet, we are. Many of the images, culture, values, and concerns reflected in every institution of this country, including the media, television, and schools tell us to "sit down, shut up, and accept what you have. It's not that bad. Be glad you have what you have. Things have changed." But what changes is a matter of who has the power. Change — when our children are not graduating from high school? Change — when young African American males are killed in the streets or ending up in prison? Feels like the past to me.

> The persistent tendency to think of dark skin as unattractive, kinky hair as "bad" hair, and African features as less appealing than Caucasian features, come from this sense of inferiority. Our lack of respect for African American experts comes from this sense of inferiority. The disastrously high Black-on-Black homicide rate is in many ways indicative of fundamental disrespect for Black life growing out of this same sense of inferiority. It is a simple fact that people who love themselves seek to preserve their lives — not destroy them. (Akbar, 1991, p. 22)

My African American students are often afraid that they are unacceptable, stupid, or not capable of making it in school because of fears of inferiority, which have been reinforced by a racist society. These students are thus afraid to write, because nothing exposes voice more clearly than written pieces. Many of my other students, who are voluntary immigrants, express themselves differently; their fear motivates them to make high marks so that they can succeed in their new country, socially, and economically.

Recently, one of my African American students asked me, in a rather defensive tone, how he was doing, and I told him, "Fine." "But I always fail English," he said, sounding depressed. This baffled me, since he is at the appropriate grade level for his age. We talked about it, and I discovered that what he really meant is that he *feels* like a failure. Since that time he has approached me several times with a self-denigrating attitude, and I have given him the affirmation he needs. He is doing well, and his attitude seems to be improving as he experiences that he is capable, and that he may be a better student than he thinks he is or than his past experiences have shown him to be. Students need to feel safe, free from ridicule and disrespect. They don't want to be rejected.

I like to use Maya Angelou's (1969) book, *I Know Why the Caged Bird Sings*, to explore the idea of voice. After extensive work in curriculum development with other ninth-grade teachers in Oakland, we chose this book as a core nonfiction work for ninth graders under the thematic umbrella, "The Individual and Society."[1] For me this is a good choice, because Angelou's life, which was fraught with difficulties — silence, loneliness, oppression, abuse — demonstrates victory over all of these and testifies to the power of courage, hope, love, and spiritual joy. It is a testament to the individual's victory over what could have been overwhelming odds. She represents a model of a person who regarded learning, reading, writing, and understanding as important, someone for whom education was the key to liberation. Students need to see this model.

When Angelou was eight years old, she was raped by her mother's lover. She was devastated — violated, silenced, and without voice in matters affecting her life. She subsequently entered a period of silence, and it wasn't until she met her first great teacher, Mrs. Flowers, that she found a reason to speak. She loved Mrs. Flowers, and she loved the poetry that Mrs. Flowers brought into her life.

The image of a teacher whom the student respects and loves so much that the student wants to communicate has had a profound effect upon me and my teaching. I learned to speak, to read, to want to communicate because I loved my teachers, beginning with my mother. It was this love that has led me into deeper understanding. I consider myself very ordinary. In fact, I think I am a slow learner, but the love of others has taught me to think and to love. It is out of deep gratitude to those teachers that I do the best I can with what I have been given. Therefore, *I Know Why the Caged Bird Sings* is a wonderful model of human accomplishment, victory, and identity for me, as well as for my students.

The problems associated with prejudice, difficult parental relationships, divorce, sexual relationships, pregnancy, abuse, and homelessness are also presented in Angelou's book, in a way that demonstrates how they can be overcome by education. This is good for my students, many of whom, regardless of race or culture, are beset by seemingly insurmountable problems in their own environments. Angelou's work shows that even tremendous problems can be conquered, that amazing things are possible, and that one can forgive the hurts of life, can acknowledge what is not good and choose to live life at the highest level, being good and true to oneself.

In the opening chapter of *I Know Why the Caged Bird Sings*, Angelou writes about a Sunday in church when, wearing a faded purple dress made from an old White woman's throw-away, she is ridiculed by the other children. Her fantasy is that these children will one day be sorry when they realize that she is really a little White girl with blonde hair, and they will then have to give her the respect she deserves:

> Wouldn't they be surprised when one day I woke out of my black ugly dream, and my real hair, which was long and blond, would take the place of the kinky mass that Momma wouldn't let me straighten? My light-blue eyes were going to hypnotize them after all the things they said about 'my daddy must of been a chinaman' (I thought they meant made out of china, like a cup) because my eyes were so small and squinty. Then they would understand why I had never picked up a Southern accent, or spoke the common slang; and why I had to be forced to eat pigs' tails and snouts. Because I was really white and because a cruel fairy stepmother, who

---

[1] This theme, "The Individual and Society," was chosen by English teachers in our district because it would cover a broad range of literary materials, from Angelou's *I Know Why the Caged Bird Sings* to Shakespeare's *Romeo and Juliet* to Orwell's *Animal Farm*.

was understandably jealous of my beauty, had turned me into a too-big Negro girl, with nappy black hair, broad feet and a space between her teeth that would hold a number-two pencil. (Angelou, 1969, p. 2)

When I read the first chapter, including this passage, to my students, their reactions are mixed. The entire class begins to brainstorm as to the effects of Angelou's self-view on the eventual outcome of her life. Students participate by offering physical, mental, and emotional characteristics that they feel would be significant to Angelou's development as a person. I write their ideas on butcher paper, and then they group related ideas into categories. They look at how her attitude affects the successes or failures of her life — in other words, they make predictions. Since most of them know nothing about her, and those with any knowledge are unsure of themselves, they have little to go on besides the book's first chapter. In one class, a great deal of giggling was generated around her physical qualities: "She got nappy hair, and she's stanky," yelled out one young man.

This remark reminded me of what it was like growing up in Louisville, Kentucky, where I had "good" hair — not as good as White folks, but not as nappy as Black folks.[2] At least that was the case until Nanny, my father's mother, took a hot comb to it. But this article isn't really about Nanny and my problems. It's not even about hair texture and skin color. Those are merely metaphors for what is really going on in the internal world of many African Americans: the sense of self-contempt and self-hatred that many of us take in stride with a sense of humor, and which are reflected nowhere more clearly than in the classroom. The student who yelled out "she got nappy hair" was voicing the self-view that many African Americans have accepted consciously or, even more unfortunately, unconsciously:

> Even today there is an unnatural equation of Caucasian physical features with beauty, intelligence, authority, and so forth. A disproportionate number of professional, educated so-called "beautiful" African Americans have prominently Caucasian features. . . . "Good hair" and "nice features" are still thought to be those characteristics most like Caucasians. Contrary to popular belief, these attitudes have not changed substantially among African American youth who have grown up since the "Black Power" movement of the 1960's. (Akbar, 1991, p. 32)

For me, this hair consciousness began on my first day of school. The day began as if it were my birthday. My Mom had been preparing me for weeks, telling me how grown up I was, how special I was to begin first grade at five years old. That morning she woke me up saying, "How's my first grader? Come on big girl. Get

---

[2] Good hair is European hair or European American hair, the kind featured in most of the television shampoo commercials, and magazine advertisements. In fact, blonde hair might be considered the ultimate. After all, "blondes have more fun."

For most African Americans, this straight hair can only be approximated through the use of chemical relaxers or straighteners. Hair is a metaphor and a reality for the differences between Blacks and Whites. White people have beautiful hair. Black people have ugly hair. Many African American people believe this consciously and/or unconsciously.

No chemical can really make a Black person White. However, because of rape and miscegenation, some Blacks have come closer to European standards of beauty. Historically, for African Americans, hair texture and skin color reflect one's proximity to European Americans and their power. The straighter the hair, the lighter the skin, the better the person. African American literature and experience are full of examples of this problematic sense of values.

up. Let's get a bath!" As I rubbed sleep out of my eyes, I was filled with nervousness, excitement, and a sense of my new-found maturity. I was the star of the day!

After Mama's breakfast of bacon, eggs, toast, orange juice, and milk, I dressed for my new adventure. I was proud to be going to first grade at five, since my birthday wasn't until November, and I had already begun reading by looking at newspapers, cutting out words, identifying them, and learning them with my Mom's help. My head was full of wonderful stories of princesses who turned frogs into princes with a kiss. Flowers fascinated me and brought me great joy. So, wearing a pretty white dress and a yellow rose from my mother's rose bush in my tightly braided shoulder-length hair, I set out for Virginia Avenue Elementary School. I was all the more joyous because it had also been my Mom's school. The principal had been her principal, and the teachers knew her. My excitement knew no limits. Besides going to school for the first time, I had my daddy beside me. I was always in love with him, because he was tall and beautiful. We walked up the street — me bursting with pride — all the way past Leonhardt's Grocery, through the Greenwood Cemetery shortcut, and on to Virginia Avenue and the school.

I don't remember my first-grade teacher. It seems that I should, and if someone told me her name, perhaps I would. My most vivid impression of my first school day — in fact of my first year of school — centers around a girl named Sherylanne. Sherylanne had really short hair in rubber bands and barrettes all over her head, and she was lighter than I in complexion. By now I was painfully aware from my neighborhood friends of being "yellow" or "high yellow" or "yellow belly," or sometimes "macaroni and cheese," a take-off on my last name, McElroy.

We hadn't been in the room half an hour before Sherylanne apparently had decided she couldn't stand me. All I remember is her coming up to me and smacking me, saying, "You think you cute you yellow thing, cause you got long hair." As she ripped the yellow rose out of my hair and stomped on it, all I could do was cry. Why did she attack me? I was mute, shocked, hurt. I didn't understand. Tears streamed down my face until Daddy came. When I asked him "Why?", he could only answer, "She's just jealous," and give me a pat on the head.

I don't remember my first-grade teacher intervening at all with Sherylanne and me. She was either unaware of what was going on, or she didn't care. And it didn't matter what color she was — we both needed her help.[3] Sherylanne needed someone to train her in how to treat other people. I needed someone to teach me how to stand up for myself. We needed help in understanding ourselves, to get in touch with our voices. Sherylanne and I needed to speak up about what was bothering us, needed to be given an inner voice of self-worth. Where was the teacher? A good teacher would have "seized the day," would have talked about "good" hair versus "bad" hair, dark skin versus light skin. My school was full of pictures of African Americans of all hues. A good teacher would have used those pictures and had us draw pictures to teach us about our heritage and

---

[3] I attended segregated schools until high school, and all of my teachers were Black in elementary and junior high.

to instill pride in us for who we were and where we came from — pride in our history. Instead, on that first day of school I waited in a state of distress, fear, and sadness for my Dad to pick me up.

A good teacher creates an environment in which the child grows and develops, replacing the environment of the child's home. A child leaves the safety of the home at five years old and is completely vulnerable, spending from four to six hours a day in a foreign environment. A good teacher tries to address the needs of the student, whatever those needs may be. A bad teacher resists those needs, blaming them on someone else at best, or ignoring them at worst. A good teacher succeeds in assisting students to handle their needs and become successful within the school system. A bad teacher fails to help her students adapt to the school environment, ignores the children, or is too self-involved, ignorant, or self-assertive to look at the individual, cultural, and human needs of the student.

I know now that Sherylanne's behavior was more than just jealousy. It was part of a predicament shared by many African Americans, one reflected in the attitudes of most of my students. I relate the story about Sherylanne not because of its personal significance to me, but to illustrate the need for teachers of children who come from an African American background to be vigilant in helping them understand that these kinds of attitudes reflect self-denial and self-hatred. Students, and young people in general, can be resilient and forgiving — often among my students, in the face of awesome odds. But resiliency does not negate the reality of how deeply African American people are affected by the forces of racism. No matter how strong people are, the power of these forces has an impact on the lives of all of African Americans, and ultimately all people. Through conscious development of personal/cultural and historical self-knowledge, people can deal effectively with the limitations placed on them by our society.

In my classroom, as I have stated earlier, many students arrive with attitudes about themselves and their appearances that are often negative. I teach directly to these problems. Beginning with the first day of school, I tell my students that it doesn't matter to me what they look like, what color they are, what country they come from, how much money they have, what kind of hairdo they have, what kind of clothes, shoes, and jewelry they own. My only concern is what they have in their heads and in their hearts. I ask them three questions: How much do you know about the English language? How well do you think? Can you communicate your thoughts intelligently in speaking and in writing? These three questions are the basis of our relationships in the classroom.

I divide all of my classes into groups of four students each, which are mixed by race and gender. I tell the students that they must leave all that old racist/sexist baggage outside my door. If they want to, they can pick it up again when they leave the room, but I don't think most of them really want that excess baggage.

The word educate comes from the Latin *educare*, which means "to lead forth." By returning students to the source — to themselves and to their inner understandings of identity, culture, responsibility, and self-worth — it is possible to "lead them forth" to an expanded view of self and of others through an English curriculum designed to give them knowledge, skill, and competence to communicate intelligently. As a teacher, it is my job to guide them through the process of learning what they will need to know about themselves and others, through reading, writing, and communication, in order to live in a larger environment, no matter what it is. Knowledge gives them power, a voice in the development of their own lives. This kind of education gives them power to make positive lives for themselves and others.

Education involves taking personal experience, objectifying it, and relating it to universal themes that are important to all people. A teacher, for example, must be aware that all children need to be loved, affirmed, and appreciated, to be given guidance, direction, and instruction. Teachers have a captive audience and a great deal of time each day to impart important basic values to their students. But at the same time that we share universal characteristics, we are also different from one another. We all have our own ancestors, culture, religion, and history, and these differences must be recognized by the teacher. We must begin by leading our students back to the cause of their attitudes in order to move them forward to understand their experience and take charge of their lives.

As an English teacher, I am aware that adolescence is fraught with the drama of life. It is the time when young people make basic decisions about the kind of people they are going to hang out with and the kind of people they are going to be. It is a time of rebellion against parents, a time of first love, and a time for making big decisions and choices about future educational, professional, and employment goals. In today's schools, many of these adolescents have lost their way, have no knowledge of who they really are, and it's our job as teachers to educate them, to help them find their way. Perhaps their parents should have given them an African American consciousness, but many parents don't have it themselves. No one can blame the children or their parents for this failure. For four hundred years, African Americans have had their history, language, culture, and self-worth destroyed by the forces of slavery and segregation. It is no secret that African American people have long been seen as less than human by the forces of White supremacy. A teacher needs to have a consciousness and understanding of these conditions in order to teach African American students successfully. All teachers, not just African American teachers, have a responsibility to help these students discover who they are. I am talking about an African American rather than African consciousness. It is no more possible to people of African descent born in America to have an African consciousness than it is for them to have a Chinese or European consciousness. Most of us have never been to Africa, and while our roots are there, we live in America.

In my class examining Maya Angelou's *I Know Why the Caged Bird Sings* — after the students have made a list of Angelou's characteristics and made projections on her life — we discuss how they feel about the words they've put on the board. This is both a pre-writing lesson and an inductive reasoning lesson, the object of which is both academic and cultural. Students use the lists of words generated by the class to come up with categories of ideas, such as prejudice, emotions, adult/child relationships, peer relationships, and self-esteem. Then they make predictions based upon their reasoning, and eventually they will write a speculative essay on the causes and effects of prejudice.

The cultural objective of this lesson is to educate students about larger concerns in the African American community: about the need for African American people to build a strong sense of self-worth and to build understanding of the causes of the current predicament in order to survive in the future. It also opens a way for students from various cultures to build their own sense of identity: by looking at the struggle of others they also can learn to understand them, and themselves.

But, before letting a class discuss what they've generated, I show the list to another class and have them make observations about the attitudes of the students who made the list. The list by one class of ninth-graders, which included the words "stanky," "ashy," and "nappy hair," drew a great deal of comment from two other classes. In a seventh-grade class, the students compared this "stanky" list to the list produced by another ninth-grade class. They did not talk about words like stanky and nappy specifically, although they noted that those words were derogatory; however, they found the second class's list to be more respectful and more mature. This prompted me to take the "stanky" list to the more "mature" ninth-grade class in order to get their reactions. They were incensed. Not only were they angry with Angelou for writing about herself that way, but one Black male stated that "she was very ignorant and ashamed of her color, and the person in your other class is even more stupider. That what's wrong with Black people."

I shared the responses from the other classes with the ninth-grade class that had originally generated the "stanky" list. The student who had yelled out "stanky" was quite subdued, but he insisted it was the truth because of what she had said about herself, which he said identified her lack of self-esteem. His statement, in defense of his previous remarks, illustrates his understanding of "self-hatred," as well as his acknowledgement of Angelou's state of being. "I think it's really sad," remarked an Asian girl, a recent immigrant from Hong Kong. "She is ashamed of who she is. She care what White people say. It disgraces her. She need to know who she is, take pride in herself. I think this [is the] result of slavery." Students agreed that a sense of inferiority still affects Blacks in many ways, and they made a variety of observations about Maya Angelou. African American students said things like, "She don't know who she is," "She wanna be White," "She hates herself." Akbar's words illustrate the underlying theme of these feelings:

> So, dark skin became equated with the reason for slavery. The skin color of the slave became associated with other kinds of subhuman traits. On the other hand, the slave master's pale skin became equated with superhuman traits. In fact, God, all the Saints and the entire heavenly hosts, became identified with the pale skin. The logical conclusion of the abused, oppressed slave was that the basis for his condition was his skin color, and the way out of his condition was to change that color." (Akbar, 1991, p. 32)

When we were growing up, everyone was color-struck and caught up in hair-consciousness. We couldn't escape it. Sherylanne is a metaphor for all the beautiful Black girls who have suffered, because they are not White, at the hands of insensitive teachers. I don't think Sherylanne liked school very much. She was a pretty girl, with long eyelashes and beautiful skin. The boys loved her — and she was pregnant at the end of sixth grade. Now that I look back on it, she may have suffered more at the hands of insensitive teachers than I did. Some teachers, then and now, refuse to teach to the circumstances of students. Instead, they teach to a curriculum as if it were set in stone. Many don't know anything about the backgrounds or life circumstances of their students, and maintain a distance that borders on indifference. How does a twelve-year-old get pregnant without anyone observing it? What kind of interest was expressed towards this girl? I am not saying that the teacher was responsible for Sherylanne's pregnancy, but I am saying that the teacher might have contributed to the girl's lack of knowledge about other possibilities for her life.

But I did have teachers who transcended such insensitivity. Helen King, my fourth-grade teacher, helped all of her students do their best. She cared about all aspects of our beings, our personal values, and our futures. Mrs. King was somebody too, a strong, successful woman, a Creole from New Orleans with brilliant green eyes that shone with love and affection; but she could snap a person in two if needed. She had sung with the New York City Opera, so our quiet times were full of arias from "Madama Butterfly," "La Traviata," "La Boheme," "I Pagliacci," "Suor Angelica," "Louise," "Meditation de Thais," and so on. Mrs. King never began a day without singing and playing on the piano James Weldon Johnson's "Lift Every Voice and Sing." We had his picture in the classroom. We also had Sojourner Truth, Harriet Tubman, Madame C. J. Walker, Paul Laurence Dunbar, Countee Cullen, Frederick Douglas, W.E.B. Dubois, Carter G. Woodson, Langston Hughes, Mahalia Jackson, and Marian Anderson staring at us daily from their pictures on the wall. Mrs. King helped us have some self-respect. She encouraged my love for music and expanded my horizons. When she asked us to listen, we listened. She loved us.

Another special teacher was Mrs. McQuinney, who had also been my mother's sixth-grade teacher. My mother, like many other African American parents, believed strongly in the rule, "Spare the rod, spoil the child." When she would spank or whip me, she would usually do it with a belt. I know some people look aghast at such punishment, but my people learned these practices as a part of their history. Slaves were beaten with whips and chains, so a belt was nothing. Anyway, Mama would always cry when she whipped me, so there would be the two of us crying together. My skin was fair enough that all marks showed easily, and my legs would welt up. We had to wear dresses to school, and I went to Mrs. McQuinney's class not thinking about the marks. But she called me to her desk one day during play time while the other kids were busy and asked, "Beverly, what on earth happened to your legs?"

"I got a whippin," I answered.

"Well, I'll have to talk to your Mama about that," she replied.

I didn't have any anxiety about her talking to my Mom, because I knew Mama respected her, and I figured I could use the assistance if it would keep me from getting any further such punishment.

That evening, while I was washing dishes and getting ready to do my homework at the kitchen table, the phone rang in the back of the house. I started my homework and was pretty involved in it when my Mom came in with big tears in her eyes. She told me Mrs. McQuinney phoned and gave her a good talking to.

Mama said, "You're too old for whipping, and I'm not going to do it again, but don't think you're going to just do any old thing. You're a McElroy and there's certain things you do and certain things you don't do." I was greatly relieved. After that I received different kinds of lessons in cause and effect, but whipping was eliminated. Obviously, Mrs. McQuinney remained one of my favorite teachers.

Home training and school training must work together to create a sense of inter-relatedness, a sense of community. Parents do the best they can in most instances. I was the eldest child and my mother was young. She was anxious for me to get an education to improve my life circumstances, and she was very strict. My mother's training of obedience, academic achievement, and self-respect was reinforced by Mrs. McQuinney, but she also helped my mother see that whipping was unnecessary; she was training my Mom as well. In this sense, training is education.

When teachers care about students, they view them within a whole context. They make contact with parents and assist them in helping the child develop a sense of pride and self-respect. By calling my mother, Mrs. McQuinney showed that she cared about both of us. By extending herself personally to my Mom, Mrs. McQuinney helped a young parent deal with the frustrations of raising a strong-willed, highly verbal child, which also helped my Mom assess some of her long-held beliefs about child rearing. These two women were connected in their concern for my well-being and for their own. They were connected, inter-related. School and home were part of one system, sharing a common interest and concern — the students.

My elementary school was a beautiful place to me. The teachers represented all the hues and shades of African Americans and were highly skilled educators. The school walls were covered with pictures of famous African Americans. My best teachers reinforced the images that I saw on the walls. They taught me my history as a Black person living in North America. They taught me to look at the beauty of my people through reading our poetry and singing our songs. I grew to appreciate the courage, strength of character, and love that African Americans had developed and demonstrated, not only during slavery, but during our constant oppression in this country. They addressed the question of purposes. They showed me that life has meaning and that learning, knowledge, enlightenment can and must be passed on from one generation to the next. They encouraged me to dream about what I could give back to my parents, to my people, to my community. Anything I thought I could do, including singing, writing, even becoming a teacher, they supported with the affirmation that it would be possible if I were willing to put in the effort. I loved them, and I wanted to be like them.

While I don't remember my first-grade teacher, I remember Mrs. King and Mrs. McQuinney vividly. These two teachers, in particular, taught me to have a sense of pride and courage. They also gave me a sense of past reality and future possibility. They helped me answer questions like "Who am I?" "Why am I here?" and "What am I supposed to do?" They gave me a voice.

Teaching is a complex and demanding profession, more complex than medicine, according to one scholar who has studied both professions. Thus, career-long op-

74

portunities for growth, renewal, and access to new information are essential. (Anderson, 1985, p. 102)

My own goal in teaching is not just to create literate, accomplished student writers who make it in the world. Although those are important goals, they are not big enough for the world in which we live today. Our students come to us with a great deal of confusion, from many different backgrounds, cultures, races, and socioeconomic situations. They are confused and frightened, and often can't express their own opinions. Many express opinions that have little personal or practical meaning for them, opinions that have been instilled in them by adults (parents, teachers, television and radio personalities, and writers). They need assistance in defining their own values and identity. They need to understand the role of the individual and of society. They need and want direction. Teachers need to understand the cultural differences of their students, especially minority students. In particular, they need to understand the background of the resistance many African American children display in relation to school and learning, as explained by Ogbu:

> In their folk theory of "making it," involuntary minorities wish they could advance through education and ability as white Americans do, but know they cannot. They come to realize that it requires more education and effort to overcome the barriers set up against them. . . . The public schools for example cannot be relied upon to provide minority children with the "right education." Involuntary minorities find no justification for the prejudice and discrimination they find in school and society, which appears to be institutionalized and enduring. . . . Involuntary minorities perceive their cultural frames of reference not merely as different from but as opposed to the cultural frames of reference of their white "oppressors." The cultural and language differences emerging under these conditions serve as boundary making mechanisms. Involuntary minorities do not interpret language and cultural differences encountered in school or society as barriers to overcome; they interpret such differences as symbols of their identity. Their culture provides a frame of reference that gives them a sense of collective or social identity, a sense of self-worth. (Ogbu, 1990, pp. 153–154)

As I began this article, I pointed out that I am greatly concerned about the number of African American students who are falling into chasms of failure in our current educational system, while teachers argue over rules of pedagogy. These students need a voice to express themselves in creative, productive ways. They need a sense of history, models of successful human beings from their race and others, and ways of dealing with pent-up emotions resulting from living in a society that has not valued them. Teachers who refuse to deal with this issue are leaving these students voiceless. As opposed to majority White students, who already have these things in place, African American students need structure, clarity, and a disciplined environment. They need challenges, and teachers must maintain high standards and expectations for them. Again, Ogbu explains:

> Minority children receive inferior education also through what occurs inside the schools, inside the individual classrooms. Among the mechanisms discovered to affect minority education adversely, none is more important than teachers' low expectations. So, also, too many minority children are treated as having educational "handicaps." A disproportionate number are channeled into "special education," a

pseudonym for inferior education. Problems that arise from cultural and language differences are inadequately attended to. The failure of school personnel to understand the cultural behaviors of minority children often results in conflicts that affect the children's capacity to adjust and learn. While minority children have an obligation to understand and relate to the culture and language of the schools, this is a two-way thoroughfare. (Ogbu, 1990, p. 156)

In "The Silenced Dialogue: Power and Pedagogy in Educating Other People's Children," Lisa Delpit states:

> The Black child may perceive the middle-class teacher as weak, ineffectual, and incapable of taking on the role of being the teacher; therefore, there is no need to follow her directives. In her dissertation, Michelle Foster (1987) quotes one young Black man describing such a teacher. "She is boring, boring. She could do something creative. Instead she just stands there. She can't control the class. She asked me what she was doing wrong. I told her she could be meditating for all I know. She says that we're supposed to know what to do. I told her I don't know nothin unless she tells me. She just can't control the class. I hope we don't have her next semester." (Michelle Foster quoted in Delpit, 1988, p. 290)

What is obvious to me in this discussion between the teacher and the student is that the teacher thinks that the student has the problem. She thinks the students should "know what to do." My belief is that if they knew what to do, students wouldn't need teachers. By contrast, when a teacher takes charge and addresses the real needs of her or his students, the response from them is very different:

> A young Black man is discussing a former teacher with a group of friends: "We had fun in her class, but she is mean. I can remember she used to say, 'Tell me what's in the story, Wayne.' She pushed, she used to get on me and push me to know. She made us learn. We had to get in the books. There was this tall guy and he tried to take her on, but she was in charge of that class and she didn't let anyone rule her. I still have the book we used in her class. It's a bunch of stories in it. I just read one on Coca-Cola again the other day." (Michelle Foster quoted in Delpit, 1988, p. 209)

In order for students to develop their voices, the teacher's voice must be clear, distinct, and above-board. Students shouldn't be expected to second-guess a teacher's instruction or motivation; they needn't be clairvoyant. Black students need the security of knowing that someone is in charge. I'd venture to say that many students, including second-language students, need to hear a teacher's strong voice in order to feel secure in developing their own voices.

My experience has shown me that students think a teacher does not care about the students if he or she does not control the class. Many of my students need a teacher who establishes him- or herself as a person who "won't take no mess." They expect the teacher to establish an environment where profanity, name calling, and violence are not allowed. To my students, the classroom environment is as important as the material we study. My students also want me to "know my stuff," to give them the reasons why they must study the material I'm teaching. They want to know how their studies are going to contribute to their lives. They want a teacher who knows something about their different cultures, histories, and backgrounds. They want a teacher who can relate to and is respectful of their parents. They want a relationship with the teacher as real human beings. Whenever I hear students say a teacher "ain't teachin notin," I know that they feel ignored, undisciplined, and unaccepted.

Recently, I ran into a former student at a yogurt shop. The young woman was distraught about her new English class in a suburban school near Berkeley, California. She said that there were only two other African American students in her tenth-grade, Advanced Placement English class of thirty-five students. She went on to tell me:

> We're studying MacBeth and I hate it. Whenever I ask that teacher to explain something, she says I should change my class, because it's obviously too hard for me. All she does is throw us into these groups where the White kids basically ignore us, and we're supposed to come up with the answers but we're scared of each other. She never deals with any of the things that go on in those groups. We work in those stupid groups while she works at her desk. When we did Romeo and Juliet with you, it came alive. That's because you related it to our lives, to what's happening around us. Not her. She treats us like we're stupid and don't belong there. She's the one who's dumb.

Needless to say, I spent a good deal of time while eating my frozen yogurt trying to convince my former student to stick in there with the teacher and Macbeth, but I must admit it really troubled me. The teacher is White, and although I am not saying that this alone is the problem (there are also Black teachers who are disconnected from their students), several aspects of what the student told me made me feel that the teacher's race contributed to the problem. She treated the student in a way that made her feel as if she were "stupid and didn't belong in an advanced placement class" without considering how the student must feel being an African American in a predominantly White environment. She asked the student on her first day of class, "Are you sure you're in the right class?" She would not answer the student or give her assistance when she asked for help. The student's perception was that the teacher did not like her and did not want to help her because she is African American.

I don't know what the teacher's perceptions are. I do know from working with European-American teachers that they often find African American students more difficult to teach: the teachers don't want to be authoritarian and yet they often believe that "Black kids seem to like that." However, my feeling is that students want an authorit*ative* not authorit*arian* teacher, a sensitive, helpful, and knowledgeable person who provides a disciplined, supportive environment for student learning. I don't think that's too much to ask.

At the end of my classes' study of *I Know Why the Caged Bird Sings*, after difficult writing assignments exploring a variety of ideas brought up in the book, one of my students wrote me this note:

> Dear Ms. Johnson,
>
> You are a meaningful teacher to me in Westlake. Although I didn't have your class till the last semester, I really learned a lot from your class. I learned how to develope [sic] my own thoughts in writing and how to write a good essay. Even though I didn't do a good job in your class but at least I tried my best! I will remember and miss you all my life!!! Forget me not.
>
> Love always,
>
> Joann Chou 6-10-91

Joann was a lot harder on herself than I ever was. She earned good marks consistently. What strikes me most about her is not that she feels that she didn't do a good job in my class, but that she knows she did her best. To me this says that Joann has high standards that she may or may not reach. However, the underlying message she carries is one of triumph: "I did my best."

I share this not because I feel good about it (although of course I do!), but to emphasize the important role a teacher has in helping students develop voice. When we help a young person find a little bit of who he or she is, then we are successfully doing our jobs. When we ignore the issues facing our students, we contribute to their failures. There were many reasons for Sherylanne's problems; no teacher could accept responsibility for all of them. But a teacher must be vigilant in order to help students think more clearly about their situations and not contribute to negative outcomes. I don't know if any teacher tried to help Sherylanne get beyond the fixation on hair and color, or whether she ever developed a sense of pride in herself and her race. I don't know if she was able at some point to give rise to her voice and speak out about her problems. I only know that the experience Sherylanne and I had in the first grade represents the teacher's failure to exert her power in a positive and constructive way — a way that would have helped us, and all her students. While the unfortunate Sherylanne dropped out of school, I graduated second in my class in high school, graduated from college, went on to graduate school, and held several positions before returning to teaching. When I graduated from high school, some said I did well because I was "high yellow" and had "good hair." I like to believe, however, that I succeeded because of my talent and hard work — like Joann Chou, I did my best. But more importantly, I owe my success to the brave, wonderful, creative teachers who gave me a sense of who I am, and a voice with which to say it.

REFERENCES

Akbar, N. (1991). *Chains and images of psychological slavery.* Jersey City, NJ: New Mind Productions.

Angelou, M. (1969). *I know why the caged bird sings.* New York: Bantam/Random House.

Anderson, R. (1985). *Becoming a nation of readers: The report of the Commission on Reading.* Washington, DC: National Institute of Education.

Delpit, L. (1988). The silenced dialogue. *Harvard Educational Review, 58,* 280–298.

Dunbar, P. L. (1990). "Sympathy" and "We Wear the Mask". In *African American Literature* (an anthology). Austin, TX: Holt, Rhinehart, Winston.

Gandesbery, J. (1970). Denying origins. *The Quarterly of the National Writing Project and the Center for the Study of Writing, 13*(2), 10–12, 20.

Ogbu, J. U. (1990). Minority status and literacy in comparative perspective. *Daedalus, 119*(2), 141–167.

Challenging Venerable Assumptions: *Jan 11*
Literacy Instruction for Linguistically
Different Students

MARIA DE LA LUZ REYES

In this article, María de la Luz Reyes identifies, discusses, and challenges widely accepted assumptions that undergird and guide literacy instruction for linguistically different students.[1] Citing examples from current research, Reyes shows how the "one size fits all" belief, and its corollary assumptions about the practice of process instruction with limited- and non-English-speaking students, mitigate against the success of these students. The author draws from the findings of a case study that provides an example of process instruction that proved to be successful not only for mainstream students, but also for those who are linguistically different. In concluding, she makes a strong appeal for efforts to tailor literacy instruction to account for the cultural and linguistic diversity of all students. For the author, such adaptations cannot be an afterthought; rather, if teaching practices are to be inclusive of all learners, they must "begin with the explicit premise that each learner brings a valid language and culture to the instructional context."

Almost without exception, teachers throughout the United States are identifying their teaching philosophies with the whole language and writing process movements. Increasingly fewer teachers admit to teaching phonics or skills-based literacy. About three years ago, for example, one of my colleagues attempted to study literacy instruction by comparing a skills-based and a whole language approach, but could find no one in the surrounding school districts who would admit to being a "skills approach" teacher. In my graduate-level literacy classes, comprised primarily of teachers, virtually all indicate that they use some form of process instruction — that is, an approach to literacy that focuses on content and process rather than on skills acquisition and form. These teachers report that they "teach whole language," "do the writing process," "use literature as a base for teaching reading and writing," and that they "don't use basal readers" and "don't teach phonics."

Whole language advocates (Goodman, 1986, 1989; Harste, 1989; Newman, 1985; Short & Burke, 1989; Smith, 1986) and classroom-based studies on writing process (Atwell, 1984, 1987; Calkins, 1986; Graves, 1983, 1985; Newman, 1985), conducted primarily with mainstream, native English speakers, claim many positive outcomes from the use of these process approaches. These benefits include exposure to wholistic, authentic literature and improvement in grammar, spell-

---

[1] Portions of this article are based on a talk presented at an Invited Symposium at the American Educational Research Association (AERA), Chicago, Illinois, April 1991.

Harvard Educational Review Vol. 62 No. 4 Winter 1992, 427–446

ing, sentence structure, and writing fluency. School districts in many states have readily accepted these claims and have responded by either promoting, permitting, endorsing, or mandating whole language approaches (*English Language Arts Framework*, 1987; Gutierrez, 1992). Textbook publishers competing for profits in this lucrative new venture are producing revised versions of basal readers — said to include "literature-based instruction," "whole language," and "writing process" — to keep in step with the process instruction rage. It is not surprising, then, that teachers are eager to implement these programs and associate themselves with the movement.

ORIGINS OF PROCESS INSTRUCTION

Both whole language and writing process are based on constructivist views of learning and rely on children's literature as a base for literacy instruction (Hiebert & Fisher, 1990). The two have distinct origins — with whole language attributed to Kenneth Goodman and process writing to Donald Graves — but in classroom practice, the distinction between the two blurs. The popularity of whole language in this country is largely attributed to Goodman and his psycholinguistic model of reading (Edelsky, 1990). Although his name is readily associated with the whole language movement, Goodman (1986) himself notes that its practice in English-speaking countries like New Zealand, Britain, Canada, and Australia predates the movement in the United States. He points out that in New Zealand, whole language is a national policy for literacy instruction in all schools.

Many teachers talk about whole language as if it were a method or an approach. Advocates of whole language, however, strongly reject the notion that it is merely a reading approach (Altwerger, Edelsky, & Flores, 1987; Goodman, 1986, 1989; Goodman & Goodman, 1981; Harste & Burke, 1977; Newman, 1985; Watson, 1982, 1989), but at the same time shy away from offering an official definition. They prefer to describe whole language as a "set of beliefs and not methods" (Edelsky, 1990, p. 8) based on and supported by "four humanistic-scientific pillars." These pillars, according to Goodman, are: 1) theories of learning, 2) theories of language, 3) "a basic view of teaching," and 4) "the role of teachers and a language-centered view of curriculum" (Goodman, 1986, p. 26).

Donald Graves, Goodman's writing process counterpart, is credited for reviving interest in writing at the elementary school level. His work began in 1972 with his doctoral dissertation research on the composing processes of seven-year-old children. Later, with funding from the Ford Foundation and the National Institute of Education (NIE), he extended his study to include children aged six through ten in Atkinson, New Hampshire, where he worked with classroom teachers Mary Ellen Giacobbe, Lucy McCormick Calkins, and Susan Sowers — all of whom are now widely known in this field. His work indicates that when children are allowed to choose their topics, they not only write more, but their selections are also broader-ranged. When children are involved in writing, they are in a constant process of "emerging text and thought" (Newman, 1985). However, when they are focused on a new style of writing, or engaged in shaping their ideas more clearly, they seem to lose control over aspects of writing mechanics that they may have previously mastered (Graves, 1983).

In essence, Graves believes that children's writing is an integrated process, an interplay of drawing, talking, writing, and reading. This focus on process, its emphasis on a learner's freedom to select topics, books, and learning activities, are distinguishing characteristics of both whole language and writing process that have been internalized by teachers, and explains why they are treated synonymously. In this article, "process instruction" is used as an inclusive term to refer to whole language, writing process, or literature-based instruction, whether used collectively or individually. The rationale is that all have at their core a focus on meaning (process or "wholeness") rather than on form (product or skills).

GRASSROOTS SUPPORT FOR PROCESS INSTRUCTION

With some exceptions, university- and college-level literacy courses have not kept pace with the widespread implementation of process instruction. Instead, process instruction has been largely a grassroots movement spreading from coast to coast. Organized teacher groups, known as Teachers Applying Whole Language (TAWL), have sprung up everywhere ("Teachers Networking," 1987) and have served as support groups for those implementing whole language. The majority of teachers not involved in these groups, however, has relied primarily on information learned from institutes, workshops, and conferences conducted by whole language and writing process advocates. In many cases, teachers attending these meetings have taught other teachers in their school districts.

While the enthusiasm of teachers teaching teachers is commendable, the short-term nature of such training presents a unique problem: it virtually assures that only the rudimentary elements of these theories can be presented, and that adaptations for linguistically different learners will not be covered. This has led to narrow application of these philosophies — often without reflection and without appropriate modifications to meet the needs of diverse learners (Barrera, 1991, 1992; Delpit, 1986; 1988; Reyes, 1991a,b; Siddle, 1986; Valdes, 1991).

The terms "wholistic," "integrated," "authentic," and "relevant" used in reference to process instruction have an instant appeal and a ring of validity, making it difficult to imagine they could be anything but a "perfect fit" for all students. Challenging the effectiveness of process instruction usually incurs immediate and general disapproval from "experts" in the field who define the prevailing teaching paradigms and would have teachers believe that all children benefit equally from the same philosophies and programs. When Lisa Delpit's article "The Silenced Dialogue" (1988) first appeared, advocates of process instruction complained of "her lack of sensitivity to teachers"; some questioned her real understanding of whole language and writing process. On first reading, even today, some of the teachers in my classes feel offended by her challenge to process instruction. Her call for a balance of process and skills instruction needed by African American students was, and still is, almost lost in the rush to defend the philosophies of process instruction.

In a similar vein, in this article, I challenge widely accepted assumptions about teaching limited- or non-English speakers and critique current implementation of process instruction that ignores culturally and linguistically supportive adaptations for these students. I also present a discussion of modifications that provide greater opportunities for success. The terms "linguistically diverse students," "language minorities," and "second-language learners" refer to students whose first language is not English and whose cultural backgrounds differ from middle-class White children.

ASSUMPTIONS ABOUT LINGUISTICALLY DIFFERENT LEARNERS AND PROCESS INSTRUCTION

As a Chicana university professor who teaches language arts, and social, multicultural foundations of education, I am often asked to comment on the effectiveness of process instruction for limited- or non-English-proficient students.[2] The assumption behind the query is that I will be able to provide examples of programs in which linguistically different students are making significant gains with whole language and writing process. Over the last five years, my inability to cite just such examples has led me to examine why these seemingly successful programs are not producing the same rate of success for linguistically different students as for native English speakers. Delpit's (1986, 1988) seminal writings discussing her dilemma with process instruction for African American students have helped my understanding. My classroom teaching experience with diverse populations, as well as my own research in the literacy development of Spanish/English bilingual students suggests, however, that there are other implicit assumptions specifically related to the delivery of instruction for linguistically different students that play an important role in student outcomes. In various ways, these assumptions contribute to the ineffectiveness of a process approach to literacy for these students. I will discuss four assumptions here, assumptions that through many years of classroom practice are treated as if they were venerable — too sacred to challenge. These are:

1. English is the only legitimate medium for learning and instruction;
2. linguistic minorities must be immersed in English as quickly as possible if they are to succeed in school;
3. a "one size fits all" approach is good for all students;
4. error correction in process instruction hampers learning.

The first two assumptions are related to beliefs that guide common teaching practices in the education of language-minority students. The last two are specifically related to a mismatch between pedagogy and learners. In concert, the four undermine the goals and spirit of process instruction and, as such, must not only be challenged, but abandoned, if linguistic minorities are to derive the potential benefits of process instruction.

THE VENERABLE ASSUMPTIONS

My assertion that process instruction is not working as effectively as might be expected and is not being tailored to the needs of linguistically different students

---

[2] Chicana refers to a person of Mexican ancestry born in the United States.

is based on some of my own work with bilingual students in process classrooms (Reyes, 1991a,b) and on the work of Rosalinda Barrera (1991, 1992) and Guadalupe Valdes (1991). These assertions are also consistent with Delpit's (1988) and Emilie Siddle's (1986) work with African American students. I will draw on these data as I discuss and challenge these venerable assumptions.

Assumption One: English is the only legitimate medium for learning and instruction.

School curricula in this country have been developed primarily for native English speakers, thereby according primacy to English as *the* language of instruction. Despite the presence of linguistically diverse learners, other languages have been treated as insignificant in the teaching equation. Challenges to English-only instruction have largely gone unnoticed by mainstream educators, although as early as the 1930s, Chicano psychologist George Sánchez (1932) wrote about the academic disadvantages of treating speakers of other languages as if they were native English speakers, especially in the administration of IQ tests. Throughout his career, Sánchez persisted in pointing out the illogical assumptions that schools make regarding the teaching of Spanish-speaking children (García, 1989) — assumptions that today apply to other language groups as well. In 1951, for example, he noted that

> the first error which such school authorities make is to confuse "English" with "education" — that is, it is evident that they assume that the entire school policy or program should revolve around the question of whether or not a given child or group of children know English. (Sánchez, 1951, p. 23)

Today, despite the existence of bilingual education programs developed for language minorities (Crawford, 1989), and even in the face of widespread linguistic heterogeneity in schools, English continues to be viewed as the *only* valid medium of instruction. An extension of this assumption is the treatment of English and literacy as if they were synonymous (Reyes, 1991a) — a practice that defines literacy in narrow, ethnocentric terms.

Results from a two-year study I conducted with approximately fifty sixth-grade Spanish-speaking students in two bilingual education classes illustrate how the first assumption negatively affected student performance in process classrooms (see Reyes, 1991b). This middle school was situated in the heart of a predominately low- to middle-income Mexican American community in a large city in the Southwest. Student enrollment was approximately six hundred, of whom 73 percent were of Mexican descent; the remainder were primarily White and African American. The teachers' pedagogical backgrounds included ongoing training in whole language methodologies provided by the district, and attendance at institutes and/or conferences presented by prominent individuals in the field of process instruction.

The teachers provided numerous opportunities for integrated reading and writing activities — primarily in English for academic purposes and in Spanish for informal, non-graded activities such as journal writing. Students also kept interactive journals (two-way correspondence between the teacher and the student) and literature logs (notebooks in which students wrote their reflections on the literary books they read). They participated in writing conferences with their teachers and with peers, and took mini lessons on writing mechanics.

Teachers modeled sustained silent reading and provided good models of conventional writing. Though the teachers were White, they were fluent in Spanish and English.

On the surface, the teachers seemed to be doing everything right, yet the exposure to good models of writing, spelling, and punctuation did not produce correct writing form or growth in the bilingual students' writing fluency. Unlike the success of these models for mainstream students reported in the work of Lucy Calkins (1986), Graves (1983, 1985), and Nancie Atwell (1984, 1987), the bilingual students in my two-year study experienced failure. At the end of two years, most were still making the same spelling and grammatical errors as in the beginning of the study. For example, in a journal entry dated September 9th, a student wrote, "My *ant* is getting married in Saturday." The teacher responded, "How was your *aunt's* wedding?" In a subsequent entry, the student again reported on her "*ant's*" wedding — ignoring the correct form modeled by the teacher. In late February of the same year she wrote, "Her mom my *ant* is a good cook." In the spring of the second year of the study, one of the teachers said of her students, who were then seventh graders, "Students keep making the same errors with spelling, grammar, punctuation, etc. It's frustrating!" (Fieldnotes, April 27, 1990).

Students' journal entries also revealed that many disliked reading and thought the books were boring, difficult, or too long. Students provided many hints that they needed help in completing the literacy assignments, but their pleas went unheeded by their teachers, who seemed to have the impression that, as students became more familiar with the process, they would get the hang of it. A sixth-grade student wrote in her journal, "I really don't like reading I try but I never get the hang of the book or I don't read far anough [enough]" (Journal entry, October 3, 1988). To another student who did not like reading, the same teacher said, "I'm sorry that you don't like reading. Could it be that you just weren't comfortable? Why don't you sit on the floor?" (Journal entry, November 30, 1988). The student wrote back, "Miss . . . I dont like siting in the floor" (Journal entry, December 8, 1988). No explicit guidance in the selection of books was provided in these cases; instead, students were advised to keep trying, in the hope that they would eventually find books they liked.

Although the classes were designated "bilingual," teachers discouraged the use of Spanish for academic tasks, which was in sharp contrast to their informal interaction and communication. For example, there were subtle yet explicit requests that students write in English. Students were also discouraged from writing their literature reflections in Spanish after reading English-language books. In myriad ways, without full awareness of these contradictions, teachers conveyed the message that English was the only acceptable language for academic tasks. In so doing, teachers had no ill intent; they were merely following the school district's policies requiring English as the medium of instruction for language arts — even for limited-English-proficient students.

In their journal writing, where they were permitted to use Spanish, some students did improve their writing fluency and wrote longer, richer entries than they did in their literature logs. The better quality of Spanish writing in the journals suggests that, if students had also been allowed to write in Spanish for academic purposes, they might have experienced success. This was not possible, however, because the local school district's policies, like official policies in the majority of school districts throughout the country, undermined the heart of bilingual education, which permits academic instruction in *two* languages.[3] The message was clear: English is the only legitimate vehicle for learning.

A problem with according legitimacy solely to English is that it offers no compelling reason for teachers to change their teaching strategies to meet the needs of linguistically diverse students, as was the case with the teachers in this study. The veneration of English leads to two popular but erroneous conclusions. First is the notion that the need to adapt is incumbent on the students, *not* on the teachers. Second is the idea that if students are not performing satisfactorily, it is their fault, and not that of the curriculum, the instruction, or the way these are implemented.

Assumption Two: Linguistic minorities must be immersed in English as quickly as possible if they are to succeed in school.

This second assumption, which stems from the first, contains the idea that non-English speakers must be moved to English usage as quickly as possible or they will not achieve academically; or, worse yet, they will refuse to assimilate or to adopt the common language and culture of the larger community (Imhoff, 1990; Hayakawa, 1986 in MacKaye, 1990). Inherent in this assumption is a deep-seated belief that limited English proficiency is equivalent to limited intellectual potential.

The push for English is commonly reflected in school policies regarding instruction for language-minority students (Fishman, 1987; Hornberger, 1990, 1992; McCollum & Walker, 1990, 1992; Saidel, 1991; Wong-Fillmore, 1991). As Crawford (1989) explains, this assumption has recently been injected with new life by proponents of U.S. English, a national organization leading the movement to make English the official language of the United States. One of the six principles promoted by U.S. English, for example, states: "The nation's public schools have a special responsibility to help students who do not speak English to learn the language as quickly as possible" (Imhoff, 1990, p. 49).

This admonition to immerse language minorities in English has been interpreted as implicit permission to police, and even to ban the use of languages other than English in schools. The *El Paso Times* recently reported, for example, that a school principal in Garland, Texas (a Dallas suburb), had imposed a ban on speaking Spanish in hallways and classrooms to prevent students from cursing in Spanish. "Under the ban imposed Friday, students caught speaking Spanish risked detention or possible expulsion" ("School backs off," 1991, p. 1). The imposition of English rules in all aspects of students' lives and an inordinate concern with teaching English even in designated bilingual programs mean that

---

[3] Although federal and state Bilingual Education Programs are transitional in nature, they allow the use of a student's primary language as a bridge to the acquisition of English (Crawford, 1989). The majority of programs, however, are "bilingual" in name only. At best, they offer minimal English-as-a-Second-Language instruction. A report by Catherine Snow and Kenji Hakuta indicates that most "foster monolingualism. . . . The bottom line of these programs has been an almost single-minded interest in the extent and the efficiency of English proficiency development" ("The good common school." 1992, p. 20).

language-minority students cannot take full advantage of innovative instructional programs in their primary languages even where Spanish/English linguistic resources are available (Reyes, 1991b).

Over-zealous interest in having children learn English as quickly as possible "for their own good" does not stand up to the body of research conducted over the last twenty years. These studies indicate that bilingual students attain higher achievement levels when allowed to begin literacy instruction in their primary language before transferring to English literacy (Collier, 1989; Cummins, 1979, 1981; Fishman, 1987; Hakuta, 1986; Krashen & Biber, 1988; McCollum & Walker, 1990; Reyes, 1987; Skutnabb-Kangas, 1981). Jim Cummins (1979, 1981) suggests that students who learn academic concepts and literacy skills in their native language can more readily and quickly transfer those skills to a second language because knowledge is grounded in the language and schema they comprehend. A recent study conducted for the U.S. Department of Education, which compared the effectiveness of English immersion, early-exit bilingual, and late-exit bilingual programs on Spanish/English limited-English-proficient students, reported the following:

> Limited-English-proficient students can be provided with substantial amounts of primary language instruction without impeding their acquisition of English language and reading skills.
>
> Limited-English-proficient students who are provided with substantial instruction in their primary language (≥40%) successfully continue to increase their achievement in content areas such as mathematics, while they are acquiring their skills in English; in contrast, students who are quickly transitioned into English-only instruction tend to grow slower than the norming population. (Ramirez, Yuen, & Ramey, 1991, p. 39)

Support for native-language instruction does not mean that students should not learn to speak, read, and write English well; indeed, they should. Using English to supplant native languages, however, makes very little sense in light of current school demographics. A more reasonable option would be to use native languages to expand the linguistic repertoire of students. In this way, students can maintain their own language while becoming proficient in the common language and in the appropriate forms of discourse of the larger community.

The point here is that when there are linguistic resources to support native languages, it makes more sense to use them to students' academic advantage than to rely on traditional practices and erroneous assumptions. Exclusion of minority voices in the learning process sends the message that non-English languages, dialects, and literatures are obstacles to the acquisition of English literacy, and fails to "affirm and legitimize diverse [cultures], knowledge, and language practices that students bring into the classroom" (McLaren, 1988, p. 215).

Assumption Three: A "one size fits all" approach is good for all students.

This refers to the assumption that instruction that is effective for mainstream students will benefit *all* students, no matter what their backgrounds may be. It is similar to the "one size fits all" marketing concept that would have buyers believe that there is an average or ideal size among men and women. This idea is appealing and lures people into purchasing garments that hang on their torsos, or cry for more room at the seams. Those who market "one size fits all" products suggest that if the article of clothing is not a good fit, the fault is not with the design of the garment, but with those who are too fat, too skinny, too tall, too short, or too high-waisted. Mass production of garments in a generic size is convenient, expeditious, and less expensive for the manufacturer. Furthermore, it makes it easier for the designer and seller to reach the greatest number of buyers *without the need to make adjustments* for differences in body structure, weight, or height.

The widespread use of whole language and writing process has led to a similar "one size fits all" approach to literacy; that is, the implementation of process instruction based on the belief that it is a "good fit" for everybody — as is — *without any modifications.* Well-meaning teachers have lost sight of the fact that mere implementation of these same programs does not necessarily translate into authentic, natural, or wholistic experiences for non-mainstream students (Barrera, 1991, 1992; Delpit, 1986, 1988; Reyes, 1991b; Valdes, 1991).

The fallacy that what works for mainstream students will work for all groups, especially with respect to whole language and writing process, is illustrated by the following lesson I observed in one of the many schools I have visited:

The teacher and the school principal described this first-grade class as a whole language classroom. Indeed, that seemed to be the case. The room was physically organized into various learning centers. Numerous examples of students' art and writing were prominently displayed on the walls and bulletin boards. There were several bookshelves with children's literature, both commercial-size Big Books and standard-size books. In front of the open carpet space, where the teacher was sitting, was a large easel with a big book written and illustrated by the class. All twenty-some children, mostly from White, middle-class backgrounds (except for three Hmong girls), were sitting on the carpet listening to the teacher's expressive reading of the children's version of "Wishy Washy Washer Woman." The activity was a lively one, with students chiming in on the oral reading wherever they could. The Hmong girls attempted to join in, but their lip movement, like dubbed foreign films, was out of sync with the rest of the native English speakers. The teacher and children showed great enthusiasm reading the book in chorus.

When the oral reading was over (approximately five minutes later), the teacher instructed the students to select a reading book for fifteen minutes of sustained silent reading time. The native English speakers quickly headed to the bookshelves to make their selections. The three Hmong girls followed suit, but the expressions on their faces revealed a great sense of uncertainty and bewilderment about the task. For a full twelve minutes, they superficially browsed through the books, picking them up, whispering in their native language, giving each other blank looks, and putting them back on the shelf, but never selecting one to read.

Meanwhile, all the other students appeared to be engaged in reading their books, either in small groups of two or three, or alone. The teacher also sat in a corner reading her own book, modeling appropriate silent reading behavior. All the while, the Hmong girls continually glanced toward the teacher and circled around the various bookshelves. One or two times, they inched near her chair trying to get her attention, but to no avail.

When the teacher finally looked up from her book, she noticed that the Hmong girls were still "undecided" about their books. She called them by name and asked, "What's the matter, can't you find a book you like?" They smiled and nodded "yes" (which in this case actually meant "no"). The teacher then added, "Would you like me to read to you?" Their little faces lit up as the teacher pulled up a chair and asked them to sit next to her. But while the Hmong girls were getting chairs, two other girls ran and squeezed in on each side of the teacher, leaving the Hmong girls on the outer fringes of the newly formed group. The English-speaking girls joined the teacher in reading aloud. Seeing that they were good readers, the teacher suggested that they (the English-speaking girls) read to the Hmong girls, and so she walked away to help another group. The Hmong girls quietly slipped away and headed once again to the bookshelves.[4]

The experiences of these Hmong children, as well as the Hispanic students described earlier, reveal that even well-meaning teachers assume that the high rate of success with process instruction reported for mainstream students will magically happen for culturally and linguistically diverse learners. As this case illustrates, that is far from the truth. It was obvious that the Hmong students were lost within the free-flowing structure and their lack of familiarity with books. It would have been more beneficial, for example, if the teacher had utilized the sustained silent reading time differently by reading to them and assisting their comprehension or by guiding them in the selection of books.

As a researcher, I have noted that when the focus of instruction is on process, even otherwise good teachers can be unsure about when to allow the process to take its natural course and when to mediate instruction. Teachers are so often caught up in the euphoria and popularity of process instruction that they find it difficult to believe that these programs could possibly need any modifications. As one teacher said to me, "Can so many people be wrong?" Indeed, how many teachers would reject or alter programs that offer so much promise for improvement in reading and writing while using whole and "authentic" literature as a base for literacy instruction? They are, after all, improvements over the old "drill, grill, and kill" reading approaches (Reyes, 1991b). The problem, however, is that carte blanche acceptance of *any* program reduces the likelihood that needed modifications for diverse learners will be made.

An equally important reason why teachers experience difficulties adjusting their teaching techniques for different learners is that the majority of them are members of the dominant culture, implementing programs designed primarily for mainstream students. Teachers implementing these programs tend to treat students of color as exceptions to the norm, as students who should be assimilated into the dominant group, rather than accommodated according to their own needs. Failure to address the needs of non-mainstream students is not due to a conscious omission but to an established tradition of ignoring differences among learners — a practice supported by designing educational programs and school policies primarily for White native-English-speaking students.

In her article about White privilege, Peggy McIntosh (1989) captures aptly and bluntly what, I believe, gets to the heart of this issue regarding failure to recognize the needs of minority students. As a member of the privileged White group, she says, "I can remain oblivious of the language and customs of persons of color who constitute the world's majority without feeling in my culture any penalty for such oblivion" (p. 11). In classrooms and schools, as in larger social

---

[4] This is an actual incident reconstructed from my fieldnotes taken in January 1989.

structures, educators and policymakers are conditioned to ignore differences or to treat them as deficiencies. They continue to adhere to the misguided assumption that benefits from programs designed for the dominant group will automatically "trickle-down" to minorities, who will also profit from the same treatment (Halcón & Reyes, 1991).

Such disregard for the needs of culturally diverse students can be seen in the selection of literature books in whole language classrooms. In a recent study, Barrera (1992) reports that in an elementary school where Mexican American children make up more than 60 percent of the student population, nothing in the so called "authentic" literature-based program is tailored to the needs of these children. On the contrary,

> the program literature is dominated by themes and characters that often do not reflect the faces, experiences, and histories of many of the children at La Vista. The children are more likely to read or hear a story about an elegant tea party among the aristocratic set or a family who can travel to Africa for its vacation or children and their pets in New Zealand than they are likely to encounter a literature selection that reflects their backgrounds and communities. There is a marked cultural homogeneity to it all that renders the children's lives and experiences invisible. (p. 230)

Spanish-speaking children, as well as other linguistic minorities, are expected to derive the same enjoyment, relevance, and authenticity from stories designed for children from New Zealand where whole language originated. Many teachers, like those in Barrera's (1992) study, strive to remain faithful to the philosophy of whole language as they have learned it, without reflecting on the learners' cultural or linguistic backgrounds. This suggests that they are oblivious to the discrepancies between the "wholistic, authentic approach" they claim to be implementing and their monocultural approach to literacy that continues to rely on traditional canons.

When teachers believe that student success is inherent in adherence to a particular philosophy, rather than dependent on their own teaching expertise, a distrust of self may occur. In this seeming distrust, teachers set aside common sense and behave as if making appropriate adjustments for different learners were a violation of the principles of whole language or writing process. Instead of adapting the program for the learner, the learner is expected to adjust to the program.

Although the philosophies of whole language and writing process do not preclude modifications for diverse learners, failure to include consideration of cultural and linguistic factors as an *integral* part of their training and literature leaves teachers with the impression that these programs are inherently good as they are. The common practice of taking a "one size fits all" approach to literacy when teaching diverse learners seems to substantiate this assertion and is consistent with conclusions reached by Barrera (1992), Delpit (1988), Siddle (1986), myself (1991b), and others.

Assumption Four: Error correction in process instruction hampers learning.

An important tenet in process instruction, in both whole language and writing process, is that learning is shaped by student input. Instruction is guided by students' "invitations," and the role of the teacher is to facilitate those invitations. Judith Newman (1985) describes it in the following way: "Our role as teachers is best seen as 'leading from behind,' supporting the language learning capabilities of students *indirectly* through the activities we offer them" (p. 5, emphasis mine). The rationale is that this allows learners to initiate and participate more actively in their own learning without imposition, and departs from the traditional transmission of information model for instruction (Atwell 1987; Calkins, 1983; Graves, 1983; Hansen, 1987; Newman, 1985; Sowers, 1986). In the writing process, for example, students are free to experiment, make mechanical errors, and use invented spelling without being stifled by teacher correction (Sowers, 1986). Advocates of process instruction often remind teachers that "an overemphasis on accurate spelling, punctuation, and neat handwriting can actually produce a situation in which children come to see the conventions of writing as more important than the meaning they are trying to convey" (Newman, 1985, p. 28). For middle-class, mainstream students, this experimentation may work well. It can, however, be disconcerting for culturally and linguistically different students who expect teachers to provide direct and explicit instruction (Delpit, 1988; Macías, 1989; Reyes, 1991b; Siddle, 1986).

In the study of sixth-grade bilingual students described earlier, for example, students assumed that their writing form was correct because the teachers had not explicitly pointed out their errors — a responsibility they felt was the teachers'. The teachers, on the other hand, truly believed that they were pointing out those errors through the mini lessons and that they were also protecting students' self-esteem by presenting the errors anonymously in the lessons. Taking examples of students' errors and embedding them in a lesson seemed to be the sensitive thing to do, but the students saw no direct connection between the topic of the lessons and their own errors. Several mini lessons, for example, reviewed subject-verb agreement, including the use of "is not/are not." A sixth-grade girl repeatedly used "ain't" in her journal for several months, until finally the teacher wrote, "Honey, what would happen if you made an effort to say 'aren't' every time that you start to say 'ain't'?" (Fieldnotes, January 11, 1989). In this case, as in others, unless the teachers explicitly and individually called a student's attention to the incorrect form found in his or her writing (something they rarely did), students ignored the errors.

In attempting to follow the spirit of process instruction, which frowns upon overt attention to form (product) over content (process), teachers generally refrained from pointing out mechanical errors outside of the small group mini lessons for fear that students would be discouraged from developing fluency and voice. This was consistent in my many observations of the classrooms. In the end-of-the-year interviews, students reacted to their spelling and grammatical errors with incredulous comments like, "Por qué no me dijo?" (Why didn't she tell me?); "It was wrong? She never *marked* it wrong" (Reyes, 1991a). One of the teachers countered that even after explicit attention to errors in individual writing drafts, two or three students still ignored them (Teacher Interview, June 7, 1989). It was clear that students' expectation of their teachers' responsibility in providing direct instruction and the teachers' version of their role in a process class were at odds.

The high regard that Hispanics hold for teachers as authority figures (Delgado-Gaitan, 1987; Macías, 1989) indicates that they rely on and expect direct instructional intervention from the teacher. Many look for it and may not understand it when it comes masked in indirect requests or disguised in mini lessons. In the examples described above, bilingual students sought the teachers' assistance; for example, "Please tell me a little bit about the book" (Reyes, 1991a). Their personal attachment to the teacher and their need for social interaction were often sources of confusion for them, because the rules of engaging in social interaction and written discourse were not made explicit. Similarly, the Hmong girls inched near the teacher for help, yet she failed to assist them in understanding the literacy task, which, no doubt, was culturally foreign to them.

The assumption that error correction hampers student learning rendered the modeling of correct form and the indirect nature of the mini lessons ineffective in teaching important literacy skills to linguistically different students. Process instruction often leads to fewer opportunities for "assisted performance" (Vygotsky, 1978); that is, for teacher assistance in helping students learn a specific skill that they cannot yet perform well on their own. Assisted performance is an aspect of teaching much needed by *all* students, but especially by those whose ways of learning require programs tailored to their linguistic and cultural backgrounds.

TAILORING PROCESS INSTRUCTION FOR SUCCESS WITH SECOND-LANGUAGE LEARNERS

My misgivings about the implementation of process instruction for linguistically different students do not mean that these programs should be abandoned altogether; rather, I appeal for appropriate adaptations that will increase their likelihood of success with diverse learners.[5] When implemented well, there is little doubt that process instruction offers the potential for more interesting and challenging learning activities than those offered by skills-approach methods. For example, all students are offered increased opportunities to engage in writing activities not commonly available in traditional skills programs. Whole language and writing process offer the potential of exposure to a rich body of authentic, full-length literature as a basis for reading and writing. Nevertheless, teachers must rise above the euphoria over whole language and writing process and recognize that these programs are not perfect or equally successful for all. They are successful only to the extent that teachers understand the theories, assume the role of mediators — not merely facilitators — and create culturally and linguistically sensitive learning environments for *all* learners. What this means is that

[5] Objection to the implementation of whole-language philosophy for White, mainstream students is also emerging. A recent article in the *Denver Post*, with the headline "'Whole-language' program in Poudre angers parents," described that parents were "outraged at the lack of basic reading and writing skills being taught to their children" ("Whole-language program," 1992) and were demanding a change.

In the same vein, *The Council Chronicle* ("Whole language vs. skills," 1992), a newspaper published by the National Council of Teachers of English, reported that eight of 169 elementary schools in Houston, Texas, decided to adopt DISTAR, a highly structured, skills-oriented reading program.

teachers must do more than "lead from behind." When students are not comprehending a task or performing well, teachers must not water down concepts, but must participate *directly* in providing assistance in understanding those concepts through questions, feedback, and scaffolding; that is, "support that enables a learner to complete a task or achieve a goal that would have been unattainable without assistance" (Gaffney & Anderson, 1991, p. 184; see also Greenfield, 1984; Tharp & Gallimore, 1988; Wood, Bruner, & Ross, 1976).

The following case study is an example of an implementation of process instruction that was successful for mainstream as well as for linguistically different students (see Reyes & Laliberty, 1992). It is also a concrete example of how venerable assumptions about teaching language minorities were challenged by the teacher's validation of students' cultural and linguistic backgrounds, by her understanding of the role of primary language in the acquisition of English, and by her adaptations of whole language and writing process to meet the needs of her learners.

The study was conducted in a fourth-grade bilingual classroom in a Colorado school. Fifty-five percent of the total school enrollment was of Mexican descent. Of the twenty-seven students in the participating classroom, fourteen were Mexican or Mexican American and thirteen were White. The purpose of the study was to examine the development of children's literacy in a process instruction classroom where students were exposed to English and Spanish. The teacher was Mexican American and fluent in both languages. Like many teachers, her background knowledge of whole language and writing process was gained primarily from attendance at whole language institutes and workshops; she had no formal literacy courses in process instruction. At the time of the study, however, she was enrolled in a Master's degree program in the social and multicultural foundations of education, to which she attributes her heightened awareness of the needs of linguistically different learners.

Several factors related to her specific teaching style and to the classroom environment she created contributed to her students' success. In examining these ingredients for success, it is important to note that the teacher's organization of instruction was diametrically opposed to the traditional teaching practices and language policies generally accepted in educating language-minority students. The most salient feature of her teaching was that she did not equate English with literacy or with knowledge. Instead of the usual overriding concern for teaching limited-English-proficient (LEP) students the English language per se, she was more interested in developing *literate* students, in nurturing a love for reading and writing, and in tapping her students' full potential. Thus, rather than making English a prerequisite for process instruction, as is usually the case, she allowed students to write in Spanish or English — whichever language was most comfortable for them. She did so with the full conviction that the transfer to English literacy would occur more readily than if writing in English were required immediately.

At the beginning of the year, ten of the fourteen Spanish-speaking students in the classroom were classified as LEP and were writing primarily in Spanish. By the end of the year, three LEP students had written their own full-length stories *in English*, similar in form and style to that of their native English-speaking peers; others had written shorter pieces, and most showed eagerness to write in English. With the assistance of bilingual peers in the class, two native English-speaking students also wrote Spanish translations of their English stories, indicating a strong interest in bilingualism and a recognition of its value. Attention to the development of literacy, rather than to the acquisition of English, not only permitted LEP students opportunities to taste writing success in their own language, it also provided them with the confidence to attempt writing in English. More importantly, it made them experts on topics derived from their own cultural experiences; for example, a little boy who emigrates from Mexico, leaving his loved ones behind, being raised by his grandparents. There was much enthusiasm and excitement about reading and writing, and no pressure on the students for deadlines or amount of work; yet, the students often requested to be "excused from recess" so they could complete a story, have a draft edited, or have a writing conference (Reyes & Laliberty, 1992).

Other important factors that contributed to the success of these linguistically different students were: a) the organization of a cooperative learning classroom where assisting others in completing academic tasks was more important than individual competition; b) the provision of explicit skills instruction within the context of learning activities and, without hesitation, to cite individual errors in a culturally sensitive manner; c) heterogeneous grouping of students by language and ability so that students could learn both content and a second language from each other; and d) use of Spanish and English literature books, supported by mediation of LEP students' reading comprehension to help them make relevant connections to universal themes. An additional support system accompanying process instruction included such things as: teacher's preselection of books; reading with a partner; oral reading by the teacher; checking for comprehension in Spanish; reading English-language books while permitting discussion and written responses in Spanish; sharing students' Spanish and English written work in the "author's chair"; and providing multiple checkpoints for correcting and learning grammar, spelling, and punctuation from the teacher, peers, and parents.

In essence, the teacher not only set high expectations for all students, without watering down the curriculum, but significantly altered her classroom organization and teaching techniques so that those expectations could be reached by both mainstream and minority students. She also demonstrated the value of cultural and linguistic diversity in concrete and authentic ways. For example, although learning English was acknowledged as one priority, *it was not promoted at the expense of the students' native language.* Each linguistic group was allowed to use its native language for academic and non-academic purposes, but each was also exposed to the second language in a classroom environment that invited respect, sensitivity, and appreciation for diversity.

The inevitable question that arises is: does a teacher have to be bilingual to be successful with non-English-speaking students? Although I would urge all teachers to become bilingual for their own personal development, for greater marketability in today's teaching work force, for facilitating learning for non-English-speaking students, and for numerous other reasons, my answer here is NO. Bilingualism is not a requirement to create the kind of classroom environ-

important: teacher as mediator of lang. + scaffolding

pair work

ment described here, although admittedly, it can be helpful. I have observed a similar case in which success for a Korean girl was made possible by a teacher who could neither speak nor understand Korean, but who encouraged an already literate student to write in her native language during the writing period rather than keep her occupied with "busy work." The teacher found bilingual Korean peers to translate the work for her and the class. This not only boosted the Korean girl's confidence, but accelerated her acquisition of English and her interest in English writing instruction. In turn, it aroused the curiosity of her native English peers for foreign languages (Teacher Interview, October 1988). More important than bilingualism is the teacher's conviction about the value of diversity — namely, that differences in language and culture are not deficits — and the teacher's courage to teach out of that conviction, even if it means violating venerable assumptions.

CONCLUSION

form still important

When cultural and linguistic factors are treated as if they were incidental to sound pedagogical theories, it implies that they are not a fundamental part of effective instruction. This often leaves the impression that, even without adaptations, process instruction is appropriate for all. Moreover, it implicitly invites teachers to relinquish their role as mediators of knowledge, ignoring the importance of form (i.e., correct reading and writing skills), which, in spite of the widespread use of process instruction, continues to be used as a measure of academic success. Leading from behind, as process instruction suggests, may not always provide teachers with an accurate gauge to monitor the effectiveness of their teaching. As a result, second-language learners' lack of success with these programs may be erroneously attributed to insufficient time for the "seeds of process" to germinate, to their need to master the English language first, or to their lack of motivation to learn.

By their failure to address explicitly cultural and linguistic diversity, process approach proponents tacitly promote a narrow, ethnocentric definition of literacy based on strategies designed for mainstream students as the model for *all* learners. To be inclusive of all learners, teaching practices, literacy instruction in particular, must begin with the *explicit* premise that each learner brings a valid language and culture to the instructional context; it is no longer sufficient to infer it. Only then can we ensure that cultural and linguistic modifications will not be *an afterthought*. Without this, we will continue to venerate outdated assumptions about the best ways to educate linguistically different learners and reduce the possibilities that could be derived from whole language and writing process.

REFERENCES

Altwerger, B., Edelsky, C., & Flores, B. (1987). Whole language: What's new? *Reading Teacher, 41*, 144–154.
Atwell, N. (1984). Writing and reading literature from the inside out. *Language Arts, 61*, 240–252.
Atwell, N. (1987). *In the middle*. Portsmouth, NH: Heinemann.

Barrera, R. B. (1991, April 7). *What about culture? A look at the literature-based curriculum.* Paper presented at the American Educational Research Association Conference, Chicago.

Barrera, R. B. (1992). The cultural gap in literature-based literacy instruction. *Education and Urban Society, 24,* 227–243.

Calkins, L. (1983). *Lessons from a child.* Portsmouth, NH: Heinemann.

Calkins, L. (1986). *The art of teaching writing.* Portsmouth, NH: Heinemann.

Collier, V. (1989). How long? A synthesis of research on academic achievement in a second language. *TESOL Quarterly, 23,* 509–531.

Crawford, J. (1989). *Bilingual education: History, politics, theory and practice.* Trenton, NJ: Crane.

Cummins, J. (1979). Linguistic interdependence and the educational development of bilingual children. *Review of Educational Research, 49,* 222–251.

Cummins, J. (1981). The role of primary language development in promoting educational success for language minority students. In California State Department of Education, *Schooling and language minority students: A theoretical framework* (pp. 3–49). Los Angeles: National Evaluation, Dissemination, and Assessment Center, California State University.

Delgado-Gaitan, C. (1987). Mexican adult literacy: New directions for immigrants. In S. R. Goldman & H. T. Trueba (Eds.), *Becoming literate in English as a second language* (pp. 9–32). Norwood, NJ: Ablex.

Delpit, L. (1986). Skills and other dilemmas of a progressive black educator. *Harvard Educational Review, 56,* 379–385.

Delpit, L. (1988). The silenced dialogue: Power and pedagogy in educating other people's children. *Harvard Educational Review, 58,* 280–298.

Edelsky, C. (1990). Whose agenda is this anyway? A response to McKenna, Robinson, and Miller. *Educational Researcher, 19*(8), 7–11.

English language arts framework. (1987). Sacramento: California State Department of Education.

Fishman, J. (1987, January). *English only: Its ghosts, myths, and dangers.* Keynote address at the Conference of the California Association for Bilingual Education, Anaheim, CA.

Gaffney, J. S., & Anderson, R. C. (1991). Two-tiered scaffolding: Congruent processes of teaching and learning. In E. H. Hiebert (Ed.), *Literacy for a diverse society* (pp. 184–198). New York: Teachers College Press.

García, M. T. (1989). *Mexican Americans: Leadership, ideology, & identity, 1930–1960.* New Haven, CT: Yale University Press.

Goodman, K. (1986). *What's whole in whole language?* Portsmouth, NH: Heinemann.

Goodman, K. (1989). Whole language research: Foundations and development. *The Elementary School Journal, 90,* 207–221.

Goodman, K., & Goodman, Y. (1981). *A "whole-language comprehension-centered view of reading development"* (Occasional Paper No. 1). Tucson: University of Arizona, Program in Language and Literacy.

Graves, D. H. (1983). *Writing: Teachers and children at work.* Portsmouth, NH: Heinemann.

Graves, D. H. (1985). The reader's audience. In J. Hansen, T. Newkirk, & D. Graves (Eds.), *Breaking ground: Teachers relate reading and writing in the elementary school* (pp. 193–199). Portsmouth, NH: Heinemann.

Greenfield, P. M. (1984). A theory of the teacher in the learning activities of everyday life. In B. Rogoff & J. Lave (Eds.), *Everyday cognition: Its development in social contexts* (pp. 117–138). Cambridge, MA: Harvard University Press.

Gutierrez, K. D. (1992). A comparison of instructional contexts in writing process classrooms with Latino children. *Education and Urban Society, 24,* 244–262.

Hakuta, K. (1986). *Mirror of language: The debate on bilingualism.* New York: Basic Books.

Halcón, J. J., & Reyes, M. de la Luz. (1991). "Trickle-down" reform: Hispanics, higher education and the excellence movement. *Urban Review, 23,* 117–135.

Hansen, J. (1987). *When writers write.* Portsmouth, NH: Heinemann.

Harste, J. (1989). Commentary: The future of whole language. *Elementary School Journal, 90,* 243–249.

Harste, J., & Burke, C. (1977). A new hypothesis for reading teacher research: Both teaching and learning of reading are theoretically based. In D. Pearson (Ed.), *Reading: Theory, research, and practice, 26th yearbook of the National Reading Conference* (pp. 32–40). St. Paul, MN: Mason.

Hiebert, E. H., & Fisher, C. W. (1990). Whole language: Three themes for the future. *Educational Leadership, 47*(6), 62–63.

Hornberger, N. H. (1990). Bilingual education and English-only: A language-planning framework. In C. B. Cazden & C. E. Snow (Eds.), *The annals. English plus: Issues in bilingual education* (pp. 12–26). Newbury Park, CA: Sage.

Hornberger, N. H. (1992). Bilingual contexts, continua, and contrasts: Policy and curriculum for Cambodian and Puerto Rican students in Philadelphia. *Education and Urban Society, 24,* 196–211.

Imhoff, G. (1990). The position of U.S. English on bilingual education. In C. B. Cazden & C. E. Snow (Eds.), *The annals. English plus: Issues in bilingual education* (pp. 48–61). Newbury Park, CA: Sage.

Krashen, S., & Biber, D. (1988). *On course: Bilingual education's success in California.* Sacramento: California Association for Bilingual Education.

Macías, J. (1989, November). *Transnational educational anthropology: The case of immigrant Mexican students.* Paper presented at the American Educational Research Association Conference, San Francisco.

MacKaye, S. D. (1990). California Proposition 63: Language attitudes reflected in the public debate. In C. B. Cazden & C. E. Snow (Eds.), *The annals. English plus: Issues in bilingual education* (pp. 135–146). Newbury Park, CA: Sage.

McCollum, P. A., & Walker, C. L. (1990). The assessment of bilingual students: A sorting mechanism. In S. Goldberg (Ed.), *Readings on equal education: Vol. 10. Critical issues for a new administration and Congress* (pp. 293–314). New York: AMS.

McCollum, P. A., & Walker, C. L. (1992). Minorities in America 2000. *Education and Urban Society, 24,* 178–195.

McIntosh, P. (1989). White privilege: Unpacking the invisible knapsack. *Peace and Freedom, 49*(4), 10–12.

McLaren, P. (1988). Culture or canon? Critical pedagogy and the politics of literacy. *Harvard Educational Review, 58,* 213–234.

Newman, J. (1985). Insights from recent reading and writing research and their implications for developing whole language curriculum. In J. Newman (Ed.), *Whole language theory in use* (pp. 7–36). Portsmouth, NH: Heinemann.

Ramirez, J. D., Yuen, S. D., & Ramey, D. R. (1991). *Executive summary. Final report: Longitudinal study of structured English immersion strategy, early-exit and late-exit transitional bilingual education programs for language-minority children* (Contract No. 300-87-0156). San Mateo, CA: Aguirre International. (Submitted to U.S. Department of Education)

Reyes, M. de la Luz. (1987). Comprehension of content area passages: A study of Spanish/English readers in third and fourth grade. In S. R. Goldman & H. T. Trueba (Eds.), *Becoming literate in English as a second language* (pp. 107–126). Norwood, NJ: Ablex.

Reyes, M. de la Luz. (1991a, April 4). The "one size fits all" approach to literacy. *Invited Symposium on Literacy and Cultural Diversity: Voices, visibility, and empowerment.* Paper presented at the American Educational Research Association Conference, Chicago.

Reyes, M. de la Luz. (1991b). A process approach to literacy using dialogue journals and literature logs with second language learners. *Research in the Teaching of English, 25,* 291–313.

Reyes, M. de la Luz, & Laliberty, E. (1992). A teacher's "Pied Piper" effect on young authors. *Education and Urban Society, 24,* 263–278.

Saidel, P. (1991, April 22-26). *Growing up in linguistic limbo — Immigrant kids lose language and family, study finds.* Pacific News Service.

Sánchez, G. I. (1932). Group differences and Spanish-speaking children: A critical review. *Journal of Applied Psychology, 16,* 549–558.

Sánchez, G. I. (1951). *Concerning segregation of Spanish speaking children in the public schools.* Austin: University of Texas Press.

School backs off Spanish-speaking ban. (1991, October 24). *El Paso Times*, p. 1.

Short, K. G., & Burke, C. L. (1989). New potentials for teacher education: Teaching and learning as inquiry. *The Elementary School Journal, 90*, 193–206.

Siddle, E. V. (1986). *A critical assessment of the natural process approach to teaching writing.* Unpublished qualifying paper, Harvard University, Cambridge, MA.

Skutnabb-Kangas, T. (1981). *Bilingualism or not: The education of minorities.* Clevedon, Eng.: Multilingual Matters.

Smith, F. (1986). *Insult to intelligence.* New York: Arbor House.

Sowers, S. (1986). Six questions teachers ask about invented spelling. In T. Newkirk & N. Atwell (Eds.), *Understanding writing: Ways of observing learning and teaching* (pp. 47–54). Portsmouth, NH: Heinemann.

Teachers networking. (1987). *Whole Language Newsletter.*

Tharp, R. G., & Gallimore, R. (1988). *Rousing minds to life.* New York: Cambridge University Press.

The good common school for all students. (1992). *National Council of La Raza, 11*(1), 19–20.

Whole language vs. skills: Is it either/or? (1992, April). *The Council Chronicle*, p. 1.

"Whole-language" program in Poudre angers parents. (1992, March 31). *The Denver Post,* p. 3B.

Valdes, G. (1991, April 7). *Background knowledge and minority students: Some implications for literacy-based instruction.* Paper presented at the American Educational Research Association Conference, Chicago.

Vygotsky, L. S. (1978). *Mind and society: The development of higher psychological process* (M. Cole, V. John-Steiner, S. Scribner, & E. Souberman, Eds.). Cambridge, MA: Harvard University Press.

Watson, D. (1982). What is a whole language reading program? *Missouri Reader, 7*, 8–10.

Watson, D. (1989). Defining and describing whole language. *Elementary School Journal, 90*, 129–141.

Wong-Fillmore, L. (1991). When learning a second language means losing the first. *Early Childhood Research Quarterly, 6*, 324–346.

Wood, D., Bruner, J. S., & Ross, G. (1976). The role of tutoring in problem solving. *Journal of Child Psychology & Psychiatry, 17*, 89–100.

The author wishes to thank John J. Halcón for his invaluable critique of this manuscript.

Partial funding for this research was provided by the Office of the Associate Vice Chancellor for Faculty Affairs, the IMPART Program, of the University of Colorado, Boulder.

A Curious Plan:
Managing on the Twelfth

PATRICIA CLIFFORD

SHARON L. FRIESEN

Patricia Clifford and Sharon Friesen are team teachers in an open-area classroom at University Elementary School in Calgary, Alberta, Canada. In this article, they capture their process of creating, with their students, a curriculum that takes its life from the interests and varied experiences of their classroom community. Using excerpts from their teaching journals, the authors recount their work with a classroom of six- and seven-year-olds, in which they continually question, challenge, and ultimately change fundamental assumptions about the education of young children. Through the voices and stories of these authors and their students, we witness the rich life of a classroom where teachers and children are passionate and vibrant learners.

The Mock Turtle went on:
    "We had the best of educations — in fact, we went to school every day."
    "And how many hours a day did you do lessons?" said Alice, in a hurry to change the subject.
    "Ten hours the first day," said the Mock Turtle, "nine the next, and so on."
    "What a curious plan!" exclaimed Alice.
    "That's the reason they're called lessons," the Gryphon remarked; "because they lessen from day to day."
    This was quite a new idea to Alice, and she thought it over a little before she made her next remark. "Then the eleventh day must have been a holiday?"
    "Of course it was," said the Mock Turtle.
    "And how did you manage on the twelfth?"
    (Carroll, 1865/1966, pp. 95–96)

INTRODUCTION: PLANNING A LIVED CURRICULUM

Every September, teachers and students gather together in our classroom to learn. Each of us, teacher and child alike, walks through the door bringing experiences and understandings that are ours alone. Yet, each person is also embarking on a journey that he or she will come to share with others. This journey is made anew every year with every class.

    Travelers prepare more or less carefully for the adventures they hope to have, but the itineraries, maps, and plans do not in themselves create the voyage. The journey is an experience, lived as just the thing it turns out to be: moment-by-moment, day-by-day, month-by-month. As teachers, we prepare for each year's journey in big ways and in small ways. We make decisions, design plans, and

Harvard Educational Review Vol. 63 No. 3 Fall 1993, 339–358

99

outline key strategies to help us set directions for the coming year. In this article, we hope to share some of our decisions, plans, and strategies, therein describing the factors we consider as we prepare for an authentically engaging journey with each new class of children.

Some travelers keep diaries, which we, too, have done, recording actual situations that took place in our classroom from September 1991 to June 1992. In terms of its multi-aged, open-area configuration, our class was like others in the primary division of our school. The number of children varied throughout the year, as families moved in and out of the community. At any time, the two of us team-taught between fifty-five and fifty-eight children in grades one and two. In many ways, our classroom would be familiar to anyone used to teaching in middle-class neighborhoods. In other ways, however, there are important differences. First of all, the children in our class vary more widely in their abilities, backgrounds, emotional and physical needs than one might expect. In this class, ten students were second-language learners. One child was in a wheelchair. Several had behavioral problems severe enough that social workers, psychologists, and psychiatrists had been involved before the children entered grade one. Some had been identified as gifted, others as learning disabled.

For twenty-five years, our school has maintained a tradition of multi-aged, open-area classrooms as part of its demonstration function for the local university. Because innovative structures and teaching practices are expected and encouraged, we were supported in our request both to teach together and to conduct action research. From the earliest days of our work as a team, everyone knew what we were setting out to do. Never content simply to replicate existing best practices, our school wanted to find out what would happen if we did what teachers at our school, University Elementary School, have always done: question, challenge, and change fundamental assumptions about the education of young children.

Using excerpts from the diaries we kept last year, we hope in this article to illustrate some of the struggles and successes in our way of thinking about teaching, learning, curriculum, and planning. We feel such examples suggest a quality of children's thought and work that some may find astounding, given the fact that our students are only six and seven years old. We feel strongly, however, that this is an example of the kind of work and thinking in which *all* children could engage and that all teachers could endeavor to bring forth. We would like to pose serious questions about how teachers can prepare themselves to create situations in which the voices of children genuinely inform the construction of each year's curriculum. For some teachers, administrators, and staff developers, these questions may be uncomfortable to hear because they call into question much of what is currently recognized as sound professional practice, practice that stands squarely in the way of the kinds of educational reform our profession needs most urgently to begin.

When schools open each year, one of the first things many teachers do is begin making long-range and unit plans that outline what they hope to accomplish by Christmas or, perhaps, for the whole year. If you are an administrator, we would like to give you some things to think about as you request such plans. If you are a classroom teacher, we would like to give you things to consider before you actually sit down to plan. If you are a teacher of teachers, we would like to give you pause as you prepare student teachers for their work with children. We would like, in short, to add our voices to the conversations aimed at ensuring that lessons do *not* lessen from day to day, from year to year, for children who have no choice but to come to school. We are committed to developing a classroom where teachers and children are passionate, robust learners. This commitment requires something more than new programs or new methods. It calls forth what we can only characterize as a philosophy of education, an attitude toward teaching and learning, and a fundamental disposition that permits teachers to live differently with the children in their care.

We are searching for a school-curriculum that acknowledges the importance of the lived experience of children and teachers; that understands growth as more than an interior, private, individual matter of unfolding development; that situates teaching and learning within the context of an educative community; and that asks hard questions about the fuzzy, feel-good legacy of much of what teachers now do in the name of "progressive" practice. Creating such a curriculum is a life's work. Perhaps it is significant, however, that neither of us came to early childhood education as our first career. One of us worked for five years as a systems analyst, and the other taught senior high school for fifteen years. For different reasons, and on different paths, we had both developed similar concerns about public education long before we actually met each other. We were worried about the boredom, drop-out rates, and general lackluster performance of many students. In that we were not alone; we were part of a growing public concern that young people in North America were not learning as much as they might. Two things were different for us, however. First, we resisted the return to traditional images and practices that seem almost inevitably to accompany criticism of schools. And second, each of us knew (again, long before we met) that attempts to reform schools by concentrating mainly on the attitudes and achievements of secondary students, the young people we had been hiring and teaching, was unlikely to succeed. Each of us had already decided that the most promising place to create genuinely new practices was with the very young.

We endeavored initially to find out something about what a classroom would look like if we called into question some of our profession's most ordinary assumptions about teaching and learning. We have now studied, taught, and written together for four years. In that time, we have learned a great deal, and we fight constantly with the temptation to try to say everything at once. In this article, we hope to make a small start by posing three important questions:

— How can curriculum remain open to children's unique experiences and connect with the world they know outside the school?

— Why is imaginative experience the best starting place for planning?

— What happens when teachers break down the barriers between school knowledge and real knowledge?

DAVID'S STORY: ON KEEPING THINGS CONNECTED

"I would ask you to remember only this one thing," said Badger. "The stories people tell have a way of taking care of them. If stories come to you, care for them. And learn to give them away where they are needed. Sometimes a person needs a story more than food to stay alive; that is why we put these stories in each other's memory. This is how people care for themselves." (Lopez, 1990, p. 48)

We met David and his parents on the first day of school.[1] They had just returned to Canada after spending seven years in Africa, where they had lived and worked among the Masai. Although he was of European descent, David had been born in Africa. He went to a village kindergarten, and played and tended cattle with the Masai children. No one in our class, including us, knew much about Africa. Though we had listened carefully to what David's parents told us at the beginning of the school year, we remembered embarrassingly little of it because we had been trying to learn about our fifty-four other children at the same time. So, as we watched David take his first tentative steps in school, we often forgot that the life David had been living until the end of August was radically different from the one he now had to negotiate in our large, complicated, noisy Canadian classroom.

Throughout September and into October, David spoke very little. He would answer direct questions briefly, but never offered to share much of himself. Once, in response to an assignment to tell a personal story, he told a small group of children how he and his family had gone camping — and had woken up to find lions crouching under their truck. The other children acted the story out, growling and shrieking with frightened delight. But aside from this story, we knew little about David. As time went on, David made a friend in class, hooking up with Jason out of mutual need. David was lonely, and he wanted to establish himself in a new country. Jason needed a companion to coerce, command, and bully. This friendship worried David's parents. David had spent all of his life nurtured within a trusting, gentle community, and he approached his friendship with Jason with the same quality of trust. David got into trouble almost daily because of Jason, and David's parents found themselves having to talk to him about the inappropriateness of some people's intentions. They were heartsick — both about what was happening to David and about the ugly lessons about "the real world" that their gentle, naive son was beginning to absorb.

One day in early October, David arrived at school with a huge book about the Masai and asked if he could show his book to the other children. This was the first time David had ever offered to share part of his life experiences with the whole class, to teach us all what he knew best — life among the Masai. David stood in front of the class with his book. He flipped to a few pictures and spoke softly — so softly that only the children near the front could hear him. We tried to offer a few details about the Masai, but we knew so little. In spite of these difficulties and limitations, the children were entranced. They had so many questions to ask David, so much they wanted to know. This was the second time we had seen the children respond with enthusiasm to David's life in Africa. This

---

[1] The names of the students we use in this article are pseudonyms for the children in our class.

time we recognized the power of the invitation that he had offered us. Here was the perfect chance to bring David into the full life of the classroom.

That afternoon, David's mother came to volunteer in the classroom. We asked her if she would speak to us about the Masai. She agreed, took her place in a small chair at the front of the group, and opened David's book. As she spoke, David stood quietly at her shoulder, gently stroking her long hair. He seemed to relax into the memories of that safe, familiar place, trusting the intimacy of his mother's voice and body to secure the connection between here and there.

As our eyes met above the heads of the children, we knew we had been waiting for this all along, without knowing it: waiting for David's life in Africa to come alive for us. Up to now, David had blended in too readily with all the other children. We had had no images to help us understand that this new country, this new classroom, held few connections with the world he had known in Africa.

Our efforts to see all children as contributing members of our classroom community is a kind of standing invitation, but we never know who will take it up, or how they will do it. It appeared that David had decided that *now* was his time, and he made the first essential move. David and his mother shared their life among the Masai with us, and in that sharing helped forge new links between David, his classmates, and us. The class was filled with curiosity, and questions overflowed the hour we spent together. Because of the intensity of the children's interest in David's experiences in Africa and the potential to find, in their pleasure, a new place for David in the classroom, we felt committed to act beyond the delights of that afternoon. We accepted eagerly when David's mother asked if we were interested in using a children's book about the Masai that they had at home.

The next day David brought us *Bringing the Rain to Kapiti Plain.* As we read the story to the class, David sat at the back mouthing every word to himself. Once again we saw David relaxed, smiling, basking in the genuine delight of hearing that well-loved story again, this time in the world of his classroom in Calgary. This book was just the beginning of the stories about Africa, for we found others: *The Orphan Boy; Rhinos for Lunch, Elephants for Supper;* and *A Promise to the Sun.* David brought in other things to share with us, such as elaborate beaded collars and knives used to bleed cattle.

Months later, when the children drew maps of their known worlds, David's map showed his house in Africa, the cheetah park, the camping place where the lions crouched under the truck, a Masai warrior. We sensed then how much of his heart was still there and were honored that he felt safe enough among us to share himself in this way, for as David now tells us, he is "a very private person." We are also keenly aware that we would have known nothing about these places had David not come into our lives. Recently, when we were reading about Mongolian nomads' living on animal blood and milk, many children remembered what David had taught them about the Masai. They speculated about why the animals didn't die when they were bled, and looked to David for confirmation that such a thing was, indeed, possible.

We continually ask ourselves: How much of the life that is lived completely outside of school is welcomed into the classroom as knowledge and experience that can enrich us all? How much of each child gets to come to school? When a child says, "This is me, and I am ready for you to know it," we feel we must try to honor this offering, not shut it out, control it, or hurry to get on with the curriculum. An invitation is more than words. Offered sincerely, invitations create obligations to welcome and to provide. Having extended an invitation to David, we felt compelled to act. David's knowledge and experiences needed to become part of the curriculum, part of the life of the group.

Bringing David into the class in this way opened up new possibilities for him, but it did something just as important for the whole class. All of the children lived the experience of a standing invitation. By observing how we attended to David and to others who also offered *their* stories, the children came to understand the importance of what each of them might bring to the journey our class had embarked on together.

Our curriculum work demands mindful, deliberate improvisation at such moments. It goes far beyond "Show and Share," which can be a perniciously inauthentic practice: "You show me yours and I'll show you mine." Children's sharing is often limited to a slot in the daily agenda. While such activity is designed to bring home into the school, the activity of sharing can, unfortunately, become an end in itself, requiring no further commitment from the teacher than to provide the opportunity for each child to bring in a favorite object or news event. That is not at all what we mean when we speak of invitations. We mean, rather, that each child's voice can be heard, and that their speaking can make a difference to our curriculum decisionmaking. Improvising on children's responses to our standing invitation demands a commitment to recognizing human relationships as a fundamental source of knowledge. At the beginning of the year we could not plan for these moments, but we were prepared for them because we knew that they would inevitably arise. We knew that the children would give us what we needed to know, as long as we remained open to the possibilities.

Determined to foster continuity between personal and school knowledge, we work in a constant state of watchfulness. Children's authentic offerings are often made tentatively. Unlike David's, they can be subtle and easy to miss, but they are nevertheless vital components of a lived curriculum. We know that when curriculum includes only the plans teachers make to deliver instruction, the child who emerges is usually what we might call a "school child," one who is either compliant with or defiant of the exercise of institutional power. It is our belief that when curriculum is divorced from real life, children often lose connections with their own memories and histories. They lose touch with who they are. They may exist in our eyes more as students than as emerging selves, and we wonder if they continue to learn in any passionate sense of that word.

LEARNING: FROM THE KNOWN TO THE UNKNOWN

Children develop most fully as passionate learners when they — like all of us — are allowed to claim fully their own experience of the world. We are not, however, talking about the type of experience that is made relevant to children through its commercial appeal or immediate access: Ninja Turtles and Barbies, video games, superheros, or cartoons. Nor are we talking about the immersion in local experience that some call "the belly button curriculum": me and my house, me and my family, me and my neighborhood. Much traditional thought in early childhood education is grounded in a view of learning as predictable development through ages and stages, from familiar to strange, from concrete to abstract, from (supposedly) simple to complex.

In one sense, we accept these assumptions. After all, David *did* want to share his daily experiences in Africa with his classmates in Canada, and we watched David blossom as he accepted the invitation to connect his life in Africa with life in Canada. In another sense, however, what happened to David is best understood as a starting point for even richer engagement. What intrigued the children was not the sharing of "me and my family." They did not want to talk about *their* daily lives in Calgary in response to David's stories. They wanted, rather, to talk about knives and arrows, about drinking blood and milk, about women who shaved their heads, and about children who tended cattle all day long, far from the gaze of watchful adults. What was familiar and well-known to David called out to the imagination in each of us. Enriched by David's knowledge, we began to experience new worlds together, creating within our classrooms the kinds of imaginative experiences that Egan (1986, 1992) describes: those imaginative experiences that engage, intrigue, interest, puzzle, and enchant; those imaginative experiences that call forth sustained and key conversations about freedom, loyalty, responsibility, strength, and human relationships. When we speak of imaginative engagement, we mean the kind of engagement that invites children most fully, most generously, into the club of knowers; not at some unspecified time in the future when they are all grown up and able to use their knowledge, but today — and each and every day they spend with us.

Egan (1992) invites us to consider that "even the briefest look at children's thinking from this perspective opens profound conflicts with some of the ideas that dominate educational thinking and practice today" (p. 653). When we learn to look at children with new eyes, we can see clearly that, by the time they come to school at age five, they have already learned about some of the most complex, abstract, and powerful ideas they will ever encounter. Simply by virtue of their humanity, they have experienced joy and fear, love and hate, trust and betrayal, power and oppression, expectation and satisfaction — all, as Egan notes, before they have even learned how to ride a bicycle (1986, pp. 28–29).

Our study of a fairy tale familiar to many of us shows how this view of imaginative experience can challenge dominant educational thinking. Early last year, the children in our class listened to *Rumpelstiltskin*, an ordinary experience in a primary classroom. In choosing that story, we were depending on the children's knowledge in important ways. We did *not* assume that they had had direct experience with princes and princesses, much less with malevolent dwarves and alchemic transformations. Indeed, if learning is understood to proceed from concrete to abstract, from familiar to strange, from daily experience to the world of wonders, then *Rumpelstiltskin* should make little sense to children. But they loved the story, debating fiercely about issues such as whether parents, like the miller, have the right to put their children in danger; whether people have the right to ask for help without pledging something in return; whether adults should be allowed to give their children away, and the grief that may follow if they participate in such bad bargains. In order for children to understand this story, they needed to know about deception, the politics of rescue, false pride, boasting, and the indomitable human spirit.

As Egan (1992) notes, "to teach concrete content untied to powerful abstractions is to starve the imagination" (p. 653). David's story is important to us because of what it tells us about hearing each child's voice and bringing each child into the life of the classroom. However, it is also important to us because of what it says about children's interest in places and times long ago and far away. The great stories of history and literature are as fascinating to the children in our class as David's accounts of Africa. Stories about Leonardo da Vinci, Columbus, Ghengis Khan, Radames and Aida, Pythagoras, and King Arthur and his court prompted the same kind of lively debate and discussion of big questions about the human condition that we saw in their response to *Rumpelstiltskin*. Retellings of *Romeo and Juliet, Beowulf*, and parts of Chaucer were as enchanting as readings of *The Lady of Shalott, The Highwayman*, and *The Rime of the Ancient Mariner*. All of these stories have engaged the imagination of generations of adults because of the engagement they demand. We have discovered that these stories touch young children with as much power. They connect each of us with the past, ground us firmly in the present moment of listening to their rich language and images, and cause us to contemplate together what life holds in store.

Thus, for us, a second important planning issue centers on the "big questions" we offer to — and accept from — our children. Without those big questions, tied to great literature that engages the imagination, the spirit, the feelings, and the intellect, curriculum is likely to be thin and unsubstantial, fully satisfying to neither teacher nor child. Arising from questions about the human condition that engage each of us because we share the planet together, the curriculum we have created with our children permits them access to intellectual and aesthetic traditions that are thousands of years old. Children often ask some of the same questions the ancients asked, and discover anew, for themselves, the power of learning both to create and to solve important, engaging questions.

We have many, many typed pages of notes we took while the children were discussing stories and films about Columbus, Leonardo da Vinci, Ghengis Khan, the Arthurian saga, outer space, Greek myths, and Chinese legends. These subjects may not be considered the usual fare offered to six- and seven-year-olds. Indeed, we had no idea in September, when we were writing our plans, the various directions our studies would take. How could we have imagined, for example, that Jason would bring us back again and again to the idea that human knowledge is really a model of how we think things work? He asked us over and over how people know when their models are wrong. And over and over, we thought about that question as a way of understanding what adults have come to call "history," "mathematics," "science," "literature," "ethics" — and "education." How do any of us find out if our models are wrong?

How could we have anticipated the amazement of Diana, a child in grade one who could not yet read, when she learned that the ancient Greeks had known the earth was spherical, but that people had subsequently *lost* that knowledge for thousands of years. They had lost precious knowledge about space, Diana's passion. She was offended by the carelessness of her ancestors, and endlessly intrigued by how we had gotten that knowledge back again. Had there been one person, she wondered, who had just stood up and said, "Look, you guys, this is how it is"? Or had there been many people at the same time who figured it out together?

Could we ever have guessed that Edward would lean over to Sharon during a reading of *The Rime of the Ancient Mariner* and whisper, "It feels like the ghost of the ancient mariner is in this room right now. Do you think he's here? Do you?" Until Christmas, Edward had hardly spoken to us. He was so withdrawn from others that he often buried his face in the hood of his kangaroo shirt and rocked back and forth during lessons and class meetings. He seldom wrote, preferring to sit by himself and draw minutely detailed mazes of miniature battle scenes, seemingly obsessed with blood dripping from gaping wounds and vicious swords. On a blustery January day, Coleridge's words had reached across time and space to touch a little boy who wanted, for the very first time, to talk to his teachers about the world inside his head. The next day, he picked up the conversation again. "Do you know," he told us, "that an imagination is a terrible thing? The pictures in my mind really, really scare me." For Edward, the thing that had frightened him most — his ability to conjure detailed, vivid images — became the vehicle through which he was able, for the first time that we could see, to connect with others in the classroom.

Would we ever have expected that, after several weeks of reading, discussion, and project work about human discoveries, dreams, hard work, courage, tenacity, and integrity, the children would have pulled together the following questions about knowledge and work, questions to which they — and we — returned again and again in the months that followed:

- Where do you go looking for knowledge?
- How do you learn the secrets of the world?
- The more you learn, the more you get to know what you have to do. Why?
- Why do things come alive when you put yourself into your work?
- What do you need to give so you can get knowledge?

The children drove us deeper and further than we could possibly have gone on our own, demanding more stories, more history, more problems, more answers. The children stretched our knowledge and our capacity to hear, in their demands, the next best step to take. We haunted stores and libraries, searching for books to bring back to them and for books to help *us* learn more physics, mathematics, mythology, history, literature. When, for example, we read the children *I, Columbus* — excerpts from the log Columbus reputedly kept on his journey to learn what he called the secrets of the world — they asked many questions. Was Columbus the only person who believed that the earth was a sphere? What must it have been like to be Columbus, certain of your own knowledge but wrong in the eyes of many of your peers? Where did Columbus get his maps from, anyway? How did he navigate once he had passed the boundaries of the known world? Where was the Sargasso Sea, and was that where the Ancient Mariner had been becalmed? Why do people say Columbus discovered America when there were people living here already?

As teachers, we saw opportunities in these questions to bring in more and more material about maps and map-making, astronomy, geography, and history.

One child brought in an article from the Manchester *Guardian* about Renaissance maps. We found stories such as Yolen's *Encounter*, which raised important issues about the effect of European contact on aboriginal peoples, and we introduced the children to the fact that the First Nations of Canada struggle to this very day with the consequences of voyages of so-called discovery that ended up on shores we now think of as our own.

During each story, lesson, and discussion, we would sit side by side at an easel at the front of the group. One of us would facilitate the children's conversation, and the other would scribe as quickly as possible, catching wherever we could the actual words of the children, and paraphrasing when the talk moved too quickly. Earlier in the year we had tried to tape-record these conversations, but the microphones let us down. First, the conversation was too complex for a machine to capture properly. Second, capturing key elements of the discussion required a teacher's judgment. Which were the comments and questions we wanted to formulate for the whole group? Which were the threads that seemed, even in the moment, to hold real promise of future exploration? Where were the moments that allowed us to make powerful connections between the mandated program of studies and the children's own questions?

At the end of days on which the children had been engaged in such discussions, we would sit at the easel re-reading and organizing what they had said and asked. We would highlight for ourselves what the next step ought to be. What had the children said that we could most profitably mine? Sometimes we knew exactly what resources we could use. We would go to our class library, the school collection, or to the public library for books and films we already knew about and bring them in for future classes. At other times, we would just go looking. If a question seemed sufficiently promising or intriguing, we would look for material we were certain must exist.

Curriculum planning that takes the voices of children seriously represents a kind of openness. As we tell stories about our classroom, we feel that teachers need to remain open to children's experience in the world and construct curricula that are deeply resonant with what each child knows, who each child is. We feel that teachers also need to understand that it is only the big, authentically engaging questions that create openings wide and deep enough to admit all adventurers who wish to enter. Three things are important in this regard. First, when children raise the kinds of questions that capture their attention in our studies of literature, history, and mathematics, it becomes possible for each of them to find compelling ways into the discussion and work that follows. Individuals cannot tell in advance when moments of connection will occur — for themselves or for others. Our experience has shown us time and again that questions about fairness, justice, knowledge, learning, courage, and oppression, sparked by stories of substance and worth, seem to free children to engage deeply with complex aspects of the world and of their own experience. There is little in traditional curricula that calls forth children's capacity for profound philosophical engagement made possible through the power of such stories.

Second, these kinds of questions are ones that intrigue adults as much as they enchant children. The conversations, the debates, and all of the work that flow out of these questions are deeply engaging for us, as teachers. The children experience our own genuine sense of excitement and commitment to the world of the mind and the spirit as they struggle with us to relive, in the present moment, dilemmas that were equally real to our ancestors. Morever, when the children see their own questions returned to them as the basis for subsequent work and study, they come to know curriculum as a living, deeply connected experience. Curriculum is not delivered to them through activities made up by others; it is created with them, inspired by the work of the community of which each of them is a valued member.

Third, the worlds made available to children through stories and philosophizing of this sort form strong links with the complicated, everyday world in which they live. When the dean of the local law school, the mother of one of our students, came into the classroom during our study of *Rumpelstiltskin* and saw a child's comment written on chart paper, she hastened to copy it down: "When parents give their child away for gold, they will regret it later on, when they've had time to think about it." She was about to make a presentation about surrogacy contracts to the legal community, and she was delighted that young children, inspired by this classic tale, had articulated so clearly the dilemma that many legal scholars were now exploring. Thus, we *must* remain open to the power of real literature, real science, real mathematics, real art to touch all of us profoundly — not only the children.

REAL KNOWLEDGE AND SCHOOL KNOWLEDGE: EXAMPLES FROM MATHEMATICS

Our understanding of what *counts* as knowledge goes beyond the view that currently dominates school curricula — a view that carries with it the assumption that school knowledge, bound up in curriculum guides and school texts, is the same as "real" knowledge. Coming to know the world as mathematicians or scientists — like becoming a reader and writer — involves authentic engagement in mathematical and scientific experiences, not the busy work that often comes to count in school as math and science or reading and writing. Many school textbooks and workbooks are organized to encourage mindless recitation. Most math curricula are organized to support the notion that accuracy in computation equals excellence in understanding. Even our province's new math curriculum, which states that problem-solving is at the heart of mathematics, relegates problems to a separate unit. Many curriculum designers seem to think that problem-solving means doing word problems. It is also clear that many teachers think that they are teaching math when they are merely covering the textbook or the workbook. Unfortunately, the result often is a student who is schooled in "school math" — a form of math that bears little resemblance to the "real math" that mathematicians, physicists, and engineers experience, or to the math that sparks the imagination and ignites a passion for understanding the world mathematically and scientifically.

We want children to experience mathematics as a powerful language of the imagination that allows them to explore big mathematical ideas like balance, space, time, patterns, and relationships. We have come to see that they enjoy thinking about these matters, exploring, debating, solving problems, and learning together. Too many school children learn only "school math," a dull, lifeless, scary, and irrelevant round of pluses and minuses that usurps the real, much more engaging, thing.

How might it look in a classroom if teachers set about to make math real? The Alberta science and math curricula both state that children in the primary grades must know certain things about time: they must know how to read both analog and digital clocks, know the days of the week, the months of the year, and something about the seasons and the phases of the moon. When we sat down to talk about how to teach this part of the curriculum, we saw that among our options were activities that would encourage children to think that time resided in a clock or a calendar. Such activities would have satisfied the curriculum objectives, but we wanted more. We wanted children to learn that time is a mysterious and puzzling phenomenon.

We felt that if we restricted an understanding of time to the narrow view of "telling time" contained within most curriculum guides, we would transmit a useful skill, but not much more. Instead, we thought that if we paid attention to what physicists ask about time, we might give children access to what is undeniably one of the secrets of the world.

Here is what Bruce Gregory (1990), the Associate Director of the Harvard-Smithsonian Center for Astrophysics, tells us about the human understanding of time:

> Galileo's accomplishment was made possible by his decision to talk about the world in terms of motion through space and time. These concepts seem so obvious to us that it is difficult to remember that they *are* concepts. Time is normally measured in terms of motion, from the swing of the pendulum of a grandfather's clock to the oscillations of a quartz crystal in a modern watch. Apart from such periodic behavior, how could we even talk about the uniformity of time? In the words of the contemporary American physicist John Wheeler, "Time is defined so that motion looks simple." Wheeler also said, "Time? The concept did not descend from heaven, but from the mouth of man, an early thinker, his name long lost." Einstein demonstrated the power of talking about space and time as though they were a unity, and in the process he showed that both space and time are human inventions — ways of talking about the world. (p. 70)

In order to let children in on some of the secrets of this way of talking about the world, we need to let them in on two other big secrets. First of all, they *must* come to understand that human knowledge is humanly constructed. As a culture, a society, a community — and as a classroom — we make decisions about what will and will not count as knowledge, and those decisions make some understandings of the world possible, as much as they render other perspectives impossible.

If we really want our children to face the challenges of the twenty-first century with confidence and skill, we must teach them not only that they can acquire current knowledge, but also that they have voices that can shape what *their* society comes to accept as knowledge. This philosophy of teaching is exemplified in the following illustrations drawn from a series of lessons and activities about time.

We began one morning by asking the children to talk to us and each other about what they knew about time. Seated on the floor in front of the easel, they began to talk. As they offered examples of how time works, we recorded the following comments:

- It's something you have to use.
- You need to wear a watch to know what time it is.
- You need it — you can be late if you don't know the time.
- You can run out of time when you are playing or when people bother you.
- Sometimes grown-ups say, "You have two minutes to do something!" They really mean get it done quickly.
- You need to know time to know how fast you run in a race. You win when you have the least time.
- You can waste time.
- It is important to tell time.
- People get worried if they think they are running out of time.
- A day and a night equals twenty-four hours.
- Time can be fast and slow.
- Time lets you know when you should be doing things.
- Time goes fast when you're playing. It goes slowly when you're not having fun.
- Everyone in the world needs to know what time is the right time. You need to synchronize time with world events, like the Olympics on TV.
- Adults are expected to tell time. Children don't have to.
- If your house is flooded, it takes a long time to get it out.
- When we're doing projects, people always ask, "How much time until lunch?"
- You can tell time by counting by fives.
- People need to be home on time.

Clearly, this long list shows that the children had many experiences with time. For example, they knew about clocks and strategies about how to read clocks, they knew time was related to astronomical and geographical phenomena, and they knew time experientially. One of the children asked, "How can you tell time without a watch?" This question was to lead to intriguing explorations into the history of time and time-keeping devices and opened the possibility to explore time and its astronomical relationships. When one child recalled that a member of Columbus's crew was charged with the responsibility of turning the hour glass over when it emptied and keeping track of how often this occurred, another remarked that at one time people used sundials. This idea of the sundial caught the children's imagination, and they wanted to know exactly how a sundial told time. Fortunately, the sun cooperated with us and we went outside to begin some preliminary investigations.

In order to understand what happened next, it is important to know something about how our day is structured. We reserve a two-hour block of time between morning recess and lunch for the integrated study of literature, social studies, science, and mathematics. This time might be devoted on one day to conversations such as the one described above, and on another it might be used for a lesson and supporting activities. Sometimes we read stories and explore the children's responses; sometimes the children conduct investigations and experiments; sometimes we all listen to a guest speaker who can shed light on a question that has emerged on previous days. Often, the children paint or perform plays.

The flexibility of this long block of time permits us to follow up promising questions and comments like the ones about sundials. On this particular day, we had enough time left before lunch to go outside to explore the daytime astronomy of the sun's light and motion. Before leaving the classroom, we asked the children to observe where their shadows were and to try to make them fall in a different direction. Once outside, they turned and twisted themselves about in the sun, succeeding only in making their shadows change shape, not direction. A group of five children called us over to where they were standing. They proudly announced that they had found a way to tell time using the sun and their bodies. The children had positioned themselves in a circle and explained that one of them was at twelve, one at three, one at six, and one at nine, with the fifth child in the center. They had formed a clock and the direction of the shadow that was cast by the center person indicated the time.

Inside again, the children made further observations and asked more questions:

- If you stood in the same place for a whole day you would see your shadow change places because the earth changes position.
- Clouds can block the sun's rays so sundials won't work on rainy days.
- Can you tell time with one "hand"?
- Why is my shadow longer than I am in the evening but shorter than me at noon?
- People can't make time go faster because they're not the boss of the world. Even if you change the hands of the clock, you aren't changing time, itself.
- How do we know what the real time is?
- How did people start to tell time?

By now, two hours had passed. What had seemed like a simple beginning had flowered into exciting possibilities for future investigations. From the children's work and conversation, we saw themes on which we could now begin to improvise.

On another day, we asked the children to name all the ways they knew to record time. We learned that they knew about months, hours, and minutes; that sixty minutes equalled an hour; that 120 minutes made up two hours; and that thirty minutes was half an hour. Time, some said, could be measured in years, seconds, days, weeks, decades (which we told them meant ten years), and centuries (which they knew meant one hundred years). There were birth years, seasons, milliseconds, generations, and lifetimes (which we all decided together usually lasted from about seventy to about ninety years.)

The next question was easy for us to ask:

"Which of these measures of time is the longest?"

We even expected an easy answer: centuries. But we didn't account for children like Michael, whose hand shot up at once.

"I know, I know," he said, "it's seasons!"

"Why, Michael? Tell us what you are thinking about."

"Well, you see, seasons keep going on and on. You can have summer and fall and winter and spring. Then you keep having them all over again, and they make a pattern. See?"

And all of a sudden, we did see: not only that we had both locked into a narrow focus when we thought centuries was the best (even the only) answer, but also that Michael understood something important about the concept of relativity: that is, that "right" answers had everything to do with the framework you adopted. We looked at other measurements on the list. We asked if some of *those* could be candidates for "longest" as well. Joseph responded that generations were even better than seasons because generations went on and on with parents and children, and then their children and their children and *their* children. It all ended up in Heaven, he added, where time went on forever and ever. This idea of generations set another conversation in motion. To how many generations could each of us belong in a lifetime? Could they ever be in the same generation as their parents? As the children they would come to have? Would they *want* to be?

And so it went — from topic to topic, question to question, insight to insight. By the end of yet another discussion, we reached a conclusion to which everyone agreed: When you talk about days, seasons, or whatever in a general way, many units of measurement could be considered "longest" because they repeat themselves in a patterned way. As Michael's and Joseph's comments indicate, duration can also be understood as cycles — a fundamentally different framework from a linear one. Moreover, the children spoke of freezing time. They gave the example of designating a time — say, Friday, June 5, 1992, 11:48 a.m. — which is the precise time we had this part of the conversation. That moment will never repeat itself, they reminded us. The instant it passes, it becomes part of history. You can never, ever go back and do *that* time again the way you can repeat summers, year after year.

As the discussion continued, thoughtful and excited murmurs passed through the group like a wave.

"You mean, if we just waste that time we can't ever get it back?"

"Like, if we just were fooling around right now, we wouldn't get to come back to 11:48 because it was gone forever?"

"No, not gone forever, because tomorrow there will be another 11:48. But *this 11:48 can't come back.*"

We pushed them by asking: "How precisely do you have to indicate a time before you know that that particular moment would never repeat itself?" Clearly, every day had 11:48's in it (and Maria reminded us that there was an 11:48 for the morning and one for the night time because there were always two 12:00's in every day). Fridays would repeat themselves, and so would Junes. But the Friday that occurred on the fifth day of June in 1992 — not 1993 or some other year — was the one that wouldn't come back. The 11:48 that belonged to only that Friday was the moment that was now part of our collective history.

This discussion was in June; we had worked hard since September to create an intellectual community. We were witnessing the work and dispositions that we had nurtured throughout the year bearing fruit. The next time the children gathered to talk about time, their observations bore the mark not only of their individual experiences of time outside the classroom, but also of the hours we had spent in exploration together. We decided to ask them what we thought was a harder question: "What is time?" This is what the children told us:

- Time is something that keeps on going.
- It helps you keep track of the events in a day and also of the day.
- It's not in a clock — it's everywhere.
- It's something we use.
- It's invisible — like air.
- It's part of our lives.
- We can't hear it, we can't see it, but we can use it and waste it.
- We live time, we make it.
- You can't speed it up or slow it down.
- Planets use time to travel around the sun.
- It's a different time in every country. When we have morning other countries have night.
- If everything stopped, we would float quickly off to the sun — like a very fast airplane ride.
- The clocks we use can be wrong — but time itself can't be wrong.
- The sun uses time — it takes Mercury less time than any other planet to go around the sun. Pluto takes much more time to orbit the sun.
- If we didn't have any time we would be dead. We wouldn't have any time to be born or to live.
- Time was in the past and it is still part of the world.

They were also left with questions:

- How do we know if our clock is wrong?
- When was math invented?
- Was there time before there was a universe? Did time exist before the Big Bang?
- Where would stars and planets "go" if time stopped?
- How did time get started?

As we went over the list, we noticed that much of what they discussed referred to the solar system. We recalled that, for a number of weeks, a group of children had worked together to create an elaborate, scaled model of the sun and the planets with all sixty of their respective moons. All of us had been involved in lively discussions about outer space, gravity, density, and light. The children brought forward into this current conversation on time some of the questions and issues they had visited before. We hadn't planned to integrate or summarize their experiences, but then Scott looked pensively at the ceiling and said, "Time is the whole universe. If there was not time everywhere, there would be no time. The only way time could stop is if the universe stopped." He formulated for all of us an understanding made possible by the history we shared together.

We were excited and honored to have been part of this conversation. These children were pursuing knowledge, making conjectures, reasoning with each other. They were asking the kinds of questions that Einstein, Feynman, Sagan, and Hawkings ask. They were coming to understand that mathematics is a way of speaking. It is a language that permits us to experience the world in particular ways. It is a tool that allows us to explore other, larger ideas. The ability to think mathematically is not simply the ability to produce number facts. It is not even the ability to solve word problems. If we want to nurture children who are passionate about science and mathematics, we have to start right (in both senses of the word) from the beginning:

> Because the discourse of the math class reflects messages about what it means to know math, what makes something true or reasonable, and what doing math entails, it is central to both what students learn about math as well as how they learn it. Therefore the discourse of the math class should be founded on math ways of knowing and ways of communicating. (*Professional Standards*, 1991, p. 54)

Did the children ever learn to tell time? Absolutely. It took only one hour for fifty of them and an additional thirty minutes for the other five to learn *that* kind of math language, too. Many of the grade one's and all of the grade two's could tell time to the quarter hour, and a substantial number mastered the grade-three objective: they could tell time to the minute. As for problem-solving, a group of children created, and then set about solving, their own problems. Nathan, for example, wanted to know how many seconds were in an hour. A group of five children who had already completed the required exercises on telling time and who were interested in solving Nathan's problem gathered around him. While the rest of the class worked in small groups with clocks and question sheets, Nathan and his friends figured out what they thought they would need to know in order to solve the problem and then set about doing the computation. This was no mean feat, considering that none of them knew how to multiply. But they *did* know that mathematics is about patterns and relationships, so they were able to draw upon what they knew about addition, set organization, and place value to solve this real and interesting problem.

There is more to our story of time. The children's questions about the beginnings of clocks led us to ancient Egypt and Stonehenge, to early calendars and struggles to align solar and lunar years, to the mythological sources naming months and weekdays.

Unfortunately, like the sands in an hour-glass, we ran out of time. But we were left with a wonderful and exciting starting place for the following September, when we teach these same children again.

CONCLUSION

These are not easy times for public education. Beset on all sides by calls to do better work on behalf of children, it is difficult not to feel defensive or defeated when others far from the daily life of a classroom call for school reform. For a long time, teachers have been charged with implementing theories developed by others. Those of us who have been teaching for a long time have seen many theories come and go, and we have worked hard to keep up with what was expected of us. Increasing numbers of us have, however, begun to sense that the educational conversation is changing in important ways. Often excluded in the past, the voices of teachers and children are being welcomed as ones that can inform both theory and practice in unique ways. For it is teachers who spend their daily lives in the presence of children; teachers who are better placed than anyone to see what can happen when they begin to think differently about their work with children; teachers who can make change happen.

In our daily work, our reflection, and our writing, the two of us have taken seriously the challenge of thinking about education from deep inside its most fundamental structures. We began our work together knowing *that* we wanted to challenge basic assumptions about primary practice. As our research proceeded, we began also to be able to talk about *how* we thought changes in teaching practice might come about. First, we came to see, in the relationships that we established with each child in our care, the importance of offering invitations to connect the life each child lived fully and completely outside the school with the life we were offering inside its doors. For us, David's story was perhaps the most dramatic and obvious of fifty-four other stories we could have told. As we sat together at the end of the school year thinking about the children and the journey on which each had embarked with us, we understood for ourselves that the successes — and the failures — of our attempts to connect with each child marked the successes — and the failures — of our work with each.

We do not think that observation will come as any great surprise to good teachers. Nor will it come as a surprise to anyone when we say that living out the implications of this understanding is an awesome responsibility. What *did* come as more of a surprise to us was to see, in our relationships with the children, the power of imagination to build connections that were not only personally gratifying, but also educationally profound. Imaginative engagement in questions and issues that were big enough to enchant each person in class, child and adult alike, created the space within which each child could move with strength and freedom. Each found his or her own ways into the conversations and the work throughout the year, and the conversation and work were glorious because each voice contributed uniquely.

Perhaps what is most unexpected about what we found as we began to explore the world with children in the ways we have described here is the extent to which they learned more than we had ever imagined possible. We heard some of them recite parts of Tennyson by heart on the playground, loving *The Lady of Shalott* as much as David had loved *Bringing the Rain to Kapiti Plain*. We did physics experiments with some, and investigated ancient number systems with others. Together, we and the children built models of the solar system, medieval castles, and the Great Wall of China. We thrilled in their retellings of ancient Chinese legends and plots of Italian operas. With each and every study, the children kept pushing: tell us more. Given access to real science, real mathematics, real literature, and art of substance and merit, they seemed insatiable.

We began this article with a quotation from *Alice in Wonderland*. Like many teachers, we are fond of Alice. Indeed, there are days when we find ourselves, like her, wandering around asking foolish questions about matters that seem quite settled to others. The Mock Turtle and the Gryphon listen patiently to Alice's bewildered inability to understand what schools are for, and we wonder what — if anything — they made of her question, "And how did you manage on the twelfth?" We wonder if they clucked their beaks, rolled their eyes, and wished she'd just go away.

Having begun to create for ourselves a completely different framework from the one presented by the Turtle and the Gryphon, however, we are no longer left to resolve the beastly paradox that so bedeviled Alice. Lessons need *not* lessen from day to day, month to month, year to year. Children and teachers *can* find new and powerful ways to come to know each other through real work that engages their minds, hearts, and spirits.

We can all, in fact, manage quite nicely on the twelfth.

REFERENCES

Aardema, V. (1981). *Bringing the rain to Kapiti Plain.* New York: Dial.

Beowulf. (1982). Oxford: Oxford University Press.

Coop, P., & Coop, C. (Eds.). (1990). *I, Columbus: My journal.* New York: Avon Books.

Carroll, L. (1966). *Alice's adventures in wonderland, and Through the looking glass.* New York: Macmillan. (Original works published 1865)

Coleridge, S. T. (1992). *The rime of the ancient mariner.* New York: Atheneum.

Egan, K. (1986). *Primary understandings.* London: Routledge.

Egan, K. (1992). The roles of schools: The place of education. *Teacher's College Record, 93,* 641–655.

Gregory, B. (1990). *Inventing reality: Physics as language.* New York: John Wiley.

Harris, D. J. (1991). *Rumpelstiltskin.* Toronto: Oxford University Press.

Lopez, B. (1990). *Crow and weasel.* Toronto: Random House.

Mollel, T. M. (1990). *The orphan boy.* Toronto: Oxford University Press.

Mollel, T. M. (1991). *Rhinos for lunch, elephants for supper.* Toronto: Oxford University Press.

Mollel, T. M. (1992). *A promise to the sun.* Boston: Little, Brown.

Noyes, A. (1981). *The highwayman.* Oxford: Oxford University Press.

Price, L. (1990). *Aida.* San Diego: Gulliver Books.

Professional standards for teaching mathematics. (1991). National Council of Teachers of Mathematics.

Tennyson, A. (1986). *The lady of Shalott.* Oxford: Oxford University Press.

Yolen, J. (1992). *Encounter.* New York: Harcourt Brace.

White, E. B. (1952). *Charlotte's web.* New York: Harper & Row.

Researching Change
and Changing the Researcher

CONCHA DELGADO-GAITAN

In this article, Concha Delgado-Gaitan describes her experience as a researcher in Carpinteria, a predominantly Mexican-American community in California. After collecting data about family literacy practices through ethnographic observations and interviews, she began meeting regularly with parents to share her findings and solicit their input. These meetings became a turning point for Delgado-Gaitan, redirecting the focus of her research from literacy activities to the process of community empowerment as she learned from these parents about their own understanding of literacy and about their concerns regarding communication with schools. Through these meetings, the parents organized as a group, in order to demand that the school respond to their needs.

The situation challenged Delgado-Gaitan to redefine her role as a researcher. After much internal debate and reflection, she decided to become involved in the empowerment of parents as an informant and facilitator. This article is the story of how this research project supported the process of community empowerment in Carpinteria, and how that process challenged the researcher to examine her own identity, to refocus her research, and to change.

Over the past twenty years or so, anthropological researchers in education have employed interpretive ethnographic theories and research tools to study learning processes from a cultural perspective. Their primary task has been to provide an adequate contextualization of the cultural phenomena related to education.

More recently, interpretive anthropology has been enriched by the convergence of such approaches as phenomenology, structuralism, transformational linguistics, semiotics, critical theory, and hermeneutics (Marcus & Fischer, 1986). This cross-fertilization has been especially useful in providing a new perspective on the "native point of view," and on the problem of depicting cultural realities in social interaction. Through critical theory analysis in particular we find a language of possibility to understand change. Critical theory allows for discussion regarding the interaction between researcher and researched in the context of the researched community. Discussion about the researcher's viewpoint has in turn been important in raising questions regarding the outsider/insider position of researcher/researched (Hirschkind, 1991; Thomas, 1991).[1]

How we perceive our role in the communities we study matters greatly because it impacts the nature of the research we conduct (Elliott, 1988; Peshkin, 1982;

---

[1] The term "position" is used in academic discourse to refer to the oppositional role we researchers assume as we conduct ethnographic research. Cast in this binary oppositional framework, the researcher is considered the outsider while the participants — the researched — are the insiders.

Harvard Educational Review Vol. 63 No. 4 Winter 1993, 389–411

Podermaker, 1967). The way we, as researchers, relate to ourselves and to the people we study was the focus of Dorinne Kondo's (1990) ethnography of the Japanese company as a family. She describes how notions of her identity as a Japanese-American woman anthropologist changed throughout her research. Kondo's thesis is that the researcher shapes his or her research and is, in turn, shaped by it. Smadar Lavie's (1991) anthropological study with the Mzeina people, a Bedouin tribe in the South Sinai Desert, also illuminates how the researcher's identity is changed through her work. In her study, Lavie depicts the Bedouin struggle with the military occupation as she tries simultaneously to define her own identity vis-à-vis the Mzeinis, who were like family to her, a Jewish-Arab woman trained as a western anthropologist at the University of California, Berkeley. Based on critical inquiry of the Mzeina, she composes a written ethnography that retraces the process by which the Bedouin identity emerged through the performances of seven allegory-telling characters; within the ethnography, Lavie's own identity is fused with the personas of these characters. Both Kondo and Lavie use their ethnic identities as a tool for participating in the cultural communities that they studied, in order to involve the research participants in constructing their ethnographies.

In the United States, Michael Apple (1993) expands the discourse of the researcher's role in local communities by building and rebuilding a space where the researcher and the participants collectively raise questions about the meaning and power of knowledge through text. Apple emphasizes the importance of the researcher/researched relationship in questioning the source of knowledge in established canons. His role in the communities he researched exemplifies the possibilities of conducting research with socially disenfranchised groups in the United States.

I am a woman of Mexican immigrant heritage. My working-class family valued education and provided me with a strong foundation for learning and succeeding in school. My ethno-cultural identity was a key motivation for my studying family-school interconnections in the Spanish-speaking community of Carpinteria, California, where I engaged myself as a researcher. I set out to understand the nature of Latino family interactions involving literacy. The question of family literacy led me to further explore family-school relationships, including communication between family and school, and community empowerment.

In this article, I describe the Carpinteria study in order to discuss my role as an ethnographic researcher. I reflect on my evolving role as an observer of the people's daily interactions; as an active participant in family, school, and community activities; and as a facilitator in a conscious, reflective process undertaken by community members and between the researcher and the community.

THE PARTICIPANT RESEARCHER: A RELATIONAL PERSPECTIVE

Sharing the same ethnic background as the participants does not necessarily make the researcher more knowledgeable about the meanings of the participants' feelings, values, and practices. Researchers often hold misperceptions about participants' feelings, values, and practices based on influences such as assumed cultural knowledge. Therefore, interpretive fieldwork strategies that bring together theory and process through dialogue between research participants and researcher promise to yield a more complete interpretation (Delgado-Gaitan, 1987; Heath, 1983; Macias, 1987; Moll & Díaz, 1987; Spindler, 1970, 1974; Spindler & Spindler, 1970; Spradley, 1979; Suárez-Orozco, 1989).[2]

Given that basic tenets of critical theory presuppose a commitment to the emancipation of groups that have been socially, economically, and politically disenfranchised in society, researchers espousing this theoretical orientation enter the field with a notion about the insider-outsider relationship that includes a commitment to change. Henry Trueba and I have developed a framework called the Ethnography of Empowerment, which provides a broad sociocultural premise and possible strategy for studying the process of disempowerment and empowerment of disenfranchised communities (Delgado-Gaitan & Trueba, 1991). I understand empowerment as an ongoing, intentional process centered in the local community, involving mutual respect, critical reflection, caring, and collective participation (Barr, 1989; Barr & Cochran, 1991). Through this process, people become aware of their social conditions and strengths: they determine their choices and goals, and thus unveil their potential to act on their own behalf. Implicit in this process is a conscious responsibility on the part of disenfranchised communities for their own behavior and a willingness to shape their behavior as they desire through social processes. The Ethnography of Empowerment framework calls for the construction of knowledge through the social interaction between researcher and researched, with the fundamental purpose of improving the living conditions of the communities being researched. Thus, this kind of ethnography redefines the fundamental priorities of anthropological, educational, and social science research.

Consistent with Paulo Freire's critical theory premise, our construct of Ethnography of Empowerment establishes the process of ethnography as a theory and method applied in disenfranchised communities that addresses the question of the insider/outsider perspectives (Delgado-Gaitan & Trueba, 1991).[3] Ethnography of Empowerment rests on two fundamental premises about the nature of

---

[2] Interpretive fieldwork strategies have, nevertheless, been criticized regarding researcher bias from several different epistemological paradigms. Questions of objectivity have been a continuing point of contention between positivists and qualitative researchers, including ethnographers. Positivists have argued that if the ethnographer becomes involved with the group he or she is studying, the ethnographer ceases to identify with the professional subgroup as his or her dominant reference group. The conventional premise here is that the ethnographer has to maintain an interpretive stance congruent with the professional group he or she represents. In contrast, the relational position attempts to depict the complexity of the relationship between the participant and the researcher. For further discussion on this aspect of interpretive research, see Chow, 1986; Geertz, 1973; Spindler and Spindler, 1987; and Wolcott, 1981.

A criticism against participant observation is that the participant and the researcher usually belong to different cultures. Critics argue that through researcher participation, such as the researcher engaging in community activities, the setting may be transformed and the goals of an "objective" field study may be altered by changing the power relations in favor of the subordinate group or of the dominant groups. Critical theorists refute this criticism by maintaining that value-neutral theories and research are nonexistent (Habermas, 1974).

[3] A central theme in Paulo Freire's work with Brazilian indigenous groups is his portrayal of community learning, in which the relationship between educators and students is a phenomenon involving a certain permanent, although not antagonistic, tension. It is this same tension — which exists between theory and practice, and between authority and freedom — that renders teaching and learning inseparable. I have extended Freire's relational thesis about learning and critical practice into

learning. First, learning among humans occurs across cultures, primarily in the home or in sociocultural units in which individuals are socialized. Second, learning ideally is purposive, and should ultimately be directed to the enhancement of cultural values. This ideal is possible when learning is embedded in the context of the learning community (Delgado-Gaitan & Trueba, 1991). These notions of social and cultural self-awareness attempt to develop a description of the ethno-historical and cultural context that makes it possible to understand the nature of oppression experienced by disenfranchised people and communities. This kind of context and description can be developed when ethnographic researchers practice dialogical research processes.

In the Ethnography of Empowerment framework, not only does the ethnographer effect and/or affect change in the communities as a result of being a participant-observer, but he or she is also influenced by the community being studied, such that the direction and orientation of his or her research may be changed.

It is within this theoretical orientation that I discuss my role as an ethnographic researcher in Carpinteria.[4] Central to this discussion is my relationship with the participants — in particular, how that relationship helped me understand myself, and how it informed my role in crafting the study and influencing change in the Carpinteria community.

Action: Establishing a Relationship

During the first five years of the Carpinteria study, I was a professor at the University of California, Santa Barbara, and lived twenty minutes from Carpinteria. My initial interest in the Carpinteria Latino community was as an extension of research that I had conducted in other Latino communities in northern California and Colorado. In particular, I wanted to observe a setting that provided successful educational programs for Latino students.

My eight years of research in Carpinteria began with an ethnographic study on family literacy in the Spanish-speaking Latino community. It evolved to encompass the parent involvement process in the Carpinteria school, which had been one of shared power between families and the school. The parent-school empowerment process, through the Comité de Padres Latinos (COPLA), illustrated a difficult but doable approach taken by a community interested in Latino children's education.

Part of the impetus for this study was my reaction to much of the research literature that focused on devastating educational conditions in culturally different communities. My observations of children and their families in ethnically diverse California communities where I had been an elementary school teacher and principal convinced me that Latino people could be more than the helpless victims characterized in many studies of school failure. I observed members of

---

my research methodology framework. Freire would assert that, through active involvement of the learner, critical theory seeks practical solutions for structural problems that are social and cultural constructions. For additional discussion on Freire's critical theory, see Freire, 1985; Shor and Freire, 1987.

[4] Except for "Carpinteria," all names used in this article are pseudonyms. The real name of the school district is used because I received permission from the school district to use it in publications.

the Latino community being active participants in the day-to-day shaping of their lives, which convinced me that active participation is for them a source of strength and empowerment.

This optimism impelled my study on family literacy (involving oral, reading, and written text in daily family life) in Carpinteria, and encouraged me to try to shatter the monolithic portrayal of Mexicans as ignorant, powerless failures in U.S. schools. My own background as an immigrant from Mexico, who grew up in California from age eight and attended school in various Los Angeles communities, further impelled me to understand the complexity of these immigrant families' lives and their relations with the schools.

I negotiated my initial entry into the Carpinteria community through the school district in order to observe literacy abilities in the Latino households and in the community, including the schools. This topic was of serious concern to the schools because many Latino students were reading at levels below school expectations. The issue of literacy was especially important for me in that literacy occupies a far more complex and important place in the Mexican community than schools sometimes understand. This discrepancy between the place of literacy in the Mexican community and the schools' understanding of its place is not unique to Carpinteria; it has, in fact, been documented by various researchers (Ada, 1988; Delgado-Gaitan, 1990; Goldenberg, 1987; Moll & Díaz, 1987). School personnel, however, often do not have the time to examine family and community literacy practices. I am familiar with school personnel time constraints through personal experiences in the schools and through interviews in the Carpinteria study.

I collected data through systematic ethnographic observations of literacy activities in the household, school, and community, and through interviews of family members over a two-year period. I recorded these observations in written field notes, and in video and audio recordings. I found that although families shared common literacy activities, such as oral storytelling by parents to younger children, letter writing to relatives in Mexico, and storybook reading of popular trade books in Spanish, variation existed in parent-child interaction around homework-type literacy tasks (Delgado-Gaitan, 1990). Observations showed that children who were placed in novice reading groups in the classroom generally faced stricter rules in the home and received more direct instructional assistance from parents. These parents believed that their children needed supervised assistance, since the teachers' reports stressed negative behavior and low performance. Children who were placed in the advanced reading groups in the classroom tended to enjoy more freedom in the way they did their homework because parents usually assisted them only indirectly by assuring completion of the task. These parents seemed to trust their children and to believe that they were responsible and knowledgeable enough to do their work; they also communicated more frequently with the teachers and received pointers on ways to assist their children.

Part of the ethnographic method I employed involved sharing data with nearly one hundred Latino families to elicit their input and insight about their own literacy practices in the home and in relation to the school. The intent of the data-sharing sessions was to solicit the insider's perspective and to make meaning

123

of their experiences. An unanticipated outcome of this relational process (which I will discuss later) altered the course of my research, while forcing participants and myself to reexamine our perceptions. Friday evening meetings at the Aliso Elementary School were the setting where the families and I analyzed their experiences; these meetings eventually redirected the study.

In Carpinteria, every noon during lunchtime, the tables in the Aliso Elementary School auditorium were filled with children who swallowed their lunches as quickly as possible before running outside to play. On some Friday nights, many Latino families came together in that same school auditorium to discuss topics related to family education as part of the Migrant Education Program. The meetings were held on a monthly basis (occasionally more often) and were already taking place when my study began. The purpose of the Program was to share information with families about immigration laws, AIDS, and other pertinent issues, such as health care for preschool children. For example, on one particular Friday evening, over seventy people, including men, women holding young children on their laps, and older children, listened attentively to a guest speaker who discussed legal rights for immigrants.

I selected those Friday night meetings as the forum to share with the families the ethnographic data on literacy activities that I had collected in their homes. At six consecutive monthly meetings, I spent over one hour of their two-hour meeting sharing my data and soliciting comments from the parents. The data included findings about parents telling stories to children, reading to children at home, and assisting with schoolwork. I presented my findings while attempting to maintain a warm and friendly, yet somewhat distant, posture; generally, parents who attended the meetings talked with me about the study findings. Their insights and meaning provoked my interest and, periodically, both confirmed and challenged my interpretations.

I began my first presentation by commending the parents for their commitment to and interest in their children's education. However, I also pointed out that some parents did not read much to their children, even in Spanish, and that a connection existed between parents who read to their children and the school's expectations and perceptions about Latino children's performance. The issue that I intended to raise with parents was diversity in family literacy practices; I believed that parents' familiarity with such ideas would provide insights about their children's performance in schools.

In presenting my data to this group, I wanted them to recognize that literacy practices at home — particularly their interaction with written text — affected their children's school performance. I was not, however, advocating that they change their reading practices as a result of my data. At that point, I merely wanted to share my findings with them and to solicit their perspective about my data. When I began studying literacy activities in the homes, my understanding of literacy practices in the Latino community conformed to those of the schools in that I believed literacy to be primarily the act of decoding written text. As the study unfolded, my understanding of literacy transcended that of the school. I expanded my understanding of literacy to include oral literacy activities, as well as the critical interpretation of the "word" (Freire & Macedo, 1987). During the process of data collection, I learned that parents demonstrate their concern for their children's success in school in ways other than reading to their children in the households. The following parent's comment illustrates one of the alternative ways in which parents expressed their concern for their children's success: "My husband and I remind our children that they have a great opportunity to go to school and they should take advantage of it so they can have the opportunities we did not have."[5]

At these meetings, parents listened attentively to the speakers, even when distracted by their young children, who often ran in and out of the auditorium. I talked about the stories that some parents read to their children. The question I posed to them was, "Do you read to your children, and if so, what kind of stories do you read?" Parents raised their hands enthusiastically and related their experiences:

> I never read to my older children, although I did encourage them to read to each other. When we moved to Carpinteria, my youngest daughter went to preschool and the teacher always told us to read to our children in Spanish so that they would learn to read in their own language. It didn't make sense to me, but I did it anyway, and now that my daughter is in the second grade I see that she likes reading much more than my other children. I think it has to do with the fact that I still read to her.

Other comments were made:

> I think it's good to read to our children like the teacher has told us, but neither my husband nor I read either in Spanish or English so it's hard to help our children. What we do is to encourage our children to stay in school and to learn. They can be educated in a way that we never could.

At the Friday meetings, during my exchange with the community, parents generally shared information about their literacy activities with their children. They reported on a variety of interactions, which included adults and children reading popular storybooks such as *Snow White*, analyzing legal documents, and writing letters to their relatives in Mexico. Occasionally, parents helped their children with particular homework assignments.

Combing through piles of field notes and tape transcripts, I identified types and contexts of literacy activities in the home and in the classroom. I analyzed video tapes to define further the nature of the literacy events. Who, when, and how parents helped their children with schoolwork emerged as an unexpected salient issue in what began as an exploration of literacy in the Latino community. This issue emerged in the process of data analysis about a month before I began to meet with parents on Friday nights, and convinced me of the need to reflect with them. The parents' immediate purpose, which was to have their children succeed in school, dominated most of their literacy practices.

I pursued the theme of the home-school connection because I was perplexed by the differences in participation of parents in their children's education that emerged during my Friday night discussions with the families. Some parents interacted more actively with their children to help them complete their homework, while some felt less able to assist their children. Regardless of the parents'

[5] All of the participants' quotes in this article have been translated by me from Spanish.

level of engagement with their children's homework, most parents felt incompetent in communicating with the school. Most of them had received only a fourth-grade education in Mexico, and they blamed their lack of formal education for their *ineffective exchanges* with the school, by which I mean those attempts parents made to relate to the school, but which in fact left them more confused. For example, in one case a boy was being retained in the first grade and the mother went to the school to talk to the teacher. The teacher told her that the reason for the child's retention was his low reading ability, and that the parents needed to help him read at home. Without further clarification, the mother assumed that her son's failure in school was her fault. Essentially, this example indicates that some parents did not know what questions to ask because of their lack of familiarity with the school system. As parents repeatedly explained to me, they often felt that they did not know what questions to ask; moreover, when they knew the questions they wanted to ask, they did not know how to ask them or of whom. Led by the developments of this phase of the analysis, I probed further into the question of how parents learned to help their children do their homework. Most of the parents who were active in the school responded that they had been taught by the preschool teacher to communicate with educators. The undereducated parents, whether or not they were active in the schools, felt isolated because they believed that as a result of their limited formal schooling, their children might not have access to the best education.

As they responded to my research questions about parental participation in schools and in their children's schooling, angry emotions flared as some parents told of going to the school to make an appointment to talk with their child's teacher, and finding that they could not communicate with anyone in the office. Not knowing how to connect with the schools had clearly traumatized some of these parents. The identification of this issue expanded my research focus from describing literacy in the Latino community to understanding its meaning to the parents, including their communication with schools.

Change: Redirected Role of the Researcher

At the third Friday night meeting with the parents at Aliso Elementary School, a father, Mr. Reyes, stood up and said that he had been listening to me present information about the Latino families in Carpinteria over the prior weeks. In his opinion, many families felt isolated, not because they did not care, but because they did not have the necessary experience to communicate with the schools. He proposed that those parents who had more contact with the schools should organize and teach those who needed it. At that point, as I stood in front of the parents, I found myself fighting to remain in the "neutral" research role. I tried to resist the temptation to advocate for forming the parent leadership group that Mr. Reyes proposed, which I could see would be instrumental in achieving their cultural adjustment goal — that is, effective, cooperative, family-school relationships. It was clear to me that some type of support group could benefit the families in their communication with the schools.

Following the meeting, I approached Mr. Reyes and asked him about his intent to organize the parents. He lamented that most administrators did not have the time to work with the community, and that those who were interested, like the Migrant Education Director, had quite an overload of work imposed on them. I asked him what might prevent him from organizing the group himself, and he responded that he could not because he didn't have a list of people to call. He questioned his own skills in organizing the group. He said that he knew other people's names, but did not have their phone numbers. Mr. Reyes looked around as if he were looking for someone, and then he said that possibly the Director of Migrant Education had a list. Instinctively, I wanted to convince him to ask the Director for a list of parents' names and phone numbers, but I refrained. Mr. Reyes indicated that he wanted to get the parents together if their phone numbers were available. His response made me question again the nature of my role as a researcher. I evaluated the appropriateness of my intervening, and I contemplated the possibility of suggesting to him how to obtain the list of parents' names and organize a meeting.

At this point, I remembered the voices of some of my teachers, who had reminded me that the ethnographer's work entails only observing and describing. However, another voice resounded even more loudly and defended the role of the researcher as politically weighted. Such a position seemed to obligate the researcher, me, to intervene when it might lead to favorable results for the participants or even when it involves a question of the researcher's moral conscience. Freire (1970) advocates for direct intervention as a way to learn about the communities' needs. These internal voices intensified my quandary about whether or not to intervene directly as an advocate. Paulo Freire's literacy work in community organizing for literacy and empowerment had long governed my research pursuits. Now I had to determine if my intervening in these families' *concientizaçao* (consciousness raising) would influence the integrity of their process of change, as well as my process of traditional "objective" research, which seemed necessary to protect, given my academic training.[6] The decision to refrain from encouraging Mr. Reyes was a difficult one.

Traditional ethnographic methodology asserts the researcher's privileged position, leading one to participate in the culture in covert ways for the mere purpose of obtaining data. Under this premise, we are still led to believe that the research process can be removed from any human contamination (Schatzman & Strauss, 1973; Strauss, 1987). Thus, I confronted an ethical question as to what my real intent would be if I participated as a facilitator in the parents' emerging organization. By now I was convinced by praxis that no research is neutral, yet the realization was academic in that I still had to consider what it meant in the context of this setting, with real human beings who were working to change their lives.

At a subsequent parent meeting, I approached Mr. Reyes and asked him about the progress that he had made in convening a meeting of Latino parent leaders. After pondering the question during the previous two weeks, I had decided to initiate this topic with Mr. Reyes. By the time of this meeting, I had reconciled my intervention with my role as a researcher. He shrugged his shoulders and said that he had not mobilized parents because he did not have their phone

---

[6] My academic training was rich in ethnography; I learned to structure rigorous and systematic observations and interviews that did not include intervention in changing the setting I was studying.

numbers. I asked, "Why don't you ask the Migrant Education Director to provide you with a list of parents you can call to a meeting?" I then suggested to him that if he called together a meeting of parents, I would like to attend. I invited myself to the meeting with the understanding that I would not act as their leader, because it was their community. I did, however, offer to share my data with the parents at their leadership meetings. By this time, I had collected a large amount of data on the literacy activities and learning contexts in the home and the schools in this research site, data ranging from bedtime stories to superintendent administrators' meetings.

The following week, Mr. Reyes called me at my home and announced that he had reached several parents who were interested in attending a meeting to discuss how they could support each other on issues of educating their children. He had arranged with the Director of Special Programs (the Migrant Education Program was part of these Special Programs) to have the meeting take place in the faculty room of Aliso Elementary school that coming Friday, when there was no Migrant Education Program meeting scheduled.

On that Friday evening, I made it a point to arrive at the site on time to observe how the event unfolded. Although I normally arrived on time, it had never been as crucial as this night, since now — with my decision to intervene — my purpose included studying the process of the meeting. Eleven parents gathered in front of the school's faculty room, which apparently had not been unlocked as the parents had requested. One of the parents went to the public phone to call the District Director of Curriculum. He learned that there had been a misunderstanding about the time at which the door had to be opened, since the school's regular custodian was out ill. Evidently no one had keys to a classroom, so a couple of the men moved a large lunch table with benches from the playground to the inner courtyard. People sat and talked about their concerns as Mexican immigrants raising children in Carpinteria.

Mr. Reyes convened the meeting by asking people to introduce themselves. He explained that the purpose of the meeting was to try to get some Latino parents together to see how they could help other Spanish-speaking parents who needed to communicate with the school about their children. He emphasized that they had been called together because of their experiences with the schools so that they could share ideas on how to organize Latino families to support each other.

At that point, I began to notice a shift in my research focus from concerns with literacy activities and processes in home and school to the process of empowerment. Parents took turns talking about their heartfelt desire to have their children get a good education so that they would have greater economic security than their parents experienced as Spanish-speaking immigrants from a low socioeconomic level. Their primary concern was with their perceived distancing of the children from the family culture. This distancing was created as children learned American values that were different from their family traditions. Mrs. Ortiz was choked by her words as she disclosed her ordeal with her daughter, who did not want to speak Spanish to them because she felt ashamed:

> Our insistence to have her speak to us in Spanish is overshadowed by her need to
> be liked in school. She's just in the sixth grade, but English is more important to

her and her friends. We need to speak Spanish, that's the language of our family. There's nothing wrong with English, but the school's not teaching them Spanish, so we should, because we will always speak it.

Such words captured me. I was also captured by the support that participants in the meeting gave each other, which in turn created a safe environment that permitted them to express their feelings. Parents' love for their children was mixed with fear and frustration because, in their efforts to help, they were still faced with unknown results and expectations. The parents shared their experiences in relating to the White, European American community and the schools, and also told their stories of challenge and commitment to their families. Their contact with the school had been more active than that of other Latino parents in the Carpinteria community, yet these parents felt the pressure of not meeting the school's expectations, such as speaking English and being familiar with the way the school operated. As Mr. Soto noted:

> I always go to the school when my son's teachers call me and want to talk to me about his problematic behavior. One day the school called me, and as usual I had to leave work and take a pay cut for that release-time to help out my son. When I got there [to the school] I waited almost an hour and no one knew where my son was or what the problem was. As it turned out, it was not my son who had been in the fight. I was quite upset and I didn't even get an apology from the school. I find this degrading and humiliating. I don't think they would do it to someone who could defend himself in English.

Mr. Soto's humiliation was addressed by others in the group who believed that although he did not know English, Mr. Soto certainly deserved more respect than the school had extended.

Stories such as the one shared by this parent consumed much of the time during this initial meeting. The underlying message to each other seemed to be that they, as parents, tried very hard to do the best for their children, and that they had the desire and commitment to support their children in their education both at home and at school. The fact that they cared about their children and their education was understood by them to mean that they were "good parents."

Mrs. Mora, who would later become the group leader for the Latino parents, stressed that the parents' life experiences were of much value and should be shared with their children. For example, Mrs. Mora was a part of the Latino Spanish-speaking immigrant community. Her educational experience was somewhat more advanced than most Latino immigrants in Carpinteria, whose formal education in Mexico did not exceed elementary school. Mrs. Mora's words — "We came because *we can*, not to see *if* we can" — frame the quintessential statement for this study of family and community, since her statement reflects the perceived reality of power by Latino families. The meaning of this claim became clear as the process of community organization unfolded. Mrs. Mora's reminder to parents of their responsibility to communicate pride and struggle to their children resonated in her statement, "Many of us do not have the formal education necessary to help our children with their demands in school, but we value and respect the family. Through our family we help our children value their own lives and education."

129

Her words impressed me as being important, but still left me doubting how knowledgeable parents were in actually helping their children succeed in school. My findings had shown that parents who actively communicated with the school had children who were more advanced readers. But here were parents who perceived their own experience as the power base of their family and, in spite of their limited schooling, recognized the importance of transmitting their cultural values and beliefs to their children. Given this opportunity to listen to parents represent their views of what education means to them, I questioned my initial analysis of the family-school relationship study, which minimized the parents' experience as a value transmitted to children and its importance to their children's overall attitude about schooling beyond their placement in the classroom reading groups (Delgado-Gaitan, 1989).

At a subsequent meeting, parents agreed to select a leader for their group. Their approach to selecting a leader demonstrated their respect for each others' abilities while recognizing their need for a person to help them make contact with the schools. The choice of a president of this parent group occupied most of the discussion. Parents described a person who could speak at least some English because she or he would have to talk with administrators who might not speak Spanish. This criterion was subsequently dismissed, as they decided that someone could have leadership skills without being English-speaking. Another practical qualification desired in their leader was that the person be able to drive a car so that she or he could attend meetings at the schools. That notion was also readily dismissed because parents felt that if the person who assumed the position of president had good communication skills and wanted the position but did not drive, she or he could find transportation.

Their expectations for leadership qualifications were defined by the collective group through a process of turn-taking, in which each person shared his or her views. The person in the leadership role had to commit to the group's position. Pragmatic qualifications such as bilingualism, knowledge about the schools, availability of time, and transportation became secondary as the commitment to the group became the primary factor that the Latino parents wanted upheld.

Mrs. Mora was nominated by a parent, and the nomination was supported unanimously. It was noted that she had been a teacher in Mexico, and that her expertise in working with schools could assist the group in their communication with the schools. Mrs. Mora was also the eldest member of the parent group and no longer had children in the school district. Although she did not drive a car or speak fluent English, parents recognized her experience as an educator in Mexico and sought to utilize her skills.

It was unclear to me why they dismissed their need for people who could communicate more effectively with the schools through the use of English. Although their recognition of Mrs. Mora's teaching experience made sense from their point of view, it seemed impractical to me to have a leader who could not communicate with school personnel. However, her position as a teacher and the group's respect for her knowledge were considered high priorities by the group. Recent interviews with the COPLA leadership have clarified this question for me further. Their decision to select Mrs. Mora as their leader was not a disqualification of individuals who were more competent in English, but rather an affirmation of their interest in being represented by someone who would articulate their values and vision as concerned Latino parents.

Parents took turns complimenting Mrs. Mora's strong and positive spirit that so inspired them all. As Mr. Soto stated, "Mrs. Mora shares our vision of how we view our responsibility to communicate with our children and with the schools. We want to put our best foot forward because we know how much it matters." The group believed that the way she spoke about family cohesiveness, interdependence, and the motivation for education reflected the Mexican community's goals for their children.

The selection of a president clearly held a different meaning for this parent group from what I had expected, given my general concepts of leadership, which were based on a model of organization and participation that was different from that which oriented this group. I was under the impression that the parents would elect a president for the purpose of attending to logistical tasks, such as scheduling meetings with the principals. My teaching, administrative, and academic experience had taught me that the president's role in an organization meant representing the group, deciding the agenda, and defining the membership of the group by its voting privileges. Yet, how this organization — eventually named Comité de Padres Latinos (COPLA) — was organized revealed an obvious cultural difference between me and the Latino families.[7] However, this difference became apparent only after I discussed my observations with them. For example, the data on family systems and interaction that I shared with them at the Friday night meetings indicated a strong sense of unity and respect for one another that transcended the immediate nuclear family and extended to relatives and other members of the community. Yet, as the parent organization evolved, I failed to account for the cultural linkages between family values and those shaping the organization.

COPLA parents' division of labor at the Canalino Elementary School — the first school they approached — showed that as organizers they wanted every participant to have an active voice in the process. COPLA parents spoke to the issue of wanting more input from a larger group of Latino parents about this new organization.

During this initial part of their organizing efforts, Mrs. Mora, now COPLA president, called me. She wanted me to address the group about the overall structure and curricular programs in the Carpinteria schools, so that I could begin to show the parents how to initiate organizational contact with the schools. I had offered my facilitator services to the parents as a way of sharing the data that I had collected, but I continued to experience a great deal of consternation

---

[7] Space limitations prevent me from expanding fully on more recent developments of COPLA. The organization has continued to mobilize in Carpinteria. It has now been active for five years, and has established a structure in each school by which one teacher provides systematic linkages between the school and the parents. With formally written by-laws, they have organized a district-wide committee, as well as satellite school-site groups in all of the elementary, junior high, and high schools. COPLA holds monthly meetings for their district-wide committee on the first Friday of each month. The school-site COPLA meetings are held on alternate Fridays so as not to conflict with those of the district COPLA. Each school has two parent representatives on the district committees, who report to the group about their activities. For additional information about more current developments in the organization and its role as a community support group, see Delgado-Gaitan, 1991.

about moving away from my role as researcher. I asked Mrs. Mora what it was that the group wanted to know and why they believed I could help. She said that COPLA parents considered me knowledgeable about the schools, and that they trusted me and considered me to be an advocate for them. Furthermore, I was qualified to inform and teach them, in Spanish, about the way that schools worked in the United States, enabling them to communicate better with school personnel.

The parents' request for my services forced me to delineate my role as a researcher and focus on whether I could participate in COPLA and maintain my role of observer without compromising the integrity of the research. Would I abandon the study and just act as a facilitator? Was it possible to act as an advocate, or broker, while researching the change process? If I was going to educate parents about schooling in Carpinteria, how would it change the direction of the study? Could I, as Rosalie Wax (1971) says, "step in and out"? Again these questions surfaced, forcing me to clarify how to participate without interfering with the parents' process.

Driven by the work of Freire and the Cornell University Empowerment Group (Allen, Barr, Cochran, Dean, & Greene, 1989; Freire, 1970, 1973), I transcended my qualms and decided to involve myself as the parents requested. In Freire's work, the principles of community empowerment recognize the researcher as an active participant who acts as a facilitator in the community's change process. One week after Mrs. Mora's request, I called her and committed my services to the group. I made my position clear to the group — I would be an informant to them, but I would not be responsible for COPLA's goals and direction.

Mrs. Mora instructed me to inform the group about the way the schools operated. I asked her what the parents knew about the schools. Although I knew something about their knowledge of the education system by having sat in on the initial COPLA meetings, it was nevertheless important to hear it from her. Mrs. Mora felt that the parents wanted to learn about school programs and about how they could help their children succeed in school.

I considered how I would share my data with them regarding the schools' organization and the classroom learning setting. We first met in the teachers' room at Aliso Elementary School. About thirty parents were present, including the eleven members of the original district-wide COPLA group. I outlined the structure of the Carpinteria school system, from preschool to high school level, as well as the academic expectations at each grade level. I described what the schools expected of children, with particular emphasis on methods to achieve high grades, and presented data that I had collected in their homes and schools. In relation to parental tasks in the home, the data that I presented illustrated that as students got to the upper grades, parents lacked the language or formal academic preparation to be able to help their children directly.

During the second COPLA meeting, I assumed that Mrs. Mora, as group president, would identify the eleven formal COPLA members as those who would make the decisions. However, when it came time to vote on questions such as whether to continue to organize COPLA at Canalino Elementary School, Mrs. Mora called for a vote from all thirty people present. Everyone raised his or her hand, and I found that everyone's vote was recognized. No distinction was made between members of the COPLA group and the parents who were attending for the first time. By doing this in her role as president, Mrs. Mora defined the importance of all the people's voices, not just COPLA members'. Everyone in the room seemed satisfied with the decisionmaking process. Mrs. Mora entertained comments from non-COPLA members about the need for an organization like COPLA, then one member parent circulated a sign-up sheet and invited parents to participate in the organization. The president's message, as well as that of other COPLA members, encouraged the other parents to learn together and to accept the challenge of this new experience for themselves and for the benefit of their children. Everyone present signed on as a new COPLA member.

The COPLA group continued inviting me to their subsequent weekly meetings to talk to them more about education in Carpinteria. A slightly different group of parents attended each meeting.[8] Twenty-five parents attended the fourth meeting of the district-wide COPLA meeting. The original eleven-member COPLA cohort was present, along with five parents who were present for the first time and nine who had attended the previous meeting. Mrs. Mora opened the meeting and introduced me. She told the gathering that COPLA parents were trying to learn how to better help their children in school by having the parents support each other, which made these meetings very important. All parents present concurred, and talked about the need to spread their message to more Latino parents.

I presented what I perceived to be a distance between the school's academic demands and what the parents provided for their children. The group then discussed the ways in which they had worked with their children. As one parent recounted, "I never know whether helping my son benefits him because there's much I don't know." Another parent recommended having a dialogue with school district administrators about their needs, so that they could agree on the best way to educate Latino children. As in previous meetings, when a vote was taken to decide whether to invite school administrators to subsequent meetings, Mrs. Mora counted everyone's vote. Consistent with COPLA's concept of inclusion, she made no distinction between parents who had attended previous meetings and those who were attending for the first time. They agreed to invite school administrators to the following meeting. I juggled feelings of optimism and apprehension. I was optimistic that the empowerment process was advancing because they had plans to include educators in COPLA. On the other hand, I was apprehensive about the sharing of power between parents and school personnel. My optimism was rooted in my belief that involving school personnel seemed to indicate progress, in that families and educators could begin a dialogue to improve learning conditions for Latino students. My apprehension, however, had to do with my knowledge and experience in communities where schools try to work with families, but often ultimately distort the power relations so that the school dictates the agenda and goals for the group.

---

[8] Essentially, every Latino parent in the Carpinteria community was a COPLA parent by virtue of the name of the organization. There were no formal requirements to become a member. As the Central District leadership committee began to organize satellite COPLA groups in every school, school personnel seemed to identify only those parents in the leadership as COPLA parents, distinguishing them from parents who only attended meetings. However, the COPLA leadership stressed that every Latino parent was part of COPLA and thus needed to become actively involved.

Even though parents had voted to invite an administrator, the strategy for extending the invitation was not addressed, and they did not decide who would contact the administration. Before Mrs. Mora closed the meeting, she invited everyone to return the following week to continue the discussion about the children's education, and encouraged them to bring a neighbor or friend since these topics were important. One COPLA member pointed out that COPLA could not speak on behalf of all Latino families unless they had the whole community's support. As people were leaving, Mrs. Mora asked for a volunteer to accompany her to the district office to speak to the Director of Special Programs. Mrs. Alonso, a member of the original COPLA group, volunteered to go because she knew the Director and she spoke more English than Mrs. Mora. I was impressed with their commitment to negotiate their needs and combine their strengths in order to communicate in a different language and culture.

Interpretation: A Question of Perception, Reflection, and Voice

My relationship with COPLA as a facilitator haunted me. I feared that what I shared with them would inevitably define the direction of their organization, regardless of how neutral I intended to be. I experienced deep concern as I realized that I had abandoned my neutral, non-influential position. In reality, what I had to do was to interpret my actions along with theirs in the change process.

I constantly reminded COPLA of their progress as a group. I consciously made my presentations at their meetings less didactic and more reflective by raising questions to the group. For example, when discussing bilingual programs, I suggested to the members that they think about questions that were important to them. They wanted to know why Spanish-speaking children did not have teachers who spoke in their language, but taught in bilingual programs. They also wanted to know why schools did not send out communications in Spanish to Latino families and why their children learned limited English in bilingual programs. These concerns provided a framework for discussing with them the observational data I had regarding the district's bilingual program. I suggested that they invite the Director of Special Programs to their meeting to deal with the part of the programs I could not address. COPLA members did invite administrators and teachers to talk to them about the District's bilingual program and other curricular matters.

To make sure that the school district was aware of my extended role as a facilitator with COPLA, I informed the administration of my changing status. My emerging role as a facilitator became a test of the community's and the school district's trust in me. The school administration felt that my role as a facilitator with the Latino families could support the District's educational goal of forging closer communication with the Spanish-speaking Latino community. The administration became even more supportive of my role in COPLA when the District Director began attending the meetings and witnessed the power of the organization.

COPLA's continued practice of acknowledging all parents who attended the meetings, without defining or limiting membership, illustrated the organization's egalitarian character and its commitment to involve everyone in the discussion. When the group and I reflected on my observations of their organizational meetings, they clarified to me the importance of the collective voice in their decisionmaking process, as expressed by one parent in this statement: "We cannot be an authoritarian elite group making decisions for others."

This attitude revealed to me a cultural gap between the parents' analysis of the situation and my own. I offered information about the way the dominant school culture might expect this parent organization to operate; that is, that a formal organization meant that the leader of the group had authority over the rest of the group. COPLA in fact had a different dynamic, one rooted in more egalitarian ways of relating to each other.

At an early COPLA meeting held to organize Latino parents at Canalino School, the parents suggested that they should meet with the principal as a group. That way they could support each other, and they would present a strong united force. COPLA parents then strategized their mobilization of the school's Latino community. I felt that their efforts were designed to involve as many parents as possible in their meetings with the school administration, and that their need to involve a large number of parents represented fear about their lack of experience. I later learned that my interpretation was clearly based on my expectation of how an effective organization should operate.

The parents interpreted their behavior during meetings in two significant ways: 1) their interactions at the meetings showed respect for each other's voice and viewpoint while minimizing the authority of the leader, and 2) their collective effort to solicit input from as many families as possible represented a commitment to a democratic voice among Latino parents. Respect and democracy defined their interaction with each other and shaped COPLA.

How was I to reconcile the difference between my insider/outsider interpretation of their mode of relating to one another and their reality? Following several meetings with the parents in which we analyzed their process, I recognized that it was not fear or ignorance of the school system that motivated their mode of organizing. Rather, it was their respect for each other's opinions, insights, and experience that defined their interactions. Even though I had observed the parents empowering themselves through the process of sharing their experience as Spanish-speaking immigrant families in Carpinteria, my outside academic and social perspectives biased my interpretation. These parents' interactions with each other were not as I had initially perceived them; that is, as "ignorant" of the mainstream ways of organizing and communicating with the schools. Rather, the parents joined forces democratically in order to resolve their problems with the school system.

Building on this sense of empowerment, and despite the insider/outsider relationship, both I as the researcher and the parents as the researched moved toward change in Carpinteria. In the dilemma of being a member/non-member of the ethnic group, I recognized that I had to remain conscious of the insiders' perspectives since, even though I belonged to the same ethnic group as the subjects of this study, I could not insure true understanding of the culturally bound practices of the parent group. My lack of understanding was due to both my acculturation into the dominant culture and my academic training.

Once I understood their way of constructing meaning in their organization, I came to understand and respect the particular process and perspective that gave their organization credibility. As an outsider, I had relied on empowerment theories advanced by Freire and the Cornell Empowerment Group to guide my facilitator activities. Those theories dictated that I could not intervene in the participants' change process unsolicited (Delgado-Gaitan & Trueba, 1991). Although my involvement in their meetings unquestionably influenced their orientation and knowledge base about the schools, the COPLA parents themselves defined their organizational goals and their sociopolitical awareness and identity. My interpretation of the empowerment process in COPLA, in which I was a participant and observer, an insider and outsider, underwent its own transformation. The experience strengthened my connection with the families. The insights I gained about the process of empowerment reframed what I initially thought to be merely a set of activities conducted by a group of Latino immigrant families who were ignorant of the dominant institutional culture, to be instead a meaningful construction of literacy that included their ability to read not only written text, but also their world as text (Freire & Macedo, 1987).

SOME FINAL REFLECTIONS ON RESEARCH FOR EMPOWERMENT

The Ethnography of Empowerment framework, supported by critical theory principles, involves methodological strategies that engage the community in the research analysis. The researcher participates concurrently in the transformation of the setting being studied. Conducting the Carpinteria study taught me that a researcher can only be an outsider; however, with insight, the researcher can encourage and foster the relational process between researcher and researched. In the Carpinteria study, the reflective analysis between the parents and the researcher impacted the direction of the study; the researcher provided the community with specific data to develop their organization, while the parents changed the researcher's perception of the meaning of their activities.

The concepts of enduring self and situated self, introduced by Spindler and Spindler (in press), provided me with a psychosocial framework to look at the nature of change experienced by the COPLA parents and myself. The concept of the enduring self permits us to understand the continuity that exists in our lives, and the way in which our beliefs, values, and practices are constructed through our cultural communities. The situated self is a conception of the self that evolves, develops, and transforms, given specific contexts and activities.[9] Our situated self represents the shifting of those values, beliefs, and practices as a result of new knowledge and new contexts. These constructs are interconnected, not dichotomous.

The relational nature of change between myself as the researcher and the researched was characterized by steps that revealed the cultural center of the enduring self of those involved by: 1) transcending fear, 2) liberating our voices through self-acceptance, and 3) transforming the situation through the situated self; that is, the self that shifts from context to context given new knowledge. In the case of the Latino parents who felt fearful and insecure because they did not know how to interact with the schools, I noticed how honest and sincere they were in sharing their feelings and confronting their fears by going beyond

---

[9] The concepts of enduring and situational self seem appropriate in this analysis, because both the Latino parents and I seemed to test our notions of self and perceptions of personhood. For a discussion of these theoretical representations, see Spindler and Spindler, 1990 and in press.

the perceived limitations — in other words, in how they encountered their enduring selves. They confronted their enduring selves through continuity with their social history. The Latino parents realized that they were whole and complete as they shared their life experiences with each other. Thus, they found continuity in the midst of a fractured immigrant experience. As parents discovered their strengths and developed new ones, they became more capable of articulating their situated selves in their new contexts, as evidenced by their formation of COPLA.

In my own case, I believed initially that COPLA parents' collective organizational behavior was based on their ignorance of political organizations. I subsequently revised my interpretation as I understood how they shared power and voice among themselves. Essentially, COPLA parents interacted with one another in ways familiar to them based on mutual respect for each other's opinions and experiences in the traditions of their own culture. I learned how important self-reflection was to COPLA parents through my own introspection about my role in their organization. Simultaneously, my personal need forced me to understand my gestalt while reevaluating my learned methods. I learned that there were no guaranteed outcomes and no failsafe methods to achieve objectives. I then understood what the process of organization meant to COPLA members, which enabled me to interact in their discourse of change. COPLA moved from conceptualizing change as a list of outcomes, to a list of books they could read to their children, to interacting with each other, to learning the process by which to inquire and access information that would lead them to obtain the resources they desired.

The relational nature of the study was evident in practice. For example, when COPLA's first president had to leave the organization, members called me to help them decide how to select another president. I met with them to reflect on why they chose a president for COPLA the first time and they thought about the reasons they needed a president. I asked them what leadership meant to them, and they were able to assess their needs in the new situation and make their own decision accordingly.

The tension between the insider/outsider perceptions raised questions about diversity and the need to understand the phenomenon in its specific context. A key lesson for me was that, as a researcher, the way I perceive the world of education is shaped by the culture in which I mainly participate, and thus is based on European American cultural constructions of self, research, and education. A broader issue that emerges from this tension is what happens when the ethnographer participates in the change influenced by the research?

When the setting is transformed in some way, as occurred in Carpinteria, empowerment is affected in favor of the community if and when the researcher can reconcile the duality between the researched and the researcher. Conceivably, a danger for the underrepresented community would exist if the researcher failed to recognize the needs of a different culture when the cultures and perceptions of the researcher and researched interact. If this is the case, we need to examine just how the value system of the researcher influences the study. Ethnographers have entered communities as participant-observers with seemingly well-grounded theories for conducting research. Knowledge of the people's language and culture may facilitate research; the researcher's own cultural background, however, may conceal biases that shape ethnographic insights about a given community. As Alan Peshkin (1982) reminds us, a close association exists among four aspects of research: the researcher, the actual research, the act of researching, and the results. To counter our own ignorance and biases as researchers, we must integrate into our research rigorous and systematic joint analysis with our participants.

The role of the researcher in relation to the researched is particularly significant when disenfranchised communities are attempting to exercise their own power. Disenfranchised groups in the United States are being rediscovered through ethnographic study, which enhances our understanding of people's real conditions in their respective communities. These groups deserve a voice as the architects of their own changing historical circumstances. Ethnography of Empowerment connects the researcher to the insider's point of view in constructing new paradigms for explicating change in the education of culturally different, underrepresented groups in our post-traditional and postmodern world.

REFERENCES

Ada, A. F. (1988). The Pajaro Valley experience: Working with Spanish-speaking parents to develop children's reading and writing skills in the home through the use of children's literature. In T. Skutnabb-Kangas & J. Cummins (Eds.), *Minority education: From shame to struggle*. Philadelphia: Multilingual Matters.

Allen, J., Barr, D., Cochran, M., Dean, C., & Greene, J. (1989). Empowerment through family support: The empowerment process. *Networking Bulletin, 1*, 2–6.

Apple, M. W. (1993). *Official knowledge: Democratic education in a conservative age*. New York: Routledge.

Barr, D. (1989). *Power and empowerment*. Ithaca, NY: Cornell University, College of Human Ecology.

Barr, D., & Cochran, M. (1991) Preparation for the empowerment process: Identifying competencies and developing skills. *Networking Bulletin, 2*(1), 26.

Chow, R. (1986). Rereading Mandarin ducks and butterflies: A response to the "postmodern condition." *Cultural Critique, 5*, 69–71.

Delgado-Gaitan, C. (1987). Traditions and transitions in the learning process of Mexican American children: An ethnographic view. In G. Spindler & L. Spindler (Eds.), *Interpretive ethnography of education at home and abroad* (pp. 333–362). Hillsdale, NJ: Lawrence Erlbaum.

Delgado-Gaitan, C. (1989). Classroom literacy activity for Spanish-speaking students. *Linguistics in Education, 1*(3), 285–297.

Delgado-Gaitan, C. (1990). *Literacy for empowerment: The role of parents in children's education*. London: Falmer Press.

Delgado-Gaitan, C. (1991). Linkages between home and school: A process of change for involving parents. *American Educational Journal, 100*, 20–46.

Delgado-Gaitan, C., & Trueba, H. (1991). *Crossing cultural borders: Education for immigrant families in America*. London: Falmer Press.

Elliott, J. (1988). Educational research and outsider-insider relations. *International Journal of Qualitative Studies in Education, 1*(2), 155–166.

Freire, P. (1970). *Pedagogy of the oppressed*. New York: Continuum.

Freire, P. (1973). *Education for critical consciousness*. New York: Continuum.

Freire, P. (1985). *The politics of education: Culture, power, and liberation*. South Hadley, MA: Bergin & Garvey.

Freire, P., & Macedo, D. (1987). *Literacy: Reading the word and the world*. New York: Bergin & Garvey.

Geertz, C. (1973). *The interpretation of cultures*. New York: Basic Books.

Goldenberg, C. N. (1987). Low-income Hispanic parents' contributions to their first grade children's word-recognition skills. *Anthropology and Education Quarterly, 18,* 149–179.

Habermas, J. (1974). Introduction. In *Theory and practice.* London: Heineman.

Heath, S. B. (1983). *Ways with words: Language, life and work in communities and classrooms.* New York: Cambridge University Press.

Hirschkind, L. (1991). Redefining the "field" in fieldwork. *Ethnology, 30*(3), 237–250.

Kondo, D. (1990). *Crafting selves: Power, gender, and discourses of identity in a Japanese workplace.* Chicago: University of Chicago Press.

Lavie, S. (1991). *The poetics of military occupation.* Berkeley: University of California Press.

Macias, J. (1987). The hidden curriculum of Papago teachers: American Indian strategies for mitigating cultural discontinuity in early schooling. In G. Spindler (Ed.), *Doing the ethnography of schooling: Educational anthropology in action.* Prospect Heights, IL: Waveland Press.

Marcus, G. E., & Fischer, M. J. (1986). *Anthropology as cultural critique: An experimental moment in the human sciences.* Chicago: University of Chicago Press.

Moll, L., & Díaz, S. (1987). Change as a goal of educational research. *Anthropology and Education Quarterly, 18,* 300–311.

Peshkin, A. (1982). The researcher and subjectivity: Reflections on an ethnography of school and community. In G. Spindler (Ed.), *Doing the ethnography of schooling: Educational anthropology in action* (pp. 48–67). Prospect Heights, IL: Waveland Press.

Podermaker, H. (1967). *Stranger and friend: The way of an anthropologist.* New York: Norton.

Schatzman, L., & Strauss, A. (1973). *Field research strategies for natural sociology.* Englewood Cliffs, NJ: Prentice Hall.

Shor, I., & Freire, P. (1987). *A pedagogy for liberation.* South Hadley, MA: Bergin & Garvey.

Spindler, G. (Ed.). (1970). *Fieldwork in eleven cultures: Being an anthropologist.* New York: Holt, Rinehart & Winston.

Spindler, G. (Ed.). (1974). *Education and cultural process: Toward an anthropology of education.* New York: Holt, Rinehart & Winston.

Spindler, G., & Spindler, L. (1970). *Being an anthropologist: Fieldwork in eleven cultures.* Prospect Heights, IL: Waveland Press.

Spindler, G., & Spindler, L. (Eds.). (1987). *Interpretive ethnography of education at home and abroad* (pp. 363–84). Hillsdale, NJ: Lawrence Erlbaum.

Spindler, G., & Spindler, L. (1990). The self and the instrumental model in the study of culture and change. *Proceedings of 1987 meetings of the Kroeber Anthropological Society* (pp. 97–124). Berkeley, CA: Kroeber Anthropological Society.

Spindler G., & Spindler, L. (in press). The process of culture and person: Multicultural classes and cultural therapy. In P. Phelan & A. Davidson (Eds.), *Cultural diversity and educational policy and change.* New York: Teachers College Press.

Spradley, J. (1979). *Participant observation.* New York: Holt, Rinehart & Winston.

Strauss, A. (1987). *Qualitative analysis for social scientists.* New York: Cambridge University Press.

Suárez-Orozco, M. (1989). *Central American refugees and U.S. high schools: A psychological study of motivation and achievement.* Stanford: Stanford University Press.

Thomas, N. (1991). Against ethnography. *Cultural Anthropology, 6*(3), 306 –319.

Wax, R. (1971). *Doing fieldwork: Warnings and advice* (chap. 1). Chicago: University of Chicago Press.

Wolcott, H. (1981). Teaching fieldwork to educational researchers: A symposium [Special issue]. *Anthropology and Education Quarterly, 14.*

I am indebted to Carpinteria community members who provided insights about the theme and the text of this article. I am also grateful to Marc Blanchard, Nancy Hornberger, Ellen Lubic, and George and Louise Spindler for their critical feedback on earlier versions of this manuscript. Parts of the project and the preparation of this manuscript were also partially supported by grants from the Spencer Foundation and the Johns Hopkins Center for Social Organization of Schools.

On Transformation:
From a Conversation with Mel King

Mel King is an activist, politician, educator, and lifelong resident of the South End in Boston, Massachusetts. His passion is transformation: finding ways to support human development, learning for life, and social change for justice. For thirty years King has been a strong and active force in the development of the Black community in Boston. His role in community education and development is expansive. He has, among many other activities, worked for his community as an elected official; served as a state representative to the Massachusetts legislature for twelve years; and run as a candidate for mayor of Boston. King has always worked with young people in and out of schools, on the streets and in community centers; he was active in organizing youths and parents to desegregate Boston's public schools. King is a member of the Rainbow Coalition, a progressive organization that is politically active at the local and national levels and has, with the presidential candidacy of Jesse Jackson, become a strong voice with the Democratic Party. His books, A Chain of Change and Liberating Theory (written with Albert, Cagan Chomsky, Hahnel, Sargent, and Sklar), document his thinking and practice on community development, education, and social change. Mel King is currently Adjunct Professor and Director of the Community Fellows Program in the Department of Urban Studies and Planning at the Massachusetts Institute of Technology.

The 1989 Editorial Board of the Review thought it would be exciting and informative to talk with Mel King about his rich experience and work in community-based education. Over the span of several months three members of the Review — Alexander Goniprow, Victoria Borden Muñoz, and Jacquelyn Ramos — interviewed Mel King at his MIT office. The interviews were audiotaped and transcribed, providing over one-hundred pages of text from about five hours of conversation. What follows is an edited version of that narrative. The richness of King's experiences as an activist, politician, and educator makes this coversation a powerful document that ivites reflection and calls to action, to transformation.

The conversation begins with the editors' questions and Mel King's responses. At the end of their first meeting, where King discussed his views on transformation, education, and community development, he also asked the editors what they thought their role was in community-based education and in transformation. They agreed that each of them would think this over and return to the next meeting with a "moment of transformation" story; that is, a time when they were transformed by something they learned, when they learned something new about themselves, their community, their work. These stories compose the last part of the conversation; they represent the valuing of everyone as equals, and the personal and political importance of change.

Harvard Educational Review Vol. 59 No. 4 November 1989, 504–519

We thought a good place to start would be by talking about some of the principles of community-based education and what these are for you.

MK: For me it starts with an understanding that the fundamental reason for community education is to facilitate the building of community. I believe that building community ought to be the rationale for all schooling. Community education has as its ultimate goal the transformation of our society. Said another way, community education is that process that leads to *peace:* of mind, between groups, between nations, and harmony with the universe. Its guiding force is human love and it is energized by the infinite possibilities that come from bringing out the collective and individual genius in all of us. Community education requires the developing of skills, awareness, techniques, analysis, and knowledge that enables a person and community to understand and change those forms, forces, systems, individuals, and institutions that prevent and deny the opportunity and resources to develop as free, healthy, productive, creative persons and communities.

So community education begins with a vision. And at this point there are four terms that I would like to offer with new definitions that ought to be the framework for thinking about community education.

The first is "democracy," which means that we value all people and all people are valued. The second is "power," and here it would mean the willingness to help others to get where you are and beyond. The third is "development," which should be seen in human terms, recognizing that the buildings, schools, roads, as Nyerere would say, are only the tools to facilitate access for expression of creativity. And the fourth term is "technology," meaning that which builds positive human relationships and enhances life — both human and environmental.

Having stated the above, my question back would be, which community are you talking about? The community of the "preferred," given our current reality, or the communities of the oppressed?

Could you say more about "the community of the preferred" and "the communities of the oppressed?" How do these two different communities intersect and where do they diverge?

MK: The reason for talking about the two groups is to help us understand that, given our vision, community education is applicable to both. The "preferred," a concept put forward by the Puerto Rican educator Antonia Pantoja, have status and power and are generally White and male and Protestant. Most of the institutions have been geared or focused to lift them up and to support their interests; in this country, the major support being the Constitution of the United States. The Constitution has served as the structure that has maintained their political, social, and economic power over people of color, women, and those who did not own the land. In addition to the Constitution, media, churches, unions, and the military have been vehicles that reinforced the relationships that exist between the two communities. The major place where they intersect is in the marketplace. And where the oppressed are exploited for the economic well-being of the preferred, whether attending to their needs at home, in business, or on the land.

Where do you begin the process of community education?

MK: I would begin by looking at who is in front of me and getting to know how they understand what is in their interest and how they see their needs getting met. And here is where I would contrast the role of formal schooling with what I would call informal schooling. It depends on whether we're looking at skills that allow one to survive and grow, or whether we're thinking about kinds of knowledge and understanding of what makes a system go and who we interface. Partly it's a skill and partly it's dealing with something inside of us.

There's something that makes me like the sunset and the sunrise and want to figure out how the trees became, how I became. There's something in me that wants to figure out why I feel the way I do about each of you and myself. I think about community-based education, and I think about my life experiences. The community around which my education was based was external (school) and was geared to make me feel that I was less valuable than the members from "other" communities. That was the formal education in school. The informal, familiar community saw the school community as both hostile and useful. Hostile, because it was a group that devalued my community. Useful, because there were some practical skills, such as learning to read, that opened us up to ideas and concepts like the right of revolution. Informal education politicized us so that we could handle the hostile and oppressive attitudes that came from formal education.

This devaluing was based on race, ethnicity, and class. I can remember very, very vividly, a seventh-grade teacher calling us "guttersnakes." She was talking about those of us who came from this particular community, and we represented thirty-three different racial, ethnic, and cultural groups. It was a very classist and racist analysis or assessment.

What we have to do is try to put ourselves in the shoes of people we are working with. This means we have to listen to them, and, as Father John Harmon said in *Cycle of Silence*, "To really listen means a willingness to change." We listen, I mean we hear words, but that's it. We need a process of openness with a belief that others can say something that is as important as the experiences that we have, no matter who they are. Some of us find it difficult to believe that others have experience beyond what we know, even about their own children.

For example, when a child goes to school for the first time. There's a woman who has birthed her child, knows when the sun shines over that her child responds this way or that way, knows they don't like oat bran, or whatever. She knows. Then somebody puts them in a classroom and says to her, "I know more about your child than you do." Teachers may know some of the technical steps for learning how to read. It doesn't mean they know more about how to get the child to learn — this mother has spent a lot of time getting her child to learn some fundamentals. Phenomenal teaching and learning were going on during those early years, and parents who come into the classroom don't want to face the teacher and hear the teacher say something negative about their child. Parents can't come in because they've been conditioned to believe that they're the problem. Teachers say, "It's in the family, it's in the home. They don't teach them how to read. They don't read with them." There was nothing in the teacher contract that said there is an agreement that people have to do these things before the children come into the classroom. There's nothing written like that. There's nothing written about education. All it says is that they have to be there from age six to age sixteen and that they have to take certain physical tests — like inoculations — in order to be able to be in this classroom. We tell them, "You must go to school." There's nothing there that says that you have middle-class attitudes, that you read to your children, that you give them the basic seven food groups for proper nutrition.

It seems to me that there has to be a vision in which you see the *genius* in *all* the people that you're working with. I'm not just talking about students, because for me education happens anytime we work with people to bring out the best in us and the best in them, believing that it exists. It requires a constant analysis of those things that help and those things that hinder. Because it is important for us to build collectively toward acquiring the techniques and skills to overcome those things that hinder and to improve upon the things that help.

How does community organizing work?

MK: What we have built in over time are reinforcing ways to devalue those folks that do not fit into the community of the "preferred." This means that the kind of education needed becomes highly political, based on overcoming things that affect how one sees oneself psychologically, and how one knows what to do, politically, in order to get access. It's not just about access, it's about transformation. If you're talking about an education, you want to have some sense of what happens with some folks. What skills do you need, economically and politically, in order to change relationships? It's all about changing relationships. We talk about skills that allow one access to the economy — to getting an income for meeting physical and psychological needs.

For instance, I did this thing at the junior high school — I do it in a lot of schools — but the most dramatic things took place at a junior high school, not too far from here. I set the stage by telling them we were going to make a book of the lives of all of us, asking them what was important to them and their families, all the things they liked and did in their life, and we were going to get photos in there and put it in a bound book in gold writing with red on the outside. Then I said, "How would you feel if you opened that book up, and you went through it, and everybody's story was in there but yours?" One young man almost jumped off the bleachers and said, "I'd be mad!" I said, "How would you feel if you were in there?" "Important!" "What about the people who aren't in there?" "They don't count?" You tell that story to any group of children and you will get pretty much the same reaction. That's why we think that it is important to have Black stories. Does that mean I didn't learn to read and write and compute because I didn't see those? No. It did mean, however, that I kind of grew up with the belief that people who were White could do more things better than people who, like me, were African American, although actually I could do things better than many of the White folks that I grew up with.

What I think one has to do is have a good analysis of what time it is, of what's going on around us, and where we are in it. This is when education becomes a highly political way of dealing with a hostile environment, and a way to overcome the effects of such an environment, and the effects of being devalued. As Vincent Harding says, "We must go beyond equal opportunity in a dehumanized society." We must be about transformation. We're talking seriously about community education that should be for everyone, both the communities of the preferred and of the oppressed. And I don't think there's any real peace of mind for White males who are so-called beneficiaries of the system. But setting that aside for the moment, who we're talking principally about here are those young people who are in situations where, unless something different happens, they continue to be devalued and to devalue themselves.

This is a very, very dehumanizing culture that we live in. There's so much pain and suffering. I don't mean there aren't any good things, but think about the pain, and suffering, the alcohol consumption, the other drug consumption, and how people feel about themselves. I'm just saying to you that if you ask me how to dialogue about community-based education, it must include trying to get you to talk about yourselves — your education, your life, your work, your analysis of what's going on.

Could you talk more specifically about what your own informal and formal education was like? \

MK: My father was part of a labor union, and was working on organizing the folks that were on the sugar boats with him, and he was the secretary in the union. My father held meetings at the house and I would look at his records of the meetings, hear the discussions about workers and management where they would talk about whether there would be a strike call for more wages and the importance of getting people to stick together. The fact that people came to meet with him made me think that what he was about was very important. In addition, he would discuss and talk about the changes. I remember when the CIO [Congress of Industrial Organizations] was formed and how his group was to become a member. He also talked about how unemployment compensation and social security programs were the result of people getting organized and going to Washington, DC. He also used to make trusses and other belts to deal with the strains and problems resulting from lifting heavy bags.

I went to a camp where I was the only Black person in the camp, maybe there was one other, and this was my first experience in that situation. My father told me about being the only Black person in a work situation, and how it was important that you don't let anybody misuse you and that you don't misuse anybody. He said that if you exist on that basis then you can go there and have a good time. He was very emphatic about not letting anybody misuse me or call me names. He was not talking nonviolence but he also was clear that we would not do anything to anybody that was not nice or fair. He talked about what it meant to work in that kind of situation. He talked about what kind of responsibilities each of us had, to get skills and to overcome. That's a heavy trip that every boy, at least that I grew up with, had to deal with, and it *is* a heavy trip.

The Afro-American newspaper, *The Pittsburgh Courier,* and other Black newspapers were in the house and we read them. I knew about Shaw and Howard and those schools when I was eight and nine years of age because I saw the photos of their athletes, and I read about the "Negro National Leagues" and the American League. Through these newspapers I learned about the Homestead Grays and Satchel Paige, a great baseball player. It wasn't just that there was material to read, but that there was material that was relevant. This helped to raise my consciousness, my awareness. The institutions that I attended were re-inforcing institutions. At the Church of All Nations we had universal services, and at the same time, a specific service for Black People. There was one for Italians, there was one for Greeks, there was one for Chinese. At the eleven o'clock service everybody came together.

A lot of other ethnic groups had reinforcing institutions. After school, the Jewish youngsters went to Hebrew School, Albanian youngsters went to Albanian School, Greek youngsters went to Greek School. But Black young people went to the settlement houses and the churches to become Americanized. We didn't have another language or another set of customs and cultures to go learn, at least in this neighborhood. But that's how the other young people got it — the perpetuation of their cultural and ethnic background to overcome the devastating piece that was in the schools. A lot of Catholic youngsters had catechism classes they attended. Some who were Italian did both. There were Black young people who went to Black churches so they had a kind of movement, but it wasn't in the main a reinforcement of some Black ideology.

On the other hand my formal education was very different. In the first month of school they passed around this little card and on it they asked you what your ethnicity was, what your national origin was, they don't do that now. I used to put down West-Indian because my father was from Barbados and my mother was from Guyana. Everybody else was from Spain, Albania, Lithuania, Greece, Italy, and so on. Since I knew how they treated people who were slaves here, I definitely didn't want to say I was from the United States because that just wasn't cool. That's an example of how the system perpetuated this value in us and devalued people. I didn't figure out until later that Barbados was the first place the boat stopped on the way from Africa, so we're all slaves anyhow. That speaks to the inappropriate education that we had just in terms of factual knowledge.

At ten and eleven, I got a little more insight from my folks, so that was cool. Just in those early formative years, even though I thought my folks and my older brother were the greatest, I had been exposed to a whole dynamic in terms of who was important — things like the father of the country was George Washington and Abraham Lincoln freed the slaves. Nobody talked about the politics of it. I stopped going to movies because I got tired of watching Tarzan outwit hundreds of African natives like they were second-graders or didn't have any intelligence at all, but that's what we were growing up with so that's what was perpetuated. It's important that we talk about that side of education; it was a very purposeful, calculated approach to perpetuating White superiority. That's what it was about — perpetuating White superiority. And here again, unless we have both communities, the preferred and the oppressed, dealing with issues of oppression and devaluation, then we will perpetuate the painful and destructive environment that is eroding our country and the world.

In your mayoral campaign you said many times, in print and through other media, that "You only win the struggle for the land when you win the struggle for the mind." How is this connected with community-based education?

MK: I'm a firm believer that you have to raise consciousness. Once you've raised consciousness, the rest may not be easy, but I can tell you that if you don't raise consciousness, then you're never, ever going to get the rest.

It seems to me that the fundamental issue is, do the young people know why they're going to school? What is it that they're told? What's the purpose of this experience? What are the politics around it? I don't know if they're told anything except, "You need to learn how to read and write so you can get a job." You tell young people that, yet they know people who can read and write and still can't get a job. You have to tell them another kind of story. I think that the politics and the social psychological dynamics of this are not dealt with sufficiently.

The system can't run faster than our minds. You can raise consciousness faster than the system. It's faster than a speeding bullet, if you would. There's nothing faster. I really believe that this consciousness-raising is where it is and that no matter what's going on out there today, that we can be aware of and process some things that we need to be about. If we are not conscious about the dynamics of the relationships that exist, then we won't even know what's happening with other institutions or the community that's off and running.

Here is where the consciousness-raising has to involve youth directly in the analysis of those issues they are facing daily, issues such as, Why are people unemployed? Why has the school budget been cut? Who makes those decisions? Why are people like them more employed or unemployed than other people? What is the impact of drugs and crime on them and their communities? Who benefits and who loses? What are responsible ways of dealing with their sexuality? What leads children to have children? What are the routes that they can travel to be all they can be? What are the opportunities? What are the deterrents? What are the strategies that must be developed and worked on? Do they have a vision of what would make themselves, their communities, and the world work?

We have to ask ourselves a lot of questions about who teaches children. Is the teacher a political person? Does that teacher like him or herself? Is that teacher someone who has dealt with the race and class issues he or she brings to that situation? I heard some people recently who spent all their time talking about these young people who come to the school, who say, "go fuck yourself" and all that kind of stuff, and I said, "All the youngsters make those comments?" There was a moment of silence. You have to say, "Are we hiring the right people to teach?" Because one thing we notice, there are people out there who relate to those youngsters and get them to do things in a very positive way. We know that. If there are teachers who are not getting students to move, then it says that we're paying the wrong people. We've got to use the political consciousness-raising approach. We have to ask ourselves, "What's *our* level of consciousness?" That begins to cut across what I think is the junk that people get into.

We need to do a lot of work and much thinking about the kinds of institutional support. If churches are an institutional support and most people aren't going to church, then large numbers of people are cut off from something that could help them. What other institutions? We don't have settlement houses that do the kind of work that we used to do, so that kind of institutional support is not there. There's a lot that's missing. If racism is a problem, and I hear a lot of young people talk about racism in the classroom, we need to ask, "Who's fighting for them?" We had a situation where there was a meeting in the community and a woman came specifically to rail out against an act of racism at her daughter's school. One teacher called her daughter a racist name, the teacher was White, and a Black male assistant principal stood by and said nothing. This Black administrator, by coincidence, was at the meeting too. The mother said, "I'm sitting here. You can't talk about bringing us together unless you're going to do something about people like him who sat by and listened to somebody call my daughter a racist name and said nothing. My daughter is devastated. She doesn't know who and where she's going to get support from." It's not just the fact that a person who is White made a statement, it's the fact that as far as she was concerned, fighting for Affirmative Action to get Black people in those positions in the school didn't mean a thing.

These things are going on, and there are all the statistics about the level of suspensions and problems that happen in the school, and we act as if these are problems just with those youngsters who are suspended. There are lots of stories about this youngster or this teacher saying "f — you." Maybe that anger didn't come out of the school experience, but there are lots of stories of anger that come directly out of the school experience, and there's little challenging of how teachers are incompetent with these kinds of problems. Hopefully, the question is "What is that community's (the professional community's) basis for their education, philosophy, program, and so on?" You've got a general body politic and the concept of the preferred. You've got that layer of administration, then the professionals in the school, and then we've got the people.

There are people who the community could hire, who are in synch with them, and who can put together a political curriculum where they help these youngsters to fight racist practices, and get the technical skills. People who would have both the youngsters and their parents fighting for access to jobs; or challenging the governor or the legislators, or recreation or housing, or whatever the programs are, because that's an important part of community-based education. It's highly political. It would make sure that those things which are impediments to students feeling good about themselves would be dealt with — whether it was inside or outside the school. They would provide some leadership. They would use those experiences as part of their lesson plans, get young people to learn how to read and write and solve problems by saying, "Here is the problem. We have a situation where there are guns in this community. Why is that? What is the story? What kind of research are we doing?"

How do you go about working with young people who want to get involved? How do you help them become prepared to determine their own destinies, to speak for themselves?

MK: There are hundreds of examples and I think it comes right back to consciousness-raising. You have to be willing to talk with them. You have to be willing to take time with them. You have to be willing to express what you mean when you say you love them and value them. It's not easy but it means putting in time and going out of your way, being where they are. "Okay, let's go see this situation. Is there some movie?" It's going to where they are, asking them questions. It's following-up on every question. It's asking them questions, getting them to be the models, and getting them in situations where they can get a pay-off for what they know. It's fundamentally valuing them as powerful and political, and as geniuses, and allowing it to be expressed.

We were very, very interested when we went to the Dorchester Youth Collaborative about a way the youths have to help raise consciousness for themselves and their peers. If somebody comes in and thinks they're going to run the place or wants to push this or that or do drugs or something and that person comes in the room, the other youths will get up and leave. A person comes to the next room, they get up and leave. Pretty soon the person gets the message.Or a person comes in and they start mouthing or doing something; "No," they say, "in here, there's a standard of behavior." They have that.

The young people said two things: "We want adults to talk to us who have been through what we've been through so that we know that we're talking to people who understand and not just going from some theory." The second thing they said was, "We want adults who are, in fact, giving us direction." They want direction.

At English High School the other morning, after I spoke, a young man said, "I want to know where the Black leaders are who are standing up for us." They want direction, they want leadership, and they also want people who can talk to them from experience. You asked about consciousness-raising. It's a dialogue, it's listening, it's putting out stuff and letting them hear what it is.

At a discussion with some of the young people at Mission High we were talking about drugs. There's a big notion about the sanction of drugs by the government. We had his discussion and they said it's bad that the government is in this role. Then they talked about somebody making money dealing drugs because they wanted to get this, that, and the other. I said, "Well, I don't understand it. Here you are saying it's bad for the government to be doing this and that there's a lot of pain that's involved. Now you're saying, it's okay for somebody to make money off that misery and that pain." I said, "That's immoral." There was silence. Then I said, "It's interesting. You blame the government, but I have never seen that stuff jump from the table into somebody's nose or mouth or arm." We have to be about community development and not community destruction.

I used to work with the youngsters on the streets doing simple things. For example, we used to go bowling and everybody had to keep score. Sometimes I knew the answers for those who were having trouble with their arithmetic and couldn't keep their score. Sometimes I made a mistake. It's something when one of your peers says, "Hey, that's 86. You put down 84." All of a sudden, they don't make that kind of mistake. We used to do that. Why bowling? I took them bowling for two reasons. One, because of the arithmetic; second, because there's always somebody who is not as good playing basketball, is a little better bowling, and so, what the person doesn't get by way of pay-off with the basketball, they get bowling. I found out that one of the kids could swim and he wasn't doing well with the football team, so I took him up to a swimming pool and we all jumped in and this dude took off and everybody said "Wow!" Not only did his standing in the group improve, but his football improved. His whole outlook improved. You do that because these things support both physiological and psychological development.

In basketball I'd get them lined up and I'd put them at half-court and say, "What's this?" They'd say, "A circle." We'd get to the free-throw line and I'd say, "What's this?" They'd say, "Looks like a half circle." "What's another name for it?" "A semi-circle." I'd throw the ball and say, "What's this?" They'd say, "A ball." "What's another name for it?" and somebody says, "A sphere." Before you know it we've done a lot of geometric figures and relationships. I said, "If you can't get it through them, you go around them. If you want to move it quickly, like a triangle, what's the quickest way?" "The straight line." "Right. Where have you seen this before?" "I think the teacher mentioned something like that in school." We get up to the board and I said, "Draw these things," and you get them to do it. I'd give lots of these little rule books and they'd have to learn the rules. What they didn't learn from reading they'd have to learn from asking. All that was real. It wasn't like somebody saying, "I don't want to read this because it's not relevant to anything." "If you don't know these rules then you don't play on my team because I want people who know what's going on on the court." There are all these ways in which you can bring the life of the community into the school, into their education, into their skill development, and into their awareness.

I think that good educators — community educators — are organizers, and they know how to use the media. They know how to point out the people at all levels who have to deal with issues in their community. *Stand and Deliver,* the movie on Escalante, a Bolivian-American math teacher who taught his students calculus, was a phenomenal piece. I think that they should show that in every school in the country the first day. If the schools don't work, you have to work the schools. You have to organize and make them deliver because you believe you're deserving of the best and if you don't, all you're saying is that you don't think you're somebody who deserves it. If you do, ask why you're only getting five pages of homework, instead of ten. If Bruce Springsteen and some of the musicians and artists are on time politically then you have to expose youngsters to them.

This is to you. You're talking about how you want to get an Ed.D. so you can do more, more what? We're talking about political organizing. If you want to learn how to do more political organizing and more empowerment and learn how to value what the people know, and move with that so that they can exercise some political control and power and get the system to respond, and be in charge of those resources and develop new methods for evaluation of them, that's fine. Those young people are still in those classrooms and when you have your Ed.D., that's not going to change. If you want to go back to teaching, you don't need an Ed.D. to do that. If you think an Ed.D. gets you to be in charge of some school so that you can organize it like East Tech, that's a different story. If you say "Yeah, I want to get that so I can be that school administrator and I want to work with teachers to get them to feel good about themselves so that they can do that kind of political organizing in community education and build those connections," then fine. Absolutely fine.

It seems to me that you want to know where the ten schools in the country are where they have young people like those you want to work with, that have programs that work, and go study them. Call them and ask them, "What do you do?" Go and study them and then be able to lay that out as what should happen, and go around and talk to the parents about that. Say, "These are the approaches, these are the examples of quality experiences." That's very important. We're able to get people working on housing just by exposing them to people like themselves who have been able to organize and develop housing. In this same way you can get people to make their schools work by getting those kinds of examples. Get the resources to put those parents on a bus so they can see how these quality experiences work. Go in, sit down, talk, meet other parents. "What did you do? How did you do it?" Join them in stopping traffic in the middle of the street every day until somebody figures out with them how to make their schools reflect their needs, hopes, and aspirations. Then we'll be on our way to real community-based education.

The following comprises the section on "moments of transformation." Each of the three HER members briefly presents a time in our lives when our thinking changed radically; when our consciousness was raised; when we came to see ourselves and the environment around us in very different terms. This section is important because it illustrates how even though we each tell a different kind of story, we each have intimately experienced transformative times. Within each different story is a common thread: the human capacity and desire for learning, community, and change.

V: My story is going to go back to when I was nineteen or so. I want to take it back to when I was a teenager. This story has a lot to do with my identity and how I thought about myself. I think that getting my consciousness raised at this particular moment in my life was critical to a lot that has happened since then. I have to talk about my mother. I went to dinner at her home. She used to live in an apartment on Dartmouth Street in the South End. I went to dinner at her home and she was involved in a court battle with her landlord because he was evicting her and my sisters and brother for condominium conversion. She was really upset and I wasn't really getting it. I was into other stuff. She was pulling her hair out and I was into other stuff. Now I think about how sometimes I pull my hair out and kids are like, "What are you worried about?" Anyway, she started kind of sharking around the dinner table — walking around like this in a circle. Have you seen my mother shark, Mel? She said to me, "Who are you then, that you don't get this? That you don't feel like you're losing a home? Who are you then, that you think you can just go on in life as if nothing is happening? Who do you belong to? What community do you belong to? What do you feel a part of? Do you think you're White?" I said, "Yeah, I think I'm White. My skin's light. I'm White." Then she sharked some more around the table. She said, "You're not. You're not White. You're Puerto Rican and you're a person of color and that means certain things. It means this is your struggle and this is your fight." At that time, it was really important for me to really understand what she was saying, to really feel it, because of course she was my mother and I knew this emotionally and intellectually. But to really feel and to take on the identity that she was presenting as my own, after years of trying to, in a way, pass, changed my world around. There are lots of different ways to pass, too, and I have other examples of that. In this one, of trying to make believe I wasn't Puerto Rican as a teenager in Boston, so that people would think sometimes I was French or Italian or Canadian, and I wouldn't say anything. I would just say to myself, "Okay, that's fine with me."

When I think of a moment of transformation I think of her saying, "You're a person of color. You're Puerto Rican and that means certain things. That means you have a responsibility, not just to your family, but to the community your family lives in and to other people that are like you." It never, ever had occurred to me before in my entire life that I would be a person of color. It just had not ever occurred to me before in my entire life that I would be a person of color. It just had not ever occurred to me, not that way. Not in that political way. I knew I was Puerto Rican. It was something else. It really transformed my relationships, it seemed to me like an overnight thing, with everybody that I knew at that time. Things became more complicated. That's when I was around nineteen. What was involved in that whole process I think is real important.

I had moved to Boston from Puerto Rico. In Puerto Rico I never thought of myself as a person of color. In Puerto Rican society, I'm light-skinned. There are privileges that light-skinned people get — more like if you're from Spanish heritage than if you're from African heritage. In my family there was a mixture. The light-skinned Spanish heritage people have the most influence in Puerto Rico. Coming from that context when I got here, it seemed that if I was ahead of the game in Puerto Rico, why am I so behind the game here? I thought of myself, and I still do, as privileged in Puerto Rico. Coming here I saw that it doesn't matter, your country of origin, or the life you had or how you were or how you felt. When you come here, you're just at the bottom in many ways.

A: A significant transformation in my life dealt with the process of deciding what type of work I would be happy doing. As a college student, I was an art major. I had enough natural talent to succeed as a student and to seriously consider art as a career. Unfortunately, at the end of my four years of study I realized that talent alone wasn't enough to make art my life's work. For whatever reason, I just didn't have the burning desire to create every day — to get up each and every morning and paint or draw. I had the talent and the skill, but the desire wasn't there. And, you have to be driven to have any hope of really succeeding as an artist.

After graduating from college, I looked for work in Boston and the surrounding areas. My bachelor's degree in art wasn't much help except for the fact that I was supposedly educated. Eventually, just to begin making some money, I took a job with an employment agency that placed accountants and auditors.

You had to do two things in the job. First, you had to try to convince companies to list their job openings with the agency. Listing a job meant that the company had agreed to pay a fee if they hired one of our referrals. The employment agency made all its money from the collection of these fees. The other part of the job consisted of interviewing people who were interested in finding work or changing jobs. The employment agency would attract people who were looking for work by placing a somewhat aggrandized job ad in the newspaper.

The agency then used an interview process to not only identify candidates for listed jobs but also to find new job openings. Everyone who came in for an interview was required to tell us where they had previously interviewed or were still being considered for a job. During my training for this job, it became very clear that filling job openings — not helping people — was the goal of this agency. Which, I guess, is OK, up to a point.

One incident in particular made a striking impression on me and my feelings for this job. Several months after I had first started working, I interviewed a gentleman who, at about fifty years old, was at an age where finding a new job becomes very difficult. He was sweating and nervous and looking for help. As usual, I began the interview to evaluate how strong a candidate he was for any of our current job listings. He had an average work background, and at his age, he wouldn't be easy to place. Consciously, I moved on to the other part of the interview where I was looking to help myself and the employment agency by finding out new leads for job openings. Like most people he was hesitant to tell me of the places where he felt he still stood some chance of getting work. I pushed and finally he gave me the names of the companies that, based on his information, we then knew were actively trying to hire someone.

He did have good reason not to trust us. In the context of making money for the agency, he wasn't of much value except for the information he reluctantly gave. And, it was the employment agency's standard practice to use this information about job openings to obtain a job listing and to send other more qualified applicants for interviews. In this way, we bettered our chances for making some money.

Although it had been building up for several weeks, I began looking for another job after that interview and left two weeks later. I just couldn't take the way we devalued people and didn't really care. It was an unhealthy work environment. The pressure to close a job listing and receive the fee ruled everything. The job really even changed my personality. It made me very unhappy and I wasn't a pleasant person to be around.

I was lucky in my change of jobs. Happenstance put me in contact with a person who administered an education program for migrant children. He hired me on a two-week trial basis and I have been there ever since, fourteen years now. Education, first as a teacher and now as an administrator, allowed me to bring both creativity and desire to my work. The artist in me truly enjoys the process and challenge of program planning and design. Because I like it, I also want to do it well.

Unfortunately, like an artist, I also tend to need to control the materials that I'm working with. This fact makes it difficult for me to work in groups. I have a hard time figuring out how to make this program-planning process work; where I get as much self-satisfaction out of the fact we've designed a good program, one that isn't done by just my own vision, but one that we've been able to work out as a group. The other part of this problem is, how often do I stop to check the assumptions of what I am working on? I do it rarely. And, because I have grown up more in the program than outside the program, there is an inherent danger of always operating on assumptions that are going to defeat my very purpose. I may not look at the problem clearly.

I don't know where to go with this now. Our conversation is making much more sense as I think about our discussion, of valuing people, of checking assumptions. Mel has spoken about the need for ongoing analysis and trying to understand. It makes sense. Sitting and listening and hearing perspectives that you don't often listen to or understand, and then be willing to change, is important.

MK: Father John Harmon says that to really listen is to be willing to change. I say that over and over again. I remember the first time I read it. I said, "Oh!" and I had all these visions flashing through me. I didn't want to change. I talked about change, and I realized what it meant just to sit back and listen. This morning I had a meeting with Angela Page at Page Academy. We were talking about how you could get more people to come. I was saying, "You have to go out and network and do more and go to schools." She said, "I need somebody to drive me because this little baby. . . ." I said, "Just call a cab company." Anyhow, a friend of mine, Ray, walks in the door and he drives a cab. I introduced them. He tells her how to go about doing it and who to call. In the interim I had said, "She works in day care." After he left she said, "We don't care for the day, we care for child. We're in child care!" It's hearing that, understanding and not being hung up with it. It's great. It's just listening. It's not just her saying that I didn't use the appropriate word, it was the impact with which she conveyed what it meant to be about child care, in the way that she said it. I realized that I had been acculturated.

In the same way, it's impossible to grow up in this culture, given the structure and what we've come from, and be White and not racist, and not feel that you are better than people of color. Am I saying every single person? No. The idea isn't to be hung up about the acculturation but to understand how devaluing happens and to figure out how to behave in a way that does not allow our negative learning to impact on decisions and how other people are treated. It's also impossible for a male in this society to grow up and not be sexist. It doesn't mean that you run for cover but it means that you are aware of the fact that you have been impacted and acculturated by this and in knowing that, you have to listen to what is being said by people who are being affected by what's been an actual, systemic problem in people's lives. I think it's important that we get that out in this kind of dialogue, and then for people to be able to move on from looking at how we behave until these are no longer issues institutionalized in our culture and in our lives. There is so much debate and defensiveness about being racist or sexist, that I think sometimes we get into discussions about guilt, which I don't believe solve anything.

For me, the rest comes because then you will maybe listen to everybody. I say "maybe" because you will still come to the situation with whatever baggage you carry, but knowing that you have the baggage. I think if we own our baggage then we know what we need to shed. In shedding it, we're more apt to change our behavior.

J: You three told some powerful stories. I've been thinking about it for the last couple of weeks — what would I talk about with you? What would I choose to share? I think, like Victoria, I want to locate myself in time, back to when I was a teenager, and the things that were going on for me.

I grew up, in what I considered then, and still consider, a culturally enriched community. By that, I mean in the neighborhood where I lived, there were all kinds of people. As a child, I never knew it meant anything to be different because that's all I knew. I saw a little bit of everybody, so, so what? It took growing up into my teenage years to recognize that being of one color or another did make a difference that was acted on in schools and other institutions.

My family comes from the Cape Verde Islands. One of the things I remember is that many people in our community located the Cape Verde Islands, because it was a colony of Portugal, somewhere south of Portugal — it is actually about three hundred miles from West Africa. Thinking about it in my adulthood has had an incredible impact on me. It was important in the smaller part of our community that we were clear that we were "colored." We weren't Black. There was a real difference. Among Black communities in that time, "colored" was probably the most prevalent word but nonetheless, for us it was different because we have another language. It also meant to be better than . . . I was clear, I think we all were, that we weren't White but we weren't Black either. Everybody seemed the same to me until I left home to go to college, and that was around the time of the Black power movement. I would have to say that for me, that movement had a tremendous impact. It was hard for me to say that I wasn't Black, everything around me, all the lives and experiences, really confused me.

I attended the University of Massachusetts at Amherst. While there I met and became a student of Dr. Johnetta B. Cole, a leading African American anthropologist, now president of Spelman College in Atlanta. Her background was in West Africa. She began to make West Africa and the whole continent come alive for me. I began to understand that we are very clearly an African people and that is something to be proud of. I looked and I reached back into the history and I began to talk to my grandparents, my grandfathers in particular. They told me wonderful stories about Black men of the sea. There's a book out now about that. The more I asked, the more I saw what was there to be proud of; things I did not learn in school. I didn't get any of that in school. It took me all the way through secondary school before I had access to images and role models outside of my family that were like me, that were positive, and gave me a great source of strength and pride.

I thought as we left here after our first meeting that my story about being a student was a little different from the ones we talked about because I was a so-called "good" student. I was the one who was put in all the special programs and given extra opportunities. It was always *just me*! I thought that was the way it was supposed to be. I didn't know anything else. For example, I remember when I was eight years old, I was put in a class to learn French. Now you tell me what this little Cape Verdean child from a low-income background was going to do with French at eight years old! As it turned out I loved languages, so a little later in school I began to study German as well. I went to my counselors and I told them I wanted to take Portuguese. They said, "You can't take Portuguese. That's a dead language. Students in the College Prep course cannot take Portuguese." I said "What? But Portuguese is a part of the language my family speaks at home. You say it's dead. We speak Crioulo — a mixture of West African languages and Portuguese." Talk about silencing people! All through public school, everything that I can remember, spoke to not acknowledging a cultural heritage that was mine, which I knew and I cherished.

As I said before, it was not until I went to college that I began to develop a strong sense of cultural identity. I would say, "I know my roots." I would talk about that until they were sick of me! "Do you know where your people come from? I know where mine come from." I worked day and night, tracing back and understanding, learning about how African countries combined and worked together to create a new nation. I was active as a college student in support of the independence struggle in the Cape Verde Islands. That was something new and different, and many people couldn't understand it even in my own community. If I had to point to a moment or a piece of time in my life that transformed me forever, I would have to say it was that time of coming into my own, in terms of understanding who I was, where I fit, what my place was, being proud of that, and wanting to talk about it and help other people find their way because of the liberating feeling I experienced.

MK: Could you three put your stories in? Just let them go as you stated them. The model that we're using is the one of valuing what we each bring, and that's what has to be the model in the schools — of valuing what each of the students and parents bring to the situation and lifting them up, telling their story, and sharing these stories. The same awareness that we get and an appreciation in each classroom, with each group, no matter what the age is, of those students.

In summary, the conversation with Mel King and the transforming experiences reported by members of the Editorial Board demonstrate the ultimate goal of true community-based education: transformation and change. The concepts of "the community of the preferred" and "the communities of the oppressed" are useful in advancing an understanding of devaluation and the attendant consequences for how people view themselves and their community.

Mel King's views on community-based education are a fitting commentary on the challenges facing educators and young people today. By sharing his views on this important and timely subject with the Editorial Board and with readers of the Review, perhaps more educators will "really listen" to what young people are saying, and then they too may be transformed.

PART TWO

_____

Histories of Institutional Change

Black Curriculum Orientations:
A Preliminary Inquiry

WILLIAM H. WATKINS

In this article, William Watkins presents a historical discussion that traces the development of six different curriculum orientations in the educational experience of African Americans. He begins by pointing out that Black curriculum development is inextricably tied to Black America's experience of slavery and oppression in the United States. Watkins then outlines the six orientations, each of which represents African Americans' differing, although sometimes overlapping, sociopolitical responses to their historical reality. The author concludes that, because of the oppressiveness and separateness of U.S. society, Black curriculum orientations will continue to develop as both a part of and separate from the mainstream curriculum movement. Finally, he suggests that further study of the relationship of ethnicity, race, and culture to curriculum may be revealing as we examine contemporary urban education.

In this article, I use sociopolitical and historical analysis to develop a preliminary outline of contrasting Black curriculum orientations. The article is intended to be foundational in nature and to raise rather than answer such questions as, How can we describe the historical curriculum experience(s) of Black America? In my argument, I will suggest that these orientations have evolved, and that they survive and impact the cultural underpinnings of the contemporary African American educational experience.

DEFINING CURRICULUM ORIENTATIONS

The 1970s and 1980s witnessed renewed interest in exploring "the curriculum." Important work in this period focused on the defining and categorizing of curriculum paradigms, conceptions, perspectives, and orientations.[1] Although modern curriculum theorists are far from achieving unanimity of definition, most include notions of objectives, subject matter, methods, activities, historical evolution, organization, and personalities in their inquiry (Schubert, 1986). Questions of what to teach, why, and how to teach remain central to the discourse.

Toward an Understanding of Black Curriculum Orientations

Curriculum theorizing in the mainstream community is the product of an interaction between natural intellectual inquiry and sociopolitical forces. Differing orientations are associated with contrasting views on the nature of the learning

---

[1] Eisner and Vallance (1974); Kliebard (1987); Penna, Pinar, & Giroux (1981); and Schubert (1986) were central among the efforts to categorize curriculum orientations.

Harvard Educational Review Vol. 63 No. 3 Fall 1993, 321–338

organism, as well as with cultural-political views on the social order. The "struggle for the American curriculum" (Kliebard, 1987) has been greatly influenced by intellectual and political interests alike. However, although vested interests were ever present, the American curriculum generally evolved in an environment free of physical and intellectual duress and tyranny.

Black curriculum theorizing, on the other hand, is inextricably tied to the history of the Black experience in the United States. Black social, political, and intellectual development in all cases evolved under socially oppressive and politically repressive circumstances involving physical and intellectual duress and tyranny. Black America's socio-educational development is thus distorted, unnatural, and stunted.[2] The Black response to servitude and exclusion has run the gamut from capitulation to accommodation to outright defiance. Thus, the way African Americans have developed their views on education, and especially the curriculum, is connected to their socio-historical realities (Bond, 1966).

Black curriculum outlooks are the result of views evolving from within the Black experience, as well as from views that have been imposed from without. The dynamics of colonialism, American apartheid, and discriminatory exclusion have been political in nature. Among their objectives have been containment, the maintenance of a cheap labor force, and all the social benefits that accrue to a society structured on privilege and stratification. I am referring to two kinds of containment: physical and sociopolitical. Physical containment includes the restriction of Blacks to certain neighborhoods and locations; sociopolitical containment involves short-circuiting radical activity. The enforcement of structural stratification is as ideological as it is forcible.

Paul-Albert Emoungu (1979) attempts to understand these imposed socio-educational ideologies undergirding Black education. He suggests that two general frameworks are salient: the educational adaptation model and the cultural-educational deprivation model. The educational adaptation model, developed by Samuel Armstrong and Thomas Jesse Jones (Watkins, 1989c) and presented in the form of the Hampton-Tuskegee philosophy, attempts to accommodate White racial attitudes. This view holds that the difference between the races is natural and normal and that, given the differing backgrounds and circumstances of the races, a differentiated education should be offered. Thus, the notion of literary education for Whites and utilitarian education for Blacks emerged.

While this adaptation model served Jim Crow America, Emoungu believes that it was later supplemented by the cultural-educational deprivation outlook. Relying on the "culture of poverty" hypothesis, this view suggests that Blacks are culturally deficient. The notion of Black pathology prescribes the construction of a culture to which Blacks adapt. In either case, Black education has evolved as a function of the sub-culture status of its people.

Black curriculum orientations are the result of complex overlapping historical forces. Although directly associated with the Black experience, the larger arena of the struggle for the U.S. curriculum cannot be ignored, both as context and in terms of the common quest to understand the learning organism. There seems to be clear evidence of at least six somewhat overlapping orientations: the

---

[2] Rodney (1974), in *How Europe Underdeveloped Africa*, offers an interesting discussion on how colonialism distorts the development of the subject people.

functionalist, accommodationist, liberal, reconstructionist, Afrocentrist, and Black Nationalist. Each of these is described below.

The functionalist and accommodationist orientations are the result of discriminatory and colonial practices. Their evolution is not dissimilar to that of other "Third World" and subject peoples whose curriculum practices are both rudimentary and imposed. A. Babs Fafunwa's (1974) discussion provides an illustration of how functionalism prevailed in Nigeria's education for a long period, while Anderson (1988) wrote extensively on accommodationist practices in the segregated South. The liberal orientation is indicative of the hope Black America held for common education in the emerging democratic industrial state. The final three orientations represent a radical response to the discriminatory colonial educational and curricular policies that have characterized much of twentieth-century America's approach to curriculum.

BLACK CURRICULUM ORIENTATIONS

Functionalism

Although records are sketchy, Black intellectual and social interaction existed even during the early days of slavery. Henry Bullock (1967) documents that slaves frequently engaged in record-keeping, skilled labor, artisanship, household management, the purchase of insurance, and other commercial activities requiring the use of intellect and reasoning. He writes:

> By the opening of the nineteenth century, permissiveness had eroded the plantation society's rational policy, and new educational opportunities had opened for a select group of slaves. As an expression of the emotional needs and rugged individualism of the planter class, the institution of slavery had become infected with a form of indulgence that was eventually to create an educated group of Blacks who would supply a leadership on behalf of their own freedom. (Bullock, 1967, p. 7)

Eighteenth- and early nineteenth-century Black education was the resulting combination of a "slave aristocracy," self-effort, religious altruism, and the involvement of benevolent Whites. The Grimke sisters of South Carolina and the Burrwell sisters of Virginia are among the best-known examples of people involved in underground efforts in Black education. Sarah Grimke wrote: "The light was put out, the keyhole secured, and flat on our stomachs before the fire, with spelling books in our hands, we defied the laws of South Carolina" (Birney, 1885, pp. 11–12). Even the harshness of chattel slavery could not eliminate the strong psychological urges of humans to interact and inquire.

Bullock (1967) argues there was enough permissiveness in slave society to allow limited education to exist and spread. But, under these circumstances, curriculum was shaped by the necessity of survival, and thus took the form of basic education to prepare individuals for human interaction. This preparation for life is at the center of the functionalist curriculum. Consistent with colonial education, functionalism is typically basic, largely oral, and frequently includes folklore as part of its curriculum. Learning occurred through imitation, recitation, memorization, and demonstration. A functionalist curriculum shuns abstractions. It is tied to the practical, the useful, and the demonstrable.

Fafunwa (1974) describes early colonial and primitive education in British West Africa as functionalist. Owing to foreign interference and domination, much of West African social, political, cultural, and educational development was distorted and unnatural (Rodney, 1974). Under such circumstances, the mostly verbal education was informal and scattered. More accurately described as allowing for rudimentary social interaction, this kind of education facilitated basic communication such as the exchange of goods, community life, and the transmission of the culture through the passing down of accumulated knowledge and ways of the group. This responsibility was undertaken by *griots* (teachers and village elders) and other keepers of the culture in West African society.

Few deny the colonial sociopolitical development of the southern United States. Slavery, that "peculiar institution" (Stamp, 1956), shaped and influenced three centuries of intellectual and social life. Although unique in its historical development, the informal curriculum of early southern Black education fell very much within a functionalist framework.

As informal Black education became more formal, functionalism remained an important outlook. The "sabbath" schools, normal schools, and all varieties of rural self-help schools maintained a curriculum aimed at social interaction.

Accommodationism

While functionalist education is linked to the limited and rudimentary interaction of an earlier period, accommodationism was a more widespread and politically charged curriculum for the emerging late nineteenth- and early twentieth-century racially segregated, industrial nation. Of all the Black curriculum orientations, accommodationism was the one most clearly associated with an imposed political and racial agenda (DuBois, 1903). Often called the "Hampton-Tuskegee" model of education, this curriculum, which emphasized vocational training, physical/manual labor, character building, and a social science package suggesting the acceptance of racial subservience for Negroes, was promoted by northern corporatists (Berman, 1980; King, 1971) and popularized by Booker T. Washington and his considerable following. Its ideological origins can be traced to the post-Reconstruction period, wherein the corporatists involved themselves in the social, cultural, and political life of the country as never before. Their objectives included re-annexing the South in an orderly way, minimizing the political and financial power of the southern planters, sociopolitically containing the newly freed slaves, and guaranteeing that the intellectual and cultural values of the country were consistent with their own.

Given these aims, schooling, and especially the curriculum, took on increased political significance. Booker T. Washington's infamous speech to a predominantly White audience at the Atlanta Exposition in 1895 (Anderson, 1988; Harlan, 1983) offered a political platform favorable to the corporatists. Washington exhorted Black America to work hard, be obedient, and avoid politics. As Harlan writes, "In the Atlanta compromise in 1895 and on other occasions he [Washington] reassured Whites that blacks would not demand an abstract 'social equality,' or intrude into private gatherings where they were not wanted" (Harlan, 1983, p. 205). Offering agricultural education, vocational training, and character building as centerpieces, this orientation is sharply distinguished from the liberal, progressive, and more militant outlooks.

Dr Th. Jesse Jones

In post–Civil War America, corporate-industrial interests influenced public and educational policy as never before (Berman, 1980). To northern political forces who wanted the country reunited under northern rule, Black education was increasingly perceived as crucial in engineering race relations in the fragile South. The emergent northern hegemonists, most notably industrialists, bankers, and others whose fortunes were tied to the new corporate industrial order, agreed that newly codified Black citizenship should not disturb the traditions of Black subservience. Hampton Institute in Virginia and its now famous Hampton Social Studies provided a curriculum model that promised incremental Black progress without social upheaval.[3] Initiated by General Samuel Armstrong and fine-tuned by Dr. Thomas Jesse Jones, this curriculum was customized for southern rural Blacks, and later exported to Africa (Watkins, 1989c).

Jones, a Welsh immigrant, emerged as one of the most powerful figures in Black education. While working toward his Ph.D. at Columbia in 1904, Jones studied under sociology professor Franklin W. Giddings. Giddings had committed much of his career to the study of race and social development. A Spencerian evolutionist, he believed that people of color had not evolved to the intellectual levels of the Anglo-Saxon and Nordic peoples. He charted a hierarchy of race that characterized African people as childlike, emotional, and lacking in ambition.[4]

Jones adopted Giddings's views of racial development. His curriculum philosophy, fully described in his *Four Essentials of Education* (1926), *Essentials of Civilization: A Study in Social Values* (1929), and essays in the *Southern Workman* (1905–1908), was presented in the language of social and individual betterment, Christian patriotism, community, vocationalism, and character development. *The Southern Workman*, an illustrated monthly founded by Hampton leader Samuel Armstrong in 1868, became an influential tool for Armstrong, Hampton, and those supporting accommodationist politics and education (Anderson, 1988). A social evolutionist, Jones believed Blacks were capable of learning but were not yet ready for an academic curriculum. In Jones's view, Blacks were an immoral and childlike people who required Western socialization prior to cognitive training.

His curriculum platform was based on the "essentials" (Jones, 1929, p. 5) of human existence. "Primitive" (Jones, 1929, p. 6) people needed to learn about health and sanitation, and to develop an appreciation of their environment and an understanding of their home and heritage, and of the processes of their physical, mental, and spiritual "re-creation" (Jones, 1926, p. 22). Building upon these innocent-sounding curriculum themes, Jones's social studies courses were designed to supplement the many daily hours of agricultural and manual labor required of Hampton students.

---

[3] The Hampton Social Studies was first serialized in *The Southern Workman* in 1906, then was printed in its entirety by Hampton Institute Press (1908). It was the prototype social science curriculum for Hampton and Tuskegee. Expansive analysis can be found in Lybarger (1983).

[4] Giddings wrote six books that explained his views on the sociology of race, education, and development. His works include *Civilization and Society: An Account of the Development and Behavior of Human Society* (1932); *Perspectives in Social Inquiry: The Scientific Study of Human Society* (1924); *Studies in the Theory of Human Society* (1906); *Democracy and Empire: With Studies of Their Psychological, Economic, and Moral Foundations* (1901); *The Principles of Sociology: An Analysis of the Phenomena of Association and Social Organization* (1896).

Courses in civics, political economy, civil government, mental and moral science, general history, and Bible study all taught of the triumph of Western civilization. Jones, an ordained minister, believed his social studies assisted God's work. As he stated, "The race must be given time to acquire habits and ideals preparatory to a forward step" (Jones, 1908, pp. 4–5).

The accommodationist curricula provided more than mere school subjects; it also laid the socio-intellectual foundations for a "backward" race. Economics study would establish a relationship between human toil and social progress. Government courses emphasized that Western democracy provided optimum conditions for the evolution of human liberty, but that democracy could not be attempted by the ignorant or irresponsible. "Race development" as a topic transcended many courses: Lessons in the Hampton curriculum took up evolutionary development, acceptance, and natural order. Slavery was part of the natural order in the United States, and the government was repressive on account of the mixed ethnic population. If Blacks would only adopt White values, all would be well.[5]

Hampton Social Studies was divided into five sections, all of which were authored by Jones and bear his ideological signature. Section one, entitled "Social Studies in the Hampton Curriculum: Why They Are Needed," is a rationale and introduction. Section two, "Civics and Social Welfare," examines the development, rationale, and machinery of government. Section three, "Economics and Natural Welfare," teaches the law of supply and demand, the virtues of capitalism, and the place of Negro labor in America. Section four, "United States Census and Actual Conditions," includes population distributions and health statistics. Section five, "Sociology and Society," examines issues of race and society, the social mind, and social organization. Sections two, three, and five are the most politically charged and most representative of accommodationist and colonial thought. The physical and manual components of the curriculum consisted of approximately six hours daily of agricultural and/or trades labor (Anderson, 1988). Manual labor in this formulation of curriculum promoted dignity and discipline. Reminiscent of prison, Hampton students were unpaid, while the products of their labors were often sold.

Religious ideology was emphasized in character education, which drew from standard Bible verse to promote thrift, piety, and obedience. Evangelicalism provided the rationale for students to become teachers — they must spread the word of Hampton.

Despite the fact that he shunned the spotlight during his lifetime (he died in 1950), and that his role in Black education has not yet been fully studied, Jones's influence should not be understated. Called by DuBois (1919) "that evil genius of the Negro race," Jones was not only an important curriculum theoretician and ideologist, he was also corporate America's point man in Black education. Leaving his professorship at Hampton in 1909, Jones built a power base as educational director of the Phelps-Stokes Fund, a foundation similar to other corporate philanthropies such as the Rockefeller, Rosenwald, Carnegie, and Du Pont Funds (Berman, 1969). The Phelps-Stokes Fund, backed by New York bank-

---

[5] These themes were gleaned by the author after reading actual lessons in *The Southern Workman*. Lybarger's (1981) discussion (pp. 52–76) has a different focus but, I believe, supports this summary.

ing money, focused on the education of Blacks in both the United States and Africa. This fund was powerful in shaping the ideology and funding of Black education. During his nearly three decades at Phelps-Stokes, Jones became a powerful force.[6] His approval meant funding, hence life, for accommodationist curriculum. His acceptance of Negro subservience influenced the South's educational and social policy for decades to come.

Liberal Education Orientations

While accommodationist orientations were linked to colonialism, segregation, and subservience, liberal outlooks were more hopeful for the prospects of education in the expanding democracy. The liberal education orientation grew out of a different group in the philanthropic community. Two tendencies were obvious within the late nineteenth-century philanthropic community. The industrial corporate philanthropists were concerned with questions of power and control in the new industrial United States. An orderly South, a productive agricultural base, access to cheap labor, and a favorable business environment were central objectives of their social philosophy. The missionary philanthropists never opposed the industrial ordering of society; however, their agenda was directed more toward social amelioration and developing human potential. Rooted in the Christian abolitionism of the pre–Civil War period, this outlook became significant in the postbellum period. The missionary philanthropic community was ideologically and practically connected to the Freedman's Bureau, the YMCA, YWCA, and assorted socially conscious church denominations. Education was an important part of their blueprint for a harmonious society (Anderson, 1988).

The curriculum was important to this community because it devoted a significant amount of resources to educational enterprises. For example, various missionary societies had established Black colleges such as Fisk University, Talladega College, Meharry Medical College, Morehouse College, Shaw University, and many others. Not unaffected by the racial and paternalistic attitudes of their times, this missionary community derived a liberal education curriculum that borrowed from the traditions of humanism, such as altruism, free expression, and the unfettered intellectual development of the individual. The undereducated Black southern community, hungry for educational advancements, was able to embrace this curriculum.

This liberal curriculum acknowledged that slavery, not race, impeded Black education, and it assumed Blacks learned by the same modality as Whites. It also focused on standard academics, with some religious and political undercurrents, in order to prepare its students for higher education. An example of the liberal outlook was the African Free School that operated in New York City throughout the nineteenth century. Its curriculum combined literature, religion, African history, and political philosophy (Rigsby, 1987).

---

[6] Jones spent most of his twenty-eight-year career as educational director of the Phelps-Stokes Fund. In that capacity, he avoided public exposure. Analysis of Jones's role in Black education can be found in Watkins (1991, 1990c, 1989c), Correia and Watkins (1991), Anderson (1988), Lybarger (1983, 1981), Berman (1980), and King (1971).

The various missionary societies influenced higher education, as well as elementary and secondary schools (King, 1971). At every level, their focus on a liberal democratic culture contrasted sharply with the racial subservience of accommodationist vocational training education. As part of the effort toward equal education, liberal curriculum offerings in Black schools and colleges were often duplicated from White schools. Anderson (1988) found that early twentieth-century liberal education in Black colleges typically offered freshmen Latin, Greek, and mathematics. Sophomores took courses in natural sciences, more advanced mathematics, and perhaps more language, often French. Juniors continued in the languages and added philosophy, history, and English to their programs of study. Seniors proceeded to more advanced philosophy and political science courses.

Black liberal education differed little from traditional liberal thought. A clear connection to Deweyan themes is evident.[7] The curriculum was designed to develop the students' analytical and critical faculties, and to help students become worldly, tolerant, and capable of significant societal participation. Black liberal education placed much significance on leadership. It strove to educate teachers, preachers, civil servants, and others who would be committed to the ideals of the liberal democratic state; these ideals encompassed gradual change, electoral politics, and planned societal transformation. The "talented tenth" concept first developed by the Reverend Alexander Crummell was supported by W. E. B. DuBois.[8] DuBois (1903) asserted that Black America would be saved by its "exceptional men" (DuBois, 1903/1969).[9]

The Black Nationalist Outlook

While liberal educators have hoped for human progress and change, nationalists and separatists have not shared such optimism. Black Nationalist outlooks began to emerge at the end of the eighteenth century. These protest views were linked to international slavery, colonization, the debasement of Africa, and the mistreatment of African peoples scattered throughout the world. As early as the 1830s, Blacks began to join with the American Colonization Society in calling for an American Negro political state in Africa. Advocating notions of "separatism," ethnic consciousness, and "cultural revitalization" (Moses, 1978, pp. 34–35), various strains of Black Nationalist thought began to evolve. The Pan-Africanist, cultural nationalist, and separatist views together voiced the Black Nationalist outlook. Prominent twentieth-century Black nationalists, cultural nationalists, and separatists with interests in education included Marcus Garvey, Noble Drew Ali, Elijah Muhammed, and Malcolm X.

Wilson J. Moses (1978) points to the rise of "macro-nationalist" theories evident in the emergence of Pan-Germanism and Pan-Slavism; he describes the

[7] Extensive discussions of Dewey's liberal progressive education views can be found in *Democracy and Education* (1916), and *Experience and Education* (1938).

[8] Moses (1978) describes how it was Crummell, not DuBois, who first used the phrase "talented tenth."

[9] Debate over the "talented tenth" (DuBois, 1903/1969) concept has raged for decades. Critics such as Marcus Garvey, Booker T. Washington, and A. Phillip Randolph viewed it as elitist. DuBois's essays on education, compiled by Aptheker (1973), appear to support the view that Blacks must turn to their intelligentsia to begin the long climb into U.S. social and political life.

objective — to unite various independent ethnic groups under the banner of collective nationalism — as part of the foundation of the Pan-African movement. He traces the development of Pan-Africanism to the "maroon" (Moses, 1978, p. 18) revolutions of Haiti, Jamaica, and Surinam during the seventeenth and eighteenth centuries, as well as the rebellions of Denmark Vesey and Nat Turner in the nineteenth century. Pan-Africanism, in general, seeks to raise Africa and promote the interests of African people regardless of location. It links the fortunes of Africa with her scattered people. Some Pan-Africanists, such as Bishop Turner and Marcus Garvey (Moses, 1978), advocated massive emigration back to Africa, while others believed the movement for African revitalization and identification could be supported from the diaspora where Black people have toiled and taken root.

The cultural nationalists believe culture is the binding force for a people's cohesion, stability, and progress. In general they view culture as the building block of civilization. Culturalist positions, while loosely defined, date back over a century, but they have become particularly prominent in the post–World War II period. Contemporary cultural nationalists describe how colonization and oppression have stripped African Americans of their names, languages, celebrations, religions, and cultural legacies. They argue for an educational system around which Black people can unite in the present day.[10]

The separatists, most notably Black Muslims, Malcolm X, and the Republic of New Africa, share common views with both Pan-Africanists and culturalists alike.[11] Their views somewhat overlap those of Black Nationalists. Shunning assimilationism, the Black separatists call for the building of a parallel society. The hope of the separatists is for African Americans to maintain a Black economic, political, educational, and cultural structure within the United States. The general category of nationalist thought that emerged in the early 1800s provided the historical antecedent for the late nineteenth-century ideas of DuBois, Turner, and others. Likewise, the early twentieth-century separatist and nationalist views of people like Garvey, Ali, and others represent the continuation of the early outlooks. Essien Udosen Essien-Udom (1962) traces the separatist nationalists to the Negro Convention Movements of the early 1800s.[12] He describes their early philosophy as anti-emigrationist; proponents favored economic self-sufficiency and the separation of the races, except for limited social contact. DuBois (1897) offered a definition of separatism culled from the writings of its proponents:

> Unless modern civilization is a failure, it is entirely feasible and practicable for two
> races in such essential political, economic and religious harmony as the white and

[10] The many works of H. Makhubuti (Don L. Lee) are representative of this outlook. See, for example, Lee's *From Plan to Planet* (1973).

[11] The Republic of New Africa (RNA) was a "militant"-styled Black separatist organization founded in Detroit in 1967. The RNA demanded that several states in the South be ceded to Blacks. The new sovereign state would be called New Africa. A brief discussion of the RNA can be found in the introduction of *Black Protest in the Sixties* (Meier & Rudwick, 1970).

[12] The Negro Convention Movement (NCM) held its first meeting in Philadelphia in January 1817, to protest proposals from the American Colonization Society to systematically remove Blacks from the United States. The NCM were indeed separatists, but they did not want to be removed. Instead, they favored relocating somewhere in the Western Hemisphere, such as Canada or the West Indies.

colored people of America to develop side by side in peace and mutual happiness, the peculiar contribution which each has to make to the culture of their common country. (pp. 10–14).

The platform of the Nation of Islam in the 1960s offers an example of separatist thinking. Examples of that program include Black-owned businesses, a separate Black educational system modeled after the University of Islam, the development of a Black military named the Fruits of Islam, and an end to Black participation in U.S. electoral politics (Essien-Udom, 1962). Its demand for a parallel society combines notions of culturalism, revitalization, and identificationist thought.

School curriculum is important to Black Nationalists because it provides a vehicle through which Black values can be imparted to young learners (Essien-Udom, 1962), who are expected to go forth and contribute to the building of Black civilization. Segregated schools, private schools, Black Muslim schools, urban storefront schools, and after-school programs have served to transmit Black values.

The Black Studies curriculum movement of the past twenty-five years represents an evolution of the Black Nationalist orientation. A survey of course titles in universities reveals courses on such topics as Black Politics, Black Economic History, the Black Aesthetic, the Black Experience in Theater, Black Art, Black Poetry, Black Literature, and Black Religious History (see Higgins, 1985). Interdisciplinary in nature, these courses range from the mundane to the exotic and represent how Black Studies has become a critical discipline in university offerings (Watkins, 1989b).

Black Nationalist curriculum may be the most extreme reaction to American racism. Its focus on separateness indicates little optimism for integration. It represents an angry break from the imposition of hegemonic ideology (Moses, 1978).

The Afrocentric Curriculum

In many ways, the nationalist and separatist outlooks may be viewed as forerunners of the contemporary Afrocentric idea. The Black Nationalist outlook is also reflected, in part, in contemporary renditions of Afrocentrism. The reclaiming of traditional African culture drives the placement of "African ideals" at the center of historical, social, communicative, and pedagogical dialogue. Ancient Kemetic (Egyptian) civilization provides a reference point for Afrocentrics to reconnect African Americans to their spiritual origins (Asante, 1987).

Afrocentrism suggests the recapturing and regeneration of a once great continent and people who may now be culturally adrift. Redemption, renewal, integrity, and a sense of community are but a few themes underlying African cultural identification. Paraphrasing Ivan Van Sertima (1990), as Black people piece together the shattered world of Africa, we make ourselves whole again.

Afrocentric theorizing rejects European and American social theories as the only legitimate models of inquiry. Eurocentric analysis is viewed as linear. Rooted in empiricism, rationalism, scientific method and positivism, its aim is prediction and control, according to Asante (1987). Afrology, or African epistemology, on the other hand, is circular (Asante, 1987), and seeks interpretation, expression, and understanding without preoccupation with verification. Afro-

168

centric orientations hold that Europeans have colonized not only the world, but also its knowledge.

Afrocentrics would generally agree that U.S. public schooling and curriculum have failed African Americans by not providing the appropriate cultural foundations for learners. Asa Hilliard (1990), a proponent of infusing African themes into the school curriculum, points to six areas in which the prevailing curriculum has fallen short:

- The significant history of Africans before the slave trade is ignored.
- A history of peoples of Africa is most often ignored.
- A history of the people of the African diaspora — for example, Fiji, the Philippines, and Dravidian India — is not taught.
- Cultural differences, as opposed to similarities of Africans in the diaspora, are highlighted.
- Little of the struggle against slavery, colonialism, segregation, apartheid, and domination is taught.
- Little explanation of the common origins and elements in the system of oppression during the last four hundred years is offered. (Hilliard, Payton-Stewart, & Williams, 1990)

Proponents of Afrocentric curriculum (e.g., Van Sertima, 1990) further assert that U.S. public schools have relied on negative pathological labels such as "permanent underclass," "at-risk," "cultural deficit," and "disadvantaged" as the theoretical rationale for educational policymaking. The Afrocentrists want validation of African *ways of knowing* (Asante, 1987), African method and content.

African methods, Asante argues, seek to legitimize expression, public discourse, feeling, myth-making, and emotion as acceptable avenues of inquiry. Unlike European paradigms, Afrocentrism seeks out transcendence — that is, the quality of exceeding ordinary and literal experience (Asante, 1987). The pursuit of knowledge goes beyond the material world. Extreme interpretations of the Afrocentric idea speak of the "Sudic" ideal (Asante, 1987, p. 185), which refers to people's quest for self-definition described as harmony with the universe. The Sudic spirit, which may be summoned by chant and incantation, offers a metaphysical energy force allowing one to achieve a high state of harmony, peace, consciousness, and insight.

Afrocentric curriculum is focused on Africa and its place in the world from the early Egyptian civilizations, circa 3000 B.C., to the present. Sample topical themes in textbooks, lectures, discussions, and assignments in Black Studies courses may include the great African civilizations, the golden age of Egypt, African religions, great leaders, lost cities and civilizations, European imperialism and colonialism, slavery and the slave trade, and the African diaspora. In addition to the better known African American scholars such as W. E. B. DuBois, Carter G. Woodson, and so on, Afrocentrists wish to popularize the lesser known African-oriented historical and sociological writings of Cheikh Anta Diop, Yosef ben Jochannan, Chancellor Williams, J. A. Rogers, Water Rodney, Eric Williams, and others.

slavery not race

Social Reconstructionism

Although the Afrocentrics are very provocative, in general they don't challenge the contemporary or historic economic arrangements of society. Social reconstructionism, however, questioned the capitalist order as a facilitator and generator of racism. Of the curriculum movements in the early twentieth century, the social reconstructionists were among the most radical.[13] Prominent among the Social Reconstructionists were George Counts, Sidney Hook, Harold Rugg, and many others. They viewed schools and the curriculum as an instrument to challenge and eventually change unjust economic, political, and social arrangements. Most of their followers were progressive educators and former members of the Progressive Education Association. Their call for democratic socialist reform and improved race relations represented a departure from the eugenicist and White racist views of many curricularists and educational theorists.

Though widely discussed and described in the mainstream literature (e.g., Kliebard, 1987), Social Reconstructionism in connection with Black education has been ignored. Although the notion of social amelioration persists in Black liberal education, curricular theorists have failed to make any further connection. It was the progressive education movement, and the more radical Social Reconstructionist movement that grew out of it, that provided a theoretical and practical context to influence Black Reconstructionist education.

Harold Rugg, a prominent progressive and reconstructionist educator, had some interest in Negro education, as evidenced in his work on the education of minorities, as well as on general racial equality.[14] Beyond that example, the most appealing aspect of progressive era reconstructionism was its platform. The ideals of a collectivist, egalitarian, reformed society found some support among the politically conscious Black intelligentsia, civil rights leaders, and labor activists (Woodson, 1933).

The existence of Black socialists, communists, and outspoken critics in the 1930s and 1940s is often overlooked.[15] A. Phillip Randolph, founder of the Sleeping Car Porters Union, was a public socialist. Angelo Hearndon, active in organizing southern sharecroppers' unions, was one of several Black communists who exerted a presence in Black political life. The ideological views of these Black critical thinkers, who were deeply concerned with education, were not inconsistent with the Social Reconstructionists. Alain Locke (1940), a prominent Black social thinker, even contributed an article to the *Social Frontier*, the journal of the Reconstructionists.[16]

While formal ties between Social Reconstructionists and radical Black educator activists were few, it can be argued that an ideological connection certainly did exist. The views of W. E. B. DuBois, the preeminent twentieth-century Black educator, were indistinguishable from the "social frontiersmen." Marable (1986) traces DuBois's early ideological influences to the radical progressive intelligent-

---

[13] See Watkins (1990b) for a comprehensive discussion of this movement.

[14] One prominent example of Rugg's concern is illustrated in a chapter entitled "Education and the Minorities: Racial and Social Conflict in America" included in the widely known Harold Rugg and William Withers, *Social Foundations of Education* (1955, pp. 264–280).

[15] For a full discussion see, for example, Robinson (1983), Record (1951), Haywood (1978), and Kelley (1987).

[16] *Social Frontier* changed its name to *Frontiers of Democracy* around 1939–1940.

sia of New York City. Having attended Harvard and studied in Europe, DuBois was able to connect with White socialists and progressives in a way other Black intellectuals could not and did not. Avant-garde socialist thinkers who befriended DuBois, such as William English Walling, Max Eastman, and Walter Lippmann, provided a strong influence on the political and social criticism of the times (Marable, 1986).

DuBois consistently supported progressive political and educational objectives. In the social arena, he was comfortable with economic and political reform, trade unionism, and democratic socialist welfarism (Marable, 1986). As a curricularist, DuBois has been described as a Black Social Reconstructionist (Watkins, 1989a). Recognizing that the Social Reconstructionists emerged from the split in the Progressive Education Association, DuBois, without affiliation, argued their cause within Black education.

In his essay "Diuturni Silenti," DuBois rebuked the medievalism of educational practices that maintained Black subservience.[17] He advocated a curriculum that would criticize capitalism, promote democracy, propagate common schooling, foster emancipatory thinking, support societal transformation, and seek a higher civilization, all of which are part of the Reconstructionist educational program.

Like the Reconstructionists, DuBois criticized the curriculum of cultural transmission and the apologia for social injustice. His curriculum placed the social studies and social sciences at the center.[18] Rigorous study was devoted to understanding and criticizing inequity, racism, class stratification, and imperialist adventure.

Reconstructionist education meant leadership to DuBois, who believed that education was useless if it did not foster change. DuBois perceived the curriculum as social capital: Black people must use education not simply to study the world, but to change it. His educational essays, collected by Aptheker (1973), are a powerful testament to these ideals. In an eloquent summary of his views on the power of education, found in his 1930 essay "Education and Work," DuBois noted: "We are going to force ourselves in by organized far-seeing effort — by out thinking and out flanking the owners of the world who are too drunk with their own arrogance and power to successfully oppose us" (Aptheker, 1973, p. 77).

CONCLUSION

Social scientists recognize the persistence of minority sub-cultures. Practices peculiar to ethnic groups continue to provide a legacy for shared experiences. Education, both formal and informal, is a significant ingredient in the historical evolution of any people. Black education, once focused in the rural South, is now at the center of the urban educational experience. Further exploration of the sociopolitical and cultural underpinnings of Black curriculum outlooks should be useful in helping to understand the Black educational experience.

[17] This essay is found in Aptheker (1973, pp. 41–60).
[18] A cluster of essays entitled "The Negro College" found in Weinberg (1970, pp. 155–200) describes DuBois's views on the importance of social sciences for emancipatory education.

What preliminary conclusions can we draw from this first effort to categorize Black curriculum orientations within the context of the field in general?

First, it must be reiterated that the nature of Black education has been highly political. Powerful economic interests have imposed colonial-style policies aimed at socialization and containment. Education and curriculum have been at the heart of broader initiatives to stabilize and control a potentially volatile population. Within that process, patterns of traditional race relations have been preserved. The result of colonial educational practices has been the marginalization and continued subservience of African Americans.

Critical theorists have argued that curriculum is a function of state and hegemonic power (Apple, 1979, 1982). From an accommodationist perspective, industrial magnates directly brokered Negro education, resulting in largely realized social engineering. For nearly a century, from Reconstruction to World War II, most rural southern Blacks were offered a curriculum far removed from the technical and intellectual demands of the twentieth century. Accommodationism was equally damaging in other areas. Not only were Deweyan notions of education as promoting democracy scorned, but indeed the possibility for any emancipatory or transformative discourse was truly stifled.

For quite different reasons, the accommodationists, as well as DuBois, argued for a Black educated class. The corporatists recognized that stabilizing any ethnic group in the United States could only be accomplished with the development of an indigenous middle class. In a politically repressive state, such a group can provide a buffer, can encourage role modeling, and can participate in sham social conciliation. While DuBois called for the Black middle class, or the "talented tenth," to lead their people forward, the corporatists cultivated a Black compradore class of clerics, educators, civil servants, and petty entrepreneurs. Accommodationist education merits further examination as it has contributed to the ideological, philosophical, and educational class differences that have continuously divided Black America.

One could argue that functionalism, common to "Third World" people, has dominated the traditional culture of Black education. Inhabitants of a hostile, even fascistic, environment take on survival modes, and functionalism has been both attainable and practical. Although functionalist curriculum emerges from the sociocultural life of a people, at some point it must serve as a springboard to more socially, politically, intellectually, and technologically advanced subject area pursuits.

The traditions of the liberal orientation are consistent with the politics of oppositionist reform. The significant Black middle class, with roots in the early twentieth-century South, has supported these curricular views. The more than one hundred historically Black colleges operating for the last 130 years (Watkins, 1990a) have produced a Black intelligentsia committed to higher education, the development of a well-rounded individual, social advancement, and incremental planned political change that liberal education fosters. The 1940s were the "golden age" of the Black colleges, a time when a number of exceptional professors and students were working together (Watkins, 1990a) at various campuses. For example, Thurgood Marshall and Spottiswood Robinson were students at Howard Law School at the same time that William Hastie and Leon Ransom were professors there.[19] During this golden age, the viewpoint of most Black scholars remained within the ideological parameters of the liberal orientation.

The notion of Black Reconstructionism requires much more investigation. Although evidence of connections between Black and progressive educators may be sketchy, the parallel traditions of Black Reconstructionist and radical social thought are clear. Further inquiry is required to uncover those in the Black educational community who implemented DuBoisian curriculum programs; who were influenced by Counts, Rugg, Brameld, and others; and who opposed the conservative corporatist formulations of Armstrong, Jones, and Washington.

Deeply rooted in early twentieth-century separatist thought, Black Nationalism as a curriculum orientation continues its pedagogical consolidation. As post–Civil Rights era phenomena, Black Nationalism and Afrocentrism continue to evolve. Subject to differing interpretations and levels of stridency, the separatist notions existing in Black social and educational thought are undeniable. Much of the future direction of urban (Black) education may depend on the contingent popularity of separatism (Watkins, 1990).

As redemptionists — that is, those who believe in redeeming or reviving Africa's culture, legitimacy, and people — the Afrocentric movement has moved decisively to launch its curriculum and, indeed, its own schools. This growing phenomenon will be carefully observed by African Americans and the educational community at large. Many questions remain to be addressed: Will this model lead to resegregation? How should Afrocentric models fit with current proposals of "globalism" and "internationalism" and "cultural diversity" in the curriculum? Can the claims for higher academic achievement be demonstrated? Beyond the questions of education and curricular reform, the Afrocentrist cultural movement will likely encounter a Black population historically divided on issues of African identification.

Black curriculum orientations have emerged and will continue to develop as both a part of and separate from the larger curriculum movement. The oppressiveness and separateness of U.S. society guarantee the continuation of this phenomenon. Our knowledge of the dimensions of curriculum continues to expand. We now know about the out-of-school as well as in-school curriculum. We also speculate that the "hidden" curriculum may be as important as the open. As a somewhat recent pursuit, the study of the relationship of ethnicity, race, and culture to curriculum may be revealing as we continue to examine contemporary urban education.

REFERENCES

Anderson, J. D. (1988). *The education of blacks in the south 1860–1935*. Chapel Hill: University of North Carolina Press.

Apple, M. (1979). *Ideology and curriculum*. London: Routledge & Kegan Paul.

Apple, M. (1982). *Education and power*. Boston: Ark Paperbacks.

---

[19] During that same era, John Hope was the president of Atlanta University where Du Bois, Mercer Cook, Rayford Logan, Frank Snowden, William Dean, and Ira Reid, leaders in their disciplines, taught. Howard University also included top scholars Alain Locke, Ralph Bunche, E. Franklin Frazier, Charles Thompson, Abram Harris, and Charles Wesley in their faculty ranks.

Aptheker, H. (Ed.). (1973). *The education of black people: Ten critiques, 1906–1960, by W. E. B. DuBois*. New York: Monthly Review Press.

Asante, M. K. (1987). *The Afrocentric idea*. Philadelphia: Temple University Press.

Berman, E. H. (1969). *Education in Africa and America: A history of the Phelps-Stokes Fund 1911–45*. Unpublished doctoral dissertation, Columbia University.

Berman, E. H. (1980). Educational colonialism in Africa: The role of American foundations 1910–1945. In R. F. Arnove (Ed.), *Philanthropy and cultural imperialism: The foundations at home and abroad* (pp. 179–201). Boston: G. K. Hall.

Birney, C. H. (1885). *Sarah and Angelina Grimke*. Boston: Lee and Shepard.

Bond, H. M. (1966). *The education of the Negro in the American social order*. New York: Octagon Books.

Bullock, H. (1967). *A history of Negro education in the south: From 1619 to present*. Cambridge, MA: Harvard University Press.

Correia, S. T., & Watkins, W. H. (1991, April). *Thomas Jesse Jones: A portrait*. Unpublished paper presented at the Annual Meeting of the Society for the Study of Curriculum History, Chicago.

Dewey, J. (1916). *Democracy and education*. New York: Macmillan.

Dewey, J. (1938). *Experience and education*. New York: Macmillan.

DuBois, W. E. B. (1897). *The conservation of race* (American Negro Academy Occasional Paper No. 2, pp. 10–14).

DuBois, W. E. B. (1903). *The souls of black folk*. New York: Signet.

DuBois, W. E. B. (1919). Opinion of W. E. B. DuBois. *Crises, 18*, 9.

DuBois, W. E. B. (1973). Education and work. In H. Aptheker (Ed.), *The education of black people: Ten critiques, 1906–1960, by W. E. B. DuBois* (p. 77). New York: Monthly Review Press. (Original work published 1930)

DuBois, W. E. B. (1969). The talented tenth. In *The Negro problem* (pp. 31–75). New York: Arno Press. (Original work published 1903 in B. T. Washington [Ed.], *The Negro Problem*. New York: James Pott.)

Eisner, E., & Vallance, E. (Eds.). (1974). *Conflicting conceptions of curriculum*. Berkeley: McCutcheon.

Emoungu, P. A. (1979). Socioeducational ideologies of black education. *Journal of Negro Education, 48*(1), 43–56.

Essien-Udom, E. U. (1962). *Black nationalism: A search for an identity in America*. New York: Dell.

Fafunwa, A. B. (1974). *History of education in Nigeria*. London: Allen & Unwin.

Giddings, F. H. (1896). *The principles of sociology: An analysis of the phenomena of association and social organization*. New York: Macmillan.

Giddings, F. H. (Ed.). (1901). *Democracy and empire: With studies of their psychological, economic, and moral foundations* New York: Macmillan.

Giddings, F. H. (1906). *Studies in the theory of human society*. New York: Macmillan.

Giddings, F. H. (1924). *Perspectives in social inquiry: The scientific study of human society*. Chapel Hill: University of North Carolina Press.

Giddings, F. H. (1932). *Civilization and society: An account of the development and behavior of human society*. New York: Henry Holt.

Harlan, L. R. (1983). *Booker T. Washington: The wizard of Tuskegee 1901–1915*. New York: Oxford University Press.

Haywood, H. (1978). *Black Bolshevik: Autobiography of an African American Communist*. Chicago: Liberator Press.

Higgins, N. (1985). *Afro-American studies: A report to the Ford Foundation*. New York: Ford Foundation.

Hilliard, A. G., Payton-Stewart, L., & Williams, L. O. (Eds.). (1990). *Infusion of African and African American content in the school curriculum: Proceedings of the First National Conference, October 1989*. Morristown, NJ: Aaron Press.

Jones, T. J. (1908). *Social studies in the Hampton Curriculum*. Hampton, VA: Hampton Institute Press.

Jones, T. J. (1926). *Four essentials of education*. New York: Charles Scribner.

Jones, T. J. (1929). *Essentials of civilization: A study in social values*. New York: Henry Holt.

Kelley, R. D. G. (1987). *Black radicalism and the Communist party in Alabama, 1929–41.* Unpublished doctoral dissertation, University of California at Los Angeles.

King, K. (1971). *Pan Africanism and education: A study of race, philanthropy and education in the southern states of American and East Africa.* Oxford: Clarendon Press.

Kliebard, H. (1987). *The struggle for the American curriculum 1893–1958.* New York: Routledge & Kegan Paul.

Lee, D. L. (1973). *From plan to planet.* Chicago: Broadside Press.

Locke, A. (1940). With science as his shield: The educator must bridge our "great divide." *Frontiers of Democracy, 6*(53), 208–210.

Lybarger, M. (1981). *Origins of the social studies curriculum 1865–1916.* Unpublished doctoral dissertation, University of Wisconsin-Madison.

Lybarger, M. (1983). Origins of the modern social studies 1900–1916. *History of Education Quarterly, 23,* 455–468.

Marable, M. (1986). *W. E. B. DuBois: Black radical democrat.* Boston: Twayne.

Meier, A., & Rudwick, E. (Eds.). (1970). *Black protest in the sixties.* Chicago: Quadrangle Books.

Moses, W. J. (1978). *The golden age of black nationalism, 1850–1925.* New York: Oxford University Press.

Penna, A., Pinar, W., & Giroux, H. (1981). *Curriculum and instruction.* Berkeley: McCutcheon.

Record, W. (1951). *The Negro and the Communist party.* Chapel Hill: University of North Carolina Press.

Rigsby, G. U. (1987). *Alexander Crummell.* New York: Greenwood Press.

Robinson, C. J. (1983). *Black Marxism.* London: Zed Press.

Rodney, W. (1974). *How Europe underdeveloped Africa.* London: Bogle-L'Ouverture.

Rugg H., & Withers, W. (1955). *Social foundations of education.* New York: Prentice-Hall.

Schubert, W. H. (1986). *Curriculum: Perspective, paradigm, and possibility.* New York: Macmillan.

Stamp, K. (1956). *The peculiar institution.* New York: Knopf, Random House.

Van Sertima, I. (1990, October). Future directions for African and African American content in the school curriculum. In A. G. Hilliard, L. Payton-Stewart, and L. O. Williams (Eds.), *Infusion of African and African American content in the school curriculum: Proceedings of the First National Conference* (pp. 87–109). Morristown, NJ: Aaron Press.

Watkins, W. H. (1989a). *W. E. B. Dubois: Black social reconstructionist.* Unpublished paper, American Educational Research Association, San Francisco.

Watkins, W. H. (1989b). Black studies. In T. Husen & T. Postelthwaite (Eds.), *The international encyclopedia of education: Supplementary volume one* (pp. 107–110). London: Pergamon. Reprinted as "Black Studies" (1991) in A. Lewy (Ed.), *The international encyclopedia of curriculum* (pp. 779–782). Oxford: Pergamon Press.

Watkins, W. H. (1989c). On accommodationist education: Booker T. Washington goes to Africa. *International Third World Studies Journal and Review, 1,* 137–143.

Watkins, W. H. (1990a). Teaching and learning in the Black colleges: A 130 year retrospective. *Teaching Education, 3*(1), 10–25.

Watkins, W. H. (1990b) The social reconstructionists. In T. Husen and T. H. Postelthwaite (Eds.), *The international encyclopedia of education: Supplementary volume two* (pp. 589–592). London: Pergamon Press. Reprinted as "Social reconstructionist approach" (1991) in A. Lewy (Ed.), *The international encyclopedia of curriculum* (pp. 32–35). Oxford: Pergamon Press.

Watkins, W. H. (1990c) W. E. B. DuBois versus Thomas Jesse Jones: The forgotten skirmishes. *Journal of the Midwest History of Education Society, 18,* 305–328.

Watkins, W. H. (1991). *A curriculum for colored people: The social and educational ideas of Franklin H. Giddings.* Unpublished paper presented at the Bergamo Curriculum Conference, Dayton, OH.

Weinberg, M. (Ed.). (1970). *W. E. B. DuBois: A reader.* New York: Harper & Row.

Woodson, C. G. (1933). *The mis-education of the Negro.* Washington, DC: Associated.

Caswell County
Training School, 1933–1969:
Relationships between Community and School

EMILIE V. SIDDLE WALKER

The history of education has many references that depict the inequities African American children experienced during the pre-integration era, but few studies that describe the positive interactions in segregated school environments. In this article, Emilie Vanessa Siddle Walker discusses the case of Caswell County Training School of North Carolina. In this study, ethnographically approached, the author explores the relationships between school and community as they existed in a segregated Black school in the South that was defined by its community as a "good" school. Specifically, Siddle Walker considers: 1) the ways in which the community supported the school; 2) the ways in which the school supported the community; and 3) the implications of these relationships both in their historical context and in informing the current school reform debates.

When court-ordered school desegregation plans were announced in 1969 for rural Caswell County, North Carolina, the local newspaper recorded the reaction of one White parent:

> We have no animosity toward the Board. They have done all they can to stall. However, we now feel that this reorganization of our public schools will destroy our high standard of education, depriving our children of the quality of education they deserve and what we all want.

What they wanted, the parent continued, "was the highest standard of education in [the] county" ("Eighteen-Member Board," 1969).

That parent's implicit denigration of the county's one Negro school was ironic.[1] The county high school for Negro children, the Caswell County Training School (CCTS), was a three-story, immaculately kept brick structure that included a gymnasium and a 722-person-capacity auditorium with a balcony.[2] The principal, Nicholas Longworth Dillard, who held a master's degree from the University of Michigan, was esteemed locally by both Black and White educational leaders for his knowledge of national educational issues. By 1954, 64 per-

---

[1] The terms "Negro," "colored," "Black," and "African American" are used interchangeably in this article. In general, the term used reflects the appropriate label given to those of African descent during the particular era being discussed.

[2] During the last decade of segregation, the name of the school was changed to Caswell County High School, even though it continued to maintain an elementary department for the local township until 1967. In the early years, it was referred to as the Yanceyville School and, after integration, the name was changed to Dillard Junior High School. For purposes of consistency, this article consistently refers to the facility as Caswell County Training School, the name by which it was known for the longest period of time.

Harvard Educational Review Vol. 63 No. 2 Summer 1993, 161–182

cent of the school's teachers had graduate training beyond state recertification requirements, and during Dillard's thirty-six-year tenure from 1933 to 1969, the school offered more than fifty-three extracurricular clubs and activities to enhance student leadership and development. Moreover, the school's educational programs had been on the approved list of the Southern Association of Colleges and Schools since 1934, and were formally accredited in 1955 after that agency began accrediting Negro schools. In contrast, the area high school for White children was smaller, older, had fewer facilities, and was not accredited.

Yet this White parent's belief that White educational systems were superior to Black, and that Negro educators could have nothing to offer White children, is an accurate reflection of many White Americans' perception, both during that era and into the present. Indeed, the history of U.S. education documents so well the inequities African American children experienced during the pre-integration era — specifically the lack of resources, the substandard facilities, and the poor response of school boards to the needs of schools (see Anderson, 1988; Brown, 1960; Clark, 1963; Clift, Anderson, & Hullfish, 1962; Kluger, 1977; Newbold, 1935) — that these images of uniform deprivation have become the dominant picture at the center of most thinking about the segregated schooling of African American children.

This perception of inequality, while not totally inaccurate, is, however, one-sided. It highlights the need and struggle for equality, but overlooks any suggestion that not all education for African American children during segregation was inferior. Sowell (1976), for example, in his description of six "excellent" historically Black high schools and two elementary schools, lists some traits common to these good schools. These traits include, but are not limited to, the commitment and educational levels of the teachers and principals, and the support, encouragement, and rigid standards that characterize the schools' atmospheres. Similarly, in Jones's *A Traditional Model of Educational Excellence* (1981), the segregated school environment is described as "one's home away from home, where students were taught, nurtured, supported, corrected, encouraged, and punished" (p. 2). These and other studies (Adair, 1984; Foster, 1990; Irvine & Irvine, 1984) suggest the presence of a positive sociocultural system in which "uniquely stylized characteristics" reflective of the student population developed independently of White control (Irvine & Irvine, 1984, p. 416), and in which African American youth were successful because of the school environment in which they were taught.

The degree to which such descriptions of segregated Black schooling might also apply to other undocumented cases is further suggested by the numerous voices in southern African American communities, which today speak forcefully of the "goodness" of their pre-integration schools. These voices do not speak of test scores and/or any measured success of school graduates in defining "goodness." Rather, they fondly recall a time when, in the words of one eighty-year-old grandmother, "colored children learnt something in school." Cecelski (1991) has captured some of this appreciation as he chronicles a little-known political struggle in which Negro parents and students boycotted their school system for a year, rather than sacrifice their schools in a locally proposed desegregation plan. Though other voices remain undocumented, the fact that they are heard so frequently in many small-town communities suggests that schooling that was valued by parents, students, and school personnel may have been more common than has been realized.

However, little is known about these unidentified good community schools. Even the paucity of literature that exists on pre-integration Black schooling focuses almost exclusively on good urban high schools, so defined because of their success with standardized test scores, the number of doctoral degrees earned by graduates, or some other easily measured outcome variables. Educators understand little of the emic perspective — that is, how and why communities considered their schools to be good. Educators also do not understand the nature of the schooling in those community-defined good schools. This lack of knowledge not only denies that there are valuable lessons to be learned from principals and teachers who successfully schooled African American children in the past (Foster, 1990), but it also ignores the fact that the communities were pleased with that education. Perhaps more significantly, this lack of knowledge also results in ahistorical approaches to school reform that deprive reformers of important contextual information that could directly impact the success or failure of select school programs. Such oversight could well decrease opportunities for African American children to succeed in today's schools.

I premise this article on the idea that segregated schools that were valued by their communities did exist, and that understanding more about the nature of those schools is important for historical accuracy and for educational reform. As I discuss below, I believe that understanding the history of education in these schools, as well as the types of parent and community participation that were present, will facilitate our ability to ask the right questions as we tackle current reform issues. This is preferable to focusing on questions that are premised on negative assumptions about African American communities.

With this in mind, I present the case of CCTS, the segregated Negro school described earlier. Situated in North Carolina's rural Caswell County, CCTS was a self- and community-defined "good" school. The belief that their school provided a good environment for learning was shared by its graduates, parents, and teachers. This belief is documented in the school's written and oral history, and remains generally consistent throughout most of its existence. In this article, I accept the community's evaluation of CCTS as a good school. I make no effort to argue that by traditional criteria, such as test scores or college attendance rates, CCTS represents the best in segregated schools in the South, or even in its region. Importantly, my description of why CCTS was perceived as a good school is not meant to validate the inequities or minimize the discrimination that existed in this and other segregated schools, where parents were overly burdened to create for themselves the educational facilities and opportunities school boards often denied them (Anderson, 1988; Bullock, 1967). Rather, I offer this case as representative of the many other southern African American schools whose communities were also pleased with their schools, but whose histories have been lost and whose value is understood now only by former teachers, principals, parents, and students.

This case, ethnographically approached, uses eighty open-ended interviews with former teachers, students, parents, and administrators, to uncover the themes of the school's goodness, and also to explore the nature of the relationships within the school environment that explain that goodness.[3] To reduce the influence of interviewee nostalgia, school documents such as yearbooks, school newspapers, handbooks, and so forth, as well as newspaper accounts, minutes of school board meetings, Southern Association reports, and other archival materials are used to corroborate emerging themes. The knowledge base derived from a triangulation of documents with interviews is used in this article to analyze one area little explored in segregated schooling — that is, the nature of the relationship between community and school. Within the context of this discussion, "community" refers to all of the African American adults who lived within the forty-square-mile county and who shared a real or imagined bond with CCTS. While some of the adults lived within the town in which the school was located, and thereby had more than the usual informal contact with the principal and teachers at the churches, stores, and other incidental meeting places, this discussion is not confined to their relationship with the school. It also incorporates the feeling of relationship and perspective of those adults who lived outside the town. Thus, the community was not defined by physical proximity. In this article, I focus specifically on the ways in which this community and CCTS supported each other. I further explore the significance of these activities, both in their historical context and in their implications vis-à-vis current advocacy for more involvement of African American parents in their children's education.

The Case in Historical Context: African Americans in Traditional Modes of Support

CCTS did not always boast the facilities or programs it enjoyed in 1969, the year it ceased to operate as a high school. Indeed, like most other segregated schools, its history was one of financial struggle, broken promises, delayed response from White school authorities, and financial burdens on its students and parents. It began as a small elementary school in a two-story house purchased by several prominent Negro citizens in 1906.[4] In the 1924–1925 school year, it expanded to a four-room "Rosenwald" structure, which teachers and community patrons had contributed $800 to complete.[5] Having previously been denied permission to expand the school beyond the seventh grade, community patrons, under the leadership of newly arrived Principal Dillard, were able in 1934 to add a high school attended by seventy-seven students, many of whom had to travel twenty

---

[3] "Open-ended interviews" is a term used to describe a questioning format that allows the researcher to ask for facts about the matter under discussion, as well as to ask the interviewee's opinion about the facts. This method was used in conjunction with Spradley's (1979) suggestions for the "ethnographic interview," which describes specific procedures to tap the knowledge base of a participant in a culture scene. Interviews lasted usually from 60 to 90 minutes; participants represented varying regions of the community and varying degrees of involvement in the school.

[4] Under a fund set up by Julius Rosenwald in 1917, Negro patrons received matching funds for any monetary or other contributions they could make towards the building of schools for Negro children. Records indicate that Caswell County school patrons participated in this program, and that their school, like the 5000 others built in the South before 1948, was known as a "Rosenwald" school. This name, of course, detracts attention from the numerous contributions made by Negro parents and educators. This emphasis on the program rather than the parents is more fully discussed by Anderson (1988).

[5] Although I refer here to the first known building, the education of Negro children in the area precedes the purchase of a school building in Yanceyville in 1906. The North Carolina Session of 1897, for example, notes the incorporation of the "Yanceyville Colored Graded School" for the education of the colored children. Moreover, the oral history records the existence of church schools throughout the area in the late 1800s.

miles to school on an open-air truck. The truck was donated by a parent, Ulysses Jones, who operated it at a loss for two years, before finally donating it to the state as collateral for the new truck the PTA promised to supply. Meanwhile, another parent, T. S. Lea, paid the electric bill, and others who had dug an unauthorized well were not reimbursed by the school board for their expenses.

Although by 1938 the over-crowded school housed six hundred children in fewer than ten rooms, and a "colored citizen [had] offered to donate to the county nine-and-a-half acres of land as a site for a new school" (Newbold, 1935), the community was forced to wait thirteen years before the new facility was completed.[6] This delay can be attributed in part to the school board's self-description of being "hindered in the making and completing of their plans by lack of sufficient funds" (School Board Minutes, November 3, 1941). However, the minutes also suggest that the county was initially unwilling to use local resources for the building of a Negro school. Further, even after local resources were appropriated, the building needs of the Negro children were merged with those of two other schools for White children.

In the meantime, while the school board passed four resolutions affirming its commitment to build a new school, Negro parents continued to provide resources for the twenty-two teachers and 735 pupils who were part of the school by the 1948–1949 school year. The 1949 yearbook notes that "while the building does not yet satisfy our patrons, they are proud of its equipment." This equipment included modern tablet arm chairs; instructional supplies, including audio-visual aids such as radios, a movie projector, a 35-mm projector, and a wire recorder; and other items they considered important for education, but which the school board refused to supply. The academically oriented school curriculum was complemented by an award-winning debate team, a band (the first in any Caswell County high school), a newspaper, and other student organizations (Caswell County, 1949).

In March of 1951, when the students and teachers finally moved into the twenty-seven-room facility described by the local paper as "modern in every respect," the new building reflected the tremendous community support that was part of its history. While the county contributed $80,000 toward the cost of the $325,000 state-funded project, the Negro citizens themselves added close to $8,000 in equipment, almost a tenth of the cost the county expended, to create the kind of facility they had envisioned in 1949 — "a physical plant second to none in the state" (Caswell County, 1949). Among the items added were an $1,800 stage curtain and colored footlights, $3,000 worth of venetian blinds for the windows, a $400 time clock to regulate classes automatically, and a $2,000 public-address system ("Dedication," 1951). The money for these items was contributed by students, parents, and other community supporters.

Between 1951 and 1969, parents continued to support the financial needs of CCTS, supplying such items as band uniforms and instruments, science equipment, a piano, and workbooks. While they engaged in many fundraising activities during those years, the most consistent and most remembered was the Popularity

---

[6] This information is based upon a letter recorded in the school board minutes from N. C. Newbold, director of the Negro Division of Education, to Holland McSwain, Superintendent of Caswell County Schools. The letter itself is dated August 29, 1938; the letter is recorded in the school board minutes under the meeting for September 5, 1938.

Contest. In this annual event, each high school class nominated a king and queen; members of the class, with the participation of parents and other community leaders, then raised money to support their nominees. In the heyday of this event, records indicate that the winning class alone contributed as much as $1,410.35 to support the school. In February of 1969, however, things began to change: Principal Dillard died unexpectedly in the midst of planning desegregation, and that fall the school was reorganized as a fully integrated junior high. After these two events, Negro parents ceased all such financial assistance to the school.

Considering a rural community where, in 1953, 58 percent of the parents were farmers, 23 percent homemakers, 6 percent laborers, and 8 percent service and domestic workers, there is a temptation to view the CCTS community's financial contributions to the school as exceptional. Their self-reliance, sacrifice, and sense of community responsibility not only created ongoing support for the school, but also provided their children with a model for the role interested parents should play. Their commitment insured that continuous resources would be provided for the education of Black children, despite the lack of adequate support from the all-White school board. Yet, the sacrifices, self-help, and support of these CCTS patrons were typical of Negroes in many communities in the South during this era. This story of self-help for segregated schools has been most notably described and analyzed by Anderson (1988), who emphasizes the fact that, although such help was helpful in improving school conditions, it also was oppressive in that it imposed a "double taxation" on Negro citizens. According to Anderson, "rural Blacks in particular were victims of [this] taxation without representation" (p. 156). They were often forced to "take from their meager annual incomes and contribute money to the construction and maintenance of public schools for the Black child because southern state and local governments refused to accept responsibility for Black public education" (p. 176). In other words, Black parents paid taxes for services they did not receive. The history of CCTS lends additional evidence to Anderson's thesis.

What has been less often discussed, however, are the other avenues of parental support that existed in segregated school environments. Although CCTS grew significantly between 1933 and 1969, the nature of the relationship between school and community remained consistent. In addition to providing financial support, parents at CCTS 1) maintained a physical presence in the school, primarily through the Parent Teachers Association (PTA) and other events to which they were invited; 2) played an "advocacy" role for the school in soliciting funds from the school board; and 3) provided invisible home-based support for the principal and teachers.

Parents in the School: Other Avenues of Community Support

In the CCTS environment, the PTA functioned as an umbrella organization that took the lead in providing financial contributions to the school, and also provided other opportunities for parental involvement in school activities. Perhaps the most obvious facet of this involvement was parents' attendance at PTA meetings. While exact attendance figures are not available, former teacher Helen Beasley remembers:

I don't know how many folks we *didn't* have at PTA! Good gracious. If the auditorium wasn't filled up, it was maybe like three-fourths. That great big auditorium would be three-fourths full with the mamas and daddies and the brothers and the sisters and the grandmamas and the aunts, and the uncles and whoever.

Though not all informants are as enthusiastic in their memories of the number of people attending and often focus instead on whether there should have been even more, they do report that the auditorium was frequently filled to capacity as Beasley relates. In absolute numbers, PTA attendance was less in earlier years, when parents were more likely to sit around a pot-bellied stove rather than gather in a formal setting; nevertheless, participation was reportedly high, especially given the distance parents had to travel and the lack of automobiles. When parents did not attend, it was usually because of transportation problems or conflicting work schedules. Lack of interest in the school or a feeling of alienation were seldom the reasons given for their absence.

Several activities were consistently part of the business portion of the PTA meeting. First, parents received reports about the school's financial and educational status. Since one of the PTA's primary missions was to help supply the school's needs, the financial report often involved the president or the principal outlining the most pressing needs. Based on these reports, parents organized collaborative plans of action with teachers and the principal, and actively engaged in completing the projects. These activities typically included overseeing a teacher's homeroom activities and reporting on that class's participation, or joining in a parent-teacher basketball game. Parents who were not active in planning often provided support by attending an event, and supplying or buying items on sale there.

The principal also regularly used a portion of the meeting to report to the parents about education, what was going on in the school such as problems drivers were having on buses, or ways in which parents could help their children succeed academically. He also reviewed his expectations for the children, the school policies, and the events planned for the year. Parents who recall Dillard's PTA reports remember how interested he was in the children. Says one parent: "[Having every child succeed] — that was his main priority."

Dillard also shared with parents his experiences at any national or regional meetings he had attended. His teachers, who were required to join their professional organization and urged to attend non-local meetings, were also expected to report to parents during this segment of PTA meetings. Today CCTS parents describe little about the educational trends that were discussed during those times, but they still remember the jokes Dillard was famous for collecting and sharing with them.

In addition to the PTA business reports and discussions, parents could also expect entertainment and refreshments. This entertainment came from various high school groups or elementary classes, who were assigned a time in the school year to make a presentation to the PTA. Teachers often repeated for the PTA the assembly programs they were periodically scheduled to have in Chapel.[7]

[7] Chapel was a weekly gathering of the principal, teachers, and students, where student talent was showcased and where the principal used the time to talk to the students about pressing issues, such as life, discipline, or any other topic he felt compelled to address. While religious services were not the

Since few parents saw these programs during Chapel, they usually played to a new audience. The refreshments that were served afterward to cast, teachers, and parents were supplied by the PTA.

When the formal portion of the PTA meetings ended, the informal talk between teachers and parents began. According to parent Dorothy Graves, these informal talks, during which the parents could find out how their children were doing in school, were among the primary reasons they went to PTA. She explains:

> You didn't go to the schools during the day or after school to talk about your children. You didn't go in unless there was a problem and the principal called you in. The time during the school day was allotted for the teaching of the student. Parents just didn't go in to school and disturb a teacher. [The teachers would say], tell your parents to come to PTA.

These informal conversations between teachers and parents sometimes took place in the classrooms, at other times in different areas of the auditorium. Most conversations began with the parent's single question: "How is my child doing?" If the teacher responded "fine," little else would be said, other than the parent perhaps saying, "Now you let me know if there's a problem." Or if there was a problem, the teacher might consult her rollbook and say, "Jeff is doing fine in English; however, he needs to work on his math." Such informal conversations continued until each parent had the opportunity to speak to every teacher he or she wished to see. Since teachers were required to attend PTA meetings, said one parent, "there was never any worry that [your child's teacher] wouldn't be there."

Besides attending the regular monthly meetings, some PTA members implemented planned tasks, such as preparing appreciation dinners for the teachers or continuing their ongoing fundraising activities. They referred to this as "working along with the teachers," and valued the time as an opportunity to get to know each other. Parents also attended major school functions, filling the auditorium for the concerts held by the high school choir and band every Christmas and spring, and the annual "operettas" held by the primary and upper elementary schools. A few parents were also involved in some classroom functions, such as providing food and setting up for a class Christmas or end-of-year party, supervising the Maypole dances in preparation for field day, or, in the case of at least one teacher, assisting in classroom instruction by playing educational games with the children. Reports indicate that parents on all socioeconomic levels were likely to participate in the events, if they were asked.

What is central to the nature of this parental presence at CCTS is the key phrase, "if asked." For example, Nellie Williamson, the teacher who had parents play educational games with the children, emphasizes that "not many did this"; those who did, she says, did so "because she had a conversation with them individually." Thus, parents who helped in the classroom or assisted with other events, were responding to teachers' notes or oral invitations. PTA meetings and student performances were other events to which parents had invitations. Says Janie Richmond, a former student and later an elementary school teacher, "the

---

focus of the gathering, talk often emphasized moral values that were consistent with the values held by the community.

184

parents supported the school" and came whenever you asked them, but they didn't schedule parent-teacher conferences, or volunteer to assist with tutoring, or concern themselves with other areas of classroom instruction. Long-time English teacher Chattie Boston concurs that "parents left curricula concerns to the teachers." The data suggest both are correct, as parents never describe themselves as having initiated visits to the school to observe or to discuss any curricular concerns. Some parents, however, did assume a political role that might be termed "working for the school." This role of advocate was historically associated with the PTA leaders. These advocates positioned themselves between the school's needs and the oversight of the school board, and on numerous occasions lobbied for additional funding for the school. No records indicate that the White school board was hostile to the Negro patrons who sought their assistance; they were generally polite, even as they postponed and denied repeated requests for funding.[8]

The leadership role these parent advocates took in going before the board to lobby for the school is termed "working" for the school because the teachers and principal seldom appeared before the board. In the political climate of the era, those employed by the school system could expect to lose their jobs if they involved themselves in questions of equity. As one parent advocate recalls, "Dillard himself couldn't afford to come out. He was a very smart leader who knew how far they would let him go." A second parent recalls, "Mr. Dillard provided prompting on preparation, who to speak to. He would give you an idea. Usually [men] would go. They would go as a group and usually have one spokesman." This behind-the-scenes prompting most often occurred with farmers who owned their own land, preachers, or private business owners. While in the earlier years these were primarily men, documents and interviews from later periods indicate that women also assumed an advocacy role. What all advocates generally had in common was that they relied on other Negroes for their income, and thus did not need to fear repercussions from the White school board.

The role of parent advocates also extended beyond the county level. Records indicate that these citizens, like Dillard, made numerous trips to the state capital to seek assistance when their requests were denied on the local level. This was particularly true of their efforts in the early years of CCTS to see that a high school be established, and later, that a new one be built. In response to these visits, and as a part of his push to get the county to build a new school, the Director of the Division of Negro Education wrote the Caswell County school board requesting that an "adequate brick building be supplied" for the Negroes. He freely admitted that his urging was the result of having been "approached by a group of very intelligent colored citizens from [Caswell] County."[9]

---

[8] The board's receptivity did, as may be expected, increase in the 1950s and 1960s. This may be attributed in part to the aftermath of the *Brown* decision, when the county sought to be certain that all its Negro schools were "equal." However, the parents also credit the efforts of a new superintendent, Thomas Whitley, whom they characterized as a "fair" man who was willing to go "as far as he could go" to promote equity.

[9] In 1921, the Negro Division of Education was established by Legislative Act in the state of North Carolina. Although headed by a White agent, the director, N. C. Newbold, has been credited with helping to "set in motion the development and standardization of secondary schools" in North Carolina (Brown, 1960, p. 49). The school board minutes in Caswell County indicate that through both letters and meetings with the board, Newbold was instrumental in pressuring the county to address the needs of the Negro community.

The importance of this advocacy role over the years was recognized and appreciated not only by other parents, but also by the students. Consider their commendation of three parents in the opening pages of the 1960 yearbook:

> The annual certainly would be incomplete if the seniors failed to salute the successful efforts of these three patrons in obtaining a modern physical education building for the school. Over a three year period they continuously appeared before the Board of Education in behalf of a new physical education building. Time and time again they made appeals and, needless to say, at times they were disappointed, but not enough to ever cease their efforts. Soon, thanks to them, this facility will be available. The students and patrons of C.C.T.S. shall ever remember with gratitude their untiring efforts. Again we salute you, Mrs. Bigelow, Mrs. Saylor, and Mrs. Little. Words will never express our appreciation.

The passage is accompanied by a portrait of the three women. While other CCTS yearbooks do not contain such elaborate expressions of appreciation, special thank you's to parents for their assistance frequently appeared in dedications and in class histories.

Perhaps the most consistent way parents supported the school — even those who never participated in PTA or related activities or assumed the role of advocate — was accomplished without the parents ever leaving home. They instilled in their children a respect for teachers, which carried with it an expectation of obedience. Says parent Nannie Evans, "I would always tell my child, 'when you go to school, remember you are supposed to obey your teachers just like you obey me at home.'"

These attitudes about obedience led students to believe that if they were punished at school for an offense, they could expect additional punishment at home. In the words of one student: "I knew not to get sent home for anything. If I did, I knew my daddy was going to whoop me good — not spank — but whoop me. I knew not to try to get into trouble." And if a child did get into trouble at school, the parent's likely response to the teacher was, "Well, if he doesn't do well, you just let me know again."

This "home training," as southern African Americans are likely to call their parents' expectations of them, reinforced school policies and provided a solid mechanism of invisible support. While the disciplinary skills of the CCTS principal and teachers will not be discussed in this article, I will point out that demands on their disciplinary skills were lessened by this seldom-articulated, yet forceful parental support. Thus, parent and school were united in their expectations of the students. As one student described the relationship: "My mommy and daddy are pushing me and my teachers are pushing me . . . oh well, I got to do good."

School Supports Community

CCTS parents provided financial and physical support, advocacy, and home-front support. From the vantage point of current advocates of parental involvement (see, for example, Henderson 1987, 1988; Rich, 1987), the parents' degree of activity might not be considered unusual. However, given the current lack of involvement of many African American parents in schools (Henderson, 1987), the degree of their support is exceptional. To what might their level of involvement be attributed?

186

Several explanations are possible. As Lightfoot (1978, 1981) has noted, African Americans have traditionally believed in the importance of education, and have made sacrifices to be certain that their children had opportunities to achieve in school. That parents valued education and therefore contributed to the support of CCTS is corroborated by records from other elementary schools scattered throughout Caswell County, where parents were also active in PTA and other school events. Thus, the parental response at CCTS might well have been the public manifestation of the parents' private beliefs about the importance of education. Another equally compelling reason for the relationship between CCTS and parents in later years might relate to existing community ties. As many parents point out, they had known Principal Dillard themselves as children, when they attended school under his leadership; they had also gone to school with some of the teachers. Therefore, school personnel were not strangers, but rather people with whom they already had a relationship.

Though parents' belief in education and the existence of community ties are both important factors in understanding the parents' relationship to the school, they offer an insufficient explanation for the levels of support provided by parents. Teachers who had not grown up in the county, for example, were equally accepted, supported, and welcomed by parents, as was Dillard, even in his early years. According to Inez Blackwell, a parent and former student, this was because new teachers quickly made themselves known to the community. "They were never stuck up," she says. "Within months," Blackwell notes, "it seemed like they had been here all the time." Thus, teachers who had previous ties with the community had little advantage over those who came into the county. Moreover, though African American parents today still believe in the power of education, their belief does not evoke the responses described at CCTS. Perhaps a more compelling explanation for the consistency of support from parents at CCTS lies in the manner in which the school reached out to and supported the parents.

For example, in his weekly Chapel talks with the students, Principal Dillard was heard to say on more than one occasion: "I'm not going to let you come up here and wear your mama and daddy's clothes out and they're out there working hard for you and you're up here doing nothing." The band director, Leonard Tillman, recalls the admonishments students received in the classroom:

> I used to tell my kids — Miss Ann doesn't need anyone to cook for them anymore. ["Miss Ann" was a term used by Negroes to describe White women who had servants.] They got frozen foods. All they got to do is throw them in the oven. Don't you think you need to stay here and get this education?

In their talks with students, the principal and teachers assumed the posture of protectors of the parents' sacrifices, and their frequent reminders of the need to get an education echoed parents' aspirations for their children.

The school also actively assisted parents. For students who wanted to go on to college, this assistance included helping them fill out forms, providing financial aid, traveling with students to campuses, and in some cases giving advice on what would be expected in college. As Aleane Rush, former student, and later president of the state teachers' association, remembers:

> [Mr. Dillard] would try to help students. . . . He would refer them personally to college contacts, friends; he was very helpful in trying to see that they would leave

Caswell County with the appropriate kind of clothing. Remember I said he knew his students. So, he would not feel intimidated, nor would the student if he said, "Now Vanessa, you can not go to Shaw with those kind of shoes on. . . . You will be in college and you are coming from CCTS, remember that. And you've got to represent yourself, your family, and your community." And when he spoke of community, he was speaking of Caswell County. And parents of those students were very, very appreciative.

In some cases, as in that of teacher and former student Deborah Fuller, the principal actually accompanied the student and parents on their first trip to a campus, functioning as mediator between the family's aspirations and the unknown expectations of college admissions. Teachers also engaged in these sorts of supportive activities, providing financial assistance through their teachers' clubs and, more frequently, offering the encouragement a student needed to go to college. Irvine and Irvine (1984) have characterized this behavior most succinctly:

> Black schools served as the instrument through which professional educators discharged their responsibility to their community. Black educators labored to help students realize their achievement goals. In this role both principals and teachers were mere but profound extensions of the interests of the Black community. (p. 417)

In effect, the authors note, parents and school had a "collective stake in the educational process of the youth in the community" (p. 419).

But the school's support was not only available for college-bound students. The principal and teachers also assumed responsibility for students who were having difficulty in school by working with the child and contacting parents about any problems. One parent remembers Principal Dillard telling her about her son's school behavior: "Well, he just loves to sometimes stand out in the hall and have a chance to go uptown." ("Uptown" is a local slang term used to refer to the town's small business district, which was located approximately one mile from the school.) Of Dillard's disciplinary approach and contact with her, this parent says, "I felt good because I felt like he was there with him and he was paying attention [to my child]." After describing the events of mischievousness that accompanied her son through his school years, she concludes, "But anyway, he finally finished . . . and I felt like Mr. Dillard had a great hand in that."

The school's protectiveness toward the children — going the extra mile to see that students succeeded — instilled in parents an adamant conviction that the teachers and principal really "cared about those children." In the words of Rachel Long, a farming parent who sent nine children through high school and college, "I think all those teachers were really close to those students. I know they were to my children." Her conviction echoes the sentiments of many. A former student, the Reverend Cephaus Lea, remembers Principal Dillard:

> He was never too busy to talk with you about your problems. Not only was he interested in you in school, he was interested when you left school. He knew all the children by name. He wasn't like some other people I've known. He loved people and he was concerned about you. And that's the kind of principal Mr. Dillard was.

While the influence of the school's ethic of caring is a story that I cannot explore fully in this discussion, I must note that parents' belief that the school cared about the success of their children might help explain the "respect" and "trust" that parents had toward CCTS and their support of it. In essence, in supporting the institution, the parents were directly supporting those responsible for the success of their children.

Principal Dillard's particular style of interacting with parents is another way that parents were drawn to CCTS. In effect, Dillard created a sense of "us" that *) uß* helped to forge the collaboration between school and community. Though he was clearly the visionary, "he did not boast [about] what he did," says one parent. "He used to always say, 'we're working together. See what we can do if we work together.' But he never did say what *he* did." This style of interaction was probably carefully chosen. In the traditional African American community, the "educated" are often viewed with suspicion if they are perceived as "above" the other members of the community; thus Dillard's approach represented an important way of reaching out, and conveyed to community members his respect for their contributions.

Perhaps the most striking way in which the school reached out was in its willingness to meet the parents on their own turf. Dillard, for example, was an avid member of community organizations and would often walk to town after school was out and take the time to talk with farmers gathered on the corner. He sang in the local choir, attended both the Methodist and Baptist churches, and frequently visited the rural churches and the homes of parents who lived out in the country. Says one parent:

> He visited my home a lot of times. He would get around. Then another thing he would do — if his children's [relatives] or somebody passed, he would try to make it to the churches to the funerals. He had a closeness to people.

Valuing community members apparently was an important part of Dillard's philosophy. Even "from the beginning, he worked with the community," reports teacher and former student Janie Richmond, whose mother worked actively in the creation of the first PTA. "Whatever project they put on, he was very diligent in working with them — picnics, fishing trips, etc. His being present helped to draw other people."

It is important to note that Dillard also used his visits in the community as opportunities to communicate. Often when invited to speak in area churches, he would speak about his belief in the value of education. Thus, parents were apprised of the goals of the school and the needs of the children in their own communities, churches, and homes. These visits and talks were supplemented by frequent notes that children brought home with information about school events or classroom needs.

Dillard expected no less community involvement from his teachers. "I would hope you would be broad enough to attend some of the area churches," he was known to tell new faculty members. In essence, he expected that if they worked in the community, they should make themselves known and become part of it. He wanted teachers who were accessible to the average parent. He also expected teachers to visit the students' parents in their homes, whether or not a disciplinary problem had arisen. "If you could see the circumstances out of which the children have come," many teachers remember him saying, "you would understand better how to teach them."

And the teachers did go — both to the churches and the homes. Fifth-grade teacher Betty Royal remembers telling parents who opened the door to her knock, "I just happened to have been in the area and I thought I would just stop by and say hello." The parents generally responded positively to these unannounced visits, having been told to expect them at PTA meetings.

Reaching out to support parents occurred in other ways, too. The school offered adults classes in agriculture, typing, and sewing, and provided guidance and counseling for adults. The school also ranked itself highly on "providing community use of the school and facilities" (CCTS Faculty, 1950). From the parents' perspective, however, the school's interest in their children's development and the teachers' community visits are the ways of reaching out that are most remembered and most valued.

Significance of School and Community Interactions in the Historical Context

Long-time residents of this Caswell County community who participated in the CCTS culture remember the interaction between school and community as a collaborative relationship, a kind of mutual ownership in which the community and school looked out for each others' needs — the parents depended on the school's expertise, guidance, and academic vision, and the school depended on the parents' financial contributions, advocacy, and home-front support. They were united in a common mission to provide a quality education for their children.

This relationship provides several important ideas to consider. While school and community members moved easily in and out of each other's domain, the participants were clear about the boundaries of their relationships. The parents' role was to attend school events, reinforce discipline at home, and to get their children to school. They also made economic sacrifices to allow their able-bodied offspring to go to school rather than keeping them home to help "take in the crop." When the students went home in the afternoon, parents made sure the children had time to do their lessons. As one student remembers, "[Our] parents didn't have any education, but after you finished your work and chores, they knew to tell you to sit down and get your lesson." The teachers' and principal's reciprocal role was to exercise authority in the school environment and address issues of curriculum and instruction.

The strength of the respect for these boundaries was reinforced by its presence across economic and class lines. For example, even teachers who had children in the classrooms of other teachers did not discuss curriculum or help their children with homework. In fact, the attitude that the teacher was completely in charge of the child once in the classroom was reflected in private conversations with their coworkers. Said one teacher, "I've got my classroom to see to. If anything happens, you do the punishing. I don't have anything to do with it." Like other parents, these teachers did support the punishment given by their child's teacher by reinforcing discipline at home. However, they did not interfere with the teacher or class activities within the school.

Unlike current situations in which parents and schools disagree about how they should support one another (Henderson, 1987), in the CCTS environment, participants shared common expectations. The distinct roles minimized conflict between school and community, as all interaction was defined by mutually accepted boundaries of authority.

Also significant are the opportunities for, and the positive nature of, the communication that was possible in the CCTS environment — unlike interaction today, in which talk between teachers and parents is almost uniformly negative, and parents indicate that they only hear from the school when there is a problem (Lightfoot, 1978; Swap, 1987). The school's fund-raising activities, for example, created opportunities for parents, the principal, and teachers to discuss how to achieve their common goals. Moreover, during some fund-raising activities, opportunities existed for role-reversal between administration and members of the school community. For example, if parents were assigned to oversee participation in a particular classroom, it meant that the teacher looked to the parents for assistance. This created a sense of teamwork and reinforced the idea that parents and teachers could both be authorities — even if they exercised power in different domains. Thus, the creation of teamwork between teacher and parent was a direct outcome of the fund-raising activity.

Also important to the school-community relationship were the informal interactions maintained outside of school. When teachers visited the churches, parents were likely to invite them to other services, such as a revival or church homecoming, and teachers in turn used these opportunities to invite parents to particular activities at the school. Students' work was not necessarily discussed in these incidental interactions.

The opportunity to engage in dialogue both in the school environment and in the community was important to the community-school relationship, but it would not have succeeded had not the principal and teachers known how to talk to the parents. Parent Marie Richmond confirms this:

> I heard [Mr. Dillard] say it so many times. He would say, "When you are in a situation, you don't go in there using a lot of big words and you know the people can't understand you.". . . He wasn't one of these people that kept so high up that he couldn't get in where a person was and understand him. I think that's why people loved him so. You could relate to him. But when you go into a place . . . and are so high and mighty, parents would stay away from you, because they feel like you think you are better than they are because maybe they didn't get any schooling. But if you know how to mix, and they feel comfortable with you, they will work with you.

The ability to adapt his language to the demands of a situation is a talent for which Dillard is consistently credited; he told his son he learned it in his job as an insurance salesman after graduating from college. Of the teachers, parents also said, "They knew how to talk to you, and that made a big difference."

The "difference" was that, when parents had the opportunity to talk with teachers and the principal, both in and out of school, they were positive exchanges in which teachers and principal communicated with language parents could appreciate and respect. That is, they used the language of the parent, adopting informal forms of language and styles of communication that created an atmosphere in which parents did not feel intimidated to speak.

This atmosphere of respect also created a positive environment for handling more sensitive problems. Teachers or the principal could begin a difficult discussion with positive comments about a child, because they knew the children so well, understood their family circumstances, and likely had some interaction with someone in the family. Moreover, because of the opportunities for positive informal talk and the school's proactive role in its relationship with parents, the parents did not view the teacher or principal as always being the bearer of bad news about their child, which diminished the potential for hostility or animosity.

The nature of the community-school relationship, strengthened by the principal's personal characteristics, eased tensions when differences did occur. English teacher Chattie Boston recalls that, if a parent came in upset over a perceived injustice done to his or her child, "Mr. Dillard didn't get excited. If the parent was excited, Mr. Dillard listened and let them talk. He let them get it off their chest." Then, she says, "he would explain the situation and when [the parent] left, everybody would be buddy-buddy."

This personal style of settling conflicts was impossible when the disagreement involved larger concerns, such as choosing a location for the new school. Such differences were resolved through an open meeting where both sides had opportunities to air their concerns, and the final decision was made by voting. But even when the community-school relationship was not completely tranquil, the dissonance did not destroy their working relationship or the individual respect between parents, the teachers, and the principal.

Segregation in Retrospect: Issues and Challenges for Today

The nature of the relationship I have described between CCTS and its community suggests some valuable lessons for education today. One suggestion is a possible change in the definition of parental involvement. Although parental involvement has been defined by researchers in a number of ways (Henderson, 1987, 1988; Rich, 1987; Swap, 1987), for purposes of this discussion, consider a definition offered by Hoover-Dempsey, Bassler, and Brissie (1987), who define parent involvement in their child's school as including: 1) parent-teacher conferences; 2) parent involvement in classroom volunteer work; 3) parent involvement in tutoring at home, such as assisting with homework; and 4) parent involvement in carrying out home-instruction programs designed or suggested by teachers to supplement regular classroom instruction (p. 423). In each of these cases, parents initiate and/or are involved in complementing the curriculum and instruction provided by the teacher.

Current definitions of parent involvement, however, do not explain the kind of support the CCTS parents demonstrated. They did not have formal parent-teacher conferences as they are now defined; they did not volunteer unless they were specifically asked; and they did not tutor at home or carry out home-instruction programs.

By current definitions, then, these parents could be deemed failures. One wonders, then, if African American parents and White teachers and school leaders are operating out of different frameworks for parental involvement. Perhaps schools apply dominant cultural definitions of good parental involvement, such as those described by Hoover-Dempsey, Bassler, and Brissie (1987), while African American parents lean towards more traditional perceptions and modes of interaction, such as those practiced at CCTS.

To explore this possibility, consider the comment of Dorothy Graves, a Black parent who observed the CCTS parents when they first attended PTA meetings after court-ordered integration began in Caswell County in the fall of 1969:

> You just didn't see any teachers hardly. What few teachers came said, "you don't walk up to teachers and ask how your child is doing; you have a conference." They said we were not supposed to ask about any [concerns] about our children [in the presence of] anyone else. We were used to when we were there at the PTA meeting, we could just talk.

This parent further explains that PTA meetings after integration seemed to focus more on bringing in resource people than dealing with the problems of the students. She notes that before integration, the students were the primary focus for PTA meetings — either discussing their needs and jointly devising plans of action, and/or watching their performances before the PTA. After integration, she remembers that less attention was paid to students and that there was more of a focus on procedures. She sums up the differences by adding, "I guess this was their method. [It seems] when we integrated we went into using their pattern and not our pattern."

This difference in handling the PTA meetings suggests that after integration a cultural mismatch occurred between school personnel and parents on at least two levels. First, for parents accustomed to using the PTA to talk informally with teachers, the absence of many teachers and the directives by those present to schedule a conference represented a system for interacting with teachers that was not familiar to Black parents. While the data are not available to document the response of Black parents to this new system, it is worth noting that Dorothy Graves, the parent quoted above, recalls scheduling only one conference after integration, as compared to monthly meetings with teachers before integration.

In addition to creating new expectations of the appropriate way to relate to teachers, the focus of the PTA in the integrated system also was perceived by Black parents to change. At the segregated PTA meetings, parents expected to discuss the needs of the school and to see their children perform — both activities that contributed to the importance of attending PTA meetings. In the integrated system, they describe a system where "your part was already outlined and you just went through the procedure." PTA was thus transformed from a parent-school gathering where meaningful input was expected, to meetings that became the "contrived occasions" that Lightfoot (1978) describes.

The data are not available to argue that the failure of African American parents today to volunteer, to schedule parent/teacher conferences, and so forth is the result of historical differences in definitions of involvement. However, the forms of support demonstrated at CCTS suggest that it is at least possible that historical models of parental involvement may differ from current definitions, and that this may be one area to consider in efforts to understand African American parents, failure to conform to expectations about school involvement. The failure to consider the possible influence of conflicting expectations about roles may result in parents, especially African American parents, being labeled deficient and uncaring.

Consider further the current literature on parental involvement, which emphasizes the parents' desire to be involved in school decisionmaking. According to Henderson (1987), "Educators, tend to relegate parents to insubstantial bake sale roles, leaving parents feeling frustrated, belittled, and left out" (p. 2). Yet the CCTS parents did not express a desire to have input in the school's curriculum decisionmaking. The same is true in Sowell's (1976) descriptions of other historically Black schools:

> The interest of the teachers in the students was reciprocated by the interest of the parents in supporting the teachers and the school. . . . Parental involvement was of this supportive nature rather than an actual involvement in school decision making (p. 36).

Sowell's finding is consistent with the type of support CCTS parents offered, and their parallel lack of discussion of curricular matters. This is not to say that parents should not now be involved in such decisionmaking. However, making decisions on curricular matters may not be a traditional parental role valued within the African American community, where community and school shared similar values and where parents trusted the teachers and principal to create the best learning environments for their children.

Moreover, while the current literature on parental involvement denigrates the bake sale and the ritualistic PTAs (Henderson, 1987, 1988), CCTS parents found comfortable avenues of support through such activities. Perhaps the value of these activities, especially their ability to create ownership and pride in the school, should be explored before they are unilaterally dismissed as trivial functions. Swap (1987) has advocated having refreshments at PTA meetings and using children in the program as examples of incentives that schools might use to help initiate parental involvement in school functions. Both of these activities made useful contributions to the CCTS PTA meetings, so perhaps the CCTS examples suggest extending the parent-school relationship beyond some current practices.

Two other ideas should also be briefly considered. The data suggest that the community-school relationship is a two-way process, that involvement should not be defined simply as how to bring the parents into the school, but also how the school can be "in" the community. It was CCTS's outreach to the community that prompted the parents to "reach in" to the school. While some studies have considered the positive results of home visits (Olmstead, 1983, cited in Tangri & Moles, 1987), too little has been done to create schools with positive attitudes toward the community, both in terms of the school's general outreach and the attitude of individual teachers. School reform leaders might do well to remember the CCTS example, and to consider ways that teachers and principal can become advocates for, rather than adversaries in, their students' communities.

Schools might also consider the benefits of implementing activities that communicate to parents a sense of caring about their children. The response of CCTS parents to their school should not be considered atypical; people generally respond well to those they believe are concerned about their loved ones. When people, or communities, perceive that this caring is no longer present, they respond with mistrust. Thus, it should not be surprising that many African American parents are now distrustful of schools in which their offspring are the ones most often punished, most frequently on the lower tracks (Braddock, 1995), most likely to have the least successful teachers (Darling-Hammond, 1995), and most likely to feel alienated and drop out of school. This care ethic would seem to be as crucial to conversations about how to induce parental involvement as is advocacy for parental voice on curricular matters.

Can all ideas applied at CCTS transfer simply and easily to today's schools? Indeed they cannot. CCTS functioned in a uniquely closed society in which the school for the Black community was one of the two major social, cultural, and educational centers, the church being the other. Together these centers served to counteract the effects of racism in a segregated society. Since that era, the nature of problems confronting children has changed, as has the structure of families. The 1990 U.S. Census Bureau, for example, indicates that Black children are less likely to live with two parents today than they were in 1967, and that families are now more likely to be polarized between the well-educated and the poor. Moreover, crack, AIDS, and guns are the serious issues confronting school personnel, as compared with alcohol, smoking, and truancy during the era of CCTS.

What we can gain from the case of CCTS is a deeper understanding of what African Americans valued in their schools during legal segregation, an understanding of the community-school relationships that allowed for the school's successful operation, and a series of ideas about school-community interaction that might spur thinking on how to achieve similar ends in new contexts. Moreover, the CCTS case provides an important framework within which to consider current problems of school reform. For example, understanding the various possibilities for parental involvement may lead to more appropriate questions when considering how to link schools and communities. A question asked frequently about African American parents in reform meetings I have attended is, "How can we get them to become involved with the school?" a question that suggests that parents have never been involved and are generally uninterested. Yet, as the evidence demonstrates, these poor, rural parents were very much involved, when one applies their definition of involvement. They only ceased to be so when the schools integrated. Thus, perhaps a more appropriate question is, "Why did they stop supporting schools and what can be done to eliminate the barriers so they will come back?" These different questions suggest a variety of different answers and strategies. Only by asking the right questions, however, are we likely to find answers that will result in meaningful and lasting solutions.

The CCTS case also suggests an agenda for new research questions: for example, how do African American parents currently view the schools? Are there still "invisible" ways they support the school that are generally unknown and unappreciated? Are African American parents and schools operating from the same expectations about appropriate community-school interactions? To what extent has the advocacy role ceased, or is it operative in other ways? For example, at the school level, do African American parents have a mode of advocacy that creates dissonance, rather than collaboration, between parents and administrators? Is it possible that the level at which they protest treatment of their children has moved from the school board to the teachers and principal in the school itself?

Serious consideration of these and other questions about the relationship between African American parents and their children's schools is important for enlightened educational policy and agendas. Seeking answers to these questions is also important in restoring voice to African American educators and parents, whose knowledge has been devalued and whose opinions have been silenced since the onset of integration (Foster, 1990; Irvine & Irvine, 1984). Most importantly, documenting the nature of community-school relationships in the segregated school is important because it begins to correct the commonly held misperception that those schools were without any merit, and that educators have nothing to learn from them. The correction of this misperception is long overdue.

REFERENCES

Adair, A. A. (1984). *Desegregation: The illusion of black progress.* Lanham, MD: University Press of America.

Anderson, J. D. (1988). *The education of blacks in the south.* Chapel Hill: University of North Carolina Press.

Brown, H. V. (1960). *A history of the education of Negroes in North Carolina.* Raleigh, NC: Irving Swain Press.

Braddock, J. H. (1995). Tracking, literacy, and minority status. In V. Gadsden & D. Wagner (Eds.), *Literacy among African American youth: Issues in learning, teaching, and schooling.* Norwood, NJ: Ablex.

Bullock, H. A. (1967). *A history of Negro education in the south.* Cambridge, MA: Harvard University Press.

Caswell County Training School PTA: 1924–1948. (1949). In *Caswell County Training School Yearbook, 1949.*

CCTS Faculty. (1950). *Evaluative criteria* (Washington Cooperative Study of Secondary School Standards).

Cecelski, D. (1991). *The Hyde County School boycott: School desegregation and the fate of black schools in rural south, 1954–1969.* Unpublished doctoral dissertation, Harvard University, Cambridge, MA.

Clark, K. B. (1963). *Prejudice and your child.* Boston: Beacon Press.

Clift, V., Anderson, A., & Hullfish, H. (1962). *Negro education in America.* New York: Harper.

Darling-Hammond, L. (1995). Teacher quality and equality: Implications for literacy among black youth. In V. Gadsden & D. Wagner (Eds.), *Literacy among African American youth: Issues in learning, teaching, and schooling.* Norwood, NJ: Ablex.

Dedication of new Caswell County school will take place tomorrow. (1951, March). *Caswell Messenger,* p. 5.

Eighteen-member board of trustees named to direct private schools. (1969, February). *Caswell Messenger,* p. 1.

Foster, M. (1990). The politics of race: Through African American teachers' eyes. *Journal of Education, 172*(3), 123–141.

Henderson, A. T. (1987). *The evidence continues to grow: Parent involvement improves student achievement.* Columbia, MD: National Committee for Citizens in Education.

Henderson, A. T. (1988). Parents are a school's best friends. *Phi Delta Kappan, 70,* 148–153.

Hoover-Dempsey, O., Bassler, J., & Brissie, J. (1987). Parent involvement: Contributions of teacher efficacy, school socioeconomic status, and other school characteristics. *American Educational Research Journal, 24,* 417–435.

Irvine, R., & Irvine, J. (1984). The impact of the desegregation process on the education of black students: Key variables. *Journal of Negro Education, 52,* 410–422.

Jones, F. (1981). *A traditional model of educational excellence.* Washington, DC: Howard University Press.

Kluger, R. (1977). *Simple justice.* New York: Random House.

Lightfoot, S. L. (1978). *Worlds apart.* New York: Basic Books.

Lightfoot, S. L. (1981, Spring). Toward conflict and resolution: Relationships between families and schools. *Theory into Practice, 20,* 97–104.

Newbold, N. (1935). *Report of the governor's commission for the study of problems in the education of the Negro in North Carolina* (Publication No. 183). Raleigh, NC: State Superintendent of Public Instruction.

Rich, D. (1987). *Teachers and parents: An adult to adult approach.* Washington, DC: National Education Association.

Sowell, T. (1976). Patterns of black excellence. *The Public Interest, 43,* 26–58.

Spradley, T. P. (1979). The ethnographic interview. New York: Holt, Rinehart & Winston.

Swap, S. M. (1987). *Enhancing parent involvement in schools: A manual for parents and teachers.* New York: Teachers College Press.

Tangri, S., & Moles, O. (1987). Parents and the community. In V. Richardson-Kolher (Ed.), *Educator's handbook: A research perspective* (pp. 519–550). New York: Longman.

This research was supported through a Spencer Post-Doctoral Fellowship from the National Academy of Education. The author also acknowledges early research support provided by the Graduate School of Education at the University of Pennsylvania and continuing support provided by the University Research Committee at Emory University. Research assistants Trudy Blackwell and Evelyn Lavizzo aided in the data collection and processing.

197

When the Walls
Come Tumbling Down

PAULA LAWRENCE WEHMILLER

In this article, Paula Lawrence Wehmiller addresses the need for restructuring our schools in ways that encourage educational reform, the integration of school and community, and the building of covenants that take to heart the eradication of ignorance and the hierarchical trappings that prevent systemic change. This article is a revised version of the keynote address given by the author at the 1991 Country Conference for School Heads in Maryland, which was sponsored by the Association of Independent Maryland Schools and the Association of Independent Schools in Greater Washington.

There were no walls around our two-room schoolhouse. The noisy old school bus came to a grinding stop at the side of Old English Church Road. As he reached for the big silver lever that unfolded the door, Mr. Gurky, our cranky but faithful driver, looked into the rearview mirror, adjusted his grey cap, and searched in the dim reflection of his charges for offenders of his unspoken rule: big guys stay seated; little children out first. Rule-breakers had to give him a half of their sandwich. Bobby Babcock once made him an eggshell sandwich and broke the rule on purpose.

My sister and brother and I had walked the mile of uphill road to the highway to catch the bus. As we passed the houses of our agemates, we separated into packs — packs of boys, packs of girls, packs of threes and fours. My best friend Gretch and I were the only ones our age from the far end of the road at the bottom of the hill, so we were a pack of two. On mornings when Gretch and her big sister Mary were late coming out of their driveway, I walked alone, sometimes listening to the big girls' conversation or eavesdropping on the boy talk. Mostly I was happy in my own thoughts and wanderings, dreaming about the day's adventures at school.

Everyone endured a fair amount of bus stop banter. Teasing prevailed among the packs. Having an older brother and sister was my built-in protection from anyone pushing me too far. The worst that I remember happening to me at the bus stop was having my Brownie cap tossed into the snow bank by one of the Vitale boys, but I was sort of proud of that. Kurtis Bugle took the most grief from everyone. He was naturally grumpy and lived in a stone house with a wall around it. We thought it looked like a fort. Whole myths were built around our lack of experience inside those walls. Like anybody else, we substituted myth for what we didn't know. Just when I began to get nervous that Kurtis was not going to take much more teasing, we would hear the whining downshifting of the school bus as it stopped to pick us up on Route 45.

Harvard Educational Review Vol. 62 No. 3 Fall 1992, 373–383

There was just one bus for all of our section of Ramapo Central School District No. 2. We picked up Adelaide and her cousin in the trailer park; pale, quiet Rose from a bungalow somewhere down a long driveway off a busy highway; and tall Juliana Clem, who saved a seat for the other tall girl, Rita. Rita got on at Mount Ivy. Billie Smith's dad had a mink farm. We were all used to the mink odor that got on with him. Everyone liked Billie, and, as far as I know, the smell was just how we knew we'd gotten to his stop.

Along the back road through peach orchard country, we had three Jackson family pick-ups. Two of the Jacksons were "ck" Jacksons. Their families both had orchards, one with better peaches than the other. The other Jaksons had lost the "c" from before the "k" in their name. They were poor and quiet.

The next few stops were on Buena Vista Road. Everyone on Buena Vista Road was related, it seemed to me. And they all — girls and boys — were good at sports. So was Jimmy Anderson, who lived right on Route 45. He was younger than my brother, Chuck, and would in time succeed him as captain of all our games. Legend had it that Jimmy's older sister was a model. I thought about that a lot. Down Pomona Road was Happy Valley Home. No one ever explained what Happy Valley was all about, why children lived there overnight without their parents. Besides my sister and brother and me, the only other brown-skinned children on the bus got on at Happy Valley. They waited outside of dark, little buildings, and it didn't seem like a happy valley home to me.

The last stop before school was Summit Park — the only development I knew about, though I didn't know the word for it back then. All I knew was that everyone who got on there was a Yankee Fan and a Republican and rooted for war. Most of us on our road were Dodger fans — Brooklyn Dodgers, that is. Our parents used words like peace and race relations. We had Russians and Quakers, painters, musicians, writers, and teachers on our road.

One hour over bumpy, winding country roads later, I was happy to see the little red schoolhouse through the now-foggy bus window. When Mr. Gurky was satisfied that his rule was in order, he opened the folded door and we all paraded off the bus — a motley and mixed parade — little children first. Through the crowded aisle, down the three giant steps I went and bounded off the bus. I felt fine in my hand-me-down dress from Jo Simons, my everyday brown oxford tie shoes and thin anklet socks. My brown, thick, curly braids bounced along on my shoulders, a little worse for wear from the humid school bus ride. I had my big, black lunch box packed by my father. The faint smells of baked beans from my thermos and a sandwich of peanut butter and bacon on pumpernickel reminded me of home and my father's enthusiasm for his own cooking inventions. I was happy to be at school.

There were no walls around the school. The school was for all of us. We were a colorful parade of people with our names, our histories, our temperaments, our looks, our fears, our smells, our haves and have nots, our novice politics, our baseball teams, and our futures, whatever they were to be. We all poured off the bus right onto the blacktop play yard of the school. Beyond the blacktopped yard was a sandy area with seesaws, then a hill down to a meadow below. Swings and kickball games, complete with rules and arguments, waited in the meadow.

Beyond the meadow was the woods and finally a stream. Occasionally our recess games even ventured over the stream. There were no walls on that side of the school either.

The school was at one with our world. I carried my treasures, my dreams, my stories, and my imagination to school and back home without ever putting them down. They were part of both my school self and myself, which were the same happy, confident person. I loved school. When I was in first grade and my sister Sara in second, we each got a matching set of shorts and halter top on promotion day for having perfect attendance. You see, I believed then that school could not possibly go on without me.

Now as I travel the country visiting schools, I no longer arrive in a rickety old school bus. Now I pull up in a cab or arrive by an airport limousine, or a teacher from the school picks me up in her Subaru station wagon, with teacher stuff strewn across the back seat and a compost heap of breakfasts-on-the-run on the floor. Sometimes I arrive on foot. But I arrive with the same sense of anticipation that I had forty years ago, the same enthusiasm for the adventure. Perhaps I still have the impression that school can't go on without me. I am still carrying my dreams and my stories and my imagination, if not the lovingly packed lunch box. But this time, as I locate the street number and find the sign that announces the school, I am almost always met with a wall. A stone wall, a brick wall, a chain-link fence, a gate. Sometimes it isn't a wall I can see, but that I can feel. The school is one world and the community around it is another.

The wall around the school tells me that inside is a school of self-importance. It is a school with a history. It had founding mothers or founding fathers, and those people had stories of their own. They had a purpose and a mission. They created a school and invited certain students and their families to become part of the school community. They worked at making it a place of excellence and strength. They created and lived their story, their school, their community. Then they put a wall up around it.

Over the last decade, educators have talked a lot about diversity. During this time we started calling ourselves "independent schools" rather than "private schools." We said we intended to create schools where students of different races, cultures, religions, economic groups, and neighborhoods could come and be a part. In some cases, by diversity we meant different talents and learning styles, people who are differently able in a variety of ways. Different from the majority. Different from the students the founders had in mind. Different from the students the original mission was written about. We said that since we have an excellent education to offer, why not offer it to students in the world beyond our walls. And so we invited diversity of all kinds to come through the gate and inside the wall.

Today I want educators to think hard about the traditions and assumptions that live on inside the walls of our schools. And as we face the twenty-first century, I want us to dare to ask what we really mean by inclusiveness and diversity. Do we mean that we want to take the walls down? Do we mean we want the school to be at one with the community? Those walls protect our institutions. They protect the assumptions that have been made for generations about what is best for students — what to teach, how to teach it, how students learn, how to prepare them for college and beyond. From the beginning, the walls defined who the insiders were — and who they were not. And the walls successfully kept who they were not out of their view. Once inside the school, there are little walls everywhere — rituals and symbols and language and habits that represent the way it has always been. Do we mean we want to look at these, carefully dismantle them brick by brick, and discard the ones that aren't relevant or that actually offend? What happens when the walls come tumbling down?

My father was a trumpet player. He had a big, beautiful tenor voice that sounded like his trumpet. Most people thought that he was a baritone. It was his big, joyful presence that made his voice sound deeper to them than it was. It was not unusual for my dad to burst out in song, often a spiritual, almost anywhere — as he took his vigorous walks up and down the hills of our country road, as he chopped wood and stacked it for the fire, while he was cooking, or as he went up and down the grocery store aisles doing the food shopping. He would burst out in song on Lexington Avenue in New York City if the song came to him and wanted singing. And, though sometimes as an adolescent I would cringe and shrink if I thought my friends were around, I look back on those bursts of singing as a source of strength and joy.

"Joshua fit the battle of Jericho, Jericho, Jericho. Joshua fit the battle of Jericho, and the walls came a-tumbling down." I can hear my dad singing that spiritual with jubilation. The way he sang it gave me the lasting impression that the story was about hard work, courage, triumph, and jubilation. For this reason, I share this story with other educators as it was given to me — as a source of strength and joy — as we face the hard work of leading our schools into the twenty-first century, as we summon the strength we need to do the job, as we invoke the courage we need to overcome the frustrations and fears, as we are rewarded by the joys and triumphs when they finally come.

The gates of Jericho were kept shut and guarded to keep the Israelites out. No one could enter or leave the city. The Lord came to Joshua and said, I have put Jericho in your hands. You are to march your army around the city once each day for six days. Seven priests, each carrying a trumpet made of a ram's horn, are to march in front of the Covenant Box. On the seventh day, you and your soldiers are to march around the city seven times while the priests blow their trumpets. Then they are to sound one long note. As soon as you hear it, command your people to give a shout, and the walls of Jericho will fall down.

Joshua heard and he ordered his people to do what the Lord had told him. He warned them not to shout until he told them to, not even to say a word as they marched around the city.

Joshua's people marched around the outside of the walls of Jericho once each day for six days, and the seven priests, marching before the Covenant Box, sounded their trumpets.

On the seventh day, they got up at daybreak and marched around the city as they had done on the six days before. But this time they marched around seven times.

And on the seventh time around, when the priests sounded one long note, Joshua commanded his people to shout.

The people made a great loud noise, and the walls of the city came tumbling down. Then all of Joshua's people went straight up the hill into the city and captured it. They were still carrying the Covenant Box with them.[1]

As I read and reread the story of the Battle of Jericho, as I began to hear the story in my own words, to let the metaphor echo in our own times, I began to understand how the disturbance, subtle and distant at first, crescendoed to the point of urgency, and, finally, to destruction. No one drew swords. There were no guns, no missiles, no obvious violence. This was a more menacing battle.[2] I can just imagine the people inside the city taking no more than a casual glance out the window, wondering why they were hearing trumpets outside there. It reminds me of being high up in an apartment in New York City when sirens are going off somewhere down in the street. At first you wonder a little. Then you dismiss it or deny it. Finally you get used to it. My friends in San Francisco all tell me that they denied the first serious rumblings of the earthquake a year and a half ago. One friend, a professor at a university in the San Francisco area, was chairing an important promotion and tenure committee meeting when the huge, heavy oak table they were sitting around began to dance noisily on its own. Volumes of important learning began to tumble from high shelves. He told me later that the scholarly members of his committee kept doggedly on with their groaning talk, only talking louder to outshout the confusion. He took the lead in ducking under the table, where I presume these distinguished faculty members did not continue their important meeting.

Each time I hear the story of Jericho, I find myself at the end wondering: What happened next in that story? When the walls of our schools come tumbling down, what happens next in our story? What are we commanded to become as institutions? How do we rebuild, re-create, reform in a wall-less school? If the walls come down, the school will be at one with the community. What profound changes will we face, and how will we face these changes in order to triumph?

Imagine for a moment the march of trumpeters parading around the outside of our schools. Whose footsteps do we hear? What are their stories and what worlds do they come from outside of our walls? When they shout and the walls come down, what changes and what challenges will they be asking of our schools?

During the civil rights movement of the 1960s, we witnessed the Battle of Jericho over and over as the schools were desegregated in the South. In the beginning there was often only one trumpeter, the footsteps of one lone child. Yes, there were prayer meetings and civil rights leaders, and of course there were the marcher's parents and siblings at home, sick with fear. Do you remember Ruby? Robert Coles told us Ruby's story in *Children of Crisis*, which is set in 1964. At age six, Ruby, born in a sharecropper's cabin and raised by her young Black parents in the industrial slums of New Orleans, walked in her clean school clothes, carrying her lunch box, past the jeering, angry, violent mob of White parents. She walked alone to integrate the school. Coles tells us of the indignities

---

[1] Adapted from the *Good News Bible*, The Book of Joshua 6: 1–20 (Nashville, TN: Thomas Nelson, 1976, under license from the American Bible Society).

[2] The image of this as a "menacing" battle with the absence of tangible weapons was given to me in a personal communication with Gay Grissom.

and obscenities inflicted on this small person, ravaging her insides. "Is it only my skin?" she kept asking her mother.[3] And I keep seeing her lunch box, filled with the only tangible signs of love her mother could send to school with her. I keep seeing that lunch box as a Covenant Box. A box with this message inside: *I want to belong.*

Coles tells us of attending a medical meeting in Mississippi in 1958. He describes a doctor at the meeting who "was just recovering from the shock of Little Rock, only to hear that New Orleans was, as he put it, 'next.' He was beyond anger, and a bit of the doctor was in him when he spoke: 'One by one the schools are taking a turn for the worse. This desegregation is spreading from city to city, and we can't seem to stop it. I think it'll destroy our schools.'"[4] No, doctor, not the schools. Just the walls around them.

Ruby's story is still being enacted every day, in and around our schools. These stories are usually more subtle. They are not necessarily stories of physical violence and tangible injury, but they are the stories of the children from diverse backgrounds whom we invite to come to our schools. They are the stories of people coming through the gates, each alone in some way, separated daily from their own stories, histories, and family strengths, from their understanding of the way life works and how to survive it. As they come inside the walls of our schools, they are severed daily from the language, the art, the songs that are the fabric of their lives.

I have a pile of favorite and beloved books that I keep near me. Passages from these books are part of ongoing conversations, like conversations with close friends understood more deeply each time we resume them. In that pile is a small volume called *Dark Testament and other poems* by Pauli Murray. One poem comes to me now. It is called "Psalm of Deliverance, (To the Negro School Children of the American South in the Year 1959)":

> Children of Courage, we greet you!
> Gentle Warriors, we salute you!
> Youthful veterans of upheaval,
> Victims of mindless resistance,
> We, the wounded and dead of former campaigns,
> Unknown, unheralded, unribboned,
> The nameless millions, native and migrant,
> We are legion and we support you!
> From restless graves in swamps and bayous,
> From slave ships, slave pens, chain gangs and prisons,
> From ruined churches and blazing lynch-trees,
> From gas chambers and mass crematoriums,
> From foxholes, ghettoes, detention camps,
> From lonely outposts of exclusion,
> We hear your marching feet and rise,
> Silently we walk beside you!
>
> *We have returned from a place beyond hope;*
> *We have returned from wastelands of despair;*

[3] Robert Coles, *Children of Crisis* (New York: Dell, 1967), pp. 75–85.
[4] Coles, *Children of Crisis*, p. 73.

> *We have come to reclaim our heritage;*
> *We have come to redeem our honor!* [5]

The "children of courage," the "gentle warriors" coming through the gates of our schools, are on this silent march. And for twenty years, as I have experienced independent schools as a teacher, a parent, and an administrator, I have walked beside them. I have witnessed the process as newcomers attempt to become a part of the life inside the school community. I see this process happening in five general stages:

In the first stage, families of students are shopping, searching for a school (and the school is shopping for or recruiting students). Of course, in this time of a depressed economy, it is a buyer's market, but in stage one, the school and the student are looking each other over.

In the second stage, student and school are narrowing their selections and choosing. Catalogues and view books serve the schools well; they give the image of inclusiveness and allege diversity, with photographs that show ballet shoes, lacrosse sticks, cellos, and *Peterson's Guide to Competitive Colleges*, strategically placed under the arms of an unrealistic representation of the number of children of color in the school. Although these are good efforts at attracting new families to the school, it is doubtful that they are actually serving the families, themselves.

In the third stage, students newly enrolled in the school and their families are finding their way in this new environment. They are trying to discern the expectations of the school. They are learning the laws, most of them unwritten: how to fit in, how to operate, how to advocate, how to survive. This is the time for handbooks, new-parent teas, picnics, back-to-school nights. Again, these traditional efforts serve the school fairly well — at least they serve the status quo.

In the fourth stage, conflicts begin to arise out of the discrepancy between the school's assumptions, values, and character, and the parents' expectations of the school — what they want and value for their children.

In the fifth stage, either resolution of the conflict results in understanding, reconciliation, and, ultimately, belonging, or lack of resolution results in a gulf of misunderstanding and injury. The student and family depart or, worse still, they just retreat, until something upsetting happens to unearth the old injury. By then, no one can imagine what went wrong to upset the injured parties.

Most schools have learned to take families successfully through the first two steps (admissions offices have recently enjoyed a strong and colorful yield from their offers). The process seems to work smoothly until about half-way through stage three. Some time just beyond the back-to-school nights and freshly printed handbooks, the process breaks down: the school has not upheld its part in getting to know the students and families they have admitted, to learn about their stories, their strengths, their gifts, and their fears.

When there are walls of ignorance between people, when we don't know each other's stories, we substitute our own myth about who that person is. When we are operating with only a myth, none of that person's truth will ever be known to us, and we will injure them — mostly without ever meaning to. What assump-

---

[5] Pauli Murray, *Dark Testament and other poems* (Norwalk, CT: Silvermine, 1970), p. 41.

tion did you make because she is a woman? What assumption did you make because he is Black? What myths were built around the neighborhood listed on the application? What myths were built around the employment of the father or the absence of the mother? What story did we tell ourselves in the absence of knowing this person's real story? Remember Kurtis Bugle, who lived near the bus stop behind a wall? We never found a way to take down the wall of our own ignorance about him and find out who he was. So we made up a myth, and I know we hurt him.

The brochures, the view books, and the admissions open houses proudly announce a philosophy of education, the philosophy of the school. With carefully wrought words and choreographed pictures, the school presents assurances that all the students and their families will belong to a fully inclusive community. But when the first misunderstanding about a homework assignment, about a casual comment or gesture from the teacher, about something said in the locker room or on the team bus — when that first misunderstanding presses its weight against the school's philosophy — those carefully wrought images may not contain enough truth to hold it up.

When this happens, you are going to wish you had mined more deeply for the truth. You are going to wish the school had a mission, not a philosophy — a mission that examines the purpose, the meaning, the school's reason for being, and then puts that intention into action.[6] A mission is the result of the choices and decisions made in the life of the school, based on what the school values. A mission holds more truth in it than a philosophy, because the truth about the school lies in how the school acts on its philosophy.

The trouble with a mission is that it is the school's truth, and it assumes that the school's truth is the whole truth. But it is really just one side, a piece of the truth. Other pieces of the truth live on the outside of the school's wall. This time, when the gulf of misunderstanding is so great that injury becomes trauma, when some terrible incident unburies itself from the store of repressed hurt feelings, even a well thought out mission with purpose and meaning will break under the weight of the explosion. It will break because in the narrow, walled-in definition of the truth, ultimately the mission serves only the school itself. The walls might just as well be restored as they were. Use some better mortar next time.

To be inclusive, to be excellent, to be who we need to be as a whole community, everyone's truth must be known. Instead of a mission, schools need to create a covenant, an agreement with the school community. It should say that each party to the agreement depends on the others to have a piece of the truth.[7] In a mission, the school defines the students who are in it; in a covenant, the members of the school community define themselves and create the definition

[6] Daniel L. Klatz, in describing his efforts to help his colleagues in independent schools articulate their purpose more clearly, introduced me to the idea of a "mission" being a stronger statement than a "philosophy."

[7] The notion of covenant as I have used it here was inspired by a lecture on the *Book of Exodus*, given by theologian Walter Brueggeman at Immanuel Episcopal Church, Wilmington, Delaware. Brueggeman explains the historical purpose and meaning of a covenant in the life of a community. I have applied his explanation specifically to the context of the educational community.

of the school.[8] A covenant is a promise to carry the gifts, the stories, the histories, the visions, the dreams of all the people inside the school. It is a promise to take down the walls of exclusion.

Consider the school where, on a field trip, a White bus driver, after several frustrating attempts to "encourage" a Black child to follow verbal instructions he'd given him to sit down, gave him a firm push into his seat. The boy, who had been expertly escalating the original request into a full-blown incident, missed the seat and landed on the floor. Now a school with the most reasonable of philosophies, respectful of families, and welcoming of students from diverse backgrounds, finds itself in the midst of a full-blown, demoralizing war. Enraged Black parents are raising issues buried long ago in their initial desire to adapt to the school. The mother of the offended child, in her rage, has abandoned every thought of courtesy and decency. All the while she is using her boy to run interference for her — holding him up as "exhibit A" at parent meetings, furthering, no doubt, the complexity of his difficulties. In the meantime, a small and tender group of teachers of color are feeling hurt and defeated and impotent. How could they have been expected to be everywhere, to take care of every child of color entering the school? And the principal, who wrote the perfectly reasonable philosophy, can't imagine how they all ended up in this mess. Now they are all mining for the truth, but the truth is so fractured, so buried in the rubble, that it is unrecognizable. No doubt everyone feels the promise has been broken.

As we approach the work of planning for the twenty-first century in our schools, we must create covenants anew. The children marching around with trumpets outside of our schools carry an important message in their Covenant Box: *I want to belong.* Moment by moment, they will challenge us to reinterpret their school's mission in their presence, in their time. They demand that the vision and the dream be theirs, too. That is what covenant is all about — the promise that their education be about them. As we create covenant, we must look at every aspect of life as it is experienced in our schools and try to find out where the walls of exclusion have been built.

The wall may be the weekly half-day pick up, when a single mother working to pay tuition couldn't possibly pick up her child. The wall may be the second-grade teacher who does not ask that a capable, bright Black boy finish his homework, but instead tells the boy's mother, "He's doing fine and we don't want to push him." Mother knows this will not do for her Black son in the world he must be prepared for; it did not do for her, and she feels frightened and sorrowful and betrayed. The wall may be the complexion of the group that leaves the third-grade room for the ten-o'clock tutoring class in the special-help room down the hall. Or, the wall may be the solid wall of photos of White former graduates in white dresses that one Black senior girl has to endure every time she goes to her locker, all the while imagining that when her class photo goes up there next year, the fancy photographer will surely not know to set the f-stop

---

[8] Abram L. Wehmiller, "The Uncommon Application," *Prism*, Winter 1991, p. 29. I am indebted to Abram Lawrence Wehmiller, whose poem "The Uncommon Application" courageously calls on each of us to "define" ourselves, not to "be defined."

on the camera low enough to illuminate her beautiful dark face. The camera will read all that white and leave her looking like an ink spot.

What negative patterns are being learned by habits and traditions inherent in even the best of pedagogical intentions? Some of the walls are subtle, some are invisible, but they all must come down.

A word about heads-of-schools as creators of the new covenants of our schools — a word about Joshua. Just before Joshua took on this Jericho job, he had a typical independent school-head job interview. The search committee had him meet with an angel who carried a sword. He asked the question of the angel that any one of us would have asked in that same situation: Whose side are you on — mine or my adversary's? The angel said he was on the side of the Lord. At that, Joshua fell to his knees and asked what was expected of him. The angel answered, "Put aside your shoes, for you are on holy ground."

My word to each of us as creators of new covenants is, "Put aside your shoes." If we are considering entering into a covenantal relationship with the members of the school community, there are parts of the way the headship has been traditionally played that will need to be put aside. It is hard to let go of some of the hierarchical trappings that this involves. But we will need to put aside some of those trappings and habits of headships and come to know — really know — the teachers, parents, and children in our school communities. We will also have to put aside our shoes and know ourselves.[9]

And here I want to share with you a piece of the truth that I call my own. I call it my own through hard learning and trials inside the walls of independent schools.

I guess it was in the fifth-grade New York State Board of Regents science curriculum that we were commanded to know that water seeks its own level. So, I memorized that. Later, when I taught first grade in New York City and the children wanted to know how water got way up in the Empire State Building, I discovered anew the magic and power of that phenomenon. Now I see that schools, like water, seek their own level, the level of the community in which they exist. Schools have a potential of their own — an institutional IQ, if you will. An incompetent, destructive leader can come in and push the school's level down, but eventually the school will come back up to its own natural level. In the same way, an innovative, strong leader can come in and push the level up — but only temporarily. Sooner or later, the school wants to come down to its own comfortable position. When a person pushes the school beyond its level, it feels momentarily pretty satisfying. As it comes back down, however, the person who led the way of change pays the price. As leaders in our schools, we had better know what the potential of our schools is, and whether or not we are pushing the schools unrealistically, beyond that potential, beyond what will hold up against gravity. As we create the covenants with which our schools will enter the twenty-first century, we must be sure they are covenants that our schools have the strength to keep; otherwise, we will surely pay the price.

The bringing down of walls is scary, tiring, frustrating work. But tearing down our ignorance, building community, knowing people and their stories and their

---

[9] Elizabeth M. Reis, *A Deeper Kind of Truth* (New York: Paulist Press, 1987), p. 63.

gifts — their truths — this is joyful work. I hope that one day soon you will be at school walking to the baseball field or striding down the hall, or fixing your lunch in your kitchen at home or walking down Whatever Avenue in Whichever City, and a song will come to you that wants singing. Don't be amazed if the refrain is, ". . . and the walls came a-tumbling down." You'll know then, as my father knew, and as I know now, that it is a song of joy.

Reading the World of School Literacy: Contextualizing the Experience of a Young African American Male

ARLETTE INGRAM WILLIS

In this article, Arlette Willis articulates the literacy schooling experiences of her son, Jake, as he engages in a struggle to affirm himself as both a literacy learner and an African American. Asserting that Jake's struggle has historical roots and present-day consequences for the education of culturally and linguistically diverse school children, Willis argues for a reconceptualization of literacy that builds on these children's backgrounds and knowledges. In the last section of the article, Willis provides the reader with some of the strategies and practices she has employed as a teacher-educator to assist her own students in expanding their understandings of the various cultures in U.S. society that children represent.

Let me share a conversation that I had with my nine-year-old son, and the context in which it occurred:

It's a cold, frosty winter morning, and everyone has left for work or school except my youngest son Jake and me. I am busy applying last-minute touches to my makeup and encouraging Jake, in the next room, to "step it up." I wonder why he is dragging around; school starts in ten minutes and we haven't yet left the house. Jake knows the routine; I wonder if something is troubling him. So, I peek around the corner and find him looking forlorn — you know, a scowl on his face, a look of growing despair and sadness. I forget about the clock and attend to him.

"Jake, what's wrong? Why are you so unhappy?" I ask.

"We have the Young Authors [writing] Contest today, and I don't have anything to write about."

"Sure you do. There are lots of things you can write about," I encourage him. (I believe people write best about those subjects they know and care about.) "Why don't you write about baseball or soccer?"

"No," he replies. "A kid at our school wrote about cancer last year, and the story went all the way to the next state [regionals]."

"Well," I answer, "maybe you should write about something funny — like when you go to the barbershop. You and your brothers are always talking about your trips there."[1]

---

[1] Going to the barbershop and getting a haircut is a bimonthly occurrence for many African American males. A number of Jake's classmates differed in their definition of what constituted a "part"; however, the other African American children in his class have a similar cultural understanding of the term.

Harvard Educational Review Vol. 65 No. 1 Spring 1995, 30–49

"Oh no, Mom, they wouldn't understand. When I just get my haircut, they always ask me, 'Why do you have that line in your hair?' 'It's not a line, it's a part,' I try to tell them. I can't write about the barbershop. They won't understand."

"Well," I say, trying to clarify what I really mean, "I don't mean write about getting a haircut. I mean writing about all the funny people that come in and the things that happen while you are at the barbershop. You and your brothers always come home tellin' a funny story and laugh about it for the rest of the week. That's what I mean by writing about the barbershop."

"No, Mom. They won't understand," he insists.

"What do you mean, 'they won't understand?' Who is this 'they'?" I ask.

"The people in my class," he replies, somewhat frustrated.

Jake continues, "You should read this story that M. wrote. It is a mystery story and it's really good. I can't beat that story. I'll bring you a copy of it if I can. I know it will win." (Sadder now that he has had time to consider his competition, Jake turns and walks toward his room.)

Wanting him to participate in the contest, I ask, "How do you know M.'s story is good?"

"She read it in class. Everybody said it's really good," he responds.

"Well, I still think you should try. You are a really good writer. Look at all the 'good stuff' you wrote in Mrs. S.'s room. You could rewrite some of it and turn it in."

Finally he answers, "I'll think about it," and we go off to school.

As I remember the conversation, Jake's tone of voice hinted at both frustration and defensiveness. I interpreted his use of phrases like "they always ask" and "I try to tell them" to mean that since he gets his hair cut every two weeks, it gets pretty tiresome answering the same questions from his classmates so frequently.[2] Furthermore, I interpreted his intonation to mean that he has had to stand his ground with other children who either do not agree with his definition of a "part," or who try to define its meaning for him.

I believe that Jake cannot bring this aspect of his life and culture into the classroom because he doesn't feel that it will be understood by his classmates and teacher. When Jake says "They won't understand," I interpret his words to mean that if his classmates cannot understand the simplest action in getting a haircut — the barber taking less than ten seconds to place a part in his hair — how can he expect them to understand the context and culture that surround the entire event. Also, I see Jake's reluctance to share something as commonplace in his home and community life as a haircut as a way of distancing this portion of his life from the life he leads at school. It seems that he has come to understand that as an African American he must constantly make a mediating effort to help others understand events that appear to be commonplace on the surface, but are in fact culturally defined.

haircut – culturally defined

Several interwoven incidents have helped me to understand the conversation with Jake. I will briefly describe them to provide the context for my under-

[2] As a Writing Workshop parent volunteer in his class, I know that Jake's class consists of ten European American boys, nine European American girls, four African American boys, two African American girls, and one Asian American girl. The class is taught by a European American woman with over twenty years of experience. Also, during this school year, there have been three student teachers (all European American women) and several other parent volunteers (also European American women).

standing of the subtle, yet ever-present and unquestioned role of cultural accommodation that occurs in the school literacy experiences of children from diverse backgrounds. I have been teaching courses in multicultural literature at my university for several years. After my fall 1993 course, I reflected, using journal writing, on my growing experience teaching multicultural literature courses.[3] Teaching these courses has led me to a more informed understanding of how, in the practice of school literacy, there are many culturally defined moments of conflict that call daily for cultural understanding, knowledge, and sensitivity from teachers. These "moments" also challenge non-mainstream students to choose between cultural assimilation and accommodation, or resistance. My journal entries centered on my readings, research, and, most importantly, my daily conversations about school life with my three sons, who range in age from nine to seventeen. In my classes, I have often shared my sons' school experiences and my reactions to them in an effort to help my students understand how teachers' daily subtle and seemingly inconsequential decisions can affect the learning of the children they teach.

A striking example of a teacher's unintentional disregard for the cultural *cultural insensitivity* history, understanding, experiences, and voice of a student occurred when my oldest son struggled to meet the requirements of a national essay contest entitled, "What it means to be an American." One of the contest's restrictions was *ex.* that students should not mention the concept of race. My son thought this was an unfair and impossible task to complete, since his African American identity is synonymous with his being American. Yet, his efforts to articulate the difficulty of the task to his English teacher were frustrated by her response that, although she was empathic, she did not have the authority to change the rules. I intervened and spoke with the teacher at length about my son's values, beliefs, and his unwillingness to compromise himself in order to compete in an essay contest in which he had little or no interest other than a grade.

My second son also had a similar experience involving unintentional cultural *ex.* insensitivity. He is a member of the school band, which was having its fall concert. While attending, I noticed that all the music the band played was composed by Europeans or European Americans. I spoke with one of the band directors, and asked rhetorically if there were any songs that the band members could perform that were composed by people of color. She responded that she had never considered the choices she made as nonrepresentative of all the students who had to learn them, while I could see little else than the absence of cultural diversity. I was pleased when the winter concert included some Hanukkah tunes. It was a start.

REFLECTIONS

Though my conversation with Jake is now months old, it has continued to haunt me. I have been deeply concerned about a noticeable shift in my son's attitude toward writing. Jake's early writing experiences in kindergarten and first grade

---

[3] In the fall of 1993 I taught a pilot course, which included multicultural education, reading methods for grades six–twelve, and literature for grades six–twelve with special emphasis on multicultural literature.

revealed that he found writing to be a natural outlet for self-expression. He often wrote for pleasure and has kept all of his drafts. Jake learned the process approach to writing in first grade and treasures his portfolio, which he had originally developed in that class. I have found him in his room revisiting a piece he had written. However, this past year I have noticed a change in his level of production. Jake no longer writes detailed accounts. Instead, he spends a great deal of time thinking about what to write and how to say it. While I believe these are laudatory traits of a good writer, his teachers often accuse him of being under-productive.

Reflecting on our conversation, I sense that Jake believes (understands?) that his perceived audience will neither value nor understand the cultural images and nuances he wishes to share in his writing. Jake is a child wrestling with an internal conflict that is framed by the sociohistorical and sociocultural inequities of U.S. society. He is trying to come to grips with how he can express himself in a manner that is true to his "real self," and yet please his teacher and audience of readers who are, in effect, evaluating his culture, thinking, language, and reality.

Jake's perception of an unaccepting audience is not unique. Several researchers have expressed similar concerns about the narrowly defined culture of acceptable school literacy and the growing literateness of culturally and linguistically diverse children (Delpit, 1986, 1991, 1993; Gutierrez, 1992; Heath, 1983; Labov, 1972; Ovando & Collier, 1985; Reyes & Molner, 1991; Sawyer & Rodriguez, 1992).[4] Why is it clearer to children than to adults that there are systematic, institutional inequalities in the decisions teachers make about the "appropriate" methods and materials used to enhance their students' literacy development?

Like millions of culturally and linguistically diverse people, Jake understands the unstated reality of schooling in U.S. society: It is built upon a narrow understanding of school knowledge and literacy, which are defined and defended as what one needs to know and how one needs to know it in order to be successful in school and society. As Barrera (1992) explains:

> The school culture can be seen to reflect the dominant class and, so too, the cultures of literacy and literature embedded within the school culture. For this reason, the teaching of literacy and literature are considered to be neither acultural nor neutral, but cultural and political. (p. 236)

The real question is, why do we as educators continue this "sin of omission" — that is, allowing the cultural knowledge of culturally and linguistically diverse children to be ignored, devalued, and unnurtured as valid sources of literacy acquisition? Excerpts from the writings of five noted African Americans help to illustrate my point.

---

[4] To me, "growing literateness" means an understanding of how language, reading, and writing fit into the communication patterns of home and school life. It can also mean the development of literate behaviors, the adoption of literate attitudes, and the confidence that allows one to define oneself as a reader and a writer.

The Past Revisited

The problem of defining one's literary self is not a new one. As noted scholar W. E. B. Du Bois argued in 1903:

> After the Egyptian and Indian, the Greek and Roman, the Teuton and Mongolian, the Negro is a sort of seventh son, born with a veil, and gifted with second-sight in this American world, — a world which yields him no true self-consciousness, but only lets him see himself through the revelation of the other world. It is a peculiar sensation this double-consciousness, this sense of always looking at one's self through the eyes of others. . . . One ever feels his twoness, an American, a Negro; two souls, two thoughts, two unreconciled strivings; two warring ideals in one dark body, whose dogged strength alone keeps it from being torn asunder. The history of the American Negro is the history of this strife, — this longing to attain self conscious manhood, to merge his double self into a better and truer self. (1903/1965, pp. 214–215)

Similarly, historian Carter G. Woodson (1933/1990) stated:

> In this effort to imitate, however, those "educated people" are sincere. They hope to make the Negro conform quickly to the standard of the whites and thus remove the pretext for the barriers between the races. They do not realize, however, that if the Negroes do successfully imitate the whites, nothing new has thereby been accomplished. You simply have a larger number of persons doing what others have been doing. The unusual gifts of the race have not thereby been developed. (p. 4)

Poet Langston Hughes (1951) expressed a similar notion:

> I guess being colored doesn't make me not like
> the same things other folks like who are other races.
> So will my page be colored that I write?
> Being me, it will not be white.
> But it will be
> a part of you, instructor.
> You are white —
> yet a part of me, as I am a part of you.
> That's American.
> Sometimes perhaps you don't want to be a part of me.
> Nor do I often want to be a part of you.
> But we are, that's true!
> As I learn from you,
> I guess you learn from me —
> although you're older — and white —
> and somewhat more free. (pp. 39–40)

Novelist Ralph Ellison (1952) writes:

> I am invisible, understand, simply because people refuse to see me. Like the bodiless heads you see sometimes in circus sideshows, it is as though I have been surrounded by mirrors of hard, distorting glass. When they approach me they see only my surroundings, themselves, or figments of their imagination — indeed, everything and anything except me. (p. 3)

And, finally, Toni Morrison (1992) refers to the phenomenon of double consciousness as "writing for a white audience" (p. xii). She asks:

> What happens to the writerly imagination of a black author who is at some level *always* conscious of representing one's own race to, or in spite of, a race of readers that understands itself to be "universal" or race-free? In other words, how are "literary whiteness" and "literary blackness" made, and what is the consequence of these constructions? (p. xii)

Like other culturally and linguistically diverse people before him (including myself and every other person of color with whom I have shared this incident), Jake has encountered the struggle of literary personhood.

Questions and concerns flood my mind: Where, I wonder, has he gotten the idea of a "White" audience — that is, the sense that his classmates and others who read his writing will not appreciate what he has to share? When did his concept of a "White" audience arise? My questions persist: How long has Jake known, intuitively perhaps, that his school literacy experiences have been tempered through a mainstream lens? Will Jake continue to resist "writing for a white audience?" When do culturally and linguistically diverse children learn that they must choose between selfhood and accommodation?[5] When do they learn that "the best way, then, to succeed — that is, to receive rewards, recognition . . . is to learn and reproduce the ways of the dominant group?" (Scheurich, 1992, p. 7). Must there be only one acceptable culture reflected in current school literacy programs? What thoughts, words, and language is Jake replacing with those of the dominant culture in order to please his audience? Will he ever be able to recapture his true literate self after years of accommodation?

As a third grader, Jake is writing, but not for pleasure. Whereas once he wrote as a way of expressing himself or as a hobby, now he does not. He only writes to complete assignments. Much of the "joy" he experienced in writing for pleasure seems to have waned. I recently read some of his writings and noted that he concentrated on topics that do not reflect African American culture. For example, his most recent entries are about his spoon collection, running track, rocks, and football — pretty generic stuff.

My fears are like those of all parents who believe they have prepared their child, having done all that they have read and know a parent should do, yet see their child struggling with a history, a tradition, that is much larger than they can battle.[6] What can I do to help my son and children like him enjoy the freedom of writing and reading? How can I help them value the culturally relevant events in their lives? How can school literacy programs begin to acknow-

---

[5] Selfhood, as used in this article, means the awareness of oneself as a person, in particular as a person who belongs to a specific culturally and linguistically distinct group.

[6] Cose's (1993) book, *The Rage of a Privileged Class*, gives examples of the frustration experienced by other middle-class African Americans who believed that by doing everything according to plan they would reap just rewards. For example, Cose quotes Darwin Davis, senior vice president of Equitable Life Assurance Society: "They [young Black managers] have an even worse problem [than I did] because they've got M.B.A.'s from Harvard. They did all the things that you're supposed to do . . . and things are supposed to happen" (p. 76).

By "history," I mean how the inequalities that exist in schools reflect a much greater history of institutionalized inequalities. By "tradition," I mean teachers' tendency to teach how they were taught. Whether history or tradition is the overriding factor in this instance, I am not sure.

ledge, respect, and encourage the diverse cultural knowledge and experiences that children bring to school?

In this article, I am speaking as a teacher educator and parent. This article is an attempt to begin conversations with my colleagues that will address cultural complexities so often ignored in literacy research and practice. For too long, the only perspective published was European Americans' understanding of literacy events. Over the past few years, other cultural perspectives have been published and, more recently, a few have questioned the connection between the theoretical notions of literacy and the historical, and daily, reality of institutionalized inequalities.

As a scholar, I can begin conversations with my colleagues about reexamining theories of literacy to include the role of culture and linguistic diversity. Moreover, teachers and teacher educators like myself can then extend these conversations to reinterpret literacy development, school literacy programs, and teacher education methods and materials to include the experiences of nonmainstream cultures. Finally, I can further extend these conversations into rethinking how we teach and practice school literacy.

BROADENING THE SCOPE

Several contemporary positions on literacy serve to enlighten our understanding of how literacy is defined in the field and how it is defined in practice. In this section, I will offer a brief look at several definitions. First, Cook-Gumperz (1986) describes two competing definitions of school literacy that are useful in framing this discussion. She states that "inherent in our contemporary attitude to literacy and schooling is a confusion between a prescriptive view of literacy, as a statement about the values and uses of knowledge, and a descriptive view of literacy, as cognitive abilities which are promoted and assessed through schooling" (p. 14). Second, a more expansive definition of how literacy is conceptualized is offered by Freire and Macedo (1987). They suggest that "literacy becomes a meaningful construct to the degree that it is viewed as a set of practices that functions to either empower or disempower people. In the larger sense, literacy is analyzed according to whether it serves a set of cultural practices that promotes democratic and emancipatory change" (p. 141). Further, they clarify their position on literacy by noting that "for the notion of literacy to become meaningful it has to be situated within a theory of cultural production and viewed as an integral part of the way in which people produce, transform, and reproduce meaning" (p. 142). Third, more general discussions of literacy define literacy as functional, cultural, or critical. Each of these concepts also refers to very different ways of thinking about literacy. *Functional literacy* refers to mastery of the skills needed to read and write as measured by standardized forms of assessment. This view of literacy is similar to Cook-Gumperz's (1986) notion of a descriptive view of literacy. The functional view promotes literacy as a cognitive set of skills that are universal, culturally neutral, and equally accessible through schooling, and is based on a positivistic ideology of learning. Further, this view is heavily dependent on the use of standardized testing measures as a proving ground for literacy acquisition. Most basal reading series and programmed reading approaches embrace the functional/descriptive view of literacy.

3 types of literacy
2. Hirsch → prescriptive
3. Freire → power

2. cultural lit: E.D. Hirsch standard Engl

2'a) a)

in Spain missing culture

Cultural literacy is a term that is most often associated with **E. D. Hirsch**'s 1987 book, *Cultural Literacy: What Every American Needs to Know.* Hirsch defines cultural literacy as "the network of information that all competent readers possess. It is the background information, stored in their minds, that enables them to take up a newspaper and read it with an adequate level of comprehension, getting the point, grasping the implications, relating what they read to the unstated context which alone gives meaning to what they read" (p. 2). Cook-Gumperz (1986) has labelled this form of literacy "prescriptive." In effect, this form of cultural literacy validates language forms, experiences, literature, and histories of some and marginalizes or ignores the language forms, experiences, literature, and histories of others. In the United States, the prescriptive view can be seen in the use of standard English, Eurocentric ways of knowing and learning, a Eurocentric literary canon, and a conventional unproblematic rendering of U.S. history. This form of the cultural/prescriptive view marginalizes the pluralistic composition of U.S. society by devaluing the language, contributions, and histories of some groups. Traditional or conventional approaches to school-based literacy take this form. McLaren (1987) argues that there is a second form of cultural literacy. He writes that this form of cultural literacy "advocates using the language standards and cultural information students bring into the classroom as legitimate and important constituents of learning" (p. 214). Cultural literacy, thus described, suggests that the language and experiences of each student who enters the classroom should be respected and nurtured. This form of cultural literacy recognizes that there are differences in language forms, experiences, literature, and histories of students that will affect literacy learning. Social constructivist theories fall into this prescriptive/cultural literacy category. These approaches to literacy emphasize the active engagement of learners in making meaning from print, the social context of literacy learning, and the importance of recognizing individual and cultural differences.

b) others are valued

3.

Critical literacy refers to the ideologies that underlie the relationship between power and knowledge in society. The work of Brazilian educator **Paulo Freire** has been influential to U.S. efforts to adopt a critical literacy position. Freire, among others, suggests that literacy is more than the construction of meaning from print: Literacy must also include the ability to understand oneself and one's relationship to the world. Giroux's (1987) discussion is worth quoting here at length:

> As Paulo Freire and others have pointed out, schools are not merely instructional sites designed to transmit knowledge; they are also cultural sites. As sites, they generate and embody support for particular forms of culture as is evident in the school's support for specific ways of speaking, the legitimating of distinct forms of knowledge, the privileging of certain histories and patterns of authority, and the confirmation of particular ways of experiencing and seeing the world. Schools often give the appearance of transmitting a common culture, but they, in fact, more often than not, legitimate what can be called a dominant culture. (p. 176)

Giroux goes on to state that:

power & prestige

> At issue here is understanding that student experience has to be understood as part of an interlocking web of power relations in which some groups of students are often privileged over others. But if we are to view this insight in an important way,

Schools = political
Crit. lit = hist, pol, cult & social dimensions of lit
= power relations in soc

Role

we must understand that it is imperative for teachers to critically examine the cultural backgrounds and social formations out of which their students produce the categories they use to give meaning to the world. For teachers are not merely dealing with students who have individual interests, they are dealing primarily with individuals whose stories, memories, narratives, and readings of the world are inextricably related to wider social and cultural formations and categories. This issue here is not merely one of relevance but one of power. (p. 177)

Similarly, Apple (1992) has argued for nearly a decade that "it is naive to think of the school curriculum as neutral knowledge. . . . Rather, what counts as legitimate knowledge is the result of complex power relations and struggles among identifiable class, race, gender, and religious groups" (p. 4). Critical literacy draws attention to the historical, political, cultural, and social dimensions of literacy. Most importantly, this form of literacy focuses on power relations in society and how knowledge and power are interrelated. Educationalists, practitioners in particular, have not yet fully grasped this position on literacy. The other forms of literacy, functional/descriptive and cultural/prescriptive, do not include, among other things, the notion of power relations in literacy instruction.

* the big difference

Philosophically, social constructivist notions (a form of prescriptive/cultural literacy) may be seen as comparable to those espoused by critical literacy. From the schema theorists of the early 1980s to the social constructivist theories of the 1990s, literacy development is understood to be a "meaning making process" — that is, socially mediated (Meek, 1982). Drawing primarily on the work of Halliday (1975), Vygotsky (1978), and Goodman (1989), a number of literacy researchers have stressed the universality of language learning. For example, Goodman's (1989) discussion of the philosophical stance of whole language is that:

> At the same time that whole language sees common strengths and universals in human learning, it expects and recognizes differences among learners in culture, value systems, experience, needs, interests and language. Some of these differences are personal, reflecting the ethnic, cultural, and belief systems of the social groups pupils represent. Thus teachers in whole-language programs value differences among learners as they come to school and differences in objectives and outcomes as students progress through school. (p. 209)

but;! Reyes

However, I argue that the role of culture in the social constructivist theories is not as well defined as it needs to be in a pluralistic or multicultural society. While it is fair to say that unidimensional views of culture would not be supported by social constructivists, it is also fair to say that the multilayered complexity of culture, especially the cultures of historically oppressed groups, is not explicitly addressed by them either. By way of example, I will examine the prescriptive/cultural literacy foundation of whole language. Goodman (1986) argues that "language begins as means of communication between members of the group. Through it, however, each developing child acquires the life view, the cultural perspective, the ways of meaning particular to its own culture" (p. 11). But this definition fails to acknowledge that in addition to acquiring culturally "neutral" knowledge, some children must also acquire a Eurocentric cultural perspective to be successful in school. It is not sufficient to suggest that the

agrees with Reyes

219

language and culture of every student is welcomed, supported, and nurtured in school without explicitly addressing the power relations in institutions, social practice, and literature that advantage some and hinder others (Delpit, 1988; Reyes, 1992). School-based literacy, in its varying forms, fails to acknowledge explicitly the richness of the cultural ways of knowing, forms of language other than standard English, and the interwoven relationship among power, language, and literacy that silences kids like Jake.[7] To fail to attend to the plurality and diversity within the United States — and to fail to take seriously the historic past and the social and political contexts that have sustained it — is to dismiss the cultural ways of knowing, language, experiences, and voices of children from diverse linguistic and cultural backgrounds. This is not to imply that programs based on such theories need to be scrapped. It does mean that social constructivist theories need to be reworked to include the complexities of culture that are currently absent. It will also mean that teacher education will need to: 1) make explicit the relationship among culture, language, literacy and power; and 2) train teachers to use cultural information to support and nurture the literacy development of all the students who enter their classrooms.

When taken at face value, social constructivist theory would lead one to assume that new holistic approaches to literacy are culturally validating for all students. An examination of Jake's home and school contexts for his developing understanding of literacy illustrates that this is not always true. That is, we need to understand where he acquired language and his understanding of culture, as well as his history of literacy instruction, to understand how he is "reading the world" of school literacy and how his experiences with a variety of school literacy forms, including holistic approaches, have not addressed his cultural ways of knowing, experiences, language, and voice.

LITERACY CONTEXTS

Home Context

Literacy acquisition does not evolve in one context or through one type of event; rather, it is a complex endeavor that is mediated through culture. Jake's home literacy environment began with our preparations for him as a new baby. He was brought into a loving two-parent home in which two older brothers were awaiting his arrival. Jake also entered a print- and language-rich environment. He was read to when only a few months old, and continues to share reading (and now writing) with family members. Like the homes of many other middle-class children, Jake's is filled with language, and a range of standard and vernacular languages is used. Our talk centers around family issues, but also includes conversations about world events, neighborhood and school concerns, and personal interests. There are stories, prayers, niceties (manners), verbal games, family jokes, homework assignments, daily Bible reading and discussion, as well as family vacations and excursions to museums, zoos, concerts, and ball parks. Daily

---

[7] Silencing, as used by Michelle Fine (1987), "constitutes a process of institutionalized policies and practices which obscure the very social, economic and therefore experiential conditions of students' daily lives, and which expel from written, oral, and nonverbal expression substantive and critical 'talk' about these conditions. . . . Silencing constitutes the process by which contradictory evidence, ideologies, and experiences find themselves buried, camouflaged, and discredited" (p. 157).

routines include reading and responding to mail, making schedules, appointments, grocery and chore lists, and taking telephone messages, all of which include opportunities for shared conversations. There is also a family library that consists of adult fiction, nonfiction, and reference materials. Conversations flow constantly and with ease as we enjoy sharing with each other.

Prior to Jake's entering school, we enjoyed music, games, songs, fingerplay, writing notes on unlined paper with lots of different writing tools, long nature walks, as well as trips to the store, library, barbershop, and church.[8] All these activities were accompanied by lots of talk to expand understanding and draw connections. In addition, Jake and his brothers each have their own bedroom libraries in which they keep their favorite books, collected since early childhood. Jake's written communications include telephone messages, calendar events, schedules, notes, recipes, invitations, thank-you notes, game brackets (Sega or Nintendo), and occasionally letters and poems.

Jake has a special interest in his collections of stickers, stamps, coins, puzzles, board games, maps, newspaper clippings, and baseball, football, and basketball cards. He also enjoys reading his bedtime story books, magazines (especially *Sports Illustrated for Kids*), and the newspaper (his favorite parts are the sports page, the comics, and the weather map).

What makes Jake's understanding of language and literacy so culturally different from his school's, although both are apparently based on middle-class standards, is that his home literacy events have been culturally defined and are mediated through his cultural understanding. Jake's world is African American; that is, his growing understanding of who and what he is has consciously and unconsciously been mediated through an African American perspective. We select our artwork, magazines, novels, television programs, music, videos, and movies to reflect interests in African American life and society.

School Context

Like most parents, I inquired about the kindergarten's literacy program before enrolling Jake in school.[9] I wanted to have some idea of how his teachers viewed literacy development and how they planned to conduct literacy instruction. My primary question was, "What approach to literacy will you use?" Jake's private, full-day kindergarten was founded by three Jewish women, two of whom taught the kindergarten class, while the third served as school administrator. The teachers informed me that they had taught for many years and were aware of the modern trends. They had therefore designed a program that included what they considered to be the strong points of several programs. Jake's classmates included twelve European Americans (eight were Jewish) and two African American children. His teachers tried to provide all the children with what they thought the children would need to know in order to be successful readers and writers in grade one. As a result, the classroom was colorful and full of print.

---

[8] "Fingerplay" is a term often used to describe actions made with the fingers as children sing a song. For example, the motions used with the song "The Itsy Bitsy Spider" are fingerplay.

[9] During my years as a classroom teacher, many parents asked what type of reading program I planned to use. While most parents do not use the term "literacy programs" or inquire about writing programs per se, they do inquire about reading. I have also found that parents are interested in the methods used to teach spelling and vocabulary.

Labels were placed on cubbyholes, activity centers, children's table chairs, and charts.[10] The reading material was an eclectic mix of basals, trade books, and a small library of children's classics.

In first grade, Jake attended a public elementary school. This classroom was a mixed-age group (grades one and two) of twenty-three children, including seventeen European Americans, four African Americans, and two Asian Americans. His teacher described her literacy program as literature-based, and she stressed reading and writing. This teacher read to the children, who also read individually or in small groups. The reading materials included recipients of the Caldecott award and other award-winning books, stories, and poems by children's favorite authors, classics of children's literature, and writing "published" by the students. The children especially liked to read folk tales. As they gained reading and writing skills, the children coauthored, published, and shared their own work. Students were also encouraged to read and write for pleasure. In all these works, I recall that very few were written about or authored by people of color, except for a few on the Caldecott list.

Jake attended a different elementary school for second grade. I eagerly met his new teacher and asked my standard question about literacy. She informed me that she used the basal approach, which she believed ensured that all the "skills" needed to be a successful reader would be covered. The particular basal series she used included "universal" themes and contained illustrations of various racial/ethnic groups but made little reference to the culture of the people. There were several "ethnic" stories, but I consider their authorship suspect, at best.[11] The series also included isolated skill development, vocabulary regulated text, several thematically organized stories, informational selections, and limited writing opportunities. This class of twenty-eight children included twenty European Americans, five African Americans, and three Asian Americans.

Not wishing Jake to repeat this basal approach in grade three, I spoke with other mothers in the neighborhood, soliciting information about the "good" third-grade teachers. After much prayer, I informed the principal of my choice. Now in third grade, Jake is experiencing what his teacher refers to as a whole language approach to literacy, which includes lots of reading and writing for meaning, working in cooperative groups, process writing, and having sustained time for reading and writing. Writing is a daily activity, and Thursday mornings are designated as Writing Workshop mornings with parent volunteers who assist students in a variety of ways, from brainstorming topics to editing their writing. The teacher allows time for individual and small group readings of trade books on a daily basis. Since my conversation with Jake, I have learned his teacher had selected the books she planned to use during the school year, ahead of time, and the children were allowed only to choose which of these books to read. All of the books were written by European American authors. Even the folk tales

---

[10] Activity centers are areas set aside for special activities. For example, the science center, math center, etc., all have activities specifically designed for children interested in learning more about a selected topic.

[11] Many stories contained in basals, like the one Jake used in second grade, are written by teams of authors seeking to control vocabulary or teach specific skills. Basal stories are often abridged or edited versions of original works, and in some instances, such as folk tales, legends, and fairy tales, are translations or a retelling of the original.

from other countries were rewritten by European Americans. Very few books by or about U.S. minorities have been read to students by the teacher, student teachers, or in the reading groups.

I cannot account for the moment-by-moment decisions Jake's teachers have had to make each day. However, I can review the philosophies behind the programs they use. Theoretically, each literacy program purports to be culturally neutral and not mediated by any dominant view of language, when, in fact, a Eurocentric, mainstream cultural view dominates. Darder (1991) argues that it is important to understand the historicity of knowledge:

> The dominant school culture functions not only to support the interests and values of the dominant society, but also to marginalize and invalidate knowledge forms and experiences that are significant to subordinate and oppressed groups. This function is best illustrated in the ways that curriculum often blatantly ignores the histories of women, people of color, and the working class. (p. 79)

Having held a conference with each of Jake's teachers and observed each class setting on several occasions, I can say without hesitation that each teacher believed that she was doing her best to meet the needs of each child in her classroom. That is, she was trying to foster a growing sense of literacy competence in each child. Yet, I don't believe that any of Jake's teachers were aware that they were also narrowly defining the cultural lens through which all children in the classroom were expected to understand literacy.

Thus, in four short years Jake has experienced a wide range of philosophies, approaches, and instruction in literacy, and, at the same time, a narrow ethnocentric view of school literacy. All of his teachers have meant to encourage his growth and development as a literate person. Why, then, have they failed to acknowledge an important part of who he is and what he *culturally* brings to the school literacy program? Reyes (1992) argues that teachers often fail to make adjustments in their approaches to literacy for culturally and linguistically diverse learners because

> the majority of [teachers] are members of the dominant culture, implementing programs designed primarily for mainstream students. Teachers implementing these programs tend to treat students of color as exceptions to the norm, as students who should be assimilated into the dominant group, rather than accommodated according to their own needs. (p. 437)

Some theorists, researchers, and teachers may suggest the counter argument; that is, that elements of the mainstream culture are apparent in all "parallel cultures" and that it is easiest to teach to the mainstream (Hamilton, 1989).[12] I would argue that to ignore, consciously or not, the culture and language that each child brings to the literacy table is to mis-educate him or her. As the research by Au (1993), Morrow (1992), and Reyes and Laliberty (1992), among

---

[12] Recently, Hamilton (1989) used the term "parallel cultures" to refer to the historical experiences of domestic minorities in the United States. "Parallel" conveys a sense of coexistence with the more dominant European American culture so loosely referred to as American culture. The term "domestic minorities" is used to refer to minority groups that have a long history in this country (African Americans, Asian Americans, etc.) but whose forefathers and foremothers lived elsewhere — except in the case of Native Americans.

others, has shown, when cultural and linguistic adjustments are made to school literacy programs, all children benefit.

You may wonder if I have tried to inform Jake's teachers of the narrowness of the literacy lens through which they seem to be defining literacy development and instruction. I admit that I have failed miserably to take a strong stand. Rather than confront them about the lack of culturally responsive literacy instruction, I have expressed my concerns for Jake's personal literacy growth. For example, I have shared multicultural book lists with Jake's teachers and offered to serve as a resource. I have honestly wanted to inform Jake's teachers of two things: one, the need to be more sensitive in their approach to the language and cultural experiences that children bring to the classroom; and two, the need to incorporate more books written by people of color to legitimize the contributions of all literate people. Yet I have also believed that expressing my thoughts might jeopardize Jake's educational future with some kind of backlash.

A STATUS REPORT

While literacy theorists, researchers, and practitioners continue to suggest that school literacy is culturally neutral, Jake's literacy experiences offer an intimate and compelling argument that, as currently practiced, school literacy has been and still is narrowly defined in terms of culture. Only the packaging is new.

Descriptions of my conversation with Jake have met with lots of head nodding and similar stories from many of my non-White students. Delpit (1988) has shared similar insights into what she correctly describes as the "silenced dialogue." The commonsense response among some people of color to school literacy (and schooling in general) has been to take a "way things are" attitude. Many people of color understand that there are inequalities in the educational system; however, we also understand that little can be done without massive school reform. So, to be educated in our current system requires accepting that "this is the way things are. If you want to advance you must learn to play the game." That is, institutionalized racism is something we all know, but see as an unavoidable part of education in U.S. society.

In sharing my analysis with my graduate students, several European Americans have questioned why I refer to Jake's school literacy experiences as being narrowly defined and inquired what is so "acultural" about his literacy education. They ask, "Aren't literature-based and whole language programs built upon notions of constructivist theory that embrace notions of culture?" Of course, my students' understanding is correct: Current holistic school literacy programs support constructivist theory. I guess that's what is so frightening.

While the rhetoric of school literacy programs suggests that culture is part of the theoretical framework, "culture" has been narrowly defined to mean middle-class European American culture. The tacit assumption is, then, that all children are being well served by the new literacy programs that are built on the "natural" language acquisition of middle-class European American children. However, natural language acquisition is mediated through the particular culture in which the child lives. The reality, then, as shared in this article, is that theoreticians,

researchers, teacher educators, practitioners, and publishers of literacy approaches and programs are frequently unaware of their assumptions.

Teacher
Ed.

Some may truly believe that they are delivering on their promise to build on
the culture and language of the child, but what they have been unable, or unwilling, to acknowledge is that school literacy, as it exists, is not universal or
reflective of the language and culture of many children. They claim that current
school literacy programs and practices are acultural. These programs, however,
clearly put some children at a disadvantage, while giving an advantage to others.
It is clear, even to a nine-year-old, that school literacy is narrowly defined. ✓ Jake

DISCUSSION

In order to meet the needs of our U.S. society, which is rapidly becoming more
culturally diverse, our literacy programs should offer more than sensitivity training, human relations, or attitudinal shifts to issues of culture and linguistic diversity. Programs are needed that will also help teachers transform their thinking
about the role of language and culture in literacy development. It is simply not
enough to inform teachers of what they do not know. Teachers need to question
"cultural bumps," or mismatches in expectations of performance in literacy development (Garcia, 1994, personal communication). As Barnitz (1994) states,
"Teachers must recognize difference as manifestations of cultural discourse
which can be expanded rather than interrupted or suppressed" (p. 587).

T. ED

What I see is an institutionalized racism that is grounded in the theories used
to discuss literacy and to inform and educate teachers and teacher educators. I
believe that we need to enhance pre-service teacher curricula and education.
The current method of dispersing concepts of diversity, inclusivity, or multiculturalism across several courses, hoping students will synthesize these issues into
a workable whole, has been ineffective. Pre-service teachers also need intensive
education in understanding the dynamic role that culture plays in language and
literacy development and in defining school literacy.

In a pre-service teacher education course I teach, I use literature authored by
domestic minority men and women as a starting point for pre-service teachers
to begin to reflect on their cultural assumptions about how they "read the word
and the world" (Freire, 1985). The method has been effective in helping many
students face their own, heretofore unvoiced, assumptions of their own culture
and the cultures of other groups.

✳

Most of my students are in their early twenties and have never really concerned themselves with issues of race. Even the students who are members of
U.S. minority groups prefer not to discuss race, ethnicity, or culture openly. At
the opening of class, for example, many of my students think that their cultural
understanding will not affect the students they teach. They believe that their
most important concern should be the subject matter and how to transmit effectively a love for their subject to their students. Some of my students also have
difficulty understanding the notion of institutionalized racism in U.S. public
education. It is at this point in the course that I begin to share the daily occur-
rences in the lives of my children. Further, some of my European American

✳ Cf. Colleague who was startled to hear that I read a
text differently

students see themselves only as "American" and do not wish to deal with their heritage. They want to minimize any tie to Europe and only concentrate on their "Americanness." Some students believe that most U.S. minority group members are poor people, and that most poor people (from all racial groups, but especially those seen most frequently in the media — African Americans and Latinos) really don't care about their children's education. Some also think that children from minority groups don't care about their own education. Most of my students have not even considered how to prepare to teach in multicultural or multilingual classrooms. They tend to live under the false assumption that they can get jobs in homogeneous, suburban school districts.

As in most pre-service teacher education courses nationwide, my students are predominantly European American women. However, in each of my classes, I have had at least one U.S. minority group member. The presence of members from these groups has helped give voice to the concerns of their various communities. My courses are elective, which I believe is important, because it means that the students in my class are interested in issues of diversity. In the best of all worlds, all students would be so inclined, but they are not.

One of the first things I do to help my students become aware of their own cultural understandings is to have them write an autobiographical essay. The essay requires them to trace their ancestry over four or five generations, and to explain their families' use of language, food traditions, and other interesting cultural habits. The essays are shared first in small groups and then with the whole class. In this way, students can readily understand that everyone is a product of their culture, knowingly or not. I too share my cultural and ethnic background. As a person of African, Native, and European American descent, yet who looks only African American, I use my background and life as a springboard for discussions of students' cultural diversity and the limited conception of "culture" in most schools. Since this is a semester-long course, we have the time to engage in many activities, such as community and faculty presentations, videos, and readings by U.S. minority members. However, I believe that some of the most productive work occurs in the small group discussions my students have with each other as they respond to literature written by U.S. minority group members. For example, recently we read a number of novels written by Asian Americans. Many of my students had not heard of the internment of Japanese Americans during World War II.

After my students and I have reflected upon the cultural assumptions from which we perceive our world (and those worlds that might differ from our own), we begin to address teachers' roles and how their cultural assumptions affect the decisions they make, their interactions with students, and their selection of teaching materials. I then give the students opportunities to use their growing understanding of cultural knowledge in lessons they design and teach. My students are all required to teach two literacy lessons during the semester. Many of them choose activities that require participants to work together in cooperative learning groups. Four examples come to mind. One student asked each of us to recall an event using the Native American concept of a "skin story" — drawing on animal pelts — to create pictograph symbols to relate that event. Another student separated class members by attributes they could not control (gender, hair color, size of feet). The "minority" group members (men in this case) were seated in the front of the classroom and were the only students the leader of the exercise asked to respond to her questions. In a third example, a student distributed a series of photographs to small groups and had each group classify the people in the photos, rating them on attributes such as who appeared most intelligent, most successful, and nicest. Finally, a student asked us to read current newspaper articles about war-torn countries and write a diary entry or letter to a government official from the perspective of someone in the country. Through such exercises and activities, my students have learned that culture is a complex issue, one that cannot be taken lightly. They learn to think and act reflectively and become predisposed to considering issues of race, class, gender, age, and sexual preference. Moreover, they understand that their decisions must be based on more than theory; they must also consider the interrelationship of power and knowledge.

I also design in-class lessons around students' responses to the authentic texts they have read. Throughout their field experiences, I have been impressed by the culturally responsive approach to literacy and literature that many of my students have taken with them into the field. For example, one of my students invited recent Asian immigrants to her eighth-grade class to be interviewed by her students. She believed that the face-to-face interactions her students had during the interviews allowed them to understand better the hardships endured by the new U.S. citizens. Another student taught *Huckleberry Finn.* She began the lesson by sharing the historical context in which the novel was written, a model I insist each student use in my class. When confronted by an African American student about the use of the word "nigger" in the novel, she was able to facilitate a group discussion on the use of derogatory terms. She believed that membership in my class enabled her to deal openly with the student and the offensive term. Her experience demonstrates that it is possible to create multicultural learning communities within classrooms that are based on critical literacy theory that validates and legitimizes all learners.

CONCLUSION

In this article, I have argued that for school literacy to begin to move beyond its "neutral" conception of culture, educators at all levels must acknowledge the role and importance of more than one culture in defining school literacy. Educators have not effectively built upon the culture and language of every child, and have set arbitrary standards of acceptance and defined them as normative. I have also argued for the reconceptualization and program development of school literacy, not to dismantle, but to strengthen, literacy frameworks. We can and must do a better job of inviting all students to the literacy table and including them in conversations on school literacy.

I had initial misgivings about sharing my conversation with Jake, as I feared that my thinking would be misinterpreted. My fears lay with the "predictable inability" (West, 1993) of some European Americans to consider honestly the shortcomings of programs they espouse as universal. In addition, I was concerned that my colleagues would view the conversation as one isolated event,

ignoring the fact that there are countless instances of narrow cultural constructions of literacy in the daily lives of culturally and linguistically diverse children.
I was also reluctant to give such an intimate look into my private world. Therefore, I hope that sharing the incident opens conversations about reconceptual-
izing and reforming school literacy. When I wonder if I've done the right thing,
I recall Jake saying to his older brothers, "I want to share a picture of my real
self."

REFERENCES

Apple, M. (1992). The text and cultural politics. *Educational Researcher, 21*(7), 4–11, 19.
Au, K. (1993). *Literacy instruction in multicultural settings.* Fort Worth, TX: Harcourt Brace
Jovanovich.
Barnitz, J. (1994). Discourse diversity: Principles for authentic talk and literacy instruction.
Journal of Reading, 37, 586–591.
√ Barrera, R. (1992). The cultural gap in literature-based literacy instruction. *Education and
Urban Society, 24,* 227–243.
√ Cook-Gumperz, J. (Ed). (1986). *The social construction of literacy.* Cambridge, Eng.: Cam-
bridge University Press.
Cose, E. (1993). *The rage of a privileged class.* New York: Harper Collins.
Darder, A. (1991). *Culture and power in the classroom: A critical foundation for bicultural
education.* New York: Bergin & Garvey.
Delpit, L. (1986). Skills and other dilemmas of a progressive Black educator. *Harvard
Educational Review, 56,* 379–385.
√ Delpit, L. (1988). The silenced dialogue: Power and pedagogy in educating other people's
children. *Harvard Educational Review, 58,* 280–298.
Delpit, L. (1991). A conversation with Lisa Delpit. *Language Arts, 68,* 541–547.
Delpit, L. (1993). The politics of teaching literate discourse. In T. Perry & J. Fraser (Eds.),
Freedom's plow: Teaching in the multicultural classroom (pp. 285–295). New York: Routledge.
Du Bois, W. E. B. (1965). *The souls of Black folks.* New York: Bantam. (Original work
published in 1903)
Ellison, R. (1952). *Invisible man.* New York: Random House.
Fine, M. (1987). Silencing in public schools. *Language Arts, 64,* 157–174.
Freire, P. (1985). Reading the world and the word: An interview with Paulo Freire. *Language
Arts, 62,* 15–21.
Freire, P., & Macedo, D. (1987). *Literacy: Reading the world and the word.* South Hadley, MA:
Bergin & Garvey.
Giroux, H. (1987). Critical literacy and student experience: Donald Graves' approach to
literacy. *Language Arts, 64,* 175–181.
Goodman, K. (1986). *What's whole in whole language?* Portsmouth, NH: Heinemann.
Goodman, K. (1989). Whole-language research: Foundations and development. *Elementary
School Journal, 90,* 207–221.
Gutierrez, K. (1992). A comparison of instructional contexts in writing process classrooms
with Latino children. *Education and Urban Society, 24,* 244–262.
Halliday, M. (1975). *Learn how to mean.* London: Edward Arnold.
Hamilton, V. (1989). Acceptance speech, Boston Globe-Horn Book Award, 1988. *Horn Book,
65*(2), 183.
Heath, S. (1983). *Ways with words: Language, life and work in the communities and classrooms.*
Cambridge, Eng.: Cambridge University Press.
Hirsch, E. (1987). *Cultural literacy: What every American needs to know.* Boston: Houghton
Mifflin.
Hughes, L. (1951). Theme for English B. In L. Hughes, *Montage of a dream deferred* (pp.
39–40). New York: Henry Holt.

Labov, W. (1972). The logic of nonstandard English. In R. D. Abrahams & R. C. Troike (Eds.), *Language and cultural diversity in American education* (pp. 225–261). Englewood Cliffs, NJ: Prentice Hall.

McLaren, P. (1988). Culture or canon? Critical pedagogy and the politics of literacy. *Harvard Educational Review, 58,* 213–234.

Meek, M. (1982). *Learning to read.* Portsmouth, NH: Heinemann.

Morrison, T. (1992). *Playing in the dark: Whiteness and the literary imagination.* Cambridge, MA: Harvard University Press.

Morrow, L. (1992). The impact of a literature-based program on literacy achievement, use of literature, and attitudes of children from minority backgrounds. *Reading Research Quarterly, 27,* 251–275.

Ovando, C., & Collier, V. (1985). *Bilingual and ESL classrooms: Teaching in multicultural contexts.* New York: McGraw-Hill.

Reyes, M. de la Luz. (1992). Challenging venerable assumptions: Literacy instruction for linguistically different students. *Harvard Educational Review, 62,* 427–446.

Reyes, M. de la Luz, & Laliberty, E. (1992). A teacher's "Pied Piper" effect on young authors. *Education and Urban Society, 24,* 263–278.

Reyes, M. de la Luz, & Molner, L. (1991). Instructional strategies for second-language learners in content areas. *Journal of Reading, 35,* 96–103.

Sawyer, D., & Rodriguez, C. (1992). How native Canadians view literacy: A summary of findings. *Journal of Reading, 36,* 284–293.

Scheurich, J. (1992). Toward a White discourse on White racism. *Educational Researcher, 22*(8), 5–10.

West, C. (1993). *Race matters.* Boston: Beacon Press.

Woodson, C. (1990). *The mis-education of the Negro.* Nashville, TN: Winston-Derek. (Original work published 1933)

Vygotsky, L. (1978). *Mind in society.* Cambridge, MA: Harvard University Press.

Disturbing 1. author's fear of backlash

2. Holistic school lit programs support constructivist theory — but fail to include voices & a study of power

3. author sees institutionalized racism backed by theory

Equity, Equality, and Biculturalism in the Restructuring of New Zealand Schools: A Life-History Approach

SUE MIDDLETON

In this article, Sue Middleton draws on interview data from the initial phase of "Monitoring Today's Schools," a research project to monitor the impact of New Zealand's educational restructuring. Unlike restructuring movements in other countries, the New Zealand movement specifically included goals of social equity and cultural inclusiveness, and Middleton focuses on the reactions of parents, teachers, and administrators to the restructuring efforts surrounding these issues. After presenting a brief historical overview of the development of and debate over equity and cultural inclusiveness in New Zealand education, Middleton presents excerpts from interviews with members of three different schools' boards of trustees, which were created as part of the restructuring effort to move more authority to the local school level. She includes their reactions to the impact of social equity and cultural inclusiveness policies on their schools and their children, and concludes by describing recent developments in New Zealand education regarding these issues.

Since the mid-1980s, governments in many Western countries have restructured their school systems. Such restructuring has produced interchanges among academics, as well as between academics and policymakers. These discussions have generated a large body of literature, much of which has been based on the reading and analysis of policy documents. As texts, policy documents are "capable of being decoded in different ways, depending upon the contexts in which they are read" (Codd, 1990, p. 133). Within university education departments, academics — including sociologists, curriculum theorists, philosophers, and historians — have brought the theories of their disciplines to bear on restructuring policies.

From such perspectives, many academics have criticized the reforms, seeing them as driven by "New Right" economic agendas (Apple, 1989; Aronowitz & Giroux, 1987; Bates, 1990; Grace, 1990). They have argued that education is being increasingly conceptualized by policymakers as an economic, rather than a social, political, or moral, activity. The language of business management, centered around the values of competitiveness, individualism, efficiency, effectiveness, and accountability, is seen as replacing the more "collectivist" concerns that have characterized education policies in many Western societies since World War II (Arnot, 1991; Greene, 1988). For example, the new policies are seen as placing little emphasis on the idea that a central task of schooling is to build and protect democracy, and that strong measures designed to promote equal

Harvard Educational Review Vol. 62 No. 3 Fall 1992, 301–322

opportunities for "disadvantaged groups" are important in bringing this about. Such criticisms of educational restructuring have emerged in the United States (Apple, 1989; Aronowitz & Giroux, 1987; Greene, 1988); in Australia (Yates, 1991); in Britain (Flude & Hammer, 1990); in Canada (Livingstone, 1987); and in New Zealand (Lauder & Wylie, 1990; Middleton, Codd, & Jones, 1990). These analyses have been useful in making visible some of the social theories behind educational restructuring, and also in making connections between the restructuring of education and policy changes in other agencies of the state.

Studies that rely too heavily on academics' readings of texts can "bracket out" — that is, render invisible — the everyday conversations, experiences, and perspectives of people in the schools. It is possible to assume from a reading of some academic critiques of policy texts that these texts characterize teachers and school administrators as passively socialized puppets of the New Right, and schools merely as sites where populations are governed through what Foucault (1980) and others (e.g., Henriques, Hollway, Urwin, Venn, & Walkerdine, 1984) have described as techniques of monitoring, surveillance, and regulation. As Dorothy Smith (1987) has observed, policy research grounded in the analysis of texts makes "a continual transcription of the local and particular activities of our lives into . . . abstracted and generalized forms" (p. 3).

If we are to gain a wider understanding of educational restructuring, we need to augment textual analyses with studies of how the restructuring processes are lived and thought about in specific local sites, such as schools. We can learn by studying the processes of administrative reform through the eyes of, and in interaction with, key protagonists in the various restructuring "dramas" as they are lived (Ramsay, 1990). We need studies that explore relationships between the theoretical assumptions of government policies and the ideas of those who are involved in the everyday implementation of those policies within the schools.

This article draws on research carried out in an initial phase of a wider study designed to monitor within schools the impact of New Zealand's educational restructuring.[1] The larger project, "Monitoring Today's Schools," has been funded by New Zealand's Ministry of Education for a three-year period. Coordinated by David Mitchell, sixteen researchers are each monitoring one school's experiences of educational restructuring over a three-year period. One objective of the project is to "give voice" to those who initially have been those most directly affected by the administrative changes — board members and teachers. A variety of methods are being used: in-depth interviews, observations of meetings, quantitative postal surveys sent to a larger number of schools, the reading of policy documents issued by the Ministry, and descriptions of texts written in schools, such as minutes and agendas, memoranda, and official forms.

[1] Although the central argument and methodology used in this article are my own, the life-history data in it were gathered as part of a wider research project, "Monitoring Today's Schools." The case studies are summarized from a larger report (Middleton & Oliver, 1990); data for the larger project were gathered and/or critical comments on the study were made by the following: David Mitchell (coordinator of the project), John Barrington, Ian Calder, Alan Hall, Barbara Harold, Mike Hollings, Richard Jeffries, Bob Katterns, Paul Keown, Robin McConnell, Clive McGee, Angela Main, Ruth Mansell, Kath Mason, Roger Moltzen, Debbie Oliver, Peter Ramsay, Cathy Wylie, and myself. Some of the material in the present article — especially that pertaining to the New Right — has not been discussed with the research team. An earlier version of this article was presented at the 1991 annual meeting of the American Educational Research Association in Chicago.

In this article, I draw on research that was carried out in an early phase of the study, an analysis of the educational life-histories and perspectives of 111 parents and teachers who had recently been elected or co-opted as members of their schools' boards of trustees.[2]

Between October 1988 and February 1989, when the interviews for this study were conducted, New Zealand state educational institutions were being required by the central government to codify their aims and practices in documents known as school charters. Among other aims and goals, schools were required to design policies to enhance equity and equal opportunities for staff as well as for students. As I shall argue below, the latter requirement differentiated Labour's reforms from those in countries where New Right ideology had become dominant. Board members' experiences of, and ideas about, these issues became central in the questions asked in the interviews. We wanted to know what the board members thought about the officially designated "equity issues." The interview data were discussed in a report entitled "Who Governs Our Schools?" (Middleton & Oliver, 1990). In this article, I draw on the section of that report pertaining to issues of race relations in education.

This article consists of four parts. In the first, I outline the major policy changes in New Zealand education since the Fourth Labour Government came to power. In the second, I provide a brief historical overview of the ways in which equity, equality, and race-relations issues have been conceptualized in New Zealand during the lifetimes of today's school board members. I also sketch for foreign readers the historical context within which such people formed their opinions. In the third section, I present case studies of biculturalism and multiculturalism as conceptualized and experienced by board members in three very different schools. And in the conclusion, I outline policy changes that have been implemented since the research was completed.

THE RESTRUCTURING OF NEW ZEALAND SCHOOLS

New Zealand's Fourth Labour Government (1984–1990) undertook a radical restructuring of school administration. Following recommendations in the "Picot Report" (Taskforce to Review Educational Administration, 1988), policymakers devolved responsibility for many major educational decisions from central government authorities to boards of trustees, composed of parents, staff, and (in secondary schools) student representatives.[3]

[2] "Co-opted" means "invited to join" (as distinct from being elected). Because school boards were required to be representative of their communities, many chose to co-opt members in order to ensure a gender balance and/or ethnic mix of their boards. Some co-opted members with needed skills, such as accountancy. A report by Harold & Mitchell (1990), which was the first report in the "Monitoring Today's Schools" project, contains the information on the numbers of board members who were co-opted after the first round of elections of school boards, and the reasons each school chose to co-opt additional board members.

[3] Unlike the United States or Australia, New Zealand does not have a federal system of government. Until 1988 there was a central Department of Education, located in Wellington, which prescribed the national common core curriculum and designed the syllabi. Decisions over the qualifications, hiring, firing, and promotion of teachers were determined on the basis of national criteria negotiated between the education authorities and the teachers' unions. Building and resource provisions and maintenance were the responsibility of central or regional authorities. The new reforms place many such decisions and responsibilities in the hands of school boards. The structure set up under Labour restricted

New Zealand's Left critics have seen the practices and rationale of Labour's restructuring as mimicking New Right reforms elsewhere — particularly in Britain (Grace, 1990; Lauder, 1990). It is difficult, if not impossible, to deny that, during the term of New Zealand's Fourth Labour Government, the New Right was highly influential in educational policy, as it was in economic and other social policy (Jesson, 1989; Jesson, Ryan, & Spoonley, 1988). Unlike the restructuring policies in Britain, however, New Zealand's changes were also premised on Labour's commitment to equity.

Labour's policies embodied contradictions between the atomized individualism of its free market economic vision and the centralized "socialism" of its conception of equity. While the New Right conceptualizes "the population" as atomized, competitive, acquisitive individuals, Labour's equity policies viewed New Zealand society as composed primarily of groups. These policies were based on the idea that certain groups, through no fault of their own, had been educationally disadvantaged, and were therefore owed compensation. Within this discourse, schools were conceptualized as sites for effecting compensatory justice (Middleton, 1990, 1992; O'Neil, 1977).

The powers and responsibilities of each board of trustees were listed in school charters, which contained detailed statements of broad objectives and specific goals. Some of these objectives were required by government and listed in "charter frameworks" that were issued to the institutions in May 1989 (New Zealand Ministry of Education, 1989). Schools' successes and failures in achieving their stated goals were to be monitored regularly by state Educational Review Officers. "Equity objectives" were to "underpin all school activities" (New Zealand Ministry of Education, 1988). All schools were to ensure that their "policies and practices seek to achieve equitable educational outcomes for both sexes, for rural and urban students; for students from all religions, ethnic, cultural, social, family and class backgrounds, and for all students irrespective of their ability or disability" (New Zealand Ministry of Education, 1988, p. 8).

These requirements were particularly strong with respect to gender (Middleton, 1992) and biculturalism. With respect to biculturalism, each board of trustees was required to accept "an obligation to develop policies and practices which value our dual cultural heritage" (New Zealand Ministry of Education, 1988, p. 6).

EQUITY AND BICULTURALISM IN NEW ZEALAND EDUCATION

Maori people make up around 10 percent of the total New Zealand population. The term "biculturalism" in the New Zealand setting usually refers to relations between Maori (the indigenous Polynesian population) and *Pakeha* (the White descendants of British and other European colonists). Biculturalism is used in various senses. In its less radical sense, it refers to "bicultural individuals," for

---

membership of school boards to parents of current pupils (most parents were elected, although co-options took place in schools without a representative balance of the genders or ethnic groups or in cases when special expertise was needed, such as parents with accountancy skills). In addition, board membership was to include the principal, one or more elected staff representatives, and, at secondary schools, a student representative.

example, *Pakeha* attempting to learn Maori language and customs. In its more radical sense, it refers to the restructuring of major social institutions, such as schools, hospitals, the social welfare and justice systems, according to Maori values. Separatist institutions — Maori-controlled and often funded with public money — are also seen as a way of achieving a "bicultural society." Maori sovereignty activists have argued that *Pakeha* are *manuhiri* (visitors) on Maori land (Awatere, 1984). The term "multiculturalism" is less widely used and has been given less political urgency than have questions of biculturalism in New Zealand's educational restructuring. Multiculturalism is often used to refer to the educational visibility and rights of cultural groups other than Maori and *Pakeha*, including such Pacific Island groups as Samoans and Cook Islanders.

These discourses have, to varying degrees, influenced the rationale and processes of educational restructuring. During the post-World War II years (the time during which many of today's school administrators attended school), equal opportunities were usually conceptualized as the provision of an identical range of educational choices for all children. Any subsequent inequalities were seen as due to lack of ability or effort. By the 1970s, the idea of "treating different groups differently" was gaining some currency. This pluralistic, or multicultural, model rested on the assumption that experiences of cultural diversity could have positive educational outcomes. Unlike the bicultural approaches, multiculturalism does not necessarily prioritize things Maori. By the late 1980s (the period of New Zealand's Fourth Labour Government), the term "equity" was also being widely used in official policy texts. The Fourth Labour Government's notion of equity rested on the assumption that certain social groups had been disadvantaged by their historical and socioeconomic circumstances, and that additional resources — for example, "targeted funding" — were needed to bring about equality of educational opportunity for members of "educationally disadvantaged" groups. This rationale has been supportive of some Maori initiatives for separatist institutions and for Maori-based programs and structures in mixed schools.

In this section, I draw on works published by New Zealand Maori and *Pakeha* scholars to sketch the dominant assumptions about culture and equity that have characterized educational policies, provisions, and debates during the lifetimes of those school board members interviewed for the study. Most members were between thirty-five and forty-five years old.[4]

During the nineteenth and for much of the twentieth centuries, policies regarding Maori education were, to varying and changing degrees, assimilationist. The speaking of Maori language, for example, was discouraged by many teachers on the assumption that it would hinder children's command of English (Barrington & Beaglehole, 1973; Benton, 1981). Until recently, few *Pakeha* were willing to admit that racism was a problem in New Zealand schools, although Maori academics and activists had been saying so for many generations (Bray & Hill, 1973, 1974). Issues of cultural inequality and institutional racism erupted into

[4] New Zealand English has incorporated many Maori words, for which there are no simple translations. The questions we asked in our interviews assumed a knowledge of commonly used New Zealand educational terms such as *taha Maori* or *kohanga reo*. The following account defines these terms and places them in their historical context.

public awareness at the very time that newly formed boards of trustees assumed their new administrative powers. Accordingly, our interviews with them captured their strong opinions on the issues.

The boards of trustees formally assumed their powers in October 1989. A few months later, February 6, 1990, marked the sesquicentenary of the signing of the 1840 Treaty of Waitangi. The Treaty was a legal, or constitutional, document signed by representatives of the British crown and many of the chiefs of the various Maori tribes. Its three clauses — existing in several, at times contradictory, Maori and English versions — addressed issues of Maori rights (Kawharu, 1990; Orange, 1987). Such rights included both property rights (to their lands, forests, fisheries, and other possessions) and "person rights" (the rights accorded to the citizens of this new British colony). The school charter guidelines required boards of trustees "to fulfil the intent of the Treaty of Waitangi makers and partners" (New Zealand Ministry of Education, 1989, p. 6).

During the 1950s and 1960s, when many of today's policymakers, school governors, and teachers were at school, the dominant ideology was that modern New Zealand was an egalitarian society (McLaren, 1973). Many *Pakeha* assumed that equal rights and opportunities for Maori and *Pakeha* already existed. School texts implied that such equality or equal opportunities had been guaranteed in 1840 with the signing of the Treaty (McGeorge, 1981). As our interviews illustrate, however, many Maori had experienced the assimilationist policies of successive governments as oppressive. With Maori language effectively banned in many schools, their educational experiences were of cultural genocide and school failure (Barrington & Beaglehole, 1973; Benton, 1981; Bray & Hill, 1973, 1974; Pere, 1983; Walker, 1985).

The dominant educational ideology of the post-World War II years was outlined in 1943 in the Thomas Report (Beeby, 1986; Renwick, 1986). This report sketched the blueprint for post-World War II secondary schooling, schools that most of today's board members themselves attended. The Thomas Report made little specific mention of Maori students or of cultural inequalities, but rather assumed that the rights and aims discussed applied equally to all individuals.

In contrast to many of today's New Right documents, the Thomas Report constituted education as a social, political, and economic activity. Influenced strongly by American progressivism (Beeby, 1986; May, 1992; Middleton, 1989), it outlined a state school system in which

> all post-primary pupils, irrespective of their varying abilities and their varying occupational ambitions, receive a generous and well-balanced education. Such an education would aim, firstly, at the full development of the adolescent as a person; and, secondly, at preparing him for an active place in our New Zealand society as worker, neighbor, homemaker and citizen. (New Zealand Department of Education, 1944/1959, p. 5)

This "well-balanced education" would be ensured by means of a compulsory core curriculum — English, general science, arts and crafts, mathematics, social studies, music, and physical education. In addition, pupils would select optional groups of subjects according to their interests and abilities. Although vocational considerations were present, these were means to the greater end of building an egalitarian democracy (Beeby, 1986):

The human values we sum up in the word "democracy" have been too much taken for granted. They are still threatened from without, and only active effort and unceasing vigilance can make them secure within. The schools thus have the overriding duty of helping pupils to understand them and live in accordance with them, in other words of assisting to build up a democratic society capable of both defending its essential values and of widening and deepening their influence. (New Zealand Department of Education, 1944/1959, p. 5)

This progressive view was characteristic of New Zealand's First Labour Government (1935–1949), which constructed a strong welfare state. It was assumed that the rights and privileges of democratic citizenship should be, and already were, the same for people of all races and cultures.

At this time, equal opportunities were to be brought about in comprehensive secondary schools provided and administered by the state. Most of the schools chose to differentiate students of different abilities by streaming (tracking) (Whitehead, 1974). Streaming was usually based on those optional subjects that pupils took in addition to the common core subjects. Top-stream students took European languages, such as Latin, French, and/or German; lower stream students took technical subjects, such as woodworking for boys and cookery for girls. The Maori language was not viewed as a top-stream subject and, if offered, was usually taught only to those in general or lower streams (Middleton, 1987; Te Awekotuku, 1988). This hierarchy of knowledge, as our interviews illustrate, served as a hidden curriculum that devalued Maori culture — and Maori pupils — within the schools of this time.

As a former British colony, New Zealand remained politically, economically, and culturally oriented to Britain in the post-World War II years. It would have been unusual at the time for the correctness of colonialism to be questioned in the schools. The content of school curricula of the post-World War II years was strongly influenced by British political ideology with respect to the Commonwealth — the former Empire (McGeorge, 1981). However, during the 1960s and 1970s — the years during the baby boomers' secondary schooling — what had been described in New Zealand's state schools since their nineteenth-century colonial beginnings as our "glorious empire" collapsed. These momentous changes led many *Pakeha* New Zealanders of the postwar generation to question previously taken-for-granted ideas about the nature of races, the supposed supremacy of British over indigenous cultures in the countries they colonized, and the resulting legitimacy of *Pakeha* domination in New Zealand.

Such critiques developed during the 1960s and 1970s of rapidly expanding educational opportunities. More Maori, working-class, rural, and women students had the chance to attend secondary schools and institutions of tertiary education (Nash, Harker, & Charters, 1990). The baby boomers' inflation of school rolls had exacerbated already existing teacher shortages, which resulted in government recruitment of thousands of young people into teaching. Many of these students were members of groups underrepresented in the student bodies of the universities and teachers' colleges — working-class, rural, and small-town origins, Maori, and women (Watson, 1966). In their education, many such students were simultaneously positioned as both successful and marginalized. Their experiences of exclusion or marginality in education made educational change seem desirable. At the same time, their opportunities to work in education and in other white-collar occupations in times of full employment made such changes also seem possible (Middleton, 1987).

As elsewhere in the Western world, these underrepresented groups developed and adopted a variety of radical critiques of education. Maori student groups such as *Nga Tamatoa* demanded Maori cultural and linguistic autonomy in education. Black U.S. civil rights struggles were closely studied by many New Zealand students and teachers. Within New Zealand, many thousands marched in demonstrations against sporting contacts with South Africa and against New Zealand's military involvement with the United States in the Vietnam War. Within such political protest movements, New Left theories that linked racism, capitalism, and colonialism gained some currency.

Within education, many New Zealanders were influenced by the neo-progressivism of the early 1970s that became so powerful among White Western students and educators in the emerging "counterculture" movements — such as free schools, deschooling, and open classrooms. As elsewhere in the Western world, there was much discussion of the neo-progressivist ideas of "pupil centeredness" and of teacher autonomy in meeting the diverse needs and interests of their pupils. In New Zealand, such ideas were not new, but they highlighted once again the kinds of progressive ideas that had influenced aspects of education policy and practices during the 1940s and 1950s.

During the 1970s, education policymakers were influenced by neo-progressive discourses, and also by Maori critiques of their people's invisibility or marginalization in education. From a blending of such ideas, there began to emerge some distinctively New Zealand models of pluralism or multiculturalism (Metge, 1982). Policymakers had long taken for granted that "equal opportunities" meant equal formal or legal rights of access to a similar range of educational choices — a form of liberalism in which "equal" means "the same" (Secada, 1989).

By the early 1970s, this notion of equality was being questioned, and equality began being interpreted as a means towards the broader social goal of parity between groups (Beeby, 1986). Bill Renwick, Director General of New Zealand Education in the 1970s, posed the question, "How in a society that values equality of opportunity and fairness can special treatment be justified for people whose attributes might otherwise be similar to others except on matters of ethnic affiliation?" (Renwick, 1986, p. 111).[5]

During the 1980s, the Department of Education began to require teachers to incorporate a Maori dimension into the various subjects of the curriculum, rather than teach Maori studies as a separate compulsory subject. This version of biculturalism was officially termed *taha Maori* (New Zealand Department of Education, 1987).

The *taha Maori* approach to curriculum has been criticized by many Maori (and some *Pakeha*) on the grounds that, while it may help to combat *Pakeha* ignorance or racism, it benefits *Pakeha* rather than Maori students. It does little, if anything, to alleviate the disenchantment, unemployment, and imprisonment of Maori youth (Smith, 1990; Walker, 1985). Achievement statistics, together

---

[5] The Director General was the chief executive in the former Department of Education, now replaced by the Ministry and much reduced in size and functions.

with historical, sociological, and biographical accounts, have provided evidence that, for Maori as a group, state schooling has served to reproduce, rather than alleviate, social disadvantage in terms of employment, political power, socioeconomic status, health, and morale (Awatere, 1984; Irwin, 1990; Smith & Smith, 1990; Walker, 1985). Many Maori have argued for, and established, their own educational institutions. These are seen as a means of reviving Maori language, of protecting cultural autonomy, and of developing curricula that teach tribal knowledge and approach the academic disciplines from Maori perspectives (Awatere, 1984; Smith & Smith, 1990; Walker, 1985).

The *kohanga reo* (literally, Maori language nests) are total-immersion Maori language preschools, initiated and controlled by Maori communities and funded by the state. In these schools, not only have the children been immersed in Maori linguistic and cultural environments, but parents, too, through their involvement, have learned the language, become involved in educational debates and activities, and become politically active in education (Irwin, 1990). Maori people have been able to exert considerable pressure on state primary schools to provide bilingual or total-immersion Maori language classes for children coming from *kohanga reo*. Separate Maori language schools (*kura kaupapa Maori*) are preferred by many Maori parents (Smith & Smith, 1990). Maori withdrawal from the *Pakeha* education system and the establishment of separate Maori education systems is the project of many Maori educational activists in the 1990s.

The 1980s saw strong protests by some Maori that the Treaty of Waitangi had not been honored, and that they had been dispossessed of Maori lands, forests, and fisheries (Awatere, 1984; Kawharu, 1990; Orange, 1987). Many Maori educators argued that Maori rights to cultural autonomy, as well as political sovereignty and economic self-sufficiency, were guaranteed by the Treaty. During the administration of the Fourth Labour Government, the treaty was written into legislation, departmental regulations, and policy documents, including the school charters. In our interviews with board members, we asked them to discuss their experiences with, and opinions on, these issues.

BICULTURALISM AND MULTICULTURALISM IN THE EDUCATIONAL LIFE-HISTORY NARRATIVES OF SCHOOL BOARD MEMBERS

Through life-history interviews, we explored with board members their reasons for joining a board of trustees, their opinions of their own schooling in comparison with that of their children, their opinions of the restructured school system, and their priorities as board members.[6] We introduced the study in the following way:

[6] In this early phase of our study, fourteen schools were participating (there are now sixteen). Because there were fourteen interviewers, we designed a questionnaire to give form to the life-history narratives. Interviewers used their discretion in deciding in which order to ask the questions. Some interviewers and interviewees preferred to begin with their own schooling and proceed chronologically; others preferred to begin with their present work on the board and then to move back in time. Because of the lack of time and resources, we were unable to tape record and transcribe the interviews (although one interviewer did this himself). The majority kept detailed notes. These were verified by the interviewees before being reported. Respondents also had the opportunity to comment on a draft of the report before it was finalized.

We are trying to find out what board members believe to be key issues in education and what they believe should be the main priorities in education. In this interview I should like to ask you about how you see your work on the board and how your views on education have been formed.

We asked them for their opinions on the social policies (equity issues) that, by their school charters, they were required to address:

There are a number of issues that boards and schools will have to deal with when working out their charters. Could you tell me what your views are on some of these issues and how they relate to your school?

The board members were invited to comment on each of the equity issues that were constituted in school charter frameworks as requiring special treatment in education. These issues included: equity in general, biculturalism and multiculturalism, the place of *taha Maori* and Maori language in the curriculum, the educational significance of the Treaty of Waitangi, equal opportunities for women and girls, education of pupils with handicaps and disabilities, the role of teachers' unions, and religion in state schools.

A major objective in writing the report (Middleton & Oliver, 1990) was to make board members' ideas and difficulties visible to one another. Although we summarized and quantified some data, the main objective of our inquiry was not to do a survey of the 111 board members. Rather, we were interested in how board members positioned themselves with respect to the various, changing, and often contradictory equity discourses — the debates then raging in the mass media, in parliament, on *marae* (Maori tribal or family meeting places), and in other public and private spaces. We were interested in the variety of views expressed by board members within each school. A school-by-school (or case study) approach enabled us to compare the boards of different types of school. In our report, we made this comparison with respect to each of the equity issues that board members would be required to address in their charters. Here, however, I explore only the question of biculturalism.[7]

Our interview data depicted school communities that embodied wide differences of opinion and perspectives on biculturalism and multiculturalism. Strong differences were evident between schools in communities with distinctive ethnic/cultural mixes. For example, the board members of the only predominantly Maori school in our study placed a higher priority on Maori language and culture than did those of the predominantly *Pakeha* schools. While most of the board members of the former placed top priority on total immersion or bilingual education, most *Pakeha* schools' board members did not see the relevance of these policies to their schools. However, although they did not see a justification for bilingual or bicultural teaching of *Pakeha* pupils, most supported the rights of access of Maori pupils to such an education. Few, if any, board members openly expressed overtly racist ideas. Most expressed liberal rather than radical or conservative views and favored some degree of *taha Maori* and/or multicultural experiences in their schools' curriculum.

Wide differences of opinion were particularly evident on the boards of the two schools with large Maori populations and predominantly *Pakeha* boards. In

---

[7] Some of the interview material on gender is discussed in Middleton (1992).

both these schools, Maori board members favored bilingual/bicultural programs, while *Pakeha* members' attitudes to these programs ranged from supportive to indifferent to hostile. Board members of one multicultural school (a school with many pupils from families of recent immigrants) were generally supportive of multiculturalism in the sense of learning about other cultures, but only if such learning were within the framework of the dominant New Zealand *Pakeha* culture. In the following section, I will discuss three schools: a large, predominantly Maori, urban school; a small, predominantly *Pakeha*, rural school; and a large school in a small town with a mixed Maori-*Pakeha* population.

CASE STUDIES

A Predominantly Maori Urban School

With the exception of one parent and one staff representative, all members of this school's board are Maori, including the principal. The school's area contains a range of income levels, including many state houses.[8] Many of the families in the school community are on welfare benefits or in low-paid jobs, and were reported to be experiencing severe financial hardship. As one board member explained, "The children here lack food, their health is poor, some children do not have more than one meal a day." Board members described ways in which poverty structured the work of the school. For example, the board established a cooked lunch scheme. Cooking school lunches provided some parents with the opportunity to contribute to the welfare of the school in a way that gave them confidence in their abilities to help.

Eighty percent of the school's present pupil population is Maori, which reflects the community's ethnic composition. Some board members mentioned the reality of daily transporting of pupils both away from and into the school. For example, some members of a fundamentalist Christian sect, who viewed *taha Maori* curricula as "paganism," were sending their children to a school out of the area (Jesson, Ryan, & Spoonley, 1988; Klatch, 1987). In contrast, several board members who lived outside the school's catchment area had chosen this school over their local school because of its Maori emphasis. One *Pakeha* board member chose it because she wanted her child to have a bicultural education. A Maori board member — a university graduate who lived in an affluent, predominantly *Pakeha* suburb — said: "I've had to drive my kids to a school with 80 percent Maori kids, Maori teachers, where Maori things are valued and our kids could speak Maori. . . . I don't settle for less than total immersion."

Commitment to total immersion and/or bilingual education was mentioned by the majority of the board members as their major reason for seeking election. The majority of the Maori board members had grown up either speaking Maori or hearing Maori spoken, but being discouraged from speaking it because of the dominant belief at the time that it would hold them back educationally. While some had attended secondary schools where Maori was taught, it was sometimes unavailable to "bright" Maori pupils, who were expected to study French and/or Latin; rather, Maori was available only to those in the lower — for example,

---

[8] These are houses owned by central government and rented to low-income earners for a nominal rent. The newly elected National Government is in the process of privatizing these facilities.

"general" — streams. In Bourdieu's (1971) terms, "Maori knowledge" was not accorded the status of academic "cultural capital" in state schools (Harker, 1990).

In contrast, this school's philosophy was grounded in a commitment to Maori language and culture. As one board member expressed it, "The language is a marker of who you are and what you stand for. This, in fact, gives kids *mana* [status, prestige, self-esteem]. . . . Being told who you are is the most important thing in the school." When asked to comment on biculturalism in their school's priorities, most of these board members emphasized the necessity of bilingualism. Several board members saw the centrality of Maori language and culture in the school as mandated by the school's commitment to the Treaty of Waitangi. "It's very much part of our mission statement: 'under the guidance of the *tangata whenua* [people of the land],' " said one *Pakeha* board member, acknowledging Maori rights as the indigenous people, the *tangata whenua*, and thereby positioning herself within the discourse of Maori sovereignty (Awatere, 1984). Maori rights to cultural autonomy through education had, within this discourse, been guaranteed by the Treaty, and this philosophy had been made "official" in the school charter's "mission statement." Although few board members at first were resistant to Maori language as a medium of instruction, one Maori board member described how she overcame her initial reservations: "When I came to the school once there was an atmosphere of love, and the feeling converted me."

The school offered students a choice of educational programs: total Maori-language immersion, bilingual programs (with Maori as a second language), and a multicultural option with English as the medium of instruction. *Taha Maori* was described by several board members as "a program to sensitize *Pakeha* people." As such, they maintained, it had its place in New Zealand education, but should be taught by *Pakeha*. The majority saw biculturalism as having a higher priority than multiculturalism, although most, as one board member expressed it, supported the rights of "Pacific Islanders, Chinese, and others. Their culture is also important." Opinions on the Treaty of Waitangi were hindered for some by their need to learn more about it; this was further reflected in their wish that their children learn about the Treaty in school: "I'd like to see it built in as part of the children's education. It should be part of the curriculum."

While most board members had tertiary qualifications and had worked in professional occupations, one described himself as an "unemployed laborer" and several had worked in manual jobs.[9] These "working class" members had close links with many of those parents who had not gained educational qualifications and who previously may have felt distant from schools. The board members had endeavored to ensure representation of "working class" as well as tertiary-educated Maori and *Pakeha* parents. To illustrate, I shall sketch two brief individual profiles.

Walter described his occupation at the time of interview as "unemployed laborer."[10] He had grown up "in the backblocks" (a remote rural area) on family land. His upbringing was steeped in Maori tradition: "At home, Maori was our

[9] Tertiary (postsecondary school) qualifications include university degrees, teachers college or other professional diplomas, certificates, and other credentials from Polytechnics.

[10] I have not given my interviewees' surnames for two reasons. First, in New Zealand, it is customary for adults in a similar age group to be on first-name terms. In this study, researchers and researched

first language. We know no English till school. We know to be humble, to look after ourselves and our elders. We respected the elders." However, at school his "Maori knowledge" was not accorded value — was not constituted as cultural capital. Furthermore, the demands of his responsibilities at home came into conflict with those at school. Walter was subjected to corporal punishment for giving the former too high a priority: "I was punished for not listening, for doing the things I wanted to do, for being late. I used to walk to school. I had to milk the cows at four a.m." His responsibilities as a worker in the family production unit — the farm — were not synchronized with the timetable of compulsory schooling, which had been structured according to the diurnal rhythms of the city (Shameem, 1990). Walter had dropped out of school early. Like several of the other Maori board members, Walter had become interested and involved in schooling as a parent through his experiences in the *kohanga reo* movement (Irwin, 1990).

While Walter had grown up as a native speaker of Maori language in a small farming community, other board members had learned the language at secondary school, at universities, and at teachers colleges. For example, Ngaire was Maori and a graduate of a university and teachers college. She was "successful" in an education profession. Ngaire's parents also spoke Maori, but unlike Walter, she was discouraged from speaking the language: "My parents were native speakers. I didn't speak Maori and had quite limited understanding. Our parents rarely spoke to us in Maori. It was so rare when they did that we'd shrug it off and walk away. They thought we should learn English." Ngaire's family was deeply involved in tribal affairs, and she attended *hui* (tribal ceremonial gatherings) regularly. Ngaire felt that her own children, brought up in cities, were missing out on the benefits of living in an *whanau* (extended family) setting.

Ngaire won a scholarship to a private church-run boarding school for Maori girls.[11] This enabled her to avoid the local high school where "the other Maori kid went" — a school she described as having "a high drop-out rate." She enjoyed the boarding school and became confident academically, in sports, and in Maori language and culture. She was able to attend university because of government studentships available in the 1960s and 1970s for those willing to "bond" themselves to teaching.[12] She studied Maori language in her degree program, and emphasized the importance of choice for her children. She saw a bicultural education as a means of maximizing such choices. As another tertiary-educated Maori woman on this board expressed it, she wanted her children

> to have very good bilingual education and be able to speak well in English and in Maori, do well at school — academically, in sports, in music — have access to as

shared many common experiences — it is unlikely that honorifics would have been used during the research process. Second, and more important, many of those whose voices are heard in this article are Maori. The politics of naming in Maori is different from *Pakeha* family traditions. To give "randomly selected" Maori or *Pakeha* surnames to informants is culturally insensitive.

[11] New Zealand has several prestigious church-run, single-sex boarding schools for Maori girls and boys.

[12] Studentships were salaries paid by the state to student teachers. Those training for secondary school teaching usually went full-time to university. Upon completion of their degrees, they would attend a secondary teachers college for one year (also on salary). The student would then be required to teach for the number of years she or he had received the salary. Ngaire had this kind of award. The scheme, devised during the teacher shortages of the 1960s and 1970s, has since been abolished.

many things as possible so at the end they can make choices — go home to the *marae*, or be a doctor.

A Predominantly Pakeha Rural Primary School

This five-teacher primary school is situated about sixteen kilometers from the nearest provincial city. The community's economic base is farming, and some families have farmed there for several generations. By comparison with many other rural communities in New Zealand, this one is economically well off. The community's ethnic mix is overwhelmingly *Pakeha*, and this small rural school board is all *Pakeha*. There are five parent representatives (two women and three men), a male principal, and a female staff representative. Several board members expressed strong feelings against what they described as "the equity rationalization." They understood equity in the terms in which it had been defined by David Lange (Minister of Education during the Picot and other committees of inquiry). For Lange, equity meant "the unequal targeting of resources" as a means of compensating groups who suffered educational disadvantage in the past (McCulloch, 1990; New Zealand Ministry of Education, 1988). Discretionary funding was to be made available to schools whose constituent parent populations were less able than the affluent to donate time and money.

This targeting of discretionary funds annoyed certain board members. As one farmer argued, "Everyone has the same opportunity if they wish to take it up. There shouldn't be different payments because of people's socioeconomic status or culture." Because of its middle-class *Pakeha* constituency, this school did not qualify for such discretionary allowances, and Barry, one of the parents, believed that it was unfair that parents in his community should subsidize those schools that did: "The parents are paying twice."

The principal and the staff representative were aware that some board members espoused such opinions on equity issues. The principal said, "There shouldn't be a question mark over this. In our school they can't see that all children don't have all opportunities. . . . The board don't see it as an issue." These staff members described *taha Maori* and "movement in the multicultural dimension" as among their priorities for educational change. These priorities indicate that they believed parent education to be essential, since the "parents need to see that change is needed." A staff member reported seeing blatant White racism in the school and commented that a previous school committee had overtly opposed staff use of Maori language greetings in the school newsletter. The principal noted that, while he personally saw biculturalism as a more urgent priority than multiculturalism, "society relates better to multiculturalism."

One board member, while opposed to targeted funding as an equity policy, believed it was important for the children in his school to have some knowledge of Maori culture. He did not, however, approve of *taha Maori* as a name for a component in the compulsory school curriculum: "The name has frightened people. We were happy with 'Maori culture' or 'Maori studies.' "

Like the vast majority of board members interviewed in this phase of our study, he supported the teaching of Maori language as an optional school subject, provided that it was economic to do so: "There will need to be sufficient people wanting to learn to have it as part of the curriculum. . . . It shouldn't be compulsory but I would like to see it available."

Four members of this board described multiculturalism as irrelevant to their school because of its almost homogeneous *Pakeha* population (there were only three Maori pupils in the school). However, some of them also felt that, should children from minority ethnic groups become a significant part of the school population, they would attempt to provide for their needs. Reservations were also expressed about biculturalism in that there was "a danger in separating the two cultures." Further, some members believed biculturalism was potentially divisive. As one parent commented, "Children should all have the same education. There shouldn't be any distinction between races. . . . The Maori claim they want equality. They want more. It's creating a split." Another parent representative argued:

It is important to look at the New Zealand community as being multicultural. The curriculum should take account of New Zealand being multicultural. We have started with a bicultural society. I don't know whether we should be distinguishing Maori and European. European consists of many peoples also.

Several members of this board made comments to the effect that, "We're all New Zealanders."

However, there was more support for including *taha Maori* in the curriculum. As one parent commented, "It will help our children have a better understanding of Maori language and culture. Both cultures need to understand each other better."

Board members were divided over the significance of the Treaty of Waitangi. Two saw it as irrelevant to the present; two others believed it needed to be looked at carefully and, therefore, they sought more information. One of these stated:

I've never read it. My understanding is through the media. It's obvious that kids need to learn about the Treaty, as it has become an issue. Originally I was not happy, but we have a treaty and can't turn a blind eye. At my age we were not taught. Our children need to be informed so they can meet the problems as they arise.

Community opposition to the Treaty, according to a staff representative, arose because it was seen as a land issue and a threat to the farm-based community.

A Small-Town Secondary School with a Mixed Maori-Pakeha Population

This secondary school has around five-hundred pupils, 40 percent of whom are Maori. The school is situated in a community with a substantial Maori population; Maori tribal politics and community activities are prominent. Its economic base is farming and other primary industries. The economic recession had hit some local businesses hard, and unemployment had increased at the time of interviews. The parent trustees of this school comprised five *Pakeha* and two Maori. There were four men (three *Pakeha* and one Maori) and three women (two *Pakeha* and one Maori). The principal and staff representative (both men) were *Pakeha*.

Although all board members expressed some degree of support for the teaching of Maori culture in this school, the board was deeply divided on the nature of, and rationale for, such teaching. For example, they differed over the extent to which biculturalism should be an aim of the school. Of the *Pakeha* representatives, two believed that the school was neglecting non-Maori children (specifically, *Pakeha* and Pacific Island children) in its move towards biculturalism; two believed that bicultural studies should be an optional part of the curriculum. One *Pakeha* said that *Pakeha* parents must accept that "biculturalism is here to stay." He spoke of his horror when, during his own schooling, he had seen teachers beat Maori children for speaking their native tongue within the school. Both Maori board members argued that biculturalism was necessary if *Pakeha* were to come to understand Maori points of view and to be able to work towards a national unity.

Several board members regarded Maori concerns and/or Maori-*Pakeha* relations as their central reasons for having stood for election. Craig, a Maori and a member of his local *marae* committee, had been prompted by his wife to stand: "She works a lot with Maori kids. I can remember the problems I had. I wanted to help our Maori kids."

Rachel, also Maori and a member of her *marae* committee, felt that parents must do more with respect to their children's education: "Especially Maori kids really need encouraging. They're held back because school's an institution run by *Pakeha*. They're intimidated by it."

In contrast, two *Pakeha* members had been approached by people in the community and on the school staff to stand in support of *Pakeha* interests "because some felt the Maori community could stack the board." One, who had lived among Pacific Island people, was also concerned with the visibility and interests of Pacific Islanders: "They're going overboard for Maori. There's others to think of; European and Island as well are important." In other words, she wanted a multicultural rather than a bicultural focus. These two board members were "also concerned that the principal had enough power and shouldn't be given a free reign." They felt that he was trying to develop an undue emphasis on Maori perspectives and Maori education in the school.

One *Pakeha* board member was strongly opposed to recognizing the Treaty as fundamental to the state's commitment to bring about biculturalism in education and in the wider society:

> I think it [the Treaty] should be burnt. Because, as far as I'm concerned, I'm a fifth generation New Zealander. And I feel I have some rights. I'm not responsible for what happened 150 years ago. It doesn't happen in other countries. We're all New Zealanders. The Maori have done very nicely in our system. The ones that are making the noise (radicals) have survived the system. So why the unrest?

This board member, himself a teacher, felt that the school's Maori bias was leading to lowered standards of conduct among the pupils:

> There should be equity, not a biased one toward Maori, which I feel it's heading toward. We're forced to accept substandard behavior from them (uniform, language, etc.). Because they're Maori, they get special treatment. Some teachers let them off, others don't. So there's lack of consistent direction from the top.

Like the vast majority of *Pakeha* board members in the study, however, he wanted today's children to have some knowledge of *taha Maori*, which he described as having "relevance to most subjects." He observed that many parents today "want their children to know things Maori but want their kids schooled in English."

DISCUSSION

Some academics have criticized New Zealand's Fourth Labour Government's educational restructuring policies, which are seen as dominated by the competitive individualism of the New Right (Grace, 1990; Jesson, 1989; Lauder, 1990); the academics have also likened educational reforms in New Zealand to those in Britain. Such interpretations have under-emphasized — or rendered largely invisible — Labour's strong agenda for bringing about social equity through the schools. Labour's policies were, in fact, multivocal in that both New Right individualism and collectivist state interventionism were evident.

In October 1990, eight months after our initial interviews with board members were completed, New Zealand had a general election. Labour lost to the National Party by a massive majority. The economy — more specifically, New Zealand's rapidly escalating rate of unemployment — was the major election issue.

During the National's election campaign, New Zealand's state schools were described as failing by international standards and needing dramatic changes, such as increased privatization, if they were to produce individuals who could compete in an international economy (New Zealand National Party, 1990a,b). In its election manifesto (New Zealand National Party, 1990b), National had conceptualized education as an economic rather than a social issue: "We are investing in education as part of our economic strategy." The object of "investing in achievement" through education was described as creating "a new environment of enterprise." Together with National's policies for industry, agriculture, industrial relations, and tourism, education was described in the manifesto as part of National's "blueprint for the Enterprise Nation." Education was constituted as an economic issue, and Labour's emphasis on equity was seen as contradictory to the kind of education needed to build "the Enterprise Nation." For example, the National Party's spokesperson on education, Lockwood Smith (now Minister of Education), announced that, "Under National, schools will be free to re-negotiate their charters if they wish to do so. They will no longer be compelled to adhere to Labour's 'Orwellian' social agenda" (New Zealand National Party, 1990b, p. 8), and further, that "Labour's social engineering at the expense of our children's future must be stopped" (New Zealand National Party, 1990a, p. 1). The construction of National's Enterprise Nation was thus conceptualized as a purely economic matter — not as an example of social engineering.

In November 1990, shortly after assuming office as Minister of Education, Smith announced that he intended to make the equity requirements in the school charters optional rather than mandatory. Teachers' unions and women's and Maori groups protested vociferously.[13]

---

[13] Although at the time of preparing this manuscript for publication the relevant legislation has not yet been changed, the new political climate is likely to result in a de-emphasis of equity issues within some schools and in less attention being paid to these issues by the state Educational Review Officers.

Our life-history interviews with board members took place several months before the election. These people, with very few exceptions, expressed high opinions of their children's schooling, preferring it greatly to their own. They said that they thought the overall standard of New Zealand education was very high. They did not describe education's core aim as competitiveness, but wanted their children to become "well-rounded individuals." And, although at the time of the interviews most boards had not yet developed equity policies for their schools, the vast majority of them expressed support for some form of equal opportunities or equity policy in their schools (Middleton & Oliver, 1990).

Should such people as the present board members continue to serve on school boards, it is likely that at least some of the bicultural provisions will remain in the charters of predominantly *Pakeha* and multicultural schools. Those predominantly Maori schools that have made commitments to stronger versions of biculturalism — total immersion and/or *kura kaupapa* Maori status — will be able to continue to do so. Those of us who are educational researchers can, by making the protagonists in the debates both audible and visible to one another, assist them in this task.

In his recent edited collection of papers, *Equity in Education*, Walter Secada (1989, p. 68) stated, "Equity in education seems to be uniquely an American notion. Most writers who write about equity and equality of education come from the United States." But, as the above examples illustrate, issues of equity have also been central in New Zealand education, not only in its official policies, but also in the everyday discussions and activities of parents, teachers, and school administrators. Labour's restructuring both localized and intensified debates about education in institutions as well as in private spaces. In Foucault's sense, it has served as "an incitement to discourse" (Dreyfus & Rabinow, 1986).

REFERENCES

Apple, M. (1989). How equality has been redefined in the conservative restoration. In W. Secada (Ed.), *Equity in education.* Lewes: Falmer Press.

Arnot, M. (1991, April). *Feminism, education and the New Right.* Paper presented at the annual meeting of the American Educational Research Association, Chicago.

Aronowitz, S., & Giroux, H. (Eds.). (1987). *Education under siege: The conservative, liberal & radical debate over schooling.* South Hadley, MA: Bergin & Garvey.

Awatere, D. (1984). *Maori sovereignty.* Auckland: Broadsheet Books.

Barrington, J., & Beaglehole, T. (1973). *Maori schools in a changing society.* Wellington: New Zealand Council for Educational Research.

Bates, R. (1990). Educational policy and the new cult of efficiency. In S. Middleton, J. Codd, & A. Jones (Eds.), *New Zealand education policy today: Critical perspectives.* Wellington: Allen & Unwin/Port Nicholson.

Beeby, C. E. (1986). Introduction. In W. L. Renwick, *Moving targets.* Wellington: New Zealand Council For Educational Research.

Benton, R. (1981). *The flight of the amokura.* Wellington: New Zealand Council for Educational Research.

Bourdieu, P. (1971). Systems of education and systems of thought. In M. F. D. Young (Ed.), *Knowledge and control.* London: Croom Helm.

Future interviews carried out in the course of the "Monitoring Today's Schools" project will be recording reactions to the further changes the new National Government is in the process of introducing.

Bray, D., & Hill, C. (Eds.). (1973). *Polynesian and Pakeha in New Zealand education: Vol. 1.* Auckland: Heineman.

Bray, D., & Hill, C. (Eds.). (1974). *Polynesian and Pakeha in New Zealand education: Vol. 2.* Auckland: Heineman.

Codd, J. (1990). Policy documents and the official discourse of the state. In J. Codd, R. Harker, & R. Nash (Eds.), *Political issues in New Zealand education* (2nd ed). Palmerston North: Dunmore.

Dreyfus, H., & Rabinow, P. (1986). *Michel Foucault: Beyond structuralism and hermeneutics.* Chicago: Harvester.

Foucault, M. (1980). *A history of sexuality: Vol. 1.* New York: Vintage.

Flude, M., & Hammer, M. (Eds.). (1990). *The Education Reform Act 1988: Its origins and implications.* Lewes: Falmer Press.

Grace, G. (1990). The New Zealand treasury and the commodification of education. In S. Middleton, J. Codd, & A. Jones (Eds.), *New Zealand education policy today: Critical perspectives.* Wellington: Allen & Unwin/Port Nicholson.

Greene, M. (1988). *Dialectic of freedom.* New York: Teachers College Press.

Harker, R. (1990). Schooling and cultural reproduction. In J. Codd, R. Harker, & R. Nash (Eds.), *Political issues in New Zealand education* (2nd ed). Palmerston North: Dunmore.

Harold, B., & Mitchell, D. (1990). *Getting started* (Monitoring Today's Schools Report No. 1). Hamilton: University of Waikato.

Henriques, J., Hollway, W., Urwin, C., Venn, C., & Walkerdine, V. (1984). *Changing the subject.* London: Methuen.

Irwin, K. (1990). The politics of *kohanga reo.* In S. Middleton, J. Codd, & A. Jones (Eds.), *New Zealand education policy today: Critical perspectives.* Wellington: Allen & Unwin/Port Nicholson.

Jesson, B. (1989). Fragments of Labour. Auckland: Penguin.

Jesson, B., Ryan, A., & Spoonley, P. (1988). *Revival of the right.* Auckland: Heineman.

Kawharu, H. I. (Ed.). (1990). *Waitangi: Maori and Pakeha perspectives of the Treaty of Waitangi.* Auckland: Oxford.

Klatch, R. (1987). *Women of the New Right.* Philadelphia: Temple University Press.

Lauder, H. (1990). The New Right revolution and education in New Zealand. In S. Middleton, J. Codd, & A. Jones, (Eds.), *New Zealand education policy today: Critical perspectives.* Wellington: Allen & Unwin/Port Nicholson.

Lauder, H., & Wylie, C. (Eds.). (1990). *Towards successful schooling.* Lewes: Falmer Press.

Livingstone, D. (Ed.). (1987). *Critical pedagogy and cultural power.* South Hadley, MA: Bergin & Garvey.

May, H. (1992). Learning through play: Women, progressivism and early childhood education, 1920s–1950s. In S. Middleton & A. Jones (Eds.), *Women and education in Aotearoa: Vol. 2.* Wellington: Bridget Williams Books.

McCulloch, G. (1990). The ideology of educational reform: An historical perspective. In S. Middleton, J. Codd, & A. Jones (Eds.), *New Zealand education policy today: Critical perspectives.* Wellington: Allen & Unwin/Port Nicholson.

McGeorge, C. (1981). Race and the Maori in the New Zealand school curriculum since 1877. *Australian and New Zealand Journal of History, 10,* 13–23.

McLaren, I. (1973). *Education for a small democracy: New Zealand.* London: Routledge & Kegan Paul.

Metge, J. (1982). Multiculturalism — Problem or goal? In National Advisory Committee on Maori Education (NACME), *He huarahi.* Wellington: Government Printer.

Middleton, S. (1987). Schooling and radicalization: Life-histories of New Zealand feminist teachers. *British Journal of Sociology of Education, 8,* 169–189.

Middleton, S. (1989). American influences in the sociology of New Zealand education, 1944–1988. In D. Philips, G. Lealand, & G. McDonald (Eds.), *The impact of American ideas on New Zealand's educational policy, practice and thinking.* Wellington: New Zealand/U.S. Educational Foundation.

Middleton, S. (1990). Women, equality and equity in liberal education policies, 1944–1988. In S. Middleton, J. Codd, & A. Jones (Eds.), *New Zealand education policy today: Critical perspectives.* Wellington: Allen & Unwin/Port Nicholson.

Middleton, S. (1992). Gender equity and school charters. In S. Middleton & A. Jones (Eds.), *Women and education in Aotearoa: Vol. 2*. Wellington: Bridget Williams Books.

Middleton, S., Codd, J., & Jones, A. (Eds.), (1990). *New Zealand education policy today: Critical perspectives*. Wellington: Allen & Unwin/Port Nicholson.

Middleton, S., & Oliver, D. (1990). *Who governs our schools?* (Monitoring Today's Schools Report No. 2). Hamilton: University of Waikato.

Nash, R., Harker, R., & Charters, H. (1990). Reproduction and renewal through education. In J. Codd, R. Harker, & R. Nash (Eds.), *Political issues in New Zealand education* (2nd ed.). Palmerston North: Dunmore.

New Zealand Department of Education. (1944/1959). *The post-primary school curriculum* (Thomas Report). Wellington: Government Printer.

New Zealand Department of Education. (1987). *The curriculum review*. Wellington: Government Printer.

New Zealand Ministry of Education. (1988). *Tomorrow's schools*. Wellington: Government Printer.

New Zealand Ministry of Education. (1989). *Charter guidelines for schools*. Wellington: Author.

New Zealand National Party. (1990a). *National: Investing in achievement* (Abridged version of National's education policy). Wellington: Author.

New Zealand National Party. (1990b). *National Party policies for the 1990s: Creating a decent society* (Election Manifesto). Wellington: Author.

O'Neil, O. (1977). How do we know when opportunities are equal? In M. Vetterling Braggin, F. A. Elliston, & J. English (Eds.), *Feminism and philosophy*. Tottowa: Littlefield Adams.

Orange, C. (1987). *The Treaty of Waitangi*. Wellington: Allen & Unwin/Port Nicholson.

Pere, R. (1983). *Ako: Concepts and learning in the Maori tradition* (Department of Sociology Monograph). Hamilton: University of Waikato.

Ramsay, P., with members of the Project CRISP research team. (1990). *There's no going back: Final report of the Curriculum Review in Schools Project*. Hamilton: University of Waikato.

Renwick, W. L. (1986). *Moving targets*. Wellington: New Zealand Council for Educational Research.

Secada, W. (1989). Educational equity versus equality of education: An alternative conception. In W. Secada (Ed.), *Equity in education*. Lewes: Falmer Press.

Shameem, S. (1990). *Sugar and spice: Wealth accumulation and the labour of Indian women in Fiji, 1879–1930*. Unpublished doctoral dissertation, University of Waikato, Hamilton.

Smith, D. (1987). *The everyday world as problematic*. Boston: Northeastern University Press.

Smith, G. (1990). Taha Maori, Pakeha capture. In J. Codd, R. Harker, & R. Nash (Eds.), *Political issues in New Zealand education* (2nd ed.). Palmerston North: Dunmore.

Smith, G., & Smith, L. (1990). Kura kaupapa Maori. In A. Jones, G. McCulloch, J. Marshall, G. Smith, & L. Smith, *Myths and realities*. Palmerston North: Dunmore.

Taskforce to Review Educational Administration. (1988). *Administering for excellence* (Picot Report). Wellington: New Zealand Ministry of Education.

Te Awekotuku, N. (1988). He whare tangata, he whare kura. In S. Middleton (Ed.), *Women and education in Aotearoa*. Wellington: Allen & Unwin/Port Nicholson.

Walker, R. (1985). Cultural domination of taha Maori. In J. Codd, R. Harker, & R. Nash (Eds.), *Political issues in New Zealand education* (1st ed.). Palmerston North: Dunmore.

Watson, J. (1966). Marriages of women teachers. *New Zealand Journal of Educational Studies, 1*(2), 149–161.

Whitehead, C. (1974). The Thomas Report: A study in educational reform. *New Zealand Journal of Educational Studies, 9*(1), 52–56.

Yates, L. (1991, April). *A tale of sound and fury — signifying what? Feminism and curriculum policy in Australia*. Paper presented at the annual meeting of the American Educational Research Association, Chicago.

PART THREE

Changing Classrooms

Opening Up the Classroom Closet:
Responding to the Educational Needs of
Gay and Lesbian Youth

ERIC ROFES

In this chapter, Eric Rofes, gay community activist and author, explores the issues surrounding the schools' failure to meet the educational needs of gay and lesbian youth. He argues that there has been an across-the-board denial of the existence of gay and lesbian youth, and that this has taken place because "their voices have been silenced and because adults have not effectively taken up their cause." Rofes goes on to present some promising initiatives that are designed to change the status quo: Project 10 in Los Angeles and the Harvey Milk School in New York City. He concludes by proposing needed changes in U.S. schools if they are to become truly accessible to gay and lesbian youth.

> Someday, maybe, there will exist a well-informed, well considered and yet fervent public conviction that the most deadly of all possible sins is the mutilation of a child's spirit.
>
> — Erik Erikson

Andy is a middle-class White sixteen-year-old who ran away from his family home in Oregon after suffering years of abuse from his father after the man read his son's love letters from another boy. Arriving in Los Angeles, Andy worked in a fast-food restaurant in the evenings and attended high school during the day, resolving to complete school and get his diploma, despite the obstacles caused by the relocation. Instead of a supportive environment at his new school, Andy found his peers hostile and harassing. Openly gay to his classmates and teachers, Andy was mocked during class time by other students, and received no support from teachers. After he was physically assaulted at the bus stop after school, Andy felt pushed to the point of either quitting school or demanding action.

Nina is a Black fifteen-year-old from Harlem. She had difficulty coping with the rejection she faced in her inner-city high school because she was up-front about being a lesbian. Her mother and brother tried to lend support, but school authorities had little assistance to offer. Name-calling, harassing notes, and verbal threats of violence, including rape, began to turn an upbeat, cheerful girl into a jumble of dysfunction and misery. As Nina faced the unpleasant task of steeling herself for two more years of such assaults, she found herself moving toward leaving school.

Gay and lesbian youth attend schools throughout the nation, and they have existed quietly throughout the history of U.S. education. These students — from

Harvard Educational Review Vol. 59 No. 4 November 1989, 444–453

every ethnic and racial background, in urban, suburban, and rural schools —
have sat passively through years of public school education where their identities
as gay and lesbian people have been ignored and denied. They have done this
because of their own fears and isolation, and because of the failure of gay men
and lesbians to effectively take up their cause. The result has been the creation
of a population within our schools who exhibit significant indications of lack of
self-esteem, emotional problems, and substance abuse.

Yet the late 1980s have seen a new, radical assertiveness by this population,
which has forced individual schools, and then entire school systems, to grapple
with the reality that gay and lesbian youth are in the schools and are not going
to go away. Almost a decade after a gay male student in Cumberland, Rhode
Island, threatened legal action if his right to bring a male date to his prom was
violated, high schools in diverse parts of the nation are confronted with informal
networks of gay youth, formal gay and lesbian student groups, students "coming
out" to teachers and classmates, and the need for appropriate AIDS prevention
information for the particularly high-risk population of gay male youth.

Ten years ago, as an openly gay schoolteacher, I found myself frequently
raising issues related to the educational and social needs of gay and lesbian youth
at educational conferences. Most often, I was challenged by other teachers who
insisted that the term "gay youth" was essentially a contradiction: youth were
sexually neutral, because sexual orientation was formed during late adolescence.
While I was facilitating social programs and rap groups for gay youth — some
as young as thirteen and fourteen years old — my colleagues in the field of
education were insisting that this population didn't exist. "It's just a phase of
rebellion they're going through," I was told.

Yet in working with other projects as a youth advocate for the Massachusetts
Committee for Children and Youth, I saw the urgent needs of this population.
I sat on a youth suicide task force and found numerous cases of young men and
women who had attempted or completed suicide where homophobia was an
issue. Some were simply taunted by their peers as "fags" or "dykes." Others had
histories that revealed deep conflict over gender issues. Some were actively homosexual and had experienced rejection from family, church, or peers.

Yet the entire field of research on youth suicide neglected to discuss any
relationship between homosexuality and suicide among young people. I was a
member of a team of advocates who consulted on a television media piece on
youth suicide that focused on four young men and women who had killed themselves during the past two years. In studying these case histories in depth, it was
clear that the trigger that sent two of the youths over the edge involved their
homosexuality — or peer assumptions of homosexuality. One young man had
been taunted as a "fag" for years. One young woman had recently been rejected
by her girlfriend and had been devastated. Yet, the final television special omitted any references to gay issues; viewers were left mystified that such wonderful
young people would kill themselves. A key clue had been censored by producers.

It has been frustrating to observe critical youth issues enter the field of public
debate, while widespread censorship results in the exclusion of the issues of gay
and lesbian youth. Street outreach workers in urban centers throughout the

nation know that a large proportion of street kids are gay and lesbian youth who have been kicked out of family homes or who have fled abusive family situations — yet academic research on this population rarely acknowledges or probes the needs of gay and lesbian youth. Social workers counseling pregnant teenage women regularly come across young women who have attempted to deny their lesbianism by having a baby — yet few programs exist that are prepared to assist these women in coming to terms with their lesbian identities. AIDS prevention counselors working with teenagers in the schools frequently find themselves educating young people about how to remain uninfected, yet without giving any training or materials to deal with the issue of male-to-male sexual activity among youth.

This across-the-board denial of the existence of gay and lesbian youth has been allowed to take place because their voices have been silenced and because adults have not effectively taken up their cause. And, except in rare instances, gay and lesbian adults have clearly taken steps to ensure that youth issues are *not* a part of the greater community agenda. The stereotypical fears of gay people "recruiting" children into our ranks have been a key barrier to significant moves toward advocacy for youth, but other factors clearly restrict these efforts as well. Many adult gay men and women have not come to terms with their own youth and have not faced the pain of those years of repression, stigma, and harassment. Working with young people would force them to confront difficult, unresolved feelings. Other gay and lesbian adults harbor many of the unfortunate and simplistic views of teenagers held by the larger adult population: adolescents should be seen and not heard. Hence the ageism of the adult gay and lesbian community has restricted efforts to develop an agenda for youth.

Professionals who work with young people — including those in the school system — are finding gay and lesbian youth issues difficult to ignore as we enter the 1990s. Part of this is due to the increased visibility of the gay and lesbian movement, but part is also due to the emerging strength of up-front, outspoken young people who are asserting their identities as young gay men and lesbians. This has resulted in more investigation of the needs of gay and lesbian youth by a wide range of youth-serving institutions. In December 1988, the Seattle Commission on Children and Youth, after extensive public hearings and investigation, issued twenty-one recommendations addressing the "special needs" of gay and lesbian youth. A survey of all public high schools in the state of Illinois has resulted in a large volume of requests from counselors throughout the state for positive information on counseling gay and lesbian youth. A task force of the Minnesota Department of Health recommended that teachers and other AIDS educators of young people ensure that students "see and hear images of gay and lesbian teenagers that are nonprejudicial" as part of a prevention plan focused on gay adolescents.

Perhaps most notable has been the development of two key educational programs focused on meeting the special needs of some gay and lesbian youth. These programs — in Los Angeles and New York City — though different in essential ways, share a commitment to keeping gay and lesbian youth within a public system of education. Formed primarily by lesbians and gay men already involved in public education or youth services, Project 10 in Los Angeles and the Harvey Milk School in Manhattan offer two models of educational programs centered on the needs of gay and lesbian teenagers.

PROJECT 10

Project 10 is run by the Los Angeles Unified School District. It began as a program designed to prevent gay and lesbian youth from dropping out of Fairfax High School. A high school teacher, Virginia Uribe, began the program in 1985 after years of observing the school's failure to serve the educational needs of students who self-identify as gay or lesbian or who express conflicts over sexual orientation. The project has evolved into a general counseling and educational vehicle for both gay and non-gay students and faculty.

Uribe developed the Project 10 model in a manner that acknowledges that different schools within her district will have different needs for programs serving gay and lesbian youth. This flexible model has four components: education, school safety, drop-out prevention strategies, and support services. The program is coordinated by Uribe, who teaches classes during the first two periods of the school day and uses the remainder of the day for Project 10 activities.

Educational components of the project include a speakers' bureau that brings gay and lesbian youth and adults into schools throughout Los Angeles, training and consciousness-raising for school staff members, and the expansion of school libraries to make positive materials on homosexuality accessible to teenagers. Project 10 also provides specific training for teachers on methods of recognizing and responding to harassment of gay and lesbian students, and has created a model back-up system that allows anti-gay incidents to be quickly reported and responded to by school authorities.

A key component of the Project 10 model involves counseling of gay and lesbian youth and of those struggling with issues of sexual orientation. Uribe facilitates informal rap groups, offers drop-in counseling, and has created a peer counseling program. Existing school programs that focused on substance abuse, suicide, and depression have been evaluated and updated to include the experiences and needs of gay and lesbian youth.

Uribe currently serves between two and three hundred youth annually. Seventy percent of the gay-identified teenagers in her school have been young men. She hopes to expand Project 10 throughout the school district, first by designating regional coordinators, and then by establishing resource centers throughout the district run by trained staff members. Project 10 has been the focus of much recent publicity throughout California. Fundamentalists have organized conservative state legislators to sponsor a bill that would cripple programs such as Project 10 by requiring schools not only to obtain parental consent for classroom discussions of homosexuality, AIDS, abortion, and other sex-related topics, but also to verify parents' permission. On the positive side, the California Democratic Party recently adopted a motion at its annual state convention, stating that the party "does hereby join the growing list of professional and civic bodies which believe that all persons regardless of sexual orientation should be afforded equal opportunity within the public educational system. We resolve that every school district in California should provide counseling for students who are struggling with their sexual/gender orientation based on the Project 10 model." Similar endorsements of the project have come from the Los Angeles City Council and the National Education Association.

Critical to the success of Project 10 has been the strength of social service organizations in Los Angeles serving the needs of gay and lesbian youth. The Los Angeles Gay and Lesbian Community Services Center has a Youth Services Department staffed by about twenty employees. The department offers seven weekly rap groups for youth throughout Los Angeles County, as well as a Youth Talkline that allows isolated gay and lesbian youth to reach out to their peers several evenings a week. The Center also operates an emergency shelter for youth and AIDS prevention programs, and provides emergency clothing, food vouchers, and case management. In addition, another organization, Gay and Lesbian Adolescent Social Services, provides two long-term residences for gay and lesbian youth, as well as a foster care placement service focused on these young people. Gay-sensitive job training, mental health, and medical services are also available to gay and lesbian youth in Los Angeles.

Uribe counts many students among her successes. Project 10 allows gay and lesbian youth to continue within the mainstream of public education in Los Angeles. She describes one young man who transferred to her school from another high school because he was being harassed due to peer assumptions that he was gay. Charlie stopped going to school and began to abuse alcohol and marijuana. His supportive father suggested he go to a therapist, who referred Charlie to Fairfax High School and Project 10. Uribe saw to it that Charlie was assigned a trained guidance counselor sensitive to gay issues and worked to see that any harassment of Charlie was confronted by teachers and other staff members. When Charlie was repeatedly attacked both verbally and physically by a classmate, the harassing student was first reprimanded, then suspended, and finally transferred to another school. As Charlie found support in his new school, his self-confidence increased. He managed to graduate from Fairfax High School and was selected to be class speaker at graduation. During his speech at the Hollywood Bowl, Uribe listened proudly as Charlie credited Project 10 with his success. He is currently in college and off drugs and alcohol.

Project 10 has begun to be considered as a model by other cities. Uribe has had inquiries from places as diverse as Roanoke, Virginia, and San Diego, California. She has assisted other school districts in creating quiet peer-support groups for gay and lesbian youth, and she has trained hundreds of teachers in responding to anti-gay slurs in the classroom. Her commitment has been to designing a program that provides the advocacy and support services that allow a gay or lesbian youth to remain in the local high school and that force non-gay peers and staff members to confront their homophobia. While she readily admits that her model might not work everywhere, she sees it as flexible and responsive to local community needs, and she believes its key components of education, counseling, and support services are critical to gay youth programs within the schools.

THE HARVEY MILK SCHOOL

Named after the assassinated openly gay San Francisco supervisor, the Harvey Milk School opened in New York in 1985 as part of a larger organization originally called the Institute for the Protection of Gay and Lesbian Youth. The Institute, recently renamed the Hetrick-Martin Institute in honor of the group's co-founders, Dr. A. Damien Martin and Emerty Hetrick, currently has a budget of over one million dollars, employs twenty-six staff members, and functions as a social-service agency with an interdisciplinary approach.

The school was founded because youth advocates working with gay and lesbian youth found that many homosexual young people were not succeeding in the New York City public schools. Many young people — especially those who were cross dressers, or young men who were effeminate, or young women who were "too butch" (tough, independent, and "masculine") — found their peers hostile, often to the point of violence. For gay youth who could "pass" and remain undetected in the school system, advocates found that the hiding process robbed students of much of their energy and vitality. Whether lesbian and gay youth were open about their identities or were closeted, societal prejudice took its toll; young gay people were often antisocial, alcohol- and drug-abusing, and/or depressed to the point of suicide.

A group of gay and lesbian youth advocates noted these difficulties and drafted a proposal to the New York City Board of Education for an off-site alternative school. It was clear to the founders that some gay and lesbian youth could survive in the public schools, but it was also apparent that many youth were terminating their formal education because they felt unsafe or alienated in the school system. There was little public interest in the project when the school opened its doors, but, in June 1985, after the *New York Times* placed a story about the school on the front page, the media swiftly beat a path to their door. Students and staff members alike faced cameras, microphones, and careful scrutiny by editorial writers nationwide.

Immediately the concept of a "gay high school" was challenged not only in the media, but also by certain members of the gay and lesbian community. Was the Harvey Milk School "ghettoizing" gay and lesbian youth? (The gay and lesbian community has long debated the pros and cons of separating ourselves from mainstream culture or integrating into it. The "gay ghetto" — an urban neighborhood with a substantial, visible gay and lesbian community — is a subject of continuing community debate.) Was it appropriate to take these young people away from their non-gay peers? What was the school attempting to accomplish?

Alternative high schools in New York City generally serve as transitional programs and attempt to mainstream young people back into society and traditional schools. At the Harvey Milk School, most of the students learn coping skills, such as how to deal with the homophobia of others while focusing on one's own educational needs. Counselors and teachers assist students in acquiring these skills, primarily through focus groups, individual counseling, peer counseling, and role playing. The aim is frequently to process the nightmares these young people have endured in the past and build confidence in facing the future.

Most of the young people at the Hetrick-Martin Institute — and at the Harvey Milk School — are between fifteen and seventeen, although youth have ranged from twelve to twenty-two. Students experience a traditional academic curriculum, but are also provided with substantial social services. Students come from a wide range of backgrounds, and most parents generally appear to approve of their child's placement in the program — often they are simply relieved that their child is back in school. Many families take advantage of the Institute's family counseling program.

There is no requirement regarding one's sexual orientation for a student to enroll at the school. Most young people find their way to the Harvey Milk School through referrals or from the criminal or family court system. Despite the arguments that this school might "ghettoize" gay youth, little formal work has been done within the New York City School System to provide in-school services to gay and lesbian youth. Hence, many gay and lesbian youth, simply refusing to deny their identities, find few alternatives outside of the Harvey Milk School. The school currently serves about twenty-four youth, with an additional two hundred served in some of the Institute's other programs, including Project First Step, an outreach program for street kids. The institute also offers a support group for HIV-positive youth and assists young people diagnosed with AIDS.

THE FUTURE OF EDUCATIONAL PROGRAMS
FOR GAY AND LESBIAN YOUTH

As someone who has worked with gay and lesbian youth for over a decade, it is clear to me that neither our school districts nor the gay and lesbian community have made significant progress in addressing the educational and social service needs of these young people. Several factors seem to serve as barriers to the development of services to meet the needs of gay and lesbian youth, including a lack of courage from adults of all sexual orientations, a lack of information available to the public about the needs of these young people, and the failure of school systems to confront controversial matters, especially in the area of youth sexuality.

The criticism faced by the Harvey Milk School provides a good starting point for evaluating an appropriate response to the needs of gay and lesbian youth. If by removing these youth from the mainstream we are placing them in an artificially supportive environment, what are educational administrators doing to change the homophobic atmosphere in our public schools? Can we guarantee safety for openly gay youth in most of our schools throughout the United States?

In a fascinating essay, "Gay Youth and the Right to Education," in the *Yale Law and Policy Review*, Donna I. Dennis and Ruth E. Harlow argue that the Harvey Milk School "presents an unacceptable solution for the education of gay youth because it does not have the resources to provide gay students with the quality of education that heterosexual students receive in regular schools."[1] The authors

---

[1] Donna I. Dennis and Ruth E. Harlow, "Gay Youth and the Right to Education," *Yale Law and Policy Review*, 4 (1986), 445–455.

note that "Courts have recognized that segregation of children on the basis of characteristics that the dominant group regards as inferior inflicts serious, possibly irreparable injury on the segregated children" (p. 454). They go on to cite *Brown v. Board of Education* in arguing for a program designed to mainstream gay and lesbian youth into our schools, and insist that a legal strategy might be the best route to take in making educational services available to gay and lesbian youth:

> We propose a litigation strategy based on state constitutions to enforce gay students' right to an equal, integrated education. Advocates for gay youth should sue, in state courts, school districts that abridge gay teenagers' educational opportunities. We urge judges to protect the right to education articulated in state constitutions by enjoining such discriminatory school practices as harassment of gay youth by teachers, the uneven enforcement of disciplinary rules, and censorship of texts of library books that show tolerance toward gay persons. In addition, judges should require school districts exhibiting pervasive discrimination to institute programs that will abate homophobia in the schools and repair the harm done by past discrimination. (p. 454)

While legal advocacy groups have yet to take up these strategies, significant work has started in random districts throughout the nation in addressing the social and educational needs of gay and lesbian youth. Often operating in complete isolation, sympathetic educators, counselors, administrators, and school nurses are leading the way by quietly making changes in the educational opportunities for gay and lesbian youth. One suburban Massachusetts school district offered a weekly support group for gay youth, but refused to acknowledge the existence of the group when a journalist called seeking information. Are these small efforts able to make an impact when their existence remains unpublicized due to fear of public reaction?

There are several things that will need to change if U.S. schools are to become truly accessible to self-identified gay and lesbian youth:

– Schools are going to have to focus on the needs of young people rather than on the demands of parents or the larger community. Rarely will a program for gay and lesbian youth receive widespread public support, particularly outside urban centers such as Los Angeles or New York City. When schools return to a focus of student-centered curricula, gay and lesbian youth will stand a chance of receiving appropriate attention.

– Issues of sexuality must move from the taboo into a public forum. It will be impossible to adequately serve the educational needs of this specific population without acknowledging the role that sexuality has had in forming the identity and culture of gay men and lesbians. During a time when schools rarely provide sex education and face pressure from certain church groups to avoid discussions of birth control, abortion, or sexuality outside of marriage, it seems unlikely that schools will comfortably move towards open discussion of homosexuality. Yet, particularly in the age of AIDS, education concerning sexual safety for young gay men should be a key part of curricula developed for this group of students.

– Teachers will need to be comfortable with gay and lesbian issues. This will not only require rigorous training, but also courageous educational leadership. Because many educators believe that homosexuality is sick, sinful, or criminal, it is tremendously difficult for them to truly adopt an "objective" stance when addressing gay and lesbian issues in the classroom. The situation is exacerbated by the tension teachers have faced for years concerning discussions of homosexuality: by allowing positive treatment of homosexuality in the classroom, teachers are vulnerable to witch-hunts by parents and school committees attempting to root out homosexual teachers. In certain parts of the nation, laws have been proposed and successfully passed that forbid positive discussion of homosexuality in public school classrooms.

– School curricula will need to be integrated to include the historical contributions of gay men and lesbians, as well as literature that reflects the experiences and culture of lesbian and gay writers. While homosexual women and men are included in current high school classes — people such as Walt Whitman, Gertrude Stein, James Baldwin, and Adrienne Rich — rarely do teachers discuss the contribution of these individuals in the context of their true lives as gay people. This "de-gaying" of U.S. literary and historical figures sends a message of shame and denial to lesbian and gay youth and is a missed opportunity to provide historical role models for our youth.

– Educators must abandon the concept that by discussing homosexuality in a positive way, they will cause young people to grow up to be gay or lesbian. Until we get beyond thinking that all our youth are heterosexual and some only appear to be gay because they are "stuck" in an "immature phase of social development," teachers will hinder the natural development of gay and lesbian young people and will rob them of their healthy adolescent experiences. Perhaps one of the saddest aspects of what our culture does to gay and lesbian youth is that a period of life that could be filled with the discovery of one's own identity in a positive and growth-filled way becomes mired in shame, denial, and self-hatred.

We are finally left to wonder, "Who will initiate the changes necessary in U.S. schools to make them more responsive to the needs of gay and lesbian youth?" The answer does not come easily. Neither gay and lesbian adults nor non-gay adults have proven themselves particularly ready to take leadership in moving schools towards a more progressive approach to educating this population.

Yet, particularly when we look at statistics regarding the spread of the HIV infection into the youth population, it is difficult to deny that the time to confront these issues is now. Many AIDS experts see young people as the third wave of individuals affected by HIV — following adult gay men and IV drug users. While it is certainly true that youth are increasingly infected with HIV due to drug use and heterosexual sexual activity, it is difficult to deny that the population of youth most at risk for AIDS has been — and continues to be — young men who are sexually active with other men.

Many of these teens do not identify as gay or bisexual and do not see themselves as especially vulnerable to AIDS or any other life-threatening illness. Reaching this population with effective AIDS prevention information has been difficult and problematic. The key element that has proven most helpful in educating gay men and IV drug users — introducing peers who have AIDS and who can discuss risk factors in becoming infected with HIV — is especially difficult to do with youth, primarily due to the long time period between exposure to HIV and development of AIDS. Many people who are developing AIDS in their early twenties are exposed during their teenage years; yet few fifteen-year-olds are able to identify with a twenty-four-year-old man with AIDS. The generation gap is just wide enough to prevent identification and to continue to foster denial. We need to find other ways to reach youth with information and get them to put that information into action to protect themselves. Since we have found limited success in the area of pregnancy prevention or substance-abuse prevention, many youth-AIDS educators see their task as particularly difficult.

And yet AIDS education will prove totally fruitless if young gay men do not have enough self-esteem and enough sense of their identities as gay men to make the effort to protect themselves. As we approach the 1990s, it is clear that we no longer have the luxury of ignoring our gay and lesbian youth; continued denial of the existence of this population will result in a devastating spread of infection with HIV. Many of us failed to respond when we heard that gay and lesbian youth were disproportionately at risk for suicide, homelessness, assault, and sexual abuse. Can we continue our pattern of averting our eyes from the tremendous threats to the lives of these children, or will we find the courage and commitment to educate and serve this special group of young people?

A Hearing Teacher's
Changing Role in Deaf Education

PATRICIA J. SAYLOR

In this article, Patricia Saylor tells of her experience as a hearing woman dedicated to learning and teaching about the Deaf community. Saylor is the founder and director of BRIDGES, a program aimed at building connections between Deaf culture and hearing culture. In her essay, Saylor offers a moving and detailed description of the program's goals by articulating her own experiences along with those of members of the BRIDGES community. As she explores a world that is largely ignored by the hearing population and describes some of the positive implications of connecting the hearing and deaf worlds, Saylor reveals the strengths and richness of the Deaf community.

A local television station has sent a camera crew to videotape the BRIDGES campers at a local skating rink. The camera is on; the light shines in my face so brightly that I cannot see my interviewer.[1] He asks, "How does it feel for the deaf to be living in a society of hearing people?"

I know I am on camera. My comments will be broadcast at 6 p.m. I smile broadly and say, "You know, I think it would be really inappropriate for me to answer that question since I am not Deaf myself."[2] He rephrases the question and asks me again. "I think it would be best to ask one of the Deaf staff members that question," I tell him, still smiling broadly, just in case he decides to use this clip.

After my third refusal, he turns off the camera and informs me that I need to answer because I am the "voice for these people." I inform him that I am not. I ask if it would be appropriate for me to answer the question, "How does it feel to grow up as a Black person in the South?" He is Black, and I am White. Finally, he seems to understand.

I offer to bring Connie or Donya over. I offer to interpret their answer to his question. Like so many hearing people, he is not willing to listen to what Deaf people have to say on behalf of their own experience. He decides not to interview them.

* * *

When Margaret Herring made her name tag at the end-of-summer picnic for BRIDGES 1990, it said, "Margaret Herring, Volunteer." Margaret had come to

---

[1] BRIDGES is not an acronym. The name describes a program created with the goal of building understanding between two cultures, the Deaf culture and the hearing culture.

[2] In this text, as is becoming customary in the Deaf Community, there is a distinction between the words "deaf" and "Deaf." The word "deaf" refers to someone who does not hear or does not hear well, and "Deaf" refers to a cultural identification with members of the American Deaf Community.

Harvard Educational Review Vol. 62 No. 4 Winter 1992, 519–534

camp two mornings a week to supervise in the locker room and dress our pre-schoolers on swim days. She called them her "deaf grandchildren," and she had been so loving and concerned about them that I reminded her, "Margaret, you're not just a volunteer, you're the *grandmother* here." A few minutes later, Margaret had crossed out "Volunteer"; her tag now read, "Margaret Herring, Deaf Grandmother." Her husband's read "Russell Herring, Deaf Grand-father."

Margaret told a reporter, "I used to have just eight grandchildren, none of whom are deaf. Now I have about fifteen more, and they are all deaf." Margaret's acquisition of fifteen deaf grandchildren in five weeks relates directly to the changes I am experiencing as a hearing educator working in the field of deaf education. I realize that she, and other Deaf people like her, have something to offer these children that I never could.

Just over a year ago, I was teaching young deaf and hard-of-hearing children in a self-contained classroom in a public school. I was able to teach the funda-mentals of reading, math, science, and social studies, but I soon realized that the thing I was not able to give these children was a strong sense of who they could be when they were grown.

This fact became most obvious to me when, toward the end of my first year of teaching, I invited Adam, one of my young deaf students, to accompany me to Washington, DC, to visit Gallaudet University, the only university for the deaf in the world. The thing he wanted to do most of all was to meet Dr. I. King Jordan, Gallaudet's first Deaf president. Dr. Jordan graciously invited us into his office and fielded questions from this six-year-old deaf child. Adam was most impressed. When we returned to school, he decided to write to this Deaf man. Weeks later, when he got his reply, he took it home and insisted that his parents frame it.

Adam seemed to be hungering for Deaf role models. While we were at Gal-laudet, every time he met someone new he asked, "Are you Deaf?" More often than not the answer was yes, and the person would ask the same question of him. When Adam said he was, the person would make a sign that best translates, "You and I are the same." And Adam would grin. He told me that when he grows up he wants to go to Gallaudet University because "there are many, many Deaf people there and just a few hearing people."

A few days after we returned, Adam asked a Deaf teacher's aide in our class-room if she liked to be Deaf. She gave him the standard Deaf answer: Yes, she liked to be Deaf and sometimes wished the whole world were Deaf. Later, Adam asked me if I liked to be hearing. What could I say? I told him that I did, but that I thought being Deaf was fine too. I was just glad that he had this wonderful Deaf woman's input as well. Most deaf kids are not lucky enough to have any Deaf role models.

Shortly after my trip to Gallaudet with Adam, the mother of another child told me that every teacher her Black Deaf son ever had was a "hearing White woman." She wanted the opportunity for him to meet adults he could admire and in whom he could see his own future. Both my experience with Adam and that mother's comments convinced me that I wanted to change the role I played in the lives of deaf children.

I decided to use my administrative talents and skills to create an environment where deaf children could find the role models necessary to develop a strong sense of themselves, and where they and their families could see the potential for the linguistic and social competence they possessed. I knew that in order to create such an environment, I would have to work in cooperation with Deaf adults.

I had some reservations about moving into this new role. If I started the program, raised the funds, and became its director, I would be one more hearing person in charge of the information and services offered to families with deaf children. The more that hearing people are in charge, the fewer Deaf role models deaf children and their families have. Even if I hired Deaf people to work with the children, I would be the primary parent-contact person, and everyone involved in the program, whether hearing or deaf, adult or child, would have reinforced the idea that the hearing people are the ones in charge, and the Deaf people are the assistants.

The choices I saw for myself were to 1) leave the field altogether, 2) continue as a classroom teacher, or 3) redirect myself into a more administrative role. I did not want to leave the field; my heart and passion are in my work. Still, my reasons were clear for not continuing in the role I had. I had considerable experience directing quality children's programs for hearing children, and believed that deaf children deserved the same kind of opportunities. So, I decided that the administrative role was the most appropriate one to choose.

Thus BRIDGES was created. BRIDGES is a bilingual/bicultural day-care and family-service organization for deaf children and hearing children with Deaf family members. The idea behind BRIDGES is simple, but in the field of Deaf Education, our practices are rather revolutionary.

BRIDGES is based on the idea that the developmental delays typically experienced by deaf children are entirely preventable. What deaf children need for normal social and linguistic development is to mingle daily in a community of Deaf, fluent signers. Deaf children with Deaf parents have the opportunity to develop sign language naturally through this kind of interaction at home, but most deaf children of hearing parents do not.

Unfortunately, the typical deaf child of hearing parents is severely delayed in language and social development. These children are not able to acquire naturally the dominant language of their families because they cannot hear it. Therefore, it is not at all uncommon for a deaf child to arrive at school with a vocabulary of fifty or fewer words, little or no emergent literacy skills, and little or no conversational language skills. This delay is in sharp contrast with their hearing peers, who have usually acquired most of the morphological and syntactic rules of their language by the time they enter school.[3] Hence, the deaf child's language delay is usually accompanied by severe deficits in social skills and in the general knowledge required to function in the world.[4]

[3] Helen Trager-Flusberg, "Putting Words Together: Morphology and Syntax in the Preschool Years," in *The Development of Language*, 2nd ed., ed. Jean Berko-Gleason (Columbus, OH: Merrill, 1989), p. 153.

[4] Robert E. Johnson, Scott C. Liddell, and Carol J. Erting, *Unlocking the Curriculum: Principles for Achieving Access in Deaf Education* (Washington, DC: Gallaudet University Department of Linguistics and Interpreting and Gallaudet Research Institute, 1989).

This early language deprivation adversely affects the deaf child's education, and may ultimately affect his or her ability to succeed and function independently as an adult. The average deaf high school graduate in the United States reads English at the third-grade level.[5] In the majority of deaf education programs, hearing teachers will speak English in the classroom while supporting their speech with a manually coded English Sign System. Some of the signs in these systems are borrowed and modified from American Sign Language (ASL) and others have been invented for educational purposes. However, given the lack of success in the current deaf education system in this country, it becomes obvious that spoken English, whether or not it is mixed with signs, is not sufficient for the education of children who cannot hear it.

With BRIDGES, I aim to create a unique environment where deaf children can develop language, cognitive, and social skills at the same rate as their hearing peers. In order to explain how this is possible, it is necessary to look briefly at the American Deaf Community.

Members of the Deaf Community in the United States do not usually consider themselves disabled, but rather part of a cultural and linguistic minority group. As a hearing person who signs, I am affiliated with, but not a member of, this culture.

Membership in the group is determined by the shared experience of being deaf (usually from birth or early childhood), by specific cultural values, and by the use of American Sign Language. There are active Deaf Communities in most major cities across the country.

The deaf child who is born into a family with culturally Deaf parents (fewer than 10 percent of deaf children fall into this category) does not experience any of the language or social delays of his or her peers living with non-signing, hearing families.[6] The Deaf child in a Deaf family is exposed to an accessible language from birth and is able to take advantage of critical periods for language acquisition that occur during the preschool years. These children, like their hearing counterparts, acquire cultural and social values and a sense of identity through language.

Later, these children typically become more fluent in English (usually through literacy) than their deaf peers from hearing families because they have a solid language base and knowledge about the world on which to build their education.[7]

Most of the deaf children born into hearing families are less fortunate. It has been my experience that fewer than 10 percent of hearing parents ever learn to sign well enough to converse fluently with their Deaf children — a statistic that is considered general knowledge within the field.

---

[5] Thomas E. Allen, "Patterns of Academic Achievement Among Hearing Impaired Students: 1983–1984," in *Deaf Children in America*, ed. Arthur N. Shildroth and Michael A. Karchmer (San Diego: College-Hill Press, 1986), pp. 161–206.

[6] Raymond Trybus and Carl Jensema, *Communication Patterns and Education Achievement of Hearing Impaired Students*, Office of Demographic Studies Series T, No. 2 (Washington, DC: Gallaudet College, 1978).

[7] Donald F. Moores, *Educating the Deaf: Psychology, Principles and Practices*, 3rd ed. (Boston: Houghton Mifflin, 1987).

My vision for BRIDGES is to create a place where *all* deaf children (from Deaf or hearing families) can thrive. I want to see them develop their social skills, their language, and their knowledge about the world around them. With these skills, they will be able to move freely in both Deaf and hearing environments.

In the last two years, although BRIDGES has taken a lot of my time, it actually has not been difficult to establish. I approached the local YMCA's executive director in January 1990. He offered me space and administrative support if I could come up with the funding for a summer pilot program, which I received from a local foundation and service clubs. I put the word out in the local Deaf Community for staff, volunteers, and students. The first year there was a Deaf staff and lots of Deaf volunteers, who were joined by a hearing assistant the following year. The enrollment goal for that first year was ten children. We had twenty-three.

Some great things happened in the summer of 1990.

The BRIDGES pilot program was a five-week-long summer camp, which provided a place where being deaf presented few barriers. Because the hearing people at BRIDGES were in the minority, nearly all of the conversations were signed instead of spoken. When the children took field trips, fluently signing adults were available to explain where they were going and what to expect. When the children participated in activities with hearing teachers, interpreters were present to make sure two-way communication was possible. Deaf children aged three to thirteen came to camp every day and swam and played and learned in an environment that was almost completely accessible to them.

Preschoolers who arrived with almost no conversational language skills made incredible gains in the few short weeks they were involved in BRIDGES. Many deaf preschoolers arrived unable to ask or answer even simple questions, to comment on their environment, or to explain what they wanted or how they felt. Once at BRIDGES, most of them followed the same pattern: for three days they made no signs, the fourth day they began to copy the teacher's signs, and by the fifth day they were having short, meaningful exchanges.

On her fifth day at camp, four-year-old Isabelle emphasized that she wanted to ride the *rabbit*, not the giraffe, on the carousel at Pullen Park in Raleigh, North Carolina. By the end of the program, she was explaining abstract concepts she could not have discussed five weeks earlier. She told her teacher, "My brother and I have the same mother and father." Upon returning to the YMCA from a field trip, she wanted to know if it was time for the "boys and girls to go home now."

This was great progress for a child who would not even maintain eye contact when she arrived!

Hearing children who came to camp took home not only sign-language skills, but also an understanding of the experiences of their Deaf family members. Both of these gains benefitted the whole family. One ten-year-old girl with a deaf brother talked about feeling left out the first week of camp. She could not understand what was being said. I pointed out that her brother probably felt like that almost all the time. She said, "You know, I never understood that before."

A Deaf mother who brought her hearing son to BRIDGES said his sign-language fluency and attitudes about using sign language improved dramatically over the five-week period. He had been embarrassed to sign to her in public before, but after BRIDGES he began to take pride in the skills he possessed.

At the BRIDGES program, deaf children not only got to see signs being directed at them, but they had an opportunity to witness groups of Deaf people discussing and making decisions. They had the opportunity to "overhear" adult conversations daily. This experience is almost never available for deaf children unless their parents are members of the Deaf Community.

I remember a trip to the North Carolina Zoological Park I made with a group of mostly hearing teachers and deaf children. On that trip, we teachers had decided among ourselves which exhibits we would visit first, and then we had informed the children.

When the BRIDGES staff took the children to the zoo, they also decided among themselves the order of the day's activities. In this case, however, the children were able to witness the negotiation and decisionmaking process, and thus were able to take advantage of the incidental learning opportunities that come with being witness to adult conversations.

Parents had an opportunity to interact with people who did not view their children's Deaf experiences as negative. One woman approached the staff on a field trip to say that her nineteen-month-old daughter was deaf. She was answered with excitement and questions about her child. It was the first time that statement about her child had been received positively. Deaf adults from all over the Community volunteered their time to participate in the program and to be role models for these children and their families.

Margaret Herring, our "Deaf Grandmother," said that she had never spent any time with deaf children, and at camp, for the first time, she felt her contributions were valued. The Deaf cultural experience of children was also affirmed by the Deaf adults with whom they had contact. Adam had announced to a Deaf visitor at his school in the spring of 1990, "When I grow up, I am going to be hearing." That summer, a local Deaf man who had heard of this comment patiently explained to him that when he was young, he had been a deaf boy, too. He told Adam, "When you grow up, you will be a Deaf man, like me." Adam could see that he did not have to go to Gallaudet University to find Deaf people who made him feel good about his identity as a Deaf person.

In spite of the positive aspects and benefits of the program for both the deaf and hearing children, it was not possible to eliminate cross-cultural issues from this environment of Deaf-hearing contact. I was still the hearing person in charge, and the parents still came to me first to discuss their children's progress and program activities. Most of the parents do not have the sign-language skills even to converse fluently with their own children, and they therefore are not able to converse comfortably with the Deaf staff members. To help solve that problem and to encourage communication between parents and teachers, I plan to add a full-time interpreter to the staff when the program is established year-round.

When the BRIDGES Program requires interpreters, we use free-lance, certified local interpreters. I am careful to avoid the role of interpreter whenever possible. It would be an easy role to take on, but while I sign fairly well, I have had no training in the skill of interpreting. I feel this policy of using only certified interpreters is crucial if we are to maintain respect for the profession of interpreting and to encourage our children and their families to become well-informed consumers of these services. In the meantime, however, there is less communication between the staff and parents than I would like to see.

Most parents at BRIDGES are able to see the value of Deaf role models for their deaf children, but still have little or no understanding of Deaf Culture or its importance to their own families. Many will not use the term "deaf" in reference to their children, and most of them continue to talk to their children showing no apparent awareness that the children are understanding only a small fraction of what they are saying. Even the parents who know some signs use them primarily as a method to supplement their speech, rather than as the primary mode of communication.

Cultural differences between Deaf and hearing people can be a source of misunderstanding. For example, it is considered polite among Deaf people to share much more personal information than hearing people are accustomed to sharing among themselves. Sometimes this cultural difference leads Deaf people to perceive hearing people as distant, and hearing people to perceive Deaf people as nosy. The deaf children get mixed signals about what kinds of behaviors are appropriate. Cross-cultural awareness can ease tension between deaf and hearing adults, and also make it easier for them to explain to deaf children why some behaviors are appropriate in Deaf groups while others may be more appropriate among hearing people.

To address these issues, the year-round BRIDGES Program will include a parent-education component taught by Deaf instructors. Topics will include ASL, Deaf Culture, and cross-cultural concerns. Through this education, we hope to help hearing parents depend less on interpreters and other hearing people for information about their children. They will begin to be able to learn about Deaf Culture from Deaf people directly. They will develop the communication skills to participate in their deaf children's lives as fully as possible. Their children will then learn that their own experiences and culture as Deaf people are valuable. I do not, however, imagine that this respect for and value of Deaf Culture will happen in every family, nor that it will happen quickly. At least the BRIDGES environment has encouraged some communication between hearing parents and Deaf staff members. So far, it has been on the level of, "Where is my child's bathing suit?" or "Do I need to pack a lunch for her tomorrow?", but it is a start. Eventually, I hope discussions about educational decisions, parenting issues, communication, and Deaf Culture will occur between hearing and Deaf people.

Cross-cultural issues are also hard to overcome in the children's relationships. The school-age children at camp divided themselves into two groups, hearing and deaf, during independent play time. The preschool children were less segregated, but many of them did not yet have the language skills for cooperative, imaginative play.

One encouraging exception was Natalie, a preschool hearing child with Deaf parents. Natalie was by far the most fluent signer in the preschool group and moved freely between deaf and hearing play groups, signing or speaking as necessary. She is a true bilingual and could choose appropriately from her available communication strategies.

As a rule, very young deaf children are not able to be bilingual in ASL and English, as is Natalie.[8] Until they learn to read, they will not have access to spoken language. They can, however, become fluent users of ASL. Their second-language skills in English will then develop rapidly when they become literate through their elementary school education. Some of them may also develop varying degrees of spoken English proficiency with speech therapy. The use of speech therapy for deaf children has had widely varied success.[9] Some may develop speech that is intelligible only to their families and close friends. A few may learn to speak clearly enough to be understood by strangers, but many do not, and so choose not to use their speech by the time they are adults. Natalie and other children of Deaf parents show, however, that true bilingualism is a very realistic goal for young hearing children. If the siblings of deaf children could learn to sign fluently and to accept Deaf and hearing ways as equal, then there would be a positive impact on the families of deaf children.

When children who enter the BRIDGES Program are already in elementary school, their linguistic and cultural identities seem to be well established. Some experiences reach across cultural barriers, but most children, like their parents, are most comfortable communicating and socializing within their own cultural group.

These cross-cultural concerns make me even more aware of my role as a hearing administrator running a program for Deaf people. In an ideal situation, I would be working cooperatively with a Deaf person to codirect the program, which would be a model Deaf–hearing partnership for the staff and families involved. It is unrealistic, however, to expect a small, local program to support two directors. We are lucky to raise the funds to support one director, rent a van, buy program supplies, and pay the staff every summer. Perhaps in the future we will be able to incorporate more Deaf leadership into the program; for now, I do all the grant writing in my spare time, and speak to foundations and service clubs when I get a chance. It is not possible, at present, to change that administrative composition.

In spite of cross-cultural concerns, the summer program seems to be an excellent start for BRIDGES. The 1990 pilot summer program has successfully served as a catalyst to move us toward our goal of year-round operation. The United Way gave us a Venture Grant of $12,000 to bring our facility up to day-care licensing standards; the state of North Carolina Division of Child Day Care Services awarded us the funds to purchase a van. We have applied for a federal grant from the Department of Education that would allow us to become a model demonstration preschool program. Although we were not awarded a grant the first year, a federal administrator tells me that every year we successfully raise local funds for the program, we will significantly increase our chances of receiving a five-year federal grant.

After the first summer of BRIDGES, I returned to teaching. This time the subjects were Spanish and American Sign Language at a local high school.

---

[8] For the purposes of this article, English is used as the example of a native spoken language.
[9] I base this assertion on discussions with Deaf adults and personal observation.

Adam's older sister had circulated a petition requesting that a sign language class be offered at her high school, and the principal asked me to teach it. I needed year-round employment, and I saw this job as a way to continue my efforts to build bridges of understanding between Deaf and hearing cultures. My ASL classes included many hearing students with Deaf family members, neighbors, and friends.

While I had some reservations about teaching ASL (in some places it is considered "politically incorrect" for a hearing person who has not grown up in the culture to teach ASL), I made it clear to my students that I was not a native signer or a representative of the Deaf Culture, but that I would share with them the knowledge and skills that I had. I assigned readings and videotapes produced by Deaf people and provided opportunities for them to meet Deaf adults in our community. We exchanged letters and made a videotape to send to other high school students from the Eastern North Carolina School for the Deaf.

I invited one of the BRIDGES Deaf staff members and some local deaf children to accompany my ASL students and me on a field trip to the School for the Deaf. The tour was conducted by a hearing woman who unfortunately showed little awareness of Deaf Culture. She proudly showed off the school's audiological technology and bragged about the speech therapy students received.

During the rest of the afternoon, my students mingled in the dorms, watched a basketball game between two Deaf teams, and attended a party some of the Deaf students had prepared for them. As we were leaving, one of the Deaf students told me that my students had the best attitude about Deaf people of any hearing visitors they had ever had to the school. The Deaf student never fully explained what he meant when he said most hearing people had a very "bad attitude" about the Deaf. I was only glad that my students did not share it. The hearing students had approached the visit with the idea that they were guests of another culture, and I was pleased to know that it showed.

I had not planned to have a second summer program for deaf children in 1991. After the initial pilot program, I was focusing my attention on the goal of setting up year-round services. The parents, however, insisted that we have another day camp.

Groups who funded us the first year were approached, as well as a few other funding sources, and we were pleasantly surprised by the response. Some of the service clubs had already set aside funds for us. Local businesses came through with printing and t-shirts. Our major funding came from two local foundations, the Durham Merchants Association Charitable Foundation, and the Mary Duke Biddle Foundation.

The 1991 summer program had an expanded staff and served more children than the year before. Most of our children returned for a second year, and some new three-year-olds joined the program. The individuals' and the program's successes were as great as the first year.

I am confident that if the federal grant comes through to cover basic operating expenses, local funds can be raised to build a playground, set up a family resource library, and continue to provide summer opportunities for school-age children.

The **BRIDGES** Program has been so successful for the deaf children, it is hard to see why our methods are considered controversial. The revolutionary aspect of **BRIDGES** is the idea that Deaf adults are the most appropriate role models for deaf children. **BRIDGES** is different from most programs for deaf children because we don't consider being "more like hearing" to be necessarily better than being Deaf.

For years, the educational establishment has operated on the principle that in order to function in the "hearing world," deaf children need to assimilate and need to be as much like hearing people as possible. The more speech skills and auditory awareness they develop, the assumption is, the better off they will be, even if this focus on "speech and hearing" takes time away from academic studies and from more fluent and effective communication options. The reality of the Deaf Community shows us that this assumption is not true.

In March 1988, four Deaf students at Gallaudet University led a successful university-wide protest to install Dr. I. King Jordan as the first Deaf president in the institution's history. I was on campus during that eventful week. I saw student leaders take charge of the campus and work with the media. They set up press conferences, established a phone bank for fundraising, and achieved worldwide recognition for their cause. They changed the course of Deaf history in less than one week. No one will convince me that they did not know how to function in "the hearing world." It is significant that all of them sign ASL fluently; not once during that week did I hear them speak. All four come from Deaf families; from an early age, all four had the support and training of the Deaf Community to learn how to function as *Deaf* people in the hearing world.

As I was preparing for the **BRIDGES** 1991 summer program, I once again realized the importance of Deaf role models for deaf children. For example, when a new staff member, Richard, was preparing to come to his first **BRIDGES** staff meeting, I gave him directions over the phone (using a TTY — a telecommunications device). He had never been to the YMCA before and was coming from out of town. He assured me that if he got lost there would be no problem; he would stop and ask for directions.

Later I realized that I did not know how he would ask. I had no doubt that he could ask for directions without a problem, but I had no idea *how* he would. It struck me once again that there was a gap in my knowledge. If a deaf child asked me the best way to approach a hearing person and request information, I would have no idea what strategies to suggest. Richard, however, has years of experience interacting with hearing non-signers and would be an excellent resource for such questions.

Deaf people not only have a wealth of knowledge about how to cope in a sometimes hostile (or at least unaccommodating) environment, they also have a rich heritage of folklore, literature, customs, and values that can be a source of pride and self-esteem for young deaf children. Usually, hearing people (including teachers of deaf children) are completely ignorant of this heritage. Only through other Deaf people can deaf children have access to this rich source of pride and tradition in the Deaf Community.

At **BRIDGES**, we don't try to ignore or "overcome" Deafness in children. Instead, we nurture them through contact with Deaf adults who can share their stories and experiences. Most professionals working with deaf children and their families have a different perspective from that of the BRIDGES Community.

A school interpreter told me that a few years ago she brought two Deaf people to a group of parents of deaf preschoolers. The Deaf women talked about their experience and frustrations growing up with non-signing birth families. They told the parents how common it is for Deaf children to not want to go home from school to families with whom they cannot communicate. One parent cried. A couple of parents were so upset that they did not ever come back to the group. The interpreter suggested that maybe parents of young deaf children are not capable of handling the truth that Deaf adults share with them about what it means to grow up deaf.

My experience with parents of deaf children has been different. I think it is sometimes a relief for parents to have someone tell them that there is nothing wrong with their child. I have found that frequent exposure to a community of Deaf adults can be very positive for the families of deaf children. By seeing the Deaf teachers on a daily basis, the parents can begin to develop trusting relationships with them. Any one of the BRIDGES Deaf staff members would tell parents that they feel very positive about their Deaf identity. Some of their attitudes about themselves are bound to influence positively the parents' attitudes about their own deaf children.

Of course, these relationships take time to develop. I still find myself, uncomfortably at times, in the role of educating parents about the Deaf Community and the impact that being Deaf will probably have on their child and their family. Eventually, Deaf people will be doing this job instead of me, but for now, I persist.

I reassure the parents that a survey of existing literature demonstrates ample evidence that deaf children exposed to a natural sign language (as opposed to a "sign system" or one of the manual codes for English that are almost exclusively used in programs for deaf children) will go through a normal language acquisition process. This process almost exactly parallels the process hearing children go through when acquiring spoken languages.[10] I tell them that communication does not have to be any more of a struggle for their children than for hearing children.

For years, parents have been told that if they let their deaf children learn to sign, it will sap their motivation to learn to talk. More recently, they have been told that their children must learn a manual code representing English, rather than the language of the Deaf Community, ASL. In actuality, the skills and knowledge they learn through ASL and through interaction with a community that shares this language will make it easier for them to learn English. It is well known by educators that Deaf children from Deaf families who learn to sign early are almost always more successful students than those who do not acquire language until they are older.[11] The English skills of these children may or may

[10] Patricia J. Saylor, "Language Acquisition in Deaf Children: A Survey of Literature," Unpublished manuscript, 1988.

[11] K. Brasel and Stephen P. Quigley, "The Influence of Certain Language and Communication Environments in Early Childhood on the Development of Language in Deaf Individuals," in *Journal of Speech and Hearing Research, 20* (1977), 95–107.

not include speaking and auditory awareness or speech reading, but literacy is a realistic goal for almost all deaf children.

I tell parents that speech skills are a "convenience" for their deaf children, but not a prerequisite for success as an independent deaf adult. I tell them about the work of the Deaf student leaders during the "Deaf President Now!" protests at Gallaudet University.

Still, parents share their fears with me. They are given so much conflicting advice. They are afraid they will do the wrong thing. They are afraid that they will lose their children to a community of which they (the parents) cannot be a part. They are afraid life will be hard for their children. They are afraid their children will live a life of isolation. They are afraid that they will look foolish and incompetent if they try to sign with Deaf adults.

Conflicting advice is nothing new for parents of young deaf children. For decades, deaf children have been subjected to one "method" after another that attempts to minimize or annihilate what many Deaf people call the "Deaf Way." A local parent advocacy organization offers a videotape that informs parents of methods for communicating with their deaf children. The methods include: oral (lipreading and speaking); auditory/verbal (similar to oral, but in which the teachers cover their mouths when they talk to the children); cued speech (eight hand shapes made near the mouth while speaking); verbo-tonal (children and teachers move in rhythm with vocalizations); total communication (speech supported by some signs borrowed from ASL and others invented by educators); the modified Rochester Method (teachers finger-spell words as they speak); and vibro-tactile stimulation (the child wears a device on his or her body that vibrates with sound). Nowhere on the tape is ASL or the existence of a Deaf Community mentioned.

There are many "methods," but really only two choices. Parents may choose to follow one of the methods that denies the importance and contributions of the Deaf Culture and language and that tries to "fix" their children. Or, they may respect centuries of precedent and learn from the Deaf Community.

From Deaf adults, they can learn that having a Deaf child does have positive aspects. Parents have an opportunity to become familiar with a culture that they otherwise probably never would have encountered. They may become acquainted with a community of people who have a strong interest in the well-being of their child. And they can learn a new language, ASL.

Nevertheless, sometimes I find it hard to help parents see any positive aspects to their child's Deaf identity when there is so much negativity surrounding hearing loss. The parent advocacy organization mentioned above also presents a handbook to parents of recently identified deaf children. The first statement in the book tells them that finding out their child is "hearing impaired" (a label that many Deaf people find offensive) will probably make them feel as if someone has died!

While I agree that it is important to acknowledge the grief that parents experience when they find out that their child is not what they expected, it seems another message might be more helpful. I imagine what a different tone the book could have taken if it started with a quote from Dr. I. King Jordan: "Deaf people can do anything, except hear!"

I value children's relationships with their birth families. But I believe that continuing to foster an attitude that perceives hearing loss as a medical condition to be fixed, rather than an attitude that Deaf Culture is something to be nurtured and valued, will sabotage the relationship between deaf children and their hearing family members. As long as the deaf child is viewed as the defective member of the family, the parents will never be able to celebrate the Deaf child's language or culture, and a significant part of that child's identity will be lost. Even if the child is able to identify with other Deaf people later in life (and many of them do, in spite of their educational programs or their parent's efforts), the parents will be left out of one of the most significant parts of their child's life. I tell these mothers and fathers that they can have support in learning the language and culture of the Deaf Community, and that if they do that, they need not fear losing their children.

It takes one visit to a local Deaf Community event for parents to see that being Deaf will not condemn their children to a life of isolation. These community members are a tight-knit group who keep up with each other like an extended family. They are thrilled to see parents learning to sign for their deaf children, and almost all will support and encourage those efforts. Margaret Herring knows that deaf babies need a Deaf grandmother, but she also knows they need to be able to communicate with their own parents. She circulates, bounces babies, and makes a point of welcoming every family that brings a deaf child to the monthly Deaf Community dinners.

I also remind the parents that my parents and I are hearing. Yet as I grew up, I began to create a community for myself that was separate from my parents. It is the nature of all children to grow up and find their own communities. The fact that their children's community includes other Deaf people does not have to make them any less a part of their birth families than I am of mine.

So, my goal with BRIDGES is, in cooperation with Deaf people, to provide an environment where deaf children will have sufficient contact with fluent signers so that they can develop ASL as naturally as possible and at age-appropriate times. At the same time, the staff will provide support for their parents and siblings in learning the language and culture of the Deaf Community. Then, by the time these children are ready to enter school, they will have had several years of experience conversing and learning about their world. Their parents will have the skills necessary to allow the deaf child to be a contributing member of the family. The child will enter school with the base of language, knowledge, and family support necessary for a successful education.

We are not there yet, but after two summer programs, we are well on our way. Roadblocks are unavoidable, but with education and time, we make more and more progress. The roadblocks often come in the form of well-meaning, but misguided, professionals. The mother of a recently deafened toddler received informational materials from a friend she had known in the Peace Corps. The friend is now a doctor, and when he found out that her baby was deaf, he wanted to help. The emphasis of all his materials was on speech and hearing aids and surgical intervention. He warned her to stay away from sign language if she wanted her son to be able to function in the hearing world.

This parent tells me that her friend is very progressive about social issues. He supports and respects ethnic and cultural differences. I guess I should no longer be surprised, but I am consistently amazed that the same level of respect is almost never given to the language and culture of the American Deaf Community.

Perhaps this man's medical training prevents him from moving beyond a medical model of hearing loss to recognition of Deafness as a cultural identity. I only hope he does not encounter many parents with young deaf children.

* * *

Isabelle's mother tells me that she thinks Isabelle has a lot to say. She can't wait until her daughter has enough language to express herself. It is a comment I remember my sister making when her daughter was just under two years old.

It is July 1991. Isabelle lies on her blanket watching intently as Connie, one of the BRIDGES teachers, signs to own her daughter, Natalie. Natalie complains about having to lie down. Connie promises her a swim with her daddy that evening. For about five minutes they share the intimate, easy, fluid conversation of those who know and understand each other well. Isabelle's eyes never leave them.

A few minutes later, Connie turns her attention to Isabelle. They talk about Isabelle's family. Connie asks how many rooms there are in Isabelle's house and with which of her siblings she shares a bedroom. Isabelle obviously understands the topic and comments on her house, but she never makes it clear exactly who shares her room.

Connie asks if her mother works. Isabelle does not understand the question, and Connie rephrases it. Isabelle finally says something about sick babies. Connie looks to me and I inform her that Isabelle's mother is a neonatal intensive-care nurse. With that information, Connie is able to continue the conversation and elaborate, "Oh, your mother works in a hospital."

Sometimes Isabelle is frustrated and looks away, but each time, Connie gently brings her back to the conversation with a more accessible topic or an explanation she knows Isabelle will understand. I am amazed at Connie's patience and the success with which she engages this child. I have never been able to hold Isabelle's attention for more than one or two exchanges.

Connie pats Isabelle on the back and tells her it is time to go to sleep. She looks over at me and says, "Isabelle needs a Deaf person to converse with her every day. If she had that, she would be able to sign like Natalie." Natalie and Isabelle are both within weeks of their fifth birthdays.

* * *

Two years ago, a four-year-old girl I interviewed for a research project told me there were three kinds of people. They were either "Deaf, like my mom, a little bit Deaf, like my dad or *not* Deaf, like me!" To her, being Deaf was not negative, it was just a fact of life, like her brown hair. It would not occur to her to think she is any better than her parents because she is hearing and they are Deaf.

I used to teach in a program that the Harvard Graduate School of Education labeled as being for the "hearing impaired." Now I teach about Deaf Studies and ASL to hearing high school students. One night each week, a group of parents with deaf children come to my home to work on their sign language skills. In my spare time, I raise funds for a bilingual, bicultural program for the benefit of deaf children and their families. I wait for the break that will allow me to implement the program full-time.

People who know what I do frequently say I am involved in the field of "Speech and Hearing." It seems odd to me that they would focus on the things that most Deaf people do not do, speak and hear. I tell them that is not my field. My field is language and Deaf Studies, a very different thing.

Author's Note: Clayton Valli, a noted Deaf Activist, informs me that the term "deafness" is something of a culturally sensitive term. Many Deaf people prefer the terms "Deaf Way" or "Deaf World." There were passages in this article where I could find no way to express adequately the meaning I was trying to convey without using the word "deafness," and I decided to leave it in. However, it is important to inform the reader that some Deaf people find the term distasteful.

Also, since writing this piece, I have accepted a job working with very young deaf children for the Central North Carolina School for the Deaf as a teacher in their Durham Satellite Preschool Program. I accepted the position in spite of some reservations about my role as a hearing person teaching deaf children. One of the major factors that influenced my decision to take the position is that I am able to work in partnership with a Deaf woman in the classroom. Many of the children served in the preschool also come to the BRIDGES Program in the summers, and their parents encouraged me to accept the position. My Deaf coworker and I together work to create a classroom environment that reflects the values of Deaf Culture.

Because You Like Us:
The Language of Control

CYNTHIA BALLENGER

Teachers often learn techniques to manage the behaviors of the children in their classrooms with the assumption that those techniques are universal, rather than culturally based. In this chapter, Cynthia Ballenger shares her process of coming to understand the cultural assumptions that lie at the heart of effectively managing her class of four-year-old Haitian children. Through multiple "conversations" with a teacher-researcher group, with Haitian teachers and parents in a day-care center, and through her work with Haitian teachers in a child development class, Ballenger learns about Haitian cultural ways and queries the assumptions that shape her own experience as a North American teacher. Her story demonstrates a model of teacher reflection on both theory and practice that can illuminate the practices of other teachers who encounter children of differing cultural, racial, or class backgrounds.

This article is the result of a year spent in conversations about teaching — difficult conversations in which I, a seasoned teacher and fledgling sociolinguist, was only rarely the informed party.[1] Mike Rose, in *Lives on the Boundary* (1989), uses the metaphor of "entering the conversation" to describe the process of learning to participate in academic discourse. In my case, there was a multitude of different conversations I was trying to enter, and in each I had a different role to play.

During that same time I was teaching preschool, as I have done for most of the past fifteen years. The school was in the Haitian community in Dorchester, Massachusetts, and primarily served the children of Haitian immigrants. I went there because in my previous work as an early childhood special education teacher I had noticed that more and more Haitian children were being referred to my class. These children were arriving attended by all kinds of concerns from the educational professionals: they were "wild," they had "no language," their mothers were "depressed." There were certainly some children I saw who had genuine problems, and yet time and time again I found that, after a period of adjustment, they were responsive, intelligent children; their mothers were perhaps homesick and unhappy in a strange, cold country, but generally not clinically depressed. During that period, however, we did make many mistakes, and I became interested in learning the Haitian culture and language in order to

---

[1] Earlier versions of this work have been presented at the Penn Ethnography in Educational Research Forum in February 1991 and the Brookline Teacher-Researcher Seminar in June 1990. My research was carried out as a member of that seminar with teachers and children at my school. In this article, all teachers' and children's names have been changed.

Harvard Educational Review Vol. 62 No. 2 Summer 1992, 199–208

see the children more clearly. After a period at graduate school studying sociolinguistics, I took a position as a preschool teacher in a bilingual school where both Haitian Creole and English were spoken and where, as I came to understand, Haitian culture was quite central. I was the only teacher at this school who was not Haitian and, although by this time I spoke Creole, I was still getting to know the culture.

During that time I was one of two instructors of a course in child development that a local college offered for Haitian people who wished to work in day-care centers. My Haitian co-instructor and I designed this course based on the model of a conversation about child rearing — a dialogue between Haitians and North Americans about their attitudes on the subject. I was also a new member of the Brookline Teacher-Researcher Seminar (BTRS), a group of public school teachers and academic researchers who are attempting to develop a common language and a shared set of values with which to approach classroom issues (Michaels & O'Connor, in press; Phillips, 1991). As a graduate student in sociolinguistics, I had done research; as a teacher, I had thought about teaching; I was now involved in trying to approach issues in ways that incorporated both of these perspectives. The work that I will report on here was part of these conversations. I will try to let the reader hear some of the different voices that I heard.

In this article, I will discuss the process I went through in learning to control a class of four-year-old Haitian children. Researchers who regard language as the principal vehicle by which children are socialized into their particular family and culture have consistently regarded control and discipline as central events — events where language patterns and cultural values intersect in visible ways (Boggs, 1985; Cook-Gumperz, 1973; Watson-Gegeo & Gegeo, 1990). When, as in my case, the adult does not share the same cultural background and the same experience of socialization as the children, one becomes very aware of learning how to enter and manage the relevant conversation. Although it can be argued that my participation in the events I relate here was in some ways informed by sociolinguistic theory, I present this more as a story than as a research report. This is my attempt to discuss this experience in a way that will not deny access to the conversation to those who helped form my understanding of it. I must stress, however, that all of these conversations would not have been possible if there hadn't been room in the preschool day for talk — the school was run jointly by the teachers and we spent considerable time each day together — and if there had not been some financial support for the Brookline Teacher-Researcher Seminar (Phillips, 1991). This support, in the form of small stipends, xeroxing, money for an occasional day off to reflect, and a sense of being valued, combined with the nature of the school where I was teaching, made my situation luxurious compared with that of many teachers faced with problems similar to mine.

THE PROBLEM

Having had many years of experience teaching in early childhood programs, I did not expect to have problems when I came to this Haitian preschool three years ago. However, I did. The children ran me ragged. In the friendliest, most cheerful, and affectionate manner imaginable, my class of four-year-olds followed their own inclinations rather than my directions in almost everything. Though I claim to be a person who does not need to have a great deal of control, in this case I had very little — and I did not like it.

My frustration increased when I looked at the other classrooms at my school. I had to notice that the other teachers, all Haitian women, had orderly classrooms of children who, in an equally affectionate and cheerful manner, *did* follow directions and kept the confusion to a level that I could have tolerated. The problem, evidently, did not reside in the children, since the Haitian teachers managed them well enough. Where then did it reside? What was it that the Haitian teachers did that I did not do?

The group of Haitian preschool teachers whom I was teaching in the child-development course recognized the problem in their own terms. As part of the course, they were all interning in various day-care centers, some with me at the Haitian school, the majority in other centers. Many of the teachers in the other centers were extremely concerned about behavior problems. What they told me and each other was that many of the children in their centers were behaving very poorly; many felt that this was particularly true of the Haitian children. They felt that the way in which they were being instructed as teachers to deal with the children's behavior was not effective. One woman explained to me that when she was hit by a four-year-old, she was instructed to acknowledge the anger he must be feeling, then to explain to him that he could not hit her. She told me that, from her point of view, this was the same as suggesting politely, "Why don't you hit me again?"

When I talked with Haitian parents at my school, I again heard similar complaints. From the point of view of many of the people I talked with, the behavior tolerated in their neighborhood schools was disrespectful; the children were allowed to misbehave. A common refrain in these conversations was, "We're losing a generation of children"; that is, the young children here now, who were not brought up first in Haiti, were not being brought up with the same values. However, when I asked for specific advice about things I might do to manage the children better, the teachers and I could never identify any behaviors of mine that I could try to change.

I took my problem to the Brookline Teacher-Researcher Seminar. The members of BTRS have come to share a focus on language — the language of instruction; children's language in a wide variety of situations; the language of science talk, of book talk, of conflict; and so on. Thus, in our conversations, the BTRS group encouraged me to approach my problem by discovering what it was that the Haitian teachers *said* to the children in situations where directions were being given. The Seminar members have also come to believe that an important part of a research project is examining where a particular research question comes from in one's own life — why it seems important, what its value is to the teacher-researcher. In many cases, this is a matter of investigating one's own socialization, a kind of self-reflection that became an important part of my investigation.

SITUATIONS AS TEXTS

I began to write down what the Haitian teachers said to the children in situations where the children's behavior was at issue. I then carried these texts to the various conversations of which I was a part: the Haitian teachers in the child development course, the North American teachers in the Brookline Seminar, and the parents and teachers at the school where I was teaching. I will present here some texts that I consider typical in their form and content, and then share some of the responses and the thinking engendered by these texts among the people with whom I had been conversing.

I present first Clothilde's account of an event at her day-care center. Clothilde is a middle-aged Haitian woman and a student in the child-development course. She has a great deal of experience with children — both from raising her own and from caring for other people's — and many of her classmates turn to her for advice. The text below is from a conversation in which she had been complaining to me about the behavior of the Haitian children in the day-care center where she was student teaching. She felt that the North American teachers were not controlling the children adequately.

One day, as Clothilde arrived at her school, she watched a teacher telling a little Haitian child that the child needed to go into her classroom, that she could not stay alone in the hall. The child refused and eventually kicked the teacher. Clothilde had had enough. She asked the director to bring her all the Haitian kids right away. The director and Clothilde gathered the children into the large common room. The following is the text of what she told me she said to the children:

Clothilde: Does your mother let you bite?

Children: No.

Clothilde: Does your father let you punch kids?

Children: No.

Clothilde: Do you kick at home?

Children: No.

Clothilde: You don't respect anyone, not the teachers who play with you or the adults who work upstairs. You need to respect adults — even people you see on the streets. You are taking good ways you learn at home and not bringing them to school. You're taking the bad things you learn at school and taking them home. You're not going to do this anymore. Do you want your parents to be ashamed of you?

According to Clothilde, the Haitian children have been well-behaved ever since. Other Haitian teachers with whom I have shared this text have confirmed that that was what the children needed to hear. However, they also said that Clothilde will have to repeat her speech because the children won't remain well-behaved indefinitely without a reminder.

The next text involves an incident at my school. Josiane, who has taught for many years both here and in Haiti, was reprimanding a group of children who had been making a lot of noise while their teacher was trying to give them directions:

Josiane: When your mother talks to you, don't you listen?

Children: Yes.

Josiane: When your mother says, go get something, don't you go get it?

Children: Yes.

Josiane: When your mother says, go to the bathroom, don't you go?

Children: Yes.

Josiane: You know why I'm telling you this. Because I want you to be good children. When an adult talks to you, you're supposed to listen so you will become a good person. The adults here like you, they want you to become good children.

Finally, we have Jérémie's father speaking to him. Jérémie is a very active four-year-old, and the staff had asked his father for help in controlling his behavior:

Father: Are you going to be good? (Jérémie nods at each pause)
Are you going to listen to Miss Cindy?
Are you going to listen to Miss Josiane?
Because they like you.
They love you.
Do it for me.
Do it for God.
Do you like God?
God loves you.

REFLECTING

The content and the form of these texts are different from what I, and many other North American teachers, would probably have said in the same circumstances. I shared these and other texts and observations with many parents and teachers, both Haitian and North American. I asked them to reflect with me on how these conversations were different and what underlay them. What follows is a blend of many people's observations and self-reflections, including my own. Here I want to note that I am assuming that the North American teachers, including myself, shared similar training and enculturation. Although we differed in many ways, I would characterize our culture — as Heath does in *Ways with Words* (1983) — as "mainstream culture." The Haitian teachers also shared some, although not all, values and assumptions. Although I am trying to distill these conversations in order to identify "typical" practices of Haitian or North American teachers, I do not mean to imply that all North American or all Haitian teachers are the same.

The Haitian preschool teachers had clear insights into behavior characteristic of North American teachers. Clothilde commented that the North American teachers she knows frequently refer to the children's internal states and interpret their feelings for them; for example, "you must be angry," "it's hard for you when your friend does that," and so on. Clothilde pointed out to me that in her speech she makes no reference to the children's emotions; other Haitian teachers I have observed also do not do this as a rule.

Rose, another Haitian teacher, also commented that North American teachers often make reference to particular factors in the child's situation that, in the teacher's opinion, may have influenced his or her behavior. For example, Michel, whose mother had left him, was often told that the teachers understood that he missed his mother, but that he nevertheless needed to share his toys. When a child pushes or pinches another child sitting next to him or her, many North American teachers will suggest that, if the child does not like people to sit so close, he or she should say so rather than pinch. Rose felt, and from my observation I concurred, that Haitian teachers rarely do this. Josiane suggested further that if she were concerned about an individual child and his or her particular problems, instead of articulating them for him or her, her goal would be "to make him or her feel comfortable with the group." If the child were misbehaving, she felt she would say, "You know I'm your friend," and then remind him or her that "we don't do that." In fact, I have seen her do exactly that many times, with excellent results.

These examples suggest to me a difference in focus between the North American and Haitian teachers. It seems that North American teachers characteristically are concerned with making a connection with the individual child, with articulating his or her feelings and problems. On the other hand, Clothilde, Josiane, and the many other Haitian people I spoke with and observed, emphasize the group in their control talk, articulating the values and responsibilities of group membership. For example, we have seen that both North American and Haitian teachers make reference to the family, but in different ways. North American teachers are likely to mention particular characteristics of a child's family, characteristics that are specific to that family and are seen as perhaps responsible for the child's individual actions. The Haitian teachers emphasize instead what the families have in common. The families do not differ in their desire that the children respect adults, that the children behave properly, and that their behavior not shame them. The children's answers, when they are given in unison as in Josiane's text above, present a vivid enactment of the sort of unity the Haitian teachers' approach may engender.

Another difference the Haitian teachers noted is the use of consequences. North American teachers typically present the particular consequences of an act of misbehavior. For example, I often say something like, "He's crying because you hit him," or, "If you don't listen to me, you don't know what to do." Haitian teachers are less likely to differentiate among particular kinds of misbehavior; they condemn them all, less in terms of their results than as examples of "bad" behavior. Clothilde is typical of the Haitian teachers in that the immediate consequences are not made explicit; she does not explain why she is against biting or punching. She instead refers to such behavior as "bad," and then explains to the children the consequences of bad behavior in general, such as shame for the family. Jérémie's father simply tells Jérémie to be good, to be good for those who love him. Josiane, too, tells the children to be good because the people who like them want them to be good. I have heard other Haitian teachers refer to the impression that bad behavior would create in a passer-by, or to the necessity of modeling good behavior for younger children. But Haitian teachers rarely mention the specific consequences of particular acts, a clear difference from North American teachers.

In the Haitian texts, one has the impression that the children share the adult's understanding of what bad behavior is. Clothilde's series of rhetorical questions, like "Do your parents let you kick?" is an example of the form that many Haitian teachers adopt when addressing children about their behavior. The children understand their role without difficulty; they repeat the expected answers in choral unison. The choice of this form — that is, questions to which the answer is assumed — emphasizes the fact that the children already know that their behavior is wrong.

[margin note: internal responsibilities / focus on prior knowledge]

In the North American control situation, on the other hand, the child often appears to be receiving new information. If there is a consensus about behavior — certain behavior is bad, certain other behavior is good — we don't present it this way. North Americans frequently explain the consequences of particular actions as if they were trying to convince the child that there was a problem with his or her behavior. As presented in school, misbehavior is considered wrong not because of anything inherent in it, but because of its particular consequences, or perhaps because the behavior stems from feelings that the child has failed to identify and control.

These differences, as I came to recognize them, seemed significant enough to account for some of the difficulties I had been experiencing in my classroom. But what to do about them?

PRACTICE

With the overwhelming evidence that these children were used to a kind of control talk other than what I had been providing, I have since begun to adopt some of the style of the Haitian teachers. I assume that I am not very good at it, that I have no idea of the nuances, and I continue to include many of the ways I have typically managed behavior in my teaching. Nevertheless, I have developed a more or less stable melange of styles, and my control in the classroom has improved significantly. In addition, I find that I love trying out this Haitian way. I was struck by an experience I had the other day, when I was reprimanding one boy for pinching another. I was focusing, in the Haitian manner, on his prior, indisputable knowledge that pinching was simply no good. I also used my best approximation of the facial expression and tone of voice that I see the Haitian teachers use in these encounters. I can tell when I have it more or less right, because of the way that the children pay attention. As I finished this particular time, the other children, who had been rapt, all solemnly thanked me. They were perhaps feeling in danger of being pinched and felt that I had at last been effective. This solemn sort of response, which has occurred a few other times, gives me the sense that these situations are very important to them.

The following anecdote may suggest more about the way in which these interactions are important to the children. Recently I was angrily reprimanding the children about their failure to wait for me while crossing the parking lot:

Cindy: Did I tell you to go?

Children: No.

Cindy: Can you cross this parking lot by yourselves?

Children: No.

Cindy: That's right. There are cars here. They're dangerous. I don't want you to go alone. Why do I want you to wait for me, do you know?

"Yes," says Claudette, "because you like us."

Although I was following the usual Haitian form — rhetorical questions with "no" answers — I had been expecting a final response based on the North American system of cause and effect, something like, "Because the cars are dangerous." Claudette, however, although she understands perfectly well the dangers of cars to small children, does not expect to use that information in this kind of an interaction. What, then, *is* she telling me? One thing that she is saying, which is perhaps what the solemn children also meant, is that, from her point of view, there is intimacy in this kind of talk. This is certainly the feeling I get from these experiences. I feel especially connected to the children in those instances in which I seem to have gotten it right.

THE LARGER CONTEXT

North American teachers generally think of reprimands — particularly of young children who are just learning to control their behavior — as put-downs, and are reluctant to give them. North American preschool teachers, in particular, will take great pains to avoid saying "no" or "don't." In contrast, I have learned from working with Haitian children and teachers that there are situations in which reprimands can be confirming, can strengthen relationships, and can, in a sense, define relationships for the child, as seems to have been the case for Claudette in the example given above.

Such an opportunity may be lost when we go to great lengths to avoid actually telling a child that he is wrong, that we disagree or disapprove. When we look at the difference between the ways in which things are done at home and at school, and the negative consequences that may result from these mismatches for children coming from minority cultural backgrounds, the area of misbehavior and the way it is responded to seem particularly important because it affects so directly the nature of the relationship between child and teacher.

I was not unaware when I began that this subject was a hotbed of disagreement: North Americans perceive Haitians as too severe, both verbally and in their use of physical punishment, while Haitians often perceive North American children as being extraordinarily fresh and out of control.[2] Haitian immigrant parents here are at once ashamed and defiantly supportive of their community's

---

[2] It must be stated that the consequences of this disagreement are, of course, vastly more painful for the powerless. Contact with schools, with social service institutions, with the police, is in many cases highly problematic for Haitian families. The Haitian family, in these situations, is frequently met with a lack of understanding that leads easily to a lack of respect. Mainstream assumptions about "proper" ways of talking and dealing with children's behavior often stand in the way of distinguishing a functioning family, for example, from a dysfunctional one, in distinguishing a child whose parents are strict in order to help him or her succeed from one whose family simply does not want to deal with the

disciplinary standards and methods. In order to represent the views of Haitians I spoke with independent of my process of understanding, I asked them to reflect again on our two cultures after they had heard my interpretations.

People, of course, offered many varied points of view, yet everybody emphasized a sense of having grown up very "protected" in Haiti, of having been safe there both from getting into serious trouble and from harm. This sense of being protected was largely based on their understanding that their entire extended family, as well as many people in the community, were involved in their upbringing. Haitian families in the United States, some pointed out, are smaller and less extended. The community here, while tight in many ways, is more loosely connected than in Haiti. This change in social structure was bemoaned by the people I spoke with, especially with reference to bringing up children. They attributed to this change their sense that this generation of children, particularly those born here, is increasingly at risk. They are at risk not only of falling away from their parents' culture, but also, and consequently, of falling prey to the drugs, crime, and other problems of urban life that they see around them.

And yet everyone I spoke with also recalled some pain in their growing up, pain they relate to the respect and obedience they were required to exhibit to all adults, which at times conflicted with their own developing desire to state their opinions or make their own choices. This pain was nevertheless not to be discarded lightly. For many of the Haitian people with whom I spoke, religious values underlie these twin issues of respect and obedience; respect for parents and other adults is an analogue for respect and obedience to God and God's law.

Many people seemed to agree with the ambivalence expressed by one Haitian lawyer and mother who told me that, while she had suffered as a child because of the uncompromising obedience and respect demanded of her in her family, she continued to see respect as a value she needed to impart to her children. She said to me, "There must be many other ways to teach respect." She was one of many Haitians who told me of instances where a child from a poor family, a child with neither the clothes nor the supplies for school, had succeeded eventually in becoming a doctor or a lawyer. In these accounts, as in her own case, it is in large measure the strictness of the family that is regarded as the source of the child's accomplishment, rather than the talent or the power of the individual.

Presumably, there is some tension in all societies between individual and community. In these accounts is some suggestion of the form this tension sometimes takes within Haitian culture. For my part, I am struck and troubled by the powerful individualism underlying the approach I characterize as typical of me and many North American teachers. It appears that North Americans do speak as if something like the child's "enlightened self-interest" were the ultimate moral guidepost. In comparison to the language used by the Haitian teachers, North

---

child's problems. Such assumptions often stand in the path of appropriate help as well. The school where I taught was often called upon to discuss cultural differences with social service groups, hospitals, and other schools. Occasionally, we were asked to provide some assistance for particular cases. But, of course, there were countless instances in which Haitian families were involved with these various powerful institutions and the families were without such aid.

American teachers' language seems to place very little emphasis on shared values, on a moral community.

The process of gaining multicultural understanding in education must, in my opinion, be a dual one. On the one hand, cultural behavior that at first seems strange and inexplicable should become familiar; on the other hand, one's own familiar values and practices should become at least temporarily strange, subject to examination. In addition to the information I have gained that helps me to manage and form relationships with Haitian children in my classroom, I also value greatly the extent to which these conversations, by forcing me to attempt to empathize with and understand a view of the world that is in many ways very different from my customary one, have put me in a position to reexamine values and principles that had become inaccessible under layers of assumptions.

I am not teaching Haitian children this year, although I continue to visit them. Next year I expect to have a classroom with children from a wide range of backgrounds. It is difficult to say how my last experience will illuminate the next — or, analogously, how my experience can be of use to teachers in different kinds of classrooms. I do believe that teachers need to try to open up and to understand both our own assumptions and the cultural meaning that children from all backgrounds bring to school. It seems to me that accommodation must be made on all sides so that no group has to abandon the ways in which it is accustomed to passing on its values. I have been fortunate that the knowledge and collaboration of so many people, Haitian and North American, were available to help me begin to understand my own experience. All of these conversations have been their own rewards — I have made new friends and, I believe, become a better teacher.

REFERENCES

Boggs, S. (1985). *Speaking, talking and relating: A study of Hawaiian children at home and at school.* Norwood, NJ: Ablex.

Cook-Gumperz, J. (1973). *Social control and socialization.* London: Routledge & Kegan Paul.

Heath, S. B. (1983). *Ways with words.* Cambridge, Eng.: Cambridge University Press.

Michaels, S., & O'Connor, M. C. (in press). *Literacy as reasoning within multiple discourses: Implications for policy and educational reform.* Newton, MA: Education Development Center.

Phillips, A. (1991, February). *Hearing children's stories: A report on the Brookline Teacher-Researcher Seminar.* Paper presented at the Penn Ethnography in Educational Research Forum, Philadelphia, PA.

Rose, M. (1989). *Lives on the boundary.* New York: Penguin.

Watson-Gegeo, K., & Gegeo, D. (1990). *Disentangling: The discourse of conflict and therapy in the Pacific Islands.* Norwood, NJ: Ablex.

Reframing Classroom Research:
A Lesson from the
Private World of Children

ADRIENNE ALTON-LEE
GRAHAM NUTHALL
JOHN PATRICK

Research on classroom discourse typically focuses on the public statements of teachers and children. In this article, Adrienne Alton-Lee, Graham Nuthall, and John Patrick describe findings from a project in which sixth-graders' public and private statements, to themselves and to peers, were recorded using individual microphones. The authors analyzed the children's utterances as data about the children's cognitive and emotional responses to the ongoing lesson. The data reflect how the children perceived and responded to subtle cultural and gender biases in the curriculum and in the teacher's presentation. Their study allows us to better understand children's actual experiences as they struggle with the overt and covert messages of the curriculum.

In this article we explore children's public and private experiences during a lesson in an intermediate (sixth-grade) classroom in Aotearoa New Zealand. In the *Handbook for Research on Teaching*, Courtney Cazden described "two interpenetrating worlds: the official world of the teacher's agenda, and the unofficial world of the peer culture" (1986, p. 451). Although children in the classroom experience both of these worlds simultaneously, the unofficial, private world has been largely hidden from teachers and researchers. By exploring both the official and public, and the unofficial and private utterances of individual children, we can open a window to the child's experience of both worlds.

We are unlikely to come to such a window with open minds. In both educational practice and research, children's talk in the unofficial world has frequently been "considered a nuisance; literal noise in the instructional system" (Cazden, 1986, p. 448). Children's talk, even when it involves engagement with curriculum content, may be judged off-task because it contravenes the rules of order in a classroom. The "official world" of the teacher's agenda has become not only the focus of classroom research, but also the lens through which children's behavior is observed and judged.

The unofficial children's talk that occurred during the class lesson we focus on in this article would have been categorized as off-task in most classroom observation schedules. There is now evidence, however, that observer judgements about children's "on-task" behavior are not a valid index of children's engagement with content (Blumenfeld & Meece, 1988; Peterson, Swing, Stark,

Harvard Educational Review Vol. 63 No. 1 Spring 1993, 50–84

& Waas, 1984), and that children's spontaneous talk during time "off-task" can contribute to their intellectual development (Dyson, 1987).

A fundamental challenge for educational researchers has been the inaccessibility of the learning processes that take place in the mind of the child. The early behaviorists resolved the issue by denying the significance, or even the existence, of internal processing. In contrast, more recent research in cognitive science and artificial intelligence has attempted to develop functional models of these internal processes. In the field of classroom research, techniques such as stimulated recall (Peterson, Stark, Swing, & Waas, 1984) and eliciting children's reports of their own internal processing strategies (Blumenfeld & Meece, 1988) have been used to provide insights about classroom learning. These techniques, however, depend on children's conscious and selective recall of their mental processing. In the study reported here, we have employed a new technique, in which children's utterances are recorded by individual broadcast microphones during the course of classroom activities. These utterances provide a unique and concurrent source of data about children's learning processes, and allow us to identify individual children's responses to curriculum content, their use of prior knowledge and experience, their existing misconceptions, and their strategies for engaging with curriculum.

In our larger research program, the Understanding Learning and Teaching Project, we have traced children's learning during their interaction with specific test item content in the course of instructional units (Alton-Lee & Nuthall, 1992a; Nuthall & Alton-Lee, 1991, 1992).[1] We have explained knowledge acquisition in classrooms as a developmental process in which children generate specific knowledge constructs as they participate in the enacted curriculum. We define the enacted curriculum as the actual ways in which students encounter curriculum content as they participate in individual, group, and whole class activities and tasks.

Utterance data can be a rich source of information about the ways in which children experience and negotiate the instructional, social, and cultural contexts of the classroom. If the purpose of educational research is to improve classroom practice, then we need to understand how teachers influence these contexts. Children's utterances, when triangulated with other data, can illuminate the hidden cognitive and cultural processes that mediate their learning and well-being.

In this article, we use several data sources from a single class lesson to demonstrate the interplay between instructional, social, and cultural contexts that influence children's experience. In particular, we focus on cultural processes mediating gender and race. We report a detailed analysis of four case-study children's experience of one lesson, using multiple sources of data: transcripts

---

[1] Our project, the Understanding Learning and Teaching Project, consists of a series of six studies of children's learning from integrated instructional units in fourth, sixth, and seventh grades (Alton-Lee, 1984; Alton-Lee & Nuthall, 1990, 1991, 1992a, 1992b; Nuthall & Alton-Lee, 1991, 1992, 1993). An instructional unit is a series of lessons and tasks through which students experience curriculum content relevant to a particular topic. The term "integrated" is used when different subject areas are integrated into the unit. For example, language, reading, and social studies were integrated into the New York City unit taught in the sixth-grade class we studied.

of the public enacted curriculum and of children's private utterances (transcribed from audio recordings); continuous observational records of case-study children; tests of short- and long-term learning outcomes; and interviews with the teacher and with the children. We explain how the utterance data helped in the development of a model of classroom learning. Finally, we consider the implications of our analysis for developing an understanding that takes into account both the psychological and sociocultural dimensions of classroom learning processes.

GATHERING UTTERANCE DATA IN THE CLASSROOM

We began each of the studies in our project by finding a teacher who was aware of the nature of the research and was eager to participate. Each teacher decided which curriculum unit we would study. We negotiated prior permission with the local Education Board and the principal, and obtained written permission from the children's parents. The purpose of the research was explained to the children, and they were given the opportunity to decide whether or not to participate.[2]

The Understanding Learning and Teaching Project now comprises a series of six studies of children's learning in schools selected for racial and social-class contrasts in student population. This article focuses on an introductory lesson taught in a sixth-grade classroom in a suburban intermediate school (sixth- and seventh-grade students only) serving a predominantly *Pakeha* (White) middle- to upper-middle-class population.[3] Four case-study children in the classroom were selected from those who had parental permission, wanted to participate, and were visibly accessible to the video camera. Any child who the teacher believed might be adversely affected by the intensive observation was not chosen as a case-study student.

Individual broadcast microphones were used to record the private and public utterances of the children. Public utterances were those audible to the teacher and the class, including comments and exclamations that were called out during the lesson and recorded on the public transcript of the lesson. Private utterances included private conversations between children and the whispers and comments that children made to themselves. Each private microphone and transmitter was encased in a small plastic box and hung by an elastic band around the child's neck and under his or her sweater. Each day the children put on their microphone transmitters at the beginning of the unit and switched on the transmitters. The children were shown how to turn off the transmitters if at any time they wished to keep their conversation entirely private. All the children in the class who wished to participate wore the microphone transmitters, but only the transmitters worn by the case-study children were live. The children rarely switched off the microphone transmitters during teacher-directed lessons. There

[2] In this article and in all our research reports, the names of the children were changed.

[3] *Pakeha* is the Maori term for White New Zealanders. We use the term as a mark of respect for the right of the indigenous people to name those who came after them. The term *Pakeha* is widely used in Aotearoa New Zealand. "Aotearoa" is the Maori word for New Zealand.

is evidence that they often forgot they were wearing the microphones, but monitored their behavior when they did remember. For example:

Child (talking to peer): Don't give me that shit! — Nice little microphone.

The children appeared to disregard the recording process after the familiarization period, perhaps because they did not receive any reactions from the researchers to what was recorded.

The Lesson

To illustrate the value of utterance data in revealing the processes that mediate children's experience in both the official and unofficial worlds, we selected a thirty-six-minute introductory whole-class lesson from a social studies unit entitled "New York City: A Study in Cultural Differences."[4] One of the teacher's goals in teaching the unit was for the children to develop more tolerance and appreciation for different races as they learned about the cultural mix in New York City. The teacher was a *Pakeha* (White) male.

Throughout the lesson the children were seated in a semicircle around the teacher, who used an overhead projector and a map as visual aids. During the first two minutes the teacher introduced the unit topic, and then the lesson itself began. The teacher began with a brainstorming activity, asking the children to respond to the question, "What does New York make you think of?" His purpose was to get "a word, a reaction, just to tune them in . . . getting them to bring to their awareness what they think about New York." The task difficulty increased slightly when he then asked, "What do you know about New York?" The teacher recorded the children's public responses on the overhead projector. The children were then asked to reflect on their responses and to consider a third question, "What would it be like to live in New York?"

After this brainstorming activity, which lasted nine minutes, the lesson continued with teacher-led discussions about New York's European settlement, its geography, the reasons for its growth, and the location of boroughs, landmarks, and prominent buildings. While discussing the European settlement, the teacher emphasized key dates as "coat hangers or signposts" to help the children with the concept of time. He made frequent comparisons between New York City and Aotearoa New Zealand in order to relate the new information to the children's prior knowledge. Throughout the lesson the teacher interspersed brief reviews in which he asked the children to recall factual details from the foregoing introductory lesson. At the end of the lesson he provided instructions for two follow-up map-labeling tasks to be done individually by the children.

Utterance Data as a Window on Children's Experience of the Lesson

We focused on four case-study children in order to trace the ways in which individual children participated in and were influenced by classroom processes.[5]

[4] For the sake of simplicity, we use the term "lesson" to describe the 36-minute teacher-directed task sequence.

[5] Although this article focuses predominantly on the four case-study children's participation in a single lesson, we traced their experience of the enacted curriculum throughout the entire unit in order to investigate their learning from their total in-class opportunity to learn specific item content (Alton-Lee & Nuthall, 1992b).

The case-study children were selected to include children of different achievement levels and both boys and girls: Ann (average), Joe (low), Jon (high), and Mia (high).[6] All four children came from families in which both parents were in paid employment. Mia and Jon came from upper-middle-class families in which both parents were professionals (teacher and lawyer, teacher and scientist); Ann's and Joe's parents were in middle-class occupations (small business management, sales, and nursing). All were *Pakeha* (of European descent). The only Maori child in the class, Ricky, was not chosen for the case study because he was one of the children who the teacher perceived would be unsettled by the observational process.

We classified each utterance of each case-study child according to whether it was public or private and whether it was related to the curriculum content.[7] Public utterances were then classified in relation to the teacher's designation within the enacted curriculum: whether the child was publicly answering the question when called upon ("public nomination"), calling out the answer without being called on ("call out"), responding in chorus with other children ("choral response"), or reading with the group ("unison reading"). Private utterances were initially classified by audience: whether the child was speaking or listening to a peer, talking to his or her self, or, in the case of one child, singing.

During the thirty-six-minute lesson, the four case-study children produced 318 utterance strings, 86 percent of which occurred in the unofficial or the private dimension of the children's experience of the lesson (see Table 1). For Ann, Joe, and Jon, public utterances comprised only 12 percent to 13 percent of their total utterances during this time. Mia engaged in much less private talk: 41 percent of her comparatively infrequent 17 utterances were public.

Table 1 also shows the number of private utterances that were unrelated to curriculum content. These were: 16 percent for Ann, 11 percent for Jon, and 10 percent (one utterance) for Mia. Mia's private utterance that was unrelated to curriculum content concerned the task, as did half of Ann's and a third of Jon's. Private utterances that were unrelated to either the curriculum content or to

[6] The achievement levels were determined using a variety of measures, including the teacher's prior assessment of each child's general achievement level and scores on the New Zealand Council for Educational Research standardized achievement tests (administered in schools at the beginning of each school year). The teacher's assessments of the case-study children's achievement levels were consistent with the children's performance on the standardized tests and with the children's actual learning from the unit, as measured by the unit test. However, the case-study children's prior knowledge, as measured by the unit pre-test, indicated a possible gender difference rather than a general achievement difference. Out of 99 items, Jon scored 76 on the pre-test, Joe scored 57, Ann scored 54, and Mia scored 53.

[7] Utterances were defined by speaker and topic. Where the topic of an utterance string remained constant within a quarter-minute interval, the utterance string of a single speaker was counted as one "utterance." We located the continuous data in quarter-minute intervals because they were the smallest practical time intervals for the synchronized transcriptions and observational data in the Understanding Learning and Teaching Project. Where the topic of an utterance changed within a quarter-minute interval, the number of topics determined the number of distinct utterances counted. Where utterance strings (for example, peer conversations) persisted across quarter-minute intervals, they were counted as additional utterances with the same topic. We use the term "utterance" rather than "utterance string" for simplicity. When the same utterance served more than one function, the content-relevant meaning took precedence in the coding. For example, Joe's utterance, "Hi Mom," was a response to the video camera and a free association to the U.S. usage of "Mom"; this utterance was categorized as content-relevant, whereas an utterance such as "look at the camera" would have been classified as relevant only to our observational procedures (in substance, off-task).

TABLE 1

Frequency of Public Talk, Peer Interaction, and Talking or Singing to Self for the Case-Study Children (36 Minutes)

Utterance Type/Audience	Number of Utterances			
	Ann	Joe	Jon	Mia
	Public talk			
Public nomination	2	3	7	3
Call out	5	11 (1)	3 (1)	1 (1)
Chorus response	2	0	1	1
Unison reading	2	0	2	2
	Private talk			
Talks to peer	23 (14)	36 (17)	26 (10)	1 (1)
Listens to peer	3	18 (11)	8	1
Talks to self	49	37	53 (1)	8
Sings	0	0	10	0
Total	86 (14)	105 (29)	110 (12)	17 (2)

Note: The number of utterances in each category that were unrelated to curriculum content are indicated in parentheses.

the ongoing tasks were infrequent, except for those by Joe; even for Joe over two-thirds of his private utterances were related to curriculum content.

BEYOND "OFF-TASK"

A comparison of the audio recordings and the observers' records revealed that fewer than a quarter of the private utterances recorded by the children's microphones were apparent to the observers. The simple finding that children's hidden classroom talk was far more prevalent than was apparent to the observers, who were each continuously watching one case-study child, reflects the children's expertise in hiding their private interactions. This is not surprising, given that private pupil talk is officially "off-task" during a teacher-directed lesson because it contravenes the rules of order. Doyle (1986) noted that in both secondary and elementary classrooms, quiet private talk between peers, although permitted in other task contexts, contravened the rules for teacher-directed lessons.

Indeed, the common assumption in the official classroom world is that during a lesson children should talk only when they participate publicly, and the teacher should nominate who talks publicly. Classroom research, however, shows a discrepancy between the official rules and actual behavior patterns. Doyle (1986) reviewed a series of studies that found that teachers are not always consistent in enforcing rules against "call-outs," and Cazden (1986) noted that in the course of curriculum enactment the rules of turn-taking are relaxed as the momentum of a lesson increases. Kounin (1970) explained that teachers risk sacrificing the instructional flow and momentum of a lesson if they engage in too many reprimands to achieve rule enforcement.

During the lesson we studied, the teacher did not consistently reprimand children for the private talk he appeared to notice. We should note that, because the teacher was attending primarily to the instructional flow, he noticed much less of the private talk than did the observers. However, the teacher enforced the rules of order when he found private talk disruptive.

The data in Table 1 indicate that much officially "off-task" talk was not only actually task-relevant, but also directly relevant to the children's engagement with the curriculum content.

Before we move on to consider the children's curriculum-relevant utterances during the teacher-directed lesson, we briefly consider a further problem with the use of "on-task" and "off-task" classifications of children's talk. This problem is the prevalence of "on-task" talk that shows preoccupation with task organization or presentation (for example, printing headings and coloring maps) but that displaces the academic work the teacher intended the task to involve.

For example, in the map-labeling tasks that followed the lesson we described earlier, the teacher had asked the children to locate New York City on a map of the world, and to identify and label the Hudson River, the Atlantic Ocean, Mexico, and Canada. The second task involved labeling the boroughs and key landmarks on a map of New York City. Compare Jon's and Ann's utterances over a parallel time period while working at these tasks:[8]

Ann:

Ann (talking to peer): Mine [felt-tipped pen] hasn't been used that much . . . it goes a bit funny.

Ann (talking to peer): Can I use your navy? Can I use your navy please? Are you going around the edge in navy blue? What are you going to do there?

Peer (talking to Ann): Blue. But not with blue felt. Blue pencil.

Ann (talking to peer): In pencil. Yeah! Can I use your green or are you using it? Rose, have you got a blue-green?

[Two minutes later]

Ann (talking to peer): Are you definitely using pencil? I'll tell you which blue I did. I'm not going to take long. Remember we had to do the map in social studies. It's not going to take as long as that.

[Two minutes later]

Ann (talking to peer): That blue works marvelous. My blue works hopeless.

Jon:

Jon (singing to self): New York! Hot in the city! Hot in the city tonight!

Jon (talking to self): New York. Hudson River. Atlantic Ocean is here.

---

[8] Throughout the article, private utterances are shown in italics and public utterances are shown in regular type.

[Two minutes later]

Jon (talking to self): Mexico. Mekiko. Mehico.

Peer (talking to Jon): Statue of Liberty, eh?

Jon (singing to self): Mehico Ga-la-la!

Jon (talking to peer): Do you like Canada? Do you like Canada, the place?

Peer (talking to Jon): Do you know their cops are the worst in the world?

Jon (talking to peer): They're nasty.

Jon (talking to self): Mounties? . . .

Jon (talking to peer): Man, I've lost track of this map. That must be the Bronx up there. Bronx, Queens. Aw man, this map's hard to follow. It's badly drawn.

Peer (talking to Jon): No it's not. It's easy . . .

Jon (talking to peer): Well, that's your opinion, Mark. New Jersey! New Jersey man [attempts accent].

Peer (talking to Jon): That's the Bronx, isn't it?

Jon (talking to peer): Yeah. That's the Bronx . . . uh, Queens is across from the Bronx.

Peer (talking to Jon): That big bit down there. Queens, Manhattan, Brooklyn, it's down there.

Jon (talking to self): Brooklyn . . .

Jon (talking to peer): Staten Island. That's it. Here it is.

These examples reveal that during the map-labeling task, Ann was largely preoccupied with the coloring process, while Jon systematically attempted to locate and label each place specified by the teacher in his instructions. A pattern found across our classroom studies is that children often become preoccupied with task presentation rather than engaging with the curriculum content. From our detailed records of children's experience of curriculum in the classrooms we studied, it is clear that off-task behavior played a relatively minor role in inhibiting learning, as compared with on-task behavior that did not involve engagement with curriculum concepts.

We now turn to the case-study children's public and private utterances during the teacher-directed lesson, a high proportion of which were directly relevant to the curriculum content (Ann, 84 percent; Joe, 72 percent; Jon, 89 percent; and Mia, 88 percent). We cannot know whether these utterances were facilitating or even mediating learning processes; some utterances may simply reflect some of the thinking processes used by the children during the lesson. Alternatively, verbalization in itself may facilitate children's learning.

INTERPRETING THE UTTERANCE DATA

We needed to develop a framework for interpreting the educational significance of the children's utterances. The prevalence of children's private talk that was not directed at *any* audience led us away from a traditional view that utterances are always a form of communication. Much of the children's talk did involve

FIGURE I

A Framework for Interpreting the Contextual Influences on a Child's Experience of a Classroom Lesson

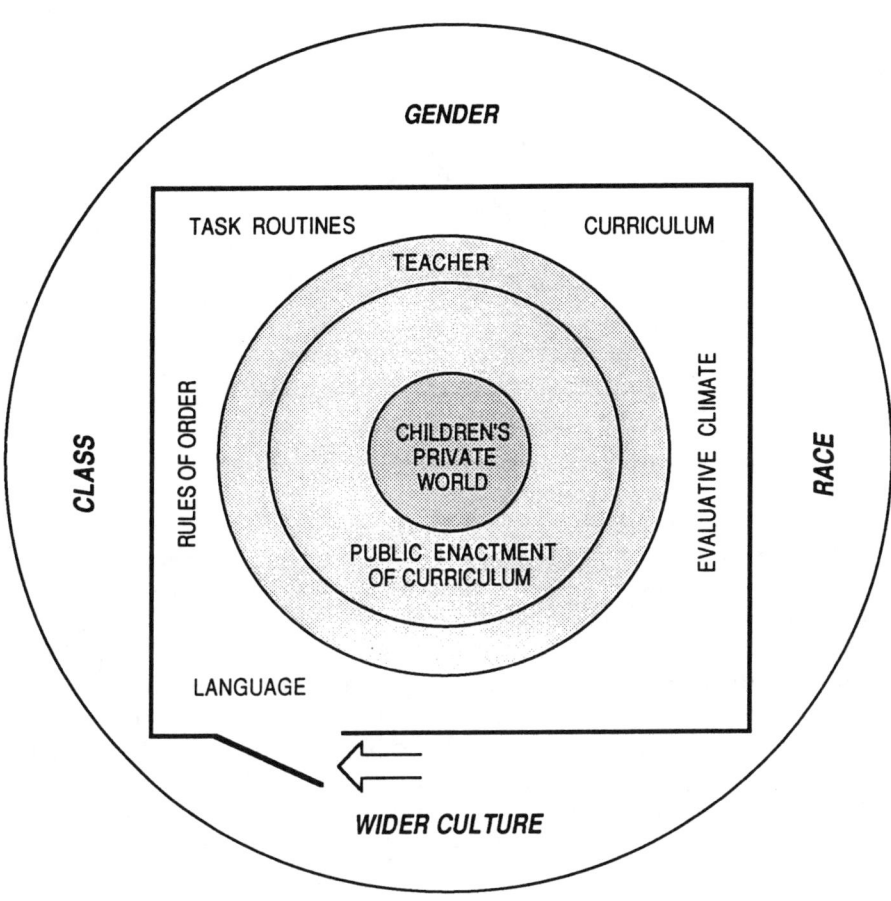

communication, but a significant proportion involved the children's personal and hidden verbal responses to the classroom processes.

We developed a framework within which utterances are interpreted as a source of information about the ways in which children are responding to the classroom context (see Figure 1). The framework is grounded in our data and evolving theoretical work in the Understanding Learning and Teaching Project (Alton-Lee, 1984; Alton-Lee & Nuthall, 1990, 1992a; Nuthall & Alton-Lee, 1990, 1991, 1993) and derived from a process of theoretical triangulation with the work of Doyle (1983) and Apple and Weiss (1983) and with recent information-processing theory (Howard, 1987). Central to our framework is a concern with the children's process of knowledge construction; this process we frame not only within the larger classroom context, but also within the wider sociocultural context of which the classroom is a part.

In this framework, the four major dimensions of official classroom culture are: the rules of order, the task routines, the curriculum, and the criteria by which children's performance is evaluated. As in any culture, many elements of these dimensions are implicit. The participants are enculturated over time (Berwick-Emms, 1989); it is the language, content, and perspectives of the curriculum that shape the classroom culture. For any particular classroom task, the task routines used by the teacher moderate the rules of order and shape the evaluative climate, creating particular contextual demands to be negotiated by the children (Doyle, 1983, 1986). The official agenda is that all children should acquire the same skills and knowledge through their participation in the classroom tasks. The teacher and children, however, have their own cultural perspectives shaped by their gender, class, and race. These cultural perspectives influence their negotiation of the classroom culture and their public and private participation in curriculum enactment. The outcomes for children include not only how much they are able to learn from the official curriculum, but also what they learn about their own identity, value, and capability. The process of curriculum enactment itself is critical because children experience and learn culturally specific ways of participating that influence their learning and their well-being.

Our framework allows us to interpret the functions of children's utterances during a class lesson. Whether or not children talk privately is in itself significant, because private utterances contravene the rules of order in the lesson context. Accordingly, it is necessary to interpret the significance of silence. How a child negotiates the classroom culture during any lesson will influence the likelihood that she or he will participate, publicly or privately, in the lesson. Children's participation is also constrained by the evaluative dimension of classroom lessons. There is risk involved in responding publicly and failing. Individual children are more or less likely to be able to lower the risk and accomplish tasks successfully because of differences in their prior knowledge, experience, and the particular skills and resources available to them both within and outside of the classroom. For children, participation in classroom lessons involves negotiating risk publicly and managing the social consequences of succeeding or failing.

In addition to whether or not a child talks publicly or privately, we must pay particular attention to the audience of an utterance. Even within the private utterance data for this lesson, there were three distinct audience categories. At the most private level, the case-study children engaged in whispers to themselves that were inaudible to peers; the second level involved private interactions with a single peer that were hidden from other peers and the teacher; and the third level involved verbalizations accessible to a few peers but not public. By identifying audience, we can learn much about the way a child negotiates the culture of the classroom and sociocultural processes.

Using this framework, we explain a child's experience during a lesson as a unique process involving three concurrent strands: 1) responding to curriculum content, 2) managing the classroom culture, and 3) participating in sociocultural processes.

Responding to Curriculum Content: Developing Knowledge Constructs

Our understanding of the way children acquire knowledge in the classroom is that they generate specific knowledge constructs as they engage in the process of making meaning out of curriculum content. The term "knowledge construct" is used to refer to a unit of knowledge that is constructed in memory as the child interprets classroom experience in relation to prior knowledge. It is less generic than a schema (see Howard, 1987) and more general than a mental model (Johnson-Laird, 1983).

We developed a model of the processes by which children generate specific knowledge constructs during instructional units by comparing the developmental progression of children's experience of curriculum content they learned with that for content that they failed to learn. Elsewhere we have described the model (Nuthall & Alton-Lee, 1991, 1992), the success of that model in predicting children's learning in three studies with children of different ages studying different curriculum areas (Nuthall & Alton-Lee, 1993), and the rationale for the methodology used (Alton-Lee & Nuthall, 1992b).

According to our model, in order to generate a specific knowledge construct, a student needs to be exposed to a sequence of appropriate, topic-relevant information within a limited period of time. Knowledge construct generation involves the child in a series of cognitive processes: obtaining information, creating associative links, elaborating the content, evaluating the truth and consistency of information, and developing metacognitive awareness (Nuthall & Alton-Lee, 1993).

The utterances recorded during the teacher-directed lesson in this study illuminate the ways in which the case-study children created associative links to their existing knowledge, evaluated the truth of their emerging understandings, and elaborated the content. It should be noted that because the lesson we focus on in this article was only an introductory one (almost seven hours of class time were spent on the New York City unit), the utterances often reflect the preliminary stages of the children's knowledge construct generation.

Creating associative links between new information and prior knowledge The following utterances are examples of the ways in which the case-study children made connections with their prior knowledge and experience as they responded to the content of the enacted curriculum:

Teacher: . . . a whole 102 stories high. Imagine running up the stairs.

Mia (whispers to self): Cross country.

. . .

Teacher: . . . and the Dutch people under a Mr. Peter Stuyvesant, who of all things had a wooden leg.

Pupil (calls out): Smokes!

Teacher: If that helps.

Joe (talking to Ricky): Smokes! Ciggies!

. . .

Teacher: . . . Staten Island sometimes called Richmond.

Ricky (talking to Joe): I used to go to that school.

Joe (talking to Ricky): Richmond school.

. . .

[Teacher asks question about subway routes on map]

Ann (talking to self): Streams. Boats. In Lyttelton they have those boats.

. . .

Teacher: It's on . . . a little wee island. What is it, Jon?

Jon: Statue of Liberty.

Bart (talking to Jon): See that island there. That's where they dump their rubbish at the tip.

Jon (talking to Bart): I know 'cause they put rubbish barges down the Hudson River.

The teacher's invitation to imagine climbing the Empire State Building by the stairs reminded Mia of the school cross-country race scheduled for later in the day. Joe associated the name of Peter Stuyvesant with cigarettes (the brand his father smoked) after the teacher publicly validated another child's use of the association as a memory device. Joe realized that Ricky was making an association between Richmond Borough and Richmond School, which Ricky had attended previously. Ann's prior experience was insufficient to help her identify the subway route on the map, but she guessed, from her knowledge of a local seaport, that the symbols represented some kind of transport route. Jon's response to the teacher's question about an island near Manhattan was not only a public answer, but also a private display (to Bart) of extraordinarily specific prior knowledge about the use of barges for Manhattan rubbish disposal.

By identifying and making associations with personal experience and knowledge, children connect the new with the familiar in order to make sense or meaning out of the curriculum. Children's success at this process depends on the extent and availability of their general and topic-specific knowledge. The following excerpt illustrates the critical role that general knowledge can play in enabling a child to make sense of curriculum content:

Teacher: Brett?

Brett: The average stay for a visitor is two days.

Julia (talking to Ann): Are you only allowed to stay for two days?

Ann (talking to Julia): No that's an average. How long they do stay.

Although not every association made by the children occurred in response to a direct cue from the teacher, these associations were more likely to occur following the teacher's questions, cues, and hesitations. When reviewing the video record of the lesson, the teacher commented, "I'm pleased to see that I'm not only getting a pause, a 'wait-time,' but also that I was consciously doing it. . . . I'm asking them to think."

In addition to the logical associations the children made between their prior knowledge and the curriculum content, they also made idiosyncratic, playful, and joking associations; this was particularly true of the boys. These associations were sometimes linked to the meaning of curriculum material and sometimes to the sound of a name or an alternative meaning. For example:

Teacher: Manhattan.

Joe (talking to self): Madhattan!

. . .

Teacher: . . . sitting right on a fault line.

Joe (talking to self): Yeah! The line going across the motorway.

Jon's singing also illustrates this process:

Teacher (introducing the unit): We'll be handing out a map of New York . . .

Jon (singing to self): Cool, New York, hot in the city! Hot in the city! Hot in the city, tonight!

Teacher: Can you have a look [at map of New York City]?

(Jon singing to self): . . . from Central Park to Shanty Town. . . . New York . . . do do!

The process of making links to the curriculum content is not always consistent with the public curriculum. Inappropriate links lead to misconceptions. The utterance data showed not only children's extant misconceptions, but also the development of misconceptions during the lesson. For example, Ann inappropriately linked the notion of East Indies (where the English explorers were intending to go when they "found" New York) and the Indians who lived in New York. As a result, she mistakenly generated the name "Eastern Indians" to refer to the Manhattan Indians.

Evaluating and validating emerging understandings The children's utterances also demonstrated that they were integrating curriculum content. This involved identifying the implications of the new material and checking its coherence and validity in relation to their existing knowledge. In this monitoring process, they might identify their own misconceptions and explore evidence or reasons to support their emerging understandings. For example:

Teacher: 1664? . . . Charles?

Ann (talking to self) : American Revol-

Charles: Ah, um the English took over from the Dutch . . .

Ann (talking to self): Oh!

. . .

Teacher: Where did we start prior to 1600?

Jon (provides sound effects of gun fire): K.K.K.K.k.k.k.k.k . . .

Jon (talking to self): No machine guns . . . wouldn't have even been pump-action muskets.

. . .

301

Teacher: Yes, it [New York City] grew to a million people. It grew to more than
. . .

Mia (talking to self): Eighty million.

Pupil: Eight million.

Teacher: What made you say eight million?

Ann (talking to peer): I guessed that because I just thought that New Zealand is three million and New York's bigger than that.

. . .

Teacher: 1609?

Mia (talking to self): The Dutch [precedes the correct answer in public lesson by half a minute].

There is evidence to suggest that this monitoring and integration process is an internalization of the model of teacher-student interactions that the children experience in the public discussion. This cycle of question-answer-reaction has been well-documented as the traditional pattern of teacher-student verbal interaction in the classroom (Aschner, 1959; Bellack, Hyman, Smith, & Kliebard, 1966). Empirical evidence indicates that students who participate publicly in the discussion cycle do not learn more than students who only listen to the cycle, and that listening to a discussion cycle is more effective than listening to a teacher lecture (see Hughes, 1973; Nuthall & Church, 1973). The utterances in this study suggest that the children are not only learning how to respond in an acceptable manner, but are also learning the teacher's role of reacting to responses. In their private utterances, both Mia and Ann responded to the teacher's cues and reacted like the teacher to their own covert utterances and to other children's overt responses. The evaluative climate of the lesson became their own internal evaluative process.

Developing and extending knowledge constructs Once children have generated a specific knowledge construct, they develop and extend its content. Because the lesson we selected was the introductory session to the unit, the children were interacting with primarily new information; thus this process was only infrequently evident in their utterances. There was one example in Ann's utterances:

Teacher: What did they use the river as?

Ann (talking to Julia): Exporting.

Teacher: Neil?

Neil: A road.

Teacher: Thank you. They used the river as a road.

The notion that the Hudson River had been used to transport people was discussed in the public lesson, but the idea was not developed to include the commercial function that Ann privately suggested to Julia.

Jon had the most relevant prior knowledge of all the case-study children (he already knew the content of over three-quarters of the items in the pre-test), so it is not surprising that his utterances frequently involved comments that developed, extended, and provided his personal perspective on the curriculum content:

> Teacher: The English took over from the Dutch, and they said, "We'll blow you up if you don't give us the island!"
>
> *Jon (talking to self): Threatened them!*
>
> . . .
>
> Pupil (in response to first question, "What does New York make you think of?"): Nukes.
>
> *Jon (talking to self): Nuclear. There's none in New York. They're all in Washington.*

As the unit progressed, these comments became more frequent. For example, in a later lesson about reasons for early immigration to New York, Jon found the teacher's explanation ironic:

> Teacher: So wars meant that some folk said, "Let's shift from Europe and go to where there are no wars," so they went to America.
>
> *Jon (talking to self): Now America's king of war.*

While there is danger in over-interpreting the utterance data, there are reasonable grounds for believing that, because they are spontaneous and private, they represent an externalization of normally covert processes; that is, that they represent spontaneous thinking aloud.

Jon's utterances during the introductory lesson reflected his higher prior knowledge: his utterances involved associative links, elaborations, evaluations of the truth and consistency of information, and metacognitive processes.[9] Ann's utterances were mainly concerned with monitoring her own misconceptions and emerging understandings. Joe frequently related the new curriculum content to his own knowledge, but did little monitoring or integrating of the new knowledge. Mia was very quiet, but her characteristic response was to monitor her own answers.

It may be that these differences between the children reflect differences in their ability to organize their experiences and generate relevant knowledge constructs. But what constitutes "ability" here? What the utterances do reveal is the critical role of cultural capital in enabling the children to engage in the process of generating constructs.[10] This is apparent in both the topic-specific and general knowledge that the children brought to the lesson, or which they gained access to by interacting with peers and with the teacher during the lesson.

The utterances also reveal a difference between the children in the extent to which they incorporated into their processing a teacher-like role of monitoring the validity of their emerging understandings. Evidence of monitoring is least apparent in the utterances of Joe, the low achiever, suggesting that monitoring

---

[9] On the unit pre-test, consisting of 99 items, Jon already knew 19 items more than Joe, 23 items more than Ann, and 24 items more than Mia.

[10] See Bourdieu (1977) for early arguments about cultural capital and habitus. There is cultural bias in the cultural experiences that are publicly linked to new information in the enacted curriculum.

one's own understandings may be particularly critical to the knowledge construct generation process.

It is important to remember, however, that with our focus on this one lesson we have opened only a partial window on the processes with which children generate knowledge constructs. Our studies indicate that such constructs are generated across a number of occasions throughout the course of a unit (Nuthall & Alton-Lee, 1992, 1993).

Managing the Classroom Culture

As is apparent in the section above, the children's ability to make meaning out of curriculum content was dependent on the extent to which they could draw upon relevant prior knowledge, skills (such as map interpretation), and experiences. When a child lacks these resources, she or he finds it difficult to manage the evaluative climate. In the following accounts, we consider what the utterances reveal about the ways in which the teacher and the case-study children managed the evaluative climate. Our findings should be interpreted with the proviso that our presence as observers almost certainly heightened the children's perception of the risk of replying.

Ann Ann appeared to manage the evaluative climate with accurate judgment about the adequacy of her answers. Her public answers were consistently correct or appropriate and her eleven wrong answers were kept private. She was able to draw on considerable relevant prior knowledge during the lesson, including her recent television viewing of a news item about the Statue of Liberty. Almost 10 percent of Ann's utterances involved her friend Julia in a shared process of interacting with the curriculum content. When Ann was overwhelmed by new curriculum content and no longer able to engage in making associations to relevant prior knowledge and experience, she used an apparently deliberate strategy of repetition of key words:[11]

Teacher: The Dutch . . .

Ann (talking to self): The Dutch.

Teacher: . . . started a town on Manhattan; they called it New Amsterdam.

Ann (talking to self): New Amsterdam.

. . .

Teacher: There are three buildings I would like you to identify: United Nations, Empire State, and World Trade Center.

Ann (talking to self): World Trade, World Trade, Empire State, United Nations, Empire State.

Ann's style of participation in the lesson indicated almost total continuous involvement in the tasks or with the content. Of all the case-study children, she was most often observed to be focused on the teacher or on a relevant resource.

---

[11] Our exploratory analyses of the relation between occurrence of utterance type and learning outcome revealed that Ann's repetition strategy was used more frequently during time she spent on content she did not learn (Nuthall & Alton-Lee, 1990).

Ann received no positive feedback from the teacher for her two publicly nominated responses, and she appeared frustrated in her desire to participate publicly more frequently. Of the four children, she was least likely to elicit teacher nomination with her hand raises: her fifteen hand raises during the lesson only elicited two teacher nominations. Ann responded by calling out her answers five times and by talking privately at a rate of two to three utterances per minute. A third of these utterances involved cooperative interactions with her friend, Julia. This private peer interaction appeared to play an important, mutually supportive role in both girls' management of the evaluative climate during the lesson. Julia sought Ann's help with strategies to remember the dates presented by the teacher. Ann shared her misconceptions with Julia. This talk was hidden, enabling Ann to give and receive peer support during the lesson, yet allowing her to avoid being seen by the teacher as contravening the rules of order.

Her management (masking) of her contravention of the rules of order was so effective that even when the teacher reviewed the video (long after the unit), Ann's private utterances were hidden, and he commented that "Ann doesn't offer as much as some of the others in terms of an active type of learning. . . . She learns just sitting and soaking it up."

Joe Joe did not appear to manage the evaluative climate as carefully as Ann: his only two wrong answers were public responses. This can be explained partly by the absence of self-monitoring in Joe's interaction with curriculum content during the lesson; he did not appear to check the validity of his own answers.

Both Joe's utterances and the interview with Joe reveal that his free associations drew extensively on his prior knowledge and experiences, particularly on his television viewing: "Oh yeah! 'The Equalizer' program. The one just starting, there was this . . . picture of a subway and there was all this yukky stuff and rubbish." His background knowledge, however, was insufficient to enable him to answer public questions correctly:

Teacher: Can you think of any city, say in New Zealand or anywhere else, that has got this type of [name]?

Joe (talking to self): No, damn!

When another boy, Sean, gave information about the average stay for a visitor to New York being two days, Joe's retort was a scathing, "How do you know that?" But when the teacher then acknowledged Sean's prior reading as a valuable source of information, Joe grabbed a book from a nearby display. Throughout much of the rest of the lesson, Joe attempted to use the book to find answers to the teacher's questions:

Teacher: What else is there in New York?

Joe (calling out): Yeah, I know! I know! It's in this book!

. . .

Teacher: What did they use the river as [in the context of discussing the commercial growth of New York City]?

Joe (talking to self): It said canoeing here.

305

Joe's determination to get right answers preoccupied him to the point that he failed to follow the meaning of the public discussion; hence his response of "canoeing" in the instance above. The process finally became public after a sequence when Joe called out and pleaded with the teacher to choose him to participate:

> Teacher: Why did New York grow, whereas the cities at the time that were a bit down there didn't grow nearly as much?
>
> Joe (calling out): I know!
>
> Teacher: You've got everything you need, Joe. Go!
>
> Joe: Well it says in this book. It may not be right, but it says that European settlers had a habit of pulling it out — of pulling something out.
>
> Teacher: Well! [pupils laugh] Let's just say you pulled it out of a book and I'm not certain what it is, but just leave it there, Joe.

The consequences of his public mistake did not seem to worry Joe excessively, and the teacher later commented, "I think it was a general humorous laugh and Joe was laughing as well. I don't think it was a ridicule laugh."

Though the social consequences of public failure were not serious for Joe, his inability to provide right answers seemed both to frustrate him and to motivate him to copy an effective strategy used by his peer — reading a book. Not only did Joe contravene the rules of order by getting the book, he also flicked through it in an attempt to get answers during the lesson. This strategy reduced the possibility of his making meaning of the ongoing curriculum content according to the teacher's agenda. During the lesson, Joe focused on the teacher or a relevant resource less than half as frequently as did both girls, though unlike them, he appeared to take great pleasure in the lesson, making jokes, word plays, and humorous free associations. He was the only case-study child to engage in more peer interactions than talk to himself.

Although a large proportion (41.5 percent) of Joe's social interactions involved a shared process of interacting with curriculum content, he also used the private world to abuse his peers. He engaged in serious breaches of the rules of order — kicking and name-calling. He was, however, very skilled at hiding his contraventions and was never individually reprimanded by the teacher. Actually, early in the lesson he was rewarded for breaking the public participation rule:

> Teacher: That is, homework as opposed to what you do while you are?
>
> Joe (calling out before the teacher opened up the turn to other children): At school!
>
> Teacher: I want to hear a voice — "at school." Brilliant!

Joe's public response during the brainstorm, "Oh, what is, yeah . . . lots of violence," was rewarded with the affirmation, "He thinks, he does!" Joe made ten more public call-outs during the lesson.

Mia Mia appeared to be the case-study child most concerned about the evaluative climate and the rules of order. Her private utterances were rare and mostly inaudible to her peers. Mia's only comment to a peer, "He always says 'Brilliant!',", concerned the teacher's feedback to other children and revealed Mia's sensitivity to the evaluative climate. He never said "brilliant" to Mia. Mia watched or glanced at the teacher or appropriate visual resource at least three times per minute, but she also glanced around at a rate of twice a minute. She appeared to be very attuned to other children's private talk — particularly to Jon's evaluative comments, even when he was not directing them to peers.

Mia contravened the rules of order for public participation only once, when she called out to the teacher that she and the other girls around her could not see the visual resource. Her desire to see the screen overcame her characteristic reticence.

When Mia raised her hand, she was less likely to elicit a teacher nomination than were the boys. However, she gave two publicly nominated responses. The teacher's response to her contribution to the brainstorm indicated that he was using a more stringent criteria for Mia than for the other case-study children. Unlike the other case-study children, Mia (for both public responses) used an interrogative intonation, suggesting that she was attempting to diminish the risk. This was surprising, given the apparently low-risk status of a brainstorming session. However, her anxiety was justified. Instead of accepting the response, the teacher probed further, thereby changing the level of risk when Mia was already the focus of public attention:

Mia: The Empire State Building, Sir?

Teacher: Something about the Empire State Building. Can I just ask another question? What do you know about the Empire State Building?

Mia: Um, it's the tallest building in the world, isn't it?

Teacher: Ah, no; it's not.

Mia (talking to self): I thought it was.

The public correction of her incorrect response was remembered by Mia a year after the New York City unit:

Interviewer: Do you remember quite well when you said something in class?

Mia: Yeah, 'cause I was wrong (laugh) so I remember that. . . . I always thought what I said was the highest building, so I was surprised when he said to me I was wrong.

Jon Of the four case-study children, Jon was the one who, when he raised his hand, was recognized most often by the teacher: approximately one out of four times that he raised his hand he was called on. He was nominated publicly seven times and called out on three occasions. Jon appeared to be less constrained by the evaluative climate and more at ease than the other case-study children:

Teacher: What's his name?

Pupil: Oh, I'm not sure.

Teacher: I should have written it down. I'm being a wee bit nasty asking you to remember these things.

Jon: Starts with a C. Was it Cooligan or something?

Neil: I know! Peter Stuyvesant.

Jon (talking to self): Oh yeah!

307

Jon (talking to Neil): How did you know it was a cigarette, Neil? Ooohhh!

In the example above, Jon was prepared to take the risk to give a public response that he knew he was unsure about. When Neil gave the correct response, Jon's self-monitoring was private. Within the unofficial peer culture, he mocked Neil for having knowledge of cigarettes, suggestively implying that his knowledge may have been acquired illicitly. Jon effectively took the evaluative focus off himself.

Of all the case-study children, Jon had the most specific topic-relevant knowledge, much of which came from television. His most frequent private utterance response to the lesson was to give an answer. Out of sixteen of Jon's private answers, only one was incorrect.

The contribution of television to Jon's learning was extraordinarily specific. The mystery of his knowledge of Manhattan barge rubbish disposal was revealed in an interview when he explained how he knew about the Hudson river:

Interviewer: How did you learn that?

Jon (laughing): "Yogi Bear" and "Top Cat"!

Interviewer: Tell me more. Educate me about "Yogi Bear" and "Top Cat."

Jon: Oh no! I don't think it was "Yogi Bear." I think it was "Top Cat." And one day he wanted to take a cruise down the Hudson River and the only way he could do that was on a garbage boat, and he got put in a garbage can or something and by accident he got taken away by the garbage man, and at the end all his friends sort of say, "Oh well, you got what you wanted T.C.! A cruise down the Hudson!" or something like that!

Another source of topic-specific prior knowledge, a magazine, was revealed in the interview with Jon:

Jon: . . . in the magazine (*Mad Magazine*) where . . . on a deserted New York subway at 3:00 in the morning . . . there's three dark figures creeping up behind with knives . . .

Jon's confidence about his own prior knowledge was reflected in his next-most frequent utterance type, which involved an evaluative commentary on the adequacy and shortcomings of public answers offered by other pupils. For example:

Pupil: It's [New York] sitting on a fault line.

Jon (talking to self) : It's not. That's San Francisco.

Teacher: OK. What did they name New Amsterdam?

Jon (talking to peer): New York. Everyone tends to forget that.

He was confident enough of his own topic-relevant prior knowledge to qualify information given by the teacher:

Teacher: The very first people who may have lived in this area would have been?

Pupil: Indians.

Jon (talking to self): Red Indians actually.

Jon's response to Charles's challenge to the teacher about historical inaccuracy in the curriculum indicated that he himself was evaluating his peers and the teacher:

> Charles: The Vikings were there [America] first because they saved all those copies of bits of paper and they said the Vikings were there in 1300.
>
> Teacher: Yes. So, what?
>
> Charles: So you said they were there first but they weren't.
>
> *Jon (talking to self): Guilty, man!*

Jon not only evaluated peer responses and the teacher's information, he also argued about public information with a male peer:

> Mia: It's [Empire State Building] the tallest building in the world.
>
> *Jon (talking to self): No, it's not. It's the second tallest.*
>
> *Frank (talking to Jon): It's not the second highest.*
>
> *Jon (talking to Frank): I know what the highest is.*
>
> *Frank (talking to Jon): There are lots of buildings higher than the Empire State. It was a few years ago it was.*
>
> *Jon (talking to Frank): It's the second highest.*
>
> [Argument continues]
>
> *Jon (talking to Frank): It's got eighty-six floors!*

Jon, like Mia, was prepared to contravene the rules of order in order to interact with curriculum content. He directly contravened the teacher's direction not to use any other resource to solve a subway route problem by using a map key to locate the requisite answer.

Towards the end of the lesson, Jon complained to a peer that he wanted to be getting on with his own agenda — writing his own story about New York. However, overall he appeared to derive great enjoyment and entertainment from the lesson:

> *Jon (talking to self attempting American accent): West of the Mississippi.*
>
> [Teacher discusses reasons for expansion of New York City]
>
> *Jon (talking to peer): It also became big because it's a sea port . . .*
>
> *Jon (talking to peer): Because the Bronx Warriors were doing good!*

Jon's private utterances gave us the impression that he was covertly directing his own movie version of the lesson, providing his version of a vocal sound track, relevant sound effects, and a commentary with corrections and modifications when he judged the enacted curriculum to be falling short of the needs of the topic.

The differences in the case-study children in their management of the classroom culture reflect not only differences in the resources they were able to bring to their participation, but also differences in the ways in which the teacher operated the official agenda for different children. Irrespective of achievement level, the case-study boys were more easily able to participate publicly, were more likely to be praised, and more likely to take the risk of offering answers of which they were uncertain. The girls were careful to keep answers they were unsure of covert. Mia's strategy of remaining comparatively silent contrasted with Ann's strategy of managing much of the lesson through hidden supportive interactions with her friend, Julia.

Participating in Sociocultural Processes: Learning within the "Lived Culture" of the Classroom

Children's responses to curriculum occur within a cultural context that is also shaped by the wider society. This cultural context is described by Apple and Weiss as the "lived culture" of the classroom: "Lived culture refers to culture as it is produced in ongoing interactions and as a terrain in which class, race, and gender meanings and antagonisms are played out" (1983, p. 27). The records of the enacted curriculum and the children's utterance data provided us with a unique perspective on the specific processes through which the lived culture was produced by the teacher and the children and influenced the children's inter-action with curriculum content during this lesson.

Cultural Bias in the Curriculum Because teachers' agendas have shaped our per-spectives on classroom practice, the unofficial world of the students has been invisible; in addition, the cultural dimensions of classroom processes in the of-ficial world have been invisible. Spender (1982) argued that the school curricu-lum is strongly biased towards a White male perspective. The content of the enacted curriculum of the lesson we studied included not a single mention of a female, but fifty mentions of males (for example, Peter Stuyvesant, Henry Hud-son, the Duke of York, Englishmen, Englishman, the "man in charge").[12] Pro-nounced gender bias is not uncharacteristic in the enacted curriculum of the social studies units we have studied in the Understanding Learning and Teach-ing Project. For the entire "New York City" unit, references to females comprised only 2.4 percent of the references to people. In the enacted curriculum for a study of the Middle Ages, references to females comprised only 3.9 percent of the references to people (81.7 percent were references to males) in more than fifty-two hours of class time (Alton-Lee, Densem, & Nuthall, 1991; Alton-Lee & Densem, 1992). The few women mentioned in the New York City unit were characteristically derogated or marginalized.[13] Clearly, if particular groups of people are omitted from curriculum content or characteristically marginalized or derogated, the curriculum conveys a message about relative cultural valuing of those groups.

---

[12] There were 112 mentions of people in which gender was not specified.

[13] The first mention of a woman in the unit and the only mention of a woman given in response to the teacher's question about occupations of New Yorkers was "a prostitute." Another female mention was of a girlfriend of a boy who was the subject of a picture book story set in New York City. The children suggested that the problems of children living in poverty in New York could be caused by bad mothers. One child explained that young mothers needed to be confined to their apartments because of the violence in the city, and a joke was made about men's ability to be more successful than women, even when they attempt suicide. By contrast, White men such as Henry Hudson and Peter Stuyvesant, portrayed as intrepid and conquering, were central throughout the main lessons in the unit.

The Role of the Teacher How does bias become so pronounced in the enacted curriculum? The school resources available to teachers and historical reference books contribute to this bias, but the teacher is instrumental in shaping the lived culture of the enacted curriculum beyond the initial selection of lesson content and resources.

During the lesson studied, the teacher unconsciously structured the children's experience of curriculum by race and gender as he identified with a particular cultural group — White men of European descent. Although he began by calling each group of people or men who lived in New York City "they," as the momentum of the lesson increased, he began to use the term "we" occasionally. The following examples, spread over a six-minute period, show the teacher's use of "we" when referring to White people:

> Teacher: The very first people who may have lived in this area may have been?
>
> Child: Indians.
>
> Teacher: They gave their names to one of the islands because they spoke of the Manhattan Indians . . .
>
> . . .
>
> [Forty-five seconds later]
>
> Teacher: When White men first came they found Indians. . . . They were called Manhattan Indians. Because White people, Europeans, we were . . .
>
> Teacher: Before we, or the Dutch people could get this island where we wanted to build our city . . .
>
> . . .
>
> [Five minutes later]
>
> Teacher: Wouldn't that have been lovely if we had have owned it [New York City]?

The teacher's use of pronouns conveyed not only his own unconscious identification with the European men who colonized New York, but also an implied positioning of the children in the class as "White people, Europeans, we." He went on to mention the Treaty of Waitangi, which was the original (broken) agreement between the Maori and Europeans (*Pakeha*) in Aotearoa New Zealand, but he did so from the perspective of a White (*Pakeha*) male strongly identified with English settlers:

> Teacher: In terms of Christchurch, what is the approximate date the first lot of boats, the first four ships — the big ones — where all of our ancestors came from? You know we all came . . .

This evidence illustrates the claim made by Apple and Weiss (1983) that "what counts as school knowledge . . . tends to embody the interests and culture of the group or groups who have power to distribute and legitimate their worldview through educational institutions" (p. 28). The teacher plays an unknowing but critical role in the hegemonic cycle, and the White male bias becomes so customary it seems normal. In this lesson, the teacher's intention was to increase the children's appreciation of cultural diversity, but his unconscious assumption of "we" to refer to White males in the official enacted curriculum was in conflict with his overall aim. Although his conscious intent was to convey tolerance and cultural inclusiveness, the teacher inadvertently excluded Maori from "our ancestors . . . we all came" (a reference to the English settlement of Christchurch) during the process of curriculum enactment.

Cultural bias can also influence the enacted curriculum through the teacher's split-second decisions about who can contribute to the enacted curriculum through public participation. If a teacher unwittingly favors the participation of a particular group of children, then that group's knowledge, experiences, and cultural perspectives shape the curriculum content. Marked gender bias was apparent in who was nominated to participate and in who participated in the lesson. The boys' perspectives on New York City were twice as prominent as the girls' in the enacted curriculum. Eighty-five (70 percent) of the public contributions were made by boys compared with thirty-six (30 percent) by girls. There were fourteen girls and fifteen boys in the class, making the average public participation rate for a girl 2.6 responses, and for a boy 5.7 responses. Our analyses of the experiences of the case-study children suggests that this imbalance occurred partly because the teacher was more likely to nominate boys. Also, the evaluative climate was more stringent for the girls with respect to the responses of both the teacher and their male peers. We consider that the bias in the curriculum content may itself contribute to the imbalance through affirming and supporting the participation of those children who are White and male.

Like curriculum-content bias, gender bias in public participation, although not usually so pronounced, has been shown to be characteristic of much educational practice (Kelly, 1988; Sadker, Sadker, & Klein, 1991). Research in Aotearoa New Zealand has uncovered pronounced gender bias even in the practice of feminist teachers (Newton, 1988) and shown patterns of cultural bias, with White (*Pakeha*) girls participating publicly more than Polynesian girls (Jones, 1985), and teachers giving more attention to both White (*Pakeha*) and Samoan children than to Maori children (Clay, 1985).

The curriculum enactment was not structured by gender just in the content and public participation. The children were physically segregated by gender, with the boys in a semi-circle at the front and the girls in a semi-circle behind. This segregation was normal in this classroom, and the teacher appeared to keep the boys close as a means of proximity control. After his introduction, the teacher began the lesson proper with the comment, "Let's boot off!" — a football analogy close to the heart of male culture, both *Pakeha* and Maori, in Aotearoa New Zealand. Although the analogy is used by the teacher inclusively — "Let [u]s" — the prior experience of the children will have been influenced by gendered practices in sporting participation. For the boys, the analogy cued prior experience as active participants. For the girls, who were most unlikely ever to have played on a football team, the analogy cued either their experience as spectators or their lack of experience.

The Role of Popular Culture in Classroom Learning The utterances highlighted the ways in which images from and associations to popular culture and the media were integral to the children's classroom learning processes and their generation of knowledge constructs. For this particular topic, the children drew extensively on prior knowledge they had gained from their television viewing. For example, in the post-unit interview, Jon described a documentary that he had watched before the unit:

> *Jon:* It [a documentary] was about the poor side and the rich side of New York, and that there was a street down the middle that divided them, 49th Street or something. Oh yeah, it was called "The Streets of New York" and it was all about crime and everything in New York.

The children did not focus only on television programs about New York City. Television advertisements and general programs also provided a common source of general prior knowledge that they linked to new curriculum content.

This background knowledge was also predominantly male-focused (for example, with references to male cartoon characters, male television stars, male police, male baseball teams, male basketball players, male gangs, male brand names). There was also a difference in the television viewing patterns of the female and male case-study children. For example, the boys reported watching more late-night American police shows than did the girls. Mia explained:

> *Mia:* Well, from the television I thought all of New York was like "Diff'rent Strokes." I thought it was all very posh and things. I had no idea about all the sort of slum areas and things.
>
> *Interviewer:* Have you ever seen anything on television about crime in New York?
>
> *Mia:* Crime in New York?
>
> *Mia:* Mmm . . . I don't think so . . . no . . . Dad doesn't like television much and especially he doesn't like American programs, so we don't watch them.

Children's Responses to Cultural Bias in Curriculum How did the children respond to the teacher unconsciously positioning them by using the pronoun "we" to mean White and male? During the following interview, the female researcher was startled when Mia showed her unconscious identification with White males in the curriculum by using the pronoun "us." This occurred when she was asked about the early settlement of New York City:

> *Mia:* I think it's the Indians. I think they were the first people to have it.
>
> *Interviewer:* Mm.
>
> *Mia:* 'Cause they just, see you don't um Indians came before sort of today sort of wearing, wearing all them facepaints and things and you sort of think of them being first there because they're before us. You can tell sort of. You think of Indians and you think of long hair and headbands and weapons . . . and . . .
>
> *Interviewer:* Yeah. And you say, you don't think of them — you think of them being there before us?
>
> *Mia:* Mm.
>
> *Interviewer:* And do you feel, when you say us, do you mean that the people who came to settle New York after the Indians were people like us?
>
> *Mia:* Mm. Mm. [nods]
>
> *Interviewer:* How were they like us?

Mia: Well, they didn't wear um, war paint and carry weapons around. They just sort of had, they wore clothes like us, sort of [laugh] civilized clothes.

Interviewer: When you say us do you think of women or men?

Mia: I think of men really 'cause like, sort of early Canterbury you have visions of people wearing sort of long suits and things. You know I don't really, yeah, that's right! I only think of the men. [giggle] I don't think of the women. [giggle]

Mia's identification with White colonists contrasted with the perspective taken by Ricky, the only Maori boy in the class. Ricky also remembered the men who colonized New York City, but spoke of them as culturally distant — "they" as opposed to "we" or "us":

Ricky: Oh well, first it was the Indians and then I think it was Englishmen, and ever since they have lived there, I think.

Interviewer: And you say Englishmen. Who are you thinking of? What sort of people?

Ricky: Well they were a bit greedy and more advanced than the Indians, so they just made towns and that started from there. They got rich and that.

The utterance data revealed that Ricky's exclusion from the White male "we" in the enacted curriculum also influenced Joe during the lesson:

Teacher: Because White people . . .

Joe (talking to Ricky): Honkies.

Ricky (talking to Joe): Shut up!

Teacher: Europeans, we were . . .

Joe (talking to Ricky): Nigger!

Teacher: Watch this way please, Ricky! — were often wanting to get things . . .

Joe (talking to Ricky): Black man! Samoan!

. . .

Teacher: East Indies.

Joe (talking to peer): Ricky, they're going to play cricket![14]

. . .

Joe (talking to Ricky): Shut up! Prove it! Get stuffed, Ricky!

. . .

[Joe kicks Ricky]

Joe (talking to Ricky): Ricky hurt his foot!

Teacher: . . . the English took over from the Dutch and . . .

Joe (talking to self): They built a ship.

. . .

Ricky (talking to Joe): Idiot! You get out!

Joe (talking to Ricky): You kicked me first you, nigger!

---

[14] Male sports teams in Aotearoa New Zealand have traditionally played cricket against West Indian teams. The topic of cricket plays a significant role in social communication throughout the country.

Ricky (talking to Joe): Did not you honky honk. I'm not a nigger you flippin' honky honk!

. . .

Joe (talking to Ricky): Shut up!
Teacher: Ricky, could you try and watch here please?

. . .

Joe (talking to Ricky): Ow! You kicked me!
Ricky (talking to Joe): I haven't! I haven't! Prove it! Prove it!
Joe (talking to Ricky): God, you're dumb! Now I'll prove that you're dumb!
Ricky (talking to Joe): Prove it! You don't know!

. . .

Joe (talking to Ricky): All right! I will! . . . What's fifty-nine divided by sixteen . . . ?

Joe immediately responded to the teacher's inadvertent exclusion of Ricky from "White people, Europeans, we" and compounded the teacher's positioning of Ricky as "other" by directing racist abuse — *"Nigger!"* — at him. His provocative challenge after he first kicked Ricky — *"Prove it!"* — suggests that he felt inviolable even from the rules of order in the classroom. Joe's confidence was well-placed. The teacher reprimanded Ricky repeatedly. The victimization experienced by Ricky culminated in a crisis when a group of White (*Pakeha*) boys, including Joe, went to the teacher after school to ask him to remove Ricky from the class because his "bad behavior" was "interfering" with their work. From the teacher's perspective, Ricky was always the child associated with trouble, since Joe was particularly skilled at hiding his racist provocation. Neither the teacher nor the observers ever heard instances of the racist abuse revealed later in the broadcast microphone transcripts, and in a later interview Ricky appeared to be surprised that the interviewer was aware of the racism.[15] When asked about the abuse he had experienced, Ricky attributed the cause of the racism to himself and revealed his solution to the problem:

Ricky: Well sometimes people be racist to me 'cause I annoy them. Sometimes they . . . That's how I know. . . . Sometimes I just get up and hit them and they stop.

Although physical abuse contravened the rules of order in the classroom, the message that superior violence prevails was conveyed by the colonial perspective on history in the curriculum content. For example, the history of New York City provided in the enacted curriculum was a military history in which the English were seen as triumphant and superior conquerors of the Dutch. Ricky referred

[15] Both the school principal and the teacher agreed to allow us to interview Ricky because of their concern about the abuse he had experienced. When Ricky initially expressed reservation about participating, he was assured by the principal that he could choose either not to participate, or to participate with the option to end the interview at any time. Ricky did choose to be interviewed, and when he was answering a question about how he learned the concept of racism, he referred to his own experience. At this point the White (*Pakeha*) interviewer acknowledged that she knew about the abuse because of the audio recordings. Ricky appeared to be deeply surprised that an adult believed him, but then began to talk openly about his feelings about the racist abuse. He prolonged the interview through a recess period (a request unprecedented in our studies), and asked that he be allowed to continue in the long-term interview.

not only to the New York City unit, but also to other social studies units as the source of his definition of "advanced" meaning possessing superior military strength:

> *Interviewer:* You say they [the English] are more advanced?
>
> *Ricky:* Oh well, the Indians just had bows and arrows I think, and they had guns.

We suggest that the cultural bias in the curriculum enactment created a climate wherein the White (*Pakeha*) boys used their culturally privileged position to speak out more, contravene the rules of order more frequently, and to derive more pleasure and entertainment from the lesson. When the teacher used the football term to initiate the lesson, Jon repeated the phrase and laughed. Mia watched Jon laughing.

The cultural climate triggered Joe's *private* racial abuse of Ricky, but allowed the boys to engage in *public* sexist behavior involving sexual innuendo and verbal harassment of the girls. One girl in the class, Sarah, had high status among the children because she was a class councilor.[16] This status appeared to enable her to respond publicly more frequently than any other girl in the class, thereby breaking the pattern of male dominance. During the brainstorming session, however, when she responded that New York made her think of breakdancing, Joe called out, labeling her "New Zealand Knickers!" (referring to underpants), making her the focus of a sexual innuendo and silencing her: she stopped participating after he made that remark. The introduction (by boys) of information involving sexual content or sexual innuendo was the major threat to orderliness during the lesson and gave rise to much joking among the boys while the girls watched. When one of the boys gave the response "flashers" (men who expose themselves) to one of the brainstorming questions, the ensuing disturbance brought the lesson to a halt. Although the teacher attempted to go on with the brainstorming session, his attempts failed and he introduced a disciplinary measure — asking the boys to stand and sit down again. The football analogy appeared apt, as the teacher managed the behavior of the boys while the girls were spectators.

The low status of women in the curriculum was also reflected throughout the unit in the private utterances of both case-study boys. For example, during the introductory lesson, Joe responded "prostitutes" to the teacher's question about the first people to settle in New York, and "prostitutes" was the first public mention of women on the second day of the unit.

The language as well as the content and perspectives of the enacted curriculum play a powerful role in structuring cultural norms in the classroom. Who is included, how they are portrayed, and how the children are positioned in relation to them convey to the children messages about who is valued in society. The consequences for the well-being of children who are not White and male are profound. Mia accommodated to the norm by identifying as a White male at the cost of her own cultural identity as a White (*Pakeha*) female. Ricky admired the White male cultural norm, but became victim to it while blaming himself

---

[16] Sarah received more votes than any other child in the class on a sociometric questionnaire we designed to identify the children's status amongst their peers.

for the victimization. We do not have data to explain the ways Maori girls experience the enacted curriculum. However, in a lived culture featuring a curriculum in which White and male is valued and privileged, Maori girls are confronting bias against both their race and their gender.

The process worked both ways: the lived culture in the classroom contributed to the focus on male experience and interests in the enacted curriculum, and the curriculum significantly influenced power relations in the lived culture. Though the teacher intended to increase the children's tolerance of cultural differences, the hidden curriculum of differential cultural valuing was more powerful in the lesson we selected than his official agenda.

THE EFFECT ON THE TEACHER

In our experience, teachers who are prepared to open up their classrooms to the intensive audio and video recording and observational processes that these studies entail do so because of their deep commitment to children and to improving their educational practice. The experience, however, can be deeply disturbing when the evidence that is uncovered shows the impact of destructive cultural processes on individual children. The teacher involved in the New York City unit said that the data had a "devastating" effect on him, and that it was

> heart-rending because I would have liked to have thought that I was tuned in to what was happening in the class. . . . I just didn't know. . . . Prior to doing this research . . . I would've said "Yes, you know, I'm fully aware of all these things whether it's the race issue or the gender issue, whatever." . . . It comes as a real blow to find that in actual fact you're not necessarily doing things that are in line with what you believe. . . . You're faced with this discrepancy.

This teacher worked with us to disseminate the early findings and to make the research integral to his and our continuing work in teacher education; he has since taken up issues of gender and race in his own in-service teacher education courses. The following quote describes his perception of the influence of the research on his practice:

> The important things in the long run are the outcomes. . . . The outcomes for me of taking part in this research are not what we originally [foresaw]. I believe that they're extremely positive because they've increased my level of awareness. They've altered my action. . . . It's altered the things that I think are important when I'm devising a curriculum. . . . It's altered the way I treat other people too.

He has also discussed the implications of involvement in the research with the teachers who have chosen to participate in two subsequent studies. They, in turn, have used the opportunity to evaluate their own curriculum reforms that address issues raised by earlier research.

TOWARDS A CONSTRUCTIVIST PERSPECTIVE ON CURRICULUM LEARNING

There are profound questions to be addressed about the value of curriculum knowledge. Traditional classroom research has bypassed the question of the

317

value, asking instead questions about quantity and efficiency. Sociologists have framed the curriculum content children learn as a commodity (Apple & Weiss, 1983) of which children get more or less — as if it is external, material, and given. But the constructivist view of learning we have taken here renders the concept of curriculum as commodity inappropriate. The findings from our analyses suggest that children do not *receive* various proportions of that commodity. Rather, they construct their own knowledge as they struggle to make sense of the enacted curriculum within the lived culture of the classroom. Unless they resist, they learn to construct a worldview that undermines their gender if they are female and their race if they are non-White. In the kind of contexts we have studied, the knowledge they construct is a Trojan horse for those children who are not White and male. Those children who fail do not receive the certification that allows them a better chance of paid employment in the mainstream of society. Those who achieve do so by coming to construct within their own minds a worldview that legitimates White male power and their own subordination.

While cultural bias in the classroom context is framed by the curriculum, it permeates the entire classroom culture. We cannot adequately explain how cultural bias influences children's experience and learning unless we include the critical role of social class in mediating classroom processes. The role of social-class membership has been extensively documented in input-output studies of educational achievement and in studies showing how parental education and out-of-school access to curriculum-relevant cultural resources and experiences advantage upper-middle-class children (Apple & Weiss, 1983; Bowles & Gintis, 1976; Densem, Wilton, & Keeling, 1988; Lauder & Hughes, 1990). Shirley Brice Heath's (1982) study of the match between children's experiences of language and books at home and at school revealed the importance not just of resources, but also of culturally specific (by race and social class) ways of linking written material to experience. Heath explains that "the *culture* children learn as they grow up is, in fact, ways of taking meaning from the environment around them" (p. 49).

Although the social-class differences between the case-study children in this study were small relative to the range of social-class differences in Aotearoa New Zealand, these class differences were reflected in the children's curriculum-appropriate prior knowledge, experience, and resource access (cultural capital), and in the ways in which they interacted with the curriculum content. When we take into account the complex ways in which class, race, and gender mediate classroom processes, we have the potential for a more coherent explanation for the contradictions and conflicts in children's experiences in classrooms.

Although Mia's race and class privileged her in the classroom, and she learned more as measured by the unit test than the other case-study students, her secondary status as a female within the classroom culture shaped her reticent way of participating and her identification with male experience. Joe was generally perceived as a low achiever by the teacher, and his long-term learning as measured by the unit test was lowest. In spite of his privileged position participating as a White male in the classroom culture, he did not have access to sufficient prior knowledge or ways of monitoring his own cognitive processes to succeed in the class discussions. He was able, however, to use his powerful position to abuse privately his Maori peer and to harass publicly his female peers with no official consequence. Ricky experienced private abuse and unjust public reprimands, but was engaged by Joe in a shared male culture, revealing the contradictions that arose from his being both male and Maori. Jon's participation in the lesson from a position of class, race, and gender privilege seems to have afforded him both freedom from the kind of anxiety evident in the girls' behavior and obvious pleasure as he sang and joked, impatiently correcting his peers. Ann's attempts to participate publicly were least successful and least rewarded, even though her private answers revealed that she successfully grappled with much of the new curriculum content despite having less prior knowledge than Jon. She participated instead by talking privately with her friend, Julia, taking refuge and offering support in a shared and hidden female world.

A child's class, race, and gender have a powerful and often contradictory effect on the way the child negotiates the sociocultural context of the classroom and shape the child's experience in the lived culture. These cultural dimensions also have a profound effect on the way the enacted curriculum is translated into the child's personal beliefs and knowledge. Our model of the way children acquire knowledge through a process of generating knowledge constructs is based on the premise that children are more or less constantly engaged in trying to make sense of the curriculum. But making sense of curriculum content in the classroom is itself a cultural process. It involves the child in making links to prior knowledge and personal experience, and in integrating and evaluating new experiences to conform to his or her developing understanding of what constitutes coherent and valued knowledge.

It is critical to understand not only the extent to which classroom learning is culturally constructed, but also the consequences for some children when they attempt to manage the problem this cultural construction may pose for them. For example: some children may reject the enacted curriculum as alien, as belonging to "them," and not "us," to be kept at a distance from personal understandings and beliefs. Some children may respond to the enacted curriculum as something to be memorized or circumvented to avoid public humiliation. Some children may actively engage in accommodating to the enacted curriculum by identifying with "them" and learning to be dismissive of their own experiences and perspectives. Some children may feel "at home" and able to pursue a model of "truth" that empowers them to evaluate and be critical of even the teacher's knowledge.

We have demonstrated that children's utterances in the private world raise fundamental questions about bias in research. To focus on the instructional dimension without attending to the lived culture of the classroom context makes invisible some of the most significant questions about both the learning and the well-being of children in classrooms. Our approach promises to allow the detailed records of children's experience to speak directly to teachers, to illuminate teaching practice, to lead to more adequate theoretical perspectives on classroom learning, and to inform theories about the role of schools in our society.

REFERENCES

Alton-Lee, A. G. (1984). *Understanding learning and teaching: An investigation of pupil experience of content in relation to immediate and long term learning.* Unpublished doctoral dissertation, University of Canterbury, Christchurch, New Zealand.

Alton-Lee, A. G., & Densem, P. A. (1992). Towards a gender-inclusive school curriculum: Changing educational practice. In S. Middleton & A. Jones (Eds.), *Women and education in Aotearoa* (Vol. 2, pp. 197–220). Wellington: Bridget Williams.

Alton-Lee, A. G., Densem, P. A., & Nuthall, G. A. (1991). Imperatives of classroom research: Understanding what children learn about gender and race. In J. Morss & T. Linzey (Eds.), *Growing up: Lifespan development and the politics of human learning* (pp. 93–117). Auckland: Longman Paul.

Alton-Lee, A. G., & Nuthall, G. A. (1990). Pupil experiences and pupil learning in the elementary classroom: An illustration of a generative methodology. *Teaching and Teacher Education: An International Journal of Research and Studies, 6*(1), 27–46.

Alton-Lee, A. G., & Nuthall, G. A. (1991). *Understanding Learning and Teaching Project: Phase Two* (Report to the Ministry of Education). Wellington: Ministry of Education.

Alton-Lee, A. G., & Nuthall, G. A. (1992a). Challenges in developing a methodology to explain "Opportunity to Learn." *Classroom Interaction Journal, 27*(2), 1–9.

Alton-Lee, A. G., & Nuthall, G. A. (1992b). A generative methodology for classroom research. In *Educational Philosophy and Theory,* special issue of *Educational Research Methodology, 24*(2), 29–55.

Apple, M., & Weiss L. (Eds.). (1983). Introduction. In M. Apple and L. Weiss, *Ideology and practice in schooling* (pp. 3–33). Philadelphia: Temple University Press.

Aschner, M. J. (1959). *The analysis of classroom discourse: A method and its uses.* Unpublished doctoral dissertation, University of Illinois, Urbana.

Bellack, A., Hyman, R., Smith, F., & Kliebard, H. (1966). *The language of the classroom.* New York: Columbia University Press.

Berwick-Emms, P. E. (1989). *Classroom interaction patterns and their underlying structure: A study of how achievement in the first year of school is influenced by home patterns of interaction.* Unpublished doctoral dissertation, University of Canterbury, Christchurch, New Zealand.

Blumenfeld P. C., & Meece, J. L. (1988). Task factors, teacher behavior, and students' involvement and use of learning strategies in science. *Elementary School Journal, 88*(3), 1–9.

Bourdieu, P. (1977). Cultural reproduction and social reproduction. In J. Karabel & A. Halsey (Eds.), *Power and ideology in education* (pp. 487–511). New York: Oxford University Press.

Bowles, S., & Gintis, H. (1976). *Schooling in capitalist America.* London: Routledge & Kegan Paul.

Cazden, C. B. (1986). Classroom discourse. In M. Wittrock (Ed.), *Handbook of research on teaching* (3rd ed., pp. 432–463). New York: Macmillan.

Clay, M. (1985). Engaging with the school system: A study of interactions in new entrant classrooms. *New Zealand Journal of Educational Studies, 20*(1), 20–38.

Densem, P., Wilton, K., & Keeling, B. (1988). Community, residential and family indicators of psychosocial retardation. *Mental Handicap in New Zealand, 11*(4), 4–26.

Doyle, W. (1983). Academic work. *Review of Educational Research, 53,* 159–199.

Doyle, W. (1986). Classroom organization and management. In M. Wittrock (Ed.), *Handbook of research on teaching* (3rd ed., pp. 392–431). New York: Macmillan.

Dyson, A. H. (1987). The value of "time off task": Young children's spontaneous talk and deliberate text. *Harvard Educational Review, 57,* 396–420.

Heath, S. B. (1982). What no bedtime story means: Narrative skills at home and school. *Language in Society, 11,* 49–76.

Howard, R. W. (1987). *Concepts and schemata.* London: Cassell.

Hughes, D. C. (1973). An experimental investigation of the effects of pupil responding and teacher reacting on pupil achievement. *American Educational Research Journal, 10,* 21–37.

Johnson-Laird, P. N. (1983). *Towards a complex science of language, inference and consciousness.* Cambridge, Eng.: Cambridge University Press.

Jones, A. (1985). Which girls are "learning to lose"? Gender, class, race in the classroom. *New Zealand Women's Studies Journal, 1*(2), 15–27.

Kelly, A. (1988). Gender-differences in teacher-pupil interactions: A meta-analytic review. *Research in Education, 39,* 1–23.

Kounin, J. S. (1970). *Discipline and group management in classrooms.* New York: Holt, Rinehart & Winston.

Lauder, H., & Hughes, D. (1990). Social inequalities and differences in school outcomes. *New Zealand Journal of Educational Studies, 25*(1), 37–60.

Newton, K. (1988). *Gender differences in classroom interaction.* Unpublished master's thesis, University of Auckland, New Zealand.

Nuthall, G. A., & Alton-Lee, A. G. (1990). Research on teaching and learning: Thirty years of change. *The Elementary School Journal, 90,* 547–570.

Nuthall G. A., & Alton-Lee, A. G. (1991, April). *Making the connection between teaching and learning.* Paper presented at the Annual Meeting of the American Educational Research Association, Chicago.

Nuthall, G. A., & Alton-Lee, A. G. (1992). Understanding how students learn in classrooms. In M. Pressley, K. Harris, & J. Guthrie (Eds.), *Promoting academic competence and literacy in school.* San Diego: Academic Press.

Nuthall, G. A., & Alton-Lee, A. G. (1993). *Understanding learning and teaching: A theory of student knowledge construction in classrooms.* Unpublished manuscript.

Nuthall, G. A., & Church, R. J. (1973). Experimental studies of teaching behavior. In G. Chanan (Ed.), *Towards a science of teaching* (pp. 9–25). Slough, Eng.: National Foundation for Educational Research.

Peterson, P. L., Swing, S. R., Stark, K. D., & Waas, G. A. (1984). Students' cognitions and time on task during mathematics instruction. *American Educational Research Journal, 21,* 487–515.

Sadker, M., Sadker, D., & Klein, S. (1991). The issue of gender in elementary and secondary education. *Review of Research in Education, 17,* 269–334.

Spender, D. (1982). *Invisible women: The schooling scandal.* London: Readers & Writers.

We acknowledge the Social Science Research Fund Committee, the University of Canterbury, the Ministry of Education, and the New Zealand Employment Service for providing funding for this project. We are deeply grateful to Roger Corbett for creating the broadcast microphone transmitters and to Greta Bowron, Anthea Warren, and Kerry Hancock for their meticulous work in assisting with the transcription and coding of data.

Promoting the Success of
Latino Language-Minority Students:
An Exploratory Study of Six High Schools

TAMARA LUCAS
ROSEMARY HENZE
RUBEN DONATO

In this chapter, Tamara Lucas, Rosemary Henze, and Rubén Donato explore cultural differences in relation to school success. They report that, for the growing numbers of Latino students in U.S. secondary schools, academic success has been elusive. Poor attendance records, low test scores, high drop-out rates, and small numbers going on to college all bear witness to schools' failure to meet their needs. But some secondary schools are providing an environment in which language-minority students and others can achieve academic success. This chapter reports on an exploratory study of six such schools in California and Arizona, and describe the key features they found to be integral to these schools' success.

By focusing on broad issues of schooling in secondary schools with large populations of language-minority students, the authors extend existing research on effective schooling, which until now has focused primarily on urban elementary schools in low-income neighborhoods. They also offer suggestions and a sense of possibility to educators seeking an effective response to the secondary education of language-minority students.

In "Effective Schools for the Urban Poor," Ron Edmonds states: "All children are eminently educable, and the behavior of the school is critical in determining the quality of the education." (1979, p. 20). This way of thinking diverges from often-cited "deficit" models of education, which account for student failure by reference to certain cultural, linguistic, and socioeconomic factors in students' backgrounds, thus making a liability out of difference. Language-minority (LM) students in particular have often been blamed for their underachievement in U.S. schools.[1] By considering them "difficult" or culturally and linguistically "deprived," schools have found it easy to absolve themselves of responsibility for the education of these students. Edmonds, on the other hand, places the responsibility for quality education squarely in the hands of the schools.

This assignment of responsibility for language-minority students has had a complex legal history. In 1973 the Supreme Court held, in the *Lau v. Nichols* decision, that public schools had to provide an education comprehensible to

---

[1] We will use the phrase "language-minority (LM) students" to refer to those who come from families where a language other than English is spoken. Such students may or may not speak English fluently.

Harvard Educational Review Vol. 60 No. 3 August 1990, 315–340

limited English proficient (LEP) students.[2] In an attempt to equalize educational opportunities for LEP students in U.S. schools, the Court stated: "Basic English is at the very core of what public schools teach. Imposition of a requirement that, before a child can effectively participate in the education program, he must already have acquired those basic skills is to make a mockery of public education" (*Lau v. Nichols*, 1973).

The *Lau* decision has had a powerful impact on the education of language-minority students. It marked the beginning of a national interest in educational equity for LM students and provoked policymakers throughout the country to respond to the special needs of this growing student population. After 1974, under pressure from the federal government, many states began to push school districts to develop programs for LM students. California, for example, passed a bill in 1976 mandating bilingual education in its public schools.[3] School districts in California with large numbers of LEP students were required by the state to demonstrate how they were going to serve those students. For the most part, however, school districts focused on LEP students in elementary schools and ignored the schooling of secondary LEP students.

However, secondary schools do enroll many students whose English proficiency is limited. For example, poor economic conditions in Mexico have caused large numbers of Mexican students to arrive in the Southwest, with or without their families. Political unrest and war have brought thousands of refugees to the United States from such countries as El Salvador, Nicaragua, Guatemala, Vietnam, Cambodia, Laos, and Afghanistan. Students of all ages often arrive with little or no knowledge of English. Because of wartime conditions in their countries, many students have had interrupted schooling and thus come unprepared not only in English, but also in content knowledge, basic study skills, and knowledge of school culture. Providing effective schooling for these students is particularly challenging at the secondary level, when students are expected to possess a wealth of implicit and explicit knowledge about how to be a student.

On the other hand, many immigrant students arrive in the United States with strong educational backgrounds; for example, those who have attended *"Secundaria"* in Mexico may have had higher levels of math than their U.S.-born peers. Secondary LM students, in other words, are extremely diverse, bringing with them educational, social, academic, and cultural experiences that may differ widely from those of members of the host culture. To assure academic success, schools must attend to this diversity through special programs and practices, and through increased sensitivity to students' needs. High drop-out rates, low standardized test scores, poor attendance records, and the small numbers of students going on to post-secondary education all attest to the failure of most high schools to meet the needs of this student population (See Arias, 1986; Brown & Haycock, 1984; Espinosa & Ochoa, 1986; Gingras & Careaga, 1989; Medina, 1988; Orfield, 1986; Orum, 1988; Rumberger, 1987; U.S. General Accounting Office, 1987).

---

[2] We will use the phrase "limited-English-proficient (LEP) students" to refer specifically to those language-minority students who are not yet fluent in English.

[3] California State Department of Education, Assembly Bill 1329, 1976. In 1982, AB-1329 was revised as AB-507.

Because we believe that schools are responsible for the quality of education students receive, and that given a good education, all students can achieve, we are interested in what makes some schools more successful than others. During the past fifteen years, some educational researchers have turned away from attempting to explain school and student failure and have focused instead on explaining success, producing a body of research known as the "effective schools" literature. This work, most of which comes from studies conducted in urban elementary schools, provides some insight into the attributes of successful schools, including strong leadership; high expectations of students; school-wide staff development; parent involvement and support; recognition of students' academic success; district support; collaborative planning; collegial relationships; and sense of community (Edmonds, 1979; Purkey & Smith, 1983).

The research on effective schools is not without its detractors, however. Critics have pointed to shortcomings in the literature, citing, for example, lack of generalizability to any but elementary schools; lack of attention to the variety of student populations and community contexts; an over-emphasis on attributes and lack of sufficient attention to complex processes and interrelationships; and a top-down strategy for school improvement growing out of the "implementation of attributes" approach (See Carter & Chatfield, 1986; Rosenholtz, 1985; Rowen, Bossert, & Dwyer, 1983; Stedman, 1987; Wilson & Corcoran, 1988).

One of the most frequent criticisms is that the effective schools literature has given little attention to what makes some schools more successful than others with language-minority students. Jennifer Bell (1989) has offered several reasons for this lack of attention. First, since most of the effective schools studies were conducted in schools that were predominantly Black and White in composition, LM students were not a major factor in overall student achievement. Second, with certain exceptions, most researchers did not consider language to be an important factor in student achievement. Third, the diversity of LM students was generally considered too difficult to account for in research design. Furthermore, since the public has been so sharply divided over bilingual instruction, research on LM students in the schools has focused primarily on the role of language in instruction rather than on the effectiveness of the whole school.

Recently, however, some studies have focused on effective schooling for language-minority students. Thomas Carter and Michael Chatfield (1986) reported on characteristics of three effective bilingual elementary schools, emphasizing processes over structures and attributes. The schools they described were characterized by such factors as: a well-functioning total system producing a school climate that promotes positive student outcomes; positive leadership, usually from the formal leaders; high staff expectations for students and instructional programs; strong demand for academic performance; denial of the cultural deprivation argument and stereotypes that support it; and high staff morale.

Bruce Wilson and Thomas Corcoran (1988) report on a number of middle and secondary schools that are successful with "at risk" students, which they define as students from poor and minority backgrounds (p. 130). Since some of the schools had sizable numbers of Latino and Asian students, we can assume that some of them were language-minority students, although the authors do not discuss the language backgrounds or English proficiency of students. The common elements of these successful schools include a positive attitude toward the students, a willingness to question conventional practices, a strong and competent leadership, a highly committed teaching staff, high expectations and standards, and an emphasis on high achievement in academics.

A number of studies have examined effective instructional practices for language-minority students in elementary bilingual programs (Ramírez, 1988; Tikunoff, 1985; Wong-Fillmore, McLaughlin, Ammon, & Ammon, 1985). However, there is little research of any kind at the secondary level, and little at either the elementary or secondary level that looks beyond effective classroom instruction to the broader issues involved in effective schooling for LM students. In a critique of the ways in which the "effective schools formula" has been applied, Stedman (1987) argues for a reconceptualization of the effective schools literature, focusing on "detailed descriptions of school organization and practice" (p. 217) and on providing "concrete guidance about what to do to make a school effective" (p. 218). Ways in which good schools foster cultural pluralism need to be documented, Stedman writes, and secondary schools need to be given more attention.

The exploratory study reported here intends to narrow these gaps in the existing research and to extend our knowledge about effective schooling. The study is based on information gathered at six secondary schools that have been recognized by local, state, or federal agencies for their success in providing a quality education for LM students, not only through effective classroom instruction but also through whole-school approaches. Because previous research, such as that described above, has primarily focused on successful instructional practices for LM students, our discussion will focus its attention on the whole school rather than on classroom practices per se.

It is important to point out that there is of course no formula or prescription for success; no single combination of variables will produce an effective school. Educators cannot simply adopt the features of these six schools and expect their institutions to become successful with LM students overnight. Schools can, however, begin to work toward such success by following the lead of these schools in ways that are appropriate and realistic for their particular school settings.

We believe that the most critical element in determining whether educators can work toward success for all students is the belief that all students can succeed. In 1979, Edmonds argued that the degree to which we effectively teach "the children of the poor" depends more on our political persuasions than on the information we gain from educational research. He asserted that we already know more than enough to successfully teach all students, and that the question is whether we *want* to teach all students. Recently, Shirley Jackson (1989) made a similar assertion. Yet many educators still appear uncertain as to whether schools can significantly influence the achievement and attainment of poor and minority youths, often claiming that parents do not support their children's educational efforts and implying that therefore schools cannot be blamed for failing to educate these children (Suro, 1990). In contrast, we hope that by presenting case studies of "living examples of success" (Carter & Chatfield, 1986, p. 229), we will not only encourage educators to believe that *all* students can succeed, but also provide them with concrete knowledge of what schools can do to help them.

BACKGROUND

In 1988, an initiative was undertaken by the Southwest Center for Educational Equity, at the request of and in collaboration with the Arizona Department of Education and representatives of six Arizona school districts, to develop strategies for Arizona high schools to serve language-minority students.[4] In surveying the literature on effective schooling, we realized that little was known about successful schooling for LM students at the secondary level. To gather information for the Arizona High School Initiative, we therefore conducted an exploratory study of schools promoting the achievement of this student population. We visited five high schools in California and one in Arizona that had large populations of Latino students and that had been recognized by local, state, and/or federal agencies for excellence.[5] Because the needs of different groups of LM students vary, and because we wanted to increase comparability of student populations across schools, we decided that schools working successfully with Latino LM students in particular would be the focus of this part of the initiative.[6]

METHODS

Selection of Case Study Schools

The selection of case study schools was complicated by the lack of consensus about what constitutes an "effective" or "successful" school. After much deliberation over which criteria were the most relevant, we decided to take a two-pronged approach to site selection, using both qualitative and quantitative criteria. First, we sought nominations from a variety of people familiar with secondary schools with large numbers of language-minority students, consulting with educators at state, county, and district levels and asking them to recommend schools that they believed were successful with those students (Wilson & Corcoran, 1988). We then contacted the principals of the recommended schools to determine whether they had received any formal recognition from local, state, or federal agencies for their instructional programs for LM students and whether they could provide us with some quantitative evidence of their success — for example, average daily attendance rates, drop-out rates, numbers of Latino LM students going on to post-secondary education, and standardized test scores that compared favorably with other minority schools. While we recognize that "effectiveness is a construct, an abstraction" (Wilson & Corcoran, 1988, p. 26) and that this process did not capture the full range of possible indicators of success, we believe it enables us to select six schools which are taking identifiable, positive steps to educate LM students.

[4] The Southwest Center for Educational Equity is funded by Title IV of the U.S. Department of Education to assist school districts in California, Arizona, and Nevada in their desegregation efforts in the areas of race, gender, and national origin.

[5] Awards and recognition included a California Department of Education Distinguished School Award, a city Commendation Award, nomination as an exemplary school for the National Secondary School Recognition Program, an award for the academic achievement of the school's graduates attending a university in the state, a U.S. Department of Education Excellence in Education Award, and selection as one of the "77 Schools of the Future" by *Omni* magazine.

[6] The term *Latino* is used here because it is the term that the majority of people we interviewed used to describe their own ethnicity, when speaking on a broader level than their individual countries of origin.

DATA COLLECTION

Data were collected at five school sites in California and one in Arizona.[7] Two to four project staff members visited each site for three days, thus providing multiple perspectives and allowing for intensive collection of information. The combined data from all six schools consisted of audiotapes and notes from structured interviews with one superintendent, two district-level bilingual program directors, six principals, six assistant principals, five school-level project and program directors, fifteen counselors, fifty-two teachers and aides, and 135 students; 124 student questionnaires (thirty-five from newcomers and eighty-nine from non-newcomers); fifty-four classroom observations; school-wide observations of the six schools; and various records and documents for each school, including policies regarding LM students, special program descriptions, transcripts for students who were interviewed, and other written information that interviewees gave us. Because we wanted above all to facilitate communication, we allowed students to use either English or Spanish for interviews and questionnaires, depending upon their preference. Students whose proficiency in English was very limited would not have been able to participate had they not been given the opportunity to use Spanish. Because the study sought to understand what contributes to the success of high school LM students, we were primarily interested in obtaining information from school staff who worked extensively and effectively with these students. Assistant principals, counselors, and teachers were selected to be interviewed if they 1) worked with large numbers of Latino LEP students, and 2) were recommended by others (administrators, counselors, teachers, students) as being especially effective with, and/or knowledgeable about, these students.

At each school, we asked a counselor, or in some cases a program director, to select students for us to interview. We requested six Latino students in each of four groups — high achievers, average achievers, students who had been doing poorly but had now improved, and students who had immigrated within the last two years. We also asked that students be non-native speakers of English. Though we succeeded in interviewing an average of twenty-four Latino LM students at each school, the distinctions among high achievers, average achievers, and "turnarounds" were not at all clear. For purposes of analysis, therefore, we grouped students only as newcomers or non-newcomers. Both groups included students from grades nine through twelve.

Sixty-one percent of the students interviewed were born in Mexico. The newcomers had arrived in the United States between the ages of fourteen and eighteen, while the non-newcomers were students born in the United States and students who had entered the United States in the early and middle grades. According to the student questionnaire, 72.5 percent of the students spoke Spanish at home, while 39 percent used Spanish at school. Ninety-eight percent of the students' fathers worked in labor- or service-related jobs, while 90 percent of the mothers worked as housewives or in service-related jobs.

---

[7] Anaheim High School, Anaheim, CA; Artesia High School, Lakewood, CA; Newcomer High School, San Francisco, CA; Overfelt High School, San Jose, CA; Sweetwater High School, National City, CA; Nogales High School, Nogales, AZ.

In the aggregate, then, the Latino students we interviewed came from working-class backgrounds. However, they represented a tremendous range of educational and cultural experiences, from those whose entire education had been in the United States to those who had attended school in several different countries before coming here. Some students, according to the questionnaire, had had interruptions of several years in their schooling due to political unrest in their countries, while others had attended continuously. Factors such as these, combined with the different cultural identities of Mexicanos, Chicanos, Nicaragüenses, and other groups, made it clear that there is no such thing as a "typical" Latino student, and that a school successful with this population would have to be sensitive to differences in students' experiences and backgrounds.

Data Analysis

Data Analysis was a recursive process which began with the design of the study. The design, influenced by previous research on effective schooling, determined who would be interviewed and what other types of data would be collected. The questions used in interviews were formulated as new issues emerged from the data. Categories for analysis, inspired at first by the effective schools literature, were continually shaped as we interviewed, observed, and gathered documents at each site. Once information-gathering had ended, intensive analysis proceeded from within-site analyses to cross-site analyses:

1. Each person who visited a site wrote a report of the data that she or he collected from interviews, observations, and serendipitous encounters. These reports brought together all of the data collected by each researcher into one organized and accessible whole. Reports included information about the school context (community, school board, student body composition and ethnicity, language census), types of Latino LM students enrolled at the school, what seemed to be working based on what was reported and what we saw, and what improvements were suggested to better meet the needs of the students.

2. All individual reports about each school were then synthesized into one case study report per school to provide "a well-grounded sense of the local reality" in that setting (Miles & Huberman, 1984, p. 151).

3. The six case studies were then analyzed in order to compare perceived realities across these schools.

In this process, we developed both concrete descriptions of what we observed and categories or themes derived from the data and informed by other studies of effective schooling (see Merriam, 1988). This process resulted in highlighting eight features that existed across sites, as noted in the introduction. Although each school is unique, the eight features represent commonalities in the ways the schools were promoting success for language-minority students. Most of the study findings are derived from interviews with staff members and students — particularly when the same or similar features were mentioned by a large number of people in different schools — and from our informed observations. In many cases, the language of the findings reflects words or phrases we heard repeatedly.

What we were told in interviews was also confirmed and concretized through classroom and school-wide observation and consultation of school records and documents.

FINDINGS

School Profiles

Five of the six schools were relatively large, with 1,700 to 2,200 students. All had minority White populations, and in all but the smallest school, Latino students constituted the largest single group — more than one-third of the school population. The four schools with the larger proportions of non-White students (Nogales, Overfelt, Sweetwater, and Newcomer) also had larger proportions of non-White staff. In none of the schools, however, was the ethnicity of the staff comparable to the student population; in all of them, a much larger proportion of staff than students was White. The percentage of students participating in a school lunch program — a rough measure of their socioeconomic status — varied considerably among the six schools. At Anaheim and Artesia, fewer than 25 percent of the students received such aid, at Overfelt and Sweetwater, about 33 percent did so, and at Nogales and Newcomer 80 percent did so. Thus, socioeconomic status of students is not a feature shared by these schools overall, although as noted earlier, the Latino students whom we interviewed were largely working class.

Key Features that Promote the Success of Language-Minority Students

Through the exploratory case studies and the analysis across cases, eight features emerged which we believe to be the most important in promoting the success of language-minority students at the six schools we visited. A more concise version of these eight features appears in Table 1, pp. 324–325.

1. Value is placed on the students' languages and cultures.
Rather than ignoring barriers to equality and perpetuating the disenfranchisement of minority students, the principals, administrators, counselors, teachers, and other support staff at the schools we visited celebrated diversity. They gave language minority students the message that their languages and cultures were valued and respected, thus promoting the self-esteem necessary for student achievement. They communicated this sense of value and respect in a number of concrete ways, translating the ideal into an everyday reality.

First, the ability to speak a language in addition to English was treated as an advantage rather than a liability. A number of White and Latino teachers and counselors who were not native speakers of Spanish had learned the language. Some spoke it well enough to understand some of what their students said; others had learned it well enough to teach bilingual content classes. Students commented in interviews that they appreciated efforts made by teachers to speak Spanish and were pleased to see that the teachers valued their language. One student noted that "when teachers are bilingual, it makes our learning easier. They treat us equally." Another described the school as *"una amiga bilingüe"* (a bilingual friend).

Although these high schools made English literacy a primary goal, they also encouraged students to enhance their native language skills in classes for those students who spoke Spanish. Four of the six high schools we visited offered Spanish courses for Spanish speakers. Of these, three of them offered both literacy skills instruction and advanced courses in Spanish. Advanced Placement (AP) Spanish classes at these schools gave native-Spanish-speaking students the opportunity to capitalize on their native language to obtain college credit. The principal at Nogales High School, where 89 percent of the students were Latino, had gone even further in demonstrating the value placed on Spanish. All students at this school were required to take five years of language instruction — four in English and one in Spanish. Students who passed a proficiency test in Spanish were free to take another language to fulfill the fifth year requirement; others had to take Spanish for Spanish speakers or Spanish as a second language, whichever was appropriate.

A less formal but no less effective way that educators showed respect for the students' language was to allow them to speak their native language when English language development was not the focus of instruction. Their philosophy was that nothing was gained from stifling a young person's desire to communicate in his or her primary language. Throughout the campuses of the high schools we visited, students were free to speak Spanish with each other and with school staff. The use of their native language was not restricted to informal settings. Five of the schools provided content courses in Spanish, thus giving students the opportunity to progress through the content areas while developing their English skills. They were not required to postpone taking advanced content courses until they were fluent in English.

Besides showing respect for students' native language, staff in these schools also celebrated the students' cultures. Perhaps the most transparent and readily accessible aspects of culture are customs, holidays, and overtly stated values. While many schools give lip service to these aspects of culture, for example, by celebrating *Cinco de Mayo* and serving tacos on that day, the schools we visited affirmed the customs, values, and holidays of the language-minority students' countries in deeper and more consistent ways throughout the year.

Teachers, for example, made it their business to know about their students' past experiences. Some had visited Mexican schools to better understand their students' previous educational experiences. A group of teachers from one school had observed mathematics teaching in a Mexican school. One of them said that understanding how Mexican students were taught math in Mexico made teaching them easier. He could say to students, "This is the way most of you were taught how to divide in Mexico. And that's OK. This is another way of doing it." Without denigrating what they had learned in Mexico, he would ask which way was easiest for them.

In addition, while faculty and staff were sensitive to the importance of students' language and cultures, they did not treat students simply as members of an undifferentiated ethnic group. They recognized students' individual strengths, interests, problems, and concerns rather than characterizing them by reference to stereotypes. The assistant principal at one school said, "Basically, Hispanic kids are no different from other kids; they want to learn. Those who

TABLE I

Features of High Schools that Promote the Achievement of Language-Minority Students

1. *Value is placed on the students' languages and cultures by:*
   Treating students as individuals, not as members of a group
   Learning about students' cultures
   Learning students' languages
   Hiring bilingual staff with similar cultural backgrounds to the students
   Encouraging students to develop their primary language skills
   Allowing students to speak their primary languages except when English development is the focus of instruction or interactions
   Offering advanced as well as lower division content courses in the students' primary languages
   Instituting extracurricular activities that will attract LM students

2. *High expectations of language-minority students are made concrete by:*
   Hiring minority staff in leadership positions to act as role models
   Providing a special program to prepare LM students for college
   Offering advanced and honors bilingual/sheltered classes in content areas
   Making it possible for students to exit ESL programs quickly
   Challenging students in class and providing guidance to help them meet the challenge
   Providing counseling assistance (in the primary language if necessary) to help students apply to college and fill out scholarship and grant forms
   Bringing in representatives of colleges and minority graduates who are in college to talk to students
   Working with parents to gain their support for students going to college
   Recognizing students for doing well

3. *School leaders make the education of language-minority students a priority. These leaders:*
   Hold high expectations of LM students
   Are knowledgeable of instructional and curricular approaches to teaching LM students and communicate this knowledge to staff
   Take a strong leadership role in strengthening curriculum and instruction for all students, including LM students
   Are often bilingual minority-group members themselves
   Hire teachers who are bilingual and/or trained in methods for teaching LM students

4. *Staff development is explicitly designed to help teachers and other staff serve language-minority students more effectively. Schools and school districts:*
   Offer incentives and compensation so that school staff will take advantage of available staff development programs
   Provide staff development for teachers and other school staff in:
   – effective instructional approaches to teaching LM students, e.g., cooperative learning methods, sheltered English, and reading and writing in the content areas
   – principles of second-language acquisition
   – the cultural backgrounds and experiences of the students
   – the languages of the students
   – cross-cultural communication
   – cross-cultural counseling

TABLE I *continued*

5. *A variety of courses and programs for language-minority students is offered. The programs:*
   Include courses in ESL and primary language instruction (both literacy and advanced placement) and bilingual and sheltered courses in content areas
   Insure that the course offerings for LM students do not limit their choices or trap them in low-level classes by offering advanced as well as basic courses taught through bilingual and sheltered methods
   Keep class size small (20–25 students) in order to maximize interaction
   Establish academic support programs that help LM students make the transition from ESL and bilingual classes to mainstream classes and prepare them to go to college

6. *A counseling program gives special attention to language-minority students through counselors who:*
   Speak the students' languages and are of the same or similar cultural backgrounds
   Are informed about post-secondary educational opportunities for LM students
   Believe in, emphasize, and monitor the academic success of LM students

7. *Parents of language-minority students are encouraged to become involved in their children's education. Schools can provide and encourage:*
   Staff who can speak the parents' languages
   On-campus ESL classes for parents
   Monthly parents' nights
   Parent involvement with counselors in planning their children's course schedules
   Neighborhood meetings with school staff
   Early morning meetings with parents
   Telephone contacts to check on absent students

8. *School staff members share a strong commitment to empower language-minority students through education. This commitment is made concrete through staff who:*
   Give extra time to work with LM students
   Take part in a political process that challenges the status quo
   Request training of various sorts to help LM students become more effective
   Reach out to students in ways that go beyond their job requirements, for example, by sponsoring extra-curricular activities
   Participate in community activities in which they act as advocates for Latinos and other minorities

fall by the wayside are those whose needs aren't being met. Who wants to fail everyday?"

Faculty and staff also knew that there is no such thing as a generic Latino LM student. Rather, people from Mexico, Nicaragua, El Salvador, Guatemala, Cuba, and other Spanish-speaking countries were known to have different histories and customs and to speak different varieties of Spanish. Mexican immigrants, Mexican Americans, and Chicanos were also recognized as different from one another, and variation among Mexican immigrants based upon socioeconomic background and educational attainment level was acknowledged. When asked

333

to describe the Latino students at the school, one teacher responded with five categories: those who are "well off, well educated, not disenfranchised; the migrant kids who have little education; children born here of parents who have immigrated here; limited-English-proficient students who have been here ten to twelve years but have lived in insular communities and had no education in Spanish; and then Central Americans."

Respect for students' languages and cultures was communicated through support programs as well as academic programs. In some schools, special programs provided tutorial and counseling assistance. Teachers and Latino students were paired in mentoring and advocacy activities, thus increasing the sense among faculty of a personal connection with the students. Extracurricular programs involved activities that were relevant to Latino cultures. In one school, students could take a PE class called *Bailes,* in which they learned and performed dances from different regions of Mexico. In another, a student-run group published a monthly newspaper in Spanish called *El Mitotero.* Begun by a teacher, the paper was quickly "taken over" by the students themselves. They formed a committee and organized a formal club with officers and by-laws, which was then recognized by the school's student association. According to the teacher who started it, the paper is "very culturally oriented — if you understand Spanish, you might understand the words, but if you are not familiar with the local Mexican culture, you will probably miss a lot of the 'double meanings' and cultural references." One issue of the newspaper was devoted to a debate about bilingual education. The newspaper staff interviewed students and teachers and then presented both pro and con sides of the debate, the former written in Spanish and the latter in English.

A final and important way in which these high schools showed respect for the students' cultures and languages was through their staffing. Faculty members who spoke the native languages of the language-minority students in the school and shared similar cultural backgrounds not only used this skill and knowledge to improve instruction for them, but also served as role models and advocates for these students. Comments of several faculty reflect their awareness of the roles they were playing. For example, the principal at Nogales High School said:

> When we hire teachers, we try to look for the best teachers, number one, but number two and most importantly, we try to get teachers that relate to our type of kids, and number three, if we can get teachers that are from this area, that are teachers that have graduated from this high school, teachers that have had to go through these problems, the growing-up problems, the educational problems from here, and have gone out and have become successful, then we have provided role models for our kids that are essential. I think probably that's one of the reasons I'm principal. We've had all kinds of principals, but I think that the community itself has tried to hire administrators that, number one, relate to our community, and number two, have been here [for a long time]. The majority of the administration from this district is from here.

A teacher at another school said, "The students are very proud and the teachers support that. It's okay to speak Spanish, to be Mexican, not to know English." He believes that students at the school feel supported by the fact that teachers speak Spanish "in public." One student had come to him and reported with some incredulity. "Mr. W. [an Anglo] spoke Spanish to me in class!" The head counselor at the same school said:

> Parents and students see us [Latinos] in leadership positions, not just in the cafeteria or as janitors. People in the school understand problems in the community and have lived it themselves. . . . For example, I understand if a student has to stay home all week to take care of kids. . . . Parents come in because I speak Spanish and can understand their problems. I'm not from a middle-class, elite, intellectual background.

A counselor at a third school said, "I have a sensitivity to these students that comes from my family background. I'm third generation here. I know what it is to leave your roots and live in a system different from that of your parents. Maybe that's why I have an urgency to push college." Students also referred to their teachers and others at the schools as role models. When asked to tell us about a faculty member who was particularly effective, one student commented, "Ms. V. has been a good role model. She speaks many languages and inspires me." Another student said, "Mr. A. encourages students to break stereotypes by being good in chemistry, physical science, and physics."

2. High expectations of language-minority students are made concrete.
Throughout the schools we visited, people recognized the importance of high expectations for Latino LM students. Such expectations form the foundation for the program features we describe. One principal put it this way: "I firmly believe that what you give to the best kids, you give to all," while taking into account special needs and equity issues. The professional staff members in the six schools we visited not only held high expectations of their students but had also taken concrete actions to demonstrate those expectations and to help students accomplish what was expected. Some of these actions already have been mentioned. For example, when students see people like themselves who have become teachers, counselors, and principals, they learn that professions like these are attainable.

Recognizing that language-minority students do not have information that mainstream students possess, school counselors who understood students' languages and cultures helped them plan their high school programs, find information about different colleges, apply to college, fill out financial aid forms, and apply for scholarships. Counselors also communicated with parents to gain their support for their children to apply for college, understanding that if going to college is a new idea to the student, it is probably completely unfamiliar, perhaps even threatening, to the parents. As one female student noted, "At first my parents weren't wanting me to go to college, but Mrs. C. [the counselor] convinced them that it was okay." College and university representatives were brought to the high school to talk with students. Former graduates of similar backgrounds who had gone to college were invited back to the high school to share their experiences and to encourage others to follow in their path.

In classes, teachers challenged students with difficult questions and problems. Complex ideas and materials were made more accessible to LM students through visuals, board work, group work, reading aloud, and clear and explicit class expectations. Teachers did not talk down to limited-English-proficient students in "foreigner talk," but spoke clearly, with normal intonation, explaining difficult words and concepts as needed.

In all the schools we visited, student success was recognized publicly. In one high school, achievement in a particular class was recognized through a ritual in which the principal came to the class and congratulated the student. In another school, LM students who did well in particular areas (for example, most improved or perfect attendance) were recognized at a monthly "Student of the Month" luncheon during which teachers who had nominated the students presented certificates to them and spoke briefly about the students' accomplishments. Several high schools had special assemblies for students on the honor roll, where parents were invited and recognized while the students received certificates. "It makes you want to try harder when you get an award," noted one student. Latino LM students received these forms of recognition just as other students did.

3. School leaders make the education of language-minority students a priority.
Strong instructional leadership has been cited as a key ingredient of effective schools (Carter & Chatfield, 1986; Purkey & Smith, 1983). Effective school leaders, usually principals, are described as actively coordinating curriculum; monitoring students' academic progress; having a clear mission for the school which they communicate to staff, students, and parents; holding high expectations for student achievement and promoting the same among faculty and staff. In the high schools we visited, the principals were, in addition, sincerely committed to educating LM students and knowledgeable about effective teaching approaches for this population. All but one of the principals were bilingual minority-group members themselves. Although each had a unique leadership style, they all demonstrated a strong commitment to raising the achievement levels of minority students, including LM students. Sweetwater's principal, a Latino himself, said:

> One of our major roles in this community is to develop a sense of confidence that we can compete in all areas, not just athletics, that we can go out there and be just as good as anybody else. I guess if I had a wish, I would like for the kids in the school to absolutely believe and know in their hearts that they are as good as anybody on this planet.

Steps taken by this principal to support the success of language-minority students illustrate the types of leadership that we found in these schools. Sweetwater's principal was given the authority by the district to make virtually all decisions at the school, including hiring teachers of his choice. He had initiated several changes in the education program for language-minority students. For example, all remedial classes were eliminated so that LM students would not receive "watered-down versions of content." When he came to the school, he discovered that bilingual classes were "remedial," that the school offered bilingual life science rather than biology and bilingual math rather than algebra. He quickly set out to "amend" the situation. Sections of physics, chemistry, and calculus were added along with summer sessions of geometry; the requirements for athletic participation were raised; the number of bilingual staff was increased from eight to thirty-three; the bilingual program was expanded to include advanced courses such as economics, biology II, and honors chemistry as well as lower division bilingual courses.

336

Although now credited with raising standardized test scores, tightening discipline, and raising the morale of students and teachers, the principal (and staff who supported his changes) encountered opposition from some staff members from the very beginning. When he eliminated the "remedial" classes in the school, for example, some teachers felt he was unrealistic; they argued that students were going to be lost in algebra. The principal recalled telling them that "students perform as well as they're expected . . . [and that] students in remedial classes in junior high school are still in remedial classes in the twelfth grade, often performing worse as time [goes] on." He believes students "will learn more in a classroom filled with students of mixed abilities than in a class composed solely of students with minimal math skills." He provided calculators for students, justifying their placement in basic algebra when others would think them more suited for remedial math: "If they're going to fail remedial math, why not have them fail basic algebra?"

We found that good leadership can and does come from program directors, department chairpersons, and teachers in high schools as well as from principals. In some schools, these individuals had taken on strong leadership roles vis-à-vis the education of LM students. At Artesia High School, for example, a separate ESL department had been formed, and it was the chair of this department who advocated most strongly for the education of LEP students. The principal at this school played a less active role in this area, though the previous principal, it should be noted, had been very active in making changes for the LM population. This example of a leader who is not a principal serves as a reminder that the strength for change does not necessarily have to come from the top. Though a strong principal who is deeply committed to the needs of LM students is certainly desirable, the principal is not the only person who can make a difference. Teachers, program coordinators, and department chairs can also take it upon themselves to be leaders in the education of LM students.

4. Staff development is explicitly designed to help teachers and other staff serve language-minority students more effectively.

As Lisa Delpit writes, "It is impossible to create a model for the good teacher without taking issues of culture and community context into account" (1988, p. 291). Teachers who are expert in the instruction of mainstream students are not necessarily effective instructors of language-minority students. For this reason, professional development was a high priority for school administrators, teachers, and other professional staff at these schools. Teachers at Nogales High School in Arizona, for example, were encouraged to get an ESL or bilingual endorsement. Teachers received a salary bonus if they held such an endorsement and incorporated ESL or bilingual methods into their curriculum plans. In addition, staff at this school and others we visited received professional development through inservice workshops and conferences. Teachers received training in the principles of second language acquisition and effective instructional approaches for teaching language-minority students, such as sheltered content,[8] cooperative learning, and reading and writing in the content areas. Teachers

---

[8] The term *sheltered content* refers to an approach to teaching content classes for LEP students in English in which the development of English language skills is emphasized along with content area development. Teachers use whatever means they can to make the content comprehensible and mean-

and other staff learned about students' cultural backgrounds and experiences. Counselors became informed about cross-cultural counseling strategies. Professional staff worked to develop their ability in the native languages of their students, enabling them to communicate more effectively with LM students and their parents.

Most important, *all* teachers and other professional staff were encouraged to participate in professional development of the sort described here, not just those who taught specific classes for this special student population. It appeared that all school staff took responsibility for teaching these students. No one expressed the attitude that one group of teachers would "take care" of LM students and that the others therefore did not need to "worry" about them. In fact, one principal had set a policy prohibiting bilingual teachers from teaching bilingual classes the entire day. He believed that bilingual teachers should teach mainstream as well as bilingual classes so they would not forget what they were preparing LM students to do.

At Anaheim High School, a five-year plan developed to improve the achievement of Latino students included a strong emphasis on staff development and teacher empowerment. When the current principal first came to Anaheim High School in 1983, she convened the ten department heads, and together they examined the effective schools literature to establish a commonality of language and philosophy before instituting changes. These teachers developed a school plan. According to the principal, "[Empowering the teachers] was the best thing I could have done. I had ten advocates for change, and the plan was theirs, not mine. . . . You can force compliance, but you can't force commitment." Later, the principal and ten department heads shared the process they had gone through with all the teachers. One of the teachers who went through the process reflected, "There is an overall drive to help kids. That's one of the unique things about Anaheim High School. That mood was set by Mrs. C., and the turn-around is now being seen." At Anaheim, staff development was conceived of as teacher-motivated, rather than the traditional top-down process. A small cadre of teachers, with the support of the principal, made it their business to learn what could be done to improve the quality of education at their school and later served as models and teachers for the rest of the staff. A similar process occurred at Artesia High School, where a strong staff development program had been developed partly as a result of the school's participation in the state's School Improvement Program.

5. A variety of courses and programs for language-minority students is offered.
Too often LM students are placed and kept in a limited selection of low-level high school courses with the rationale that their English is not proficient enough to allow them to cope with more advanced classes. Often these classes are overfilled, leaving students with few opportunities to interact with the teacher adequately (Brown & Haycock, 1984). Yet LM students, like all students, do best when they have the opportunity to take a wide range of courses, including advanced courses that challenge them intellectually.

---

ingful to the students: for example, simplified speech, vocabulary work, visuals, hands-on activities, and highly structured lessons (see Northcutt & Watson, 1986).

In these high schools, those who did not yet speak or write fluent English nonetheless were given the opportunity to progress in content courses appropriate to their academic level. Educators in these high schools did not assume that English proficiency matched content knowledge or cognitive skills. They recognized the fine but critical line between programs that failed to prepare LM students for college and those that facilitated their transition to an English language curriculum while providing continuing academic challenge through a variety of bilingual and sheltered courses. If, for instance, a student from Mexico had passed fundamental math and algebra in her country and had limited proficiency in English, she was able to take a geometry class taught in Spanish or one that used sheltered English methods. Advanced-Placement Spanish offered strong Spanish speakers the opportunity to receive college credit for studying Neruda and Cervantes, just as native-English-speaking students could receive advanced credit for studying Wordsworth and Hawthorne. Bilingual economics and bilingual honors chemistry allowed those who possessed the required content-area background to move beyond basics, doing advanced work in these areas while developing their English language competence. In addition to offering a wide range of courses to LM students, two of the schools also had special programs to facilitate their transition to mainstream classes, and another had a program to identify those who qualified for participation in the school's GATE (Gifted and Talented) program.

Special programs were also in place in all the high schools to promote LM students' academic and social growth. These programs have the net effect of extending learning time through before- and after-school activities, a feature which Wilson and Corcoran believe may be the "critical difference between a mediocre school and an excellent one" (1988, p. 58). In an advocate program, teachers were paired with students as tutors and advocates. BECA (Bilingual Excellence in Cognitive Achievement) provided tutoring, career planning, and multicultural awareness for both limited and fluent English-speaking Latino students at one high school. UCO (University and College Opportunity) encouraged and prepared underrepresented minority students in another high school to go to college. The Tanner Bill Program (or "SAT Program," as it was known in one school) had a similar goal, though it targeted Latino students in particular. AVID (Advance Via Individual Determination) was a college-prep program for disadvantaged students in one high school that included one class specifically geared to LEP students. These are only a few of the special programs that either targeted or included LM students. A more complete listing appears in Table 2 along with names of the schools where the programs were offered.

6. A counseling program gives special attention to language-minority students.
In our interviews with students, one question asked them to identify the teacher or other staff member who had helped them the most. Many students referred to counselors as being key to their adjustment to the new environment and to their clarification of future goals. "At the beginning of the year," said one student, "I wasn't into school. Then I talked to Mrs. B. [a counselor] and got into it. My mom said she was proud of me." In the schools we visited, there was at least one bilingual Latino counselor who was able to communicate effectively with newcomers as well as with longer term residents and understood the so-

TABLE 2
Courses, Programs, and Activities for Language-Minority Students at Six High Schools

Academic Courses and Programs
- *ESL:* focus on English language development.
- *Transitional ESL/Booster courses:* for students who have completed the ESL sequence but need some extra help in order to succeed in mainstream English classes.
- *Sheltered English content classes:* content classes with English language development built in (includes advanced classes).
- *Spanish-language content courses:* content classes taught in Spanish (includes advanced classes).
- *Spanish for Spanish speakers:* basic literacy and advanced Spanish skills.
- *Math and reading labs (computer-assisted instruction):* work on basic skills at individual pace.

Support Programs
Some of these programs serve only Latino and/or LM students; most include but are not limited to Latino LM students. Some focus on helping students develop advanced skills; others focus on more basic skills.*
- *Advocate Program:* Teachers volunteer to be paired with students, act as advocates and tutors. (Nogales)
- *BECA (Bilingual Excellence in Cognitive Achievement):* tutoring, career planning, multicultural awareness for Latino LM students. (Overfelt)
- *UCO (University and College Opportunity Program):* to encourage and prepare underrepresented minorities to go to college. Students are assigned to a special counselor, go on field trips to colleges. (Overfelt)
- *AVID (Advance Via Individual Determination):* college-prep program for disadvantaged students of all ethnic backgrounds. Uses peer and college tutors. One class in the program is specifically geared to LM students. (Sweetwater)
- *SAT Program, funded by the Tanner Bill:* for Latino students who have potential for academic success. Teachers are specially trained, classes are small (25 students), teachers act as mentors for 10–12 students, parents are involved. (Anaheim)
- *MESA (Math, Engineering, Science Achievement):* college-prep program for disadvantaged students of all ethnic backgrounds with emphasis on science and math. (Overfelt)
- *PLATO (Programmed Logic for Automatic Teaching Operations):* This computer-based dropout program allows students to attend school part of the day and work part-time. They use computers for individualized instruction, get career and college counseling. Students can receive regular diploma. (Sweetwater)
- *High-Risk Program:* for students who have failed a class or two and/or have attendance problems. Students are assigned to work with mentor teachers who have had training to participate. All participate voluntarily.
- *Chapter 1 program:* for students in low socioeconomic brackets who have scored below the 36th percentile on the CTBS or equivalent. Focuses on basic math and language arts and the use of computers; 20 students per class. (Anaheim)

Extracurricular Activities
- *Bailes:* a group of students who learn and perform dances from different regions of Mexico. (Anaheim)

TABLE 2 *continued*

- *La Prensa Latina*: a student journalism group that produces a Spanish-language newspaper called *El Mitotero*. (Sweetwater)
- *International Club*: a student group that sponsors events to increase intercultural awareness. (Artesia)
- *Celebration of cultural events and holidays* such as *Cinco de Mayo* by the whole school.
- *MECHA (Movimiento Estudiantil Chicano de Atzlá)*: a group that represents the interests of Chicano, Mexican-American, and Mexican students on college and high school campuses. (Sweetwater)
- *Sports*: Soccer and baseball are emphasized over football.

*Schools where these programs were operating are listed in parentheses.

ciocultural backgrounds of the students. This person was also well informed about post-secondary educational opportunities for language-minority students — scholarships, fellowships, grants — and could guide the students in getting and filling out the appropriate forms. He or she could also communicate with parents about students' successes and problems in school and the value of a college or university education.

One case we heard of involved a twelfth-grade student who lived with her aunt and uncle because her parents were in Mexico. The parents were reluctant to let their daughter, who had been accepted at a reputable college, move away from the family. The counselor took it upon herself to call the parents and talk it over with them, eventually convincing them of the wisdom of letting their daughter take this opportunity. In a school with no bilingual counselor who cared as much as this one did, this student — and presumably others like her — would have missed her opportunity and become another statistic of the low college attendance of minority students.

Simply having one or more bilingual counselors on the staff who are sensitive to students' cultures does not necessarily mean that LM students have access to that counselor, however. In talking with counselors and students, we learned about the importance of having an effective method of assigning students to counselors. Schools used a variety of methods, including assignment by class level, alphabetical order, special needs, and various combinations of these. Those that were most effective made sure that language-minority students were assigned to a counselor who could communicate with them, was knowledgeable of post-secondary opportunities for language-minority students, and was sincerely committed to helping all students succeed in school and beyond.

In the better counseling programs, case loads were relatively low, and bilingual Latino counselors were specifically designated for Latino LM students. At Sweetwater, in order to encourage counselors to guide all students toward postsecondary education, the procedures used to evaluate counselors took into account the test scores of the students with whom they worked, the number of students who applied to college, and the number of students who received college/university grants and scholarships. The head counselor said that four or five years before, they had realized that some people on the counseling staff were doing a much better job than others. They all sat down together and decided that helping students get money for college and go to college would be the priorities of the staff. The approach was later adopted for the whole district. It is a competitive approach, but "we work together. A counselor might say, 'What did you do that I didn't?'" At Artesia High School several Latino LM students indicated that their counselors worked with them on future plans, made sure they were doing well in classes, and advised them about the courses to take so they would have the option of going to a university. A College Aspiration Partnership Program (CAPP), developed by the counseling department at this high school, paired the school with several colleges and universities in the surrounding area. Language-minority students met with representatives of these institutions to learn the requirements for entry and procedures for applying for scholarships and other student support funds.

At Newcomer High, which unlike the other schools serves immigrant students for only a year before they make the transition to regular high schools, college counseling is not as large a component of the counselors' roles as helping students, many of them refugees, deal with the emotional and physical traumas they have experienced in leaving war-torn countries and coming to the United States. The counselors there, two of whom speak Spanish and one of whom speaks Chinese, see themselves as nurturers and facilitators of cultural adjustment. One of them described her roles: "I wear many hats; at times I'm a mother, a referral service to agencies, and I may have to be a comedian when needed." A student, commenting on her first day at the school, said, *"Para mi no fue tan extraño. La Señora S. me presentó a los compañeros."* ("For me it wasn't so strange. Mrs. S. introduced me to friends.") It is the counselor's job, as well as that of teachers, to acquaint students with the expectations of the school system, particularly those areas that differ from one culture to another. Students learn, for instance, that in most U.S. classrooms student participation — including asking questions of the teacher — is expected and desired and that one shows respect to Anglo teachers by making eye contact while they are speaking. In addition to dealing with cross-cultural issues, counselors at Newcomer had to be experts at referring students to appropriate agencies for medical or psychological traumas which could not be handled at the school.

We realize that for schools which are only now beginning to see an increase in language-minority and LEP populations, it may be difficult to find qualified counselors who share the students' linguistic and cultural backgrounds. Until such counselors are found and hired, however, it is advisable to at least have a counselor who speaks the students' native language, who has been trained in cross-cultural counseling techniques, and who can bring to students' attention special funding and scholarship opportunities.

7. Parents of language-minority students are encouraged to become involved in their children's education.

The parent participation feature was the least developed component of the high schools we visited. The principals, counselors, and teachers at all of the schools commented that more needed to be done to increase the schools' interaction with the parents of LM students. Yet they had taken steps to encourage parents to take an active part in their children's education. Several schools had Parent

Advisory Committees that met monthly and included parents of LM students. These committees typically reached out to other parents for assistance with parent-sponsored multicultural activities. Some schools regularly sent newsletters to parents in their native languages.

Newcomer High School held a parent night once a month. Students and teachers in the school worked together to plan presentations about various aspects of the school's education program, including ways parents could help their children be better students. When we visited the high school, students were being prepared in their reading class to present to parents a play that dramatized some ways of "monitoring and motivating one's child," the topic for that month's meeting. The play was to be performed in Spanish, Chinese, Burmese, Vietnamese, Tagalog, and English. Afterwards, students would read several poems to parents — "Exile" by Pablo Neruda; "The Truth" by a student; and "The Road Not Taken" by Robert Frost. Finally, students would sing "The Impossible Dream."

The Tanner Bill program for Latino students at Anaheim High School required that the teachers and parents of participating students meet twice a month. In addition, the program coordinator held evening meetings several times a year in the neighborhoods of the students in the program. Representatives of colleges and universities in the area attended these meetings to inform parents of the college programs offered by their institutions, the entry requirements, and the scholarships and other support services available to language-minority students. Generally, the college and university representatives who attended spoke the parents' native language(s).

Nogales and Anaheim held early morning pancake breakfasts and invited parents to attend before they went to work; eight hundred people had attended Anaheim's most recent breakfast when we visited the school. Nogales also held monthly student-of-the-month breakfasts for parents and students in which a student in each department was honored, as well as an Honors Assembly each quarter in which parents were asked to stand up and be recognized with their children. More than 750 people attended the most recent Honors Assembly. Overfelt High School had a full-time community liaison who spoke Spanish and offered ESL classes for parents on the school campus. Parents of Overfelt students had also come out on weekends to paint the school. Several schools contacted parents by telephone to check on students who were absent or to inform parents when a student had become ill and was returning home. The person making the contact spoke the parents' native language.

Although we did not interview parents, comments from students indicated that many Latino parents were very supportive of their children's education. The language barrier, lack of familiarity with the U.S. educational system, and their own lack of educational experience made it difficult for some parents to help directly with homework; however, they encouraged their children in other ways to pursue the education they had not had the opportunity to receive. One student reported, "For my mom, the only thing is school. She said I could do anything; 'All I want is for you to finish school.' She pushes that I get educated. She herself dropped out and got married and regrets it. I dropped out too for awhile; it tore my mom and me apart." The theme of "becoming somebody" is a strong thread in the students' talk about their parents and their own goals for the future. "My dad is always telling me to work and study, to be somebody," said one. *"Quiero seguir estudiando para llegar a ser alguien en la vida"* ("I want to keep studying so that I can become somebody in life"), said another. These comments by students attest to the strong desire among these Latino parents to do whatever they are able to do to gain a good education for their children. The schools we visited were working hard to find ways of making the schools accessible to parents.

8. School staff members share a strong commitment to empower language-minority students through education.

The most fundamental feature of all, and the most difficult to describe in concrete terms, is the commitment we heard about from most if not all of the school staff and students we interviewed. This commitment goes beyond the value the staff places on students' languages and cultures and beyond the high expectations staff members hold for language-minority students. One can value the language and culture of a student and expect that student to be successful, yet still remain passive when it comes to promoting that student in the world. Commitment and empowerment of students involve staff members reaching out, giving extra time to further the goals of a few students, and taking part in a political process that challenges the status quo. In the words of Jim Cummins, "minority students can become empowered only through interactions with educators who have critically examined and, where necessary, challenged the educational (and social) structure within which they operate" (1989, p. 6).

Such commitment manifested itself in various ways at the schools we visited. Teachers and other staff at the schools were described as having students' best interests at heart and giving extra time and energy after school and during lunch or preparation time to counsel as well as teach them. For example, the Coordinator of Special Projects at Overfelt High School said that he had found the teachers there to be very eager to learn how to work effectively with language-minority students. He said that they considered it "a very serious endeavor" to be sensitive to the needs of such students, and that they frequently requested training of various sorts to help them become more effective. At all of the schools, students mentioned teachers who had given them special help and attention, often crediting them with providing personal counseling as well as academic support. Typical student comments included the following: "The teachers here don't just teach; they care about you" and "Teachers stay after school to explain what we didn't understand."

Activities at these schools promoted participation and empowerment of Latino students outside the classroom as well. Through participation in MECHA groups, Latino clubs, Spanish language newspapers, soccer teams, and other activities sponsored and advised by school staff, Latino students developed awareness and knowledge of their cultures and language as well as a sense of community and cooperation with other Latino and non-Latino students.[9] School staff involved in these activities took their commitment beyond the classroom to help develop students as whole people. Through the *Ballet Folklórico* group at

---

[9] MECHA, or *Movimiento Estudiantil Chicano de Atzlán*, represents the interests of Chicano, Mexican American, and Mexican students on college and high school campuses.

Anaheim, for example, students not only learned and performed various Mexican dances, but also learned about the different regions in Mexico where dances originated, and presented this information in performances as well. They thus deepened their own and others' knowledge and understanding of Mexican culture and history.

Besides their work in the school setting to promote the achievement and success of Latino and other language-minority students, staff at these schools also participated in various community activities, attended meetings, and held positions in their communities through which they acted as advocates for Latinos and other minorities. An assistant principal at Nogales High School, a Latino from the community, had been the mayor of Nogales. A teacher and MECHA advisor at Sweetwater High School, also a Latino, was elected to the City Council of National City in 1989. The principal at Anaheim High School described her work to develop an advocacy base in the community through her ongoing participation in a variety of community events and activities. She had gotten support from Anaheim graduates in the community, some business people, and many parents — both Latino and Anglo — by participating in community activities herself. Some of these people had spoken out at school board meetings advocating programs and services that were crucial to the success of the district's language-minority students. Sensitive to the fact that the way certain issues are discussed can trigger negative reactions and therefore interfere with the achievement of desired goals, she worked to communicate effectively with different audiences. Above all, she said, "I have not been naïve in thinking I can do it all by myself; I spent the first year getting a sense of who supported the equity issues that I'm concerned with."

It was evident at these schools that teachers, counselors, administrators, and other staff were highly committed to promoting the success of language-minority students in school and beyond. Besides promoting the achievement of such students, they acknowledged the educational and social structures that surround the students and challenged these structures in productive ways through concrete actions such as those described above. By taking their advocacy into the community, those who held elective offices and participated in community groups challenged negative attitudes and policies that may have been creating obstacles to the improvement of education for minority groups. Those who initiated and sponsored activities to expand LM students' knowledge and understanding of their own cultures and languages helped them develop a sense of identity and community that knowledge of their own backgrounds can provide. Those who were putting their extra energy into helping students with their academic work were fighting to raise the low achievement records of language-minority students. This commitment and accompanying action provided the framework within which the attributes and processes we have described above were developed and carried out.

CONCLUSION

The eight features we have described appeared to be key to the success of language-minority students at the schools we visited. While the study was exploratory in nature, we believe it provides educators with a working model of effective education for language-minority students at the secondary level. These eight features can be thought of as a set of general recommendations, or perhaps as a checklist against which to compare other schools or programs.

Many of the key features we have described mirror features in the effective schools literature. The notions of high expectations, parent involvement, strong leadership, and staff development are common threads throughout the many studies that have been conducted. In addition, those studying schools with large numbers of minority and bilingual students found, as we did, that support services, a positive attitude toward students, and commitment to helping students achieve were crucial factors in the overall success of the schools. In these areas, our report offers further confirmation that, in order to be successful with language-minority students, high schools must place a high priority on services and attitudes that go beyond academic instruction.

But this study makes several additional contributions. The first of these is the focus on secondary schools with large numbers of LM students. Second, wherever possible, general features across schools have been operationalized through concrete examples of practices in particular schools. Much of the effective schools literature lists general attributes, but does not take the next step in describing ways of actually carrying out these broad manifestos. We have tried to provide not only food for thought but also suggestions for concrete action. Third, we have emphasized an integrated approach to secondary programs for language-minority students. The schools we visited provided strong academic preparation for these students in three areas — content knowledge and understanding, English language skills, and primary language skills. They also helped students develop their pride and identity as individuals, as members of ethnic groups, and as participants in a multicultural society by showing respect for students' languages and cultures, holding high expectations of students and acting upon them in concrete ways, guiding them in preparing for their futures, encouraging their parents to become involved in their schooling, and promoting student empowerment in school and in the larger community. This multifaceted approach manifested itself at all levels of the curriculum and throughout academic, support, and extracurricular programs at these schools.

Finally, this study strongly suggests that the diversity among students cannot simply be ignored. While the schools recognized the importance of integrating language-minority students with mainstream students and of providing equally challenging instruction for all students, they did not try to minimize differences among mainstream and Latino students or among Latino students themselves. Approaches to schooling that value linguistic and cultural diversity and that promote cultural pluralism were welcomed and explored whenever possible (see Stedman, 1987). Students' languages and cultures were incorporated into school programs as part of the effort to create a context in which all students felt valuable and capable of academic success (see Cummins, 1989).

Though this study was exploratory in nature, we hope the findings will guide further research. Many more secondary schools with large numbers of language-minority students need to be visited for longer periods of time to determine whether the features which emerged in the six schools we studied apply to other similar schools. The features themselves need to be examined in greater depth so that educators can understand them more fully and apply them in appropriate contexts. For example, a study of parent involvement in language-minority student schooling should include extensive interviews with parents themselves as well as with students and school staff. Longitudinal studies of secondary schools with large numbers of language-minority students could increase our understanding of the processes schools go through in providing and maintaining effective schooling for such students. Schools with different populations of students also need to be examined — for example, students of different ethnic and language backgrounds, students who have lived in the United States for various lengths of time, students who are immigrants, refugees, and native-born citizens. Nevertheless, the study has extended our knowledge of what makes schooling work for a rapidly growing segment of the school population. We hope that this working model will also provide inspiration and a sense of possibility to educators who are seeking an effective response to the needs of secondary language-minority students.

REFERENCES

Arias, B. (1986). The context of education for Hispanic students: An overview. *American Journal of Education, 95,* 26–57.

Bell, J. (1989, February). *Merging the research on effective instruction for LEP students with effective schools' research and practice.* Paper presented at the Annual Conference of the California Association for Bilingual Education, Anaheim, CA.

Brown, P. R., & Haycock, K. (1984). *Excellence for whom?* Oakland, CA: Achievement Council.

Carter, T. P., & Chatfield, M. L. (1986). Effective bilingual schools: Implications for policy and practice. *American Journal of Education, 95,* 200–232.

Cummins, J. (1989). *Empowering minority students.* Sacramento: California Association of Bilingual Education.

Delpit, L. D. (1988). The silenced dialogue: Power and pedagogy in educating other people's children. *Harvard Educational Review, 58,* 280–298.

Edmonds, R. (1979, May 5). Effective schools for the urban poor. *Educational Leadership, 37*(1), 15–27.

Espinosa, R., & Ochoa, A. (1986). Concentration of California Hispanic students in schools with low achievement: A research note. *American Journal of Education, 95,* 77–95.

Gingras, R. C., & Careaga, R. C. (1989). *Limited-English-proficient students at risk: Issues and prevention strategies.* Silver Spring, MD: National Clearinghouse for Bilingual Education.

Jackson, S. (1989, May). Luncheon address, *Symposium on Excellence in Mathematics and Science Achievement: The Gateway to Learning in the 21st Century.* Sponsored by the Southwest Center for Educational Equity, San Francisco.

Lau v. Nichols, 414 U.S. 563, 566 (1973).

Levin, H. M. (1987). Accelerated schools for disadvantaged students. *Educational Leadership, 44*(6), 19–21.

Medina, M. (1988). Hispanic apartheid in American public education. *Educational Administration Quarterly, 24,* 336–349.

Merriam, S. B. (1988). *Case study research in education: A qualitative approach.* San Francisco: Jossey-Bass.

Miles, M. B., & Huberman, A. M. (1984). *Qualitative data analysis: A sourcebook of new methods.* Beverly Hills, CA: Sage.

Northcutt, L., & Watson, D. (1986). *SET: Sheltered English teaching handbook.* San Marcos, CA: AM Graphics and Printing.

Orfield, G. (1986). Hispanic education: Challenges, research, and policies. *American Journal of Education, 95,* 1–25.

Orum, L. S. (1988). *The education of Hispanics: Status and implications.* Washington, DC: National Council of La Raza.

Purkey, S. C., & Smith, M. S. (1983). Effective schools: A review. *The Elementary School Journal, 83,* 428–452.

Ramírez, D. (1988, April). *A comparison of structured English, immersion, and bilingual education programs: Results of a national study.* Paper presented at the Annual Meeting of the American Educational Research Association, New Orleans.

Rosenholtz, S. J. (1985). Effective schools: Interpreting the evidence. *American Journal of Education, 93,* 352–388.

Rowen, B., Bossert, S. T., & Dwyer, D. C. (1983). Research on effective schools: A cautionary note. *Educational Researcher, 12*(4), 24–31.

Rumberger, R. W. (1987). High school dropouts: A review of issues and evidence. *Review of Educational Research, 57,* 101–121.

Stedman, L. C. (1987). It's time we changed the effective schools formula. *Phi Delta Kappan, 69,* 215–224.

Suro, R. (1990, April 11). Education secretary criticizes the values of Hispanic parents. *New York Times,* pp. A1, B8.

Taylor, S. J., & Bogdan, R. (1984). *Introduction to qualitative research methods* (2nd ed.). New York: Wiley.

Tikunoff, W. (1985). *Applying significant bilingual instructional features in the classroom.* Rosslyn, VA: National Clearinghouse for Bilingual Education.

U.S. General Accounting Office. (1987). School dropouts: Survey of local programs (GAO/HRD-87-108). Washington, DC: GPO.

Wilson, B. L., & Corcoran, T. B. (1988). *Successful secondary schools.* New York: Falmer Press.

Wong-Fillmore, L., McLaughlin, B., Ammon, P., & Ammon, M. S. (1985). *Learning English through bilingual instruction. Final Report to the National Institute of Education.* Berkeley: University of California.

The authors wish to extend their thanks to all of the staff and students of the schools we visited. We greatly appreciated the hospitality and friendliness with which we were received and the unique perspectives which people took the time to describe to us in interviews. We also want to thank our colleagues Marie Mayen, Leticia Pérez, Huynh Dinh Te, William Tikunoff, Sau-Lim Tsang, Betty Ward, and Harriet Doss Willis for their work on various stages of this project and their support throughout. The information reported here was collected as part of a plan for providing technical assistance to Arizona secondary schools. The technical assistance project was conducted by the Southwest Center for Educational Equity, which is funded by the U.S. Department of Education, Office of Elementary and Secondary Education, under Title IV of the Civil Rights Act of 1964. The contents of this article do not necessarily reflect the views or policies of the Department of Education.

"You Can't Just Say
That the Only Ones Who Can Speak
Are Those Who Agree with Your Position":
Political Discourse in the Classroom

MELINDA FINE

In this article, Melinda Fine describes the classroom dynamics surrounding the discussion of controversial issues in a middle school classroom. Through observation and interviews, she creates a detailed portrait of the interactions among teachers and students, revealing that while discussions of emotionally charged social and political issues are often heated and difficult, they can still be constructive. Fine maintains that students are more resilient and able to handle disagreement than is often believed. She concludes by arguing that education in a democracy requires that teachers and students learn to deal constructively with political and social differences.

Cambridge, Massachusetts, lies just across the Charles River from Boston. Known best for its stately, well-kept colonial homes and the ivy-clad brick buildings of Harvard University, this three-hundred-and-fifty year old city is generally perceived as a White, middle-class, intellectual enclave. While this perception is at least partially true, this densely packed city of almost 100,000 is in fact far more heterogeneous than its popular image suggests. One-fifth of all Cambridge residents are foreign-born, and one-half of these arrived during the past decade. A majority of the city's African Americans, as well as immigrants from Cape Verde, Brazil, Southeast Asia, Central America, and Haiti, tend to reside in neighborhoods that look quite different from the tree-lined streets and white-trimmed mansions surrounding Harvard University.

The Medgar Evers School is located in one of the poorer neighborhoods of Cambridge.[1] Here, mostly Black, Latino, Haitian, and Asian families live in multifamily homes that are usually close together, and often in need of paint or new siding. Many of Medgar Evers' students come from the large housing project just across the street; 44 percent of the student population qualifies for free or reduced-price lunches. Because of the city's desegregation program, however, the school's roughly six hundred K-8 students are more racially balanced than the neighborhood in which the school is located: in 1992–1993, the school was 43 percent White, 34 percent African American, 16 percent Asian, and 7 percent Latino.

---

[1] At the request of school administrators, the names of the school and its students and teachers have been changed.

Harvard Educational Review Vol. 63 No. 4 Winter 1993, 412–433

Medgar Evers is a long, three-story, beige concrete building of irregular geometric design. Surrounded by few trees, the school appears cold and austere when viewed from the street. Once inside, however, one gets an entirely different impression. Classrooms, offices, the school library, and the auditorium spin off from an airy central space that is open from the third floor to the basement. Sunlight streams in through skylights on the school's slanted roof, infusing all three floors of the building with light. Terracotta-tiled floors, clean hallways, notices for bake sales and other school events, as well as abundant displays of student artwork make the school feel cheery and welcoming. An enormous map of the world hangs on a wall across from the school's central office. This map is covered with push pins, each connected to a string that leads to a flag representing the country pinpointed. "We have children and families in our school representing *at least* sixty-four countries of the world," a card next to the map states. "We want to encourage children to become familiar with the world map, to identify all of the countries of origin, and to help celebrate our diversity!"

I have visited a classroom in this school nearly every day for the past four months, acting as a participant/observer while carrying out research for my doctoral dissertation in education. I have come to study how the teacher and students in one classroom grapple with an interdisciplinary social studies unit called "Facing History and Ourselves."[2]

This program seeks to provide a model for teaching history in a way that helps students reflect critically upon a variety of contemporary social, moral, and political issues. It focuses on a specific historical period — the Nazi rise to power and the Holocaust — and guides students back and forth between an in-depth historical case study and reflection on the causes and consequences of present-day prejudice, intolerance, violence, and racism.[3]

Facing History's decision to use the Holocaust as a case study and a springboard for exploring contemporary issues is complex and merits some discussion. When middle school teachers in Brookline, Massachusetts, created Facing History and Ourselves in 1976, relatively few Holocaust curricula existed. Perceiving the Holocaust to be a watershed event of the twentieth century, these teachers felt that their students should, indeed, learn about such a critical historical moment. At the same time, however, they felt that the Holocaust's "meaning" to students must lie not only in understanding its unique historical dimensions, but also in grappling with its more generalizable lessons about human behavior. Historically examining the escalation of steps through which individuals living under Nazi rule were made to follow Hitler — from the use of propaganda to influence one's thinking, to the threats against one's economic and personal security, to the use of terror to compel obedience — course designers sought to help students identify how opportunities for resistance were gradually eroded with the demise of German democracy and the rise of a totalitarian state. Using historical understanding as a catalyst for more personal, critical reflection, they intended to foster students' awareness of the social conditions that can under-

---

[2] Information about this curriculum can be obtained from Facing History and Ourselves, 16 Hurd Road, Brookline, MA 02146 (617-232-1595). The organization develops and disseminates curricular materials and runs an extensive training program to prepare teachers to teach the curriculum.

[3] Throughout this article, the term "Holocaust" is used to refer to the Nazi genocide of Jews.

mine democracy and promote their sense of moral and political responsibility as future citizens.

It might well be asked whether these goals could not also be achieved by undertaking a different, perhaps more relevant case study — of the Middle Passage (the transatlantic slave trade), for example, or the genocide of Native Americans. No doubt they could be. Program designers, teachers, and promoters do not argue that the Holocaust is the only genocide — or even the most important genocide — to teach about. In fact, Facing History has developed other curricular materials that deal more directly with these "closer-to-home" events, and the Facing History Resource Text includes a chapter on the Armenian Genocide.[4]

Program advocates do contend, however, that discussions about contemporary racism and violence may in fact be facilitated by focusing on a period of history more tangential to the cultural backgrounds of the course's ethnically diverse students. As Larry Myatt, a longtime teacher of the course and the director of an inner-city high school in Boston, says, Facing History offers "a way to talk about these issues in a *removed* way so that we don't hit people over the head with a two-by-four and say 'racism!' 'scapegoating!'"[5]

In keeping with the program's educational priorities, the semester-long curriculum is structured to move back and forth between a focus on "history" and a focus on "ourselves." Initial chapters of the program's resource book encourage thinking about universal questions of individual identity and social behavior. From here the course moves on to its more specific case study of prejudice and discrimination: an examination of the history of anti-semitism, beginning as far back as ancient Rome. Students undertake a rigorous, multifaceted study of German history from 1914 to 1945, examining, for example, the impact of Nazi racial policies in education and the workplace, the nature of propaganda, and the various roles played by victims, victimizers, and bystanders during the Third Reich. These lessons provide critical historical content and serve as structured exercises for thinking about the choices that individuals, groups, and nations faced with regard to action and resistance. These exercises, in turn, prepare students for later discussions about how they themselves can assume responsibility for protecting civil liberties and becoming active citizens.[6]

Facing History's complex intellectual content is undergirded by a pedagogical imperative: to foster perspective-taking, critical thinking, and moral decision-making among students. It is specifically geared toward adolescents who are developmentally engaged in a fierce (and somewhat contradictory) struggle to become distinct individuals *and* to fit in with their peers. These students, curriculum developers argue, have the most to gain from a course that "raises the problem of differing perspectives, competing truths, the need to understand motives and to consider the intentions and abilities of themselves and others."[7]

---

[4] See Alan Stoskopf and Margot Stern Strom, *Choosing to Participate: A Critical Examination of Citizenship in American History* (Brookline, MA: Facing History and Ourselves, 1990); Margot Strom and William Parsons, *Facing History and Ourselves: Holocaust and Human Behavior* (Watertown, MA: Intentional Educations, 1982).

[5] See Melinda Fine, "Collaborative Innovations: Documentation of the Facing History and Ourselves Program at an Essential School," *Teachers College Record, 94*, No. 4 (1993), 776.

[6] Strom and Parsons, *Facing History.*

[7] Strom and Parsons, *Facing History,* p. 14.

Rather than shying away from the conflicts that are inevitably generated when a diverse group of adolescents work to clarify their own beliefs and values, teachers encourage students to view complexity and conflict as potentially conducive to personal growth and social exchange.

I chose to observe the implementation of Facing History and Ourselves in the Medgar Evers school for specific reasons — reasons undoubtedly operative in my interpretation of the course and, consequently, important to acknowledge here. First and foremost, I am a supporter of the program's goals. Educational efforts to foster moral and social responsibility are difficult undertakings, not only because of the conflictual nature of the material inevitably confronted with the students, but also because of the embattled position many such education programs — including Facing History — find themselves in today. I consider them socially necessary, nonetheless.

I also find compelling Facing History's claim that using historical subject matter somewhat tangential to the lives of racially diverse students may quite effectively reach and motivate students in multicultural urban settings. For this reason I have observed Facing History courses in several urban schools over the past few years, while completing my own doctoral work and serving as a research consultant to the Facing History organization.[8] My professional collaboration with Facing History has deepened my understanding of the program, but also demanded that I be vigilant in pushing myself to view its classroom practice in a critical light.

Consequently, while at the Medgar Evers school, I observed class daily for an eleven-week period. I hoped to learn how students and their teacher interpreted issues raised by the course, recognizing that their interpretations would no doubt shift during the semester and assuming, too, that they would at times produce conflict among classroom participants. I intended to describe how these conflicts were negotiated within the classroom.

To carry out my objectives, I felt that I needed to know as much as possible about the students, their teacher, and the school culture that surrounded the classroom study. I needed to have all classroom participants speak freely with me, and thus I needed to be known and trusted by them. These requirements dictated a qualitative, descriptive, phenomenological, and self-consciously personal approach to my subject, involving, among other things, participant/observation, in-class and post-class writing, lengthy individual interviews with students and their teacher, and ongoing review of students' written work.

My relations with the teacher and students were open and friendly. Over the course of the semester, I was invited to a bar mitzvah, sock hop, viola recital, and soccer match, and after the school year ended, I received a letter from one student asking me out to lunch. Since my intent was to get to know classroom participants and to let them get to know me, I never tried to hold myself aloof or maintain the stance of a completely distant, "objective" observer. Though I

---

[8] See Melinda Fine, "Facing History and Ourselves: Portrait of a Classroom," Special Issue: "Whose Culture?" *Educational Leadership* (1991/1992), 44–49; Fine, "Collaborative Innovations," pp. 771–789; Melinda Fine, "The Politics and Practice of Moral Education: A Case Study of Facing History and Ourselves," Diss., Harvard Graduate School of Education, 1991; and Melinda Fine, *Habits of Mind: Struggling Over Values in America's Classrooms* (San Francisco: Jossey-Bass, 1995).

didn't, for the most part, participate actively in class discussion, I nonetheless tried to act in a style compatible with the school's "open" atmosphere. My constant, in-class writing was obvious to all present (in fact, students often teased me about how quickly I wrote), and I did comment on topics when asked by either the teacher or students. I also frequently asked, and was told, about students' basketball games, dances, baby-sitting, and dates. In turn, students asked and were told about me: that I was a teacher, an activist, and at that time a graduate student, and that I was writing a book about them.

I identify what I did and where I stand in relation to Facing History not to suggest that researcher "bias" qualifies the validity of my observations — as if some wholly neutral position were a preferable point of departure or even possible to attain. I believe all researchers stand in some relation to their subject; the reader simply deserves to know where I stand before watching these classroom events along with me.

* * *

It is an unseasonably hot day in May. The twenty-three students in Marysa Gonzalez's seventh/eighth-grade class sit fanning themselves with their spiral notebooks as late-morning sun pours into the classroom through a large, partially closed window on the far side of the room. Of the twelve girls and eleven boys in this room, six are African American, four are Asian, and thirteen are White, one of whom is a Latina. Nursing her latest sports injury, Jess limps to her seat clad in navy blue shorts and a University of Michigan tee-shirt. Abby sports a summer-bright turquoise shirt, matching socks, and white stretch pants. The top piece of her shoulder length, sandy-blond hair is pulled back in a clip, and her bangs remain loose and hanging. Sandra's clothing and hairstyle are almost identical. Alan and Josh each sport marginally punk hairdos. Alan wears an earring in his left ear. Chi-Ho's pressed, beige cotton shirt remains buttoned at both the neck and cuffs, and he removes his thick, black-rimmed glasses every now and then to wipe the sweat from his brow. Jamal and Amiri both wear oversized tee-shirts and baggy cotton pants.

The teacher, Marysa Gonzalez, searches intently through piles of paper on her desk. A handsome Latina in her late forties, her style is informal and unpretentious: she wears light khaki slacks, a loose-fitting red cotton shirt, and no makeup. Her long black hair, pulled back in a loose braid, is streaked with grey.

It is the eleventh and second-to-last week of the Facing History course. Using students' understanding of the Holocaust as a lens through which to approach more immediate concerns, Marysa focuses the remaining class discussions around contemporary political problems in order to highlight students' own social and political responsibilities. This way of bringing closure to the course is in keeping with the final chapter of the Facing History Resource Text:

> This curriculum must provide opportunities for students to explore the practical applications of freedom, which they have learned demand a constant struggle with difficult, controversial, and complex issues. . . . This history has taught that there is no one else to confront terrorism, ease the yoke and pain of racism, attack apathy, create and enforce just laws, and wage peace but *us*. . . . We believe that participating in decision-making about difficult and controversial issues gives practice in listening

to different opinions, deciphering fact from opinion, confronting emotion and reason, negotiating, and problem-solving.[9]

Marysa circulates around the uncomfortably hot classroom handing out the syllabus for the week. Listing all reading and homework assignments for the next five days, the syllabus begins with a quote from radical community organizer Saul Alinsky, which is directly relevant to this week's discussion: "Change means movement, movement means friction, friction means heat, and heat means controversy. The only place where there is no friction is in outer space or a seminar on political action."

Intended as a comment upon political conflicts in the world at large, Alinsky's remark is equally telling about classroom dynamics. Over the next several days, students will view provocative documentary films about individuals and/or organizations holding controversial and differing political beliefs. These films (and related readings) are intended to impress upon students the importance of clarifying one's own political beliefs and raise complex questions about how a democratic and pluralistic society should best handle the conflicts generated by political diversity. In discussing these films, political differences within the classroom itself will be illuminated and debated, and dilemmas raised by the course's intellectual content will be mirrored in the lived curriculum of classroom dynamics.

From my perspective, these classroom dynamics reveal tensions about conflicting values and ideologies among teachers, students, and the Facing History curriculum itself, demonstrating the enormous complexity of the endeavor to catalyze critical, moral thinking among adolescent students. On the one hand, the Facing History program advocates bringing forth multiple points of view, developing students' understanding of multiple perspectives, and promoting tolerance among diverse peoples of often differing backgrounds. In the classes I have observed, teacher practice is to a considerable extent in keeping with these curricular values; teachers often actively engage with students of diverse political perspectives and encourage them to remain fair-minded and open to at least hearing alternative points of view. On the other hand, the program unequivocally rejects moral relativism, condemning social attitudes and beliefs that in any way repress or discriminate against individuals or social groups. Tensions inevitably arise when teachers and students differ in their feelings about which beliefs actually further or hinder these stated curricular objectives. Whose standards should determine what is morally "right" or "wrong"? Do these determinations align with an individual's own political beliefs? How should beliefs that some regard as "wrong" be handled in the classroom? What are the repercussions of silencing these viewpoints or, alternatively, allowing them to be voiced freely? As the recent controversy over New York City's "Children of the Rainbow" curriculum demonstrates, these questions are increasingly the subject of national educational debate.

Marysa and her students also clearly struggle with questions such as these. A close look at how they are dealt with here — within the safety of a trusted school community — may help to illuminate how they are negotiated within a broader

---

[9] Strom and Parsons, *Facing History,* pp. 383, 387.

social context. What follows, then, is a portrait of classroom life. It is intended not as an evaluative critique of the Facing History program's success or failure in meeting its stated goals, but rather as an analytic exploration of the dynamics encountered in attempting to do so. As a matter of both research inquiry and writing style, social science portraiture investigates, describes, and analyzes characters, settings, and events in context and in relation to one another, and is informed by an awareness of the researcher's own relationship with his or her subject.[10] Equally important, portraiture offers a style of writing designed to engage the reader in the particular experience described and, in so doing, give him or her a sense of a larger whole. I offer the following in the spirit of what the writer Eudora Welty has noted in another context: "One place comprehended can make us understand other places better."[11]

* * *

Friday, May 11

"Remember yesterday? What did we see?" Marysa asks about a film in which the subject of political difference is raised. Sandra answers, "A story about a man who taught his students that the Holocaust never happened, and that Jews wanted to rule the world." Abby adds, "He also said that all the banks and the finances were controlled by Jewish people." "Yeah," agrees Alan, "he thought there was an international Jewish conspiracy."[12]

Students take turns passionately describing "Lessons in Hate," an early 1980s documentary about Jim Keegstra, a popular and charismatic mayor and teacher in a small town in Alberta, Canada, who taught anti-semitic beliefs to students for more than a decade. The film extensively documents Keegstra arguing that the Holocaust was a "hoax" that in no way singled out Jewish people. He also argues that the French revolution was a product of the "international Jewish conspiracy"; that John Wilkes Booth, the man who shot Abraham Lincoln, was a Jew; and that Jews caused the American Civil War. Young, vulnerable, and with little access to alternative beliefs or perspectives, Keegstra's students uncritically absorbed his teachings, or, in a few cases, adopted them ambivalently in order to receive a passing grade. More problematic still, Keegstra's statements were tacitly accepted by the school's principal and faculty, and by most of the town's council and citizens. When the mother of one student finally challenged Keegstra's teachings, she was vehemently opposed by members of her community. The school board eventually fired Keegstra, but not until after a long and difficult battle had been waged that painfully divided members of the small town.[13]

---

[10] See, for example, Sara Lawrence Lightfoot, *The Good High School: Portraits of Character and Culture* (New York: Basic Books, 1983). For an excellent discussion of the similarities and differences between portraiture and other forms of social science inquiry, see Marue Walizer, "Watch With Both Eyes: Narratives and Social Science: Sources of Insight into Teachers' Thinking," Diss., Harvard University Graduate School of Education, 1987, pp. 12–47 and 101–129.

[11] Eudora Welty, *The Eye of the Storm: Selected Essays and Reviews* (New York: Vintage Books, 1979), p. 129.

[12] All quotations of in-class comments are from written notes taken while class was in session.

[13] "Lessons in Hate," distributed by Intersection Associates, Cambridge, Massachusetts, and available through the Facing History and Ourselves Resource Library.

The Keegstra film raises questions about how a community can tolerate conflictual beliefs among its members while still maintaining cohesion. Showcasing the struggles experienced by both Keegstra and those who oppose him, it demonstrates how difficult it can be to stand up for one's beliefs, regardless of their content. After what they have read, seen, and been taught throughout the semester, Marysa's students are outraged that anyone could minimize the horror of the Holocaust, much less deny its very existence. Distancing themselves from their Canadian peers, some make disparaging remarks about Keegstra's seemingly docile and gullible students:

Abby: It seems like these people just *feed* on people who are torn apart. They just suck them up by providing them with an excuse to hate! They probably want to find a way to place the blame on someone else just to explain their own situation.

Marysa: Exactly! What's the vocabulary word which describes that? (Several students shout out, "scapegoating!") Well, what can you do to help people when they're in this condition? What can you do to turn their beliefs around?

Josh: Kill them!

Marysa: What?! Kill them?!

Josh: Yes. If they say those things, and if they start a war or something, you have to fight back.

Alan: But if you go out and fight these people, and you kill six hundred or seven hundred of them, it won't stop *anything*! More will just come and fight back!

Marysa: What I'm *really* trying to push is that this is not just a problem that happened in history, a long time ago — the Dark Ages, when I was born. These issues are *here*, in the present. And you're a part of it. You have to be aware of it so *you* are not brainwashed or indoctrinated in the future.

For the next several minutes, students discuss the apparent differences between their own multicultural community and Keegstra's ethnically homogeneous school and town. Marysa asks students to identify similarities between Nazi doctrine and what Keegstra taught, and Abby brings up the international Jewish conspiracy theme. Drawing this argument closer to home, Marysa suggests parallels between the historical claim that Jews have controlled the financial industry and the present-day fear that Japanese increasingly dominate the U.S. economy. Chi-Ho raises his hand and quietly drops a bombshell: "I think that a Jewish international conspiracy *does* exist, but not quite as much they say. So many people are talking about it, it must be some way true." "What?!" several students exclaim at once. Josh stares in disbelief at the boy who sits next to him, suddenly a stranger. Susie and Jess yell out in disbelief. Marysa responds in a strained but consciously even-tempered voice, "Chi-Ho, why do you think this?" Chi-Ho answers in a somewhat muffled voice, "I don't know, but I do." Marysa continues, "Don't you think that if there was a conspiracy it could have stopped the Holocaust?" "No, I don't," Chi-Ho replies, "because it's more recent. It's developed since the fifties only, I think." Marysa responds emphatically, "Chi-Ho, we need to talk!"

Animated one-on-one conversations spring up between students who sit next to each other in all corners of the room; the whole class seems to be buzzing. Abby raises her hand and (deliberately or not) turns up the heat several notches.

She says, "I'm against what some people are doing with Israel, with the way it was established and with killing the Palestinians and everything. But that's different from an international Jewish conspiracy." "*What* are you talking about?" Josh exclaims furiously. "We weren't even talking about that!" Sandra adds critically, "What are you against now, Abby?" Abby answers, "I'm against the way the country was set up." Marysa asks incredulously and slightly sarcastically, "The UN vote?" Abby replies, "Not that, but what happened to the Palestinian people *through* that. Elie Wiesel and people like that were involved, and millions of Palestinian people were massacred and forced to leave their homes, just like in the Holocaust."

All hell breaks loose. It seems like everyone begins yelling at Abby, and Chi-Ho's earlier remark is left by the wayside. Abby steadfastly holds her ground. Though her words remain strong and her claims unqualified, she slumps further and further into her seat with each new attack by her classmates. She strikes me as being both scared and defiant. Confused about historical facts, Josh defends the state of Israel.

Josh: They were *attacked* in an eight-day war!

Abby: Well, it's still not right to be killing people to set up a country!

Josh: That's exactly what *we* did to set up *our* country!

Abby: So? I'm against *that*, too! I don't believe in that either!

Sandra (becoming increasingly exasperated): Well, what *are* you for? What *do* you believe in?

(Alison and Susie nod emphatically in agreement.)

Abby (matter-of-factly): I believe in control by the people.

Marysa: But how do you determine which people should have control, Abby? In the film we saw, the Canadian teacher thinks he should have control, 'cause he thinks he's right. How are you going to decide who gets to speak and who doesn't?

Students debate the conundrum of free speech for the remaining few minutes of class. Though Marysa has (perhaps self-consciously) shifted discussion away from a contentious and personalized debate, the classroom atmosphere remains charged.

I am scheduled to interview Abby later on this same day. As students get ready for lunch, I watch Abby self-consciously gather her books, seeming proud yet uncomfortable about being isolated. Calling out to her, I suggest that we can discuss the points she has raised during our interview, if she is interested; she smiles appreciatively.

Sandra, Alison, and Angela note my overture and come up to speak with me on their way out of the room. "Look, I don't know much about the Jewish religion, or any religion, really," Sandra says, "but isn't it true that in the Bible it says that the land was originally Jewish land, and that's why they wanted it? Or, why didn't the Jewish people just go to a different country?"

I try to answer as best as I can, explaining that Jews, Christians, and Moslems have all lived on the land, and that all have laid claim to it at different periods of history. "But doesn't the Bible say that the Jews were there *first?*," Angela retorts, "and then the Moslems came when the Jews went to Egypt?" Trying to grant each group its legitimacy, I speak to the importance of finding contemporary political solutions to the problem. Seeing myself more as a participant/observer than an arbiter of divergent viewpoints, I refuse to choose sides despite the girls' best efforts to make me do so. The three girls head off for lunch less angry, but still visibly confused.

Josh leaves class upset by the comments made by both Abby and Chi-Ho. He speaks to Marysa for almost an hour after class, refusing to sit next to Chi-Ho and demanding that his seat be changed. In keeping with the curriculum's intent to foster students' ability to listen to alternative perspectives, Marysa tells me later:

> I tried to explain to Josh that Chi-Ho was the same person Josh thought he was before he made that statement. I told him that the way to respond to problems is not to refuse to speak to someone, but to talk together to try to figure it out and to help people to change their beliefs.

But "talking together" is not always easy. True to Alinsky's comment, "frictions" caused by Abby and Chi-Ho seem to circulate around the class as a whole (several students shout at Abby and Chi-Ho); between students and their teacher (Marysa expresses unequivocal disapproval of both students' comments); and, perhaps most poignantly, within students' individual relationships (friendships between Josh and Chi-Ho as well as Abby and Sandra are strained).

Marysa leaves class as upset as many of her students and uncertain about how to proceed. In fact, her confusion seems to have been manifest in her classroom dealings. Confronted with views she finds repugnant and even dangerous, she does, nevertheless, encourage students to remain open-minded, independent in their thinking, and respectful of difference. She even engages Abby and Chi-Ho in a critical debate, urging them to clarify their thinking and to defend their controversial points of view. At the same time, however, Marysa implicitly undermines the views of both of these students. By publicly acknowledging her disagreement with Abby and Chi-Ho, she uses her implicit authority as the "teacher" (the one empowered to design seating plans, assign homework and grades, and so forth) to undermine, rather than muzzle, these students' perspectives. Given the power differential between teacher and student, the critical debate between them is unevenly weighted.

For example, Marysa challenges Chi-Ho's remarks before the full classroom community, but then seeks to remove them from the public arena. "Chi-Ho, we need to talk," she says after only a brief exchange, simultaneously displacing disagreement to the private realm and suggesting that, once there, she will set the record straight. Moments later Marysa chooses not to intervene when several students jump on Abby, and her own questions of Abby sound slightly facetious. Finally, she eventually steers discussion away from the Middle East and toward freedom of speech in the midst of an unresolved debate.

Admittedly uncomfortable with the arguments raised and feeling unequipped to handle them, Marysa avails herself of her proximity to the Facing History and Ourselves national office and calls in staff member Steve Cohen to address the controversial issues raised by Abby and Chi-Ho. While I believe Marysa is making good use of an available resource, I also wonder whether she is bringing Steve in to quell controversy and, in essence, to set the record straight. A balding, wiry man in chinos and tennis shoes, Steve visits class a few days later.

Monday, May 14

"Why did Hitler choose to focus on the Jews?" Steve asks to open this morning's complex agenda. Alan replies, "He said that they were in charge of the money." Jess adds, "He said they were the people who put Germany in the economic state they were in." "Well, why did people believe it?" Steve continues. Abby says, "It's like that quote, 'If you tell a lie big enough and long enough, people will start to believe it.'" Steve asks, "Do you think that's true, from your own experience?" "Well, I've always been someone who doesn't like to just go along with what other people are saying," Abby replies, "but *yeah*, if you hear something long enough, it affects you . . . you kind of forget what your own principles are."

Steve bounces around the room, weaving around students' desks and speaking quickly in an animated voice that is often squeaky with excitement. Focusing directly on each student with whom he speaks, and referring to each by name, he engages the class in a discussion about how basic emotions and stereotypes take over when you "forget your own principles" and are "no longer able to think." "I want you to think about how stereotypes and propaganda work," Steve explains, "because, as you know, Hitler didn't invent anything new. Before Hitler, there was plenty of hatred of Jews." He continues with the following example:

In the 1890s, a book appeared, and it was called . . . *Protocols of the Elders of Zion.* (Steve writes the title of the book on the board, and students copy it into their journals.) It appeared in Russian in 1890. And it explained that there was an *international* group of Jews who used to get together and meet in a Jewish cemetery in Prague, at night, and they would plan *everything* that was going to happen in the world. (Josh taps Chi-Ho on the shoulder, as if to suggest that he should listen closely.) This book was republished in England in 1919. It was republished in the United States in the 1920s — in a newspaper owned by Henry Ford, one of the two or three most important men in the country! In England it was published in *the* most important newspaper — the *Times* of London. And the most interesting thing about this book is — it's a fraud! It's complete nonsense! It's made up! (Josh again prods Chi-Ho and whispers something to him; Chi-Ho smiles awkwardly.)

How do you know it's a fraud? Well, in the 1890s, this book was written by members of the Russian police force. (Steve writes "1890 — Russian police force" hurriedly on the board.) And how do you know that? Well, because this book was actually *copied* (Steve's voice cracks in excitement) from a book that was written in 1864 in France that didn't blame *Jews*, but that said the ruler of France, Napoleon III, was trying to take over the world (he writes "Napoleon, 1864" on the board). And everywhere where Napoleon appears in *this* book (Steve points to the original text), the word *Jews* appears in this one (he points to the words "Elders of Zion"). Think about this for a second! A French book in 1864 was copied by the Russians in 1890. The British copied the Russians. And the Americans copied the British. And it's a complete fraud! It's hocus pocus! It's untrue! It's a *lie*. And millions and millions of people believed it. (Pause). How come?

Susie: Because nobody told them any differently.

Alan: Because they believed it was written by someone who knew!

Josh: A lot of people want to blame somebody else for all of their problems.

Chi-Ho: Because then you're not responsible for what happens to people.

"Exactly!" Steve exclaims. "There are a lot of things that happen that are really beyond our control. An idea like this says — even if it's someone you hate, *somebody* is in control. Somebody is in charge of what's going on. And even if things are *lousy,* it's nice to be able to say, it wouldn't be lousy if it weren't for these bums. Let me show you how this happened in real life! This should take about five hours, but I'll do it in three minutes. You ready?" Students nod that they are.

For the next several minutes, Steve gives a remarkably clear and concise account of the infamous turn-of-the-century case in which Alfred Dreyfus, one of the few Jewish officers in the French Army, was falsely accused of giving military secrets to the Germans, convicted in two trials, and sentenced to prison on Devil's Island. "Many people said, 'How could Dreyfus have done it alone?' And others said, 'Aha, he didn't! He was part of this!' " (Steve points again to "Elders of Zion" on the board).

Abby asks, "Is that thing called the international Jewish conspiracy?" Steve explains: "In France, they called it the 'Syndicat.' And they referred to it as the 'international Jewish conspiracy.' There's a tremendous *power* in this kind of idea. Why were people so willing to believe it of Jews? Would they have believed it if this was . . . about Catholics? Would that have been popular in Europe?" "No," answers Sandra, "there are a lot of Catholics, so it wouldn't be as easy as singling out one Jew." Abby interjects, "What things you believe in will also depend upon the family you grow up in." Steve agrees, and draws the thorny issue of an international Jewish conspiracy to a close by reinforcing the curriculum's valuation of critical thinking. He says, "One of the things you're going to have to decide is whether you're going to believe what people say, or whether you're going to try to figure it out on your own."

Chi-Ho has remained conspicuously silent throughout this entire discussion. Often quiet in class, his behavior today is not unusual. Today's lecture, however, is given in response to his earlier remark, and it would seem to call for his participation. While only Josh makes a point of publicly acknowledging the connection between the previous class and today's by tugging at Chi-Ho's shirt-sleeve and whispering to him repeatedly, other students shoot furtive glances in Chi-Ho's direction. Chi-Ho seems to studiously ignore all meaningful looks. Though he appears to be listening throughout class and assiduously copies Steve's blackboard notes into his journal, he does not acknowledge that today's lecture was, however subtly, directed at him.

This is by no means the case with Abby when the second item on today's agenda is discussed. Referring to a set of maps of the pre- and post-World War I period, Steve shows how the world has changed since the fall of the Ottoman Empire. He points to the Middle East region and says: "There are White people, Black people, and Brown people living here. It's a whole Rainbow Coalition! After World War I, one of the major questions was — should people like this be able to rule *themselves*? And the winners of the war — France, Britain, and the United States — say 'No!' They give them independence with training wheels, and the winners of the war are gonna be the training wheels! These people end up living in countries which are *invented* after World War I. It's all a product of politics! Well, what kinds of problems might the 'training wheels' encounter?"

"They had to make sure the new boundaries wouldn't get people mad because they don't want to start another war," Alan answers thoughtfully. Nora adds, "They needed to keep people together with their own people so they'll be content." Drawing his finger across a large section of the map, Steve describes how Transjordan was ruled by the victorious British until 1948. "And who lived here?" he asks simply, pointing to Palestine. "Palestinians," Abby replies. Steve continues, asking, "Who were they, and what was their religion?" "They were Arabs," Abby responds. "They were Moslems, Jews, and Christians," corrects Steve. "To be a 'Palestinian' meant literally to live in Palestine. And they all lived under British rule."

For the next several minutes, Steve helps the class review what happened to Jews in the years leading up to and immediately following World War II. Josh remembers that Jews tried to get out of Europe, but often had no place to go. Angela believes many headed for Palestine because they had "religious ties there." Nora comments that it was often impossible to return to their homes because "they were taken by people, like their neighbors." Zeke adds that their possessions were taken, too.

"Lots of Jews live in detention camps for two or three years after the war," Steve explains. "The Jews in Palestine want the European Jews to come there, but the Arabs and Christians don't want them to. The British have control of Palestine and they don't know what to do with it. Since the British can't figure it out, they give the problem to the United Nations, which functions as an international government with representatives from different countries. This is the U.N.'s big moment! Well, in 1947 the U.N. votes to divide Palestine again, into a state for Jews and a state for non-Jews."

"Is this when the eight day war took place?" Josh interjects, reviving his previous comment. "No," Steve answers, "that took place later." Nora comments, "The U.N. is made up of representatives from all different countries, right? So, what did the Palestinian representative do?" Supportive and genuinely impressed, Steve exclaims, "That's a great question! There wasn't one, since Palestine was under British rule." "Well," Nora continues, "did the majority of the non-Jews in Palestine agree with the decision?" Steve responds, "Absolutely not! The majority of people were not happy. So in 1948 a war occurs — it's a small war compared to World War I and World War II — and in that war, the *Jewish* side of Palestine manages to survive, but the *non-Jewish* region gets taken — not by Israel, but by 'Transjordan.' . . . The Jewish part becomes Israel, but the non-Jewish part becomes Jordan and Egypt."

Abby is getting frustrated with Steve's version of history. She breaks in in a loud and exasperated voice, "But there was lots of violence between the Jews and non-Jews! A lot of people were killed! People were kicked off their homes. It was just like in the Holocaust!" Steve acknowledges the complexity of the situation, but is direct in his rebuttal. Calmly and with authority, he asserts, "That's not quite true; part of it's true, but it's *very* complex. There were broadcasts telling people to leave their land, and many people *wanted* to leave because they wanted to get away from the war. When the Israeli government came in, they didn't know what to do with the Arab land. The people that fled their homes *do* end up living in camps, but that was the choice of the Jordanians, not the Israelis."

Abby objects, saying, "But they shouldn't have had to leave in the first place!" "They *chose* to leave," Steve responds, "There's *no* question that this displaced people and that people lost their homes who didn't want to. But there's also *no* question that extermination was *not* the policy. . . . The other thing is that many Jews in these Arab countries also lost *their* homes. One of the things that happens in times of war is that international human rights are *completely* neglected. This should make us think very closely about the policies of international government — they're *not* extermination policies, but they're also not policies that make it very easy for people to live their lives in the way they would like to." Abby isn't satisfied. "But if the Palestinians hadn't been kicked off . . ." she begins. Steve breaks in, "Do you mean the Palestinian non-Jews?" Accommodating Steve's language, Abby continues, "OK, if the Palestinian non-Jews hadn't been kicked off, why should they be so angry about not having their land?" "Oh, well! They've spent the past forty years living in camps and wanting to be on their parents' land!" Steve responds.

Most students have remained silent yet attentive during this exchange. Sandra sits close by Abby and does not come to her aid, despite Abby's frequent, beseeching looks in her direction. Josh only half-hides a smirk, seemingly pleased that Steve is taking Abby on. He now contributes to the discussion, "But there was another war!" and Steve replies, "There have been *lots* of wars. The tension Abby speaks to developed more after the land was taken in 1967. Many people believe that land should be exchanged for peace. There's a large Peace Now movement in Israel today saying that those territories should be given back to the Palestinian Arabs."

"But they *won* the war!" Josh repeats emphatically. "I learned that in Temple!" Steve responds by briefly highlighting different points of view within contemporary Israeli (Jewish) society. He is careful to distinguish between current policies and those on which the state was founded. Though he admits the existence of conflicting perspectives within contemporary Israeli society, he leaves less room for alternative interpretation when it comes to the founding of the state ("The tension Abby speaks to developed more after the land was taken in 1967," he says, and he suggests that Palestinians were not "kicked off" their land but "*chose*" to leave it). Though Steve is by no means alone in articulating this perspective (and in distinguishing it from current Israeli policies), it nonetheless reflects only one particular viewpoint in a complex and contentious historical debate.[14]

Some of Steve's other interventions are also grounded in a particular political stance. While acknowledging that the founding of the State of Israel was accompanied by some human rights violations, he denies that those violations were systematic or a matter of official policy. Moments later, he "corrects" Abby's language by recommending that she refer to Arabs as "Palestinian non-Jews" — a categorization that is itself not politically neutral, and arguably comparable to

---

[14] See, for example, Zachary Lockman, "Original Sin," in *Intifada: The Palestinian Uprising Against Israeli Occupation,* ed. Zachary Lockman and Joel Beinin (Boston: South End Press, 1989), pp. 185–204.

referring to Blacks as non-Whites or women as non-men. Like Marysa in the earlier classroom incident, Steve acts in somewhat contradictory ways, eliciting students' diverse viewpoints on the one hand while undermining the legitimacy of those with which he disagrees on the other.

Class nearly over, students begin to close their notebooks and put them inside their desks. Marysa and Steve turn to each other and begin speaking privately in the front of the room; they express pleasure and relief at having gotten through a potentially difficult session without drawing too much fire.

That neither Steve nor Marysa entirely transcended their own political beliefs in interpreting and responding to political differences within the classroom is not surprising; I would argue that no one can do so. These beliefs are a part of our internal make-up, as operative within these teachers as they are within my own interpretations of their practice. I did not leave my own political beliefs at the door when I entered the classroom; they were within me as I observed each class. These perspectives no doubt influenced how I interpreted classroom tensions between eliciting and muting student voice. As a Jewish woman strongly committed to a peaceful resolution of the Israeli-Palestinian conflict, I felt strongly opposed to Chi-Ho's remarks and to Abby's more extreme comments, even though I disagreed with how the teachers at times responded to both of these students.

Interviews conducted individually with Chi-Ho, Abby, Josh, and Sandra shortly after these classes took place support my interpretation of these classroom events as political in nature.[15] By "political" I mean to suggest not only the content of the classroom debate (in which a diversity of political views were expressed), but also the process by which it was negotiated (whereby controversial voices were silenced by those with greater authority and power). In these instances, power was exercised between students and their teachers; between Marysa and Steve; and among the students themselves. So, too, the relations among these players were hierarchical: some were given (or assumed) more authority to speak than others. And, depending on one's point of view, opposing positions were granted legitimacy or invalidated. In the process, some students felt silenced and subordinated, while others felt empowered and privileged.

In the course of our interviews, Chi-Ho and Abby express discomfort at feeling "unheard" and "misunderstood" in class, while Sandra and Josh enjoy the fact that these students were silenced. Expressing frustration with being "misunderstood," Chi-Ho remarks, [Josh] wouldn't listen! . . . [It felt] terrible . . . I was disappointed. I *really* think that Marysa didn't really listen to me very carefully, and, if she *did*, she would understand what I meant."

Abby's response to the classes under study is multifaceted. She initially admits to being confused by Steve's alternative reading of historical events and expresses concern for (what she imagines to be) *his* discomfort. Portraying *herself* as the agent of her silencing (rather than Steve), Abby notes:

I *really* was confused by what he said, because, from what *I* had read (because my parents have a lot of books about that), it *really* was the total *opposite* of what he was

---

[15] All interviews with students were tape recorded. Students' verbal emphases are indicated in the text in italics.

saying. And, I mean, I *didn't* want to make a scene, so I didn't really, you know, say as much as I could have? I *didn't* want to totally contradict him, 'cause it would have made him feel uncomfortable. So I just kind of left it.

Moments later, however, Abby suggests that this self-censorship was not entirely voluntarily. Though she hesitantly adopts Steve's terminology, she nevertheless defends her own perspective and argues that he was unable to hear it:

> I thought about it a lot *during* and *afterwards* and, I *really* think that his point of view was *really, really* closed-minded! I mean, he thought about what I had to say, but he basically said it was totally wrong! . . . I was *trying to tell him* that from what *I've learned*, the situation between (pause) Palestinian non-Jews and the *Jews* was *very* oppressive, and one-sided, and it was really an awful situation! And he kind of *glorified* it in a way, and made it sound like it wasn't as violent as it really was!

While Abby eventually admits to having modified some of her own thinking in response to Steve, she seems frustrated that he has not done the same:

> I didn't really mean *millions* because there weren't that many Palestinian non-Jews in the country. . . . *He* was right, because I thought about it and it wasn't really *extermination*. But they *really* wanted them to move off that land! And it was *their* homeland in the first place! And I *meant* that by taking them out of their home, as the Nazis did with the Jews, they put them in something that was like a *camp* where they weren't allowed to have any *human* rights that most people take for granted. I agree with him that the methods weren't exactly extermination but I *don't* agree with him when he says it wasn't as bad as in the *first* steps [of the Holocaust].

In contrast, neither Josh nor Sandra expresses discomfort with classroom dynamics, but they instead express pleasure in Steve's having silenced those with whom they disagree. Sandra notes with satisfaction, "When Steve came in and told Abby, 'You're wrong!' well, it was kind of funny, because she got like, *really mad.*" Josh similarly notes, "Steve, he's great! He came in and he said this is total nonsense." Whispering "Don't tell her, but Abby talks a lot!" Josh takes pleasure in describing a contentious class in which his own beliefs reflect majority opinion while Abby's are seen as marginal. "I like when people make sure people know what's going on," he says later of Steve's also having put Chi-Ho in his place.

These excerpts suggest a confluence between my interpretation of classroom dynamics and students' experience of the course. Though students differed among themselves in their feelings about classroom dynamics, they shared my belief that both Marysa and Steve conveyed their own sense of "right" and "wrong" to the class and made sure, as Josh says, that "people know what's going on."

Tuesday, May 15

The day after Steve Cohen's visit, students return to the issue of contemporary political conflicts as originally intended by the curricular text. Walking toward the back of the class with a videotape in hand, Marysa begins: "We've talked about the thirties and the forties, and we've seen a movie about something happening in Canada in the eighties. Now we're going to look at our own home, the U.S. This documentary film is about the Ku Klux Klan teaching kids *your* age.[16] Imagine if you grew up in a town, an all-Black town, say, and you *adored* your teacher, and he told you all about all the horrible things Whites did — many of which I think are true. Would it be easy to believe it?" "It would be real easy," Jamal answers without hesitation, " 'cause he'd be my role model." "That's why indoctrination is so scary," Marysa continues, "and so important to understand. If you hear something again and again from someone you believe in, and you don't hear anything else, even though it may be one person's perspective, you'll probably believe it. . . . So in a way the diversity around you here, and the strengths from the differences of opinion you hear, and the strengths of the educational system you're in, encourage you to question and to learn different points of view. Try to think about that while you're watching this." Marysa pops the video cassette into the VCR, Angela hits the lights, and students settle down to watch TV.

"Klan Youth Corps" is a 1982 film about how the Ku Klux Klan recruits and trains American youth. Filled with riveting footage of actual night-time cross-burning ceremonies and stirring appeals made by the Klan's Imperial Wizard, the film documents 10- to 17-year-olds receiving instruction in racist ideology. The Imperial Wizard implores, "We will kill. We will stand in the streets. We will do what we have to to stop the niggers and the communists, won't we?" A counselor warns preteens at a Klan Youth summer camp that "many of the things you read in school are not the truth — they're just lies." And row upon row of cleanly scrubbed White boys and girls stand at attention and recite the Klan Youth Corps pledge in unison: "I pledge to practice racial separation in all my social contacts and to keep my forced contacts with other races on a strictly business basis. I pledge to oppose the false teaching that all races are equal or the same. I pledge that I will immediately go to the aid of any White person being attacked physically or verbally by a person of another race. I pledge that I will fight for the complete separation of all races in America and I will recruit others to do the same." The film is as direct as it is unnerving.

Marysa stops the tape and hits "rewind," while Angela turns on the lights. "Why don't people arrest the KKK?" Alison immediately asks. "They're protected by the First Amendment," Marysa replies. "Also, in a small town like that, people aren't going to stand up to it 'cause they'll probably believe it!" comments Alan. "They can pass out literature and wear their robes," Marlene adds, "but until they kill someone, or get caught killing someone, you can't do anything." Nora comments, "I understand that they're protected by the First Amendment, but I also think that they might abuse it. You never know how far they'll go."

Acknowledging that there's a big controversy about this, Marysa mentions the case in which members of the American Nazi Party won the right to march in Skokie, Illinois, after having been defended by the ACLU on the grounds of freedom of speech. The proud son of a prominent civil liberties attorney, Josh corrects Marysa matter-of-factly: "Freedom to assemble." Marysa continues, put-

---

[16] "Klan Youth Corps," distributed by the Anti-Defamation League of B'nai B'rith, New York, New York, and available through the Facing History and Ourselves Resource Library in Brookline, Massachusetts.

ting forth the traditional civil liberties argument, "If you stop *them*, who decides the next group that cannot speak?" Abby and Marysa debate this point:

Abby: I think society should be able to decide who should not speak.

Marysa: But "society" can fluctuate from time to time, group to group.

Abby: But the majority of society is not in support of oppression.

Marysa: What about people under Hitler?

Abby: If Hitler hadn't had the right to free speech, people wouldn't have believed him!

Marysa: Where do you draw the line? How do you decide who can and who can't speak? The First Amendment protects *everybody's* rights.

Abby: But millions of people don't agree with them!

Marysa: Let's say we wouldn't let socialists or communists speak.

Abby: But they're not oppressing other people!

Marysa: Capitalists feel they are.

Abby (laughing): Well, they're *wrong!*

Marysa: Abby, there's a bit of tunnel vision here that we have to speak about. You can't just say that the only ones who can speak are those who agree with your position!

As in the case of the two earlier classes described, this resource film and the discussion that followed raises the dilemma of how a democratic community that values free speech, diversity, and the open exchange of ideas can fairly address unpopular, controversial, or "wrong" points of view. Should those who voice these views simply be silenced, as Abby believes with regard to the KKK and to others who hold "oppressive" beliefs? And as Marysa — the individual holding the most power within the class — rejoins, who should define what constitutes "oppression" and be empowered to enact this silencing? As we have seen, answers to these questions are no simpler to find in the microcosm of the classroom than they are in Skokie, Illinois. Students' experiences of how issues raised by the film are handled in the classroom are contradictory. On one hand, they talk about valuing open-mindedness, a plurality of opinions, and the importance of free expression; on the other, at times they seek closure to controversies and rest easier in being told which opinions are "right."

For example, Sandra pays Steve a high compliment consistent with her valuation of "keeping an open mind": "You know, Steve doesn't just read one book and say, 'Well, this one book is right,'" she tells me during our interview. "He's the kind of person who reads lots of things, in depth." She criticizes Abby, in contrast, for failing to do the same: "Abby, she's not having an open mind! She's just so set about what she wants to believe."

But while Sandra values open-mindedness in theory, she herself finds it difficult to sustain. Overwhelmed by the diversity of opinions offered on the Middle East, she asks me to provide closure to this contentious debate, saying, "There's that issue about how the people were moved out. And Abby says some of the same things that were used in the Holocaust were used *there*, like murdering people, and some women were raped. And, then Steve said that they were *asked* to leave, and they left voluntarily. So I don't know which to believe! Because

Abby said she's read it in books, and that Steve just learned it in *conservative* books, and, see, I don't know! So who is more, who is *more right?*" Disquieted by my refusal to grant either position full legitimacy, she eventually consoles herself in the best pluralist tradition: "There could be Steve's point of view, and [Abby's] point of view, and then mix them together and there could be something that they could come to."

Josh's approach to the problem is negotiated differently. At first glance he seems desirous of silencing those with whom he disagrees. He argues for "killing" people who hold beliefs like those of Holocaust revisionist Jim Keegstra and he appears equally dismissive of Abby's point of view. A longtime friend of Chi-Ho's, however, he is torn between an impulse to shut his friend out altogether (as manifested in his desire to move his seat) and an impulse to engage him in struggle (as manifested in his ribbing of Chi-Ho in class). He ultimately supports the second position, though he clearly has difficulty doing so. Evoking the words of his much revered father, Josh says, "I've been taught that you do not start violence with people, and that the only way to prove yourself as a great person is to talk to people, to make them see that what they're saying is *so wrong.* This is what me and my father used to disagree on, but I'm beginning to believe him."

Abby seems to embody most dramatically the tensions between valuing open-mindedness and taking a clear moral stance. Reflecting the political priorities of her parents, she argues passionately in favor of social change and sees eliciting different points of view as essential to achieving it, saying, "I *really* believe that there needs to be some change in the world today! And I think a *really* important part of *change* is understanding what someone else is *thinking.* . . . If you just *come* out, *say* what you think, and give *no* regard to what the *other* person is thinking, then that will create anger. And *resentment.* And they won't really be open to change." Knowing that the points of view of her fellow classmates are important in this regard, Abby continues, "I'm usually one of the only ones who is really speaking up, and I *really* want to know what other people think about what I'm saying . . . so maybe I could either argue it out, and *really* try to tell them what my point of view was, or just hear what other people are thinking about. . . . Because if they don't *speak,* I'm totally, totally closed off from anything that they're thinking about."

But while Abby campaigns eloquently for lively debates in which multiple points of view are brought out into the open, she argues equally well against granting each view legitimacy. Far from falling into a relativist trap, she asserts, "I *do* believe that there is *always* a *right* thing! And a lot of people have the impression that it's just your *opinion.* And your point of view. And they don't really give a chance to have one be right. It's just always 'They should be able to say that because that's their *opinion.*' And I really, really *don't* agree with that!" Directly challenging the civil libertarian line promoted by Marysa in reference to the KKK, she charges, "I think that the *right* thing should always be promoted and the people who think *otherwise* should not be allowed to speak!"

* * *

Students' contradictory yearnings for both closure and openness may be irresolvably in tension. Teachers' efforts to foster tolerance for alternative perspectives may be similarly at odds with their efforts to promote moral thinking. The ambiguities, conflicts, and tensions that arose during these three classroom sessions demonstrate the enormous challenge of debating contemporary social and political issues in the classroom.

There are those who oppose interjecting contemporary issues into the classroom for precisely these reasons. Conservative activists like Phyllis Schlafly, for example, have in the past attacked the Facing History and Ourselves program precisely because it encourages adolescents to reflect critically on current social issues. Condemning the program in national public hearings in 1984, she charged that it (and other so-called "therapy education" initiatives) could "depress the child" by "forc[ing] [him] to confront adult problems which are too complex and unsuitable for his tender years."[17] By causing the child to be "emotionally and morally confused," they could, she felt, lead to the "high rates of teenage suicide, loneliness, premarital sex, and pregnancies" that plague contemporary society.[18]

The Department of Education's National Diffusion Network — an agency that reviews curricula and funds their dissemination — reflected Schlafly's concerns in 1986–1988 when it denied funds to the Facing History program. The Department's action sparked a Congressional hearing and heated debate among public-policy makers, educators, and other concerned citizens.[19]

But one need not look as far back as the mid-eighties to find opposition to classroom discourse on contemporary social and political debates. Only recently, the New York City Board of Education ousted Chancellor Joseph A. Fernandez, largely because of his support for initiatives that included AIDS education, condom distribution, and a curriculum that advocated tolerance for diverse social groups, including homosexuals. According to Carol Ann Gresser, the New York School Board's newly elected chair, parents were upset by Fernandez's promotion of a "social agenda" in the schools. "You can't bring into the classroom issues that haven't even been decided by the society," she said.[20]

I would argue exactly the opposite: one cannot possibly avoid bringing into the classroom issues over which society is still divided because students themselves are well aware of these issues and hungry to discuss them with their peers. The liveliness of the classroom sessions presented here testifies to students' investment in just such debates. While these students were at times discomfited by what transpired in class, they were also vitally invested, excited, and engaged in the struggle. Though Sandra begged for closure, she tolerated not getting it; though Josh demanded separation from Chi-Ho, he remained sitting next to his friend; though Marysa opposed Abby, she engaged with her in open debate; though Abby felt intimidated, she hung in and held her ground. In short, while tempers were high, feelings impassioned, and intellects fiercely engaged, the group never closed down or fell apart. Highly conscious of their differences and the fault lines that divide them on specific issues, the class remained a community throughout. Their ability to do so reflects the skill with which Marysa created an environment of relative trust and safety within the classroom, and Facing History's engendering of personal, critical reflection no doubt contributed to that effort. But the strengths and capacities that students bring with them into this or any other classroom — their hunger to sort out where they stand and their ripeness for engaging in just such debates — must also be taken into account.

Thus, though opponents may argue that the inevitable consequence of such classroom interactions is either political indoctrination or the promotion of moral relativism, I would contend that neither is a necessary outcome nor an accurate characterization. What does seem inevitable is ambiguity and conflict — on this point, at least, advocates and opponents both agree. But here, too, programs encouraging engagement with social, moral, and/or political issues may offer a possible passageway through trouble — not by denying conflict through positing an unproblematized, homogeneous ideal, but by helping students to take well-thought-out stands and to listen closely to each other. Hopefully, by doing so they will learn to tolerate more fully the conflicts they will inevitably encounter in the world beyond the classroom. At their best, what programs like Facing History and Ourselves may offer students is not a blueprint for creating a single ideal community, but practice in making webs between multiple ones. And that is essential to education in a democracy.

Elementary School Curricula and Urban Transformation

PAUL SKILTON SYLVESTER

In this article, third-grade teacher Paul Skilton Sylvester describes how he practiced critical pedagogy in his urban Philadelphia classroom. Conceptualizing education as a means for changing social structures rather than merely replicating them, Sylvester created a classroom economy, which his students called "Sweet Cakes Town," as part of a larger study of the neighborhoods surrounding the school. In Sweet Cakes Town, students and teacher studied and lived "real world" situations such as unemployment, nepotism, successful entrepreneurship, homelessness, injustice, and cooperation in their exploration of social transformation.

"I want to get off welfare; I've been on food stamps all of my life!" Derek said to no one in particular. It was payday. Every Friday, each of my third graders received a paycheck or welfare payment. After cashing their checks at the classroom branch of the Fidelity Bank, they could spend their money, open their businesses, or report to work.

This was Sweet Cakes Town, a name chosen by students for the child-sized, red-brick neighborhood they created out of cardboard boxes in our classroom. (None of the students could explain to me why they seized upon one boy's odd suggestion for this name.) In this town, the businesses, government, and union were owned and run by the students. The economy of Sweet Cakes Town was not make-believe; Sweet Cakes dollars were legal tender for real goods and real services. Using money they earned from classroom jobs, students participated in the economy according to their individual interests. They could buy and manage businesses, rent a chess board at the toy store, rent paints at the Art Supply Store, borrow a book from the Free Library, plant seeds at the Wonderful World of Plants Store, sell one of their own paintings at the Art Gallery, rent an outfit at the Value Plus Clothing Store, get their hair corn-rowed at Shawntay's Beauty Salon, or feed the rabbit at the Sweet Cakes Zoo.

Derek's dilemma of finding a way off welfare was real both inside and outside the classroom.[1] The students' Philadelphia neighborhood had suffered the trauma of de-industrialization during the 1970s and 1980s, and 93 percent of our students were on public assistance (most recent figures available at time of writing) (School District of Philadelphia, 1991, p. 239). As in most eastern cities, factory closings compounded the historical effects of racial discrimination, leaving many African Americans and Latinos economically isolated.[2]

---

[1] Students' names have been changed for confidentiality.

[2] Many of my assumptions about the causes of our urban situation come from the work of William Julius Wilson. Recently, he provided a concise summary of his landmark work: "I argue in *The Truly Disadvantaged* [Wilson, 1987] that historic discrimination and a migration flow to large metropolitan

Harvard Educational Review Vol. 64 No. 3 Fall 1994, 309–331

As an elementary school teacher attempting to engage my students in real social and economic issues, I needed clear illustrations of what critical pedagogy could look like in the mainstream, K-12 public school systems of this country. In reviewing the current literature on education for social reform, I found a great deal of information on the theory of critical pedagogy, including work in the fields of adult literacy, higher education, feminist pedagogy, international development, and education for employment. Unfortunately, most of this was written in an abstract fashion, with little explanation of how one could make it work in an actual classroom.

Educational anthropologist John Ogbu (1978, 1988) has shown how students' views about their chances in the economy affect their school performance. Ogbu has found that as some African American children grow older, they tend to engage in nonacademic activities and "become more aware of how some people in the community 'make it' without good school credentials or mainstream employment" (1988, p. 332). He has shown that such beliefs about success can lead to life strategies that undermine their school achievement. Similarly, in a study of twelve hundred Los Angeles high school students, Roslyn Arlin Mickelson found a significant relationship between the "economic returns" students anticipated from their education and how well they performed in school (1984, p. 112).

One could infer from Ogbu's findings that education cannot address the impoverishment in inner cities until changes have occurred in the economic opportunity structure. My own view, however, lies closer to that presented by Michael W. Apple and Lois Weis:

> If education can be no more than an epiphenomenon tied directly to the requirements of an economy, then little can be done within education itself. It is a totally determined institution. However, if schools (and people) are not passive mirrors of an economy, but instead are active agents in the processes of reproduction and contestation of dominant social relations, then understanding what they do and acting upon them becomes of no small moment. For if schools are part of a "contested terrain" . . . then the hard and continuous day-to-day struggle at the level of curriculum and teaching practice is part of these larger conflicts as well. The key is linking these day-to-day struggles within school to other action for a more progressive society in that wider arena. (Quoted in Erickson, 1987, p. 351)

In this article I describe one example of how education can address the inequality of a post-industrial society. I describe the evolution of a curriculum created with my students that involved the hands-on study of our neighborhood, as well as the creation of a child-sized model of the neighborhood in our classroom. I believe that the crucial element in the success of this curriculum was not in my personality as a teacher, but in the students' own creative power, which I tapped into by encouraging them to question, investigate, and interpret their

---

areas that kept the minority population relatively young created a problem of weak labor-force attachment within this population, making it particularly vulnerable to the ongoing industrial and geographic changes in the economy since 1970. The shift from goods-producing to service-producing industries, increasing polarization of the labor market into low-wage and high-wage sectors, innovations in technology, relocation of manufacturing industries out of the central city, periodic recessions, and wage stagnation exacerbated the chronic problems of weak labor-force attachment among the urban minority poor" (Wilson, 1990, p. 6).

experience of the world. As our classroom neighborhood evolved, it represented the opportunity for Derek and his classmates to imagine and actually live in, for a few hours a week, a future that defied the too-familiar statistics of their real-life chances.

In the second section of this article, I describe changes in the roles played by three students in the class. Finally, I discuss the implications of this curriculum for social transformation among the ghetto poor.[3] Overall, two questions guide this discussion: 1) How do we as teachers educate so that we do not replicate existing social inequalities? and 2) How do we avoid the twin pitfalls of a) stressing the obstacles to economic success, thereby encouraging defeatism, and b) stressing the possibilities for economic success and thereby encouraging the view that those who have not "made it" have only themselves to blame?

A CURRICULUM FOR URBAN TRANSFORMATION

Identifying the Problem and Becoming Part of the Solution

My interest in using education to address urban inequality began in the 1960s, as I was growing up in the suburbs of Detroit. I saw a city increasingly split between affluent suburbs where I saw only White people, and a run-down inner city where I saw mostly Black people. It was not until 1989, however, that I felt that I was making the least bit of progress in understanding what had been happening to Detroit. That year my parents gave me William Julius Wilson's *The Truly Disadvantaged* (1987) as a Christmas present, with the inscription " . . . that you may be part of the solution."

Wilson's *The Truly Disadvantaged* showed me our city through an economic lens in a time when much of the popular rhetoric blamed urban problems on the moral deficiencies of the poor (e.g., the need for "values"). Looking at the problem from Wilson's perspective, I wondered what role, if any, an urban elementary school teacher could play in helping to create the solution.

I had recently completed my teacher training at the Bank Street College of Education in New York City where, in the tradition of John Dewey and the Progressive education movement, curricula are developed around in-depth studies of various aspects of students' experiences. I began to think that if students were to overcome the obstacles presented by changes in the economy — or better yet, to play a role in breaking down these obstacles — they would first need practice imagining how they might do it. I began looking for a way to bring together students' experience of the economic conditions Wilson described with the integrated, experiential education I learned at Bank Street.

Around the same time, I was getting my feet wet as a teacher new to Philadelphia. In a curriculum guide issued by the school district, I found the suggestion to pay students classroom dollars for being "good classroom citizens" (School District of Philadelphia, 1989, pp. 34–39).[4] In this curriculum, students were to fill in a pay sheet, deciding whether they should receive pay for fulfilling the

[3] In response to Gans's (1990) suggestion that the term "underclass" is no longer useful due to the pejorative connations it has taken on through misapplication, Wilson (1990) has suggested the substitution of the term "ghetto poor."

[4] For other classroom uses of "micro-societies," see McCarthy and Braffman (1985), and Richmond (1989).

responsibilities of attendance, homework, getting along with others, and other classroom "jobs" (p. 36). The writers of the curriculum pointed out that this project could be extended in endless directions.

What I liked about this idea was that it seemed to provide the possibility of bringing economic experience into the classroom. The problem I had was that in the real world, one does not get paid for being a good citizen, but rather for doing one's job; those who are richest are not always the best citizens. With this in mind, I reframed the economic system so that children were paid for "the job of being a good student" rather than a good citizen; I structured the classroom economy to run parallel to an experiential economic study of the outside neighborhood; and I used students' questions and experience about both economies to chart the direction of our study.

The Evolution of the Classroom Economy

When the classroom economy first began, all student jobs were "government work" and I, the teacher, was the only boss. I began paying students for the job of being students, which included classroom jobs (e.g., distributing corrected work), academic performance, behavior, and a personal goal of their choosing (e.g., "I will get a job"). Students voiced no opposition to the power I reserved, which might be attributable to the reality that teachers are always the boss. A job chart at the front of the room listed government jobs, their rate of pay, and the name of the person currently holding each position. I later added a second chart listing "private sector" jobs. To apply for a job, students filled out an application. On the job application, students gave reasons why I should hire them and included their previous work experience and names of references. I returned these applications with written explanations for their acceptance or rejection. Students became familiar with the boss's criterion for a strong application. They learned, for example, that last year's teacher made a better reference than one of their friends, and that it was better to cite one's success at the last job than to state that one needs money. I once observed a boy start an application, then crumple it up to start over, saying, "I forgot, neatness counts!"

Students designed the money that we used. On the different denominations we had pictures of Rosa Parks, "Homey the Clown," Don King, and a student's mother. We printed the money on different colors of paper using our hand-cranked rexograph.

In our class, the students' schedule was highly structured, with the basic subjects being studied at the same time each day. In some progressive classrooms I have known, activities tend to be "decentralized," with two or three different groups engaged in different lessons at the same time. One group might be reading with the teacher, another working on dioramas, and still another testing each other on their spelling words. In contrast, my students seemed to do best when working as a class. Although students' ability levels varied greatly, there seemed to be a feeling of momentum when the entire class worked on an exercise, with the faster or more advanced students tutoring the others. Within this rather traditional routine, students had a great deal of input into the curriculum, great flexibility in the approaches they used to complete their work, and great responsibility when they earned it. Academic work and social behavior became the basis for the ebb and flow of the responsibilities and trust earned by students. When a child was responsible, I hired him or her for the most important work, such as collating homework packets. When the class as a whole earned my trust, we took more ambitious walking trips, such as to the local pond.

In the last ten minutes of every day, each child evaluated his or her "job of being a good student" by filling out a pay sheet. On the top half of the pay sheet was a grid for the student to fill in, with one column for each day of the week and a row for each aspect of the "job of being a student": their school work, behavior, and "government" job. Based on their self-evaluations, students wrote in how much they should be paid. I provided some parameters, such as that school work paid a maximum of twenty-five dollars per day. At the end of each column was a row for them to total each day's pay. On the bottom half of the sheet was a space for them to write their personal goal for the day. On Friday afternoons, I paid the students. They then had the chance to use their money to buy the use of activities. Yet, before they could spend their wages, they were required to pay rent for their desk and taxes needed for municipal salaries. Students who were unable to pay rent or taxes went on welfare.

Each month I asked the students, "How can we make the classroom more like the neighborhood?" Their responses directed our explorations. The first time I posed this question, students answered that we should start stores in the classroom. When William asked how much a store costs, I turned this question back to the class by asking them where we might go to find the answers. In the discussion that followed, we decided that we would take a walking trip to the soul-food restaurant named "Ziggie's Barbecue Pit," which was located on the same block as our school.[5]

The next day, with Ziggie forewarned of the invasion, we set out to learn about starting a business. Ziggie's was a dimly lit, homey establishment, with hundreds of snapshots decorating its walls. With students and parent chaperons sitting on the stools at the lunch counter and on the seats from Ziggie's long-deceased Chevy van, the press conference began. The regular customers listened with curious attention as Ziggie patiently answered the questions students posed to him. After a half-hour of talking with Ziggie, we returned to the classroom, and I asked the students what they had learned. From our conversation with Ziggie they recalled: *start small and save; buy wholesale for cheap and sell retail for less cheap;* and the motto of the patient entrepreneur, *little by little.* The students' over-sized thank you letter is still hanging on the inside of Ziggie's door.

After talking about the goods and services already available in our classroom, the students discussed what stores we should have in our classroom economy. For example, because we used educational games and puzzles in our classroom, the students decided that we needed a toy store. Once we knew what stores we needed, student builders painted red bricks on boxes large enough to be used as storefronts. Using a razor-blade knife, I cut "windows" out of the boxes so that the merchants could stand behind them and sell their wares through the open-

---

[5] In many schools, the spontaneity of going on field trips is curtailed by the time it takes to issue and receive signed permission slips. The Philadelphia school system helps teachers to avoid this problem by issuing permission slips that allow children to go on neighborhood walking trips throughout the year.

ing. Positioned around the perimeter of the room, these storefronts framed our carpeted area. Store names painted by students hung from the ceiling over each establishment. Two potted trees, donated by a company that rents large indoor plants to corporations, added to the realism of the "neighborhood."

In January, in my role as "the government," I auctioned off the Arts Supply Stores, Fidelity Bank, the toy store, Value Plus Clothing Store, an Art Gallery, and the Sweet Cakes Zoo. This "privatization" provided material for a lesson on the law of supply and demand. The students subsequently decided to add more businesses to Sweet Cakes Town. With each new proposal, we were propelled out of the classroom and into the neighborhood, visiting businesses and a factory, inviting visitors to be interviewed, collecting specimens from the neighborhood pond, and doing research at the public library.

After each trip, students drew in a few more neighborhood landmarks on a 5-foot-by-4-foot "working map" of the neighborhood that hung on our wall. Earlier in the year, students had made maps of our classroom, the school, and the area directly surrounding the school. Once we had some shared understanding of what the map of the neighborhood would look like, I laid out the larger street grid on our working map. Following each trip, two or three students would make additions to this map in pencil, then compare them to an aerial photograph of the neighborhood (purchased from the local regional planning commission) before making their additions permanent.

In January, when we first added stores to our economy, I created a form that asked students to subtract their rent and taxes from their earnings on their pay sheets in order to find their gross and net pay. From this point on, their paychecks included only the net figure. By gradually increasing the complexity of these forms, the students had meaningful applications of math problems at a level that was both challenging and attainable. I once overheard a boy say to himself after correctly filling out his pay sheet, "Ya, I'm all that."

Retail buying time on Friday afternoons was as exhilarating as anything I have experienced as a teacher. I watched in anxious amazement as students followed their own purposes, whether they were working at their store or spending their money. Without anything else to do, I might rent a hat at Value Plus, or go to the Men's Styling Shop, where Derek would spray water on my head, style my hair, and then slap the chair with a towel as I got up, as barbers often do. During this time, the zoo keepers even let Frances the rabbit wander about the classroom. The amazing thing to me was that usually retail buying time worked; that is, students went about their business and didn't require me to play the role of disciplinarian.

On those occasions when retail buying time did start to get wild, I followed the advice of a wise teacher trainer, Barbara Moore Williams, who once told me, "Don't lecture — let the kids tell you what the problem is. The kids know it all!" When it got too noisy, I would call things to a halt using the traditional hand in the air and a finger over my lips. The students would do the same, and pretty soon it would be quiet. Then I would ask, "Why did we have to stop?" One of the kids would explain, "Because Tyree was running." Then I would ask, "What's the matter with running?" Somebody would say, "It's too wild for the classroom." I would say, "What's going to happen if I see running again?" They would say, "We'll have to stop retail buying time." This generally worked for us.

After a few months of learning from people in the neighborhood, students wrote nominations for neighborhood citizenship awards (e.g., "My neighbor, Mr. Davis, watches over the children on the block to make sure they are safe. He is like a guardian angel."). We invited those people, as well as all those whom we had interviewed in our study, to come to the classroom to receive awards for their contributions.

Along with studying their neighborhood, the mandated curriculum called for third graders to study the city of Philadelphia, the state of Pennsylvania, the United States, and the world. We began to study the city after about four months of studying our neighborhood, and later, we studied the state. Our point of departure for both of these projects were first-hand investigations of other neighborhoods. We visited the outdoor Italian market as an example of the diversity of Philadelphia, and the community of Landsdale as an introduction to rural Pennsylvania. In both of these studies, we established correspondence between our class and third-grade classrooms in the other neighborhoods. Throughout these units, the Sweet Cakes Town economy continued to develop within our classroom.

Economics and the Classroom Neighborhood

I structured the Sweet Cakes Town economy to mirror some of the changes that had occurred in the economy of the students' neighborhood in North Philadelphia.[6] For example:

- I listed high-paying jobs, such as gerbil cage-cleaning, but then explained to the kids that this job had moved to a classroom in the suburbs. We talked about how many of the jobs that used to be in the cities are now outside the cities and the strategies that adults use for overcoming this problem.
- I hired fourth-grade students who would work for nothing just so that they could get out of their class. These were our immigrant workers. My students responded to this by encouraging them not to work unless they were paid.
- I sent one student a letter via Sweet Cakes mail relating the bad news that a great aunt had died. Enclosed was the inheritance check, which gave us the opportunity to discuss the fact that some people start off with more capital than others. Students reacted to this with quiet resignation.
- Students also dealt with recessions, layoffs, wage inequities, and alliances of capital.

Each of these obstacles was taken as a challenge to be overcome, rather than a defeat to be endured. After we read a biography of Cesar Chavez, student workers created their own union, which they named JBS Local 207 (standing for John Barnes School, room 207). It took a while for them to coordinate collective action. At first when I lowered their wages, one of them said, "I'm on strike," to which I replied, "OK, who wants her job?" At this point, many of the students raised their hands, and the striker backed down. Trying to make this as realistic as possible, I lowered their wages again and again. Eventually they realized that

---

[6] Philadelphia, like most Eastern, industrial cities, had been decimated by the loss of manufacturing jobs in the last two-and-a-half decades. In the period between 1975 and 1979 alone, the city lost 128,000 jobs, or one out of six (Katz, 1986, p. 276).

their individual good was dependent on each other, and except for two die-hard scabs, the workers waged a strike. The union leaders and I reached a bargain over lunch, and later the bargain was ratified by the rank and file.

Our classroom neighborhood study gave us an economic frame of reference for discussing a variety of real-life situations. For example, a work period was interrupted by two students yelling back and forth, "Your mother's homeless!" "No, your mother's homeless!" I intervened, and said that I was angry about their interruption and felt that we needed to discuss it as a class. We agreed that there were two issues at hand: one was that the two students were angrily arguing about something; the other was that homelessness was being used as an insult. I decided that the two students and I would discuss their dispute privately, but that the issue concerning homelessness would be addressed as a class.

I began this discussion by asking the students what kept people from being able to pay their rents. Jameel said, "They won't go out and get a job." We compared this explanation to what we experienced in our classroom economy, namely, the effects of intervening factors such as lay-offs, businesses relocating to the suburbs, jobs not paying enough, and people not having enough money to start a business. I emphasized that if a person is homeless, it is not something of which the person should be ashamed, but something of which our country should be ashamed. Individual students volunteered examples of honest and hardworking people they knew who were homeless. Only later did I learn that one of the students present for this conversation had recently moved to a homeless shelter with her family. I marveled at this, because even with such turmoil in her home life, she was excelling as a student, consistently making the honor roll.

It seems to me that impromptu discussions of economic issues complemented more structured discussions of inequality. For example, during the year, I used Margaret Davidson's (1986) biography of Martin Luther King, Jr., as one of our reading texts. In previous years, my students had always responded to King's fight against prejudice, but seemed to have trouble connecting their own lives with King's call for economic justice. This year, however, perhaps because of our classroom economy, students had an experiential vocabulary for talking about the economic factors behind inequality.

We also looked at language differences in an economic context. Knowing of the stigmatization of non-Standard English (NSE) in our society, I wanted to raise my students' awareness of the role that language differences play in social relations, but to do so in a way that did not demean the language style used in their homes. Assimilation was never the goal. Instead, I wanted them to see that one possible use of learning Standard English (SE) was *infiltration:* crossing over into a world where non-Standard English is not valued and using Standard English to achieve their own goals, while understanding that to do so need not mean giving up their identity as African Americans or their loyalty to their home communities.

I therefore initiated discussions of the relative effectiveness of SE and NSE in different contexts. Students identified quotes from poetry we had studied and speeches by African American leaders as "SE" or "NSE." Then we labeled quotes by students in the class in the same way. Finally, students identified a list of various situations with the type of English that would be most appropriately used there (e.g., speaking at home, writing a rap, asking for something from the principal, or applying for a job at a bank). I encouraged students to see language differences as options that could be invoked to suit their purposes in a given context, rather than as a once-and-for-all choice (Erickson 1987).

On a number of occasions, I saw informal evidence that these exercises might be raising students' awareness of their uses of language. For example, one afternoon as we were working on a science project, a boy with writing disabilities was dictating to me his observations about a snail that we had brought back from the neighborhood pond. The student said, "He ain't movin." As I started to write, he hurried to say, "He is not moving." I asked the boy if he was changing to Standard English and he looked at me perplexed. This suggested to me that while such labels as "Standard English" may have eluded him, this student had gained some practical awareness that he was able to switch codes and that he had knowledge of their appropriate contexts.

Democracy and the Classroom Neighborhood

As John Locke would have wanted it, the government of Sweet Cakes Town evolved naturally as problems arose between individuals. It seems that Lateef, the owner of the Value Plus Store, had been hiring new clerks each week rather than paying the old ones. Just when mob action seemed imminent, I separated the parties and suggested that we start a court. A judge was elected, jurors and lawyers picked, and for the time being, playground justice was held off. Before the trial, which was held a few days later, I invited an African American lawyer to coach both the prosecution and the defense. Witnesses were sworn in on a coloring-book Bible found in a student's desk. In lieu of the black robe, the judge wore a black velvet evening gown on loan from Value Plus. At one point during the defendant's testimony, Judge Jameson blurted out, "Oh, he is *so* guilty!" giving us a chance to explore the notion of "innocent until proven guilty." In the end, Lateef was convicted and forced to pay all back wages.

Occasionally an offense was committed without the perpetrator ever being discovered. On a day when I was absent and the students had a substitute teacher, someone scrawled graffiti across the red-brick front of our toy store. At the beginning of the following day, I asked the students to answer the following questions: "What feelings are people showing when they hurt the classroom neighborhood? Who does it hurt? Does it solve the problem? What are other possible solutions?" In this way, I tried to get students to see that destructive behavior, like doing graffiti, is sometimes an expression of misplaced feelings like anger, which could be better used to solve the problem. The effective uses of anger came up again in our discussion of the L.A. riots that followed the Rodney King verdict. "Solve the problem!" became our class mantra.

Another day, we had problems with loitering students starting trouble during retail buying time. I overheard one girl explain, "I don't want to shop. I'm savin' my money for a business." Some students decided that we needed a "no loitering" law and called for the election of a government. I suggested to the students that they conduct a poll regarding which citizens should be allowed to vote. The boys said that girls should not vote, and the girls said that the boys should not vote. I used these experiences to provide a meaningful context for discussing the women's suffrage movement and the history of African Americans' struggle for voting rights in the United States.

As a result of these history lessons, the class decided on universal suffrage. With signs hanging from the ceiling, they designated each group of desks as a different city council district. They elected a city council representative from each table group and a mayor for the whole town. I asked each student to submit ten laws to their city council person. Student suggestions included "No more pay increases for city council" and "No air pollution."

Once when I asked how we could make the classroom more like the neighborhood, students suggested that we add roads and garbage collectors. "Who's going to pay for all this?" asked one realist. I turned this dilemma back to them and asked, "Who pays for these services in the outside neighborhood?" We discussed this, as well as the local controversy over the privatization of municipal services.

To learn more about how tax money was used, two student delegates and I telephoned Philadelphia's City Hall. Afterwards we received a pie chart of the city's expenditures in the mail, which I simplified for use with the children. This provided the basis for a discussion of students' views on spending priorities for city governments. Students created their own pie charts showing how they thought Sweet Cakes dollars should be used, and these suggestions were given to the mayor of Sweet Cakes Town. In our discussions about public and private services, students offered a variety of opinions about which services should be paid for with tax money and which should be handled privately. Eventually, the government paid for roads made out of black contact paper marked with yellow lane dividers, and instituted trash collection.

The mayor of Sweet Cakes Town was popular for nearly a month, until students realized he had hired only close friends to fill virtually all the government jobs, with some friends holding four jobs. We talked about how this happens in real life and discussed what options voters have when they feel their elected officials are not acting on their behalf. The mayor was roundly defeated in his bid for a second term.

By the time students decided that the town needed a mayor, they were already in the habit of going to the source for their information. Philadelphia's Mayor Rendell graciously accepted the children's invitation and came to Sweet Cakes Town to be interviewed about his job. During his visit, students gave him a large bar graph showing the results of the poll they had conducted to survey their parents' attitudes toward the mayor (at that point, the mayor was enjoying an 80 percent approval rating). As a final gesture of thanks, the mayor of Sweet Cakes Town gave Mayor Rendell the papier-mache "key" to our city.

The final project the citizens of Sweet Cakes Town undertook was a community works project: the students agreed to address the problem of small grocers in the neighborhood selling "crack." By writing a newspaper about Sweet Cakes Town and selling it on the street, they raised money for DARE, an anti-drug group. This project had to be squeezed into a single week, as the end of the school year was closing in on us. Our last day of school was a triumphant one. We returned to the streets of our neighborhood to sell the *Sweet Cakes News*, telling stories from students' study of the neighborhood. The response from the community was tremendous: in about two hours we sold 250 copies of *Sweet Cakes News* at 25 cents apiece. The students also gave copies to the merchants who had helped them during the year.

At the end of the year I asked students to carry the storefronts of Sweet Cakes Town to the trash. They asked to keep them, explaining to me that, if I didn't object, they would like to use them to start concession stands in the neighborhood. I didn't object.

Student Experience and the Standardized Curriculum

A series of questions guided the Sweet Cakes Town curriculum. Each day, when students filed into the classroom, an "opening exercise" sheet awaited them on their desks. The opening exercise typically included a few problems reviewing yesterday's math lesson and a single question concerning the neighborhood study, such as, "What are some things that money cannot buy?" which did not have a single "right" answer. These questions formed the basis of our morning discussions. Sometimes they served an instrumental purpose ("What special rules will we need for our trip to the pond?"); other times, they prepared us for the arrival of a visitor from the neighborhood ("Write one question that you have about the job of a dress designer."). By linking the questions from one day to the next, we developed themes while keeping students' experience and opinions at the heart of our study. For example,

> *Monday:* In the Sweet Cakes Town system of jobs, what leaves you feeling bad, sad, or angry?
>
> *Tuesday:* In the outside neighborhood system of jobs, what leaves people feeling bad, sad, or angry?
>
> *Wednesday:* In the outside neighborhood, what are some *bad* things some people do if they are having a hard time making money?
>
> *Thursday:* In the outside neighborhood, what are some *good* things some people do if they are having a hard time making money?

After ten minutes devoted to this opening exercise, students had an opportunity to volunteer their answers, which I recorded on chart paper, and a discussion usually ensued. With this format, I found that students would listen to each other more patiently and give thoughtful responses based on their considerable life experience. I tried to let students' questions and interests guide our study as much as possible, but this was negotiated in the context of the requirements that I faced and my own beliefs about what should be taught. My principal gave me great support and flexibility, but also insisted that the objectives of the curriculum be met, and that students be prepared for the standardized tests. Unfortunately, a new standardized test was implemented during the study of Sweet Cakes Town, making comparison of students' scores to previous years problematic.

To keep track of what mandated objectives we had met, I kept a list of them in my planbook and marked each one as we studied it (Donnan, 1988, p. 3).[7]

---

[7] See Elliot Wigginton (1989) for another framework for bringing together students' interests and mandated curricula.

Topics from social studies, such as "interdependence in the community," arose relatively naturally. But when other required topics did not come up, I looked for opportunities to raise them during the course of our investigation. For example, students were not clamoring to learn about commas, so with Raquel's permission, we began a writing class with the question, "Where are commas needed in Raquel's thank you letter to the people at the clothing store?"

Overall, I found that some of the most difficult issues of our study came from the students' own experiences in the community. The proper response to violence was an issue that confounded my easy answers. After discussing problems of urban violence, Black-on-Black violence, and the uses of political nonviolence, and after doing countless role plays of conflict resolution, I would be reminded again of how complicated my students' lives were. In a bit of writing that makes me laugh even while it saddens me, Macio wrote:

> Being violent is bad to people. They steal from people. It is too bad that people are stealing from my mom. Me and my brother is going to kick some butts.

When I first began teaching in cities, I taught the gospel of nonviolence with less humility than I do today. Since then, I think that I have gained some understanding of my students' anger (and my own). I have a greater appreciation for how painfully difficult it can be to overcome anger and find solutions.

STUDENTS AND CITIZENS

Our class had, on average, twenty-four students, which was typical for third-grade classes in our school but down from thirty-four children the previous year. (This reduction was due to a vote by teachers in our school to use discretionary federal funds to reduce class size.) During the year, six students transferred in and eight transferred out. Of the entire class, one boy was Latino, and all others were African American. While Sweet Cakes Town evolved, not only was there turnover in student population, but students' roles within the town changed. Most students switched professions every month or two. Workers quit or were fired. Partnerships came and went as easily as third-grade friendships. Everyone held a job for some period, and no one held only one job. I will now describe three children who seemed to benefit socially and academically from their experiences in Sweet Cakes Town. While some students showed less personal and academic growth during the year, the experiences of these three students were not atypical among the group.

Derek

Derek, the boy quoted earlier who wanted to get off welfare, was handsome, funny, keenly observant of social interactions — a gifted mimic. At the beginning of the year, Derek requested to sit alone; he told me outright that he did not get along with other children. He was vehemently protective of his work being seen by the other students, but had a habit of yelling out humorous commentary to those very peers he held at a distance. A burly eleven-year-old, he could read at a kindergarten level. Despite this, or because of this, he refused to see a reading tutor. In the early stages of our classroom neighborhood, Derek created the character of "Kool Homie." Homie had a haircut known as a high-top fade, a big gold chain around his neck, sometimes a hat, and the local expressive walk. Week after week, Derek would pay for the clothes to dress up as Kool Homie, and act out stick-ups and muggings.

It was during this time that I heard Derek pronounce that he wanted to get off welfare, and that he had been on it all his life. Since Sweet Cakes Town did not have food stamps, I believe Derek was expressing the connection he saw between his life outside of school and his role in Sweet Cakes Town. In an effort to get off welfare, Derek applied for the job requiring the highest skill and receiving the highest wage: the filer of corrected work. The job paid forty Sweet Cakes dollars per day. Because he lacked experience, he did not get the job. Later that day another boy told Derek to apply for another job paying only $10.00 per day. Derek replied, "Who wants some $10.00 job! I don't want to get off welfare. . . . I applied to be a filer. That shows I want a job. Now I'm stayin' on welfare for the rest of my life. . . ."

I discussed with Derek the fact that he had not gotten the higher paying job for which he had applied because he lacked experience. We discussed strategies that people use to overcome this problem in the outside world, and Derek decided to volunteer as a work distributor for a week before applying to be a filer once again. Though he didn't get the filing job, he succeeded in being hired to water the plants (a job that paid a moderate wage).

With the money that Derek saved from his job, he was able to start the classroom branch of the Fidelity Bank. Making the most of our trip to a neighborhood bank, occasional lunch meetings with me, and hypothetical banking problems in math class, Derek proved greatly successful as a banker. He offered checking and savings accounts, as well as high-interest loans. As his business increased, he took on two partners. At the same time, he showed marked increases in social and academic confidence. However, though he regularly completed his math work, being older and bigger than the other children and barely able to read, he rarely attempted any language arts work in the classroom for fear of losing face.

One day in April, the kids told me that Derek had sold the bank. Because of the success he had had with the bank, I wondered why. When I talked with Derek, he would give me no explanation. A former teller, however, confided to me that Derek had sold the bank because people were bouncing checks: Derek thought this meant that he was in trouble. With the money from the sale of the bank, Derek bought the Value Plus Clothing Store and ran it successfully until the end of the school year.

Later in the year, I recommended that Derek be evaluated by our school's instructional support team (IST), a cross-disciplinary team charged with finding remedies when the school was failing to meet a child's needs. Derek was said to have a normal IQ, but also deficits in information processing, perceptual organization skills, and fine visual-motor perception and integration. As part of the IST effort to find support for students with learning problems within regular education classes, Derek was given intensive tutoring, which — this time — he accepted. When this tutoring failed to help him, the members of the IST, of which I was a part, recommended that Derek be switched to a special education class the following year.

Shawntay

Shawntay was a quiet, amiable girl. She did not cause trouble or draw attention to herself, but often did not finish her work. I found that as a teacher, I needed to keep deliberate track of her progress. Shawntay had good social skills, but remained peripheral to the social network. Moreover, I worried that her academic progress was hindered by low self-esteem. Like Derek, she too had been "held back" in first and second grades and now, in third grade, she was developing as an adolescent. In the early part of the year, the school psychologist found that Shawntay was dyslexic, but it was decided that she should remain in our classroom, where she seemed to be making progress.

Shawntay was the student who bought the bank from Derek. After the purchase, she found herself having great responsibility, but lacking a good understanding of how to run a bank. When people came to her asking for "their money," she neglected to keep track of how much she was giving out. When we realized the problem, she arranged to pay Derek to take time out from his new business to train her in banking (our first highly paid consultant). Although Shawntay learned to run the bank, she never really seemed to take a liking to it. She sold the business after a few months.

With the money she made from selling the bank, Shawntay opened a beauty parlor in May. Here she thrived. Shawntay's Beauty Parlor offered hair braiding, manicures, and make-up consultation. She did a brisk business, and soon her idea for a beauty parlor was copied by Tyree, who began a styling salon for "men." Shawntay's business career proved to be a springboard for political life; now, as an esteemed leader among the girls, she was elected to a seat on the city council. In the process, she showed marked improvement in her math skills, going from B's to A's.

William

William was a thoughtful, quiet boy who was well-liked by his classmates. In reading and math he performed on grade level. He had gotten an A in reading for the previous year, even while getting an F in behavior. My journal notes from the beginning of the year describe William as "sullen" and "sulky." Sometimes, William would become emotionally removed and perform a "go-slow" for an afternoon. William occasionally gave me a glimpse of the experiences he was having outside of school that might be draining his vigor. In response to a homework assignment asking students to write a true story about their neighborhood, William wrote the shortest of stories, but one that told volumes:

> One day on a weekend my best friend's dad got shot. I didn't know that he would get killed because he was good to people.

Despite such troubles, William came alive when we started the classroom economy. He was the first to apply for a job and the first to hold more than one government job at a time (at one point he held four). During this time William saved his money, keeping it in a big "knot" in his front pocket. It was he who inquired how much a business cost and, not suprisingly, he was the first to buy a store of his own.

Over the course of the year, William demonstrated a great entrepreneurial spirit. William's first store was the toy store, for which he hired his long-time friend Tyree as manager. With their profits, the two bought the Art Supply Store and hired Ray as a manager. William was the town's first mayor (it was his fall from power that I mentioned earlier). William's first appointment was again his friend Tyree. On Fridays, William and Tyree stayed in the classroom during recess to calculate revenues and expenditures for that fiscal week. Eventually, William and Tyree completed them on their own. One day when they requested to use silent reading time to finish their calculations, I heard William say to his buddies, "Don't bug me — I'm busy!" As he left that day I told him that he had done a good job on the budget. He grinned from ear to ear as he walked out through the gate of the schoolyard.

After William was defeated in his bid for re-election, he returned to running his businesses with Tyree. In the springtime, they started a plant store where students could plant seeds and then pick up their plants a week or so later.

LEARNING FROM SWEET CAKES TOWN

In this section, I return to the first of the questions with which I began this article: How can we teach children so that we do not simply replicate the existing social inequalities? Following are the seven primary insights I gained from my experiences with my students in our development of Sweet Cakes Town.

— Creating opportunities for repeated, meaningful applications of academic skills
As has long been recognized by educational advocates among the poor, "self-efficacy" is a hollow term when one lacks the skills necessary to accomplish one's goals (Freire, 1993, p. 59; Lukas, 1986, p. 36). But, too often, "skills" and "knowledge" have been dichotomized, as if the two needed to be taught separately, as if the meaningfulness of a task could not increase the process of skill acquisition. Besides running counter to empirical research (Sticht, 1987), this dichotomization contradicts the common experience many of us have of learning deeply and quickly something that we care about.

Sweet Cakes Town involved students in what I call "meaningful drill." For example, at the end of each day, students computed their daily pay using multiplication and addition with carrying. At the end of each week, they also calculated their weekly pay, using addition with carrying and subtraction with borrowing. This was not math taught as practice for some task that the students might face in future years, but real math applied to make things happen in their present lives. Traditionally, most of what are called "applications" of math skills, such as story problems, ask students to pretend that they are using skills in a real situation. Unfortunately, it is all too possible for a student to go from kindergarten through twelfth grade and never use math for a real purpose. In Sweet Cakes Town, the calculations were as real as the privileges that the students could buy with their money. Similarly, I believe students' involvement in issues that mattered to them dramatically enhanced their acquisition of hard skills in reading, writing, science, and geography. It seemed that students learned skills faster in Sweet Cakes Town because they needed them, and they routinized their new skills by using them every day.

— Providing opportunities for students to imagine themselves in new roles

For years, sociologists have told us that schools prepare lower socioeconomic status (SES) students to become lower SES adults, and upper SES students to become upper SES adults. Though this problem is partly a sin of omission, there are other dimensions to it that I will address later. Schools have failed to broaden their students' range of possibilities, leaving students to choose from the limited options that they see around them.

Options that Derek saw were playing "Kool Homie," standing on the street corner, or being a thief. Though Derek was not satisfied being on welfare, other options did not seem accessible to him. There were obstacles in his way, such as his lack of experience, the lack of role models to teach him how one gets experience, and, not least of which, a school system that had failed to find successful ways to teach him. I believe he needed to develop a strategy and to know that others (such as the lawyer who visited our classroom) have succeeded in overcoming the obstacles that face African Americans from the inner city.

By allowing students to imagine themselves in new roles, Sweet Cakes Town was, I like to think, a dream that we as a class dreamed together. The power of dreams to transform a life is explained by Ernst Bloch:

> Dreams come in the day as well as at night. And both kinds of dreaming are motivated by wishes they seek to fulfill. But daydreams differ from night dreams; for the day dreaming "I" persists throughout, consciously, privately, envisaging the circumstances and images of the desired, better life. The content of the daydream is not, like that of the night dream, a journey back into repressed experiences and their associations. It is concerned with an, as far as possible, unrestricted journey forward, so that instead of reconstituting that which is no longer conscious, the images of that which is not yet can be phantasied into life and into the world. (quoted in Simon & Dippo, 1987, p. 102)

Derek, Shawntay, William, and most other children in the class proved eminently successful at daydreaming new futures — as a banker, the owner of a hair styling salon, or an entrepreneur.

— Helping students to divorce academic success from "acting White"

As has been observed by Fordham and Ogbu (1986), success in school is often perceived by African American children as "acting White," which makes having a positive racial identity and succeeding in school seem mutually exclusive. Erickson (1987) has pointed out that this perception can be exacerbated or ameliorated depending on the behaviors of teachers and school personnel. He cites a comparative study of two classrooms: in one, the teacher frequently corrected the students for using "Black English"; in the other, the teacher did not correct students' language (Erickson, 1987, p. 346, citing Piestrup). At the end of the year, students who had frequently been corrected were speaking a *more* pronounced dialect in the classroom. Students who were *not* corrected were using language that was closer to "Standard English."

Erickson explains this data using contrasting metaphors of a "boundary" and a "border" (used first by Barth, 1969). In the classroom where Black English was stigmatized, a boundary was created between the world of the student and the world of the teacher. With each correction, the students' *defense* of their own cultural style grew, raising the wall a bit higher. The ultimate impact of this boundary was a sacrifice of the mutual trust that is needed for a student to risk attempting new academic tasks. In contrast, in the classroom where Black English was not stigmatized, this boundary became a border that the students could cross in both directions without threat of giving up an aspect of their cultural identity (Erickson, 1987, p. 350).

Whereas Fordham and Ogbu (1986) have shown the effects of a closed labor market on African Americans' attitudes about education, Erickson's (1987) analysis shows how the actions of people in schools can affect these attitudes. In our classroom, one way we incorporated the observations of Fordham and Ogbu and Erickson into the neighborhood study was in the treatment of language difference. I presented both Black English and Standard English as options that were appropriate and useful in certain contexts (Ladson-Billings, 1992). More generally, I attempted to show that academic skills are tools in the ongoing struggle for equality (Freire, 1993; Ladson-Billings, 1990). As educators, we need to find new ways to show students that achieving academic success can be "acting Black."

— Allowing students to take pro-active stances in relation to those in power

In Sweet Cakes Town, the students not only had the chance to imagine themselves as grown-ups in roles of power, they also had power right then and there to influence the classroom study, each other, and me as their teacher. In the drama of the classroom economy, they experimented with strategies for using power: as workers who sue a corrupt boss, as exploited union members, who strike for a fair wage, or as constituents who rally for a new mayor. In other words, as modern-day Davids, they found that the Goliaths of their day were within their range.

But beyond these chosen roles, Sweet Cakes Town also gave students a chance to experience new relationships between themselves and the authority figure with whose power they are most familiar: their teacher. Writers discussing such diverse topics as social reproduction, critical pedagogy, the hidden curriculum, process consultation, and education for empowerment have observed that having a passive role in educational institutions prepares students for taking a passive role vis-à-vis authority figures later in life: that is, a role as object rather than subject (Bowles & Gintis, 1976, p. 56; Freire, 1982, p. 59; Giroux, 1977, 1978, pp. 148–151; Schein, 1988, p. 9; Sleeter, 1991, p. 15). In contrast, problem-posing education replaces this vertical relationship between teachers and students with a horizontal one, a dialogue (Freire, 1982). In the case of Sweet Cakes Town, students were part of the process of guiding the course of study.

In our classroom, as students created a model of the neighborhood, they were *encoding* aspects of their culture (Freire, 1986). Derek's character Kool Homie was a code packed with elements of the situation faced by some African American men. Derek had an understanding of how one might portray himself as an African American male in a closed economy. I shared with Derek my belief that he could make it in the mainstream economy. In our daily discussion of Kool Homie, jobs, and strategies for getting jobs, the two of us came to a new understanding of his relationship to street corner life, as well as to how he could envision a different relationship.

Problem-posing education provides an opportunity to prepare the next generation for relationships qualitatively different than those we know between authorities and subordinates, such as bosses and workers or government leaders and constituents. Such changes are well-suited to current innovations in management practices, as U.S. corporations begin to realize the loss inherent in treating human beings like machines and move to less hierarchical, more team-oriented approaches to management (Byrne, 1993; Stewart, 1992, 1993).

For my students to play a role in changing their relationships to authority figures, they had to learn how to get, keep, and use power to participate in defining these relationships. The need for such practice will be developed below in my next-to-last recommendation.

— *Creating curricula that treats reality as something to be questioned and analyzed (Giroux, 1979)*

When teachers change their students' role in acquiring knowledge, I believe they also change the nature of the students' relationship to that knowledge. In more traditional forms of education, knowledge is deposited into the minds of uncritical students (Freire, 1982). Henry Giroux has pointed out that in such "banking" pedagogy, knowledge is treated as a set of objective "facts" (Giroux, 1979). He says that

> knowledge is divorced from human meaning and inter subjective exchange. It no longer is seen as something to be questioned, analyzed and negotiated. Instead, it becomes something to be managed and mastered. In this case, knowledge is removed from the self-formative process of generating one's own set of meanings, a process that involves an interpretive relationship between knower and known. (Giroux, 1979, p. 250)

Such "banking" instruction has been contrasted with a "mining" pedagogy, where teachers view their task as drawing knowledge *out* of the student, rather than depositing it within (Ladson-Billings, 1990, p. 340). Ira Shor (1980) says that when students are allowed to bring their experience into the classroom, teachers are able to help students see the familiar and accept it in a new light: "By identifying, abstracting and problematizing the most important themes of student experience, the teacher detaches students from their reality and then re-presents the material for systematic scrutiny" (1980, p. 100).

For example, when two students taunted each other, saying, "Your mother's homeless," I believed that the students had internalized the popular ideology of blaming the victim. Consequently, I related that example to their experience in Sweet Cakes Town, showing that factors outside of an individual's control sometimes interfere with a person's ability to pay the rent.

Similarly, as students in Sweet Cakes Town studied their environment, they created their own understanding of how their community works and where its hope lies. The structures of knowledge that they created were not isolated, abstract, and theoretical, but interrelated, concrete, and practical. To borrow terms from Lev Vygotsky (1978), the informal knowledge of their experience was organically connected to the formal knowledge of school learning. Or, from Pierre Bourdieu's (1977) perspective, the students used the "cultural capital" *from* their community to create "dividends" to *take back* to their community.

— Creating opportunities for students to develop strategies and hope for overcoming barriers to economic success in the mainstream

So far in this discussion, I have talked about aspects of my curriculum aimed at changing conditions internal to the students: their perceptions about their role in the world, their perceived relations both to those in power and to knowledge itself. But urban, African American children of lower socioeconomic status also face obstacles to success that are external to them, obstacles that they will need to understand if they are to stand a chance (Sleeter & Grant, 1986). First, there are those obstacles Black people have always faced in the United States: prejudice, residential ghettoization, poor education, lack of capital, and lack of networks to obtain capital, to name a few. Secondly, postindustrial changes in the economy have constructed new obstacles to economic success for those isolated in the inner cities: lack of jobs, jobs moving further out of the city where there is no public transportation, lack of access to job information networks, jobs that require higher skills, or, I would add here, that require them to speak differently than they do at home.[8] In the face of these obstacles to economic success, there are new self-destructive alternatives, such as crack cocaine, which also threaten to pull them down. As teachers, we want to say to our students, "If you try, you will make it," but we know that it's not that simple, and to say it is that simple is to imply falsely that those who did not make it did not try.

This brings me to the second of the two questions with which I began: *How do we avoid the twin pitfalls of a) stressing the obstacles to economic success, thereby encouraging defeatism, and b) stressing the possibilities for economic success, thereby encouraging the view that those who did not make it have only themselves to blame?* Some might argue that it is better to teach the bootstraps "myth," believing that a false hope is better than none. This, of course, would ultimately leave students unprepared for the obstacles ahead. Our students face the stark realities of the inner cities every day. As teachers we must face our responsibility to abandon the innocuous social studies curricula that do not take into account the abandoned buildings and crack vials that students pass on any walking trip to the fire station. We must help our students cope with their present problems, and prepare them to overcome future obstacles. I believe that children who are economically isolated in U.S. inner cities need to be educated about the structural obstacles to their success, while also being taught that with strategic planning and collective effort these obstacles are surmountable.

---

[8] The split between low-wage (goods producing) and high-wage (service producing) sectors of the economy was not addressed in the curriculum, but would be wisely included in future neighborhood studies.

— Offering opportunities for students to experience social structures as impermanent and changeable for the sake of those people who live within them (Freire, 1993)

In the students' creation of Sweet Cakes Town, they had the opportunity to question why certain conditions exist, and to try out new approaches in such areas as legislation, taxation, social services, and labor/management relations. Here the importance of the imagination in social change becomes clear. I would like to explain this connection with a passage written by Northrop Frye (1964) about the literary imagination. What Frye says about the literary imagination I find equally applicable to the social imagination exhibited by my students in the creation of Sweet Cakes Town. While he wrote this in 1964, referring to the imagination of Canadians, I have taken the liberty of inserting the United States of our time:

> Just as [the material world] looks real, so this ideal world that our imaginations develop inside us looks like a dream that came out of nowhere, and has no reality except that we put into it. But it isn't. It's the real world, the real form of human society hidden behind the one we see. It's the world of what humanity has done, and therefore can do, the world revealed to us in the arts and sciences. This is the world that won't go away, the world out of which we built the [United States of 1964], are now building the [United States of 1994], and will be building the quite different [United States of 2004]. (Frye, 1964, p. 152)

My students found that they could change their roles in Sweet Cakes Town, as well as alter its social structures. Thus we see that the template for the society of the future need not be what the students have seen, but what they can imagine.

REFERENCES

Barth, F. (1969). *Ethnic groups and boundaries: The social organization of culture difference.* Boston: Little, Brown.

Bowles, S., & Gintis, H. (1976) *Schooling in capitalist America.* New York: Basic Books.

Bourdieu, P. (1977). *Reproduction in education, society, and culture.* London: Sage.

Byrne, J. (1993, December). The horizontal corporation. *Business Week,* pp. 76–81.

Davidson, M. (1986). *I have a dream.* New York: Scholastic.

Donnan, C. (1988). Following our forebears' footsteps: From expedition to understanding. In V. Rogers, A. D. Roberts, & T. P. Weinland (Eds.), *Teaching social studies: Portraits from the classroom* (pp. 3–11). Washington, DC: National Council for the Social Studies.

Erickson, F. (1987). Transformation and school success: The politics and culture of educational achievement. *Anthropology and Education Quarterly, 18,* 335–356.

Freire, P. (1982). *Pedagogy of the oppressed.* New York: Continuum.

Freire, P. (1986). *Education for critical consciousness.* New York: Continuum.

Freire, P. (1993). *Pedagogy of the city.* New York: Continuum.

Frye, N. (1964). *The educated imagination.* Bloomington: Indiana University Press.

Fordham, S., & Ogbu, J. (1986). Black students' school success: Coping with the "Burden of 'acting White.'" *Urban Review, 18,* 176–206.

Gans, H. J. (1990). Deconstructing the underclass: The term's danger as a planning concept. *Journal of the American Planning Association, 56,* 271–277.

Giroux, H. A. (1977). The politics of the hidden curriculum. *Independent School, 37,* 42–43.

Giroux, H. A. (1978, December). Developing educational programs: Overcoming the hidden curriculum. *Clearing House,* pp. 148–151.

Giroux, H. A. (1979, December) Toward a new sociology of curriculum. *Educational Leadership,* pp. 248–253.

Katz, M. B. (1986). *In the shadow of the poorhouse: A social history of welfare in America.* New York: Basic Books.

Ladson-Billings, G. (1990). Like lightning in a bottle: Attempting to capture the pedagogical excellence of successful teachers of black students. *Qualitative Studies in Education, 3,* 335–344.

Ladson-Billings, G. (1992). Reading between the lines and beyond the pages: A culturally appropriate approach to literacy teaching. *Theory Into Practice, 31,* 312–320.

Lukas, J. A. (1986). *Common ground: A turbulent decade in the lives of three American families.* New York: Vintage Books.

McCarthy, L. P., & Braffman, E. J. (1985). Creating Victorian Philadelphia: Children reading and writing their world. *Curriculum Inquiry, 15,* 121–151.

Mickelson, R. A. (1984). *Race, class, and gender differences in adolescent academic achievement attitudes and behaviors.* Unpublished doctoral dissertation, University of California, Los Angeles.

Ogbu, J. (1978). *Minority education and caste.* New York: Academic Press.

Ogbu, J. (1988). Variability in minority school performance: A problem in search of an explanation. *Anthropology and Education Quarterly, 18,* 312–335.

Richmond, G. (1989). The future school: Is Lowell pointing us toward a revolution in education? *Phi Delta Kappan, 71,* 232–236.

Schein, E. H. (1988) *Process consultation: Vol. 1. Its role in organizational development.* Reading, MA: Addison Wesley.

School District of Philadelphia. (1989). *Social studies grade three.* Philadelphia: Office of Curriculum.

School District of Philadelphia. (1991). *Superintendent's management information center, 1990-1991.* Philadelphia: School District of Philadelphia, Office of Assessment.

Shor, I. (1980). *Critical teaching and everyday life.* Boston: South End Press.

Sleeter, C. E. (1991). Multicultural education and empowerment. In C. E. Sleeter (Ed.), *Empowerment through multicultural education* (p. 15). Albany: State University of New York Press.

Sleeter, C. E., & Grant, C. A. (1986). Success for all students. *Phi Delta Kappan, 68,* 297–299.

Simon, R., & Dippo, D. (1987). What schools can do: Designing programs for work education that challenge the wisdom of experience. *Boston University Journal of Education, 169*(3), 101–117.

Sticht, T. (1987). *Cast off youth: Policy and training methods from the military experience.* New York: Praeger.

Stewart, T. (1992, May). The search for the organization of tomorrow. *Fortune,* pp. 92–99.

Stewart, T. (1993, December). Welcome to the revolution. *Fortune,* pp. 66–77.

Vygotsky, L. S. (1978). *Mind in society.* Cambridge, MA: Harvard University Press.

Wigginton, E. (1989) Foxfire grows up. *Harvard Educational Review, 59,* 24–49.

Wilson, W. J. (1987). *The truly disadvantaged.* Chicago: University of Chicago Press.

Wilson, W. J. (1990, February) Studying inner city dislocations: The challenge of public agenda research. 1990 Presidential address. *American Sociological Review,* pp. 1–14.

Those who know my teaching know that it has been a wildly uneven road to any success. As any teacher, I am indebted to the wisdom and generosity of others. Credit and thanks must first go to my students, and the many members of the community who supported us. For reasons of confidentiality, all of the above must go unnamed. I am also indebted to the wisdom of my mentors: Scott Tiley, my fifth-grade teacher; Virginia Miller of Bank Street College; Fran Motola of PS 87; Joan Billen, formerly of the Bank Street School for Children; Ewa Pytowska, of the Intercultural Training Resource Center; Barbara Moore Williams of the School District of Philadelphia; the principal of my school. Lastly, I am indebted to the many people who patiently helped me with the preparation of this manuscript: Nancy Brooks, Frederick Erickson, David Kinney, Michael B. Katz, Karl Otto, Ellen Skilton Sylvester, and my family.

About the Contributors

ADRIENNE ALTON-LEE is a Professor of Teacher Education and Dean of Education at Victoria University of Wellington, Aotearoa New Zealand. She is also Associate Editor of *Teaching and Teacher Education: An International Journal of Research and Studies*. Her research focuses on children's learning in classrooms. Her recent published works include "Predicting Learning from Student Experience of Teaching: A Theory of Student Knowledge Construction in Classrooms" in *American Educational Research Journal* (with G. Nuthall, 1993).

CYNTHIA BALLENGER is a Senior Research Associate at TERC in Cambridge, Massachusetts, and a member of the Brookline Teacher-Researcher Seminar. Her research focuses on science learning among linguistic-minority students, Haitian students in particular, and in researching science teaching with these students' teachers. She is author of *Language and Literacy in a Haitian Preschool: A Perspective from Teacher-Research* (1994).

LILIA I. BARTOLOME is Assistant Professor at the Harvard Graduate School of Education. Her research interests focus on the study of home/school cross-cultural language and literacy practices, and on oral and written classroom discourse acquisition patterns of language-minority children in U.S. schools. She is author of "Effective Teaching Strategies: Their Possibilities and Limitations" in *Cultural Diversity and Second Language Learning* (edited by B. McLeod, 1994), and *The Misteaching of Academic Discourse in a Bilingual Classroom* (forthcoming).

PATRICIA CLIFFORD is a Teacher at Ernest Morrow Junior High School in Calgary, Canada. Her study of how imaginative engagement gives young children access to knowledge and skills not generally available to them through standard curriculum has led her to research whether these methods might be generalizable to other student populations, in particular adolescents in a high-needs environment. She is author of *Hard Fun: Teaching and Learning for the 21st Century* (with S. Friesen, in press).

CONCHA DELGADO-GAITAN is Professor of Education at the University of California, Davis. Her professional interests focus on sociocultural studies in anthropology and education, specifically transcultural representations of childhood and oral traditions of children in culturally diverse communities. Her publications include *Crossing Cultural Borders* (with H. Trueba, 1991) and *Protean Literacy: Extending the Discourse on Empowerment* (forthcoming).

RUBEN DONATO, Assistant Professor of Educational Foundations, Policy, and Practice in the School of Education at the University of Colorado at Boulder, is interested in the history of American education. He is author of *Ethnicity and Education: Mexican American Education During the Civil Rights Era* (forthcoming), and of a number of articles on Mexican American experiences in U.S. public schools.

MELINDA FINE is an educational research, evaluation, and program development consultant. Her professional interests include research and development of educational programs to foster social responsibility and moral development, educational equity for girls, and violence prevention. She is author of "Facing History and Ourselves: Portrait of a Classroom" in *Educational Leadership* (1992) and *Habits of Mind: Struggling Over Values in America's Classrooms* (1995).

SHARON L. FRIESEN is a Teacher at the Ernest Morrow Junior High School in Calgary, Ontario. Her research focuses on creating a curriculum for adolescents in a high-needs environment that is based on the students' interests and experiences, and on whether this approach is generalizable across age groups. She is author of "Possible Beginnings: The Power of Story" in *Early Childhood Education* (1991) and *Hard Fun: Teaching and Learning for the 21st Century* (with P. Clifford, in press).

ROSEMARY HENZE is a Research Associate at ARC Associates in Oakland, California. Her research interests center on the education of language minorities and indigenous language revitalization. She is on leave from the University of Hawaii at Manoa, where she is an Associate Professor in the ESL Department. Her most recent publication is "To Walk in Two Worlds — or More? Challenging a Common Metaphor of Native Education" in *Anthropology and Education Quarterly* (with L. Vanett, 1993).

MEL KING is Adjunct Professor and Director of the Community Fellows Program at the Massachusetts Institute of Technology Department of Urban Studies and Planning. In addition to teaching, King is a self-described "community developer" — a community organizer, activist, and political innovator committed to working for peace, justice, and development. His published works include "A Framework for Action" in *Challenging Uneven Development: An Urban Agenda for the 1990s* (edited by P. W. Nyden and W. Wiewel, 1991).

TAMARA LUCAS is Project Director of The National Center for Restructuring Education, Schools, and Teaching at Teachers College, Columbia University. She is interested in educational reform and restructuring for diverse student populations. Her articles include "Reframing the Debate: The Roles of Native Languages in English-Only Programs for Language Minority Students" in *TESOL Quarterly* (with A. Katz, 1994).

BEVERLY McELROY-WALKER (formerly McElroy-Johnson) is a mentor teacher at Havenscourt Junior High School in Oakland, California. Her professional interests focus on staff development in the area of portfolio assessment and mainstream English instruction. She was awarded the 1995 Marcus Foster Distinguished Educator Award.

SUE MIDDLETON is Associate Professor in the School of Education at the University of Waikato in Hamilton, New Zealand. Her areas of research include sociology of women's education and life-history methodologies; she is currently working on an oral history of educational theories in New Zealand from the perspective of teachers. She is coeditor of *Women and Education in Aotearoa 2* (with A. Jones, 1992) and author of *Educating Feminists: Life-Histories and Pedagogy* (1993).

SONIA NIETO is Professor of Education in the Cultural Diversity and Curriculum Reform Program at the University of Massachusetts, Amherst. Her professional interests focus on multicultural and bilingual education, and the social and cultural context of education. She is coeditor of *The Education of Latino Students in Massachusetts: Research and Policy Implications* (with R. Rivera, 1993) and author of *Affirming Diversity: The Sociopolitical Context of Multicultural Education* (2nd edition, forthcoming).

GRAHAM NUTHALL is Professor of Education at the University of Canterbury, Christchurch, Aotearoa New Zealand. His professional interests focus on research on teaching, and children's learning and cognition in classrooms. His published works include "Predicting Learning from Student Experience of Teaching" in *American Education Research Journal* (with A. Alton-Lee, 1993) and "Understanding Student Thinking and Learning in the Classroom" in *The International Handbook of Teachers and Teaching* (edited by B. Biddle, T. Good, and I. Goodson, in press).

JOHN PATRICK is a Senior Lecturer at the Christchurch College of Education, Christchurch, Aotearoa New Zealand. His research focuses on teaching skills and the influence of learners' self-concepts on learning. He is coauthor of "Take Your Brown Hand Off My Book: Racism in the Classroom" in *SET: Research Information for Teachers* (with A. Alton-Lee and G. Nuthall, 1987).

MARIA DE LA LUZ REYES, Professor of Education at California State University Monterey Bay, is interested in literacy for second-language learners and equity issues in higher education. She is currently completing a study on Chicanas in academe. She is coauthor of "Emerging Biliteracy and Cross-Cultural Sensitivity in a Language Arts Classroom" in *Language Arts* (with E. A. Laliberty and J. A. Orbanosky, 1993) and *A Tapestry of Language and Culture: Weaving the Literacy Web* (with J. D. Comas and P. Mason, forthcoming).

ERIC ROFES is a graduate student in Social and Cultural Studies at the Graduate School of Education of the University of California at Berkeley. He has been a teacher and codirector of the Fayerweather Street School in Cambridge, Massachusetts. His current research interests include charter schools, HIV prevention among gay men, and gay issues in schools. He is author and editor of *The Kids' Book of Divorce* (1981) and *The Kids' Book About Death and Dying* (1985).

PATRICIA J. SAYLOR is Director of BRIDGES, a bilingual/bicultural program for deaf and hearing children in Durham, North Carolina. She is also on the staff of the Central North Carolina School for the Deaf where, together with a Deaf colleague, she works with preschool deaf and hard-of-hearing children and their parents. Her primary professional interests are language acquisition in young deaf and hard-of-hearing children, and the influence of early language experience on future academic achievement.

PAUL SKILTON SYLVESTER, a doctoral student at the University of Pennsylvania and a former elementary school teacher, is currently an educational consultant and action researcher at the Center for Urban Ethnography in Philadelphia. His professional interests include elementary school curricula, urban school reform in a post-industrial economy, and classroom management. He is author of "Sources of Strength: Elementary School Students Doing Oral History" in *Strength and Diversity* (edited by E. Pytowska, 1991).

EMILIE V. SIDDLE WALKER is Assistant Professor in the Division of Educational Studies at Emory University, Atlanta. Her professional interests focus on learning environments and the social context of education, as well as the history of education. She is coeditor of *Facing Racism in Education* (with N. Hidalgo and C. McDowell, 1990), and author of *Their Highest Potential: A Case of African-American Schooling in the Segregated South* (in press).

WILLIAM H. WATKINS, Associate Professor at the University of Utah in Salt Lake City, is interested in curriculum history, sociology of African American education, and political sociology of curriculum. He is author of "The Social Reconstructionists" in *The International Encyclopedia of Curriculum* (edited by A. Lewy, 1992) and "A Shared Legacy: Pan-Africanism and the Politics of Education" in *Pan-Africanism Revisited: Class, Culture and Consciousness in the African Diaspora* (edited by S. LeMelle and R. D. G. Kelly, 1994).

PAULA LAWRENCE WEHMILLER is an independent educational consultant living in Wilmington, Delaware. She works with teachers, administrators, students, and parents, guiding them in their struggle for inclusivity and excellence in their schools. Her articles include "Face to Face: Lessons Learned on the Teaching Journey" in *Tyson-Mason Papers* (1992) and "Sojourners in Our Schools, Strangers within the Gates" in *Proceedings* of the Annual Meeting of the National Association of Principals of Schools for Girls (1993).

ARLETTE INGRAM WILLIS is an Assistant Professor at the University of Illinois at Urbana-Champaign. Her professional interests include secondary reading methods, multicultural literature, trends and issues in reading research, and the history of reading in the United States, especially as it concerns access to literacy by people of color. She is editor of *Teaching and Using Multicultural Literature in Grades 9-12* (in press) and author of *A Critical History of Reading Research* (in press).

About the Editors

GLADYS R. CAPELLA NOYA recently completed a doctoral degree in the Teaching, Curriculum, and Learning Environments Program at the Harvard Graduate School of Education. Her dissertation addresses young people's perceptions of teachers' influence on their class participation and learning. For the past three years Capella has worked as a research associate with Nitza Hidalgo in her ethnographic study of Puerto Rican family support for young children's school success. She has also been an elementary and secondary school teacher in Puerto Rico and the Boston area.

KATHRYN GEISMAR is a developmental psychologist and doctoral student at the Harvard Graduate School of Education. She has worked with Carol Gilligan and Annie Rogers on their pioneering work with adolescent girls, focusing on fostering girls' resiliency and courage through artistic expression. A former elementary school teacher, Geismar is currently focused in her research on the topic of recovery from sexual abuse, and on the development of violence prevention and intervention programs within the Cambridge, Massachusetts, public schools.

GUITELE NICOLEAU is a doctoral candidate in Administration, Planning, and Social Policy at the Harvard Graduate School of Education. The focus of her research is community education and lifelong learning, with a particular interest in educational practices that enhance the participation of marginalized voices in framing the discourse of educational policies. A native of Haiti who grew up in the United States, Nicoleau is currently writing her dissertation on the implementation of a community-based AIDS education program with Haitian adolescents in an urban community in Massachusetts.